FileMaker Pro 10

THE MISSING MANUAL

*The book that
should have been
in the box®*

FileMaker Pro 10

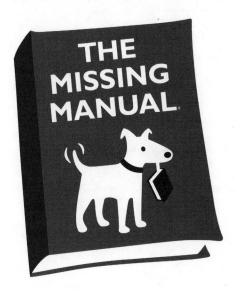

Susan Prosser and Geoff Coffey

POGUE PRESS™

O'REILLY®

Beijing • Cambridge • Farnham • Köln • Sebastopol • Taipei • Tokyo

FileMaker Pro 10: The Missing Manual
by Susan Prosser and Geoff Coffey

Published by O'Reilly Media, Inc., 1005 Gravenstein Highway North, Sebastopol, CA 95472.

O'Reilly books may be purchased for educational, business, or sales promotional use. Online editions are also available for most titles (*safari.oreilly.com*). For more information, contact our corporate/institutional sales department: (800) 998-9938 or *corporate@oreilly.com*.

Printing History:

January 2009:   First Edition.

ISBN: 978-0-596-15423-3
[M]

Table of Contents

Part Three: Multiple Tables and Relationships

Part Five: Scripting

Part Six: Security and Integration

Part Seven: Appendixes

The Missing Credits

About the Authors

Susan Prosser (co-author) is a Southern farm girl who grew up far from the nearest small town, so she's as surprised as anyone to have developed a knack for creating software. But as she's a serial obsessive, moving from one interesting skill to another, it makes weird and satisfying sense. Despite being adept using her hands, she leaves the maintenance of her five bicycles to her husband and wrench, Paul, who gallantly changes flat tires at the side of the road (mostly) without complaint.

She's certified in three versions of FileMaker, has presented at FileMaker's Developer Conference, and has been a trainer slash curriculum developer for over 15 years. Susan is the president and head developer at DBHQ (*www.dbhq.net*), which builds custom software for business, medical, education, and entertainment clients. Send email to *susanprosser@gmail.com* to talk about FileMaker or share fond memories of Gang of Four, XTC, and Shriekback.

Geoff Coffey (co-author) is co-owner of Six Fried Rice (*http://sixfriedrice.com*), where he writes about, teaches, and builds software with FileMaker Pro. With Susan Prosser, he's co-authored all four editions of *FileMaker Pro: The Missing Manual*. On the technical side, Geoff is a FileMaker Pro expert, and puts his skills to regular use building custom software for customers. He also specializes in Web application development, and built his first database-connected dynamic Web site in 1994 using FileMaker Pro and AppleScript. Since then, Geoff has created production Web systems in just about everything out there from Perl CGI to Cold Fusion to JEE, but his current favorite for small-to-mid-size sites is Ruby on Rails.

Although Geoff has an MBA from Arizona State University and a degree in Computer Science from Northern Arizona University, FileMaker Pro is his first true love. This fact is disputed by his wife of 15 years, with whom he has two practically perfect children, Isabel (10) and Sophia (7). You can find Geoff online at *http://sixfriedrice.com/* or email him at *geoff@sixfriedrice.com*.

About the Creative Team

Nan Barber (editor) is associate editor for the Missing Manual series. She lives in Massachusetts with her husband and G4 Macintosh. Email: *nanbarber@gmail.com*.

Nellie McKesson (production editor) lives in Jamaica Plain, Mass., where she makes t-shirts (*http://mattsaundersbynellie.etsy.com*) and plays music with her band Dr. & Mrs. Van Der Trampp (*http://myspace.com/drmrsvandertrampp*). Email: *nellie@oreilly.com*.

Sohaila Abdulali (copy editor) has published a novel, several children's books, and many short fiction and non-fiction pieces. She is Director of Communications for AIDS-Free World, and she teaches South Asian Cultures at New York University. She lives in New York, and can be reached through her Web site at *www.sohailaink.com*.

Karen Shaner (technical reviewer) is an editorial assistant for O'Reilly Media. She's a grad student at Emerson College in Boston pursuing a MA in Publishing and Writing. In the little free time she has, Karen goes dancing (especially contra and West African), spends time with friends, sings with a Praise Band, and tries to experience all that Boston has to offer.

Jammie Turner (technical reviewer) is a resident of Columbia, SC. She has earned a Bachelor of Arts and Master of Arts Degree from the University of South Carolina. She has worked for the University of South Carolina for 10 years. She currently works for the USC School of Music as an Undergraduate Student Services Coordinator and relies solely on File Maker Pro to run her student and financial databases.

Julie Grady (indexer) has been a professional indexer for the past 10 years. She has a degree in English Literature from Boston University. She lives with her husband and three children in Sarasota, Florida.

The Missing Manual Series

Missing Manuals are witty, superbly written guides to computer products that don't come with printed manuals (which is just about all of them). Each book features a handcrafted index; cross-references to specific pages (not just chapters); and RepKover, a detached-spine binding that lets the book lie perfectly flat without the assistance of weights or cinder blocks.

Recent and upcoming titles include:

Access 2007: The Missing Manual by Matthew MacDonald

AppleScript: The Missing Manual by Adam Goldstein

AppleWorks 6: The Missing Manual by Jim Elferdink and David Reynolds

CSS: The Missing Manual by David Sawyer McFarland

Creating Web Sites: The Missing Manual by Matthew MacDonald

David Pogue's Digital Photography: The Missing Manual by David Pogue

Dreamweaver 8: The Missing Manual by David Sawyer McFarland

Dreamweaver CS3: The Missing Manual by David Sawyer McFarland

Dreamweaver CS4: The Missing Manual by David Sawyer McFarland

eBay: The Missing Manual by Nancy Conner

Excel 2003: The Missing Manual by Matthew MacDonald

Excel 2007: The Missing Manual by Matthew MacDonald

Facebook: The Missing Manual by E.A. Vander Veer

FileMaker Pro 8: The Missing Manual by Geoff Coffey and Susan Prosser

FileMaker Pro 9: The Missing Manual by Geoff Coffey and Susan Prosser

Flash 8: The Missing Manual by E.A. Vander Veer

Flash CS3: The Missing Manual by E.A. Vander Veer and Chris Grover

Flash CS4: The Missing Manual by Chris Grover with E.A. Vander Veer

FrontPage 2003: The Missing Manual by Jessica Mantaro

Google Apps: The Missing Manual by Nancy Conner

The Internet: The Missing Manual by David Pogue and J.D. Biersdorfer

iMovie 6 & iDVD: The Missing Manual by David Pogue

iMovie '08 & iDVD: The Missing Manual by David Pogue

iPhone: The Missing Manual by David Pogue

iPhoto '08: The Missing Manual by David Pogue

iPod: The Missing Manual, Sixth Edition by J.D. Biersdorfer

JavaScript: The Missing Manual by David Sawyer McFarland

Mac OS X: The Missing Manual, Tiger Edition by David Pogue

Mac OS X: The Missing Manual, Leopard Edition by David Pogue

Microsoft Project 2007: The Missing Manual by Bonnie Biafore

Office 2004 for Macintosh: The Missing Manual by Mark H. Walker and Franklin Tessler

Office 2007: The Missing Manual by Chris Grover, Matthew MacDonald, and E.A. Vander Veer

Office 2008 for Macintosh: The Missing Manual by Jim Elferdink

PCs: The Missing Manual by Andy Rathbone

Photoshop CS4: The Missing Manual by Lesa Snider King

Photoshop Elements 7: The Missing Manual by Barbara Brundage

Photoshop Elements 6 for Mac: The Missing Manual by Barbara Brundage

PowerPoint 2007: The Missing Manual by E.A. Vander Veer

QuickBase: The Missing Manual by Nancy Conner

QuickBooks 2008: The Missing Manual by Bonnie Biafore

QuickBooks 2009: The Missing Manual by Bonnie Biafore

Quicken 2008: The Missing Manual by Bonnie Biafore

Quicken 2009: The Missing Manual by Bonnie Biafore

Switching to the Mac: The Missing Manual, Tiger Edition by David Pogue and Adam Goldstein

Switching to the Mac: The Missing Manual, Leopard Edition by David Pogue

Wikipedia: The Missing Manual by John Broughton

Windows XP Home Edition: The Missing Manual, Second Edition by David Pogue

Windows XP Pro: The Missing Manual, Second Edition by David Pogue, Craig Zacker, and Linda Zacker

Windows Vista: The Missing Manual by David Pogue

Windows Vista for Starters: The Missing Manual by David Pogue

Word 2007: The Missing Manual by Chris Grover

Your Brain: The Missing Manual by Matthew MacDonald

Introduction

For many people, the word "database" conjures up an image of a computer and a vast collection of information that requires a computer and a technical degree to access. But databases are all around you—a phone book, a cookbook, and an encyclopedia are each databases. So is the stock page in your newspaper. In fact, if you look up the word "database" in a dictionary (which is a database, too), you'll probably read that a database is just a collection of information, or data.

Ideally, the information in a database is organized so you can find what you're looking for quickly and easily. For example, a Rolodex has information about people organized alphabetically by name. You can find any person's card because you know approximately where it is, even though there may be *thousands* of cards to look through. But physical databases have major limitations compared to those stored on a computer. What if you want to get a list of all your associates in California? A Rolodex isn't organized by state, so you have to flip through every card one by one to get a list. The first database programs were created to help you avoid that kind of tedium. And FileMaker Pro is an easy-to-use, but powerful, database program.

The term *database program* means a computer program designed to help you build a database so you can store information you need. A database stored on a computer isn't much different in theory from one collected on Rolodex cards or other forms of paper. It contains lots of information, like addresses, Zip codes, and phone numbers, and organizes that info in useful ways (see Figure I-1 for an example). But since it's stored on a computer, you can organize the *same* information in numerous ways with ease—say, by name *or* by state. Computers make searching databases a whole lot faster. That list of associates in California you took hours to generate from a Rolodex? A computer can do it in less than a second.

Figure I-1:
FileMaker Pro lets you do just about anything with the information you give it. You can use it like a Rolodex to simply store and retrieve information, or run your entire business with this one program. FileMaker's built-in number crunching and word processing tools let you track people, processes, and things, creating all your reports, correspondence, and collateral documents along the way. Here are two examples of real-world FileMaker databases created for very different kinds of businesses.

This book will teach you how FileMaker Pro stores your information, and how you can rearrange that information to get the answers to meaningful questions, like which employees are due for performance reviews, who's coming to the company picnic, and which amusement park has the best deal on Laser Tag so you can throw a party for your top 50 performers. You won't have to learn to think like a programmer (or know the arcane terms they use), but you will learn how to bend FileMaker Pro's hidden power to your will, and make it tell you everything it knows about your company, your stock portfolio, or how much you've spent on the replacement parts for the '58 Bonneville Sport Coupe you're rebuilding.

Why FileMaker Pro?

If you're reading this book, you've already decided to use a computer database instead of the mulched-up tree variety. *Choosing* a database program from the many options on the market is overwhelming. Some are enormously powerful but take years to learn how to use. Others let you easily get started, but don't offer much help when you're ready to incorporate some more advanced features. Here are a few reasons why FileMaker Pro is a great choice for most folks:

- **FileMaker Pro is the ease-of-use champion.** While other programs use jargon words like *query, join*, and *alias*, FileMaker Pro uses simple concepts like *find, sort*, and *connect*. FileMaker Pro is designed from the ground up for non-technical people who have a *real* job to do. It's designed to let you get in, build your database, and get back to work.

- **FileMaker Pro can do almost anything.** Some other database programs are simple to use, but they're just plain simple, too—they can't do the kinds of things most businesses need to do. FileMaker Pro, despite its focus on ease of use, is very powerful. It can handle large amounts of data. It lets lots of people on different computers share data (even at different locations around the world). It even meets the needs of bigger companies, like integrating with high-end systems. And it's adaptable enough to solve most problems. If your home-based crafting business is taking off, and you need to figure out how much it costs you to create your top-selling items, FileMaker can do that. But if you're a large school district tracking dozens of test scores for more than 50,000 students in grades K-12, and you have to make sure those scores are tied to federal standards, then FileMaker can handle that, too.

- **FileMaker Pro works on Macs or PCs.** If you use both types of computers, FileMaker Pro makes the connection seamless. You can use the exact same databases on any computer, and even share them over the network simultaneously without a hitch (Chapter 18).

- **FileMaker Pro is fun!** It may sound corny, but it's exciting (and a little addictive) to have such a powerful tool at your fingertips. If you get the bug, you'll find yourself solving all kinds of problems you never knew you had. You might not think that getting married is an occasion for breaking out a new database, but you'll be amazed at how helpful it is. You can make a mailing list for your invitations, track RSVPs, note which favorite aunt sent you a whole set of bone china (and which cousin cheaped out by signing his name on his brother's gift card), and you can even record what date you mailed the thank-you notes.

- **Everybody uses it.** Perhaps best of all, FileMaker Pro is very popular—more people buy FileMaker Pro than any other database program. And the program's fans love it so much they're actually willing to help you if *you* get stuck. You can find user groups, Web sites, discussion boards, chat rooms, mailing lists, and professional consultants all devoted to FileMaker Pro. This is one case where there's good reason to follow the crowd.

What's New in FileMaker Pro 10

FileMaker Pro 10 is a single software package that serves two fundamentally different types of people: users and designers. Users are the folks who need a database to help them organize and manage the data they work with in order to do their jobs. Developers create the databases that users use. No matter which category you're in (and lots of people fall into both categories, sometimes popping back and forth dozens of times a day), you'll find that FileMaker doesn't play favorites. The features you need for both roles are equally accessible.

FileMaker Pro 10 includes many features that make day-to-day work in FileMaker easier than ever:

- When you create a new file, you see a redesigned **Quick Start** screen with more options. You can still create a new database from one of FileMaker's many templates, create a new file from scratch, open an existing file, or use the Learn More button to get help before you even start. You can create a new database from even more sources than ever before, like Excel .xlsx files, or FileMaker's little sister Bento (version 2 only). (For the scoop on Bento, see the box on the next page.

- All 30 **Starter Files** have gotten an interface-lift for a younger, fresher look, and the 13 most popular starter files have many new features. All the old features have been retained, though, so you can still use your existing databases and designs. The new designs also bear a strong family resemblance to Bento.

- The largest cosmetic change also brings you new power. The **Status toolbar** has gotten a complete overhaul, and now lives at the top of the screen. All tools have a new look and new abilities, and show tooltips when you hover over them with your mouse. Plus, you can customize each toolbar so it displays only the tools you use.

- Fields now have **Find icons** in Find mode. This extra feedback helps prevent you from entering data when you should be entering search criteria.

- You can make onscreen and printed reports more easily than ever. The **Saved Find Requests** tool holds a pop-up menu that lets you choose from your recent finds, and save custom finds.

- The toolbars and menus now include **common font sizes**, like 11 and 13 points. Now you don't have to create a custom font choice just to change a font to one of those common sizes.

- When you're doing data entry in a found set that's sorted (say you're adding names to your company's bulk mail list, and you want to see the records sorted by Zip code), **new records automatically appear in sorted order**. You don't have to keep re-sorting.

- **Sub-summary values get updated in real time** if you add records or edit data while you're viewing a subsummary report. No need to go to Preview mode to view the updated math.

FREQUENTLY ASKED QUESTION

Hello Bento

What's this Bento program I keep hearing about? Should I be using that along with FileMaker Pro? Or maybe instead?

Well, if you use Windows, you don't even have the option of using Bento, so quit worrying. It's Mac OS X only. But if you're a Mac fan, read on.

You can think of Bento as FileMaker Pro's much, much younger sister. FileMaker's been around since 1985. And even before that, it had a previous life under the name Nutshell in DOS (an ancient operating system that didn't even have pictures). So FileMaker has a lot of mileage under its belt and is a mature, stable player in the professional database world.

FileMaker Inc. introduced Bento in January 2008. It's an inexpensive ($49) program whose goal is to get you up and running in minutes without any previous database experience. Its greatest asset is how effortlessly you can create databases with information you already have in your Mac OS X programs like iCal, Address Book, and Apple Mail. As with

FileMaker, though, you can customize Bento for special applications like cataloging your home inventory, your Mom's antique salt shaker collection, or even what you discussed with your clients on their weekly appointments. The name Bento refers to a Japanese lunchbox, with tidy little compartments to hold various kinds of food. And in fact, using Bento is as easy as dragging and dropping to arrange and fill onscreen compartments.

But if your needs change, or your business grows (say you hire another person who has to share your database), you might need to step up to FileMaker, which permits multiple users and has a powerful scripting engine to automate processes and create brand new features. In that case, you might have to play with the big kids and move your Bento data into FileMaker. So if you already have FileMaker, you don't need to rush out and buy Bento. But you may have occasion to import data from Bento into FileMaker—see page 696 to learn how.

Database developers will appreciate these new features that help create databases (or improve those you already have):

- You can now specify an SMTP server instead of relying on your users' email clients when you use the **SMTP-based Send Mail** script step for sending email.

- **Insert into Tab Order** lets you edit a layout's tab order by typing the new object's position in the order. All the other objects in the tab order automatically adjust to accommodate the new object in your specified order.

- **Script Triggers** let you have a script run when someone clicks a button or does some other specific action in your database. Almost any object on a layout can run a script trigger, as can layouts themselves. So you can, for example, run a script that checks data entry for accuracy when someone edits data in a field, or automatically perform a find whenever the person navigates to a layout.

- **Ipv6 Support** lets you address internal networks with the new, expanded protocol, plus the *Get (HostIPAddress)* function returns IPv4 and Ipv6 addresses as appropriate.

- With **more layout themes,** you can start databases more quickly and with more polish.

- **New calculation functions** let you use Unicode text and numbers, track information about the actions that trigger scripts, and more.

- Save time when you create a new script, with a **Default Script** that gives you a jumping-off point for commonly used script steps.

- An improved **Print script step** lets you save a specified target printer instead of choosing a printer every time.

- You can now launch **PHP Site Assistant** from the Tools menu, and you don't have to click through the Server's start page to get there.

- If you want to put data into a field using a script (maybe you're checking a user's data entry before you let her create a new record), you can now set the data without hard-coding the field's name with the new **Set Field by Name** script step. That way, you can use the same script for many different purposes instead of writing a new script for each field into which you need to put data.

- When you're creating scripts that run under a variety of conditions (over the Web, on a FileMaker Server, or standalone), you can use the new **Show Compatibility** pop-up menu to see at a glance if your scripts will work .

- With the new **Install OnTimer Script Step,** turn FileMaker into an automated processor that can run repeated tasks, like verifying and approving orders submitted through your Web site. It runs a script at the interval you set.

- If you use Windows, you'll appreciate the convenience of creating scripts while viewing your database in the background, since the **Manage Script dialog box no longer opens maximized,** covering your work area.

If you use FileMaker Pro Advanced for its developers' tools (and if you aren't using it, you should), your professional life just got a whole lot easier. Here's a partial list of its new features:

- When something goes wrong with your files, **Advanced Recovery Options** give you more control over the diagnostics and repairs FileMaker Pro Advanced can perform on damaged files.

- To use FileMaker Pro 10's new features more effectively and troubleshoot them quicker, see them each listed in the **Database Design Report (DDR).**

- If something's going wrong with a script, debugging is easier now that the most recent error is no longer cleared from the **Get (LastError)** function display.

- **New calculation functions** let you find out more about your database and the data it stores. You can monitor Script Triggers with *Get (TriggerModifierKeys)* and *Get (TriggerKeystroke).* *Char( )* and *Code( )* give these functions even more power by pinpointing which characters are sent to scripts when they're triggered. *GetFieldName( )* and *SetField by Name( )* give you the power to address fields with a calculation.

If you share your FileMaker files with other databases like Oracle and SQL, or even Excel and Bento documents, you'll like the new features that make collaboration easier:

- **External Data Sources** you can use now include Oracle 11g, MySQL Community Server 5.1, and Microsoft SQL Server 2008.

- ESS now lets you use Windows **Single Sign-on.**

- You can make data entry in FileMaker more predictable by creating **Value Lists** from fields in ESS tables.

- When you use **Microsoft SQL Server's datetime fields**, you can now parse out only the date or only the time from those fields.

- If your boss doesn't use anything but **Excel 2007/2008**, you can now import and export FileMaker data to that format.

- If you've got a client who doesn't use anything but Bento, you can import her email list with **Bento 2** compatibility.

If you share databases over the network, then you'll be glad to know about FileMaker Server's new features. Here are the highlights:

- FileMaker Server can now **send email** without a robot machine to handle your emailing chores.

- If you use multiple FileMaker servers, you no longer need a robot or human intervention to handle **imports/exports**—Server can now move data in and out of its hosted files without opening a file on a client machine.

UP TO SPEED

What About the Big Guys?

The word *database* is a little abused in the computer world. Both FileMaker Pro and MySQL—an open-source database that you can use free, if you have the skills, manpower, hardware, and know-how—are considered database programs, but they're about as similar as chocolate cake and dry flour. In reality, two kinds of database programs are available. One kind is very powerful (as in run-the-federal-government powerful) and very complicated. This type of database program just holds data, and computer programmers use sophisticated, and expensive, tools when they build big systems for big companies.

The other kind of database program—sometimes called a *desktop database*—is less powerful and a lot easier, but it actually has more features. In addition to holding lots of data,

these programs provide an interface to access, organize, and search the data. This interface includes the menus, graphics, and text that let you work with the data, much like any other computer program. In other words, you don't need a computer science degree to create a powerful database with a desktop program like FileMaker Pro.

And with FileMaker Pro 10's powerful ESS connection feature, you can now have the best of both worlds. You (or even better, an IT person who's a database nerd) can create and administer an SQL database, and then you get to use FileMaker to create a snazzy interface for the SQL data. Your nerd colleague would say you're using FileMaker as a "front end" to the SQL database. You can just call it common sense.

The Very Basics

You'll find very little jargon or nerd terminology in this book. You will, however, encounter a few terms and concepts that you'll see frequently in your computer life. They include:

- **Clicking.** This book offers three kinds of instructions that require you to use the mouse or trackpad attached to your computer. To *click* means to point the arrow cursor at something onscreen and then—without moving the cursor at all—press and release the clicker button on the mouse (or laptop trackpad). Right-clicking works the same as clicking, but you use the right mouse button instead. (If you use a Mac and don't have a right mouse button, press the Control key as you click.) To *double-click*, of course, means to click twice in rapid succession, again without moving the cursor at all. And to *drag* means to move the cursor while keeping the button continuously pressed.

  When you're told to *Ctrl-click* something, you click while pressing the Ctrl key (the *Control* key on the Mac) on the bottom row of your keyboard. Such related procedures as *Shift-clicking* and *Alt-clicking* work the same way—just click while pressing the corresponding key.

Note: On the Mac, the key that does most of the Alt key functions is the Option key. Macs also have an extra key called the Command key, which has a cloverleaf (⌘) on it. When the Mac keystroke is different from the one in Windows, this book gives it in parentheses.

- **Menus** are the lists of commands you pull down from the words at the top of the FileMaker window. (On the Mac, they're always in the bar across the top of the screen.) You have two equally valid ways to choose from these pull-down menus with your mouse: Click once to open the menu, and then click again to choose a command; or click and *hold* the button as you drag down the menu, and then release when you get to the desired command. Use whichever method you find easier.

- **Keyboard shortcuts.** Every time you take your hand off the keyboard to move the mouse, you lose time and potentially disrupt your creative flow. That's why many experienced computer jockeys use keystroke combinations instead of menu commands wherever possible. Ctrl+P (⌘-P) opens the Print dialog box, for example.

- When you see a shortcut like Ctrl+Q (⌘-Q), which closes the current program, it's telling you to hold down the Ctrl (⌘) key, and, while it's down, type the letter Q, and then release both keys.

If you've mastered this much information, you have all the technical background you need to enjoy *FileMaker Pro 10: The Missing Manual*.

About This Book

FileMaker Pro comes with a PDF manual and an impressive online help system. These resources are actually pretty helpful—if you're a programmer, that is, or if you've been working with FileMaker for a while. Between the manual and the help system, you can figure out how FileMaker works. But you have to jump back and forth between page and screen to get the complete picture. And neither source does a great job of letting you know which features apply to the problem you're trying to solve.

This book is designed to serve as the FileMaker Pro manual, the book that should have been in the box. It explores each feature in depth, offers shortcuts and workarounds, and explains the ramifications of options that the manual doesn't even mention. Plus, it lets you know which features are really useful and which ones you should worry about only in very limited circumstances. Try putting sticky tabs in your help file or marking the good parts with a highlighter!

FileMaker comes in several flavors, and this book addresses them all. FileMaker Pro, the base program, takes up most of the book's focus. FileMaker Pro Advanced is an enhanced version of the program. Like the name promises, it contains advanced tools and utilities aimed at making development and maintenance of your databases easier. Its features are covered in Chapters 12 and 19. FileMaker Server lets you share your databases more safely and quickly than FileMaker Pro's peer-to-peer sharing. Learn about Server in Chapter 18.

About the Outline

FileMaker Pro 10: The Missing Manual is divided into seven parts.

- **Part One: Getting Started with FileMaker.** Here, you'll learn about FileMaker Pro's interface and how you perform basic tasks, like entering data and then sorting through it again. You'll also find out how FileMaker Pro stores your data inside fields, and then organizes those fields into units called *records*. You'll see how to *define* fields, and make them do some of the data entry work for you.

- **Part Two: Layouts.** Just as your actual data is organized into fields and records, the appearance of your database is organized into layouts. FileMaker Pro provides a whole raft of tools that make creating layouts fast and powerful. You'll find out how to use layouts to make data entry easier, and how to create layouts that list and summarize your data.

- **Part Three: Multiple Tables and Relationships.** When you're storing lots of different types of data in a database, it's helpful to organize types of data using FileMaker's tables. And when you have more than one table, you need to figure out how the information in one table relates to the information in another. You'll learn how to create, connect, and manage multiple tables, and how to set up complex relationships that show you just the data you need to see.

• **Part Four: Calculations.** Most databases store lots of numbers, but the most important information in your database comes from performing some kind of math on those numbers. You'll learn how to use FileMaker Pro's more than 200 functions to do the math for you. Surprisingly, you can also use functions on fields that don't contain numbers. For example, some functions work with text, dates, and times. And some of the most powerful functions are the logical functions, which can perform tests on your data, and then give you results based on what they find out.

• **Part Five: Scripting.** Because you have to do so many things with a database that are repetitive, tedious, or just plain boring, FileMaker Pro provides a way for you to automate those tasks using scripts. You'll start with simple steps that teach you how scripting works, and learn how to make scripts for people to use. You'll see how to use scripts to work with fields and records, or with windows, or even with entire database files. And you'll explore more complex techniques, like making scripts pass information to one another, and nesting scripts within other scripts.

• **Part Six: Security and Integration.** FileMaker knows your data's important enough to keep it safe from prying eyes. In this section, you'll learn how to protect your database with passwords, and how to use privileges to determine what folks can do once they get into your database. This part also teaches you how to move data into and out of your database, and how to share that data with other people, and even with other databases. In the final chapter, you'll see the design and development tools provided in FileMaker Pro Advanced to speed creation time and give you more control over how your database works.

• **Part Seven: Appendixes.** No book can include all the information you'll need for the rest of your FileMaker career. Well, it could, but you wouldn't be able to lift it. Eventually, you'll need to seek extra troubleshooting help or consult the program's online documentation. So, at the end of the book, Appendix A explains how to find your way around FileMaker's built-in help files and Web site. It also covers the vast online community of fans and experts: People are the best resource for fresh ideas and creative solutions. Appendix B lists FileMaker error codes.

Living Examples

Each chapter contains *living examples*—step by step tutorials that help you learn how to build a database by actually doing it. If you take the time to work through these examples at the computer, you'll discover that these tutorials give you invaluable insight into the way professional developers create databases. To help you along, online database files provide sample data, and completed examples against which to check your work.

You can get these files any time from the Missing CD page (see "About Missing-Manuals.com" on page 12). To download, simply click this book's title, and then click the link for the relevant chapter.

Macintosh and Windows

FileMaker Pro works almost precisely the same in its Macintosh and Windows versions. Every button in every dialog box is exactly the same; the software response to every command is identical. In this book, the illustrations get even-handed treatment, alternating between Windows Vista and Mac OS X by chapter.

One of the biggest differences between the Mac and Windows versions is the keystrokes, because the Ctrl key in Windows is the equivalent of the Macintosh ⌘ key.

Whenever this book refers to a key combination, you'll see the Windows keystroke listed first (with + symbols, as is customary in Windows documentation); the Macintosh keystroke follows in parentheses (with symbols, in time-honored Mac fashion). In other words, you may read, "The keyboard shortcut for saving a file is Ctrl+S (⌘-S)."

About → These → Arrows

Throughout this book, and throughout the Missing Manual series, you'll find sentences like this one: "Open your Home → Library → Preferences folder." That's shorthand for a much longer instruction that directs you to open three nested folders in sequence, like this: "In the Finder, choose Go → Home. In your Home folder, you'll find a folder called Library. Open that. Inside the Library window is a folder called Preferences. Double-click to open it, too."

Similarly, this kind of arrow shorthand helps to simplify the business of choosing commands in menus, as shown in Figure I-2.

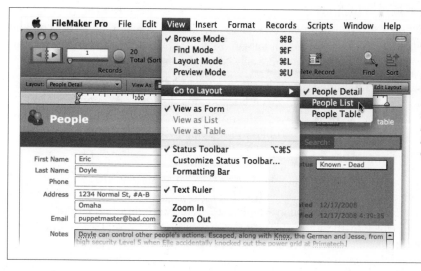

Figure I-2:
When you read in a Missing Manual, "Choose View → Go to Layout → People List," that means: "Click the View menu to open it, in that menu, click Go to Layout, and then, in the resulting submenu, choose People List."

About MissingManuals.com

At *http://missingmanuals.com*, you'll find articles, tips, and updates to *FileMaker Pro 10: The Missing Manual*. In fact, we invite and encourage you to submit such corrections and updates yourself. In an effort to keep the book as up to date and accurate as possible, each time we print more copies of this book, we'll make any confirmed corrections you've suggested. We'll also note such changes on the Web site, so that you can mark important corrections into your own copy of the book, if you like. (Go to *http://missingmanuals.com/feedback*, choose the book's name from the pop-up menu, and then click Go to see the changes.)

Also on our Feedback page, you can get expert answers to questions that come to you while reading this book, write a book review, and find groups for folks who share your interest in FileMaker Pro.

While you're there, sign up for our free monthly email newsletter. Click the "Sign Up for Our Newsletter" link in the left-hand column. You'll find out what's happening in Missing Manual land, meet the authors and editors, see bonus video and book excerpts, and so on.

We'd love to hear your suggestions for new books in the Missing Manual line. There's a place for that on missingmanuals.com, too. And while you're online, you can also register this book at *http://oreilly.com* (you can jump directly to the registration page by going here: *http://tinyurl.com/yo82k3*). Registering means we can send you updates about this book, and you'll be eligible for special offers like discounts on future editions of *FileMaker Pro 10: The Missing Manual*.

Safari® Books Online

 When you see a Safari® Books Online icon on the cover of your favorite technology book, that means it's available online through the O'Reilly Network Safari Bookshelf.

Safari offers a solution that's better than e-books: it's a virtual library that lets you easily search thousands of top tech books, cut and paste code samples, download chapters, and find quick answers when you need the most accurate, current information. Try it for free at *http://safari.oreilly.com*.

Part One:
Getting Started with
FileMaker

1

Working with a Database

FileMaker Pro databases can be as simple as a list of your antique saltshaker collection or as complex as a company-wide system for purchasing, sales, inventory, invoicing, shipping, and customer tracking. But all of them essentially *work* the same way. This chapter gives you a tour of FileMaker's major features and gets you up and running on your very first database.

FileMaker's vast assortment of tools and options can make its window as intimidating as a jumbo-jet cockpit. But the program's menu commands, dialog boxes, keyboard shortcuts, and other options stay largely consistent across all databases, so everything you learn in the next few pages applies to almost every database you'll ever use.

Note: Because a database usually solves a *problem* of some kind, some FileMaker experts call a database a *solution*, as in, "I can create an inventory solution for your bakery, but it's going to cost you some dough." Usually, *database* and *solution* mean the same thing, although the term *solution* sometimes implies a system of several connected databases (more on that in Part 3).

A Very Quick Database Tour

Every FileMaker Pro database has two major working parts. First, the data you're storing. And second, the tools that help you view and manage your data. Since data can change radically from file to file, you'll start this tour focusing on the elements you find in nearly every FileMaker database—the tools. And since the first database you create won't have any data in it yet, the tools take center stage at first.

Those tools—buttons, controls, and pop-up menus—help you fill your database with data. And once you have data in the file, your tools help you find the specific data you need.

Every database window has the same basic structure—the *content area* in the middle is where the data goes, and as you can see in Figure 1-1, a handful of special items around the edges of the window.

Tip: You can download a sample database from the Missing CD page at *http://missingmanuals.com/cds*.

Figure 1-1:
Every database window has the same apparatus around the edges—what's inside the window is up to you. Compare this window with the one shown in Figure 1-2. Both windows have a status toolbar, zoom controls, and a Mode pop-up menu. The content area is the only difference.

Content Area

The content area is where you put the information (data) that makes your database work for you.

When you create a new FileMaker database, you start with something that looks a little like Figure 1-2: It's plain, with just a few boxes for storing data. That's because you haven't added any content yet, and you haven't started arranging your data in a way that mirrors your needs. In Figure 1-3, you can see that data's been entered, and the fields have been rearranged so that they look more like information you'd expect to see outside your database. For example, address fields look like addresses on envelopes. (In Chapter 4, you'll learn more about changing the way your data looks.)

Scroll Bars

Just as with most windows on your computer, you can resize FileMaker's windows. And if you make your window too small to display all the data in the content area, scroll bars appear so you can see the stuff outside the current window size.

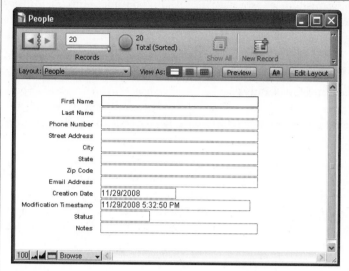

Figure 1-2:
Unlike the stark emptiness shown in Figure 1-1, this database has fields for entering information, and some even have something in them before you start to type (see page 104 for more information on auto-enter fields). These fields are arranged in a column, just the way FileMaker throws them on the screen when you first create them. Compare this screen to Figure 1-3 where the fields are resized and rearranged to create a more pleasing interface to showcase your data.

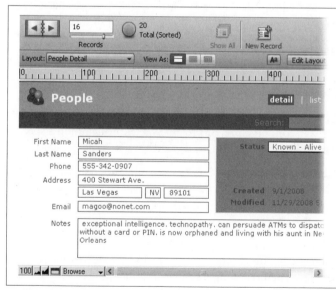

Figure 1-3:
The zoom level in this window is set to 100 percent, but you still can't see everything in the window, as evidenced by the scroll bar along the bottom edge. You've got three options for viewing more information. You can reduce the zoom level so everything fits in the window, or make the window larger (if you have the monitor real estate), or you can drag the scroll bar to scan across the screen.

FileMaker's scroll bars work just like the ones in any other program—drag them to see any areas of the screen that aren't visible. Use your keyboard to scroll up and down. Press Page Up to scroll up one screenful, and Page Down to scroll the other direction.

If your mouse has a scroll wheel, then notice that it scrolls differently based on where you put your mouse cursor. That's FileMaker's *contextual* scrolling. The wheel scrolls through the window when the cursor is inside the window's content area. It scrolls through the records in your database if you run the cursor over the book icon in the status toolbar (see page 19). And if you put your cursor over a field that has a scroll bar (see page 23), then the scroll wheel scrolls through the text in the field.

Zoom Controls

One of FileMaker's neatest features is the *zoom control*. No matter what you're doing, you can always zoom in for a closer look or zoom out for the big picture. This feature works no matter what mode you're in—even when you're previewing a printout.

To use FileMaker's zoom control, click the Zoom In button for a closer look (each click zooms in a little more). You can zoom in up to 400 percent, so that everything is four times bigger than normal. If you click Zoom Out, everything shrinks, to as small as one quarter of its normal size. The Zoom Level shows your current level, and clicking it takes you back to 100 percent. Clicking the Zoom Level a second time returns you to the *last zoom* level you were viewing.

Note: Since you probably don't need to examine the words and numbers in your database on a microscopic level, you'll probably use the zoom control mostly in Preview mode to fit the whole page on the screen, or to adjust the contents of your FileMaker window to the most easily readable size (depending on the resolution of your monitor). You might notice, though, that some fonts don't enlarge well, so they're actually most legible at 100 percent.

Understanding Modes

Each of FileMaker's four *modes* is a work environment unto itself, specially designed to help you view, edit, organize, or present your information in a specific way. Switch modes depending on what you need to do.

- **Browse mode** is the one you see when you first open a database, since it's the one you use most often. In this mode, you can add, change, and view data in your database. Browse view is the view shown in Figure 1-3, and it's where you'll spend most of this chapter.

- When you have a lot of data, looking through it all for a particular bit of information can be tedious. Use **Find mode** to let FileMaker do the looking for you. You tell FileMaker what you're looking for in Find mode; when it's done looking, FileMaker returns you to Browse mode, and shows what it found. For more details on finding specific records, see page 31.

- In addition to using databases (viewing, finding, sorting, adding, and changing data), you can use FileMaker to *build* databases. **Layout mode** is where you design the screens (or *layouts*) that present your database information to best advantage. Part 2 is all about Layout mode.

- Although computers make maintaining and manipulating mountains of information a breeze, you still can't avoid paper. Eventually you'll want to print something out, like a set of mailing labels or a paper backup of all your records. If you're ever curious about what something will look when printed, then switch to **Preview mode**. It shows a one-page-at-a-time view of your data exactly as it'll appear when printed.

The Mode pop-up menu is the easiest way to change modes (Figure 1-1). To use the Mode pop-up menu, just click it, and then choose one of the four modes. Your FileMaker window instantly switches to the new mode. You can also glance at the pop-up menu to see which mode you're currently in. (The Mode pop-up menu is the most popular way to mode-hop, but you have plenty more; see the box on page 20.)

Status toolbar

Changing modes may be confusing when you're getting started, but the Status toolbar gives you constant feedback about the features available in your current mode. So as you switch modes, you see the tools in the Status toolbar changing, too. In fact, the Status toolbar changes so much, you'll soon find that you barely have to glance at the Mode pop-up menu any more, because you can see the tools you need for the job at hand. Figure 1-4 shows the Status toolbar in each of its four modes. When you're familiar with these tools, you can do all the major tasks necessary for any FileMaker database.

Note: Don't be alarmed when the menus across the top of your screen change a bit when you switch modes. That's just FileMaker being smart. Some commands aren't useful in some modes, so the program doesn't clutter up your screen—or your brain space—with menus when you don't need them. For example, the Insert and Format menus change from black to gray (meaning *unavailable*) when you enter Find mode. The Request menu, though, appears *only* in Find mode.

FileMaker also gives you several ways to find out which mode you're *in*. The Status toolbar, Mode pop-up menu, and Mode tabs reveal the current mode, and the View menu indicates the current mode with a checkmark. So when you return to FileMaker after checking email, you've got plenty of ways to reorient yourself. See Figure 1-4 for pictures of some of these mode-changing tools.

Opening and Closing Database Files

Each database you create with FileMaker Pro is stored in a *file* on your hard drive—just like your Microsoft Word documents, Excel spreadsheets, and all the PowerPoint presentations you've ever created. This file contains all the information about how the database is structured, plus all the information stored inside it, which means you can open, close, copy, or back up a database as you would any other file. But if you need a bit more explanation, then this section explains how to do those tasks, and some quirks that are particular to FileMaker files.

Figure 1-4:
Use this illustration as a cheat sheet for locating all FileMaker's most commonly used features. In Browse mode (top), you can click the "New record" button, and then start entering data. Find mode (second from top) lets you look for records—say all your clients who live in Iowa—with all the tools you need to create brand-new requests or to select a recent or a Saved Find. Or if you inspect a report before you print it using Preview mode (third from top), then you get handy tools for saving the report as a PDF or for exporting the data to Excel, as well as plain old printing. The Edit Layout button lets you change the landscape of your database with access to text, field, and object formatting features (bottom).

UP TO SPEED

Changing Modes

Switching between FileMaker's four modes is so common that you have many ways to do it. The Mode pop-up menu (see Figure 1-1) is just one way. The Status toolbar, along the top of your screen, is convenient if your mouse is already up there. Or, from FileMaker's View menu, you can pick a mode.

The keyboard shortcuts are speediest of all:

- Press Ctrl+B (⌘-B) to switch to Browse mode.

- Press Ctrl+F (⌘-F) to switch to Find mode.

- Press Ctrl+L (⌘-L) to switch to Layout mode.

- Press Ctrl+U (⌘-U) to switch to Preview mode.

If you ever forget these shortcuts, check the View menu to refresh your memory.

Opening a Database

To open a database, open FileMaker Pro, and then choose File → Open Database.
FileMaker's Quick Start window appears. There you'll find tools to help you create
new databases or open existing ones. Select the file with which you want to work
(see Figure 1-5). If you prefer, you can find the file using Windows Explorer (Windows) or the Finder (Mac OS X), and then double-click its icon.

When you open a database, you see one or more windows on your screen. If you
open the People database that you downloaded at the beginning of this chapter,
then you see one database window. (See page 38 for more information on multiple windows.)

Figure 1-5:
*FileMaker's Open File dialog box is
pretty standard stuff, but notice
the pop-up menu near the bottom
left that helps you find specific
kinds of files on your hard drive. If
you choose "FileMaker Pro files"
as shown here, then all non-
FileMaker files in the window
below are grayed out, so you can
easily ignore them as you're
looking for the database you want
to open.*

Closing a Database

To close a database, choose File → Close or press Ctrl+W (⌘-W). This command
actually closes a window, and if your database has only one window, you've closed
the whole database. But you can open more than one window into a single database (see page 38), and if you do, then you need to close each window individually
before the file is closed. When you have more than one database open, you can't
always easily tell which windows go with each database.

If you're not sure what to close, you have an easy way to close all the windows in
all the databases you currently have open. Press Alt (Windows) or Option (Mac),
and then click the trusty File menu. In Windows, the command is still called Close,
but despite the name, it too closes all open windows. In Mac OS X, the Close command is gone, replaced by a more powerful Close All. Choose it, and FileMaker
closes all its open windows, which also closes all your open databases.

Adding Records to Your Database

Now that you understand the basic components of a FileMaker database, it's time to start adding your own information. Whether your database contains information about individual persons, eBay auctions, products you sell, student grades, or whatever, FileMaker always thinks of that information in individual chunks called *records*. Each record contains everything the database knows about that person, auction, product, or student.

Since you need to store many smaller pieces of information in each record (like a person's phone number, address, birthday, and so on), FileMaker can give each record an almost infinite number of *fields*—the specific bits of data that define each record and make it unique.

For example, each person in a database of magazine subscribers gets her own record. First name, last name, phone number, street address, city, state, Zip code, and her subscription's expiration date are all examples of fields each record can include.

The techniques in this section work the same way whether you're creating a new database for the first time, or adding to an existing one.

Note: All records in a database must contain the same fields, but that doesn't mean you have to fill them all in. For instance, in your saltshaker collection database, you might not know the year a particular shaker was manufactured, so you can leave that field blank.

Creating a Record

Adding a new record is simple: Choose Records → New Record or press Ctrl+N (⌘-N). (Since you'll be creating lots of records in your FileMaker career, memorize this keyboard shortcut.)

Note: When you're adding new records, you must be in Browse mode (see page 18).

Entering Data

Once you create a new record, you can enter information about the person you want to keep track of—that's where those fields come in handy. To enter information in any field in a record, just click it, and then type. What to type? As Figure 1-6 illustrates, each field in this database has a label to its left indicating the type of information the field contains. Each field's border has turned to dotted lines—a confirmation that you're doing data entry.

Note: A label is just a bit of text that appears near a field. It's meant to help you figure out what kind of data belongs in the field. See the box on page 24 for more on recognizing fields and labels.

Figure 1-6:
Fields can look like just about anything, but in the People database, they're pretty simple. When you click in the content area, dotted borders indicate the fields you can edit. The field you're currently editing gets a solid border. With the miracle of conditional formatting (page 206), the fields in the People database are shaded as you type in them, which helps keep you oriented when you're entering information in a screen full of fields.

Moving between fields

Efficient data entry is all about typing something in a field, and then moving right to the next field. Lather, rinse, repeat. You can use the mouse to click the next field, but unless you're eager to burn that extra half a calorie, you may want to try a quicker, less exercise-intensive way, like the following:

- Press the Tab key to move to the next field. If you're not in any field, then the Tab key puts you in the first field.

- Press Shift-Tab to move to the previous field. This time, if you're not in any field, then FileMaker puts you in the *last* field.

Note: If you're wondering who decides which field is *next* or *previous*, dig this: *You* do. When you design a database, you get to set the *Tab order*, or the order FileMaker follows when you press Tab or Shift-Tab to move among fields. See page 184 for details.

Fields for Lots of Text

FileMaker fields can hold *a lot* of text. Technically, each field is limited to two gigabytes of data *per record*, which is a fancy way of saying, "Way more than you'll ever need."

To see for yourself, in the People database, click in the Notes field. When you do, a scroll bar appears at the right side of the field. If you type lots of notes, then you can scroll through them. (When you design a database, you get to decide which fields have scroll bars, as discussed on page 166.)

You can enter text into a field in all the usual ways, like typing on your keyboard or pasting text you copied from another field or another program.

The Many Faces of a Field

Fields always appear inside the content area, but other than that, they can have amazing variety. FileMaker Pro's content area is one place you can let your creative urges go wild. You can design your database to make fields look almost any way you want. A field can have a label to the right of—or below or above—where you enter text, or no label at all.

A field can be white, blue, green, or any other color. The same goes for the border around a field. In fact, if mystery is your thing, then you can make your field invisible—no label, no border, and no color. (But here's a tip: If you want

happy database users, then make sure they can tell where the fields are and what goes in them.)

Usually, if you click in a blank space in the content area, then all the fields appear with the dotted outline shown in Figure 1-6, but you can't count on this (you can turn this feature off, as described on page 236). So don't expect every field to look the same.

See Chapter 3 for more detail on customizing and beautifying the fields in your database.

Note: Even if a field doesn't have scroll bars, you can still add lots of text. As you type, FileMaker just makes the field grow to hold whatever you type. When you leave the field, it shrinks back to its normal size, hiding anything that goes outside the edges. Don't worry, though, the text reappears when you click back into the field.

Reverting a record

After you edit a record, you may decide you've made a mistake and wish you could put things back they way they were before. That's no problem for the Revert Record command. Its purpose is simple: Choose Records → Revert Record, and FileMaker throws away any changes you made since you first entered the record. This trick comes in handy when you accidentally modify a field by bumping into the keyboard, or realize you accidentally entered Steve Jobs' address in Bill Gates' record. Just revert the record, and you can be confident that whatever you did has been forgotten.

Commitment, or on the Record

To get *out* of all fields—so you're not in any field at all—press Enter (use the one on your numeric keypad, not the one that makes line breaks), or, in the content area, click a blank spot. This process is called *committing* the record. No, you're not sending the record away for a little quiet time; rather, you're telling FileMaker you're ready to commit to the changes you've made. (If you don't want to commit to the changes you've made, then you can choose Records → Revert Record to get out of all fields and discard those changes. This command is explained more above.)

When you first click a field, you've *opened* the record. Imagine an old-fashioned file cabinet, where you have to open someone's file before you can change something in it.

As long as you have a record open, you're *in* the record. You can be in only one record at any given moment, and that record is said to be *active*. Rounding out this technobabble, when you've committed the record, you're *on* the record but you're not *in* the record. Believe it or not, getting this terminology straight will make things easier later on.

The Revert Record command is available only when you're in a record (see the box on page 24) *and* you've made changes. If you don't have the record open, or you haven't made any changes since you last committed the record, then the Revert Record command is grayed out.

Note: Committing a record is easy: You just press Enter or click somewhere in the window, and File-Maker dutifully saves the record without a peep. Once this happens, you can no longer choose the Revert Record command. (How's that for commitment?) If you want a little more control, then you can tell File-Maker to ask you for confirmation before committing a record. You'll learn how to do that on page 236.

Editing a record

You're not stuck with the data you enter in a record if something changes. For example, when people move, you can change their address data. Just click in the field that changes, select the data, and then start typing the new information. (If you try this on the sample People.fp7 file provided on the Missing CD page, then you'll notice that a field called Modified changes when you commit the record's changes. You'll learn what that field is for later.)

Tip: To edit a record, you may need to find it first. See page31for details on the Find feature.

Duplicating a record

While no two people are alike, it may not always seem that way from their contact information. For instance, if you want to include three people from the same city in your database, the data in the City field is the same for each person.

The Email and Phone fields won't be the same, but they may be close. It's time for a little organized laziness: Instead of making new blank records and retyping all that stuff, just choose Records → Duplicate Record (see Figure 1-7). FileMaker displays a new record containing all the same information as the record you chose to duplicate. (FileMaker copies everything from the first record into a new one for you.) Now you can just edit the information that needs to be changed.

Tip: Be sure you don't accidentally leave in the first person's email address or phone number, lest a message or phone call get misdirected later.

Deleting Records

Getting rid of a record you don't need is a breeze. FileMaker Pro gives you three commands that let you delete one record, a group of records, or even *all* the records in your database.

Figure 1-7:
If you go looking for your duplicated record later, you may be surprised where you find it. Here, the records weren't sorted, so the new record is added at the end of your database, no matter where the original started out. So if you have seven records in your database and you duplicate record #3, then the duplicated record is #8. Notice the thin black line just to the left of the last record in this list. That's FileMaker's way of telling you which record is active. See the box on page 39 to see what happens when you duplicate a record while records are sorted.

Warning: You can't undo deleting a record, since FileMaker saves changes automatically (see page 44). So when you delete a record (or all the records in a database), make sure you're ready to part with the information.

- **One record.** Choose Records → Delete Record to delete the record you're currently on. FileMaker asks if you're sure you want to delete the record, lest you accidentally send, say, your best client's address to the trash bin. If you've indeed written her—or anyone else—out of your life, then, in the message box, simply click Delete to complete the purge.

- **Multiple records.** FileMaker has a helpful command that trashes any group of records of your choosing. Before you use this command, you have to tell FileMaker which records to delete. You do that with the Find command (page 31). Then once you have the set of records to be deleted, choose Records → Delete Found Records. Again, FileMaker gives you a chance to change your mind with a message box that tells you how many records you have in your found set, and asks you to click either the Delete All or the Cancel button.

- **All records.** In some cases, you may want to delete all the records in a database. Maybe a colleague wants an empty copy of your database for his own use. Or perhaps your database holds data you just don't need anymore, like test results you're about to reproduce. You can easily accomplish complete record elimination with two menu commands: Just choose Records → Show All Records, and then choose Records → Delete All Records.

Note: In reality, the Delete Found Set and Delete All Records commands are one and the same. But File-Maker knows whether you're in a subset of your database or looking at all the records, and changes the wording of the menu command accordingly. It's just another bit of feedback that helps you get the results you need.

Once you get used to deleting records, you may get tired of FileMaker's nagging you about being sure you want to delete. You can bypass the dialog box by holding down the Shift (Windows) or Option (Mac) key when you choose Records → Delete Record. Or, if you're a fan of keyboard shortcuts, you can type Ctrl+Shift+E (⌘-Option-E) to get the same results.

Understanding Browse Mode Error Messages

As you just learned in the section on deleting records, FileMaker gives you frequent feedback about what you're doing. The program's not being a control freak (although after the umpteenth dialog box it's understandable if you feel that way). FileMaker's just trying to keep you informed so you can make good choices. So you sometimes see dialog boxes that FileMaker calls *error messages*. Unlike the Delete warning, when you get an error message, all you can do is click OK. There's no real choice to make, but you usually have to take some kind of action after you've dismissed the error message.

No records present

When you create a database, FileMaker creates the first record for you, so you can start typing right away. But when you start a database using a template (page 92) or if you've deleted all the records in the database so you can start fresh, you're not so lucky. If you try clicking in a field, you get the error message shown in Figure 1-8. Luckily, that error message tells you exactly what you need to do: Choose File → New Record first.

This minor annoyance is forgivable, since it's so easy to work around (and frankly, most databases don't stay empty for long). Unfortunately, another common error message is twice as annoying.

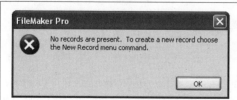

Figure 1-8:
It's annoying to start typing only to get an error message before the first character is dry on the page. But FileMaker's just trying to tell you something akin to "Put some paper in this typewriter before you start typing madly away." (You do remember typewriters, don't you?)

Typing in a record

If you try typing something *before* you've clicked in a field, then FileMaker warns you with the box shown in Figure 1-9. It may seem overly protective to warn you that you're not actually entering anything anywhere, but in this day of multitasking and distractions, it's helpful to know that FileMaker doesn't let your information disappear into space as you type it.

So, annoyingly, you have to dismiss an error message every time you accidentally bump a key, but you can't get rid of the error message for good. Just remember that you have to be *in* a field before you can start typing. (And take that book off your laptop's keyboard, eh?)

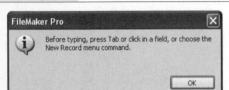

Figure 1-9:
In this communiqué, FileMaker asks you to tell it where to put all that data your 110 wpm typing power is delivering. Until you click in a field, your information has nowhere to go.

UP TO SPEED

Lost in the Wilderness

The sample file you're using in this chapter has an assortment of *buttons* in its content area (like the Delete buttons in Figure 1-7). These buttons can look like tabs, text links, or just about anything else (a few even look like buttons). A click on one of these may show you things you're not familiar with—maybe even make you feel like you've lost your place.

To avoid an accidental left turn when you try to commit the record, try not to click a button. Instead click somewhere in the empty white area around the fields.

If you've already clicked a button, and now you're lost in the wilderness, finding your way back doesn't require a trail of breadcrumbs.

Just follow these steps, in order:

- If you see a button in the Status Toolbar called Continue, click it. (If you don't see that button, don't worry—just skip to the next step.)

- If the Mode pop-up menu doesn't say Browse, click it, and then, from the menu that appears, choose Browse.

- In the Status toolbar, beside Layout, you should see a pop-up menu. Choose People Detail to get back to the main layout.

You should now be back in your comfort zone. Phew!

Navigating Your Database

Once you've entered a few dozen—or a few hundred—records into your database, the next challenge is to get back to a specific record. But first, you need to learn how to *navigate* through the records in the database. Hint: It's not called Browse mode for nothing, you know. The Status toolbar gives you several tools that help you get where you need to go.

Tip: As you go through this section on navigating, it helps to have a database open in front of you so you can follow along and try some of these techniques. You can download a sample on the Missing CD page at *http://missingmanuals.com/cds*.

Navigating Record by Record

In the People database, you can add as many records as you want. To tell File-Maker which record you want to look at, you have three options:

- The **book icon** lets you flip from record to record one at a time. Pretend your database is a book, with each record on its own page. To get to the next record, click the right-hand page. To go back, click the left-hand page. If you can't go any further in one direction, then the appearance of the icon's "page" changes, as shown in Figure 1-10.

- The **slider** is kind of a turbo-charged version of the book icon. Instead of clicking once for each record, you can advance through a bunch of records by dragging. If you know approximately where you want to go (like "around halfway" or "about one-third from the end"), then the slider is the quickest way to get there. The slider is most handy when you want to get to the beginning or the end of the database. In that case, just drag the slider as far as it goes in either direction.

- The **Current Record** indicator serves two purposes. First, it shows you which record you're on. Second, if you know which record you *want* to be on, then you can simply type in the record number to jump to it. Beside the Current Record, the Found Set display also shows you how many records you have in your database.

Note: All navigation methods let you move within what FileMaker calls a *found set*, which lets you look at a specific set of records at one time. Learn more about finds and found sets on page 31.

Book
icon
Current
record
Pie
chart
Found set
display
Status
toolbar
14
14 / 19
Found (Sorted)
Records
Layout
bar
Layout: People Detail
View As:
People
Layout
pop-up
Slider
View
buttons

Figure 1-10:
In addition to displaying the controls for switching records, the Status toolbar indicates where you are in the database. You're looking at the seventh record in the found set of records. And the pie chart tool tells you that your current found set is showing 14 of the 19 total records in the database. If you click the pie chart, then the found set switches to show you the five records that aren't in the current found set.

Numbers Sometimes Lie

As you create the records in your database, FileMaker numbers each new record as you add it—with a record number that appears next to the book icon (see Figure 1-10). You may think that this number is a great way to locate a particular record later: "I need to give Jim over at Dunder-Mifflin a call to reorder supplies. I put his contact information in record #79. I'll just go to that number." Since record numbers may change as you add and delete records from a database, or if you sort them in a different order (page 36), the record number isn't necessarily a reliable way to identify one particular record.

For instance, if you delete the first record in a database, every record below it moves up one slot. Now, what used to be record #2 becomes record #1, what used to be #3 is now #2, and so on. Jim could've transferred out of the Scranton branch before you find his record that way. If you want to assign every record its own number, and have that number stay with the record forever, then you want *serial numbers*. Serial numbers are discussed on page 108.

Keyboard Shortcuts

FileMaker also has a few keyboard shortcuts to make record navigation painless. If you haven't used a database program before, then you'll notice that some keys act in ways you may not expect—like the Enter key, as described below. Still, spending a little time getting used to using these keystrokes saves you hours of time down the road.

- To go to the next record, press **Ctrl (⌘)–Down arrow**.

- To move to the previous record, press **Ctrl (⌘)–Up arrow**.

- To activate the Current Record indicator without using the mouse, press **Esc**. Now type a record number and press Enter to go to that record. (This shortcut works only when you're not in the record; see the box on page 24.)

- Pressing the **Enter** key *commits* the record, rather than inserting a new line in a field, as you may expect based on what the Enter key does in other programs. To insert a new line in FileMaker, press **Return**.

***

Note: Some keyboards don't have a Return key—instead, two keys are labeled Enter. In this case, the Enter key that's near the number keypad commits the record, while the other (normal) Enter key enters a blank line in the field.

***

- Pressing **Tab** moves you from one field to another. (To indent a line, you have to *type* a tab character into a field, by pressing Ctrl+Tab [Option-Tab].)

Finally, bear in mind that you can change which key moves the cursor on a field-by-field basis when you're designing a database, as you'll learn in Chapter 3. For instance, FileMaker lets you decide that Return—not Tab—should move you from field to field. If you make that choice, then Tab types a *tab* into a field, and Return doesn't insert a blank line. Unfortunately, you can't tell which key does what by looking at a field; you just have to try some of these keys to find out.

Finding Records

When your database really gains some size, you realize that even keyboard shortcuts aren't the fastest way to get to the record you want. You need to *tell* FileMaker to pull up the record for you. For example, you have a season ticket holder whose last name is Bennet, who just renewed her subscription for a year. You need to find her record and make the update, and you don't have all day.

Once you have hundreds of records in your People database, it could take ages to find the one you want by clicking the book icon. Instead, switch to Find mode, and then tell FileMaker what you're looking for, and the program finds it for you. This section explains how to use Find mode to search for a record or group of records, and how to edit your search if you don't get the results you anticipated. (If you downloaded the example file discussed on page 16, you can open it, and try out Find mode now.)

You can get to Find mode in four ways:

- From the Mode pop-up menu, select Find.

- Choose View → Find Mode.

- In the Status toolbar, click the Find tool.

- Press Ctrl+F (⌘-F).

The Mode pop-up menu, Mode tabs, and View menu all indicate what mode you're currently in. Once you're in Find mode, your window should look like Figure 1-11.

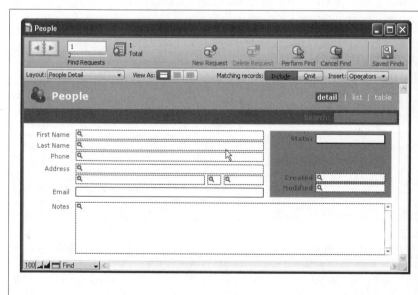

Figure 1-11:
Because Find mode looks so much like Browse mode, FileMaker gives you lots of feedback about the mode change. Instead of data, the fields now show magnifying glass icons to remind you that you're typing search criteria, not new information. The borders around the fields have a dashed line instead of Browse mode's dotted line. Notice that the Status toolbar has changed. Now you have a Perform Find button, and even better, a Saved Finds tool that lets you store frequently used find criteria. That way, you don't have to remember and recreate complicated finds. (See page 62 for details.)

Even though it may look like you're editing records in Find mode, you're actually not—you're editing *requests* instead. Requests are just descriptions of data you're looking for, so FileMaker can find them for you.

To make a request, enter enough information to tell FileMaker what you want. It then looks for records that have the same information you entered, much like searches you conduct using other programs, like a Google or Dogpile search.

Performing a find

To find every person in your People database whose last name is Sanders, do this:

1. **Choose View → Find Mode (or use any of the other methods described above to get to Find mode).**

   Magnifying glass icons show up in all the fields you can use for searching, indicating that you're in Find mode.

2. **Into the Last Name field, type Sanders.**

   This part works just like Browse mode: Click the field, and then type. (Remember, you aren't editing a record—you're editing a *request*.)

3. **In the Status toolbar, click the Perform Find button. (Or choose Requests → Perform Find, or press the Enter key.)**

   FileMaker finds all records that have "Sanders" in the Last Name field, and then puts you back in Browse mode so you can flip through the found set.

You can see how many records you found by looking at the count in the Status toolbar, as shown in Figure 1-12.

Figure 1-12:
After a find, the Status toolbar shows how many records match your request. Here, FileMaker found three records with the last name of Sanders. You can flip through these three records to your heart's content, but you can't see any records not in your found set. To see the other records, click the pie chart or choose Records → Show Omitted Only. FileMaker swaps your found set, and shows you the other records in your database. Then, when you're ready to look at all your records again, click the Show All button. If you can't see the Show All button, stretch your window. The Status toolbar drops some tools in smaller windows, but they reappear when the window's wide enough.

Tip: If your find didn't come out exactly the way you wanted, don't just return to Find mode. If you do, then you have an empty request, and you have to start all over again. Instead, choose Records → Modify Last Find, which takes you to Find mode, and then displays the request you used last. Now you can make any necessary modifications, and perform the find again.

FastMatch

In the previous find examples, you had FileMaker search for records by telling it what to look for. But sometimes you're already looking at a record that has the right information in it—you just want to find more that match.

Say you need a list of everybody in the People file who has a superpower. Flip to any record with the word "superpower" in the Notes field. Drag to select the word "superpower". Right-click (Control-click) the highlighted text.

From the shortcut menu that pops up, select Find Matching Records (see Figure 1-13). Shazaam! Faster than you can say "Ordinary people," FileMaker shows you a found set of all your contacts with superpowers.

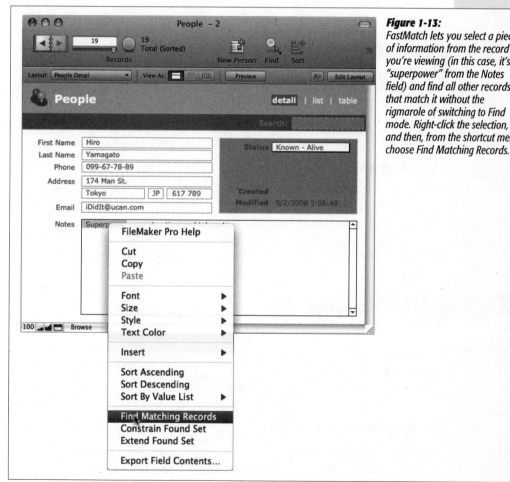

Figure 1-13:
FastMatch lets you select a piece of information from the record you're viewing (in this case, it's "superpower" from the Notes field) and find all other records that match it without the rigmarole of switching to Find mode. Right-click the selection, and then, from the shortcut menu, choose Find Matching Records.

Understanding Find Mode Error Messages

Just as it does in Browse mode, FileMaker warns you if something goes wrong when you're trying to find specific records. You might see three main types of errors. Read on to see why each one occurs, and what you need to do to correct the error.

No records match

If FileMaker can't find any records that match your request, then you see the message pictured in Figure 1-14. You might see this error if you're looking for a record that doesn't exist in your database, or maybe you've misspelled the search criteria. Click the Cancel button to return to Browse mode, or Modify Find to try again. You end up back in Find mode, with your original search terms showing so you can check your typing or enter new search terms.

Figure 1-14:
If FileMaker can't find any records that match what you're looking for, then you see the message pictured here. If that's all you needed to know, just click Cancel, and you wind up back in Browse mode as though you'd never performed a find.

No valid criteria

If you don't type anything into any of the fields before you click Perform Find, then FileMaker doesn't try to find records with all empty fields. Instead, it warns you that you didn't enter any search terms. But it uses the terms you see in Figure 1-15. Just as with the No Records Match error, you can click Cancel to return to Browse mode, or you can click Modify Find to try again.

Figure 1-15:
You see this message if you don't enter search terms in at least one field before you click the Perform Find button. Sometimes, though, you might really want to find records that don't have data in them. In that case, you can enter "==" in a field. FileMaker finds blank fields, and now you can start entering the missing data in those records. Chapter 2 gives you lots more detail on special search symbols and other tricky finds.

Accidental data entry in Find mode

Even with the magnifying glasses (Figure 1-11), Find mode looks so much like Browse mode that you can easily forget which mode you're in. It's a real drag if you *think* you're in Browse mode, and you start entering data. You can make quite a bit of progress entering records and never realize your mistake. When you finally do figure it out, it's a rude awakening: None of the requests you've just entered can be turned into real records; you must reenter them all in Browse mode.

FileMaker gives you a warning if it thinks you're entering data in Find mode. See Figure 1-16 to see what you're in for. If you create more than 10 find requests while in Find mode, then FileMaker shows this message. If you've been entering data in Find mode by mistake (at least you're finding out now, not after you've typed for 3 hours), just click No, switch to Browse mode, and then start over with your data entry. If you know you're in Find mode, and you really want to add all these requests, then just click Yes. FileMaker doesn't bother you again.

Figure 1-16:
If you create more than 10 requests in Find Mode, then FileMaker wonders if you're actually trying to enter data. If you're setting up a magnificently complex find, then you may be annoyed. Just click Yes and keep up the good work. But if you just forgot to switch back to Browse mode, then this warning can save you lots of lost keystrokes.

UP TO SPEED

Refining Your Finds

When FileMaker looks for records, it expects them to match your find request *exactly*. For example, if you put "Mohinder" in the First Name field, and "Suresh" in the Last Name field, FileMaker finds only Mohinder Suresh. Mohinder Ashtapur doesn't cut it, and neither does Arup Suresh. FileMaker ignores any fields that are empty in your request, so it doesn't matter what Mohinder's title is, because you didn't include a Title field in your find request.

Although FileMaker insists that every field in each found record match each field in your request, the data *inside* each field doesn't have to be a perfect match. The next chapter explains how FileMaker decides when a match is good enough, and how you can change its decision-making process.

Finding the right records can be a real balancing act. Be too specific and you may not find anything at all; be too vague and you find more than you can handle.

Here are some rules of thumb for creating find requests:

- Since FileMaker matches field values flexibly, you can often save typing and improve accuracy by being brief. For example, if you're looking for someone named "Rufus Xavier Sarsaparilla," just type *ruf* in the First Name field and *sar* in the Last Name field. Chances are you'll find the right guy, and you don't have to worry about spelling out the whole name.

- Enter data only in fields you're sure you need. For example, even if you know Rufus lives in Montana, you don't have to put Montana in the State field in your find request.

- If you find more records than you wanted, just go back to Find mode and enter data in more fields to narrow the search. Better yet, read Chapter 2, where you'll learn about the many powers of Find mode.

Sorting Records

Your Rolodex is limited to an alphabetical (by last name) arrangement, but a File-Maker database has no such limitation. You can sort the records in any order you want, as often as you want. You can even do a sort within a sort, as you'll see later in this section.

Understanding Sorting

Don't confuse sorting with finding. When you sort, FileMaker doesn't change the records in your found set. Instead, it rearranges the records you're viewing into a new order. For example, if you need a short-term loan, you might sort your contacts by annual income. FileMaker still shows all your contacts, but with Uncle Moneybags at the very top of the list.

The process always begins the same way: Choose Records → Sort Records or click the Sort button in the Status toolbar. You see the Sort Records dialog box shown in Figure 1-17, with all available fields listed on the left. You tell FileMaker how to sort by moving a field to the list on the right.

Note: By "available," FileMaker means only the fields showing on the current layout. If the field you want to sort by isn't in the list, then, from the pop-up menu above the list, choose the second item. Instead of Current Layout, the option starts with Current Table. (Learn more about tables in Chapter 7.)

Figure 1-17:
The Sort Records dialog box offers a lot of options, but the two lists on top and the first two radio buttons are critical to every sort you'll ever do in FileMaker. You pick the fields you want to sort by and the order in which they should be sorted, and then click Sort. That's the essence of any sort, from the simple to the most complex.

Here's how to sort your found set of records by Last Name:

1. **In the Status toolbar, click the Sort button. Or choose Records → Sort, or press Ctrl+S (⌘-S).**

   The Sort Records dialog box (Figure 1-17) appears.

2. **From the list on the left, select the Last Name field, and then click Move. (Or double-click the field name.)**

   The field name appears in the Sort Order list on the right.

3. **Click the Sort button.**

FileMaker sorts the records in the traditional alphabetical-by-last-name order.

You can browse the sorted found set using any of your favorite navigation methods.

Beyond the Simple Sort

FileMaker figures that if you've sorted your data once, you'll probably want to sort it the same way again, so once you've done a sort, the dialog box retains the last sort order you set up. That's a nice shortcut if you want to repeat the last sort, but if you want something new, just click the Clear All button, and then start with a clean slate.

Each sort field has an *order* associated with it. The most frequently used are "Ascending order" (Alphabetical from A to Z) and "Descending order" (Alphabetical from Z to A). You can click one of these radio buttons *before* you click Move, and the field has the setting by the time it makes it to the Sort Order list. More often than not, though, you move the field over before you think about the order. In this case, from the Sort Order list, just click to select the field, and then pick the order. Each field in the Sort Order list shows a bar chart icon representing the order assigned to it, which matches the icons next to each radio button.

If you change your mind and don't want to sort after all, click Cancel, and File-Maker forgets everything you've done while in this window.

The Status toolbar lets you know if your records are sorted (no surprise there). Below the Record Count, it says Sorted if you've done a sort, and Unsorted otherwise. (See the box on page 39 to learn more about sorting.)

Multiple Sort Fields

FileMaker lets you pick more than one field to sort by, which comes in handy when you have lots of records with the same data in some fields. For example, you might often have several people in your database with the same last name. If you just sort by last name, there's no telling in which order the like-named people fall. In this case, it would be ideal to sort by last name first and then, when the last names are the same, break the tie using the first name.

To set this up, simply add the First Name field to the Sort dialog box after the Last Name field. The sort field order is important: The first field you want to sort by (called the *primary* sort field) has to be at the top of the list, followed by each sub-sort field in order. In this example, the Last Name field is the primary sort field, followed by First Name. You can see the results of this multiple sort in Figure 1-18. If you don't click the fields in the right order in the Sort dialog box, then File-Maker provides a convenient way to shuffle them around. Drag the arrow to the left of any field in the sort list to rearrange it as needed.

Tip: If you change your mind about one of the fields in the Sort Order list, click it. The Move button changes to say Clear, and a click removes the selected field from the list.

Figure 1-18:
The records in this window are sorted by Last Name and First Name. The last names are in alphabetical order, and when several people have the same last name, they appear together alphabetized by First Name. The Status toolbar shows you're viewing Sorted (as opposed to Unsorted) records. Once you've done a sort, the Sort dialog box remembers the sort order, so if you forget how the records are sorted, just press Ctrl+S (⌘-S) to check.

Multifield sorts can get as complicated as you like. Sometimes, they're a little tricky to get right, particularly if you're sorting by more than two or three fields (Figure 1-18 shows a report that uses multiple sorts).

If you do a multifield sort and then discover you didn't get quite what you expected (because you had the fields in the wrong order), just choose Records → Sort Records again, move the fields in the Sort Order list to the right places, and then click Sort.

Note: Sorting records when you're creating a report can change the way FileMaker tallies data. See page 279 for info on creating layout parts that use sorted data to make sophisticated reports.

Same Database, Different Views

So far, you've spent all your time in the same People window, slogging through one record at a time. It'd be handy to see several records at once, or maybe even to compare data by viewing it twice on your screen. This section will help you find ways to break out of the single window, single view mindset.

FREQUENTLY ASKED QUESTION

Feeling Out of Sorts?

When I haven't sorted my records, the Status toolbar says "Unsorted". What order is that, exactly? Is it completely random?

Remain calm. When the records are unsorted, they're in creation order. The first record you ever created (and haven't deleted yet) shows first, followed by the next one you created, and so on. Creation order is FileMaker's natural order for the records. Once you sort the records, they stay in that order until you sort again or explicitly unsort them. (In the Sort dialog box, use the Unsort button.)

Whew, that's a relief. But if I create a new record while I'm viewing a list that's sorted, I can't always tell where the new record will appear.

Yes, that can be disorienting. The record lands in a different place in the list depending on how your data is sorted. If it's sorted by Last Name only, and then you duplicate a record that has a lot of the same last names (Sanders, in the People database), then the new record appears at the end of all the Sanders records. But if you have a multisort (page 37) by Last Name and then by First Name, then the duplicate record appears right after the original. In other words, FileMaker creates the new record *within* the sort order you've chosen.

That's not all, though. If you edit the data in the first name or last name field, then FileMaker resorts the list as soon as you commit the record. The record you've just edited stays active, but you may have to scroll your list to see where its landed. Test this out by duplicating the Jessica Sanders record while the data is sorted by Last Name and then First Name. Then change "Sanders" to "Anders" and watch what happens.

Viewing a List

In the People file, you've probably noticed the "detail" text near the content area's upper right. Turns out, that's giving you feedback about the data you're currently viewing. If you click on the word "list" (it's written in lowercase letters just because the database developers like it that way), then the scene switches to a list of all the records you're currently viewing. When you're in this new list view, you can click the Show All button, or perform a Find or sort the records.

Tip: The word you're clicking is called a "button," which is just a tool that you can configure yourself. See page 267 to learn how you can create custom buttons for your database. You can also see the View menu for the menu commands that switch views of your data.

Viewing a Table

Since it's a database, FileMaker has lots of power that spreadsheets don't have. But lots of people prefer to see their data in columns and rows that look like a spreadsheet. That's what the "table" button does for you. Click on the button to view your found set in Table view, and then see page 47 for more information on how you can customize this view of your data.

Creating a New Window

At any time, you can get yourself another window by choosing Window → New Window. You get an exact copy of the window you were just looking at. It's the same size and shape, just offset a little down and to the right of the original. And it has the exact same set of records you were browsing, along with the same current record. What's the big deal, you ask? The big deal is that you can switch to another record or do something completely different in the new window, without affecting what's displayed in the first one.

When you have multiple windows open, you can change most of the settings you've seen so far for each window. For example, if you want to compare two contacts side by side, then you can show one contact in each window.

Note (Windows Only): If your original window is maximized, the new window lands right on top of it, not to the lower right.

Multiple windows are useful when you're working with one set of found records (see page 32) but you need to do another search. You can perform a find in a new window without disrupting your work in the original window. Say you've been fiddling with the Find command to come up with a list of all your contacts with superpowers, and then suddenly get the paperwork you need to edit the detail on another record. Although you can enter data on the list layout, all the fields you need may not be available. Just create a new window, and then look up the record you want to edit (see Figure 1-19). Your superpower group is safe and sound in the first window. (See the box on page 43 to see what problems can happen when you edit the same record in multiple windows.)

Note: If you have two windows open, both of them *are* connected in one way. If you edit the data in one window, the changes show up in the other window (or every window you have open, if you're working with multiple windows). Since FileMaker's windows display only the records in your database, a second window doesn't mean you have a second database—instead, both windows share the same data.

Hiding Windows

If you have a window just the way you want it (for example, showing a list of customers Assistant Manager Dwight Schrute left behind when he went to work for Staples), but it's in your way onscreen, then you can *hide* it instead of closing it. When you close a window after using the Find command, your results disappear. Hiding a window makes it disappear from your screen, but keeps the information stashed in a handy place in your computer so you can get it back if you want it. It's a great timesaver when your screen is crowded—or when you want to keep prying eyes away from your information.

Figure 1-19:
*The back window shows
several records in the List
View layout's People
database. But the
window in the front
shows one record in
Detail view. You can also
tell that the front window
was spawned from the
back window because its
name has a "-2" added
to it. You can flip through
records in the front
window in their detailed
glory and leave your list
intact in the background.*

To hide the current window (that's the one displayed at the front of your screen),
choose Window → Hide Window. To bring it back again, choose Window → Show
Window, and then, from the list, pick the window you want. In order for this to
work, you have to remember the *name* of the window you hid (its name appears in
the title bar, across the top of the window).

Warning: You may be in the habit of using your operating system's built-in features for dealing with
windows, like minimizing them to the Mac OS X Dock. These techniques work just fine in FileMaker, but
they can play havoc when a FileMaker *script* needs to control the same window. If you're using any of
these little software robots to automate tasks, as you'll learn in Chapter 13, it's best to stick to FileMaker's
own window commands.

Closing hidden windows

On page 21, you learned to close a database by closing all its windows. As with
most rules, there's an exception: Even if you close all visible windows, the database
itself may still be open—in a hidden window.

The easiest way to close all FileMaker's open windows, hidden ones included, is to
press Alt (Option), and choose File → Close (File → Close All on Mac OS X). The ordinary Close command closes every window, hidden or not, when you press this key.

Automatically Arranging Windows

If you have a lot of windows on your screen and don't feel like rearranging them
yourself, you can use one of several commands that arrange the windows for

you—or at least try to. Using FileMaker's Window menu, you can choose one of three commands: Tile Vertically, Tile Horizontally, or Cascade. Each command rearranges the windows in a different manner, as shown in Figure 1-20.

Figure 1-20:
FileMaker offers three automatic window arrangements: Tile Horizontally, Tile Vertically, and Cascade. Choose Tile Horizontally or Tile Vertically to shrink every window enough that they all fit onscreen with no overlapping. If you choose Cascade, then FileMaker makes every window the same size, and puts each a little below and to the right of the one above. The window that was active when you chose Cascade lands in front.

The Window menu commands are a great place to start when you have so many windows open, you don't even know which one you're looking for! However, 99 times out of 100, these automatic rearrangements somehow seem to make every window the wrong size, and put each window in the wrong place. So use these commands with the understanding that you may *still* have to do some rearranging yourself.

POWER USERS' CLINIC

Record Locking

If you try editing a record in one window while it's showing in another window, then your changes don't appear in the second window as you type. In order for the changes to appear, you must first commit the record (see the box on page 24). Once you do, the changes appear everywhere else.

Here's a hypothetical example. Suppose you start making changes to Jim Halpert's contact information in one window, but you're interrupted by a phone call before you finish. To help the caller, you need to look something up in the database. Since you're a savvy FileMaker guru, you make a new window, and look it up there so you don't have to lose track of the changes you're making to Jim. (He's getting all Dwight's former customers.)

Unfortunately, by the time you finish the phone call, you've forgotten that you already started editing Jim's record. Now you go to Jim's record *in the new window* to make the changes.

Bear in mind the record is already half-changed but uncommitted in the first window.

What happens if you start making changes now? Which set of changes wins?

To avoid the problem of which changes "win," FileMaker automatically performs *record locking* for you. If you try to edit a record that's already being edited in another window, you see an error message that reads, "This record cannot be modified in this window because it is already being modified in a different window." Yes, it's frustrating to get this message, but just remember that automatic record locking really is your protection against major problems. (This is especially true when you have multiple users accessing your database at the same time—see Chapter 18.) This message is your friend.

Saving Your Database

Everybody knows it's important to save files early and often. So you're working along in FileMaker entering information about your office birthday roster, and as good habit dictates, you type the keyboard shortcut that saves in practically every program in the known universe (that'd be Ctrl+S on Windows and ⌘-S on the Mac). Up pops the wrong dialog box. This one's asking you how you want to sort your data! What gives?

Don't worry, FileMaker has you covered. The program automatically saves all your work in a *cache*, which is part of your computer's RAM (Random Access Memory). Then, periodically, FileMaker transfers the information from the cache to your hard drive, where it's less likely to be lost in case of a crash.

You can control how much work is held in cache before it's saved to your hard drive, as described in Figure 1-21. In Windows, choose Edit → Preferences, and then click the Memory tab. On the Mac, choose FileMaker Pro → Preferences, and then click the Memory tab.

Figure 1-21:
Specify the size of FileMaker's cache and how often your work is moved from the cache to your hard drive. (Nerds call that flushing the cache.) A larger cache yields better performance but leaves more data in RAM. If you're working on a laptop, then you can conserve battery power by saving cache contents less frequently. Just remember, in case of a power outage or other catastrophe, the work that's in cache is more likely to be lost than what FileMaker has saved to your hard drive.

Saving a Copy of Your Database

Chances are the data in your database is important. (Would you really go to all this trouble if it weren't?) Although FileMaker automatically saves your work as you go, what if the database file itself gets lost or suffers some digital harm? It's in your best interest to *back up* your database periodically. You can perform a backup by simply copying the database file. For example, you can copy it to a CD, email it to a friend, or duplicate it and tuck the copy away in another folder. The easiest way to make a backup is to choose File → "Save a Copy As". You see the typical Save dialog box. Just make sure that "copy of current file" is selected as the Type option. When you click OK, FileMaker makes your copy in the background, and you can continue working in the original file.

But if you want to start working in the copy you've just made, then select the "Automatically open file" option before you click OK. FileMaker makes the copy of your file, and then helpfully opens it for you. FileMaker doesn't close the original file for you, so if you're finished with the original, choose it from the Window menu, and then close it to avoid confusion. Now only your new copy of the file is open.

If you want to make a copy of your database to send to an associate in another office, choose the "Create email with file as attachment" option. FileMaker copies your file, and then launches your email program, creates a new email, and attaches your newly minted file copy to it. All you have to do is provide an email address, type your message, and then click Send. See page 662 to see how you can use similar options if you want to send data to your associate only in another format, like Excel or a PDF file.

Warning: You should always make sure a database is *closed* before you copy its file using any of the desktop methods (like Edit → Copy in Windows Explorer or the Mac's Finder). If you copy the database file onto another disk while it's open in FileMaker, then the copy you make may be damaged or missing information.

Saving a Clone of Your Database

There's no ban on cloning in FileMaker. Clones are clean copies of your database, but without the data. Clones are really useful, like when you've designed a killer database for running sales in your Dart and Billiards Supply Shop, and you want to send the files to all your franchisees without giving away your store's sales data. Just make clones of your files, and then give them to your proud new owners. To make a clone, choose File → "Save a Copy As", and then make sure "clone (no records)" is selected as the Type option.

Using FileMaker's Help Menu

As helpful as this introduction to databases has been, you may want to use File-Maker's onboard help to get more information (Figure 1-22). There you find commands for FileMaker's Help application and for online help at FileMaker's Web site. See Appendix A for more information on getting help from those sources, plus help from third parties.

Note (Mac only): The quickest way to get help, outside of sitting beside a willing guru, is to use the handy search field at the top of the Help menu. To get help, just start typing the subject you need help with. As you type each letter, the Help application changes its menu items to display topics it thinks you might need. When you see the item you need, select it from the menu, and Help appears, showing the page for the term or topic you chose.

Figure 1-22:
Here's the Help menu on a Mac in its pristine state, and showing its initial menu items. As you type a search term, FileMaker searches its Help application to create a set of custom commands that may relate to your search terms.

Note: If you bought FileMaker in a box, you'll find there's no printed manual. Not to worry, there's a lengthy PDF document included on the CD. Open the PDF by choosing Help → Product Documentation → User's Guide.

Organizing and Editing Records

In the first chapter, you learned how to use FileMaker's basic tools and get around your database. But you've just begun to scratch the surface of FileMaker's power. Now it's time to learn how to see, sort, move, and shape your information in myriad ways. For example, you may want to print a list of names and address for all the folks in your database who live in the western U.S. In an invoicing database, you may want to find everybody who's ordered 16-pound offset widgets in the last month so you can email them a special offer for widget accessories. In a student database, you may need to print a report of all third-grade students who were involved in lunchroom disciplinary actions during the first semester.

Whatever your needs, you can build on basic techniques to view your data in ever more sophisticated ways. After all, slicing, dicing, and analyzing your data is the whole point of storing the information in a database.

Views

In your People database, you learned how to add and edit data with only one record onscreen at a time (see page 22). This view is a common way to look at your information, but as you saw at the end of Chapter 1, it's only one of three ways to look at a database: Form view, List view, and Table view.

The one-at-a-time approach to viewing records is called *Form view*. In *List view*, you see the same arrangement of your records in, well, a list. If they don't all fit in the window, then you can use the vertical scroll bar to scroll through them. If you've used a spreadsheet program like Microsoft Excel, then *Table view* looks familiar—it looks a lot like a spreadsheet, with one row for each record, and one column for each field.

To switch among views in any FileMaker database, use the View menu. Choose View → As Form, View → As List, or View → As Table. You'll see what each view looks like as you learn about them on the following pages.

Note: The Chapter 1 version of the People database had custom buttons that let you switch views of your data, but that's not the only way to customize the views of your database. You can even turn *off* certain views if you want. If your database holds mostly digital photographs, it wouldn't make sense to look at in Table view, so you can make sure no one ever sees it that way. (You'll learn how in Chapter 5.) If you can't choose View → As List in the People file you have open, then download the Chapter 2 version of the file from the Missing CD page at *http://missingmanuals.com/cds*.

Form View

In Form view, you see only one record at a time. If you want to see the next record, click the pages of the book icon, press Control–down arrow, or use some other method of switching records (see page 29). Most of the database work you did in the first chapter was in Form view, so it should be very familiar by now. You can use Form view when you have a lot of information to see about one record, or when you want to focus on just one record without being distracted by all the others.

Tip: The Status toolbar has handy buttons for switching between views of your data. The tools are well designed so you can easily guess which is which, but if you're not sure, just point your mouse to any button to see a handy tooltip that explains what the tool is for.

List View

List view works *almost* the same as Form view. All the fields are arranged exactly as on a form, but if you stretch or scroll your window, then you see that your records appear one on top of the other, like a long list of forms. You can sort or find data in List view, but since you have more than one record onscreen at once, you need to know which record you're in. You can tell by the thin black line along the left edge of the window (see Figure 2-1) at the edge of the active record.

When you're working with a *group* of records—updating one field in several records or browsing through all your records in search of something—List view comes in handy.

Table View

If List view doesn't provide enough of a change for you, try Table view (Figure 2-2). It appeals to spreadsheet fans since it offers a consistent rows-and-columns design, the ability to sort with the click of a button, and the freedom to rearrange columns by dragging them around. Of course you can add, edit, delete, and find records in Table view, just like the other two views.

When you put your layout into Table view, any graphical embellishments disappear. Instead, FileMaker displays the fields of your layout in a no-nonsense, spreadsheet arrangement (Figure 2-2).

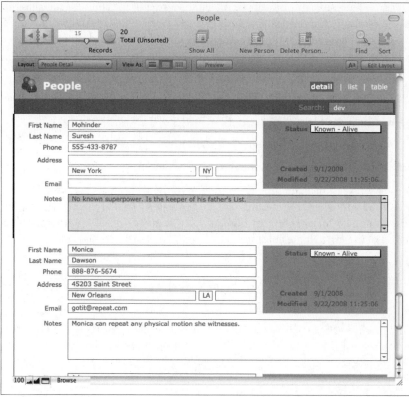

Figure 2-1:
When you switch to List view, your records look just like Form view, but you can scroll down through them with the scroll bar. A thin black line shows you which record is active, so you can edit it. And just like in Form view, you can click a record's fields to edit information if you need to. The feedback is just like Form view, too. Fields get a dotted line around them to show the record is active, and the active field has a solid border and a blinking cursor.

Figure 2-2:
This database is the same one shown in Figure 2-1, showing the same active record, but this time the layout is in Table view. The data in the Status field is too big to fit, so all you can see is a column of question marks, and the mouse is hovering over the dividing line at the right edge of that column, or field. If you drag this line, then the column expands. You can also gain a little room in the window by shrinking the State and Zip Code fields. The field labels are now column headers that act as clickable buttons, letting you sort the data by a specific field.

Each column represents one of your fields, and the order of the columns matches the order you go through the fields when tabbing (see page 184 to learn how to change the tab order). For example, the first column is the field you wind up in when you press Tab for the first time. Another Tab takes you to the second column.

In Table view, you can move columns around by dragging them. To switch the First Name and Last Name columns, for example, do the following:

1. **Point to the words Last Name, and then hold down the mouse button.**

   FileMaker darkens the column header to show you it's selected.

2. **Drag the column to the left of the First Name column.**

   You see a black line extending from the top of the window to the bottom. This line shows you where the column lands when you let go. All the other columns shift around to make room. In this case, you want the black line to appear to the left of the First Name column.

3. **Let go of the mouse button.**

   FileMaker moves the Last Name column to its new home, shifting other columns to the right to make room.

The column headings also make it easy to *sort* your data, if sorting by a single field is all you need. However, if you use the column headings to sort by Last Name, that doesn't automatically sort the First Name field, too. So if you need to do a multifield sort, then you need the Sort dialog box (page 36).

Modifying Table view

Table view is handy for scanning through a lot of data quickly. It's the only view where the Status toolbar shows a Modify button that lets you customize the view. Out of the box, Table view shows every field you see in Form view, but you may prefer to see less information when you're scanning tables, and you can do that with the Modify Table View command. For example, the Created and Modified fields may not be useful to you in Table view, so you can remove them; they still show up in Form View. Here's how to change the fields you see in Table view:

1. **In the Status toolbar, click the Modify button.**

   The Modify Table View dialog box appears with all the fields from your Form view listed and checked.

2. **Click the checkbox to the left of the fields you don't want to see, like Creation Date, Modification Timestamp, and Notes, as shown in Figure 2-3, for comparison.**

   In the background, you can see the fields disappear from Table view as you click each one.

3. **Drag the arrow to the left of each field name to rearrange the columns.**

   The fields move as you rearrange the list.

4. **Click the OK button when you're done.**

The dialog box disappears, and you're back to an unobstructed Table view.

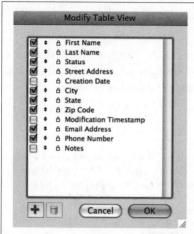

Figure 2-3:
Modify Table View lets you move columns and even keep them from appearing. There's a Plus button on the lower left that lets you add fields that aren't available in your current table. If that thought intrigues you, read Chapter 7 to learn about using more than one table in a single database.

As powerful as the Modify Table View dialog box is, FileMaker gives you even more ways to exert control over this view. Here's how to find those hidden gems:

1. **Choose View → Layout Mode, or press Ctrl+L (⌘-L).**

FileMaker switches to Layout mode, showing you the structure of your Form view. Although this window is where you usually go to change the way Form view looks, you can also change Table view in this mode.

2. **Choose Layout → Layout Setup.**

The Layout Setup dialog box appears. You can ignore all these settings for now, but see page 236 if you want to know what these options do.

3. **Click the View tab.**

The Views options appear. If you want to, you can turn off the options for Form or List view so this layout is available only in Table view. But that's not what you're after right now.

4. **Beside the Table view option, click the Properties button.**

The Table View Properties dialog box appears (Figure 2-4). Options in this dialog box let you turn off the ability to move or resize columns and the clickable sorting of the column headers.

5. **Click the Vertical option to remove the checkmark.**

This setting shows lines beneath each row, but not between each column.

6. Turn on the "Use custom height" option, and then, in the measurement field, type *25*. If necessary, from the increment pop-up menu, choose pixels.

This setting makes each table row a little taller.

7. Click OK to close each dialog box until you're back in Layout mode, and then switch to Browse mode.

If your layout isn't set to save changes automatically then you may have to click an OK button in a dialog box to save the changes you've just made. When you're done clicking OK, you see all the changes you made to the table. See the box on page 266 to learn more details about Table view properties.

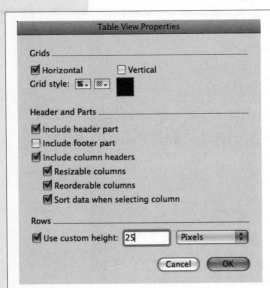

Figure 2-4:
The Table View Properties dialog box gives you control over how the view looks while you're in Browse mode. Of course, those changes also effect how the screen prints. Switch to Preview Mode to see how the layout will print. You probably need to make changes to the layout to make it print-worthy, so check out the section beginning on page 224 to see how to design a layout for printing.

By controlling the appearance of your different views, you can start to see how much customization power FileMaker gives you over your data in Browse mode. And now that you've gotten your feet wet in Layout mode, be sure to read Chapter 4 to learn how to control the look and behavior of the Form layout itself. Now, though, it's time to learn some sophisticated ways to find specific records.

Advanced Find Techniques

In Chapter 1, you learned about using Find mode for simple searches. But the more records you have in your database, the more you need advanced finding techniques to avoid wasting precious minutes clicking the book icon 1,057 times in a row just to find the record or records you want to display, edit, or print. File-Maker's Find tools give you the power to track down the one record in 100,000 you need *right this minute*, or the five records with missing phone numbers that you created a week ago Tuesday.

Modify Last Find

FileMaker always keeps track of your most recent find criteria, even if it's been a while since you did the search. So if you have to run another copy of your last report, or you just need to see if any new records match since the last time you did the find, all you have to do is choose Records → Modify Last Find. FileMaker does the equivalent of entering Find mode and typing in your find criteria. You can edit the criteria if you want, or just click the Find button, and you're done.

Modify Last Find (Ctrl+R or ⌘-R) isn't just a speedy way to recreate a find, though. You might have a found set of records, but you can't remember the search criteria. Choose Modify Last Find, and then read the requests to see. Then you can click the Cancel Find or the Perform Find button. Either way, you're right back in your found set.

Multiple Requests

You can tell FileMaker to search for more than one item at the time. But depending on how you enter your search terms, you can get very different results.

Searching with AND conditions

If you want to find everybody in the People database who has superpowers and lives in New York, a computer geek would say that you need to do an *AND search*. This odd term means you're asking for records where the city is New York *and* the Notes field contains the word "superpower". Just New York alone, or superpower alone, doesn't get the job done. An AND search is more restrictive than a single-field search because more of your search terms have to match before FileMaker puts a record into your found set. Though it's complex to think about, you can easily set up a multiple request search. Here's how:

1. **Choose View → Find Mode or, in the Status toolbar, click the Find tool.**

   FileMaker opens a new find request.

2. **In the State field, type *NY*.**

   You're telling FileMaker to find all records for people who live in the state of New York. That's your first *request* or search term.

3. **In the Notes field, type *superpower*.**

   This second request makes your search terms more restrictive. FileMaker knows that it has to show only those records that match both search terms you've entered.

4. **In the Status toolbar, click the Perform Find button.**

   FileMaker shows you the two records that match both your search terms.

Searching with OR conditions

If an AND search is more restrictive than a single criteria search, an OR search is less restrictive. That is, you almost always find more records with an OR search, since a record has to match only *one* of the many search terms you set up in order to get into the found set. To convert the previous example to an OR condition, think of it like this: "I need to find everybody who *either* lives in New York *or* has superpowers." So superpower-wielding folk who live in Nebraska (or anywhere, for that matter) show up in your found set, as do regular-Joe New Yorkers.

To create an OR condition, you add one small step to the process you just learned. Before you type the second search term, create a new request by choosing Request → New Request. Notice that the New Request command is the same one that creates a new record when you're in Browse mode. Different modes, different menus, same keyboard shortcut—Ctrl+N (⌘-N). Once you've typed your second request, you can use the book icon to flip back and review or edit the first one.

Tip: You can make your search criteria as complicated as you like, with dozens of requests, even mixing AND and OR terms within the same search. Just remember that you put a new term in the same request for an AND condition, and you create a new request for an OR condition.

Finding by Omitting

FileMaker's normal search behavior is to *include* in the found set everything you type in search fields. You can confirm this fact in Find mode by looking at the Include and Omit buttons in the Status toolbar (Figure 2-5). Every time you start a search, the Include button is automatically selected.

The Omit button comes in handy when the records you're looking for can best be described by what they aren't. For example, "Every person who isn't from California" is a lot easier to say (and to search for) than "Everyone from Alabama, Alaska, Arizona, Arkansas, Colorado…" In this case, you can get what you want by creating one find request, with California in the State field. Then, before you perform the find, just click the Omit button, which you can see in Figure 2-5. That's all there is to it. When you click Perform Find, FileMaker starts with every record in the table, and then throws out all the records with "California" in the State field, so you're left with everything else.

Omit also works with multiple find requests. If *all* your requests have the Omit option turned on, then all the records that match *any* of your requests are thrown out. Whatever's left over goes in your found set. If you have a mix of requests with and without Omit turned on, then FileMaker goes through them in order. If the first request isn't an omit request, then FileMaker finds all the matching records. If your first request is an omit, then FileMaker finds every record that doesn't match, and then moves on to the next request. That request may add new records to the found set, or remove records that are already there. In fact, a record can be found by one request, omitted by the next, and then found again by the third, so the record is ultimately included in the found set since the last request added it. In the end, you're left with a found set in which every record matches at least one of your requests.

Figure 2-5:
The Omit button tells FileMaker to do an "un-find." You can see the Omit button near the right edge of the Status toolbar. And of course, it appears only when you're in Find mode. In this example, the Omit button tells FileMaker to show you all the records for people who don't live in California. Once you get used to this inverted logic, you see that it's often easier to create an Omit search than the complicated Include search you have to come up with if you use FileMaker's normal Include behavior.

Refining a found set with Omit commands

FileMaker gives you a few menu commands to help you fine-tune your found set. Sometimes, after you've done the best find request you can, you still end up with a couple of records in the found set that you don't really want to see. FileMaker offers three commands that make tossing out misfit records as easy as pie:

- **Omit Record.** Go to the record you don't want (using the book icon, for example), and then choose Records → Omit Record. This one-off command tosses the record out of the found set, reducing your found count by one. Don't confuse it with the Omit button that shows up in the Status toolbar when you're in

Find mode (see page 54), which tells FileMaker to omit all the records that match your find request. The Records → Omit Record command omits just the single record you're sitting on.

- **Omit Multiple.** If you have a whole stretch of records you don't want, then use Records → Omit Multiple. It omits a contiguous group of records from the found set, starting with the current record. For instance, if you want to omit 10 records in a row, then navigate to the *first* record of the 10. Choose Records → Omit Multiple, and then, in the dialog box that appears, type *10*. Click Omit, and the job is done.

- **Show Omitted Only.** You can use this option when you're printing two separate lists—one of the California customers, and one of everyone else, for example. Once you've printed the California records, your found set happens to be exactly what you *don't* need. Choose Records → Show Omitted Only. This command effectively puts every record that's *not* in the found set into the new found set, and takes every currently found record out.

Note: You can also use Show Omitted Only if you forgot to turn on the Omit box in your find request. Instead of going back to Find mode to fix your request, just choose Records → Show Omitted Only, and you get the same effect.

Over-Omitted

If you try to omit more records than possible (for example, you're on the third-to-last record, and you ask FileMaker to omit 12 records), then FileMaker complains. But don't take offense: It's also nice enough to fix the problem for you. When you click OK, FileMaker returns you to the Omit dialog box, and changes the number you entered to the maximum number possible. You need only to click Omit again to get what you probably wanted in the first place.

Use this feature to your advantage. If you know you're looking at the last record that should be in your found set, you could try to do the math the dialog box needs. But that's more

trouble than it's worth. Just choose Records → Omit Multiple, and then enter something really big, like 999, or 9999999. When you click Omit, FileMaker complains, does the math for you, and enters the right value.

This routine may sound contrived, but it's fairly common among FileMaker pros. Imagine you're doing a direct-mail campaign and you can afford to send only 1,200 postcards. Your find request, however, produces 1,931 potential recipients. Rather than do the math, just go to record 1201, and then use this Omit Multiple trick.

Constraining and Extending the Found Set

When you perform a find normally, it effectively throws away any found set you had before, searches through all the records in the database, and then produces a *new* found set. But you can also tell FileMaker to *constrain* the found set (that is, search within your last find results) or *extend* it (add matching records to the current found set).

Constraining the found set

Suppose you've just created a great product, and you want to send out some free samples to see how people like it. You can't afford the postage to send everyone in your database a sample, so you decide to start with a smaller sampling—just people who live in New York.

Problem is, a simple find reveals that your database has too many New Yorkers listed. Some quick math in your head reveals that it's still too expensive. How about sending samples to just the New Yorkers who have superpowers? You *could* go back to Find mode and construct a request to find based on both criteria instead (by putting *New York* in the City field and *superpower* in the Notes field), but FileMaker gives you an easier way. After all, you've already got all the New Yorkers in your found set. You really want to search *inside* this found set for all the records with *superpower* in the Notes field.

Here's how the whole procedure goes:

1. **Switch to Find mode and, in the City field, type *New York*, and then click the Perform Find button.**

   FileMaker shows you a found set of all your New York residents.

2. **Switch to Find mode again using your favorite method.**

   Be careful *not* to choose Records → Show All Records, and don't do anything to tamper with the current found set, or else the Constrain search won't work. You're now in Find mode again, ready to enter a request.

Note: In Find mode, you can't see your current found set. You just have to remember that you last searched for "AZ" in the State field. If you need to see the found set, just switch back to Browse mode, and then flip through the records or choose Records → Modify Last Find.

---

3. **In the Notes field, type *superpower*.**

   Since the found set already has only New Yorkers in it, you don't need to repeat that information.

4. **Choose Requests → Constrain Found Set.**

   FileMaker searches out the people with superpowers, but this time it looks only in the current found set. In the end, you get what you want with less typing.

At this point, you're probably thinking that Constrain Found Set is just like doing an OR search. In fact, an OR search is usually easier. But sometimes, you don't know all the conditions you need until you do a search and scan through the list of found records. And if you've just done a complex search with seven conditions, or tricky spellings, you don't want to have to retype all that stuff, so Constrain Found Set saves the day.

Warning: Once you're in Find mode, FileMaker is itching for you to perform a find. If you press Enter, it assumes you want to throw away your last found set and make a new one. Once it's gone, you have no way to return to the old found set and constrain (or extend) it. Likewise, from the Requests menu, if you accidentally choose the wrong command, there's no going back. If you want to constrain or extend, then be sure you choose wisely or you have to start all over again.

Extending the found set

Extending the found set works a lot like constraining it. This time, though, you're asking FileMaker to perform a new find (through all records in the database), and then *add* the records it finds into your found set. You end up with all the records you already had, plus any new ones found. Suppose you've already found your *New York* folks, and you want all the *Texans* as well.

1. **In Find mode, in the State field, type *TX*.**

   So far, you're doing exactly what you would do in every other find.

2. **Choose Requests → Extend Found Set.**

   This time, FileMaker looks through every record in the database for any Texas natives. Each time it finds one, it adds it to your existing found set. When it's done, you have all the New Yorkers *and* Texans in one found set.

Refining Searches with Find Operators

Normally, FileMaker uses a pretty simple rule to decide whether a field value matches the field in your request (the *criteria*): If every word in the criteria appears at the *beginning* (within the first few characters) of any word in the field, then File-Maker considers it a match.

For example, if you put *for* in the Note field in a find request, any of these notes match:

- All for one and one for all.

- We will forever remember.

- Back and forth it went.

On the other hand, neither of these match:

- Wherefore art thou, Romeo?

- Before there was art, there was an artist.

Note: This match-the-beginning mode of operation may seem odd, but it's surprisingly useful. Imagine you're looking for someone named Ahrmshulla Maharajapuram in your database. Of course, you could find the record by typing the full name, but chances are you'll get the same results if you search for *Ah Maha* instead. Since Ahrmshulla starts with Ah and Maharajapuram starts with Maha, FileMaker finds her with this abbreviated request, saving you from all that typing—and remembering how to spell the full name.

How do you tell FileMaker that you're looking for "for" *wherever* it appears in a word, not just at the beginning? You can use a special *operator*—a character that has special meaning in a Find request—to stand for part of a word.

The Insert Operators pop-up menu, which appears in the Status toolbar when you're in Find mode, lets you add these special characters to your searches, thus gaining more control over FileMaker's decision-making process when it's looking for records. Read on to find about more special operators.

The wildcard (*)

In the "Wherefore art thou Romeo" example, use the * wildcard operator, which stands for "anything." It tells FileMaker that you don't mind if there's something *right before or right after* the "for." If you type **for** as your find criteria, then File-Maker displays records that contain "therefore," "before," "George Foreman," and so on. (Of course, if you want things that only start with "for" [forthwith, forsaken or forced], then you can type *for** in the find request.)

Less Than (<), Less Than or Equal To (≤), Greater Than (>), and Greater Than or Equal To (≥)

These operators tell FileMaker to use your criteria as a maximum or minimum rather than a direct match. For example, the criteria *<David* finds every person whose name comes before David alphabetically. ≤David is just about the same, but it includes any Davids as well.

People use these operators more frequently to find numeric or date information rather than text. For example, *<10* in a field that expects numbers finds real numbers less than 10 (like 9). FileMaker performs the correct function with dates and times as well, in which case Less Than means *before* and Greater Than means *after*. You'll learn more about field types in the next chapter.

Exact Match (=), Literal Text (""), and Field Content Match (==)

The rule FileMaker uses automatically for determining a match is pretty loose. But sometimes you want exactly what you say: "Smith," not "Smithers" or "Smithey" or "Smithsonian." In this case, use the Exact Match operator (=). In this example, type *=Smith* in the Last Name field, and then perform your find.

If you want to exactly match *more* than one word, put the words in quotes. This Literal Text match is also good for criteria that contain punctuation, like "Mr. Smith."

Note: Like French fries, quote marks come in two varieties: curly and straight. If you're someone who notices this kind of thing, then you may wonder if it matters which kind you use. It doesn't. Usually File-Maker turns your quotes curly for you, but you can turn off smart quotes for a database in the File → File Options dialog box.

For the ultimate in specificity, use the Field Content Match operator (==) instead. Exact Match requires that each *word* in your criteria match one or more words in the field. Literal Text seeks to match only what's in the quotes *anywhere* in the field. Field Content Match insists that the entire field matches the criteria text exactly. For example, =*Smith* matches "Smith," "Mr. Smith," and "Smith-Johnson." However, ==*Smith* matches only "Smith" in the field and nothing else.

> **Note:** Literal Text doesn't actually match text *anywhere* in the field. The criteria text must match starting at the beginning of a word. For instance, a search for "Mr. Smith" matches "Mr. Smith" and "Mr. Smithers," but if you search for *"r. Smith"* (no M) instead, then you get the "no matches found" error.

Range (…)

The Range operator is like the "Greater Than or Equal To" and "Less Than or Equal To" operators combined. The criteria "1/1/2009…6/15/2009" matches those two dates and everything in between. Just like the other operators, the Range operator is smart enough to understand numbers, dates, and times, as long as the field contains that kind of data.

Duplicates (!)

You might find it hard to get the hang of the Duplicates operator (!). When you put ! in a field in Find mode, FileMaker finds records with *duplicate data* in that field. In other words, it looks for records with the *same* value in that particular field. The same as *what*, you ask? The same as *any other record*. Think of it this way: If you have only *one* person in your database from Idaho, and you perform a find with *!* in the State field, then the person from Idaho doesn't appear. That's because—when considering the State field alone—the person from Idaho has no duplicates. On the other hand, if you have 11 people from Oklahoma and six people from Georgia, they'll *all* be found because they all have duplicates (each one has 10 others [or five others] just like it, statewide). In order to figure out what's up, sort the new found set of 16 records by the State field to make sure all the Georgians are grouped together, followed by all the Oklahomans. Then you can more easily compare them to the proper duplicates.

Unlike most other operators, the ! operator is always used alone in a field in Find mode. You never put *! Smith* in the last name field. Instead, you just put *!* all by itself.

Today's Date (//) and Invalid Date or Time (?)

Like the ! operator, these operators can go in a field in Find mode all by themselves. The double slash is convenient shorthand for the current date. If you're looking for all the payments due today, you can type // in the Due field more quickly than "February 22, 2010".

Finding Duplicate Records

Every database user eventually makes the mistake of entering the same data twice. Maybe you assume a person isn't in your database and add him, only to discover months later that he was there all along. The ! operator can help you hunt down this sort of thing.

If you want to find *whole records* that are exact duplicates, then you have to put *!* in every field when you're in Find mode. But it isn't at all uncommon for "duplicate" records to be slightly different. Maybe you updated the phone number in one but not the other, for instance.

Or perhaps you misspelled the street name the first time you entered this person, and spelled it right the second time. Finding exact duplicate records doesn't catch these kinds of so-called duplicates.

If you're looking for duplicate records, you're usually best off putting the ! operator in as few fields as possible. Try to pick fields that tend to be entered the same every time, and stand a good chance of identifying an individual person. You can use just First Name and Last Name, for instance.

The Invalid Date or Time operator (?) is another helper when it comes time to clean house. It's possible to end up with the wrong kind of data in fields that are supposed to hold dates or times (like "N/A", "Never", or "Next Week"). Put ? in the Due field, and FileMaker finds every payment whose due date isn't valid, giving you an opportunity to fix them. (You'll learn more about fields that hold special kinds of data in Chapter 3.)

Note: You can mix and match these operators in any combinations that make sense. For example, to find everything after today's date, just search for *>//* instead of *>4/1/2010*.

One Character (@), One Digit (#), and Zero or More Characters (*)

These operators are like the wildcard characters you sometimes see in other programs. You already saw the Zero or More Characters operator (*) at the beginning of this section. It simply tells FileMaker you're willing to accept some text—*any* text—in place of the * operator. If you're not ready to go that far, you can instead permit just one character (letter, number, or punctuation) with the One Character (@) operator. When matching numbers, you can be even more specific, permitting just one numerical digit with the One Digit (#) operator. Here are a few examples:

- **smith** matches "Smith," "blacksmith," "Smithsonian," and "blacksmiths"
- **smith* matches "Smith" and "blacksmith," but not "blacksmiths" or "Smithsonian"
- *smith@* matches "smithy" but not "smithers"
- *@*smith* matches "blacksmith" but not "Smith" or "blacksmiths"
- *smith#* matches "smith1" and "smith2" but not "smithy"

Note: As discussed at the start of this section, when you do a Find, FileMaker matches the *beginning* of a word in the field. But as soon as you add these wildcard operators to your search, it becomes a little less lenient: FileMaker insists on a complete word match. You can see this in the second example above. You might expect **smith* to match "blacksmiths" but it doesn't because FileMaker now wants the whole word to match.

Relaxed Search (~)

The last operator, called Relaxed Search (~) applies only to searching Japanese language text. It instructs FileMaker to consider characters to match if they make the same sound, even if they aren't exactly the same character. Alas, in English, spelling always counts (you can't expect "~korn" to match "corn").

Using the Find Pop-up Menu

Once you've figured out how to create the complex find to get that end-of-month report showing, say, all females in a 10–Zip code range who've emailed you, but who haven't made a purchase in the last quarter, you can use the Find pop-up menu (Figure 2-6) to recreate that find if you need it again. If you've done the find recently (within your last 10 finds), then it appears in this menu. Plus, you see another way to access the Modify Last Find command (page 53). Best of all, Save Current Find lets you save as many frequently used finds as you need.

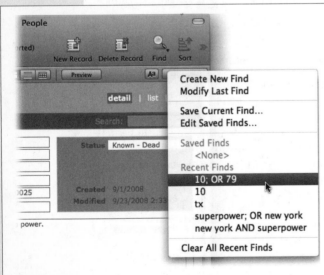

Figure 2-6:
The Find pop-up menu appears when you hold down the mouse button on the Find icon instead of clicking on it. The menu gives you an easy way to manage finds that you have to perform repeatedly. Although you can't see the name of the field (or fields) you've searched in the Recent Finds section of the menu, each item gives you as much data as it can. The highlighted search found all Zip codes that start with either "10" OR "79". There's no indication of that in the menu, so you have to rely on your memory for that bit of the puzzle. If it's all too confusing, the "Clear All Recent Finds" command lets you start from scratch.

Saving finds

You can most easily save a find when you perform it first. When you perform a find, FileMaker remembers the criteria you set. (For a challenge, see page 558 to see how to save a find you *haven't* performed yet.) To get started, search for all Zip codes that start with either "10" or "79" (see page 54 for help creating an OR condition search). Then follow these steps:

1. **In the Status toolbar, click the Find icon, and keep the mouse button pressed.**

   The pop-up menu appears, with the Find you just performed at the top of the menu's Recent Finds section.

2. **Choose Save Current Find.**

   The Specify Options for the Saved Find dialog box appears. FileMaker suggests a name for your saved find.

3. **In the Name field, type *End of the Month Report*.**

   Type a name to help you remember what the find does. Consider putting the field you're searching somewhere in the name. You have 100 characters to work with, but a lengthy name can make the menu unwieldy.

4. **Click Save.**

   Press the Find pop-up menu again, and you see the saved find.

Now you can test the new find by choosing it from the pop-up menu. FileMaker does all the work: It enters Find mode, enters the search criteria, and then performs the find. You can also enter Find mode, and then, from the Saved Finds pop-up menu, choose a saved find. In that case, though, FileMaker enters your criteria, but you have to click Perform Find. Using this method, you can create a find that's slightly different from the saved request—just edit the request any way you like before clicking Perform Find.

Note: Saved Finds are specific to a single account in your file. To see your saved finds, log in with the account under which you created the finds. Chapter 16 tells you about accounts and privileges.

Editing saved finds

If you have a saved find that needs tweaking—maybe the end of the month report needs to include a new set of Zip codes from now on or maybe you just made a mistake when you set it up—use Edit Saved Finds. You can choose the command from the pop-up menu, or by choosing Records → Saved Finds → Edit Saved Finds (Figure 2-7). Either way, you see a dialog box that shows you all your saved finds, and lets you create a new find without performing it first. You can also delete or edit finds.

To edit a saved find:

1. **From the Find pop-up menu, choose Edit Saved Finds.**

   The Edit Saved Finds dialog box appears (Figure 2-7).

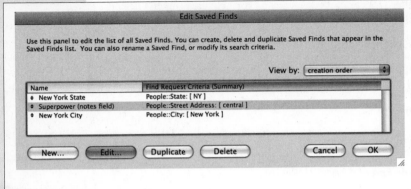

Figure 2-7:
The Edit Saved Finds dialog box shows all your saved finds. You can sort the list with the "View by" pop-up menu. You can sort alphabetically by name, by creation order or in a custom order, by dragging the arrow to the left of each find's name. Use the Duplicate button as a starting point for creating a new find that's similar to one you've already saved. The Delete button cleans up finds you won't be using any more.

2. **Click the "Superpower (notes field)" find.**

   The selected find appears highlighted, and the Edit button becomes active.

3. **Click Edit, double-click the Superpower find, or simply press Enter.**

   The Specify Options for the Saved Finds dialog box appears. If you're changing the action of the find, it makes sense to change its name. In this case, though, you're repairing a find that wasn't set up correctly, so leave the name the same.

4. **Click the Advanced button.**

   The Specify Find Requests dialog box appears. The actions that create the find requests are in a list. In this case, there's only one action, which is equivalent to a request in a manual find.

5. **Click the Find Records action, and then click the Edit button (or double-click the action).**

   The Edit Find Request dialog box appears. Here you can change the way this specific request does its work. Currently, it's set to search in the Address field for the word "central".

6. **Click the action in the top list, and then scroll the Find records list until you see the Notes field; then click it.**

   You're telling FileMaker to search the StreetAddress field instead of the Notes field. The Change button becomes active as soon as you edit the request. The change doesn't take place until you click the button or press Enter, though.

7. **In the right-hand list, click the criteria, and then type *superpower*.**

   You've entered the second part of the changed request, which is to search the field for the word "superpower". See Figure 2-8 for the settings.

Figure 2-8:
This dialog box changes a find request from searching the Street Address field for the word "central" to searching the Notes field for the word "superpower." The Action pop-up menu lets you choose between "Find Records" and "Omit Records". In a single request, you can search more than one field, which is like setting up an AND condition in Find mode. Multiple requests within a single find are the same as an OR condition in Find mode.

8. **Click Change, and then click OK in all the dialog boxes until you're back on your People Detail layout.**

   If you click Cancel on the last dialog box, then FileMaker warns you that all your changes will be discarded. Use this technique when you're not sure if your settings are correct. Since the Delete button doesn't warn you before it deletes a find request or a saved find, you can use this technique instead as a fail-safe. When you click Cancel, FileMaker discards all the changes you made while the dialog box was open.

Try out the edited search, by choosing it from the Find pop-up menu or by choosing Records → Saved Finds → "Superpower (notes field)". This process involves a lot of steps, but once you understand the Edit Find Request dialog box, the process is easy. You can use a slight variation to create a new saved find without performing it first. Just choose Edit Saved Finds, and then click New instead of selecting an existing find and editing it.

Tip: Practice creating finds from scratch comes in handy when you start scripting static finds (page 559). Several find script steps use the Specify Find Requests and Edit Find Request dialog boxes you've just seen.

Editing What's in Your Fields

Once you've found the records you want to work on, it's time to learn timesaving and creative ways to revise and format your record text. Each field is actually like a mini–word processor, with features that you're familiar with if you've ever written a letter on a computer. You can do basic things like select text, and cut, copy, and paste. You even have a Find and Replace feature, and flexible text formatting powers.

Drag-and-drop Editing

In addition to copying and pasting, you can drag text from one place to another. But first, you have to turn it on in FileMaker's preferences, like so:

1. **On Windows, choose Edit → Preferences. On Mac OS X, choose FileMaker Pro → Preferences.**

   The Preferences dialog box appears.

2. **Select "Allow drag and drop text selection".**

   If you don't like using drag and drop, just come back here and turn it off.

3. **Click OK.**

   The dialog box disappears.

Now that dragging is turned on, here's how it works:

1. **Make a new record (Records → New Record).**

   Now you've got a nice clean work surface.

2. **In the Notes field, type** *FileMaker has editing super powers.*

   Next you'll drag to fix it.

3. **Double-click the word "super".**

   The word is highlighted to let you know it's selected.

4. **Drag the selected word between "has" and "editing".**

   Figuring out where dragged text is going to land can be tricky. If you look closely, you see that in addition to the text you're dragging, a little vertical line moves along under your arrow. You can see this in action in Figure 2-9. (Unless you have excruciatingly precise mouse movements, you probably have to fix the spaces between words. Unlike most word processors, FileMaker isn't smart enough to figure out where they go for you.)

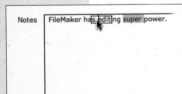

Figure 2-9:
When you turn on "Allow drag and drop text selection" in Preferences, FileMaker lets you drag selected text around with the mouse. Here, the word "super" is being moved after "has" by dragging. The little vertical line under the arrow shows you exactly where the text will go when you drop it.

Note: You can also drag text from one *field* to another. Instead of *moving* the text, FileMaker *copies* it. In other words, once you let go of the mouse button, the text is both where it started *and* where you drop it. If you want this behavior when dragging *within* a field, then hold down the Ctrl (Option) key while you drag.

Find and Find Again

Unlike the Find/Replace window in most other programs, FileMaker's doesn't politely step aside. If you try to click in your database window to switch back to it, then FileMaker just beeps at you. In fact, you can't do *anything else* but find and replace unless you close the Find/Replace window first. You can always move the Find/Replace window around the screen by dragging it, but if your database window is big, or your screen is small, the Find/Replace window can really get in the way, keeping the very results it's finding hidden behind it. Here are a few pointers to help you cope:

Make sure the Find/Replace window is as small as possible by dragging the resize handle in the lower-right corner. Like most windows, it's resizable, but its smallest size is almost always big enough.

If you close the Find/Replace window (click Close or press Escape), then FileMaker keeps the last-found item highlighted. Since FileMaker remembers all your settings, you can always open the Find/Replace window again, and then continue searching where you left off.

Wouldn't it be great if you could click the buttons in the Find/Replace window without having it open onscreen? Fact is, you can. In the Edit → Find/Replace menu, you see two handy commands: Find Again and Replace & Find Again. (They're grayed out unless you've done a Find/Replace operation, though.)

Choosing these menu commands is just like clicking the Find Next and Replace & Find buttons in the Find/Replace dialog box.

FileMaker also offers one more convenient shortcut. If you have some text already in a field, and you want to find *the next* occurrence of the same text, then you can choose Edit → Find/Replace → Find Selected. This one command does the same thing as copying the text, opening the Find/Replace window, pasting into the "Find what" box, clicking Find Next, and then clicking Close. All the other options in the Find/Replace window stay just as when you last used them.

Best of all, these handy commands all have keyboard shortcuts:

- To find the next occurrence (Find Again), just press Ctrl+G (⌘-G).

- To replace the currently selected text, and find the next occurrence (Replace & Find Again), press Ctrl+Shift+G (Option-⌘-G).

- To find other occurrences of the selected text, press Ctrl+Shift+H (Option-⌘-H).

Using the Replace Command

Sometimes the whole reason you performed a find is to change something in several records. Maybe you just noticed that your data entry person put "New Yorq" on all the records she entered. The first step to fixing them is to *find* them. Once your found set includes the proper records, you could change the City field one record at a time (especially if you're billing by the hour). But you use your time better if you use the Replace Field Contents command. Here's how it works:

1. **Click the City field (it doesn't matter which record), and then correct the spelling to "New York".**

   You've just fixed one of the records. All the others in the found set need the same fix. (Make sure you're still in the City field or the next step won't work.)

2. **Choose Records → Replace Field Contents.**

The Replace Field Contents dialog box appears (Figure 2-10). It has a handful of options that may not make sense to you yet. That's OK; just choose the first one: "Replace with". The new data you just typed is listed beside this option.

Replace Field Contents

Permanently replace the contents of the field "City" in the 5 records of the current found set?

- ● Replace with: "New York"
- ○ Replace with serial numbers:
  - Initial value: `1`
  - Increment by: `1`
  - ☐ Update serial number in Entry Options?
- ○ Replace with calculated result: (Specify...)

(Replace) (Cancel)

Figure 2-10:
The Replace Field Contents dialog box has three options: "Replace with", "Replace with serial numbers", and "Replace with calculated result". You're concerned only with the first option right now. It replaces the contents of the current field in every record in the found set with whatever's in the current record when you click Replace. So, in the current record, type what you want to be in every record before you call up this dialog box. (You'll learn about serial numbers in Chapter 3 and calculations in Chapter 9.)

3. **Click Replace.**

FileMaker now updates the City field in *every record in the found set*. When it's done, you're still sitting on the same record, but if you use the book icon to click through the records, then you see that they've all been changed.

Warning: The Replace Field Contents command can be very dangerous. It really does change every record in the found set, even if that wasn't your intent. Make sure you're absolutely certain you have the right found set before clicking Replace, because you can't use the Undo command afterwards.

Find and Replace

Like your word processor, FileMaker has a Find and Replace feature. Also as in your word processor, you can (and should) use Find and Replace tools as often as possible to automate your editing process and eliminate retyping.

Suppose one of your clients is called Lehman Brothers. For one reason or another, they decide to change their name to Nomura. Unfortunately, you have 27 folks in your database with the old name, and the name is sprinkled in Company Name fields, Notes fields, and so on. You could look through your records one by one and fix them yourself, but you're never going to become a database guru that way. Instead, do a Find/Replace operation.

FileMaker fields can hold a lot of information, and people often put things like letters, emails, product descriptions, and other potentially long documents into a field. In cases like this, the Find/Replace command is just as useful as it is in your word processing program.

Since FileMaker has fields and records to worry about, though, its Find/Replace dialog box is a little more complicated than what you may be familiar with. Luckily, the concepts are simple, as shown in Figure 2-11. The Find/Replace dialog box lets you search a field, a record, or all records for a little snippet of text. It can also replace every occurrence of that text with something new—either one at a time, or all at once.

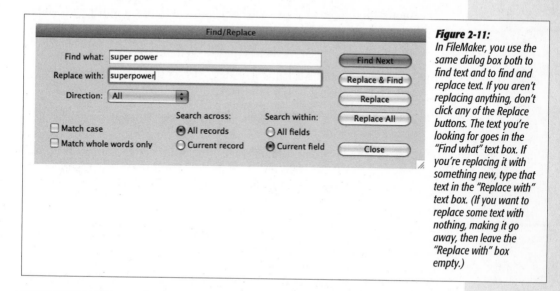

Figure 2-11:
In FileMaker, you use the same dialog box both to find text and to find and replace text. If you aren't replacing anything, don't click any of the Replace buttons. The text you're looking for goes in the "Find what" text box. If you're replacing it with something new, type that text in the "Replace with" text box. (If you want to replace some text with nothing, making it go away, then leave the "Replace with" box empty.)

Note: Don't confuse Find/Replace with Find mode. Find/Replace is for finding *text* in one or more fields and one or more records. Find mode is for finding *records*. You'll probably use Find mode much more often than Find/Replace. For the full story, see the box on page 72.

Here's FileMaker's version of Find and Replace:

1. **Choose Edit → Find/Replace → Find/Replace.**

   The Find/Replace dialog box opens, as shown in Figure 2-11.

Tip: Turning on "Match case" ensures that FileMaker looks for an exact uppercase and lowercase match. For example, when "Match case" is turned on, "Kite" and "kite" don't come up as a match. If you turn on "Match whole words only", FileMaker eliminates partial word matches. For example, "Drag" matches "Drag" and not "Dragon."

2. **Under "Search across", select "All records."**

   You've just told FileMaker whether you want it to look through all the records in the found set.

3. **Under "Search within", select "Current field."**

"Current field" refers to the field you were editing when you opened the Find/Replace dialog box. If you weren't clicked into a field when you opened the dialog box, FileMaker still lets you select the "Current field" option, but it complains when you start the find, so if you want to search a specific field, close the dialog box, click in your intended field, and then reopen the dialog box. You can select any combination of Search across and Search within. Here's how that shakes out:

- **All records and All fields.** FileMaker looks through every field in the window for a match. When it's done, it moves on to the next record.

- **Current record and All fields.** FileMaker looks through every field in the window, and then tells you it's finished.

- **Current record and Current field.** FileMaker looks only in the current field. When it reaches the end of the text in that field, it stops.

- **All records and Current field.** FileMaker looks through the current field, and then moves to the next record. It keeps looking through records for more matches, but it pays attention only to the current field.

4. **From the Direction pop-up menu, choose All.**

The Direction pop-up menu controls which way FileMaker goes when it starts its search. To figure out what that means, imagine a long string running through your database. One end is tied to the first letter of the first field of the first record. The other end is tied to the last letter of the last field of the last record. This concept is pictured in Figure 2-12.

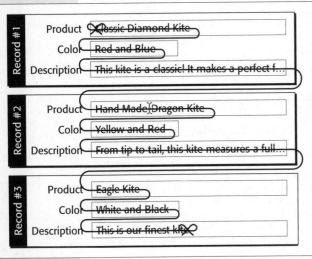

Figure 2-12:
The Find/Replace command expects you to give it a direction. To decipher what that means, you have to do a little visualization. Here's a picture of the imaginary string, starting at the beginning of the first record, and stopping at the end of the last. When you click into a field, and the insertion point sits there blinking in front of a letter, it's marking a spot on the imaginary string. If you're not clicked into a field, then FileMaker decides to mark the string right before the first letter of the first field of the current record. In this example, your cursor is sitting right there between "Made" and "Dragon".

- **Forward.** FileMaker starts looking at your current spot on the string, and moves *forward* (towards the end of the string). When it gets to the end, it beeps.

- **Backward.** FileMaker starts looking at your current spot on the string, and moves *backward* (towards the beginning of the string). When it gets to the beginning, it beeps.

- **All.** FileMaker starts off just like a Forward search. When it reaches the end of the string, instead of beeping, it skips to the start of the string, and keeps looking. It finally beeps and stops when it gets back where it started.

Now that you're through setting all your Find/Replace options, it's time to decide which button to click:

5. **Click Find Next.**

- **Find Next** starts FileMaker looking. When it finds a match, it highlights the match right in the field. The Find/Replace window stays put, so you can click Find Next as many times as necessary to find what you're looking for, and then click Replace to change it to your replacement text. Click Find Next again to go to the next match.

- If you feel the need to work more quickly—say you've done Find Next and Replace a couple times, and everything looks in order—click **Replace & Find** instead. It replaces the current match, and then finds the next one all in one step. Repeat as many times as necessary.

- If you're sure you want *every* match replaced, then click **Replace All**, and FileMaker does the entire find-replace-find-replace dance for you. File-Maker always asks you if you're sure about Replace All first, just in case. For instance, if you have some clients whose last name is Anderson and others whose company name is Anderson, you may *not* want to use the Replace All option. You need to check each occurrence individually to make sure you don't accidentally change someone's last name.

6. **When you're done with the Find/Replace window, click Close.**

Warning: Find/Replace has no undo, and since you can replace across all records and fields, it can be dangerous. Be careful with this command. Also, it can take a long time because it looks through the individual words in each field. If you're searching across all records, and you have lots of records, be prepared to wait a while as FileMaker does its magic.

Changing Text Appearance

Much like a word processor, FileMaker has commands to set the font, size, style, or alignment of the text in a field. When a field is active, or you've selected some text in a field, you can choose from any command in the Format menu. Also like a word processor, you apply formats to paragraphs of text and you can even create tab stops within a field.

Find with Replace vs. Find/Replace

You may be wondering how Find mode combined with Replace Field Contents is different from Find/Replace (discussed earlier in this chapter). In fact, they're very different, but deciding which to use can be confusing. Here are some guidelines:

- Find mode is significantly faster at finding things than Find/Replace. In Find mode, FileMaker uses something called an *index*, which lets it find 10 matching records out of 293,000 in an instant. Find/Replace, on the other hand, looks through the fields the same way you would: one by one. It's faster than you, but it still takes time.

- Replace Field Contents always operates on one field across the entire found set. Find/Replace, on the other hand, also lets you replace across all fields in just the current record, as well as all fields and all records in the found set.

- Replace Field Contents always replaces the *entire* contents of the field. You can't replace every occurrence of "teh" with "the" for example. You can only give a new value that replaces whatever's in the field.

- Most important, Replace Field Contents assumes you've already found the records you want, and always modifies every record in the found set. Find/Replace adds a second layer of searching, as it scours the record or the found set looking for matches.

So why would you ever use Replace Field Contents? Sometimes you really do want to replace everything in the field every time, just like in the Company Name example on page 68. Also, Replace Field Contents is *significantly* faster at changing lots of records than Find/Replace. It takes just a few seconds to accomplish what Find/Replace would spend several minutes doing.

In general, if you want to find records, use Find mode, but if you want to find certain bits of text, use Find/Replace. Likewise, if you want to replace everything in a field in *every* record, use Replace Field Contents, but if you want to replace little bits of text, use Find/Replace. (If you want to replace little bits of text across thousands of records, study first, or be prepared to take a vacation while your computer thinks about it.)

Finally, you have no reason not to mix Find/Replace with Find mode. Since Find/Replace searches records only in the found set, you can establish a good found set *first* to make your Find/Replace go faster. (For example, if you're replacing "teh" with "the" in the Notes field, then you may as well find all the records that have "teh" in their Notes fields first, since Find mode is so much faster than Find/Replace.)

Text Formatting

You can use all the usual commands (font, size, style, alignment, line spacing, and text color) individually, or in a handy one-stop Text dialog box. You also have a very useful Text Formatting toolbar (Figure 2-13) that can stay on top of your screen so you can change text at will.

Each of these text formatting commands lets you override the standard formatting for a field on a record-by-record basis. That is, changing a word to bold on one record doesn't affect any words in any other record in the database. So while it can be handy to make the occasional note stand out (like "NEVER PAYS HIS BILL!"), professional database designers rarely use these commands to format individual chunks of text. Instead, they change the formatting in every field of the database by changing the field itself while in Layout mode. You'll learn how to do that in Part 2.

Tip: For specifics on how FileMaker lets you format text in individual records, see the screencast at *http://missingmanuals.com/screencasts*.

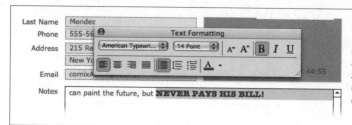

Figure 2-13:
The results of a session using the Text Formatting toolbar. The First Name field shows the formatted text, and the toolbar shows the font, size, style, and colors chosen. You can access the toolbar by choosing View → Formatting Bar.

Tip: If you change your mind about formatting, and want to put the text back to its normal state, here's a trick that lets you do it with four quick keystrokes: Select all the text (Ctrl + A or ⌘-A), cut the selection (Ctrl+X or ⌘-X), paste it right back in the field (Ctrl+V or ⌘-V), and finally Undo (Ctrl+Z or ⌘-Z). The pasted text comes back with its ugly formatting at first, but the undo doesn't remove the *text*, it removes the *formatting*. The same trick works if you paste data in from another source, like Word or Excel. If the text comes with formatting you want to lose, just do an undo right after you paste.

Paragraph Formatting

FileMaker doesn't stop with text (or *character*) formatting. It also has some paragraph formatting tools that come in handy. Well, they're handy if you can find them. You have to go through the Text Formatting dialog box to get there. To see the dialog box in Figure 2-14, choose Format → Text. When that dialog box appears, in the lower-left, click the Paragraph button.

There you see all the stuff you'd expect to be able to do to a paragraph in a field. You can align the paragraph, indent it from the left or the right, or give it a first-line indent. You can change line spacing or add space above or below a paragraph. There's even a handy Apply button so you can check out your settings before you close the dialog box. Finally, a Tabs button gives you access to another dialog box, this time for setting tab stops.

Remember, just like text formatting commands, any paragraph formatting you apply in Browse mode changes only the record and the field that's active when you choose the command. This ability comes in handy sometimes, but people use the Layout cousins of these commands far more often.

Warning: In the Text Format dialog box, when you click Paragraph, FileMaker immediately applies any formatting settings you've made. To avoid unintentional reformatting, make sure you don't have any text selected when you choose Format → Text. (Better yet, bypass the Text Format dialog box altogether by choosing Format → Line Spacing → Custom instead.)

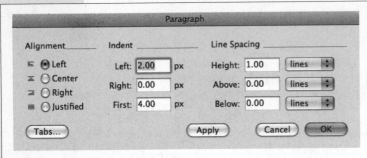

Figure 2-14:
This hidden dialog box can make text in a field more legible. In your sample database, you may have noticed how the text stands a little away from the left edge of the field border (see Figure 2-13). That was done on the layout, but you can add this effect to a field in one record with the settings shown above.

The Text Ruler

The Text Ruler (View → Text Ruler) is a visual version of the Paragraph formatting dialog box. Use it to set indents and tab stops. The ruler has an arrow icon for the Left, Right, and First Line indent settings (Figure 2-15), which you just drag to the spot on the ruler where you want the indent set. You'll learn how to set tab stops on page 74.

When you turn on the Text Ruler, FileMaker adds a space along the top of the window to hold the ruler. When you're in a field, the ruler itself appears in the portion of this space directly above the field, with the zero point on the ruler lined up with the left edge of the field. (When you're not in a field, the ruler just measures the width of the content area.)

Figure 2-15:
Like most word processors, FileMaker has a text ruler that lets you position margin markers right where you want them. When you drag the Left indent arrow, it moves the First Line arrow with it, so first drag the Left indent arrow where you want it, and then move the First Line arrow. If you want to move the Left indent arrow without moving the First Line arrow, then hold down the Alt (Option) key while you drag.

Formatting Tabs

Since a field can hold just about any kind of text, you might eventually need to use tab stops *within* a field. For example, you could have a nice large field into which you paste rows of text from a spreadsheet. To make things line up properly, you can set tab stops for each column of text. To move the insertion point to the next tab, press Ctrl+Tab (Option-Tab). This is a special keystroke, obviously, because in FileMaker pressing Tab jumps you to the next *field*. See page 159 to learn how Field Controls make plain old tabs work the way you're used to.

Like most word processing programs, FileMaker gives you two ways to create tab stops: the Text Ruler described on page 74, and the Tabs dialog box.

Setting tabs in the Text Ruler

To insert a new tab stop, simply click anywhere in the ruler. A small right-pointing arrow appears where you clicked, representing a *left* tab stop. (The arrow shows you what direction text goes when you start typing.) FileMaker also supports other kinds of tab stops, but to get them, you have to visit the Tabs dialog box, described next.

Setting tabs in the Tabs dialog box

The Tabs dialog box is a laborious way of setting tabs, but it gives you more options because you can control all aspects of each tab stop manually. Here's the drill:

1. **Choose Format → Text.**

   The Text Format dialog box appears.

2. **Click Paragraph.**

   The Paragraph dialog box makes its entrance.

3. **Click Tabs.**

   Ta-da! You found the Tabs dialog box (Figure 2-16).

Figure 2-16:
The Tabs dialog box lists all the tab stops set for a field in the list on the right. You can also adjust a tab stop, delete it, or add a new one. Each stop has a Type, Position, and Fill Character. To change the settings for any existing stop, first select the stop, and then edit the settings, and click Set.

Note: If the Text Ruler is showing (Figure 2-15), then you can get to the Tabs dialog box quickly. Just double-click any tab stop in the ruler. The Tabs dialog box opens with the clicked tab preselected.

To make a new tab stop, simply select the appropriate options, and then click New. A new entry appears in the list named after the Position you specified. The Apply button lets you see the results of your settings without closing the dialog box. You can create up to 20 tab stops, after which the New button becomes disabled. If you try to add a tab stop at a ruler position where one already exists, then the new stop simply replaces the old one.

Once you've created a tab stop, you can edit or delete it at will. Drag a tab around on the Text ruler to move it, or drag it off the bottom to delete it. Use the dialog box's Clear button to delete a tab, if you prefer that method.

TROUBLESHOOTING MOMENT

Units

In the figures in this chapter, the Indent options are specified in inches (you see "in" next to each text box). FileMaker actually has a setting for the unit used here and other places. FileMaker comes factory-set to inches, but it's nothing if not flexible. You can use inches, centimeters, or pixels–the choice is yours. If you're used to the metric system, by all means tell FileMaker to use centimeters. Or choose pixels for *really* precise control over text positioning. Here's how to change how FileMaker displays measurements:

If the Paragraph dialog box is open, click Cancel. The remainder of these steps work only if your database's main window is in front.

- Choose View → Layout Mode. In this mode, the content area of the window changes somewhat. Don't be alarmed…and don't click anything in the window. (If you accidentally change something, that's OK. FileMaker soon asks if you want to save.)

- Choose Layouts → Set Rulers to open the Set Rulers dialog box.

- In the Units pop-up menu, choose Pixels. (If you'd rather use different units, you can select anything you like. You can always repeat these steps later to get things back.)

- Click OK, and then choose View → Browse Mode.

You should be back where you started now. If you get a message asking if you want to save your changes, click Don't Save; this question refers to any accidental changes you made to the layout itself, not to the change of ruler units.

Checking Spelling

Before printing out your database or otherwise sharing it with the greater public, you want to make sure your spelling is correct. Nothing screams "amateur" louder than a City field that reads "Chciago." All the spell checking commands are found under the Edit → Spelling menu.

Spell Checking with Menu Commands

Sometimes you want to fly through data entry, and then do your spell checking later. If this is your preference, you have three choices:

- Choose Edit → Spelling → Check Selection to spell check selected text only. This method comes in handy when you're pretty sure a short passage, or even a single word, is wrong. Highlight the text you want to check, and then choose the menu command.

- To check the entire record, choose Edit → Spelling → Check Record.

- Finally, you might want to check spelling on many records at once. In this case, choose Edit → Spelling → Check All. When you choose this option, you're telling the spell checker to look at every field of every record in the current found set (choose Records → Show All first if you want to check *every* record in the database).

No matter how many records you're checking, FileMaker opens the same Spelling dialog box shown in Figure 2-17.

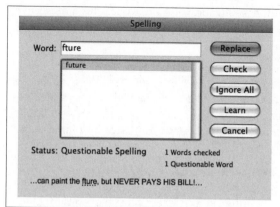

Figure 2-17:
The spell checker found a typo–"fture". You can see the misspelled word in the Word box, and underlined in red in the box at the bottom of the window. If FileMaker figures out the correct spelling, then, in the list under the Word box, it selects the spelling. And if you're the type who calculates your gas mileage every time you fuel up, you'll be delighted to discover that FileMaker keeps track of how many words you've spelled wrong so far, and tells you at the bottom of the window.

Note: Even if, by the magic of planetary alignment, you have no misspellings, FileMaker still opens the Spelling dialog box. In this case, though, it says "Status: Finished Spelling" in small print in the middle of the busy window. You're supposed to spot this right away and know the program's done. Of course, if you're like most people, you stare blankly at the screen for 30 seconds trying to figure out what went wrong first. Save yourself the confusion: Check the Status line when the window first appears. If FileMaker is finished, click Done.

At the bottom, the Spelling window says Status: Questionable Spelling. The Word text box displays the word in question. Things can proceed from here few different ways:

- Usually the correctly spelled word appears in the list. If it does, click the correct spelling, and then click Replace. (Or just double-click the correct word.)

- If you don't see the right spelling, correct it yourself. Type the correct spelling into the Word box. To confirm that your new spelling is correct, click Check; the status line changes to say Correct Spelling if you got it right. Otherwise, you're back where you started, with a misspelled word and a few suggestions below it.

- If you spelled it right originally, but FileMaker doesn't agree, click Ignore All to tell FileMaker to skip this so-called misspelling. Better yet, click Learn to teach FileMaker the word so it doesn't bother you in the future. (Clicking Learn adds the word to your current user dictionary, which is explained below. Ignore All only ignores the word temporarily; if you quit FileMaker and come back later, then it thinks the word is misspelled again.)

- If you change your mind and want to stop the spell checker, just click Cancel. This doesn't undo your changes; it just closes the dialog box.

- When the spell checker has finished, the status line changes to say Finished Spelling, and the Replace button says Done. Click the Done button to close the dialog box.

Spell Checking as You Type

FileMaker's spell checker also works automatically as you type. This *visual* spell check is a per-database setting, so you control it from the File Options dialog box. Choose File → File Options, and then click the Spelling tab. You find two options that you can mix and match to help you spell better, run faster, and jump higher. Well, you'll spell better, anyway.

The first option is "Indicate questionable spellings with special underline." If you miss your word processor, this one makes you feel right at home. You see that familiar red line underneath any word FileMaker doesn't like the looks of. Plus, if you right-click (Control-click on the Mac) the underlined word, and then, from the shortcut menu, choose Suggested Spellings, then FileMaker offers suggestions for spelling the word properly. From the same menu, you can also tell FileMaker to learn the word or ignore it.

If red lines don't get your attention, then you can turn on "Beep on questionable spellings", and FileMaker makes your computer beep when you type a space after a misspelled word. Unfortunately, it's just the same old alert beep that your computer makes in all kinds of other situations—so you can easily miss it. But in combination with the red line, this pair can be a formidable reminder to spell better.

Note: Visual spell checking can be handy. But often in a database your data entry includes things that don't need to be spell checked (inventory codes, abbreviations, email addresses and the like). Luckily, when you design your own databases, you can turn off the as-you-type version of spell checking for any particular field. See page 161 for details.

Managing Spelling Dictionaries

FileMaker comes with spelling dictionaries for various languages, and you can easily choose among them. Just choose Edit → Spelling → Select Dictionaries. The Select Dictionaries window lets you choose the language to use for all spell checking operations. You can see it in Figure 2-18.

User dictionaries

Remember from page 78 when you clicked the Learn button to teach FileMaker a
new word? When you did so, behind the scenes, FileMaker actually added that
word to the *user dictionary*, which is separate from the normal dictionary that
comes with FileMaker.

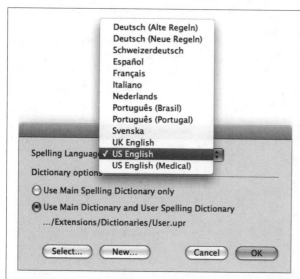

Figure 2-18:
*Out of the box, FileMaker uses a Spelling Language
that matches the language of your operating system.
But you can use a different language if you prefer.
Just select it from this pop-up menu. As you can see,
FileMaker even has a medical language dictionary
that keeps it from balking at all your ER terms. Use the
New button to create as many user dictionaries as
you want, and then select the one you want to use for
a particular database.*

You can even have multiple user dictionaries for different purposes. For example,
if you have two databases, one that tracks your apparel products and one that
stores information about tools, it might make sense to keep two user dictionaries.
The tools version might include words like "mm" and "pcs" while the apparel version would have "XXL" and "CottonPoly".

Note: In reality, it's nine times easier to just use one user dictionary, so you don't have to worry about
which one is selected. It doesn't hurt to have thousands of words in your user dictionary, but not having
enough makes spell checking more time consuming. Nothing's more boring than wading through the
same dozen correctly spelled words over and over. But, if you want more than one dictionary, you can
have it.

Printing and Preview Mode

It's a cruel fact of life that eventually you need to put your data on paper. You
might want mailing labels for all your customers in Canada, or a special printed
form prefilled with patient information for insurance filing. Sometimes you just
need your data with you when you're away from your computer. As you'll learn in
Part 2, you can arrange the data any way you want in FileMaker, and make certain

Rewriting the Dictionary

You've already learned how to add to your dictionary using the Learn button in the spell checker. Well, if you've ever wanted to just *tell* it what words you want it to skip, you can. Just choose Edit → Spelling → Edit User Dictionary to open the User Dictionary dialog box. Here you can add new entries to the dictionary (type the word, and then click Add), or remove existing entries (select the word, and then click Remove).

You can also export all the entries to a text file where you can edit them to your heart's content. When you click Export, FileMaker asks where it should save the export file. The file is a plain text file with one word on each line, which you can edit in a text-editing program.

If you already have a file that has words you want, then you can import those words into your user dictionary in one shot. For instance, if you use a lot of technical terms, then you might be able to download a list of terms from your industry and load them into a dictionary. The file has to have each word on its own line, so if it's in some other format,

then you need to clean it up first. (For example, use your word processor's Find/Replace function to turn a comma-separated list into one with a carriage return between each word.)

Also, make sure the file is plain text. A Microsoft Word file (.doc) or other special format won't work. (Making a plain-text file on Windows is a breeze: Just use Notepad, the simple text-editor program in the Accessories folder in your Start menu. On Mac OS X, however, you need a little more care. You can use Text Edit—it's in your Applications folder—but you must tell it you want plain text. Just choose Format → Make Plain Text before you save the file.)

Using the Import and Export features together can be particularly useful. You can export your user dictionary, edit it manually in the text-editing program (where making lots of edits might be easier), and then import it back in.

layouts that are particularly suitable for printing. But for now, remember that File-Maker lets you print *anything* you see onscreen (just choose File → Print). Its Print dialog box has a few special options. Figure 2-19 shows the Windows version. You can see the Mac OS X version (which requires a little more digging) in Figure 2-20.

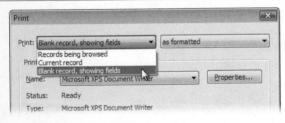

Figure 2-19:
FileMaker's Print dialog box gives you all the standard options, plus a little more. The Print pop-up menu (at the top in the dialog box in Windows) lets you tell FileMaker which records to print.

- **Records being browsed** tells FileMaker to print every record in the found set. To print all your Canadian customers, find them first, and then choose this option.

- **Current record** prints just the current record, which comes in handy when you just want to print *one* thing: your doctor's contact information to keep in the car, perhaps, or maybe Aunt Edna's candied yams recipe.

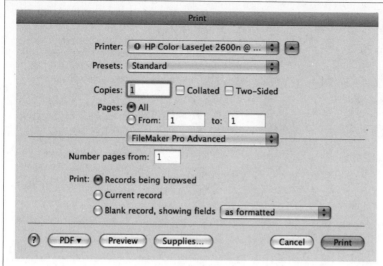

Figure 2-20:
*On Mac OS X, FileMaker's
special print options are tucked
away in a secret place. You
have to choose FileMaker Pro or
FileMaker Pro Advanced from
this unnamed but very
important pop-up menu. In this
example, you can see the field
styles you can pick from if you
elect to print a "Blank record,
showing fields".*

- **Blank record, showing fields** tells FileMaker to print what's onscreen with no data at all. You can change the look of each field to a box or an underline if you want (from the pop-up menu shown in Figure 2-19 and Figure 2-20, just pick your choice). Choose this option if you want to hand out pages for people to fill out with a pen (it's a kind of antique writing device), and later type their responses into the real database.

To see how the printout is going to look without committing trees to it, you can use *Preview mode* (Figure 2-21). You access Preview mode via the View menu, the Mode pop-up menu, or the Mode tabs (see page 20).

Preview mode shows you what your database looks like as though it were printed on paper. For instance, you can see whether FileMaker's going to chop off any information to fit on the page (anything beyond the width of the page simply isn't printed). Preview mode also indicates the margins, and lets you flip through the file page by page using the book icon.

Note: When you first go to Preview mode, the page count says "?" instead of the number of pages. File-Maker doesn't know how many pages it'll print until you force it to count them. If you drag the Page Slider all the way to the right, then FileMaker shows the last page. On its way there, FileMaker counts the pages, too. The process may take some time in a large document, but FileMaker catches up eventually.

On some computers and printers, you can reduce the printout by a percentage. When you do, Preview mode shows the page proportionately larger or smaller so you can see how the content area fits on the page. (Which options you get depends upon the computer, operating system, and printer you're using.)

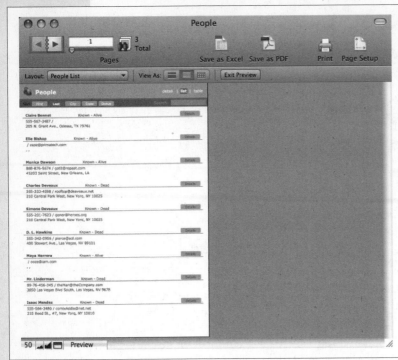

Figure 2-21:
Here the People database in List view is zoomed out to 50 percent of its actual size. The whole page fits in the window, and you can see some clues that you're in Preview mode. First, the book icon has a pair of binoculars on it. Flipping through book pages here shows you the pages of your potential printout. The Exit button has changed to read "Exit Preview".

Tip: Preview mode also has some green, tree-saving tools: Instead of printing, you can use one of the buttons in the Status toolbar to save the records you're viewing as an Excel file or a PDF. But if you do have to print, the Page Setup and Print dialog boxes are just a click away. Those standard page setup options affect Preview mode. If you change the paper orientation, then your print preview changes right away.

Beyond Text: Container Fields

Text and numbers are the backbone of most databases, but you can also store graphics, and other multimedia files in your database. For example, you can store a photograph of each employee right along with his personnel record, or add product shots to your inventory database. In either case, you can use the graphics much like data. You could print picture badges or product catalogs using your new container fields. (See page 99 to learn how to add container fields to your database.)

Unlike all the other field types, container fields don't expect (and don't accept) typed text. Instead, you use a menu command to insert just about any file you want, including pictures, sounds, animation, music, and movies. You can even put any file from your hard drive into a container field, like a PDF file or a Word document.

Note: The People database you downloaded at the beginning of this chapter has a layout called Container Fields, which you can use to follow this section. See Figure 2-22.

The Insert menu shows four commands: Picture, QuickTime, Sound, and File. Once you select a command, and then a file, you can also choose whether to store the file inside FileMaker, or just store a reference to the file. In the next sections, you'll learn how you can use these commands to get what you need.

Figure 2-22:
A container field can hold any file, but what you see on the layout depends on what you place in the field. If you put a picture into a container field, then FileMaker shows you the picture. If you record a sound file, then FileMaker gives you a special speaker icon that plays the sound when clicked. Movie files give you the typical play, pause, fast-forward, and rewind controls, just like movies on the Web. For any other kind of file, FileMaker just shows you the file's icon.

Pictures

A *picture* can be in any of more than a dozen formats, including the common kinds like JPEG, GIF, PNG, TIFF, PICT, and BMP. FileMaker also accepts Photoshop and PostScript (.eps) files. When you put a picture in a container field, the field displays the picture itself.

The following methods for copying, pasting, and inserting pictures into container fields are the same whether you're inserting a movie, a PDF, text, or another type of file. You see the same type of Insert dialog box for navigating your hard drive each time.

Copy and paste

The most obvious way to put a picture into a container field is to paste it in. You can copy a picture from just about anywhere, click once in the field, and then choose Edit → Paste (Ctrl+V or ⌘-V).

You can also copy data from the container field back into another program. Again, simply click once on the field, and choose Edit → Copy (Ctrl+C or ⌘-C) or Edit → Cut (Ctrl+X or ⌘-X). Whatever was in the field is now ready to paste into another field, record, or program.

Tip: Although you can't *type* text into a container field, you can *paste* it in a pinch. You can't edit the text once it's in the field, but you can export it (page 88). Once the text is back in a word processor, you can edit the text again.

Insert → Picture

Copy and paste is simple, but that method doesn't let you store only a reference to the file. Instead, you can insert the file directly into the field without ever leaving the comfort of FileMaker. Here's how:

1. **Click the Picture field.**

   You've now entered the record, and the Picture field is active.

2. **Choose Insert → Picture.**

   The Insert Picture dialog box appears. This window looks almost exactly like a typical Open File dialog box in Windows or Mac OS X. You can use it to find the picture you want to insert.

3. **Select the "Store only a reference to the file" option.**

   The file isn't stored in FileMaker, which can make your file sizes balloon, especially when you're storing lots of graphics. See the box on the next page for more information.

4. **Click Open.**

   FileMaker grabs the picture, and then puts it in the Image field.

Even though you've stored only a reference to the file, you can still see the graphic displayed in the container field. But remember that the real contents of the field is a text version of the path you showed FileMaker when you placed the file. So if the file is edited, then you see the changes, but if the file gets moved, you can't see the file unless you insert it again, this time from the new location.

You see why it's important to create a set of business rules for storing graphics. That is, if you're planning to store a lot of graphics or other files in your database, then you need a predictable folder structure, preferably on a shared volume or a file server. When you're ready to place a graphic, you upload it to the server first, and then you insert it, making sure to store a reference (and not the file itself). That way, the file is visible to everyone (as long as everyone has access to the server), and the file isn't likely to be moved.

Note: If you need to insert *lots* of pictures into a database, then you can save yourself a lot of trouble by using the File → Import Records → Folder command. See page 693 for the full explanation.

QuickTime

FileMaker uses QuickTime to help it deal with multimedia files, so you can insert any file type that QuickTime supports. Since QuickTime is frequently upgraded, the exact list of formats FileMaker supports also changes. If you're having trouble, check Apple's Web site for the list that matches your version of QuickTime.

When a container field holds a QuickTime file, you normally see the movie's *poster frame*, which is usually just the first frame of the movie. When you click the movie, a standard movie controller appears (like the one in Figure 2-22), so you can play, pause, fast-forward, and rewind it. The controller also has a button to adjust the volume and a little knob that shows you where you are in the movie.

Just as with a picture (see page 84), you use the Insert → QuickTime menu command to select a QuickTime file from the hard drive. If the command is not available, then check to make sure you have QuickTime installed on your computer.

Note: Unlike pictures and files, FileMaker *never* stores QuickTime movies in the database. Instead, the program remembers where the original file is on your hard drive, and then loads the data from it as needed. As with other files that are stored as references, if you move or delete the original file, then you see a message in your container field telling you FileMaker can no longer find the file. And as with other lost files, you need to show FileMaker where the files been moved with another Insert command.

POWER USERS' CLINIC

To Store or Not to Store

When you insert a picture or file (see page 84), the dialog box includes an option to "Store only a reference to the file". When this option is turned off, FileMaker copies the actual file into your database. You can move or delete the original file, and the data still appears in the field, because the database now contains all the file's information within itself. If you turn on "Store only a reference to the file", then FileMaker doesn't copy the file into the field at all. Instead, it just remembers data about the file you select, including its name and the path to the file. Each time you look at this record, FileMaker finds the original file so it can display the data. In this respect, it works like a shortcut or alias. If the file gets moved, deleted, or renamed FileMaker can't display the file, but you see a short message that tells you the file can't be displayed.

You don't have a simple rule for when you should store the actual file, and when you should store a reference instead. Some people store files because it's easier, which is especially true when multiple people are using the database from different computers. However, here are a couple of reasons you might want to store a reference instead:

- Storing many *larger* files can make your database get big—really big—which can cause a number of problems. Performance can suffer, it takes longer to back up, and moving a huge database file from one place to another is a real pain. If you're trying to email the database to your home office, your ISP may not appreciate (or allow) a 3 GB attachment, for example. If the inserted files aren't critical to the record data, it may make sense to leave them out of the database so you can work with it more easily.

- Sometimes you want to catalog files inside FileMaker even though they might change over time. For example, if you want to put promotional images into a database so they're easy to locate, then you probably *don't* want to make editing those images difficult. If you store a reference to these images, then you can still edit the originals any time. As long as you haven't changed their names or locations, when you look in FileMaker, you see the latest edits.

Sound

A *sound* is a recorded bit of audio. You can insert, copy/paste, or even record sounds right into the field. Use sound files to keep audio notes with a project record, or record your practice speeches, and save them for when you're famous. When a container field holds a recorded sound, it displays a little speaker icon; double-click it to hear the recorded sound.

Recording sound

The Insert → Sound command doesn't bring up the same dialog box as the other Insert commands. Instead, it shows the Record dialog box (Figure 2-23). If your computer has a microphone attached, then you can record any sound directly into the field.

Figure 2-23:
Select a container field, and then choose Insert → Sound (or double-click the container field) to record audio. Click the Record button to start, and then click the Stop or Pause buttons as needed. Use the Play button to check your recording. Most computers let you record any sound your computer can play. For example, you can usually record sound from audio CDs in your CD-ROM drive.

The Record dialog box is simple, but capable. The speaker icon provides feedback about what the microphone is picking up, by showing little sound waves. The more sound waves you see, the louder the recording. In fact, the speaker icon lets you check for sound waves even when you're *not* recording, so use it to do a quick sound check ("Testing, testing, 1, 2, 3").

Note: The Insert → Sound command records sound directly into the field. If you already have a sound file (an MP3 for example), then choose Insert → QuickTime instead. In general, if the data you're putting in the field has a *time component* (meaning it happens over time, like video or sound), treat it like a QuickTime file. Sound formats need to be compatible with your version of QuickTime to display the player controls, though.

Here's how the buttons work:

- The **Record** button starts the recording session. Click it when everything is set up: Your CD is playing, or you've cleared your throat, reviewed your notes, and are ready to speak.

- The **Stop** button stops whatever you're doing. If you're recording, then the session stops immediately, and you can't add to it. If you're playing back recorded audio, then the playback starts again at the beginning the next time you click Play.

- The **Pause** button pauses either a recording or a playback session. Click it a second time to resume either operation.

- The **Play** button plays whatever you've recorded.

- Click **Cancel** to return to FileMaker, and delete your recording.

- Click **Save** to make your recording permanent. Once you click Save, you see the sound icon in the container field, and you can double-click the field to play the audio.

Tip: If the record dialog box doesn't appear, make sure you have an audio input device that works with your computer, that your computer has a sound card, and that the audio device is set up properly. For setup, use the Hardware and Sound Control Panel (Windows Vista) or Audio Devices Control Panel (Windows XP) or the Sound System Preferences (Mac).

File

A container field can also hold a *file*. Since FileMaker doesn't know what the file is supposed to be, it simply shows you the file's name and icon. Unfortunately, you can't do anything with a file like this while it's in FileMaker. You can't edit it. You can't even open it and view its contents. Rather, the container field simply holds the file for you.

GEM IN THE ROUGH

PDFs in Mac OS X

You'll find that the ability to store pictures, movies, sounds, and files in your database comes in handy on many occasions. For example, if you're a recruiter, you can store resumes in Microsoft Word or PDF format right in the database alongside the info about a particular candidate. In fact, the Adobe PDF format is so common that you may want to use FileMaker to keep track of PDF files—the brochure, flyer, or documentation for each of your products, the prospectus for each of your investments, or a floor plan for each of your properties.

You already know you can use the Insert → File command to store the PDF document right in a container field (and get it back out again later to look at it). But if you're on Mac OS X, you can do one better. Choose Insert → Picture, and then select a PDF file. FileMaker shows you the PDF (the first page of it, anyway) right in the container field. If your document has more than one page, then you need to export the PDF out of the container field (see below) to read the whole thing.

Or, try this unexpected twist: You can read multipage PDFs right in FileMaker if you use Insert → QuickTime instead. This time, when you click the container field itself, the standard QuickTime movie controls appear. Using these controls, you can flip through the pages in the PDF: Fast Forward goes to the next page, Rewind goes to the previous page. If you press Play, then FileMaker flips through the pages one after the other until it reaches the end of the document.

If you need to search within a PDF file, try this. Open the PDF file, select all the text, copy it, and then paste it in a regular text field. That way, FileMaker can search the text field, but you can view the PDF in all its glory in the container field.

If you can't use the file in FileMaker, why put it there at all? Sometimes people need to keep track of lots of files. But keeping large numbers of files in a folder on your hard drive can be a real drag since they can be slow to search and hard to reorganize. With FileMaker, you can keep the files right alongside other important data. For example, you can store project specifications (in Microsoft Word format) and diagrams (in Visio format) in your database along with tasks, team members, and timelines.

The most common way to place a file into a container field is with the Insert → File command. On Windows, you can also copy a file on the desktop, and then paste it into a container field. When you insert a file, FileMaker makes no effort to figure out what's *in* the file. If you choose a picture, then you still get just the name and icon. If you want to *see* the picture itself in FileMaker, then you must choose Insert → Picture, as described on page 84.

Exporting data from container fields

Inserting files into container fields is all well and good, but it's just as important to get them back out again. To use the file in another program, click in the container field, and then choose Edit → Export Field Contents. FileMaker asks you where you want to put the file, and what to name it. Click Save, and FileMaker creates a new file that's an exact copy of the one you put in the container field.

Note: If you turned on the "Store only a reference to the file" option (see the box on page 85) when you added the file, then you don't need to get it back out again (after all, the file is on your hard drive somewhere). Instead, double-click the container field to open the original file in the appropriate program.

POWER USERS' CLINIC

Getting the Most Out of Your Fields

The Edit → Export Field Contents command isn't limited to container fields. With very few exceptions, you can export the contents of almost any field to a file (if you can't click in the field, then you can't export its contents, nor can you export a sound you recorded in FileMaker). To understand why you can't click in some fields, read about field behavior in Chapter 6, and about security in Chapter 16. You can also read about exporting data from more than one field at a time on page 677.

Here are some examples of how to export to your advantage:

- Use Edit → Export Field Contents to create a file without having to retype what you've stored in File-Maker. But if you just whiz by the Export Field Contents dialog box without looking, then you miss a couple of options that save you buckets of time. If you want to watch a QuickTime video at a size larger than the skimpy container field, just click the "Automatically open file" option as you export the contents of your field. FileMaker creates a duplicate video file for you, and then opens a QuickTime player for your viewing pleasure.

- In fact, FileMaker is smart enough to open the right program for whatever you've exported. You get a text editor for plain data, a PDF viewer for a PDF, or

a graphics viewer for graphics. You don't have to scramble around looking for a program that can handle your file, because FileMaker figures it out for you.

- If you want to spread the wealth around—let your colleagues know about a customer who always makes a big order at the beginning of the new quarter, say—then turn on the "Create email with file as attachment" option when you export a field's contents. FileMaker makes a file, and then launches your email program, starts a new email, and attaches your new file to the email. All you have to do is type in a name, subject, and some text, and then send the email on its merry way. FileMaker uses a regular email program for this process, though, so if you use only a Web browser for email, this feature's so handy that it might make you jump off the fence and get a proper email program.

Let FileMaker really impress you by clicking both options at once. You get a copy of the file open for reference and a fresh, shiny email nearly ready for sending. If you've got the screen real estate, you can look at both these little jewels while you're checking out the FileMaker record that spawned them.

Building a New Database

You really get FileMaker to work for you when you build your own databases. Lots of programs out there can help you keep track of one thing or another, but when you build your own database, it "thinks" the way you think, and works the way your business works. You can custom-craft it to capture, organize, and display the information you need to know, when you need to know it.

In this chapter, you'll learn to outfit your People database from the ground up. Creating a database always starts the same way: You set up a *table* (which resembles a spreadsheet) and outfit the table with *fields*—containers that you customize to hold the types of information you want to store in your database.

Tables and Fields

So you're getting tired of your job, and you decide it would be exciting to get into the private investigator business. You found an office, ordered business cards, secured a phone line, and purchased some snazzy furniture. But have you thought about how you're going to *run* your business? Chances are, you could use some help from a database. And when you build a database, you need to first to think about *what kind of information* it's going to track. For example, a private investigator may want to keep track of people—names, phone numbers, aliases, passport numbers, and so on. Someone in retail, however, may want to track inventory—product names, descriptions, item numbers, prices, quantities, and similar details.

Tables: The Foundation of Your Database

You already know that whatever information you put in your database goes into fields—and that's where your database building begins. These fields in turn comprise a *table*. Tables are at the heart of the database, holding all the information and keeping it organized. Everything else in a database works in service of the tables in some way, letting you edit, extract, or view the information.

Conceptually, a table has rows and columns. The fields you create become the columns in the table. As you add records, you add new rows to the table. It's called a table because it stores information in a tabular form, just like the table of values at the back of a college math book. When you first start out with FileMaker, you may not even be aware that tables exist, but you have one anyway. FileMaker always creates one table for you when you make a new database, and that's where it puts all your information. It doesn't matter how your database *looks*—even if you never see any rows and columns, you still have a table inside.

Note: In this chapter, you're going to build a database based on a single table. As you've probably guessed, a database can have more than one table. A database can also have no tables at all—instead, it can work with tables from other databases. You can even hook several tables together so they can share data and keep track of *relationships* between records. That's why FileMaker Pro is called a *relational* database program. In Part 4, you'll learn all about multiple table databases and hooking multiple databases together.

Figuring Out What Fields You Need

You decide the first thing your new business needs is a database to keep track of the people you deal with. Figuring out what fields your table should have is one of the most important decisions you'll make. To make the right choices, think carefully about *what* you need to track.

You have a lot of detail to consider when you plan a database. As you work, you may find it helpful to take some notes or even draw a picture. You'll learn more tips for this kind of planning in Part 4. For starters, use these guidelines:

- **Records** are *things*, like people, buildings, invoices, payments, products, or orders. If a single record holds information about more than one thing, you're probably making a mistake. For example, in the database you're building now, the records represent *people*. If you later want to keep track of the invoices you send to your customers, you don't want to add fields like Invoice Number, Amount, and Due Date to this table.

  Why not? Because if you did that, each person's record would have room for only one invoice. If the same customer makes another purchase, you'd have to create a new record for each invoice *and* enter the person's information all over again. Even worse, when the customer gets a new address or phone number, you'd have to change it individually in *every* record.

Note: If you have to keep track of more than one thing, there's a solution: Have more than one table—one for people and one for invoices, for example. If your business starts branching out, you may even need more than one database. You'll get into that in Part 4.

- **Fields** are *attributes* of the item in each record. First Name, for example, is an attribute of a person. Most things have lots of attributes, and that's why most records have lots of fields. Unfortunately, there's some gray area here. For instance, is Company Name an attribute of a *person* (the company he works for), or is it a separate *thing*? The answer depends on what you want to do with the Company Name information. Again, Part 4 will help you work through these tough issues. For now, a simple rule to follow is, if you're tracking only one attribute of a thing, then it's usually safe to make it a field. For instance, if you just want to keep track of the company a person works for, and don't plan to use the company's main address, phone number, or Web address, then you probably need only a simple Company Name field on each record.

UP TO SPEED

Think Table

You must understand the concept of a *table* when you're creating a database. In any particular table, every record has room to store the *same kind* of information. If you see a field called Email Address on one record, there's a place to put an email address on every record. If you want to record someone's birth date, then you need to add a field for it. When you do, every record gets a Birth Date field— if you type in a birthday on only one record, then the other records have an empty Birth Date field.

When you're deciding what fields to put in your database, it helps to imagine a real table, or a spreadsheet.

Spreadsheets have rows, which are the records, and they have columns, which are the fields. If you have a column in one row, obviously, it's there for every row. If you add a new column, even after you've added 100 rows, that column is available to all the rows at once. See Figure 3-1.

Figure 3-1:
Even if you never see your data arranged this way in FileMaker, it's helpful to think of your data in terms of a table or a spreadsheet. If you visualize your data arranged in columns and rows, then you can more easily figure out which fields you need to create in a new database.

So far, you know that your database will track people, and its fields will include any important attributes about a person. You may be tempted to have Name, Address, Phone Number, and Email Address as your fields—but you'd be making a mistake. What happens when you want to find all the people in Washington State? A search for Washington in the Address field finds them, as well as everyone on any Washington street and everyone in a town called Washington. Same goes for first and last name. You need a little experience and some careful thought to pick just the right fields. It's usually a bad move to have different kinds of information in the same field. Instead, think about what elements—no matter how small—are important to how you'll search, sort, analyze, or otherwise access your records later. In database lingo, those bits of information are *individually significant*, and each one should get its own field.

For example, the first line of a person's address often contains several pieces of information: a street number, street name, direction (north, south, east, west), and an apartment, building, or suite number. Should these all be separate fields, or is one field enough to hold the whole street address? Are all these bits of data *individually significant*?

UP TO SPEED

Explore Starter Solutions

When you first launch FileMaker Pro, the Quick Start dialog box shows you lots of ways to get started exploring the program. If you choose "Create a database using a Starter Solution", then you see a list of templates that come free with FileMaker Pro. They're grouped in general categories, like Business, Education and Personal, and cover common database uses, like Home Budgets, Music Libraries, and Contact Management.

These starter files are a good showcase of FileMaker's features, but because they're templates, they aren't meant to meet *your* specific business needs. Even if you think about starting small, these files may need a lot of retrofitting to work well as your business grows. Pro developers rarely use these templates, preferring to start creating from scratch. However, poking around in these files is a great way to spark ideas about features you want to learn how to create.

So feel free to take a look at a few starter files, and then come back to this book to learn how make a solution that's 100 percent tailored to your business rules and procedures. Here's how:

1. To create a new database from a Starter Solution, choose File → New Database.

The FileMaker Quick Start dialog box appears (Figure 3-2). If it doesn't appear, then check your preferences. Select the "Show FileMaker Quick Start Screen" option, and then try again.

2. In the New Database dialog box, from the pop-up menu, select the "Business—People & Assets" category.

The list shows each template in this category. You can, of course, choose any template that looks like the database of your dreams, but in this example you're looking for Contact Management.

3. Select Contact Management, and then click OK.

You see a standard Save dialog box.

4. Name the new database, and then save it somewhere on your hard drive.

The new database appears onscreen.

You can start entering data and exploring the file right away. As you move through the chapters in the book, you'll be able to understand what you're seeing under the hood of these starter solutions.

Most people use just one field for the entire street address, since they don't have reason to divide it into smaller elements and work with them separately. But suppose your work requires you to send different marketing materials to different people depending on which part of town they live in. You need to isolate people by street name (all the people on Hawthorne Street) or by ranges of street numbers (1000 to 1400 Elm). In this example, street name and house number are individually significant, and you want to create a separate field for each.

For your People database, you start off with fields to hold all the basics: First Name, Last Name, Phone Number, Street Address, City, State, Zip Code, and Email Address.

Defining Fields

As you know by now, every FileMaker database starts with a table. And since fields and tables are so fundamental to a database, FileMaker asks you to create them as soon as you start. FileMaker assumes your needs are pretty simple, and starts right off asking what fields you want in this single table.

1. **Choose File → New Database.**

   Up comes the FileMaker Quick Start dialog box (see Figure 3-2).

Figure 3-2:
The FileMaker Quick Start window gathers all the things you're likely to want when getting started into one place. See the box on page 94 to find out how it works.

2. **Select the "Create an empty database" option, and then click OK.**

   FileMaker asks you what to name your new database, and where to put it.

3. **Call this database People since that's what you're going to track.**

In the Save As box (Mac OS X) or the "File name" box (Windows), type *People*, and then click Save.

FileMaker creates the new file, and automatically adds the .fp7 file name extension to your database name.

Note: That's not a typo. The extension .fp7 from FileMaker Pro 7 is the same for version 10. Good thing, too: It means people who still have versions 7, 8 or 9 can use your version 10 files, although some of the new features don't work for them.

UP TO SPEED

The Quick Start Window

You can get to the FileMaker Quick Start window (Figure 3-2) in two ways: First, unless you turn it off, this window is the first thing that greets you when you launch FileMaker. Later, you can return at any time by choosing File → New Database. If you don't see it, you may have turned if off. Just choose Edit → Preferences (Windows) or FileMaker Pro → Preferences (Mac) and turn on Show FileMaker Quick Start Screen.

From this one window, you get instant access to three handy features:

- On the left edge, click the Create Database icon to see various options for making new databases. You've already seen how to make a brand new database. Turn on the "Create a database from an existing" radio button to make a database out of data you already have. You can create a database from an Excel spreadsheet, a tabular data file, or a Bento database.

- Choose "Create a database using a Starter Solution" to start with one of FileMaker's built-in templates instead of building your new database from the ground up. (See the box on page 92 for more on templates.)

- Click the Open Database icon to open an existing FileMaker database. From here, you can get a list of recently opened databases, manage a collection of favorites, and find and open databases available on your local network (see Chapter 18 to learn how to share your database on the network).

- Finally, click Learn More for access to online tutorials and instructional videos about building FileMaker databases.

If you'd rather not see this window anymore, just turn on "Do not show Quick Start again", and then click OK. If you change your mind later, then you can bring it back again in FileMaker's preferences window, as explained above.

Just as promised, FileMaker asks you what fields you want—you see the Manage Database dialog box shown in Figure 3-3. This little beauty is where you build and manage tables. You have a tab for the tables themselves, a tab for the fields in those tables, and a tab called Relationships, where you tell FileMaker how different tables work together. For now, you can simply ignore Tables and Relationships. Your one free table has already been created (it's called People, just like the database), and you're ready to give it some fields.

Figure 3-3:
In the Manage Database dialog box (File → Manage → Database), the Fields tab is where you go to tell FileMaker about the fields in your database. The field list shows all the fields in the selected table. Here, you haven't created any yet.

Since you've already decided what fields you want, all that's left is to tell FileMaker what you've planned. First, create a field to hold a person's first name:

1. **In the Field Name box, type *First Name*.**

   Every field has a name—you can choose almost anything you want. (For some guidelines, see the box on page 98.)

2. **In the Type pop-up menu, make sure Text is selected.**

   Every field has a *type*, which you'll learn about shortly. You're creating Text type fields right now because a first name is textual.

3. **In the Comment box, type *This is the person's first name* to help you remember what goes into the field.**

   Every field can have a comment to help you, the developer, remember what it's for. In this case, it's pretty obvious, so you could certainly leave the comment blank instead.

Note: Field comments don't show up when someone's *using* the database. You see them only in this window. If you need extra information on the screen for the database's user to see, then you want to *customize the layout,* as explained in Chapter 4.

---

4. **Click Create.**

   FileMaker creates the First Name field and adds it to the field list.

Now that you've created the first field, the rest are a snap. Following the same steps as above, create Text fields with the following names:

• Last Name

• Phone Number

- Street Address

- City

- State

- Zip

- Email Address

- Status

- Notes

When you're finished, the field list should look like Figure 3-4. (See the box on page 112 to learn why your Zip field must be a text field.)

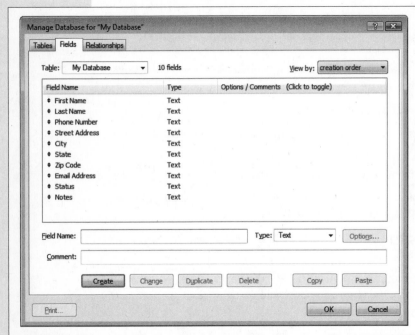

Figure 3-4:
Once you've created the necessary fields, the field list should look like this example. You may not see the field comments in the third column—this column can show comments or options. To switch between these two possibilities, click the column header. In this example, the fields' comments seem redundant. When your fields have descriptive names, comments may not be necessary. But as you start to create fields that perform math (Part 4) or help with behind-the-scenes work (Part 5), you'll find comments more helpful.

Changing a Field's Name

While you're here, you may as well try some more field-defining tricks. Say you want to change the name of the Zip field to Zip Code. It's very easy:

1. **In the field list, highlight the Zip field.**

   FileMaker fills in the Field Name, Type, and Comment boxes with the information about the Zip field.

2. **Change the field name to *Zip Code*, and then click Change.**

When you have a field selected in the field list, the Change button becomes available. Instead of creating a *new* field called Zip Code, FileMaker just changes the selected field, making its name Zip Code instead of just Zip.

Tip: If you select a field and make modifications to any of the settings at the bottom of the Manage Database window, FileMaker guesses you may want to click Change. If you try to select *another* field without clicking Change, FileMaker asks if you want to Save first. Clicking Save is the same as clicking Change: It updates the selected field with the new settings.

Duplicating a Field

The Duplicate button creates a new field that's an exact copy of what's selected in the field list. The new field's name says *Copy* at the end, which is the only difference.

Fields can have many special options in addition to the name, type, and comment. You'll learn about them later in this chapter. Duplicate comes in handy when you want a second field with many options in common with the first. Just click Duplicate, and then change the new field's name.

Deleting a Field

As you create your fields, you may get partway through your list, and then decide to name *all* your fields differently, say, or combine two fields into one. You may find it easier to delete some fields and start fresh than to painstakingly modify each one. To delete a field, highlight it, and then click Delete.

Reordering the Field List

The field list in the Manage Database window is for your eyes only—people *using* the database to enter, search, and edit data never see this list. Nonetheless, as the number of fields grows, keeping the list tidy makes your job easier. That's why FileMaker gives you complete control over the order in which the fields are listed.

If you're the type who likes-it-the-way-you-like-it-doggonit, you can drag each field individually to put them in exactly the order you want. To the left of the field you want to move, just click the tiny double-arrows, and drag straight up or down.

If you're a little more laid-back about such things, you can just tell FileMaker to arrange them for you. Either click one of the column headings to sort by the information in that column, or make a selection from the "View by" pop-up menu. In either case, fields jump into order. You can arrange them alphabetically by the name of the field (Field name), in the order the fields were originally created (Creation order), or in groups by the type of data the field holds (Field type). For example, if you can't remember what you called a field, but you know you created it recently, from the pop-up menu, choose "Creation order", and look for your field near the end of the list.

FREQUENTLY ASKED QUESTION

Field Naming Conventions

I've seen databases with all kinds of funny field names. I've seen all caps, no spaces, lots of odd prefixes, and plenty of funny punctuation. How should I name fields?

People can get downright philosophical discussing the best way to name fields, and it seems everyone has an opinion. So how should you name your fields? Well, here are some of the common suggestions, as well as some discussion about why you would or wouldn't want to follow them.

- Field names should have a prefix or suffix indicating their type.

  FileMaker Pro developers often indicate the type of field in the field name. The reasoning is simple: You often have to pick a field from a list when you're building a database. All you see is its name, and you often want to know the type as well. In that spirit, people may name the First Name field something like "tFirst Name" where that "t" at the start means "text."

  For most ordinary databases (in other words, not the really complicated stuff), you can usually figure out the type of a field by its name. For example, a field called Birth Date is probably a date field, while First Name is almost certainly text. You also don't often care about a field's type. For these reasons, you can usually ignore this advice and keep your field less cluttered.

- Field names should have a prefix or suffix indicating their purpose.

  When a table starts to get a lot of fields, it can really be hard to keep track of which one does what. For example, a big database that keeps track of products can have dozens of fields.

Some would be about inventory levels (like "Quantity on Hand", "Quantity on Order", Quantity Desired, and Quantity Back Ordered). Others would be about pricing (like Base Price, "Price for 10 or More", "Price for 20 or More", "Price for 30 or More", and so on). Some people like to come up with special codes to represent different types of information, to keep the field names more compact: QTY In Stock, QTY Order, QTY Desired, QTY Backorder, QTY Average. Again, for most databases this problem doesn't occur very often. Consistent field names usually tend to develop their own English-language prefixes anyway (like all the Quantity fields). It's true, though, that field names can start to get long, and long names are more difficult to work with. In this case, abbreviations make good sense.

- Some database programs aren't so flexible with names. To be safe, FileMaker field names should follow the same rules as everybody else.

  This rule usually *doesn't* apply. After all, why settle for names like "FNAME" and "LNAME" when FileMaker happily accepts "First Name" and "Last Name" instead? Well, there's one exception. If you plan to use ODBC or JDBC to access your FileMaker data from other applications (you know who you are), you're better off avoiding spaces and punctuation, and starting a field name with a letter rather than a number, since these other systems aren't as tolerant as FileMaker when it comes to field names.

Once you've told FileMaker to organize your fields, you can get *back* to the last manual ordering by choosing "Custom order".

Warning: If you tell FileMaker to sort the field list, and *then* move a field manually, the *new* order becomes your custom order. If you've put things in an order you like, make sure you always switch *back* to it before you move any fields.

FREQUENTLY ASKED QUESTION

Field Naming Problems

When I try to name my field "Customer Order/Preferred Delivery", FileMaker gives me some guff about not being able to "easily" use the name in a formula. Should I worry?

Well, maybe. Later on, when you read about calculation fields (see Part 4), you'll see that you can add the contents of two fields together, for example, or multiply the contents of one field by the contents of another. In fact, you can make field contents do just about any arithmetic dance you want them to do. When you perform math on fields, you're probably using number fields, but you can also do a surprising amount of work with calculations on text fields.

The specific problem with the field name above is that pesky "/" sign, which, in the language of math, means *divided by*. So if you try to use the contents of that field to do math, FileMaker gets confused about where the field name ends and the calculation begins.

This problem isn't insurmountable, though. FileMaker *can* use these sorts of fields in mathematical expressions, but it has to muss up your formulas with geeky codes, making it harder for you to read and edit them later. The exact list of symbols and special words to avoid in field names is long and pretty esoteric (you can see it in the error message FileMaker shows when it doesn't like a name). Rather than memorize the list, if you ever see this message, just consult its advice, and adjust your field name accordingly. It really makes things easier as your database grows more complex.

Printing Field Definitions

When you click Print, FileMaker prints all the details about the fields you've selected. The printout resembles the field list, except that it's expanded to make room for *everything* about a field. You can print such a list if you want to keep your field names and types handy while you're working with your database, or if you need to send a list of fields to an associate so she can send you the right information.

Note: You have to select at least one field for the Print button to become clickable. Then, when you click Print, you'll get details for any field that's highlighted. To print just a few, Ctrl+click (⌘-click) each field you want to print. If you want a printout of *all* the fields in the table, first select one field, and then choose Edit → Select All. Now every field is selected, and the Print button prints them all.

Click OK when you're done creating and changing fields. FileMaker adds your fields to the database window. Congratulations! You've just built a database. It isn't pretty—as Figure 3-5 proves—but it works. The Status toolbar shows that your database has one record. Add data for a few records, using any of the techniques you learned in Chapter 1. You can even find, sort, print, and Find/Replace in this simple database.

Field Types

Every field you create has a *type*, which determines what kind of information it holds. All the fields you just created are *text* fields—they're designed to hold various kinds of text. FileMaker actually has eight different field types, each designed for a slightly different kind of data. For just a moment, you'll step away from the database you're building to get a brief introduction to each field type. You'll actually use these field types in various databases throughout the rest of this book.

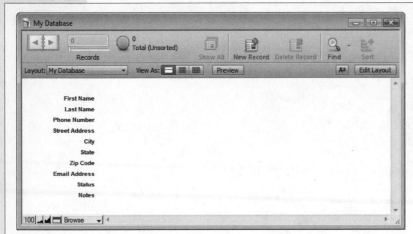

Figure 3-5:
Your first database! It has the same features as every other database you've seen, and you should have no trouble adding and editing records. It may not be pretty, but it works. You'll learn how to improve its looks in the next chapter.

You specify a field's type when you create it by selecting an option in the Type pop-up menu. The pop-up menu also shows handy keyboard shortcuts for each field type, so you can quickly create a series of fields without clicking the mouse.

Text

Text fields are the most common type—they hold any kind of text information, like a name, phone number, or email message. A text field can store up to one billion letters, numbers, or symbols, so there's plenty of room for any realistic purpose. Whatever you type into a text field shows up just as you typed it, and you can use any of the formatting options described in Chapter 2.

Number

As if it isn't obvious, *number* fields hold numbers. Like a text field, you can type in just about anything you want, but as soon as you leave the field, FileMaker does its best to turn your data into a number, and that's what it shows you. It's not as obvious that not all numerical values are numbers. Use a number field if you're going to be performing *math* with the numbers in your database. But for things like Zip codes and telephone numbers, use text fields instead. See the box on page 112 for an example and explanation.

Numbers can be very large or very small, and they're *very* precise. The actual limits are thus:

- Numbers must be between 10^{800} and -10^{800} (it's actually 9.99999999…e799, because -10^{800} itself isn't included). If you're counting something reasonable—say, the number of protons in the universe—you'll be just fine.

- You get 800 significant digits in all. If you don't know what that means, ask a high-school algebra student.

- Only the first 400 digits are indexed in all, significant or otherwise. So if you're searching for numbers, then you have a little less precision to work with.

Use the Keyboard

You can get to almost everything in the Manage Database window's Fields tab from the keyboard alone. If you're a speed freak, you can avoid the mouse almost entirely. Here's how:

- On Windows, use the Tab key to move among buttons, text boxes, and pop-up menus.

- On Mac OS X, press the Tab key to move between the Field Name, Comment, and field list. (Unfortunately, FileMaker doesn't honor Mac OS X's Full Keyboard Access settings.)

- While the field list is active, use the up and down arrow keys to select the next and previous fields.

- Hold down Ctrl (⌘) while pressing the arrow keys, to move the selected field up or down in the list.

- Use the keyboard shortcuts for each field type. (Look in the Type pop-up menu to see them.)

- Press Alt+N (⌘-O) to see the field options dialog box for the selected field.

- Press the Delete key to delete the selected field. Then, when you're asked if you're sure you want to delete the field, press D.

- Press the first letter of a button name in any of FileMaker's alert message boxes instead of clicking the button.

- Press the Escape key, then the Discard button to close the Manage Database window, and throw away all your changes.

FileMaker's number-handling capability is absolutely top-notch. If your work requires very precise mathematics, you'll be thrilled. For example, FileMaker can handle much larger numbers, and much more decimal point precision than Excel.

You can enter numbers in FileMaker as you would in most any program. Type the number and any symbols that define it, like a negative sign or a decimal point. You can also use *scientific notation*. For example, if you have a burning desire to count the air molecules in your living room, you can put 6.02E23 into a number field, which is a lot easier to type than 60,200,000,000,000,000,000,000,000. Of course, the exponent part (after the E) can be negative if really small numbers make your socks go up and down.

Date

Shocking as it may seem, a *date* field holds a date. FileMaker thinks of dates in numerical form by month, day, and year. You can put various punctuation marks *between* these numbers, but most people use a slash, a dash, or a period. For instance, 2/25/1975, 2-25-1975, and 2.25.1975 are all valid dates. If you type a date the wrong way, then you see the error message in Figure 3-6.

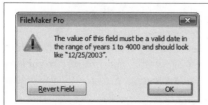

Figure 3-6:
If FileMaker doesn't like the date the way you entered it, it tells you so. The message ends with an example of a correctly formatted date.

Tip: If your date's in the current calendar year, then you can save time by typing just the day and month. FileMaker fills in the current year for you. Don't add that second punctuation mark, though, or FileMaker barks at you. Save even more time with the Insert → Date command. Just press Ctrl (⌘) and the hyphen key (–) at the same time.

FileMaker accepts dates from the year 1 (AD) to the year 4000. If you enter a two-digit year (like 09 or 87) FileMaker guesses you're being slack, and puts either 19 or 20 in front. Which one you get can be hard to guess so to avoid mistakes, you're always better off entering all four digits. If you really want a two-digit year (because you're entering a date from ancient history) then enter it like this: 6/17/0034.

UP TO SPEED

System Formats

Your computer's settings determine how FileMaker wants numbers, dates, and times entered into fields. For example, in the United States, 7/12/2007 means July 12, but in Europe, it means December 7. In Windows, you change the settings in the Date and Time control panel. In Mac OS X's System Preferences, you use the International pane. When you create a database, FileMaker notes your operating system settings and uses them. If you open the same database on a computer with different settings, then you get a message asking if you want to use the system format, or the format stored with the database.

If you don't want this message to appear, go to the File Options dialog box, and then make your preference known.

1. Choose File → File Options. This window lets you control a handful of settings for the current database.

2. Select the Text tab.

In this tab, the Data Entry section lets you control how the database handles varying format settings. The first two radio buttons prevent the message box from showing up. The third is for when you *want* FileMaker to ask every time.

Time

You can probably guess what goes into a *time* field. Time fields actually serve two purposes, though. First, you can enter a time of day, like 4:30 p.m. or 1:27:03 a.m. But you can also enter a *duration* instead, like 123:38:22 (meaning 123 hours, 38 minutes, 22 seconds). Even though this sequence isn't a valid time of day, it's an acceptable time value.

You can easily enter times. They always go in like so: hours:minutes:seconds, and the seconds can also have a decimal part for fractions of a second. If you don't need seconds, then you can just type in hours:minutes. Likewise, if you don't need minutes either, then you can just enter a number of hours.

If you're entering a time of day, you can put an AM or PM after the time if you want, or you can use 24-hour notation.

For durations, you don't have to limit yourself to a 60 minute hour. A time like 0:82:17 is perfectly valid (it means 82 minutes, 17 seconds, and is exactly equivalent to 1:22:17). (On page 262, you'll learn how to force a field to always show a valid time value in the format of your choice.)

Note: When entering time values, you *always* start with hours. If you're trying to enter just 12 minutes, 37 seconds, then you have to enter *00:12:37* or *0:12:37* so FileMaker doesn't think you mean 12 *hours*.

Time values are also quite precise. If you're recording track event times for your school, you can enter *00:00:27.180* for 27 seconds, 180 milliseconds. You can put up to six digits to the right of the decimal point.

Timestamp

A *timestamp* field is kind of like a date field and a time field combined. It holds *both* a date *and* a time. You use this kind of field to record when an event occurred, or when it will occur. You may be tempted to use two fields (a date field and a time field) for something like this, but that road only leads to heartache and pain when you start using FileMaker's *calculation* features with your fields. If something happens on a specific date and time, you should use a timestamp field for it.

Timestamps support the same less-than-a-second accuracy as time fields. They show up as a date followed by a time with a space in between. All the rules for date and time entry apply: 2/25/1975 2:45 AM.

Container

Use container fields to store graphics, movies, sounds, or files—text documents, spreadsheets, PDFs, or even other FileMaker files. Chapter 2 (page 82) has the full story about what you can put in container fields.

Note: Unlike with text and other kinds of fields, you can't sort records using a container field, and you can't perform finds on them. (But you can create a text field with keywords you enter manually that lets you find and sort.)

Calculation and summary

Unlike the other field types discussed so far, *calculation* and *summary* fields don't hold your stuff at all. Instead, they make up their own values based on the settings you give them. For calculation fields, you can specify a special *formula* it uses to determine its value. For instance, if you had a field called Birth Date, you could create a calculation field that shows the person's age. The Age field automatically updates to stay correct as time goes by, so you don't have to change it. You'll learn all about calculations in Part 4.

Summary fields are the strangest of all. They aren't even associated with a record. Instead, their value depends on the values of other fields across some set of records. For instance, a summary field could show you the number of people in the database who are from California, or the total dollar value of all outstanding invoices for a customer. You'll learn about summary fields in Chapter 6.

Advanced Field Options

At this point your database is simple, but entirely usable. In fact, you could stop reading right now, and you'd be able to build super-simple databases to solve all kinds of problems. But FileMaker's Manage Database dialog box's Fields tab has lots more settings to make your database even smarter, easier to use, and more consistent.

Auto-Enter Options

All your fields are completely empty when you create a new record. Often, but not always, that's what you want—a completely blank slate. But suppose most of your clients are from Phoenix. It would be nice if FileMaker could put Phoenix in the City field for you—you can always change it later. In fact, this situation is so common that every field has a group of *Auto-Enter* settings where you can tell File-Maker to automatically fill in certain fields in helpful ways (see Figure 3-7).

Figure 3-7:
FileMaker has several options for automatically entering information into a field. Most happen just once–when the record is created. The Modification, "Calculated value", and "Looked-up value" options, however, can automatically enter information in fields at other times as well.

When you first create a field, all the Auto-Enter options are turned off, so the field starts off empty. To get your database to automatically put your city and state in each new person record, follow these steps:

1. **Choose File → Manage → Database.**

   Or press Ctrl+Shift+D (⌘-Shift-D). The Manage Database window appears.

2. **Click the Fields tab. In the field list, select the City field, and then click Options.**

   Even quicker, just double-click the field. The Field Options dialog box emerges.

3. **In this window, click the Auto-Enter tab.**

   Now you see FileMaker's Auto-Enter options (Figure 3-7), in all their glory.

4. **Turn on the Data checkbox.**

   The big empty text box next to the Data checkbox had been unavailable, but now that you've turned this option on, you can type anything you want into it, and FileMaker puts that in the field on each new record. (You can always change the value yourself after you create the record.)

5. **In the empty box by the Data checkbox, enter *Phoenix* (or your city of choice). Then click OK.**

   The dialog box disappears, and you're back in the Manage Database window, looking at the field list. In the field list, the Options/Comments column shows "Auto-enter Data" by the City field.

Note: If you don't see this information, click the Options/Comments column heading. Clicking this column switches it from showing comments to showing options. Another click switches it back.

You can repeat the steps above for the State field (providing an appropriate state this time). When you're finished, in the Manage Database window, click OK to return to your database.

Now, when you make a new record (in the Status toolbar, click New Record, or choose Record → New Record), the City and State fields are filled in for you.

Creation values

When a record is *first created*, FileMaker can enter some information about the circumstances under which it was created. It can record the date, time, or timestamp at the moment of creation, or who created the record.

In your People database, it may be helpful to keep track of the date and time you first added each record, so you can tell how long you've been working with someone. You can even use this information in Find mode to seek out new customers, old customers, or customers you met on a Tuesday.

Setting up this field up is a two-step process. First, make a new timestamp type field: In the Manage Database window, in the Field Name box, type *Creation Timestamp*. Next, from the Type pop-up menu, choose Timestamp, and then click Create.

Missing Fields

Normally, when you add new fields to a database, they show up automatically in the database window so you can work with them. However, you can tell FileMaker not to show them. If you do, it's your job to put the fields in the window yourself (which you'll learn to do in the next chapter). If FileMaker isn't showing you the fields, you need to fix your Preferences:

1. Open Preferences by choosing Edit → Preferences (Windows) or FileMaker Pro → Preferences (Mac), and then select the Layout tab

2. Make sure the "Add newly defined fields to current layout" checkbox is turned on.

When this option is turned on, fields automatically show up in Browse mode as soon as you create them. You don't see any fields you created before you turn this option back on, though. See page 200 to learn how to use the field tool to drag new fields onto your layouts. Eventually, you'll probably want to turn this option off and manage your layouts manually.

Once you have a date field, you need to tell FileMaker to automatically enter the creation date:

1. **With the new field still selected in the list, click Options.**

   The "Options for Field" dialog box reappears.

2. **Turn on the Creation checkbox.**

   You use this option for any data specifically related to the creation of a record like, say, the date and time it was created.

3. **From the Creation pop-up menu, choose "Timestamp (Date and Time)".**

   In this case, you want the field to contain the date and time the record is created (the timestamp).

4. **Turn on the "Prohibit modification of value during data entry" checkbox.**

   Because this field automatically gets the right value, you never need to change it manually after a record is created. Editing this data would probably be a mistake, so you can tell FileMaker not to allow it. Figure 3-8 shows the finished product.

5. **Click OK, and then, in the Manage Database window, click OK again.**

   You're now ready to test your new field. Any existing records don't have the timestamp, because they were created before the field. But if you create a record now, then FileMaker automatically fills it in.

Note: If you already have a lot of records in your table before you create the Creation Date field, you can enter dates manually by turning off the "Prohibit modification of value during data entry" option temporarily. Just be sure to turn it back on when you're done to prevent future mistakes.

Figure 3-8:
*Turn on the Creation option, and then choose Timestamp
(Date and Time) to get a field that holds the record's moment
of birth. Actually, save yourself a little time and skip the
checkbox altogether. It turns itself on automatically when you
choose an option from the pop-up menu.*

Modification values

It's useful to know when a record was *created,* but it's even more useful to know when it was *last changed.* That way, you can quickly find everything that temp you hired last week messed up, or see how stale the info you have on your buddy is. But "change" is such a pedestrian word, hardly suited to the highbrow world of database development, so FileMaker calls it *modification* instead. Making modification info available in your database is a familiar exercise:

Make a new field called *Modification Timestamp.* In the field's Auto-Enter options, turn on the Modification checkbox, and then, from the pop-up menu, choose "Timestamp (Date and Time)".

You might hesitate to turn on the "Prohibit modification of value during data entry" option this time. After all, you want this field to change every time you enter data in a record. But don't fret. This checkbox keeps *you* from typing into the field, but FileMaker can still update its value for you. So by all means, turn the "Prohibit modification" checkbox on. Manually changing this field is just as much a problem as changing the Creation Timestamp field.

Note: In Part 5, when you learn about scripting, you'll discover other ways to change a field that don't involve data entry. The "Prohibit modification" option applies only to the process of a human being interacting with a field in Browse mode.

Serial number

Back in Chapter 1, you learned that record numbers can change as records get deleted or sorted. If you want to assign a unique number to your record, you can use the "Serial number" Auto-Enter option. In FileMaker, a serial number is a field whose value goes up for each new record. Typically, it goes up by a count of one, so the first record might be 1, 1001, or INV0001. In the second record you create, the serial number field would be 1, 1002, or INV0002. The numbers don't have to go up by one with each new record—you can provide any "increment by" value you want. But the value always goes up by some fixed amount.

In the Field Options dialog box, once you turn on the "Serial number" checkbox, you can specify the "next value", which is the value FileMaker uses for the next record that you create (actually, the starting value). The "increment by" value tells FileMaker how much to add with each new record.

You can specify non-numerical values for "next value" if you want. For example, if your field is a text field, you can put INV00001 in the "next value" box. Your first record would then get INV00001, followed by INV00002 and INV00003.

The Generate radio buttons under "Serial number" control *when* the serial number is assigned. If you select "On creation", then as soon as you create a record, FileMaker puts the serial number in the field. If you then decide you don't want the record, and you delete it right away, then that serial number value has been *used up*, and the next record you make has a new value. In almost every case, losing a serial number poses no problem at all, and it's convenient to have the serial number value available before you commit the record (as you'll see when you start using relationships in Part 3).

If you instead select "On commit", the serial number doesn't show up in the field until you exit the record. In other words, you can delete without committing, and you don't use up any serial numbers. Unless you have a good reason (there aren't many), you should use the "On creation" option.

You use serial numbers most often when connecting multiple tables (Part 3). Serial numbers also come in handy when the items in your database don't have a convenient name. In a database of invoices, it can be tough to talk about one particular invoice. ("You know, that one we sent last Thursday. No, not that one, the *other* one.") People generally use serial numbers to clarify things.

Value from last visited record

Some databases need a lot of repetitive data entry. For example, if you're entering scores into a grade book database, you have to enter the same assignment information and date for each student's paper—only the grade changes. In cases like this, FileMaker's "Value from last visited record" Auto-Enter option is exceptionally handy. When you turn on this option, each time you make a new record, FileMaker automatically fills in those fields with the same data as in the record you last created or edited.

Embracing Commitment

The word *commit* refers to a semi-technical database concept. When you create a new record, you haven't actually added a record to the table yet. Instead, you get a blank record on the screen, and the information you enter is stored in a temporary working area in your computer's memory. When you exit the record, the information in that working area is *committed*—or written—to the database.

When you edit a record, the same principle holds: As soon as you enter the record, it's copied to the working area. While you edit it, you're actually editing this copy. When you exit the record, FileMaker puts your edited copy back in the table. In general, think of *committing* a record as the same thing as *exiting* a record. When you exit the record, you commit it.

Just as with the Data option, you can easily change the values FileMaker enters after you create the record. When you do, the next record you create copies the new, changed values from the record you just edited. Entering multiple sets of repetitive information becomes a breeze—you modify the Assignment field only once per set of papers, for instance.

Calculated value

Sometimes you want to take advantage of the power of calculations, but you also want to be able to change the field if you need to. Since calculation fields always create their own (unchangeable) value, they don't fit the bill. Instead, you can create a normal field and have FileMaker automatically enter a calculated value into it. You can then change the value later if you want. You'll learn how to create calculations in Part 4.

Looked-up value

As you've already heard, FileMaker lets you connect multiple tables together in various ways. When you've done that, you can tell FileMaker to automatically fetch a value from some record in another table and plop it in the field. This feature is called a *lookup*, and you'll learn about it in Part 3.

Validation Options

Auto-enter options tell FileMaker to enter data for you. *Validation* options sort of do the opposite: They tell FileMaker what *not* to let you put in a field. You decide what kind of information *should* go there, and FileMaker warns you when you enter something that doesn't look right.

In your People database, you may want to make sure the Zip Code field always looks like a real Zip code.

1. **Open the Field Options dialog box for the Zip Code field.**

   You should be an expert at this by now. In the Manage Database window's Fields tab, just double-click the field.

2. **Select the Validation tab.**

As you can see in Figure 3-9, you have a lot of choices when it comes to field validation.

Figure 3-9:
The "Options for Field" dialog box's Validation tab lets you check for errors before placing information into fields. You can, for example, make sure only numbers are entered, or that the first name is no more than 30 characters. You can apply as many validation rules as you want, and FileMaker checks each one whenever someone modifies the field.

3. **Turn on the "Strict data type" checkbox, and then, from its pop-up menu, select Numeric Only.**

These settings tell FileMaker to expect only numerals in this field.

4. **Click the "Maximum number of characters" checkbox, and then enter 5.**

You can do better than just require numbers. This option tells FileMaker to accept no more than five digits in the Zip Code field.

5. **Turn on the "Display custom message if validation fails" checkbox.**

FileMaker automatically shows a message when a value in a field doesn't match the validation settings, but it's often more considerate to give the message in your own words. That's what this setting does.

6. **In the text box below this checkbox, type** *The Zip code you entered doesn't look right. Are you sure that's what you want?*

FileMaker displays this message if the validation fails. (For a little guidance on what these messages should say, see the box on page 113.)

7. **Click OK and OK again.**

You're back in Browse mode and ready to test. Try entering too many characters into the Zip Code field, and you see your message when you exit the field, as shown in Figure 3-10.

Figure 3-10:
If you enter a bogus Zip code in your database, you see your custom message. Click Yes to keep the invalid Zip code. If you want to fix it, click No and you'll be back in the field. If you click Revert Field, the field value changes back to what it was before you started editing.

Note: It's true that the validation settings you selected in the previous steps aren't perfect. For example, they don't allow Zip+4 codes (46077-1039). At the same time, they would let you enter something like *123*, which isn't a valid Zip code at all. To handle such nuances of the simple Zip code, you need to use the "Validate by calculation" option, which lets you set much more specific validation standards. You'll learn about FileMaker's calculation features in Part 3.

Making validation stricter

Your Zip code validation options work pretty well, but there's a pretty glaring problem: anybody can enter just about anything they want, and then click Yes to tell FileMaker to accept the invalid data. It may help prevent mistakes, but it does nothing to require good information. Sometimes that's just not strict enough.

To make FileMaker more insistent, revisit the Options for Field dialog box's Validation tab, and then turn off the "Allow user to override during data entry" checkbox. Since this change removes the user's choice when entering data, you also want to reword the custom message you entered. Change it to *The Zip code you entered is invalid. Please correct it.*

With these settings in place, if someone enters a spurious Zip code, then he sees a slightly modified error message, as shown in Figure 3-11.

Figure 3-11:
When you turn off the "Allow user to override during data entry" validation option, FileMaker no longer lets anyone click Yes to accept an invalid value. So any custom message you provide should not be phrased as a question. Instead, express the error as a simple statement or suggestion.

Note: The Validation tab has two more options related to this one. Under "Validate data in this field" you can choose Always or "Only during data entry". Data entry has the same meaning here that it had for auto-enter options. If you switch to the more strict Always setting, FileMaker enforces your validation rules even when data is modified by a script (Part 5). The Always option also enforces validation when you import data in bulk (Chapter 17).

FREQUENTLY ASKED QUESTION

Numbers and Text

You have to set an awful lot of validation options to make sure people enter only Zip codes into a text field. Can't I just make the Zip Code field a number field instead?

No, you can't. Zip codes are numerical values, but they're not *numbers*, and that makes a big difference as far as File-Maker is concerned. For example, number fields don't recognize leading zeros—like the ones at the beginning of 00501 and scores of other perfectly valid Zip codes. If you enter *00501* in a number field, FileMaker thinks you meant to type the number *501* and "helpfully" removes those extra zeros when you exit the record. That's just not going to get your mail to Holtsville, New York anytime soon.

The Numeric Only validation option lets the field stay a text field (which preserves all entered characters) but still accept only numerical digits on entry, which is exactly what you want for a Zip code.

Some people also assume that a phone number should be stored in a number field. Wrong again. Phone numbers contain not only numerals but also dashes, parentheses, and sometimes other special characters—all mere text to FileMaker. As a general rule, make a field a Number field only if it's a simple number, like someone's height in inches, or the price of a bag of potatoes.

Validation Requirements

When you added validation to the Zip Code field (see page 109), you asked File-Maker to accept only numbers and allow only five digits.

But data type and character count are just two of the eight kinds of validations FileMaker has up its sleeve. In the Field Options dialog box's Validation tab, you have six more checkboxes. Most of them work much the same way: They check what you type against some specific condition. But one option, "Validate by calculation", offers a completely flexible way to describe exactly what you're looking for. Unfortunately, to use it, you need to learn how to perform *calculations* (mathematical or logical formulas) with your FileMaker data. They're covered in Part 4. Until then, here's what the other options do:

Strict data type

This option lets you pick four specific validations. You've already seen Numeric Only, which insists every character in your text field be a number. 4-Digit Year Date tells FileMaker to expect a date value, and that the year must be four digits long (2007 instead of 07). This choice works with text, date, and timestamp fields.

UP TO SPEED

Validation Messages

Custom validation messages (like the one in Figures 3-10 and 3-11) give you a chance to communicate directly with whoever uses your database. If you don't provide a custom message when you set up field validation, then FileMaker uses a generic message of its own. This message explains the validation option that's being violated in language only a software engineer would love. This message may be confusing to whoever's using your database. By writing your own messages, you can explain things in a way that relates to the exact type of information with which you're dealing. Custom messages make your database a pleasure to use, and give it a professional quality.

Bear in mind, though, that although you can turn on as many validation options as you want, you can provide only one custom message. Unless you can depend upon your database users to the correct format, your message must explain exactly how to fill in the field. A message that says, "Your widget description is invalid" gives your database users no indication of how to fix the problem, and prevents them from getting their work done.

"Time of Day" tells FileMaker that only time values that represent real clock times are acceptable. Since time fields can hold any number of hours, minutes, and seconds, you can enter something like *237:34:11* to mean "237 hours, 34 minutes, 11 seconds." But if the field is *supposed* to be the time of your lunch meeting, that value doesn't make sense. This option prevents its entry. It applies to text and time fields (timestamp fields *always* require a time of day).

Not empty

If you insist on having *something* in a field, select the "Not empty" validation option. That option makes FileMaker complain if you try to commit the record without entering *something*. This option and "Validated by calculation" are the only options that let you validate Container fields.

Unique

The "Unique value" option prevents you from putting the same thing in a field for two different records. It comes in handy for things like product codes, account names, and course numbers.

Existing value

"Existing value" is just the opposite of "Unique value"; it doesn't allow any value that isn't already in that field on some record in the database. Imagine you've been using a Book database for a while, and you've built up a representative list of Category values. You can turn on the "Existing value" validation option for the Category field to be sure any books you add in the future get one of the categories you've already specified, so that typos are instantly identified.

This option doesn't make sense until after you've put data in your database. Like all the field options, you're free to turn it on or off whenever you want.

Member of value list

You often have a field that can contain any one of a predetermined set of things. In your database, for example, you may want to ensure that the State field contains a valid abbreviation for one of the 50 United States. Here's where the "Member of value list" option shines.

FileMaker lets you create *value lists*, which (not surprisingly) are lists of values: Red, Green, Blue; or Small, Medium, Large, for instance. You can make as many value lists as you want:

1. **Open the Field Options dialog box for the State field.**

   Your trusty mouse can probably scramble the maze on its own by now.

2. **On the Validation tab, turn on the "Member of value list" checkbox. Then, from the associated pop-up menu, choose Manage Value Lists.**

   FileMaker shows you the Create Value Lists dialog box.

3. **Click New.**

   FileMaker creates a new empty value list, and shows it to you in the Edit Value List window (shown in Figure 3-12).

4. **In the Value List Name field, enter *State Abbreviations*.**

   Each value list needs a unique name.

5. **Make sure the "Use custom values" radio button is selected, and then, in the list box under it, type *state names*.**

   As usual, you need to ignore several available options for now, and focus on "Use custom values". Each item in a value list must be on its own line. You can paste into this box as well, so if you find a list of states on the Internet, you can save yourself a lot of typing.

Figure 3-12:
*Value lists play a
frequent role in
FileMaker. In this case,
you're creating a value
list to dictate exactly
what a person's allowed
to type in the State field.
Each line in the "Use
custom values" box in
one possible entry. (The
finished database for this
chapter has a value list
with all these
abbreviations. Download
it at http://
missingmanuals.com/cds.)*

6. **Click OK to close the Edit Value List window.**

   The Manage Value Lists window now shows your new value list.

7. **Click OK again to close the Manage Value Lists dialog box.**

   Back in the Field Options window, the value list you just created is now selected in the "Member of value list" pop-up menu. If you want, you can also enter a custom message.

8. **Click OK twice more, until you're back to your database.**

   As Figure 3-12 attests, FileMaker loves piling up dialog boxes. Once you OK them all, try entering a value in the State field that *isn't* in the value list. File-Maker lets you know you've messed up.

In range

"In range" lets you specify a minimum and maximum allowable value. FileMaker then protests if you enter a value outside this range. This method works for all the standard data types, since they all have a concept of order. For example, if you specify a range of *Adam* to *Johnson* for a text field, validation fails for *Schultz*. Range validation is most common, however, with number, date, and time values. You can require the Age field to be between 0 and 100, for example, or the Birth Date to be between 1/1/1900 and 12/31/2010.

Maximum number of characters

As previously mentioned, this option enforces a limit on the number of characters you can enter into a field. FileMaker fields can normally hold a huge amount of text. This option lets you keep things under control. You can use it to require specific kinds of information, like the five-digit Zip code above, or to prevent abuse of the database (for example, by limiting the First Name field to 30 characters so someone doesn't get carried away and paste the complete works of Shakespeare into it).

WORKAROUND WORKSHOP

Minimum Number of Characters

For some strange reason, FileMaker doesn't provide a simple validation option to enforce a minimum number of characters in a field. If you need this sort of thing, then you have to dip into validation calculations. Luckily, the calculation to do it is really simple. Here's a validation calculation for requiring at *least* five characters in the field:

```
Length(My Field) >= 5
```

To use this calculation, turn on the "Validate by calculation" option. In the window that appears, type this calculation.

You have to change "My Field" to the name of your field. If you want a number other than five, simply change it in the calculation. When you're done, click OK.

If you want *more than* five characters, change >= to >. If you want *exactly* five characters (no more, no less) then change >= to =. You don't need a lot of expertise for this calculation. If FileMaker gives you an error, and you can't figure it out, just click Cancel, and then try again. (See Part 4 for much more on using calculations.)

Storage Options

It's time to get a little technical. Sorry. In the Field Options dialog box, the Storage tab (see Figure 3-13) lets you control aspects of a field related to the nebulous concept of *storage*. Like a highly organized attic, FileMaker both holds onto your information *and* makes it easy to take out again. There are lots of details involved in how FileMaker compartmentalizes and maintains that information.

You can actually tell FileMaker to store only one value in a field, no matter how many records you have, or to allow one field to hold *more than one value* in each record. Strange, but true. Also, you get control over *indexing*, as described in the next section.

Global storage

"A field that uses global storage contains only one value that is shared across all records." So says the explanatory text in the dialog box, but what's that in English? When you use the "Use global storage" option, everything you learned about tables goes out the window. A *global field* isn't like a column in the table at all. Rather, it's a single bit of storage that can hold one value, no matter how many records you have. In other words, if you change the contents of a global field on one record, then FileMaker instantly changes it in every other record as well. Now every record has the same value for that field. (You'll learn a lot more about *why* you would want to do this on page 363.)

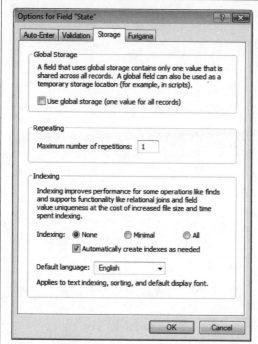

Figure 3-13:
The Storage tab is where various behind-the-scenes field settings lurk. Here, you can make a field global so it has only one value for the whole table, or make it repeating so it has several values in each record. Many of these options are most useful when writing scripts (Part 5) or for very advanced purposes.

Repeating fields

A field can hold only a single value, right? Well, not really. If you want to, you can turn any field into a *repeating field*. These fields can hold more than one value, each kept in a separate spot (and each shown in its own little box in Browse mode). In the Field Options dialog box, you specify the maximum number of values the field can hold. When would you want to use repeating fields? Almost never. See the box below for more info.

Note: The last tab in the Field Options dialog box applies only to Japanese text entry, and isn't covered in this book. Fortunately, should you ever need to add furigana to your kanji, you can read how right in the dialog box.

Indexing

Since you're reading this book, you're probably hoping FileMaker can help you search through volumes of information faster than you could do it yourself, especially as your database grows from a simple electronic Rolodex to a humongous mailing list. When you're looking for the three people out of 5,000 whose birthday is February 29, FileMaker can find them in an instant because it doesn't really look at the birthday field on each record one by one. Instead, it uses the field's *index* to skip straight to the appropriate records. It's similar to the way you'd use a book's index to go directly to the pages that mention the topic you're interested in, rather than skimming every single page in the book.

WORKAROUND WORKSHOP

Repeating Fields Aren't Your Friends

With very few exceptions, repeating fields cause more trouble than they're worth. The truth is, they exist only because years ago when FileMaker was a youngster, it wasn't a *relational* database. That means it didn't have any way to tie multiple tables together so that they could share information and make connections between things in each table. When you were learning about how to pick fields, you were introduced to the concept that you need a table for each kind of thing you're keeping track of. In a database that's not relational (called a *flat file database*), you have no good way to track lots of different kinds of things in one database, so FileMaker had repeating fields to let you store more than one thing in a single record. For example, you could have an Invoice table with one record for each invoice. The individual items on the invoice need a place to live too, so you would create repeating fields. That way, each individual invoice could hold, say, 20 items.

But this is the 21st century, and FileMaker's come a long way. Nobody in her right mind would build an invoice database that way anymore (they'd hook together two tables instead—see Part 3). Since FileMaker had repeating fields 10 years ago, and since it's really friendly about supporting all your ancient databases, it still supports repeating fields today.

That said, repeating fields are *occasionally* useful when writing calculations (see Part 4) and scripts (see Part 5). Other than that, you should avoid them like the plague for a few reasons:

- Repeating fields are uniquely FileMaker. If you want to take data out of your database and put it in some other program (like a spreadsheet or another database program), repeating fields can produce one serious pain in the neck. Likewise for getting data from other programs *into* repeating fields.

- Repeating fields are inherently limited: If you create a field with 20 repetitions, then you get 20 spots for data. If you need less, you're looking at empty fields all the time. If you need more, then you have to modify your fields and make room on your screen. A relational database, on the other hand, can grow and shrink as needed without modifying the database structure at all.

Note: FileMaker uses a field's index in other ways, too. You need an index if you want to use the "Unique value" option in the field Validation screen. You also need indexed fields to create relationships in your data, as explained in Part 3.

FileMaker's indexing feature takes its own computerized notes on your fields *in advance*, so that when you enter Find mode (see page 31), the hard work's already been done, and your finds go that much faster.

Just like a book, you can have a field without an index. When FileMaker needs to find records based on what's in that field, it has to check every single record—a process that can take noticeably longer in big databases. But indexing has tradeoffs, as explained in the box on the next page.

The Dark Side of Indexing

If indexing makes searching faster, why not just index every field?

Indexes have disadvantages as well. An index is useful only if it's up to date. When you change a field value, FileMaker has to store that new value in the table. If the field is indexed, FileMaker has to change the data you've typed, and it *also* has to update the index so that it knows about the changes to the field. Updating the index takes time (not much time, mind you, but it does take time).

When you're editing records in Browse mode, you *never* notice because updating the index for a handful of fields takes

FileMaker less time than it takes you to realize you've pressed Enter. But if you're entering *lots* of information (like when you're *importing* records, as discussed in Chapter 17), then the index updating can slow things down noticeably.

Also, indexes take up space. A database that has indexing turned on for every field could be much larger than the same file without indexes. For most users, this isn't an issue, but if you have a very large file, and saving space is a priority, you can turn off indexing where you don't need it, to save space.

Automatic indexing

The good news is you almost never need to think about indexing. FileMaker has a really smart way of dealing automatically with indexing: Every field starts out with no index at all, to save space and keep things as lean as possible. Later, while you're working with your database, if you do something that would be made faster with an index, like use the field in a find request, then FileMaker automatically turns indexing on for you. That first find is slow since FileMaker looks through records one by one and builds the index (showing a progress bar in really big files), but once the field is indexed, subsequent finds happen quickly. You almost always want this automatic behavior.

Controlling indexing manually

In very large databases, there may come a time when you want to adjust indexing manually. For instance, if you know you only very rarely search by a person's middle name, you can tell FileMaker not to index that field. Searches are slow, but that's OK since you hardly ever do it. Click the None radio button to turn indexing off completely.

If you want to be able to search efficiently in a field, turn on All instead. The third choice—Minimal—creates a smaller index for the field. This index has everything FileMaker needs for relationships and field uniqueness, but not enough for fast searching. If you *don't* need to search in a field, but you *do* need it indexed for other reasons, choose Minimal.

When None is selected, you can keep FileMaker's automatically-turn-it-on-when-I-need-it behavior by turning on "Automatically create indexes as needed."

Note: FileMaker uses the field index when you do a find from Find mode, but *not* when you use the Find/Replace command. The index points FileMaker to *records*, and since Find/Replace doesn't find records (it finds text inside a record or records), the index does it no good. Therefore, when you do a Find/Replace, you don't make FileMaker automatically index a field. Several actions trigger indexing, including using the field in a find request or value list, turning on Unique or Existing validation, and using the field in a relationship. You'll learn about relationships in Part 4.

POWER USERS' CLINIC

Put Automatic Indexing to Use

FileMaker's ability to automatically index a field when it becomes necessary doesn't just save you the trouble of thinking about all this stuff. You can also use it to your advantage in some situations. Sometimes people need to distribute databases full of information.

For example, suppose you have a large parts catalog that's stored in a database, and you want your distributors to be able to use the database themselves to find parts. You can make a real FileMaker database available on your Web site for them to download, complete with your 10,000 parts records.

If there's a lot of information about parts, then that database is pretty big. To make the download more palatable, tell FileMaker not to index *any* of the fields. But leave "Automatically turn indexing on if needed" turned on. This way, the database is as small as possible when people download it. Once people get it, they can start performing finds, and FileMaker automatically indexes fields, making searches faster, and ballooning the size of the database.

Indexing language

To keep its indexes as small and tidy as possible, FileMaker doesn't actually store all a field's text in the index. Instead, it performs a little cleanup on the field values first. Most notably, it gets rid of the notion of uppercase and lowercase letters: "Peter" and "peter" become the same entry in the index.

The index also splits the field value up into individual words and removes any characters that aren't generally part of a normal word. In order to do that, it needs to know what language the text in the field is in. If your computer's regional settings are for English, then FileMaker's field indexes use English, too. Usually, that's exactly what you want. But in some cases, FileMaker's following the same language rules as your computer can cause a problem. For example, if you enter another language in a field without changing the index, then your searches can give you unexpected results. If you search in an English-indexed field for *lang* (German for "long"), then you get both "lang" and "länger" ("longer"), but if you set the index to German, you only get "lang". (In German, "ä" is a different character from "a".)

You can select a different language from the dialog box's Indexing section's pop-up menu. A field's language setting also comes into play when you sort records. To use the example given above, when you're sorting in ascending order (from A–Z), "länger" comes before "lang" in a field indexed as German (in accordance with rules for German alphabetizing), but after it if the field's index is set to English.

Note: If the Language pop-up menu is unavailable, the field is probably not a text field. You can specify the language only for text fields.

Unicode Indexing

One language option, called Unicode, isn't a language at all. This setting tells FileMaker to forget everything it knows about languages, and use the internal code numbers for each character as is. When indexing with this language option, FileMaker doesn't remove any special characters from the index, and it doesn't ignore uppercase and lower-case letters.

A find in such a field is *case-sensitive*. When sorting, File-Maker also uses the character code numbers. Whichever code is lower comes first in the sort order, so capital "Z" comes before lowercase "a."

You rarely want your searches and sorts to be case-sensitive, but if you do, you have the option. You're more likely to use Unicode indexing when you want to easily search for punctuation. For example, a field that holds text from a business-to-business Electronic Data Interchange (EDI) document can be well served by Unicode indexing so you can easily find the records that contain "~BIG."

Seeing the index

When a field is indexed, you can get a glimpse of what's in it, and even put it to use. Just click in an indexed field in Browse mode, and then choose Insert → From Index. You see the window in Figure 3-14.

Figure 3-14:
Left: When you choose Insert → From Index, FileMaker shows this window, complete with one line in the list for each unique value in the field. These represent the "value index" you can turn on in the Storage tab.

Right: Turn on the "Show individual words" checkbox in this window to see the word index instead. This time, you get one line for each unique word.

This window is handy when you want to quickly enter something you know you've entered in a previous record. Just select the entry you want, and then click Paste to have the value inserted into the current field. This trick works in Find mode too, where it lets you quickly see a list of things for which you may want to search.

Part Two: Layouts

2

Understanding Layouts

In the last chapter you created your first database, and it really works. Unfortunately, it doesn't *look* all that great. For example, the Street Address field is the same width as the State field, even though street addresses are usually much longer than state names. The Zip Code field is *much* longer than it needs to be. And unless you're a real minimalist, the whole thing just looks boring (see Figure 4-1).

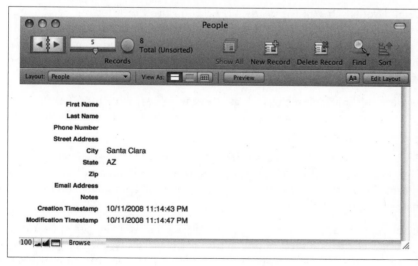

Figure 4-1:
This database works, but it could work—and look—better. What if you want to see lots of people at once? What if you want to print address labels for all these people? What if you want to arrange these fields in logical groups so they're easier to figure out? This database can't do any of those things, but if you give it a few new layouts, you can do all of them—and lots more.

You have other things to worry about as well. You have no good way to see lots of people at one time—in a nice list, for example. A list would also be handy for printing. As it stands, you have to print a whole page for each person in the database if you want a hard copy.

The FileMaker concept of *layouts* solves all these problems and more. While the Manage Database window lets you define the structure of your database (its fields and tables), layouts let you design the look and feel.

What Is a Layout?

If the tables form the heart of a database, layouts give it a face. When you design a layout, you feel like you're working in a graphics program: You can change the fonts, paste in your logo, make the background light fuchsia, and drag the fields around as though they're little onscreen Lego blocks. A single database can look like a White Pages, a "Hello! My Name Is" name tag, a glossy brochure, or a library card catalog index card. FileMaker displays the same information—but *how* it displays that information is up to you.

Better yet, a single database can contain as many layouts as you want; each shows the data in a certain way for a specific purpose. Figure 4-2 shows the People database with two possible layouts.

Types of Layouts

You can make layouts for just about anything. As far as FileMaker is concerned, a layout is a layout, but many of the layouts you'll create fall into a few common categories:

- **Detail** layouts show all (or nearly all) fields on the screen for one record at a time—a full employee profile, for example. You use Detail layouts for most, if not all, of your data entry. If you have a lot of fields, you can even create more than one Detail layout: Contact Info, Emergency Info, and Payroll Info, for example.

- **List** layouts show multiple records at one time, in a scrolling list. These layouts usually show *less* information from each record than a Detail layout so more records can fit on the screen.

- **Report** layouts are designed for printing (see page 224). These layouts usually show multiple records in a list form, often with a title at the top and summary information at the bottom. Reports can even have groups of data and intermediate summaries or running totals.

- **Envelope and Label** layouts format the data so that you can print it directly onto an envelope or a sheet of peel-and-stick labels. This layout makes addressing envelopes to people in your database a breeze. FileMaker can automatically create layouts for many envelope sizes and common label formats.

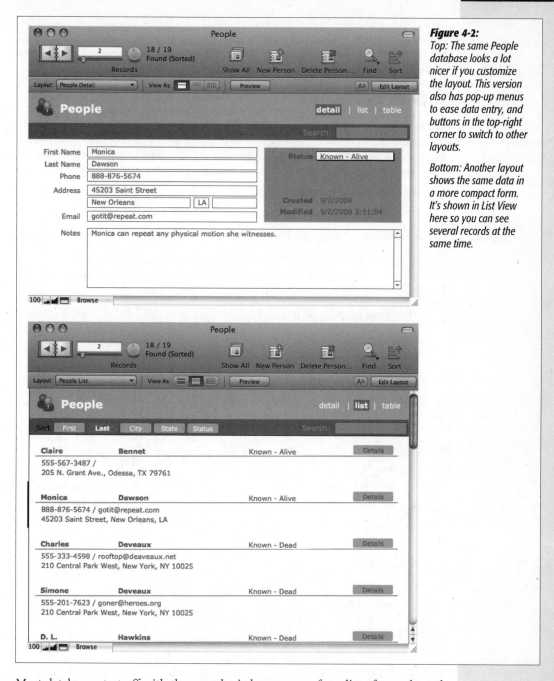

Figure 4-2:
Top: The same People database looks a lot nicer if you customize the layout. This version also has pop-up menus to ease data entry, and buttons in the top-right corner to switch to other layouts.

Bottom: Another layout shows the same data in a more compact form. It's shown in List View here so you can see several records at the same time.

Most databases start off with the most basic layouts: one for a list of records, and one for a more detailed view. That way, you can quickly scroll through lots of records without getting data overload, and then jump to a more detailed layout for closer inspection.

Over time, you often add more layouts to meet specific needs. When thinking about layouts, you should be thinking about how you'll want to see the data—what kinds of information should be onscreen at the same time, for example—and how you want to *print* your data.

Making a New Layout

As you build FileMaker databases, you'll make a lot of layouts. For the most customized look and behavior, you often build layouts from scratch, adding the various parts and pieces one by one. But for the most common layout types, FileMaker can ask a few questions, and then do a lot of the dirty work for you.

Your People database, for instance, could really use a List layout so you can print lists of people for use on the go. It takes a few steps, but it's really not difficult at all:

1. **Choose View → Layout Mode.**

   The FileMaker window changes dramatically. You're now in Layout mode, which has dozens of tools, commands, and buttons to help you create masterpieces. You'll learn loads more about Layout mode soon.

2. **In the Status toolbar, click New Layout/Report.**

   You can also choose Layouts → New Layout/Report or simply press Ctrl-N (⌘-N). FileMaker pops open the New Layout/Report dialog box pictured in Figure 4-3.

Figure 4-3:
When you tell FileMaker you want to make a new layout, this dialog box is the first thing you see. In addition to a name and table, you tell FileMaker what kind of layout you're making. It then asks you questions relevant to the type you choose, and makes a basic layout for you. If you want to work from scratch (as you'll do on page 190), then choose "Blank layout".

3. **In the Layout Name box, type** *People Report.*

This name shows up in the in the Layout bar's Layout pop-up menu (unless you turn off the "Include in layout menus" checkbox), so it should be something clear and relatively short.

4. **In the "Select a layout type" list, click List/Report.**

The List/Report item is highlighted.

5. **Click Next.**

The window changes to look like Figure 4-4.

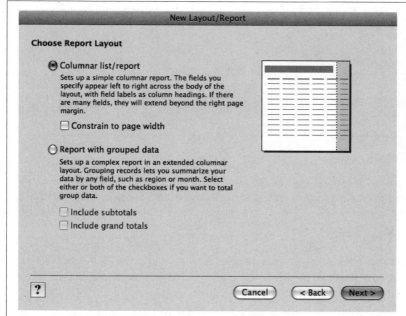

Figure 4-4:
Once you tell FileMaker you want a List/Report type layout, it starts in with the questions. You'll fly through seven screens in all before you're done. This first one wants to know what kind of list you need. For now, choose "Columnar list/report". You'll learn about reports with grouped data in Chapter 6.

6. **Make sure "Columnar list/report" is turned on, and then click Next.**

Now FileMaker needs to know what fields you want to include on the layout (Figure 4-5).

7. **Select the First Name field, and then click Move.**

The First Name field is added to the list on the right. It'll be added to the new layout as well.

8. **Repeat step 7 to add these fields: Last Name, Phone Number, and Email Address.**

You can also double-click a field to move it more quickly. When you're done, you should have four fields in the right-hand list.

Figure 4-5:
This step in the process lets you decide which fields to include on the layout. You select one or more fields from the list on the left, and then click Move to add them to the list on the right. Every field you move is included on the new layout. If you select a field in the list on the right, then the Move button changes to a Clear button, and a click removes the field from the list.

9. **Click Next.**

   FileMaker now asks you how you want to sort your list. Of course you already know you can sort any found set of records any time you want. So don't bother with this step.

10. **Click Next again.**

    This time, FileMaker asks you to select a theme. It gives you a couple dozen boring and mostly ugly themes to pick from. Feel free to choose any you like, or keep it simple, and choose Standard.

11. **In the list, select a theme. If you can't decide, just choose Standard. Then click Next.**

    Now FileMaker shows you some options to add header and footer information to your layout. You have a lot of choices to pick from here, so feel free to explore. For this layout, which isn't intended for printing, you can simply leave everything set to None.

12. **Leave every pop-up menu set to None, and then click Next.**

    FileMaker offers to create a script for you. If this were a printed report, the script might be handy: It automatically selects the new layout, sorts it, and shows it in a print preview mode. (You'll learn all about scripting in Part 5.) But you don't need any of that for a simple list.

13. **Make sure "Do not create a script" is turned on, and then click Next.**

    You're finally done with all the Q&A. Now FileMaker just wants to know if you intend to edit your layout further, or if you just want to see it in Browse mode right away. Reading this window, choosing and appropriate option, and clicking Finish takes about twice as long as just switching to Browse mode yourself, so feel free to consider this window a complete waste of your time.

14. **Make sure "View the report in Browse mode to display and edit records" is turned on, and then click Finish.**

    FileMaker shows you your shiny new List layout. You can see it in Figure 4-6, too.

Figure 4-6:
Your new List layout. It embodies FileMaker's staid design sensibilities, but by golly it shows a list of people. Feel free to scroll, find, and so on.

Views

FileMaker's concept of *views* is closely related to layouts. So close, in fact, that people often get the two confused. While you can make as many layouts as you want, FileMaker has exactly three views: Form view, List view, and Table view. Each is really just a different way to look at any particular layout.

You've already seen views in action: Your new People List layout uses *List view* while the original layout (called simply People) uses *Form view*. You can look at a layout with a different view at any time: "From the View" menu, choose "View as Form", "View as List", or "View as Table". Figure 4-7 shows the result.

When you switch views, FileMaker remembers the change, and associates it with the current layout. So if you come back to your layout later, then you'll see it with the view you last used. Typically, you pick one view that makes most sense for a layout, and keep it that way.

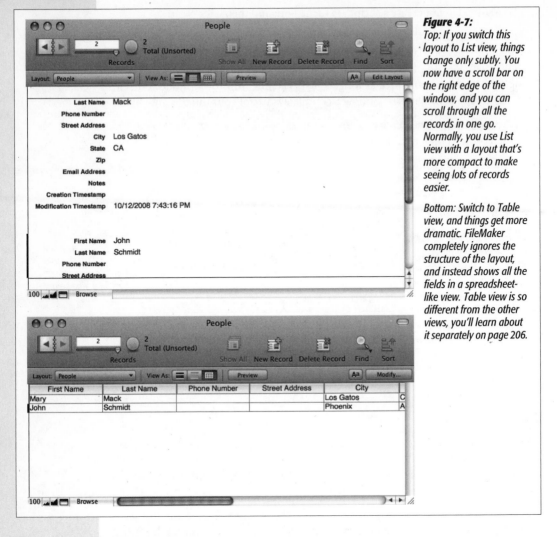

Figure 4-7:
Top: If you switch this layout to List view, things change only subtly. You now have a scroll bar on the right edge of the window, and you can scroll through all the records in one go. Normally, you use List view with a layout that's more compact to make seeing lots of records easier.

Bottom: Switch to Table view, and things get more dramatic. FileMaker completely ignores the structure of the layout, and instead shows all the fields in a spreadsheet-like view. Table view is so different from the other views, you'll learn about it separately on page 206.

The Layout Bar

Your database now has two layouts, and FileMaker makes switching between layouts a breeze. Right below the Status toolbar, you find the handy Layout bar (Figure 4-8).

Note: The Layout pop-up menu doesn't necessarily show *every* layout. You can actually tell FileMaker to hide certain layout names in this menu. You'll learn how on page 191.

To switch layouts, from the Layout pop-up menu, just pick the one you want. It couldn't be simpler. The Layout bar also lets you easily switch between views. Just click one of the three View As buttons (they're labeled in Figure 4-8).

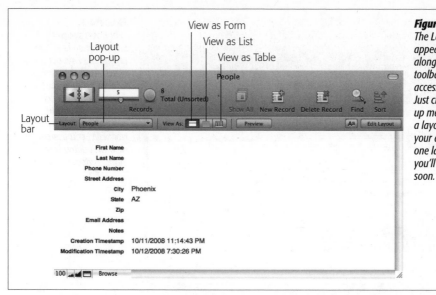

View as Form
View as List
View as Table
Layout pop-up
Layout bar

Figure 4-8:
The Layout bar—which appears and disappears along with the Status toolbar—gives you speedy access to all your layouts. Just click the Layout pop-up menu, and then choose a layout to switch to. Alas, your database has only one layout right now, but you'll be changing that soon.

Renaming a Layout

Now that you've discovered the Layout pop-up menu, you might feel like your layout names are imperfect. After all, the menu gives you these choices:

- People

- People List

It would be better if the first layout had a more meaningful name, like *People Detail*. To rename a layout, you need to revisit Layout mode. The Layout bar makes this easy too:

1. **At the right end of the Layout bar, click the Edit Layout button.**

   The window switches to Layout mode. You can tell at a glance because the Layout bar turns black. It also gets several new buttons, including the one identified in Figure 4-9.

2. **Click the Layout Setup button (Figure 4-9). It looks like a little pencil.**

   If you're not the toolbar type, you can also choose Layouts → Layout Setup. Either way, you see the Layout Setup dialog box, shown in Figure 4-10.

3. **In the Layout Name box, type *People Detail*.**

   This name more clearly indicates that this layout shows full details about a person.

4. **Click OK, and then, in the Layout bar, click Exit Layout.**

   When you click Exit Layout, FileMaker asks if you want to save the change you've made to the layout.

Layout Setup
button

Figure 4-9:
When you switch to Layout mode to edit a layout, the Layout bar turns black. This strong visual cue helps you know where you are. It also adds several buttons, most of which you'll learn about later. To rename a layout, click the Layout Setup button, shown here.

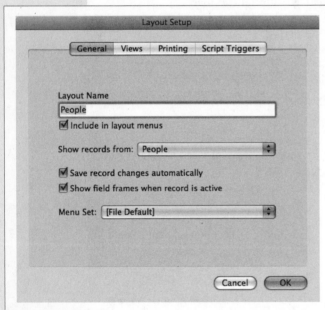

Figure 4-10:
The Layout Setup dialog box has countless under-the-hood options for your layout. You can configure which views should be allowed for the layout, how big the print margins are, and which menus appear in the menu bar. And, as in step 3 on page 133, you can type to change the layout's name.

5. **Click Save.**

   Now the Layout pop-up menu shows the new layout name.

Found Sets and Layouts

FileMaker is smart enough to know that the People List and People Detail layouts are showing the same records. In fact, you might use the People List layout to quickly find someone you want, and the switch to People Detail to make some changes.

To make switching back and forth as smooth as possible, FileMaker remembers which record you're looking at, and which records are in your found set as you switch layouts. Prove it to yourself:

1. **Switch to the People List layout.**

   Nothing new here. You see your records in a list.

2. **Perform a simple find. For instance, find someone by first name.**

   The list changes to show only the matching records.

3. **Click one of the records.**

   Even when you're in List view, FileMaker has the notion of a *current record*. Since you can see several records at once, the program indicates which one you last clicked with a little black marker along the left edge of the record. You can see the marker in Figure 4-11.

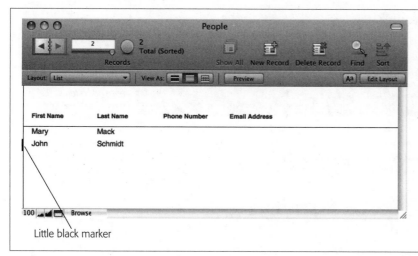

Figure 4-11:
When you're in List view (or Table view), FileMaker puts a little black marker next to the record you last clicked. That's the current record, as far as FileMaker's concerned.

4. **Switch to the People Detail layout.**

   Notice that the record you're looking at is the one you clicked when on the List layout. Also, if you use the book icon to change records, then you see that you have a found set just like you did on the List layout. If you perform a different find now, and then switch back to People List, FileMaker lists the records that match the new find as well.

Because FileMaker keeps all this in sync, you can use multiple layouts with ease. When you want to find things, use whatever layout makes it easiest. Need to print a sheet of labels? On the List layout, find what you want first, and then go to the Labels layout and print.

What Makes a Layout

A layout is made up of layout parts—sections that each behave a little differently when displaying or printing multiple records. Even the simplest layout has at least one part, and each part has objects on it. One kind of object is a field, which you've seen plenty of so far in this book. Each field in your database has a little label beside it that tells you which field it is. These labels are another kind of object: They're text objects. It just so happens those objects all belong to a part called the *body*, and if you need to talk about your layout, you'd say they're *on the body*.

Parts tell FileMaker how to treat the objects inside them when it displays or prints the layout. To see parts in action, go to your People List layout, and then switch to Layout mode. Figure 4-12 shows its parts and objects.

Note: FileMaker gives you *lots* of ways to get to Layout mode. Namely, you can choose View → Layout Mode, or, in the window's bottom-left corner, use the Mode pop-up menu (page 31). Finally, in the Layout bar, you can click the Edit Layout button. All these methods do the same thing.

Figure 4-12:
Every layout is made up of parts like the Header part (which appears once at the top of the screen) and the Body part (which appears once for each record in List view). These parts hold various objects. This layout has only Field and Text objects, but FileMaker lets you add many different objects to your layout, from pictures and shapes to Web browsers.

Part Types

FileMaker has eight different kinds of parts in all. Every layout uses at least one of these parts, and often several—although not all databases need all eight kinds of parts. Most types can occur only once on each layout (like a header), but some can appear several times:

- **Title Header.** The title header part holds things you want to appear only at the top of the very first printed page. Use it for a descriptive title, larger column labels, a company logo, or you can even make it the height of your paper, and it acts as a cover page.

- **Header.** The header part prints at the top of every page—unless you also use a title header, in which case the title header is on page one and the regular header is at the top of all other pages. In Browse mode, the header shows up at the top of the window. Here's where you might put a date and time, small title, smaller column labels, and anything else that you want on every page of the printout.

- **Leading Grand Summary.** This part prints below the header but above the records themselves. It's meant to contain totals and similar fields that add up, average, or otherwise *summarize* the data.

Note: Leading grand summary and all the other "summary" parts are how FileMaker creates advanced *reports*. Reports, which help you compile and analyze your data, are nothing more than layouts designed for the job, as you'll learn in Chapter 6.

- **Body.** The body shows the actual record information. In List view, or when printed, it repeats once for every record.

- **Sub-Summary.** These parts help you add things like subtotals to complex reports. You'll learn all about this in Chapter 6.

- **Trailing Grand Summary.** If you prefer totals and overall summary information at the *bottom* of a report, then they go in this part.

- **Footer.** The footer prints at the *bottom* of every page—unless you also use a title footer, in which case, the title footer appears on page one, and the regular footer appears on all other pages. The footer also appears at the bottom of the window in Browse mode. The footer's a perfect place for page numbers, copyright notices, and anything that ought to appear at the bottom of every page of your printout.

- **Title Footer.** The Title Footer part shows at the bottom of just the first page. Use it for special footer info that needs to show only once.

Figure 4-13 shows a layout with seven parts—one of each type except Sub-Summary.

Parts in Form view

When in Browse mode, and viewing the layout as a form, you see every part (sub-summary parts are a special exception, as you'll learn in Chapter 6). You never use *all* these parts on a layout you plan on viewing in Form view. In general, if you only ever want to view a layout as a form in Browse mode, then you really need only a Body part, although if you plan to print, then you may want a Header part as well so logos, menus, and other user interface items don't repeat for every record you print.

Parts in List view

List view is a *list* because it shows several records at once. FileMaker accomplishes this magic by repeating the Body part once for each record. The database in Figure 4-13 has three records, so in effect, the Body part repeats three times. It has several other parts too, which appear in the same order they appear in Layout mode. (Any title header or title footer doesn't appear in Browse mode.)

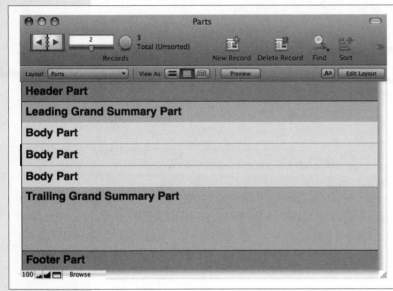

Figure 4-13:
When you view a layout onscreen in List view, FileMaker arranges the parts like this example. Any title header or title footer doesn't show up. The header sticks to the top of the window, and the footer sticks to the bottom. The leading grand summary appears right before the first record, and the trailing grand summary right after the last. The Body part repeats once for each record in the found set.

Parts in Preview mode

A quick glance at Preview mode might lead you to believe that it shows only the title header and the title footer (exactly the opposite of List view), but that's not entirely true. Turn your eyes to Figure 4-14 for the whole story.

Just like List view, the grand summary parts place themselves before the first record and after the last record. Finally, scrolling in Preview mode just scrolls the current page. If you need to see other pages of your report while you're in Preview mode, use the Book icon to move around.

When to use them

While it's perfectly legal to put any parts on any layout, you've probably figured out that some arrangements are more common than others:

- Detail layouts usually have just a Body part, or some combination of header, body, and footer. These layouts may show only a single record, so there isn't much point to Summary parts since you have no list of data to summarize.

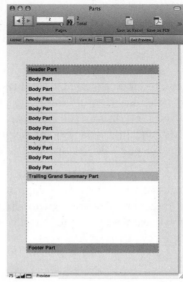

Figure 4-14:
Left: In Preview mode, the title header and title footer are at the top and bottom of the first page. The leading grand summary appears right before the first record, and FileMaker adds a copy of the body for every record until it fills up the page.

Right: Every page thereafter shows the header and footer instead of the title header and title footer. If you don't have a title header, then you get the regular header on the first page, too (and the same goes for the title footer). Also notice that the trailing grand summary appears after the last record.

- List layouts usually have a header and a body, and sometimes a footer. Occasionally, you want a trailing grand summary on your List layout as well, since it can show summary information after all the records without taking up precious space like a footer.

- Printed reports come in many forms. People often use all the parts shown above on a report: a large title header for the first page, and a smaller header for each additional page; a leading grand summary that shows below the title header and before the first record; a Body part for each record; a trailing grand summary to show totals from all records; and a footer to show page numbers and the like.

- Envelopes and layouts often need headers and/or footers just to get the record data to align properly on the printed page. These parts are generally empty.

- You may have a List layout that you use to browse your records, but you often print it as well. Make the layout do double duty by adding a title header or title footer. They'll show only when you print, and you can save valuable screen real estate.

Layout Objects

Parts aren't so useful by themselves. Parts control how the items in your layout arrange themselves on the screen or on the page, but they need to have *things* in them to be really useful. You call those things *layout objects*. Layout objects come in seven flavors: Text objects, lines and shapes, images, fields, portals, tab controls, and Web viewers

Note: Portals are all about relationships, and you won't learn about relationships—or portals—until Part 4.
You'll take up tab controls and Web viewers a little sooner—look for them in Chapter 5.

Text objects

Almost every layout ever created has included text objects: little blocks of text that
are the same on every record displayed using that layout. Think about what happens when you move from record to record. The text labels for each field stay the
same, even though the data inside each field changes with every record. Text
objects give you one form of stability in the ever-changing world of database
records.

When you design a layout, you can control every aspect of a text object, from the
words in it to the font, size, style, color, line spacing, tab stops, and so on. (In fact,
everything you learned in Chapter 2 related to formatting text in fields applies to
text objects on layouts as well.)

Tip: FileMaker's spell checker works in Layout mode too. Just choose Spelling → Check Layout. It looks
and works just as it does in Browse mode—except that it checks text objects on the current layout. Also, the
visual spell-checking feature (see page 76) works in Layout mode as well, so watch for dotted red underlines if you're a chronic misspeller.

Lines and shapes

If you need simple graphic embellishments in your layouts, FileMaker has built-in
tools for making them. For example, you might want to put a box around a person's address information, and another around the Notes field, so they're visually
separated. You can draw lines, rectangles, ovals, and round-cornered rectangles
right on your layout. You can also control the line color, thickness, and pattern for
lines and shapes; and the fill color and pattern for shapes.

Images

If simple shapes can't properly convey your artistic vision for your layout, you
have recourse: You can paste any picture right onto the layout. You can also insert
a picture from a file on your hard drive. Database developers often add icons,
logos, and other decorations this way. For example, you might add your company
logo to the top-right corner of your layout, or put a cute little envelope icon by the
Email Address field. Just remember a little of this "eye candy" goes a long way. If
you get carried away, then you can actually create so much visual clutter that people using the program are confused, instead of enlightened. Also, large images can
make your layouts slow to load, especially when you share the database over a network (which you'll learn how to do in Chapter 18).

Fields

A layout without fields is just a picture. Perhaps it's a very complex picture that changes as you switch from List view to Form view, and has an entirely different effect when printed (thank you, parts!), but it's a picture nonetheless.

To get *data* into your layout, you add field objects. For instance, if you make a new layout in the People database, and you want to show the person's address, then you can add the Street Address, City, State, and Zip Code fields to the Body part of the layout. If the field is in the Body part (the most common place), then it shows data from the current record (or each record when you view the layout as a list). In list view, fields in Header, Footer, or Grand Summary parts show the values from the first or last record in the found set. In Preview mode (or when printing), headers and footers show data from the first or last record on each page.

Note: You don't usually put ordinary fields in Header, Footer, and Grand Summary parts. These parts usually contain global fields, summary fields (see page 279), page numbering, dates, or text and pictures.

With a firm understanding of layouts, views, parts, and objects, you're ready to get down to business. The next section shows you how to put all these ideas to work in your own databases.

Customizing a Layout

Enough exposition. Chances are, you're *aching* to get back to building your database. Building layouts is, by far, the most creative part of being a FileMaker Pro developer. You have the freedom to make subjective personal decisions about the style, arrangement, and even behavior of your database.

The Look

Some people choose to put a lot of work into the design side of things, using other graphics tools and an artistic eye to make gorgeous hand-crafted layouts. Others think, "What's the point?" and are perfectly content with the spare black-and-white layouts that FileMaker creates all by itself. You may wind up somewhere in the middle: You want something more than what FileMaker gives you, but you don't have the patience or skill to treat every layout like a work of art.

Luckily, you're completely in charge. A FileMaker layout can look like just about anything you can imagine. Just remember that with all this flexibility, you can easily make *bad choices*. Layout design isn't just about how things *look*. You need to think about how people will use the system. Have you arranged fields in meaningful groups to make it easier to find what you want? Is there too much visual noise?

Is it hard to tell which field holds which kind of information? These questions are especially important if many other people use your database. As you work in Layout mode, step back every now and again, and try to view your layout with a new eye. Does it make sense?

Figure 4-15 shows your People database with two possible layouts. They both have a lot in common, but the one on the bottom is decidedly harder to build, owing to its custom graphics and meticulous embellishments.

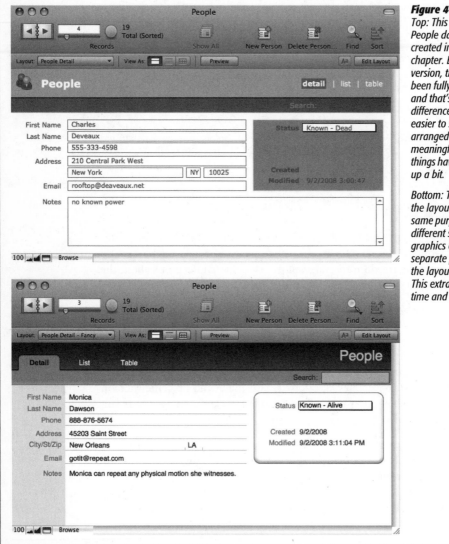

Figure 4-15:
Top: This is the same People database you created in the last chapter. But in this version, the layout has been fully customized, and that's made all the difference. Fields are easier to spot, things are arranged and grouped in meaningful ways, and things have been dressed up a bit.

Bottom: This version of the layout serves the same purpose, but with a different style. Custom graphics created in a separate program give the layout a richer feel. This extra finesse takes time and effort.

Throughout this chapter, you'll build the version on the top in Figure 4-15.

Note: To see how the dressier layout (on the bottom in Figure 4-15) was created, check out the screen-cast on the Missing Manuals Web site (go to *http://missingmanuals.com*, and then, on the left, click the Screencasts link).

Layout Mode

You already caught a glimpse of Layout mode when you were renaming the People layout on page 133. Layout mode has a lot more going on than the other modes you've seen. For example, the Status toolbar is drastically different, and the Layout bar makes an appearance. Even the available menus and commands are different: two new menus (Layouts and Arrange) have appeared, the Records menu is gone, and you find many new commands in each menu.

Inside the database window, things have changed as well. Fields now show their names, and include a dotted *baseline*. You can see dashed black *page break* lines, and labels for every layout part. Figure 4-16 marks each of these changes.

Figure 4-16:
In Layout mode, things look a little different. The Status toolbar now lets you flip through layouts instead of records. It also includes a large collection of tools (you'll learn about these soon). Fields look different in Layout mode too: They have borders and text baselines, and instead of data, each one shows its name. Finally, parts are clearly labeled, and a dotted line separates them.

Tip: Since the kind of work you do in Layout mode is so different from Browse mode, any changes you make to the Status toolbar don't show here. Instead, you can customize the Status toolbar's Layout mode version separately from the Browse mode version. (The same goes for Find mode and Preview mode.) Just choose View → Customize Status Toolbar. You get a different collection of possible toolbar buttons in Layout mode as well.

The Status Toolbar

You don't have to look too closely to see that the Status toolbar has changed significantly (Figure 4-16):

- Instead of the current record number and record count, the Status toolbar now shows the current layout number and the layout count. You can now use the book icon to flip through layouts instead of records.

- A handful of tools—little square buttons with icons on them—appear. (Read on to find out what they do.)

- In the bottom-left corner of the window, a new control called the *part label toggle* has joined the usual zoom controls and Status toolbar control. You'll see this widget in action on page 179.

- The Layout bar, with its associated menus, buttons, and icons, is in full view.

- The Mode pop-up menu now shows that you're in Layout mode.

Note: You may need to make your window wider to see everything the Status toolbar has to offer in Layout mode. If the window isn't wide enough, then FileMaker intelligently hides the least useful tools so things don't crash into each other. As usual, on the Status toolbar's far-right edge, you can click the arrow to see a pop-up menu of the missing items.

Arranging Parts

The process of building a layout isn't always linear. Most people tend to bounce from task to task as they mold the layout to match their vision. You might arrange some parts, organize fields, do some decorating, and then revisit the fields. It is, after all, a creative process.

But usually, you first get the parts roughed out. Since you don't know exactly how big things are going to end up, it isn't critical that you get the parts exactly the right size right away. But you do want to decide which parts you'll be using, get them in the right places, and take a guess at how big they need to be.

Note: FileMaker lets you move objects only into parts. Sometimes, as you're arranging things, your layout can get cramped, so it's helpful to start with parts that are a little bigger than you really need. You can shrink them up again later when you've finished laying things out.

If you view your People Detail layout in Layout mode right now (Figure 4-16), then you see FileMaker has given you three parts: a header, body, and footer. If you were to print some records while on this layout, the header would appear on the top of each page, and footer on the bottom of each page. Right now, though, the header and footer are both completely empty.

Since this layout is designed to be seen on screen in Form view, headers and footers may not be important to you. But you might consider using a title header just in case you decide to print this layout. That way the graphical embellishments you see on the top of the layout in Figure 4-15 print only at the top of the first page, leaving more room for record data, and using less ink. Here's how to fix it up:

1. **If you haven't already, go to the People Detail layout, and then switch to Layout mode.**

   You're now ready to work on your layout.

2. **Choose Insert → Part.**

   The Part Definition window appears (Figure 4-17). It wants to know what kind of part you want to add to the layout.

Figure 4-17:
The Part Definition dialog box shows up when you add or modify a layout part. It includes a radio button for each of FileMaker's part types. You also get myriad checkboxes, most of which don't apply to a title header. You'll get a chance to use each of these options in time.

3. **Make sure Title Header is turned on, and then click OK.**

   FileMaker adds a title header part to the very top of your layout. (When you use the Insert → Part command, the part is automatically inserted in the spot that makes sense. In this case, since this is a title header, it goes at the very top of the layout.)

4. **Drag the Title Header part label straight down to make the title header larger.**

   Use Figure 4-18 as a guide.

Figure 4-18:

Top: To resize a part, you can simply drag its part label. (If you're deft with the mouse, you can actually drag the thin dotted line that extends from the label.)

Middle: As you drag, FileMaker shows an outline of the label, plus the new divider line. This line crosses right over the content of the layout, which can be disorienting. But when you're done, FileMaker moves everything down to make room for the larger part, so things will be neat as a pin.

Bottom: When you're done, the part is bigger, and everything else is still intact.

Now that the title header is in place, you can get rid of the header and footer parts. This step is a snap:

1. **Click the Header part label once.**

   FileMaker highlights the label to indicate that it's selected.

2. **Press the Delete or Backspace key on your keyboard.**

   Since this part is empty, it disappears right away.

Warning: If you delete a part that has things on it (like the body part on your layout), then FileMaker asks you for confirmation. If you agree, then the part *and everything on it* is deleted. Exercise care when deleting parts.

---

3. **Click the Footer part label to select it, and then press Delete or Backspace again.**

   Once again, the part disappears.

For more tips on arranging parts, see the box below.

FREQUENTLY ASKED QUESTION

Part Manipulation

Sometimes when I try to drag a part label up, it won't go. It seems to get stuck. What am I doing wrong?

Suppose you want to make a part *smaller*? You can probably guess how: Just drag the part label up instead of down. But sometimes you'll be surprised to discover it won't go as far as you want.

FileMaker doesn't let a part be smaller than the stuff on it. For example, if you try to shorten the body part on your People Detail layout, then you discover you can't go farther north than the bottom-most field. Once the part separator touches this field, it simply doesn't go higher no matter how far you drag, because FileMaker doesn't want you to accidentally end up with the fields on a part you didn't intend.

You can most easily fix this problem when you simply move things out of the way before you resize the part. For instance, if you want a shorter body, move the fields around first, and then shorten the body.

If you want, you can press Alt (Option) while you drag instead. When you do, FileMaker changes the way it moves parts. Instead of moving everything below the part up or down to compensate for its new size, everything stays put, and just the dividing line between the two parts moves. In this way, you can move part boundaries right through other objects to, for example, resize the body to encompass newly added fields that landed on the footer.

When you're done, your layout should look like Figure 4-19.

Laying Out Fields and Labels

Now that you have the parts where they belong, you can start moving and resizing objects, and adding new things to the layout. Obviously, the exact steps you take depend on what you want your layout to look like. But the kinds of steps you take are always the same.

Moving objects

Since FileMaker has no idea where you want things on the layout, you can spend a lot of time moving objects around. Luckily, if you've used a computer any time in the last 20 years, this is a snap.

When you're in Layout mode, you can select any object simply by clicking it. When you do, it scores four *handles,* which you can see in Figure 4-20.

Figure 4-19:
Once you've added a title header and removed the header and footer, your layout should look like this example.

Figure 4-20:
In Layout mode, when you select an object, a small square handle appears on each of its four corners. In this picture, the First Name field is selected. These handles server two purposes: First, they let you know at a glance what's selected. Second, you can drag them to resize an object.

Selecting Lots of Objects

Selecting objects on a layout is such a common task that FileMaker gives you several ways to do it. You can always click an object to select it, but you can use any of the following methods as well:

If you want to select more than one object (so you can operate on them all at once), select the first object, and then press the Shift key, and click each additional object. As you click, each object joins the selection. If you accidentally select an object, Shift-click it again to deselect it.

To select *everything* on the layout, choose Edit → Select All or press Ctrl+A (⌘-A).

You can even select every object of a certain type (every field, for example). First select one object of the type you want. On Windows, press Shift, and then choose Edit → Select All. On Mac OS X, press Option, and then choose Edit → Select Same. FileMaker selects every object that's similar to the one you selected yourself.

If you have more than one object selected when you choose this command, then FileMaker selects every object like any of the selected objects. For example, to select every field *and* every text object, select one field and one text object, and then choose this command.

Finally, you can easily select objects that are close together on the layout using the rubber band technique. When you click an empty place on the layout and drag, FileMaker shows a dotted rectangle called the rubber band. Once you release the mouse button, anything inside the rubber band is selected. If you press Ctrl (⌘), then the rubber band gathers up every item it *touches*, not just the objects it completely surrounds.

To move an object, just drag. A little outline follows you as you go, and when you release the mouse button, the object snaps to its new home.

In a new database like this one, the *Object Grids* are turned on, meaning FileMaker lets you move the object only in 6-pixel increments. This feature is timesaving—it's easier to quickly drag dozens of objects around and keep them lined up if they stick to a grid of some kind. But sometimes you need a little finer control. You can bypass the grid in three ways:

- If you just need to temporarily skirt the grid, press Ctrl (⌘) while you drag the object. As long as the key is down, you can drag the object smoothly to any spot on the layout.

- Choose Arrange → Object Grids to turn the grid off more permanently. (You can always turn it on again any time you want by repeating this menu command.)

- Press any of the arrow keys to move the selected object 1 pixel in any direction. You can press a key repeatedly to carefully nudge an object into place.

On the other hand, sometimes you need a little more help. FileMaker has a handful of special commands to make lining things up a breeze:

- If you have several objects that should be lined up, but aren't, you can snap them to attention with the options in the Arrange → Align menu. Figure 4-21 shows an example.

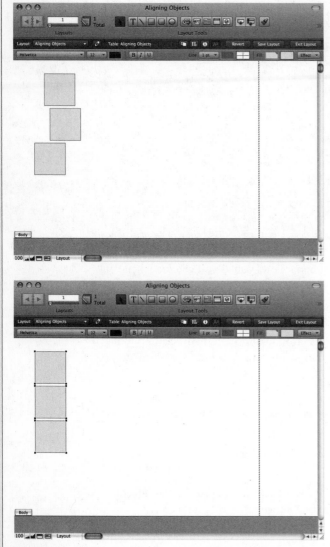

Figure 4-21:
Top: These objects are all a-jumble, and lining them up one by one could be pretty tedious. But there's a better way. First, select them all (see the box on page 149 for help). Then choose Arrange → Align → Left Edges.

Bottom: When you run the Align command, FileMaker makes sure the left edge of each item is in a neat line. You can line things up on the left, right, bottom, top, or middle.

- Sometimes the objects are aligned properly, but not evenly spaced. FileMaker has a magic tool to solve this problem too, as shown in Figure 4-22.

Figure 4-22:
Top: This time, the trouble is spacing. You want these objects evenly spaced. Once again, select them all first. Then choose Arrange → Distribute → Vertically.

Bottom: When you do, FileMaker makes sure there's an equal amount of space between each item. If you're spreading things out side to side, choose Arrange → Distribute → Horizontally instead.

- Sometimes you just need some visual aid. For instance, if two objects are far apart, and you want to line them up, it can be hard to see which way to go. File-Maker's T-Squares come to your aid in this situation. You can see them by choosing View → T-Squares (Figure 4-23).

- For the ultimate in precision, you can use the Object Info palette. To see this helper, choose View → Object Info, or turn to Figure 4-24. You can even control what units the palette uses. Just click the unit label (in, cm, or px) beside any box. Each time you click, the labels switch to another kind of unit so you can work comfortably.

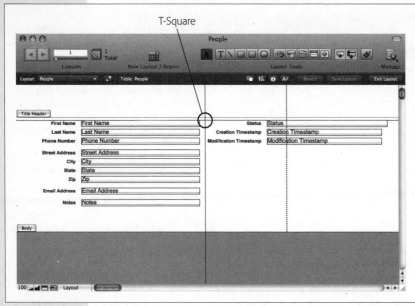

T-Square

Figure 4-23:
When you choose View → T-Squares, FileMaker adds a horizontal and vertical black line to your layout. You can move these lines by dragging them, and they show you how things line up. When you drag an object near a T-Square, the object snaps to it as though it's magnetized, making this a quick way to line up several objects.

Figure 4-24:
The Object Info palette (View → Object Info) lets you position and resize the selected object numerically. First, make sure you have the object selected. Then, in one of the boxes, enter any number you want. They set the left, top, right, bottom, width, and height respectively.

Using these various tools, you can start to position the objects on your layout appropriately. Your first task is to move the fields and labels around so they look something like Figure 4-25.

Resizing objects

As mentioned in Figure 4-16, you can resize an object by dragging one of its handles. Once again, FileMaker shows you a dotted outline while you drag so you know how big the object will be when you let go. Once again, the Object Grids (page 149) constrains your freedom here, and you can bypass them by pressing Ctrl (⌘) while you drag.

Figure 4-25:
Your next step is to put the fields roughly where they belong. In this picture, the Status and Timestamp fields are off to the side, and the other fields are grouped in a meaningful way.

Exercising Constraint

FileMaker developers often resize and move layout objects. Bearing this in mind, FileMaker has a few tricks up its sleeve to make things easier. You already know how to hold down the Shift key to constrain mouse movement (see page 147). Here are a few more goodies:

- Press the Ctrl (Option) key while creating or resizing a rectangle, rounded rectangle, or oval to make a perfect square or circle. When working with a line, this key makes it perfectly horizontal, perfectly vertical, or exactly 45° from one of these directions.

- With an object selected, press any of the arrow keys to move the object 1 pixel in the appropriate direction.

- Make a copy of an object by holding down the Ctrl (Option) key while you drag it. Add the Shift key to the mix to make sure the object stays aligned with the original.

- Use the Duplicate command to create a new object that's 6 pixels to the right and 6 pixels below the original.

- Choose Align → Object Grids to turn another alignment feature on or off. Instead of moving with pixel-by-pixel freedom—which can make things nearly impossible to line up—things on the layout automatically align themselves to an invisible grid as you drag them. You can set the spacing of this grid by choosing Layout → Set Rulers, and then adjusting the "Grid spacing" value.

As if that weren't enough, you can use the Object Info palette introduced above to move objects as well. If the palette says the left edge of an object is two inches from the ruler origin, then you can type 4 instead to move it farther into the layout.

The Arrange menu has some love for object resizers. With multiple objects selected, from the Arrange → Resize To menu, you can choose an option to quickly resize them all. You have several choices. Choose Smallest Width to make every selected object as narrow as the smallest of them. Choose Smallest Height to adjust the height of the objects instead of the width. Rounding out the Smallest options, choose Smallest Width & Height to do both at once. Each of these has a counterpart that makes the selected objects *bigger* instead. For instance, choose Largest Width to make every field expand to an equal width.

Finally, the two bottom boxes on the Object Info palette (View → Object Info; Figure 4-24) adjust the width and height of the selected object precisely.

Using these powers, you can now resize the fields on your layout (and move them a touch more). Figure 4-26 shows how your layout looks as things continue to come together.

Tip: Sometimes when you're resizing fields, you might find it hard to judge how big a field should be, especially with date, time, and timestamp fields, where too little space cuts things off, and too much is never used. In Layout mode, choose View → Show → Sample Data, and FileMaker fills your fields with type-appropriate data. If you already have records in your database, then it shows real record data. Otherwise, FileMaker just makes stuff up. Either way, though, you can start to get an idea of how much will fit in the fields you're sizing. When you're ready to see the field names again, just choose View → Show → Sample Data again.

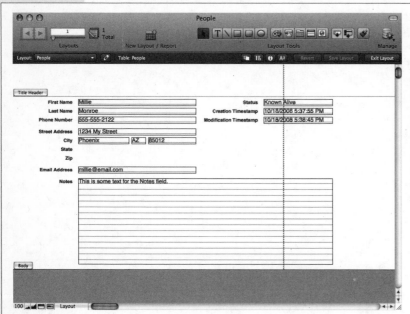

Figure 4-26:
After a little resizing, your layout is starting to come together, structurally. The City, State, and Zip fields have been squeezed and lined up in typical address fashion. The Notes field is now big enough for a thorough treatise. And the Status and Timestamp fields are no longer excessively large.

Working with text

With your fields in the right place, you can now turn your attention to the text on the layout: the field labels. You can easily edit the text, add new text objects, and modify fonts, sizes, and styles.

Editing text. This layout's two timestamp field labels could use your help. Right now they say "Creation Timestamp" and "Modification Timestamp", but those names are a bit nerdy for your average user. Instead, you label these fields "Created" and "Modified". You'll also change the "City" label to say "City/State/Zip" since these three fields are all on one line.

1. **Choose the Text tool.**

   The tools are in the Status toolbar, as Figure 4-27 attests.

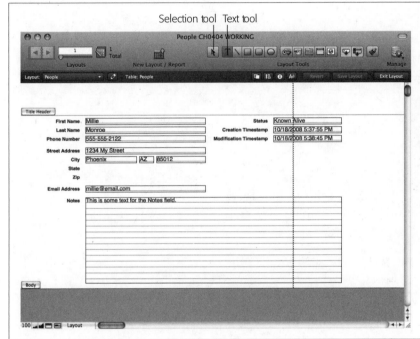

Selection tool   Text tool

Figure 4-27:
To use a tool in the Status toolbar in Layout mode, just click it. Normally, FileMaker keeps the Selection tool active, but in this picture, the Text tool is selected (you can tell because it's darker than the rest). If you change your mind, click the Selection tool again.

2. **Click the Creation Timestamp field label once.**

   The object gets a dotted outline, and a blinking insertion point appears at the spot you clicked. You're now editing the text object, and everything you know about editing text applies, as discussed in the box on page 156. You can type, use the Delete and arrow keys, and even drag or double-click to select text. Click anywhere outside the dotted line when you're done editing.

Note: By almost every measure, a field label is just like any other text object. But the labels FileMaker creates for you have one hidden property that makes them special: When you change a field's name in the Manage Database window, its label automatically changes to match. As soon as you *edit* the text in a field label, though, this magical bond is broken. This break may be a good thing or a bad thing depending on your point of view. Editing your field labels manually lets you pick just the right name, given the available space, and the nature of the layout. On the other hand, you may find that keeping your field labels and field names in sync helps you keep things straight in your head.

3. **Choose Edit → Select All or press Ctrl+A (⌘-A).**

   All the text in the text object is now selected.

4. **Type *Created*.**

   FileMaker replaces the selected text with the new text you type, just like a word processor.

UP TO SPEED

Formatting Text

Fields and text objects have one thing in common: They both show text. As such, it comes as no surprise that you can change the font, size, and style of this text. First, select one or more objects. Then go to the Format menu. The first seven submenus let you manipulate the text formatting of the selected object.

- The Format → Font menu shows fonts installed on your computer. (In Windows, you may need to choose Format → Font → More Fonts, and then add the fonts you want to your font list. In Mac OS X, every font you have installed is automatically listed.)

  You can dress up your text in any font, size, and style you like. But don't forget that the computer your database is *used* on must have the font installed. You have fancy $300 fonts on your computer, but your employees may be using the database on stripped-down PCs. You want to pick a font that comes standard with your operating system so everybody sees the same lovely letterforms.

- From the Format → Size menu, you can choose a size. If you don't see the one you want, choose Format → Size → Custom instead. In the window that appears, type any number from 1 to 500.

  If you're designing a database on the Mac for use on PCs, then you need to make all your text objects just a little larger than you (and FileMaker) think they need to be, because PCs display fonts larger than their Mac brethren do. Ideally, check your layouts on a PC, because any text object that isn't wide enough flows over onto another line, which probably isn't what you intended.

- FileMaker includes all the standard styles (bold, italic, and so on) in the Format → Style menu. You can pick from three different types of underlines (Word Underline underlines words, but not the space between them, and Double Underline puts two lines under your text). You can also choose Upper Case, Lower Case, or Title Case to determine the case of text no matter how you typed it.

- The options in Format → Align Text let you align the text left-to-right and top-to-bottom. For instance, if you choose Bottom, then the text sticks to the bottom of the text object when you make it taller. This setting makes sense only if you type multiple lines of text into a text object. For instance, you may have a paragraph of explanatory text you want to show on the layout to help people.

- Choose Format → Line Spacing → Double to apply double-spacing (or choose Format → Line Spacing → Custom to specify the spacing more precisely).

- To color your text, point to Format → Text Color. A color palette appears, and the color you select is applied to the selected text.

- The Format → Orientation menu applies only to text in Asian languages, and lets you run text either vertically or horizontally.

You can apply each of these options to an entire text object (just select the object first) or to a run of text *inside* the object. To style just a portion of the text, use the Text tool to select a portion of the text first. In this way, you can mix fonts, sizes, and styles inside a single text object.

---

5. **Click anywhere in the layout *outside* the text object you're editing.**

The dotted outline and insertion point disappear, and the object isn't selected. You're done editing its text.

Now repeat these steps, changing the Modification Timestamp object to say *Modified*. Finally, repeat the steps once more to change the City object so it reads *City/State/Zip*.

Tip: Sometimes it can be difficult to line up text objects since different letters have different shapes. When is a word that ends in a lowercase "i" lined up with a word that ends in a "w"? If you find yourself in this boat, choose View → Show → Text Boundaries. When you do, a faint gray box appears around every text object. You can use this box to see how things line up more easily. The boxes show up only in Layout mode, so you can leave this option on all the time if you want.

Adding new text. If you flip back to Figure 4-15, you see a few pieces of text that aren't field labels. In the header section of the layout, a large bold "People" label lets you know what this database holds. Adding this to your layout is a snap.

First, select the Text tool. Then click anywhere on your layout. When you do, File-Maker makes a new text object and sets you up to edit it directly. The object appears wherever you click, so you're probably best off clicking in the header near where you want it to end up. Once you click, you can begin typing. Type *People*. Then click outside the text object to tell FileMaker you're done editing. Finally, style the text as you see fit. In Figure 4-15, it's 18-point bold. (You can leave the text black for now. You'll take care of colors shortly.)

The finished layout also includes three text objects on the right side of the header: *Detail, List,* and *Table*. These objects are actually buttons to help you switch layouts easily. You won't create these until Chapter 6.

UP TO SPEED

Find and Replace Revisited

Layout mode retains some features you've already learned from Browse mode—albeit slightly modified to make sense to a database designer rather than a database user. For example, you might want to find and replace text on a layout, on occasion. Imagine you've decided to call the Zip Code field *Postal Code* instead, since you're planning a big drive in Canada. You can use Find/Replace to fix every field label on a layout in just one shot. When you're in Layout mode, the Find/Replace command searches through text on the layout itself rather than the data in fields and records.

The slightly pared-down dialog box you see when you choose Edit → Find/Replace → Find/Replace in Layout mode looks and works just like its Browse mode counterpart, aside from the lack of "Search across" and "Search within" options.

The other commands on the Edit → Find/Replace submenu—Find Again, "Replace and Find Again", and Find Selected—also work exactly as they do in Browse mode. (See page 68 for details on the ins and outs of Find/Replace.)

In Figure 4-28, you can see the layout with text changes in place.

Figure 4-28:
Your layout is coming along nicely. In this iteration, two field labels have been tidied up and you've added a title—People—in the Header part.

Removing objects from a layout

You often have objects on your layout that you don't need anymore. Sometimes you add an object, and then later change your mind. You might even create a text object temporarily just to jot down some notes, or peek at a field that's normally not showing, or add a box to help yourself line things up.

But most often, you delete things because FileMaker created them for you, and you no longer need them. That's the case right now with the State and Zip field labels. They're no longer by the fields they label, and those fields are already labeled sufficiently by the City/State/Zip text object.

Luckily, removing a text object couldn't possibly be easier. Just select the object (or objects) you want to delete, and then press the Delete or Backspace key on your keyboard. Instantly, the selected objects disappear.

To continue your work on the People layout, go ahead and remove the State and Zip field labels now.

Working with fields

With sizes, positions, and labels dialed out, you can now turn your attention to the fields. If you compare your layout with the goal laid out in the top window in Figure 4-15, then you see that your fields don't quite live up to expectations. You'll fix them up now.

Note: You can use all the same font, size, style, color, and other formatting commands for text objects on fields, too. Just select a field object, and then go to town with the Format menu. But since fields don't contain real data until you go to Browse mode, you can format only the entire field. If you want to format parts of the text *inside* the field, you need to do it in Browse mode.

Field borders. In Browse mode, the fields in your People database are currently just floating blobs of text with no defined edges. So your first task is to give the fields visible borders. Adding borders to fields is a snap. First, select the field or fields in question. (In this case, go ahead and select *every* field.) Then choose Format → Field/Control → Borders. You see the dialog box in Figure 4-29.

Figure 4-29:
When you choose Format →
Field/Control → Borders, this
window appears. Here, you can
add borders and baselines to
your fields. Just turn on the
checkboxes corresponding to
the borders you want. You can
also set the color, pattern, and
line thickness of the field
borders using the "format"
pop-up menus.

In the Field Borders dialog box, turn on the Top, Left, Bottom, and Right checkboxes. Then click OK. You don't see much change at first because field borders appear in Layout mode even when they're turned off (you can toggle them on and off by choosing View → Show → Field Boundaries). But if you switch to Browse mode, you see that each field now has a thin black border.

Field behavior. Previewing the People database in Browse mode reveals another problem. You can click into (and type into) the Created and Modified fields. But these fields are strictly informational: You should be able to *see* them and *search* them, but you don't need to edit them, because FileMaker fills in the dates automatically when you create or modify a record. In fact, even though FileMaker lets you type into them, if you try to commit the record, then it displays an error message because when you created these fields, you told FileMaker to "prohibit modification of field value" (page 106). Instead of letting people try to edit these fields and get a rude error message, you want to make it so they can't click into these fields in the first place.

If you're sharp-eyed, you might also notice that FileMaker is running its spell checker on the Email Address field. When you type in an email address, which is almost never a proper word, it gets a distracting red underline.

You can fix these problems (and more) by modifying the *field behavior*. To change it, first select a field, and then choose Format → Field/Control → Behavior. You can see the resulting dialog box in Figure 4-30.

Figure 4-30:
The Field Behavior dialog box (Format → Field/Control → Behavior) lets you control how the field acts in Browse mode. The most common setting is the first set of checkboxes, "Allow field to be entered". But each option here is useful under certain circumstances.

FileMaker lets you control five aspects of a field's behavior:

• The "Allow field to be entered" checkboxes prevent folks from being able to click into the Created and Modified fields. When you turn the "In Browse mode" box off, then clicking into the field in Browse mode doesn't work, turning the field into a visual display of data, minus human interaction. Since you often want a field that can't be edited, but can be searched, you'll most often turn off "In Browse mode" and turn on "In Find mode". But you're free to turn on or off either checkbox in any combination that suits your needs.

Note: When you can't enter a field, then you can't select its text to copy and paste. So if you want to let people copy the information from an uneditable field, then you can leave a field enterable, but remove their ability to edit using field options (page 159) or security (page 631).

• Normally when you click into a field, the insertion point appears right where you clicked. But sometimes you *always* want to edit the entire field value. For instance, you might have a set of records you update monthly with new sales totals, and you're always typing over what's there with new numbers. In cases like this, turn on "Select entire contents of field when entered". Now, when you click into the field, FileMaker preselects the entire value, and you can simply start typing to replace what's there. You can always click a second time to get an insertion point, or start making a new selection. Figure 4-31 shows this subtle difference in action.

• The "Set input method" option deals with text entry in Asian languages. When this option is on, you can control which text "input method" is used for this field. If you need this ability, you know what it means. If not, just ignore this option.

- Turn on "Do not apply visual spell checking" to turn off the dashed red lines that appear under misspelled words in that field. Many fields hold data that the spell checker doesn't like, like part numbers, email addresses, and launch codes. Since the red underlines are just a distraction in these fields, you can turn them off. You can see the change in Figure 4-31.

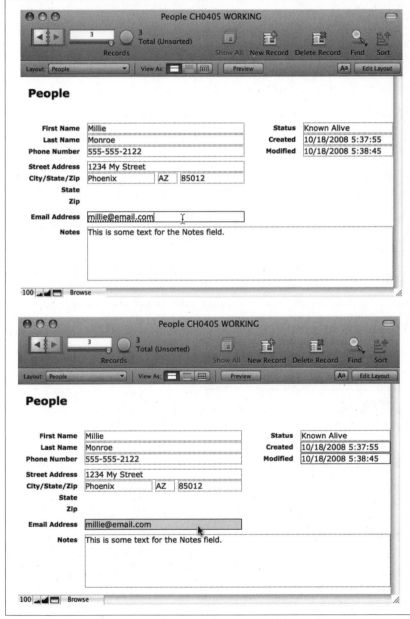

Figure 4-31:
Top: When you click a field, the flashing insertion point appears right where you clicked. In this image, you clicked at the end of the email address. Also notice that FileMaker has underlined the address because it thinks it's misspelled.

Bottom: By changing field behavior (Format → Field/Control → Behavior) the Email Address field now behaves differently. A click selects the whole address, making it a breeze to copy or replace. And the visual spell checker has been disabled for this field, so you're no longer bothered with an underline. Also notice that there's no longer a dotted outline around the Created and Modified fields, because they're not enterable anymore.

• As you learned early in this book, you can press the Tab key to jump to the next field when in Browse mode or Find mode. The Return key (or the Enter key by your main keyboard) inserts a new line into the field, and the Enter key by the number keypad commits the record, and takes you out of any field. But if you prefer, you can configure any or all of these keys to go to the next record instead. Just turn on the appropriate checkbox under "Go to next object using". If you turn a checkbox *off*, then the key goes back to its normal behavior, so if you turn off the "Tab key" checkbox here, then the tab key inserts a tab into the field instead.

To tidy up your layout, follow these steps:

1. **Click the Creation Timestamp field to select it.**

   The selection handles appear to let you know you're on the right track.

2. **While pressing Shift, click the Modification Timestamp field.**

   Because you pressed Shift, the Creation Timestamp stays selected, and the Modification Timestamp field is selected too.

3. **Choose Format → Field/Control → Behavior.**

   The Field Behavior window (Figure 4-30) appears.

4. **Turn off the "Browse mode" checkbox, and then click OK.**

   This prevents folks from accidentally typing in these fields.

5. **Select the Email Address field, and then choose Format → Field/Control → Behavior again.**

   The dialog box appears again, but this time you're configuring the Email Address field.

6. **Turn on "Select entire contents of field when entered".**

   An email address is exactly the kind of thing you often copy, but rarely edit.

7. **Turn on "Do not apply visual spell checking".**

   It would be awesome if FileMaker could tell you when you've mistyped an email address, but the spell checker just doesn't cut it. There's no sense spell checking something that's never going to be correct.

8. **Click OK, and then switch to Browse mode.**

   You can now try out your changes. Refer to Figure 4-31 if you're not sure what you're looking for.

Field controls. The Field Behavior dialog box is by no means the limit to what you can make a FileMaker field do. In fact, if you flip ahead to Figure 4-34, then you see that the Status field is something entirely different: a pop-up menu. In fact, a field can take on any of several forms, collectively referred to as *controls*. A control is something you click to manipulate the field data in some way. (Think about an airplane cockpit, whose instrument panel is covered with controls: switches, dials, and readouts of various types.)

FileMaker supports all the standard user interface controls you're used to, like pop-up menus, checkboxes, and radio buttons. It also offers pop-up calendars. And if you want to type with just a little assistance, it has *auto-completion*, which works just like the address bar in your Web browser: As you type, FileMaker gives you options based on other values you've typed in the field before.

All this power lives behind the Format → Field/Control → Setup command. You can see the resulting dialog box in Figure 4-32.

Figure 4-32:
The Field Control Setup dialog box (Format → Field/Control → Setup) lets you configure the type of control people use to enter data into the field. You'll discover a lot of power behind this little window.

In general, picking a type is simple: First select the field you want to change. Then choose Format → Field/Control → Setup (or just press Ctrl+Shift+F or Option-⌘-F). Finally, from the "Display as" pop-up menu, make your choice.

But if you choose a pop-up menu, or radio buttons, or checkboxes, how does File-Maker know what choices to let someone pick from? The answer lies in something you've seen just briefly so far: a *value list* (basically, a list of text values). You made a value list of state abbreviations on page 114 as part of the validation for the State field—one of many good situations for a value list.

When you choose one of these choice-oriented field control types, you also pick a value list. FileMaker then lets anyone using the database choose from among the values you specify. To try it out in the People database, you can make your Status field into a pop-up menu offering a list of the following choices:

• Known – Alive

• Known – Dead

• Missing

Here's how:

1. **In Layout mode, on the People Detail layout, select the Status field.**

   As usual, you need to tell FileMaker which field you want to change first.

2. **Choose Format → Field Control → Setup (Ctrl+Shift+F or Option-⌘-F).**

   The Field/Control Setup dialog box appears.

3. **From the "Display as" pop-up menu, choose "Pop-up Menu".**

   A few new options appear in the dialog box, as shown in Figure 4-33.

Figure 4-33:
When you choose to display your field as a pop-up menu, FileMaker gives you a few new choices. Most importantly, you must pick a value list from the "Display values from" pop-up menu. You can also turn on "Include 'Other...' item" to allow entry of other values" if you want your pop-up menu to include an extra choice called "Other..." that lets someone enter anything she wants. The second checkbox lets you add an "Edit..." item to the menu so database users can edit the choices in the menu at will.

4. **From the "Display values from" pop-up menu, choose Manage Value Lists.**

   The Manage Value Lists dialog box appears. This window lists all the value lists you've created (you probably have only one right now). It's perfectly OK to use the same value list in more than one place, but in this case, you don't have one with the values you want, so you'll make a new one.

5. **Click New.**

   The Edit Value List window appears, ready for you to configure a fresh value list.

6. **In the Value List Name box, enter *Statuses*.**

   You can name a value list just about anything you want. But for convenience in the future, name it something meaningful.

7. **Make sure "Use custom values" is turned on.**

   Once again, you want to specify a custom list of values. You'll learn about the other types on page 342.

8. **In the box under "Use custom values", type** *Known – Alive, Known – Dead,* **and** *Missing,* **each on a separate line.**

Make sure you press Return between each value so FileMaker knows you have three separate items in your value list, not one long item.

9. **Click OK, and then, in the Manage Value Lists window, click OK again.**

Closing both dialog boxes gets you back to the Field/Control Setup window. In the "Display value from" pop-up menu, your Statuses value list should be selected. If it isn't, select it now.

10. **Click OK.**

Your Status field looks a little different now. It has a small drop shadow, making it look like an old-school pop-up menu.

If you switch to Browse mode now, your pop-up menu should be fully functional. Figure 4-34 shows how it looks.

Figure 4-34:
Your layout now has a functioning pop-up menu. The field looks different on the layout, with a drop shadow making the field appear to pop out of the screen a little. When you click the pop-up menu, a list of choices appears.

Your layout could use a few more field control enhancements while you're here:

• The Notes field is big, but is it big enough? You can add a scroll bar with just a few clicks. Then, if you happen to need more space, FileMaker lets you scroll through all the text you add.

• Chances are you're going to put the same stuff in the City field over and over, with a few occasional exceptions. If you turn on auto-completion, then File-Maker helps you type the common values, but stays out of your way when you type something unusual.

- The State field, on the other hand, is always a standard state abbreviation (the validation sees to that), so a pop-up menu is usually great. But when you know the abbreviation you want, it's much faster to simply type it than to pick from a list. Nevertheless, the list is helpful if you can't remember whether Alaska is AK or AL (it's AK). FileMaker has another control type—the drop-down list—that's sort of like a combination pop-up menu and Edit box. It lets you either choose from the list or type for yourself.

Note: You rarely use *every* field control option in any one layout, and the layout you're creating now is no exception. Fear not, though. You can read about each field control option in detail on page 242.

First up, here's how to add a scroll bar to the People database's Notes field:

1. **Select the Notes field, and then choose Format → Field/Control → Setup (Ctrl+Shift+F or Option-⌘-F).**

   The Field/Control Setup window makes another appearance.

2. **Turn on "Include vertical scroll bar".**

   You're done; simple as that.

3. **Click OK, and then switch to Browse mode and behold the glory of your creation.**

   Your Notes field now has a little scroll bar along its right edge (Figure 4-35). (If you don't see this, you don't have field borders turned on. See page 159 for the steps you missed.) If you type enough data to fill up the Notes field, the scroll bar kicks into action, making it a snap to scroll up and down through as much text as you can throw at it.

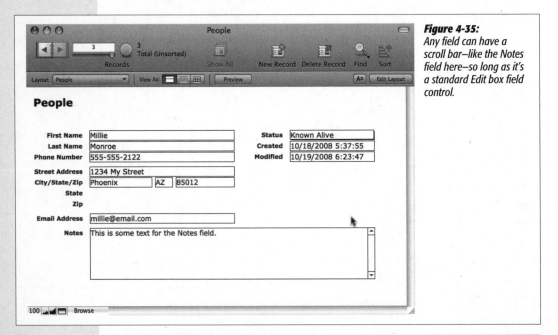

Figure 4-35:
Any field can have a scroll bar—like the Notes field here—so long as it's a standard Edit box field control.

Now you can add auto-completion to the City field. Select the field, and then choose Format → Field/Control → Setup (Ctrl+Shift+F or Option-⌘-F). This time, turn on "Auto-complete using previously entered values". When you test this control, make sure you create some records first, if you don't have any. The auto-completion is based on data in other records, so if you have no records, you don't get any completions.

Assuming you do have cities entered in other records, when you start typing in the City field, FileMaker automatically fills in the full city name that starts with whatever you type. If it isn't right, you can just keep typing. If it *is* right, press Tab, and FileMaker accepts the whole value.

Now it's time to tackle the State field. You know the drill: Select the field, and then press (Ctrl+Shift+F or Option-⌘-F). In the Field/Control Setup window, from the "Display as" pop-up menu, choose the "Drop-down List" option. From the "Display values from" pop-up menu, pick your State's value list (it's probably already selected since it's first in the list). While you're here, turn on "Include arrow to show and hide list". That adds an arrow icon to the field to indicate it has a drop-down list. Finally, click OK.

Once you've made this change, you may need to make the State field a little bigger to accommodate the arrow icon. You can make room by shortening the City or Zip Code field. Figure 4-36 shows the result of these changes.

Figure 4-36:
A drop-down list works a lot like a pop-up menu. Click the arrow, and you get a list of options. But unlike a pop-up menu, you can type directly into a drop-down list. For something short like a state abbreviation, typing is often faster than picking from a list, and the field's validation ensures no bogus entries get through.

You've now mastered field controls. You're almost ready to start decorating your layout visually, but before you add too much more, you'll make one more major improvement.

Autoresize

Now is a good time to step back from layout design, and scrutinize your work in Browse mode. Although the layout isn't much *prettier* than it was before, it does have a nicer feel. Things are aligned, grouped, and sized in a pleasing way. Your fields are more helpful to the data entry process than ever before.

But what about space efficiency? What happens if you make your database window bigger or smaller? Well, there's no need to guess. Have a peek at Figure 4-37 to see the not-so-great news.

Figure 4-37:
Top: When you resize the database window, FileMaker seems to make the worst choices possible. A smaller window leaves things out—like parts of the Notes, Status, Created, and Modified fields.

Bottom: A bigger window, on the other hand, is just a waste of space. You don't get any extra room where it counts (in the fields) so your window just takes up extra space for no good reason.

Obviously the behavior you see right now is not what you want. It isn't that File-Maker's dumb, though; it just needs a little guidance from you. Every object on the layout has a hidden set of *anchors*. These anchors connect the object to one or more sides of the window, so when you move and resize the window, the objects know how to move. Out of the box, FileMaker anchors each object to the top and left, meaning if you move the bottom or right edges (by making the window bigger), then nothing happens.

But you have complete control over these anchors. The Object Info palette (View →️ Object Info) holds the key. Its bottom half includes four checkboxes (complete with cute little anchor icons). Turn on a box, and the selected object or objects gets anchored to the associated side, as shown in Figure 4-38.

Figure 4-38:
Top: The Object Info palette (shown floating in the bottom-right corner) has checkboxes to anchor the selected object to any side of the window. Right now the selected object is anchored to the bottom and right.

Bottom: In fact, each object's anchors are configured slightly differently (the text in each box tells you how it's anchored). As you can see, the objects anchored to the bottom stay at the bottom of the window, even when you make it larger. The object in the middle has no anchors, so it stays in the middle.

You have a lot of ways you can anchor an object, and each combination is useful in one situation or another. You can even anchor an object on competing sides (both top and bottom, or both left and right, or even all four). When you do this, the object doesn't just *move* as the window gets bigger—it *grows* too, as Figure 4-39 shows .

Figure 4-39:
When an object is anchored on the left and right, it stretches side to side as the window grows. Likewise, an object that's anchored top and bottom gets taller. Of course, you can anchor an object on all four sides if you want. Then it grows in both directions as the window gets bigger.

Getting the desired results as you resize a window takes a little getting used to. The easiest approach is a four-step process:

1. **Figure out which objects should grow.**

   For instance, would it make sense for the First Name field on your layout to get *taller*? Probably not. If you let something get taller, the best candidate is probably the Notes field, since you expect it to hold a lot of text. Likewise, the Status and Timestamp fields don't benefit from extra width, so you don't want to let them grow wider. But the remaining fields could all be bigger, space permitting.

2. **Resolve conflicts among expanding objects.**

   You can have some objects stay left, some move right, and some grow. But FileMaker doesn't let any two objects grow wider in the same horizontal space, because they'll bump into each other. For instance, the City, State, and Zip Code fields all occupy the same horizontal space. So you need to decide which one should get the extra width. The obvious choice is the City field, since State and Zip Code always hold short values.

Note: If you have a series of side-by-side fields, then you might want them all to get a little wider together. But FileMaker doesn't give you that power, so you have to be choosy. In the worst case, you can make your layout big enough to accommodate any reasonable data, and skip resizing windows altogether.

---

3. **Apply the anchors.**

   This process is tedious, but you can use the rubber band technique (page 149) to grab collections of objects, and then set them all at once.

4. **Test.**

   95 percent of the time, you'll miss something the first time through. So switch to Browse mode periodically, and try resizing the window. You'll instantly spot the objects that are misbehaving, and return to Layout mode to fix them.

The best anchoring approach for your layout may be as follows:

- Anchor the First Name, Last Name, Phone Number, Street Address, City, and Email Address fields on the top, left, and right. This way, the fields stay near the top of the window, and grow wider as you make the window bigger.

- Anchor the State, Zip Code, Status, and Timestamp fields on the top and right, but not the left, so they slide out of the way as the other fields get wider. You also need to anchor the Status, Created, and Modified text labels to the right for the same reason.

- The Notes field will be anchored on all four sides. It's the one field that holds a lot of information, so it benefits the most from the extra space.

Here's how to make it happen:

1. **Select the First Name, Last Name, Phone Number, Street Address, City, and Email Address fields.**

   It's probably easiest to press Shift, and click the fields one by one. The fields should all have selection handles.

2. **If the Object Info palette isn't showing already, choose View → Object Info.**

   The palette appears somewhere on your screen (usually in the bottom-right corner).

3. **In the Object Info palette, turn on the right anchor checkbox.**

   The top and left anchors are already on (if they aren't for some reason, then turn them on so that the top, left, and right anchors are all on).

4. **Using the rubber-band technique, drag a box around the Status field, the time-stamps, and their three labels. Figure 4-40 shows how to do this.**

   Now the collection of fields and labels on the right side of the layout are all selected.

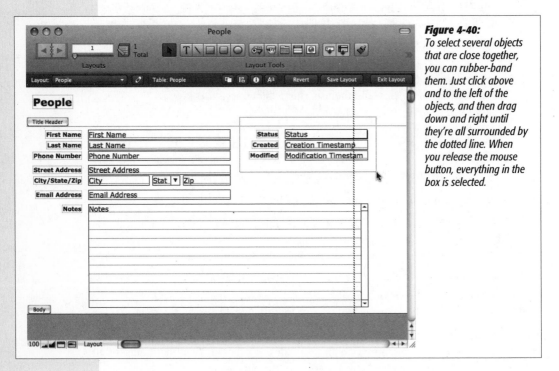

Figure 4-40:
To select several objects that are close together, you can rubber-band them. Just click above and to the left of the objects, and then drag down and right until they're all surrounded by the dotted line. When you release the mouse button, everything in the box is selected.

5. **In the Object Info palette, turn off the left anchor, and turn on the right anchor.**

   Once again, the top anchor should already be turned on, so make sure you have just the top and right anchors in play.

6. **Select the State and Zip Code fields, and then anchor them to the top and right.**

You can leave the Object Info palette open, so it's just a matter of select, configure, select, configure until the job is done.

7. **Select the Notes field, and then turn on its bottom and right anchors.**

This object should now be anchored on all four sides.

That should do it. If you try your layout in Browse mode now, it should use space wisely when you make the window bigger. You can see for yourself in Figure 4-41.

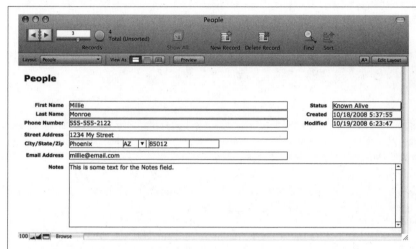

Figure 4-41:
Now when you make the window bigger, the fields get bigger too. The fields on the right bump right into the edge of the window, which most people think looks funny. You'll fix this when you decorate your layout in the next section.

If you make the window *smaller* now, though, then you see that the fields don't shrink beyond a certain point. FileMaker never lets the objects in Browse mode get smaller than they are in Layout mode. This fact lets you establish a minimum size for your layout to keep things from getting too small, but it limits your flexibility. In general, design your layouts to be as small as they reasonably can be. That way, people who use your database can decide how big things should be by adjusting the window size. You could probably make your People Detail layout a little more flexible by shrinking the stretchy fields down a little, like the picture in Figure 4-42.

Decorating a Layout

The layout you've created in this chapter is easy to use, has helpful field controls, and even adapts beautifully to any reasonable window size. Even so, it's still lacking in the looks department. You're going to fix that now.

In general, prettying things up involves five aspects of your layout:

- **Fonts.** You can get creative with fonts for headers, field labels, and even field data. But remember, any font you choose has to be installed on any computer where your database is used, or FileMaker substitutes some plain font instead.

Figure 4-42:
This version of the layout looks essentially the same in Browse mode, with one subtle difference: People can make the window smaller if they want. If you make the window big, though, you get the same roomy fields you had before.

Tip: If you want to use just a touch of text in your tastiest font, you can make a picture containing the text in a graphics program, and then paste it into FileMaker. You can't edit the text directly in Layout mode, so this method is best for things that don't change like company logos.

- **Colors.** FileMaker loves color. You can color layout parts, text, field data, and even the background of fields and text objects.

- **Effects.** You can apply three simple effects to any object: Drop Shadow to get a simple gray shadow, Embossed to make the object look like it sticks up off the page, and Engraved to make it look like it sinks down into the layout.

- **Shapes.** For clean, simple graphical embellishments, FileMaker lets you draw lines, squares, rectangles, circles, ovals, and even rectangles with rounded corners right on the layout. So you can make separator lines, boxes to hold related content, or simple logos and graphics.

- **Pictures.** If you need something more than simple geometry, then fire up your favorite graphics program and go nuts. FileMaker can import PNG, GIF, and JPEG images, and place them right on the layout, where they can be moved around and resized. And you can paste any graphic on your clipboard right on the layout too.

Coloring a part

The first thing you'll do to your layout is color the title header, giving the top portion of the layout a background color that sets it off from the rest of the layout. Any time you work with colors and effects in Layout mode, you first need to show the *Formatting bar*. This little buddy lives right below the Layout bar you've grown to love. But normally, when you first get started, it's not showing. To call it up, choose View → Formatting Bar, or you can click the Formatting bar icon shown in Figure 4-43.

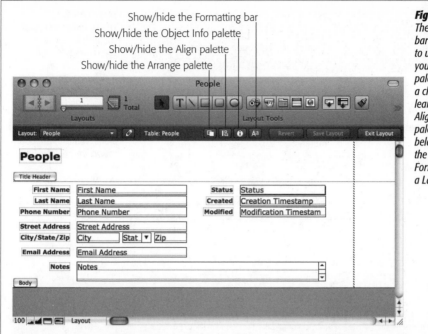

Show/hide the Formatting bar
Show/hide the Object Info palette
Show/hide the Align palette
Show/hide the Arrange palette

Figure 4-43:
These icons in the Layout bar give you quick access to useful options. Did you know the Object Info palette (page 151) is just a click away? You can learn more about the Align and Arrange palettes in the box below. The last button on the right opens the Formatting bar, which is a Layout mode essential.

POWER USERS' CLINIC

Perfect Palettes

You've already spent some time with the Object Info palette to anchor objects on your layout (page 151). But Layout mode offers a few more palettes for your one-click convenience:

- The Arrange palette (View → Arrange Palette) offers a series of tiny icon shortcuts for many commands in the Arrange menu. Hover over an icon to see a tooltip describing its function.

- The Align palette (View → Align Palette) has shortcuts for the alignment and resize tools in the Arrange menu. Once again, the tooltips tell you what all those icons mean.

When the palettes first appear, they're in a gray bar at the very top of the screen. But you can grab the dotted handles on the left edge of either palette, and then move it anywhere you want. Once you pull it out of its gray bar, it gets a title, a close box, and a resize handle in the bottom right corner. If you resize the palette, then the icons intelligently rearrange themselves. You really have control over how you organize your work area.

Finally, you can turn each of these palettes on or off using buttons in the Layout bar (as shown in Figure 4-43), which is usually quicker than using the menu commands.

Once you click the icon, the Formatting bar appears right below the Layout bar. You can see it in Figure 4-44.

With the Formatting bar in view, coloring the title header part is a breeze:

1. **Click the part label (the little gray box that says Title Header) to select it.**

   When you select the part label, it highlights.

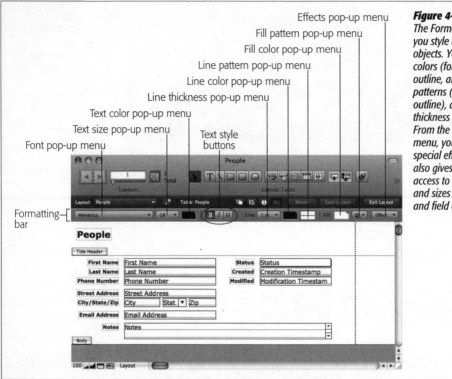

Effects pop-up menu
Fill pattern pop-up menu
Fill color pop-up menu
Line pattern pop-up menu
Line color pop-up menu
Line thickness pop-up menu
Text color pop-up menu
Text size pop-up menu
Text style buttons
Font pop-up menu
Formatting bar

Figure 4-44:
The Formatting bar lets you style the selected objects. You can set colors (for the fill, outline, and text), patterns (for the fill and outline), and the thickness of the outline. From the Effects pop-up menu, you can also add special effects. This bar also gives you speedier access to fonts, styles, and sizes for your text and field objects.

2. **In the Formatting bar, from the Fill Color pop-up menu (Figure 4-44), choose a color.**

Instantly, the part fills in with the selected color.

Applying color to text

If you selected a darkish color for your title header, then you may want to make the *People* text object white instead of black so it's easier to read.

1. **Select the *People* text object.**

You know the drill: Now it has handles.

2. **In the Formatting bar, from the Text Color pop-up menu, choose a light color or white.**

Once again, the change happens instantly. Your text is now colored.

While you're at it, you can color your field labels if you want. Be creative!

Adding lines and shapes

FileMaker's shape tools are simple but effective. You can see them in Figure 4-45.

Figure 4-45:
The collection of tools in the Status toolbar includes lines, rectangles (including the always elegant rounded rectangle), and ovals. Select a shape, and then drag to draw the shape on your layout.

Each tool works in the same way. First, click the tool to select it (highlighting its icon). Then drag the layout. As you drag, an outline of the shape you're creating follows your mouse. When you release the button, FileMaker puts the shape in place.

Once you've added a shape, you can use the Formatting bar to style it:

- The Line options (thickness, pattern, and color) style the border around the shape. If you don't want a border, then set the thickness to zero.

- The Fill options (color and pattern) style the inside of the shape. If you want the shape to be transparent, then click the Fill Pattern pop-up menu, and choose the double-overlapping-square icon, which is FileMaker's way of saying "clear."

- From the Effects pop-up menu, choose a special effect.

- For your layout, you need three shape embellishments, as shown in Figure 4-46.

In general, it's easiest to work from the bottom up. In other words, if one shape overlaps another, put the one that gets covered up on the layout first, and then add the second over it. Of course you can always shuffle how things stack up at any time using these four commands in the Arrange menu:

- Arrange → "Bring to Front" makes the selected object over anything that overlaps it.

- Arrange → Bring Forward moves the selected object up a notch in the pecking order. It covers one thing that overlaps it, but something else may still cover parts of it.

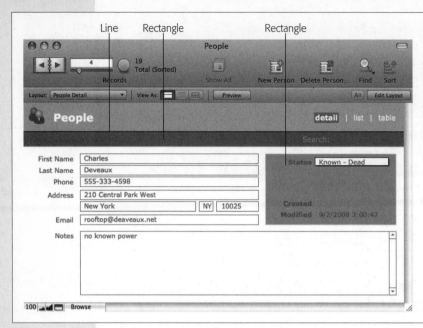

Line   Rectangle   Rectangle

Figure 4-46:
The finished layout benefits from four shapes. A rectangle and thick line separate the header from the body. And the Status and Timestamp fields are separated from the rest of the layout by a rectangle.

- Arrange → "Send to Back" and Arrange → Send Backward work in exactly the opposite way, pushing the selected object behind things that overlap it.

So to get started, you'll add the rectangle that spans the top of the layout:

1. **Since the header part label covers the area you want to work in, click the part label toggle (Figure 4-47) to flip it out of the way.**

   The part labels turn sideways so they don't overlap the layout. Also, if you don't have enough room in your title header part, drag its line down to make space. It's easy to shrink it later, and you want plenty of room to work with right now.

2. **In the Status toolbar, select the Rectangle tool.**

   When you click this tool, its icon highlights. If you ever decide you don't want a shape after all, then you can just click the Selection tool again (the arrow icon).

3. **Drag from the desired top-left corner to the bottom-right corner of the rectangle.**

   A rectangle appears where you dragged. It probably has a clear fill and thin black border, but if you've played with the Formatting bar, it may look different. You'll style it next.

Tip: It is often hard to tell exactly how big you want your shapes, or where you want them positioned, before you actually see them in place. Don't stress. You can easily move or resize them (or even delete and start again), so you don't have to be perfect out of the gate.

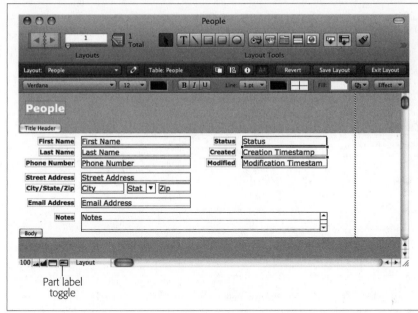

Figure 4-47:
The part label toggle lets you flip the part labels up and out of your way. Unfortunately, if your part is small, then the label may be cut off. To see the full label, just click this icon again. This way, you can quickly switch depending on your needs.

Part label
toggle

4. **From the Line Thickness pop-up menu, choose *None*.**

   The border around the shape disappears. Be careful: with a stray click, you can deselect a shape a shape with no border and no fill, and then you may have a hard time selecting it again. The rubber-band technique is usually the easiest way, but a click exactly on its (invisible) border also selects it.

5. **From the Fill Color pop-up menu, choose a color of your liking.**

   The rectangle fills with the selected color. The sample database uses a darkish brown, but use any color you like; it's *your* database.

6. **Using the mouse or arrow keys, nudge the rectangle into place.**

   It should be flush to the left edge of the window, and positioned nicely below the People text object. Feel free to shuffle the text around too, to make things look nice.

7. **Using the selection handles, resize the rectangle so it has the shape and size you want.**

   The right edge of the rectangle should be a little further right than the Status and Timestamp fields.

8. **In the Object Info palette, turn on the right anchor.**

   This shape should stretch when the window gets wider, so it always spans the window.

Figure 4-48 shows how things look now.

Figure 4-48:
The first rectangle is now in place. If you try things out in Browse mode, then you see it now defines the width of the layout, so the field no longer runs into the side of the window. Using a shape or line like this to mark off the width of the layout is a common way to keep your resizing elements reigned in.

Next, using the Line tool, draw a line along the top of the rectangle. Set its color to a darker version of the rectangle, and make its thickness *2 pt*. Anchor it on the top, left, and right.

Note: You may have a hard time getting the line exactly the width of the rectangle. If you use the Arrange → Resize To → Largest Width command, then you'll find the line is a little wider than the rectangle. That's because FileMaker's resizing prowess doesn't take line thickness into account. Since the rectangle has no border, and the line is relatively thick, the difference is visible. You can most easily fix it when you click near the end of the line, and then zoom in (View → Zoom In) a few times. Once you get a close look, you can manually shorten the line so it matches. Sometimes it's easier to see what you're doing if you make it significantly shorter first, so it doesn't cover the corner of the rectangle, and then slide it back into place.

Finally, you need to add the box around the Status and Timestamp fields:

1. **Select the Rectangle tool, and then drag a rectangle around the Status and Timestamp fields.**

   The rectangle covers right over the fields, which is probably not what you had in mind.

2. **Choose Arrange → "Send to Back".**

   The rectangle is now *behind* the fields and labels. Much better.

3. **From the Line Thickness pop-up menu, choose "1 pt".**

   Chances are the rectangle had a two-point border, so this setting puts it back where it belongs.

4. **Give the rectangle a background color and line color as you see fit.**

   You're the boss here.

---

5. **Select the Status field, and then set its fill color to white.**

   The Status field probably had a clear fill, so the background showed through. Now it has a white fill, which looks more normal. (The Creation Timestamp and Modification Timestamp fields aren't enterable, so you may want to make them something other than the same white as the enterable fields.)

6. **Move or resize the rectangle and fields so they look something like Figure 4-49.**

   Whenever you do work like this, you inevitably get the rectangle in the wrong place, or make it too big, or have fields that don't line up right. Fine-tuning is always the last step.

7. **Anchor the rectangle on the top and right (but not the left or bottom).**

   The rectangle slides right along with the fields that live inside it.

8. **Remove the borders from the Timestamp fields (Format → Field/Control → Borders).**

   Now that these non-enterable fields are tucked into a little box, they don't really need their borders anymore.

9. **If you want, color the field labels so they look nice against the rectangle background.**

   When you're done, the layout should look like Figure 4-49. If you need to, do any fine-tuning to get everything in place.

Figure 4-49:
With lines and shapes in place, your layout looks like this. Stop and admire your work. You've created the real deal: an attractive and functional database.

Locking the Layout Tools

After you create a text object with the text tool, the selection tool is automatically activated. FileMaker assumes you want just one text object, and saves you the trouble of switching back to the selection tool. If you anticipate creating several objects of the same type, give the tool icon a *double-click* instead of a single-click. The icon on the button turns white to let you know the tool is now locked. With a locked Text tool, you can create as many text objects as you want: Click to create the text box, type the text, click again for another text box, and so forth. When you're finished, click the selection tool again to make it active, or just press the Esc key.

If, for some reason, you don't like FileMaker always switching back to the Selection tool on your behalf, then you can instruct it to lock the drawing tools automatically—so even a single click keeps a tool active until you say otherwise. In Windows, choose Edit → Preferences; in Mac OS X, choose FileMaker Pro → Preferences. In the Preferences window, select the Layout tab, and then turn on the "Always lock layout tools" checkbox. If you're like most people, you may want to switch this checkbox off after a few minutes of working with it; just revisit the Layout tab of the preferences window, and then make the change.

Adding pictures

The final layout has a little people icon in the top-left corner. You can find this icon (called People-Icon.png) on the Missing CD page at *http://missingmanuals. com/cds*.

You can add an image like this to the layout in two ways:

- If you created the icon in a graphics program, and you can copy it to your clipboard, then simply paste it while in Layout mode. It appears on the layout as an object that can be moved at will.

- If you have the image in a file on the disk (like the People-Icon.png file), then you can insert it directly into the layout. You'll use this technique in the upcoming steps.

Once you've downloaded the icon files (or located an image of your own), follow these steps:

1. **In Layout mode, choose Insert → Picture.**

   A standard Open File dialog box appears.

2. **Make sure "Store only a reference to the file" is turned *off*.**

   Just as with a container field, if you turn this setting on, then FileMaker doesn't copy the file into the database. Instead, the program loads the file from its current location on your computer, and then displays it. If you later move, rename, or delete the picture file, then FileMaker can't find and display it. You almost never want that scenario with a layout graphic.

3. **In the dialog box, navigate to the file you want to insert, select it, and then click Open.**

   The icon appears somewhere on your layout. You may have to look around for it. It appears wherever you last clicked.

4. **Move the icon to the top-left corner of the layout, moving the People text object out of the way as necessary.**

You're done now. The layout looks like Figure 4-50.

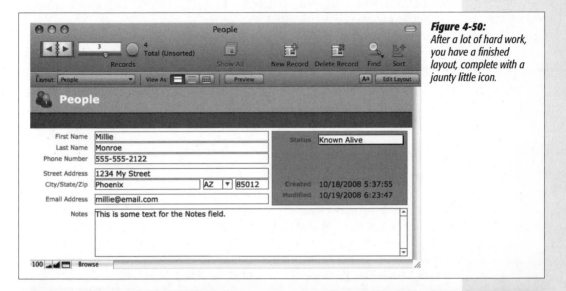

Figure 4-50:
After a lot of hard work, you have a finished layout, complete with a jaunty little icon.

Fine-Tuning Aids

When you do the kind of fine-tuning work it takes to finish up a layout, you need (and probably want) all the help you can get. For instance, it sometimes helps to have rulers to guide your work. You also might want to group objects together, or lock them in place while you fine-tune things around them.

FileMaker can show two kinds of rulers:

- Choose View → Graphic Rulers to see a ruler running along the top of the layout, and another along the left edge. As you move and resize items, markers on the ruler shows you how they line up.

- Choose View → Test Ruler to see a second ruler across the top of the layout. This ruler kicks into action when you start editing a text object. As explained in Chapter 2, the text ruler lets you set indent levels and tab stops, which work perfectly in Layout mode too.

In addition to these rulers, you can also add dotted *ruler lines* to the layout itself. These lines show only in Layout mode, and serve to help you gauge how things line up visually. To turn them on, choose View → Show → Ruler Lines.

If you have a group of objects that you're done tidying up, and you want them to stick together, select them all, and then choose Arrange → Group. For instance, you can group the box, Status field, and Timestamp fields. Then, if you need to move them, you can just drag the whole group around as if it were one object. To break the group apart again, choose Arrange → Ungroup.

Other times, it's hard to work with small items because you can too easily accidentally select bigger objects nearby. You can select that bigger object, and then choose Arrange → Lock. With the object locked into place, you can't select or move it. When you're done, you can click once on the item, and then choose Arrange → Unlock to bring it back to life.

Determining Tab Order

When you press Tab while editing a field, FileMaker automatically jumps you to the next field. But what does *next* mean? Normally, FileMaker moves through fields in a left-to-right, then top-to-bottom direction. That works well in many cases, but sometimes it falls short. For instance, on your People Detail layout, when you tab from the First Name field, it doesn't go to the Last Name field next. Instead, it goes to the Status field (a pop-up menu, so you can't type into it even if you want to), which is probably not what you want.

The solution to this predicament is to customize the *tab order* yourself. In other words, you tell FileMaker exactly what order it should tab through the fields on the layout.

Customizing the Tab Order

FileMaker lets you completely customize the tab order for any layout. To fix the tab order on the Detail layout of your People database, first choose Layouts → Set Tab Order. A few things happen onscreen: You see the arrows indicating tab order, and the Set Tab Order dialog box appears (Figure 4-51). You tell FileMaker what order to use by putting appropriate numbers into the tab order arrows. Put a *1* in the arrow that points to the button or field that should get your attention when you first press Tab. Put a *2* in the next object in line, and so forth.

Chances are, all the arrows that point to fields already have numbers in them reflecting FileMaker's automatic tab order. Clearing and typing into each arrow can thus be a form of digital torture. To ease the pain, FileMaker offers up the Set Tab Order window, which appears at the screen's bottom-right corner. This window lets you make a few targeted bulk changes to the tab order.

First of all, you can clear the numbers from every arrow by clicking Clear All. This trick is great because once all the arrows are empty, then you no longer have to type. Just click each arrow (or the field it points to) in succession, and FileMaker enters the numbers for you.

If you click Add, and then choose from the "Add remaining" pop-up menu, you can add unnumbered fields to the order. FileMaker numbers them for you using the same right-to-left, top-to-bottom philosophy that the automatic tab order uses. This option comes in handy if, for example, you want to set up a specific tab order for a few fields first, and then use the automatic ordering for all fields thereafter.

When you're done making changes, either in the window or by editing the arrows directly, click OK. If you decide you've caused more harm than good in this tab order editing session, then click Cancel instead, and the tab order reverts back to the way it was before you opened the Set Tab Order box.

Figure 4-51:
When you choose Layouts → Set Tab Order, the Set Tab Order window appears. Meanwhile, FileMaker also adds arrows to the layout while this dialog box is open. From here, you can make bulk adjustments to the tab order, clear it, and start over, or manipulate the numbers one by one to get exactly the order you want.

Fixing the Tab Order in the People Database

On the People database, on the Detail layout, you want to fix the tab order so that Last Name comes after First Name. You can approach this task in several ways, but the following steps show you a trick that makes it easier. You may be tempted to Clear All, and then renumber all the arrows yourself. But since you're *removing* only a field from the tab order (the Status field) you can save yourself the trouble. Here's how:

1. **Choose Layouts → Set Tab Order.**

   The Set Tab Order window and its flock of arrows appear.

2. **Click the arrow pointing to the Status field, and then delete the number.**

   The arrow pointing to Status is now empty. Your order also now goes straight from 1 to 3, skipping right over 2. Pay no attention to this problem (that's the trick).

3. **Click OK in the Set Tab Order window.**

   If you switch to Browse mode and try out your tab order, then you see that you can now tab right from First Name to Last Name.

This trick works because FileMaker establishes the tab order by following the numbers in the arrows in order. It doesn't give a hoot whether those numbers are contiguous. You've fixed your layout with a minimum of clicks.

The same basic trick applies if you need to *insert* a field into the tab order too. For instance, if you add a new field that should go between 2 and 3 in the tab order, just give it the number 3 spot. When you do, FileMaker automatically bumps number 3 up to 4 (and so on) for you.

Preserving the Automatic Order

As long as you never choose the Set Tab Order command on a particular layout, FileMaker automatically manages the tab order for you. For example, if you add a Middle Name field to the layout, and place it between the First Name and Last Name fields, it automatically goes into the right spot in the tab order—between First Name and Last Name. If you switch the positions of the First Name and Last Name fields, Last Name becomes the first field in the tab order, and First Name comes next.

Once you click the Set Tab Order window's OK button, though, FileMaker hands full responsibility thereafter over to you. If you add a new field to the layout, then it just gets stuck to the *end* of the tab order, no matter where you put that field on the layout. If you move fields around so that the tab order makes absolutely no sense, FileMaker doesn't care. It keeps the tab order exactly as you specified in Set Tab Order.

Building Basic Layouts

The last chapter introduced a lot of layout concepts, but you really worked only on one layout. Most databases use many layouts, each designed for a different task. Your People database has a great detail layout, but what else could it use? For starters, a few design tweaks might make your list of people easier for you to work with onscreen. And how about a way to print your contact information? You might want to print mailing labels or envelopes, too. You probably have some ideas about what *you'd* like your database to do, and FileMaker itself has some ideas of its own to help you along.

In this chapter, you'll learn about more of FileMaker's powerful layout features. You'll also learn how to optimize a layout for printing.

The Lowdown on Layout Types

When you created the List layout in the last chapter, you used FileMaker's Layout Assistant to speed the process along, but FileMaker fans are split on whether the assistant is the best option. Some people love the quick start you get from File-Maker, but others prefer to build a layout by hand, starting with a clean slate. You'll get to try your hand at the start-from-scratch approach later in this chapter.

But whatever your preference, the Layout Assistant is critical for some layout types—like labels and envelopes—where lining everything up yourself can burn a lot of hours (and paper). So before you start building a layout, you'll get a brief introduction to each of the kinds of layouts FileMaker can build for you. To use them, in Layout mode, choose Layout → New Layout/Report.

Standard Form

The "Standard form" choice creates a layout just like the one FileMaker creates automatically when you start your database—a simple detail layout (see page 126). This time, though, you get to decide which fields to include. You also have some control over the fonts and colors. FileMaker calls these design controls "themes."

Columnar List/Report

If you want to show lots of records on the screen or page at one time, then choose "Columnar list/report" instead. You used this option in the last chapter to build a quick List layout (page 126). You still get to pick which fields to include and what theme to use, but FileMaker sets up the new layout as a list of records with columns of data, one per field.

Table View

When you select "Table view", FileMaker creates a layout much like "Standard form", but the layout is set to Table view automatically. Actually, the pros (yourself included) know that in Browse mode, you can choose View → "View as Table" to see *any* layout in Table view, so you rarely need to create a separate layout of this type. But if you're new to this whole database thing and want a layout that looks and acts like the spreadsheets you're accustomed to, then the Table View layout is your fastest way there.

Labels or Vertical Labels

If you ever need to print a sheet of peel-and-stick labels from your database—to make nametags for every attendee to your conference, or address labels for all those follow-up letters—the Labels layout type is your best friend (it's shown in Figure 5-1). FileMaker is smart enough to know how to set up a layout for any of the standard Avery label types. You just pick your type, and FileMaker does all the work, producing a layout properly structured for your label dimensions. It even puts the fields you specify on the layout so that they flow together nicely. The layout may look strange to you at first, because each field is surrounded by << and >>. (These are merge fields—see page 195 for an explanation.) If you're not using Avery labels, then you can plug in your own measurements.

Note: The "Vertical labels" type applies only to people with Asian language text in their databases. This type rotates this kind of text to create *vertical* labels.

Envelope

If you'd rather print right on the envelope than stick a label on it, use the Envelope layout type. FileMaker creates a layout specially designed to print on a Number 10 envelope (see Figure 5-2). You can even customize it with your company's logo and return address, just by adding text and pictures to the layout.

Figure 5-1:
When you create a Labels layout, FileMaker lets you pick a standard Avery label size, or key in specific dimensions (you can usually find the right numbers included with printable labels). FileMaker then creates the layout with everything in the right place to print on the labels perfectly.

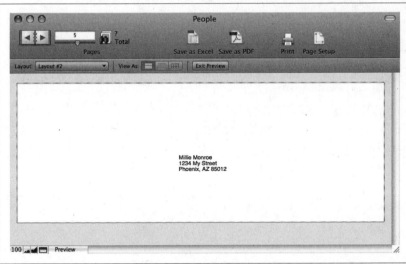

Figure 5-2:
You can address envelopes in a heartbeat to everyone with a layout like this one. Just find the people you want, load a stack of envelopes in your printer, and then print them out.

Since every printer handles envelopes a little differently, the layout needs a little adjusting to print perfectly. Luckily, it's almost always a cinch to put things right. You can usually just delete the Header part from the layout. Also, don't forget to choose the right paper size (File → Print Setup on Windows; File → Page Setup on Mac OS X) and orientation for your envelope. On more persnickety printers, you may have to leave the header in place, and adjust its height. Getting things lined up always involves a few test prints, but once you've got it working, you never have to fuss with it again. (Well, until you get a new printer.)

Blank Layout

The last type, called Blank layout, is both the simplest and the most flexible. You get a layout with a small header and footer, and a big body. It has nothing on it at all. If you like setting things up by hand, or your layout doesn't rightly match any of the types above, drawing a blank may be your best choice.

Creating a Layout from Scratch

FileMaker's built-in layout types are nice for quick and dirty work, but if you want your database to look great *and* work exactly the way you say, you may need to do some heavy customization. In fact, you'll often find it easier to start with a blank layout, and then add exactly what you need, than to try to slice'n'dice a standard form into the avant-garde arrangement you have in mind.

Adding a New Layout

However they may end up, all new layouts start the same way. Open a database, switch to Layout mode, and then choose Layout → New Layout/Report. You see the window shown in Figure 5-3—the New Layout/Report dialog box.

Figure 5-3:
The New Layout/Report dialog box (Layout → New Layout/Report) is the starting point for layout creation. Most importantly, you get to decide what type of layout you want, and what it's called.

In this box, you tell FileMaker a few basic facts about the new layout you have in mind. (You can always tweak these settings later.) From top to bottom, here's how it works:

- **Show records from.** For now, you can just ignore this pop-up menu. (It lets you choose a table, but you have only one table so far.)

- **Layout Name.** Enter a name for your layout here. You can use any name you want, but you have to keep it to 100 characters or less.

- **Include in Layout menu.** Use this checkbox to tell FileMaker whether or not your new layout shows up in the Layout bar's Layout pop-up menu. Most new developers turn on this option for every layout, to make sure they can always find their work. As your databases get more advanced, you may have special layouts that you want people to access only under certain circumstances. When you get that fancy, you can turn this checkbox off so folks can't switch to the layout any time they want.

Note: Every layout shows in the Layout pop-up menu when you're in Layout mode. This checkbox controls what shows up when you're in other modes.

To get a feel for building a brand-new layout, you'll create a layout in the People database like the one shown in Figure 5-4.

Figure 5-4:
The new List layout shows some information about a lot of people. As in all good List layouts, you can scroll through the records in the found set. Unlike your everyday, ordinary list, though, this layout doesn't have a strict columnar design.

In this chapter, you'll repurpose the plain-vanilla People List layout you made in the previous chapter, and create a Report layout for printing. To avoid chaos and confusion, rename the existing layout People Report. (If you don't remember how to rename a layout, see page 133 or visit Layout → Layout Setup.)

Now you're ready to make your new People List layout:

1. **Open the People database (see page 10 for download instructions). In Layout mode, choose Layout → New Layout/Report.**

   The New Layout/Report window pops up.

2. **In the Layout Name box, type a fitting name, like People List. Then, from the "Select a layout type" list, choose "Blank layout".**

   The Next button changes to Finish, since you don't have any more choices for a blank layout.

3. **Click Finish.**

   FileMaker returns you to your database, and shows you the new blank layout.

Matching Two Layouts

This layout needs a header almost exactly like the one on the People Detail layout. Unfortunately, you can't copy and paste the Header part (see page 136) itself, but you *can* copy everything on the header, and paste it on this new layout.

Before you do, you need to make this header the same size as the other so everything fits properly. As with many things in FileMaker, you have at least two good ways to perform this task. Which one you use depends entirely on your personal taste.

Matching part sizes with the Object Info palette

If you're a numbers person, this method is for you. Using the Object Info palette (see Figure 4-24), you can resize or reposition any layout object with pixel-perfect precision. To learn how to tackle it, on the People layout, you first check the exact size of the Header part, and then adjust the new header so its size matches.

1. **Switch to the People Detail layout.**

   You can switch using the Layout pop-up menu, or simply by clicking the book icon's left-hand page.

2. **If the Object Info palette isn't showing, choose View → Object Info.**

   You may have a hard time spotting the palette, since it's small and often lands way at your screen's bottom-right. You know it's out there if, in the View menu, you see a checkmark next to Object Info.

3. **Make sure the palette is measuring in pixel units.**

   You should see "px" by each number in the palette. If you don't, then click the unit you do see repeatedly until "px" shows.

4. **Click the title Header part tag to select the part.**

   The Object Info palette updates to show measurements for the Header part. The last field—with a double arrow pointing up and down—is the height. Jot down the height number you see there.

5. Switch to the new List layout, and then select the header by clicking its tag.

The Object Info palette now measures this part.

6. Type the number you got in step 5 into the Height field on the Object Info palette, and then press Enter.

The part doesn't move while you type; you have to press Enter to see your change take effect. When you do, the Header part resizes and now perfectly matches the header on the People layout.

If you prefer less typing and more mousing, you can use the T-squares instead.

Matching part sizes with the T-squares

In the last chapter, you learned about the T-squares (see page 151). These handy liner-uppers don't just help you keep objects on the layout straight. T-squares can also help you make sure parts and objects are in the same place on *different* layouts. Start on the People Detail layout, and then follow these steps:

1. If the T-squares aren't showing, then choose View → T-Squares.

The T-square lines appear.

Tip: On a busy layout, the T-squares can be hard to spot. If you know they're showing, but you can't *find* them, just turn them off, and then back on. When you do, they reappear smack-dab in the center of the layout.

---

2. Position the horizontal T-square between the title header and the body.

The T-square floats above everything else on a layout, so it covers the dotted part boundary line perfectly.

Note: If you're having trouble getting the lines to match perfectly, the Object Grids may be holding you back. Choose Align → Object Grids to tell FileMaker to let you move the T-squares exactly where you want them.

---

3. Switch to the new list layout, and then drag the Header part tag into the right place, using the T-square as a guide.

Since T-squares stay in the same spot as you switch layouts, you can rest assured your new header is just the right size.

Now that the header is the right size, you can fill it with the necessary objects. You could drag objects into the header manually, just as you did in the last chapter when you built the People layout. But you've already done that work once. Why not take advantage of it here as well? You can easily reuse these items: Copy and paste them from the People layout. You use copy and paste *a lot* when you design layouts.

1. **Switch back to the People layout. Select the graphic, "People I Know" text, and "[details]" text.**

   You can Shift-click or use the rubber band to select both objects. If you have a horizontal line on your layout, then select it, too.

2. **Choose Edit → Copy.**

   Nothing changes on the screen, but FileMaker copies the objects to your operating system's clipboard.

3. **Switch back to the list layout, and then choose Edit → Paste.**

   The objects appear on the new layout, probably in the wrong place.

4. **Drag the objects (as a group) into their proper place in the header.**

   Since they're all selected, if you drag one object, then the others follow.

Tip: To give your database that professional touch (or if you're just a stickler for details), you can use the T-squares or the Object Info palette to be sure everything's in the same place on both layouts. If you do, just check *one* of the objects. If you move them all as a group, and one of them is in place, then they all are.

Finishing the header

Your Header part is nearly complete. To finish it, give it a colored fill (see page 174). Your layout should look something like Figure 5-5.

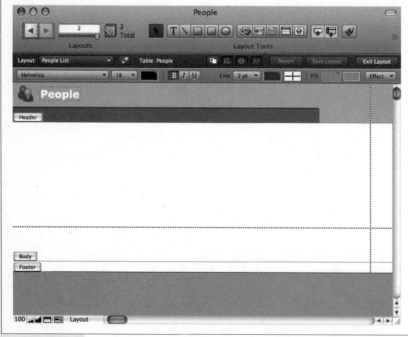

Figure 5-5:
Now that you've gussied up your header, it looks something like this example. The header's looking good, but the body could still use some work—it's empty right now. Since the body of the list layout repeats over and over for each record, the body should avoid wasted space. In Browse mode, the list scrolls so you can see all the records in your found set.

Set Up the Body

Now that the header is in place, it's time to work on the body—and learn a few new tricks. You'll add the First Name and Last Name fields to the layout, and make them flow nicely together. You'll also tell FileMaker to show the record number next to each person's name.

Making data flow with merge fields

Knowing what you know now, if you set out to build this layout yourself, you'd probably jump right for the field tool and start dragging the new field on the layout. But look closely at Figure 5-6 first.

When you put a field on a layout, you're putting it *exactly* where you want it. No matter what record you're on when you look at the layout, that field value is in the same spot. Usually, that's where you want it to be, but sometimes—like in the new list layout—you want something a little more flexible. You want the Last Name field to start where the first name ends. Since some first names are longer than others, this spot changes from record to record.

In FileMaker, you solve this problem using *merge fields*. Merge fields work a lot like a mail merge in a word processing program. You create an ordinary text object on your layout (not a field object), and then tell FileMaker to merge different field values into the text. For example, to put the first and last names together on your new layout, you create a text object like this:

```
<<First Name>> <<Last Name>>
```

Merge fields always show up in Layout mode with angle brackets around their names, just like <<this>>. When you look at this text object in Browse mode, though, you see the value of the First Name field, then a space, and then the Last Name field. Since all these values show up in a single text object, FileMaker sorts out the exact positions for you.

Tip: Although you can *type* the merge field into a text object exactly as it is shown above, this method can be error-prone. If your field data isn't showing in Browse mode (and you see the <<Field Name>> instead), you probably misspelled the field name. Even a stray space or missing punctuation is more than FileMaker's willing to ignore. You'll usually find it's easiest to let FileMaker type the name for you by using the Insert → Merge Field command. That's the process you'll use here.

Merge fields have a downside, though: They're only for display. You need a real field if you want people to be able to get in there and change its contents. Your database already has a layout with real fields just for editing data (the detail layout), so in this case, merge fields are just what the doctor ordered.

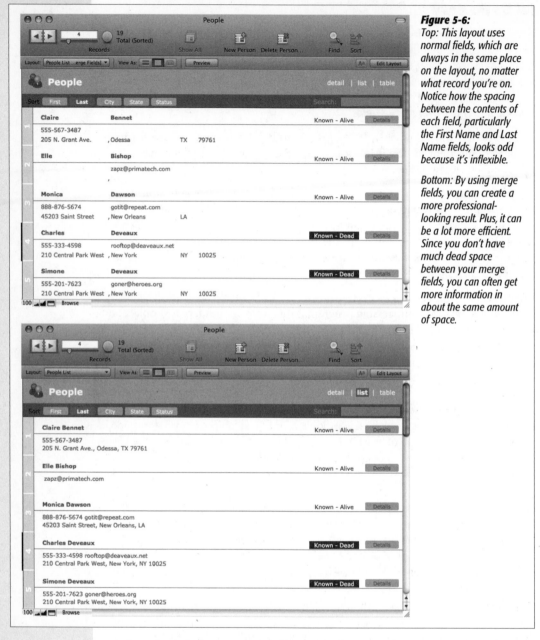

Figure 5-6:
Top: This layout uses normal fields, which are always in the same place on the layout, no matter what record you're on. Notice how the spacing between the contents of each field, particularly the First Name and Last Name fields, looks odd because it's inflexible.

Bottom: By using merge fields, you can create a more professional-looking result. Plus, it can be a lot more efficient. Since you don't have much dead space between your merge fields, you can often get more information in about the same amount of space.

Putting merge fields into a text object is easy:

1. **In the Status toolbar, click the text tool.**

   FileMaker activates the text tool; it changes your mouse arrow to an I-beam, and darkens the text tool button.

2. **Click somewhere in the Body part.**

   A new editable text box appears, ready for you to type.

3. **Choose Insert → Merge Field.**

   The Specify Field dialog box appears, listing every field in your database.

4. **Select the First Name field, and then click OK.**

   FileMaker inserts <<*First Name*>> into the text object for you.

5. **Type a single space.**

   Since you don't want the first and last name *right* next to each other, you've just added a space.

6. **Choose Insert → Merge Field again. When the Specify Field dialog box returns, select the Last Name field, and then click OK.**

   FileMaker adds the Last Name merge field to the text object.

You now have a text object that shows the first and last names with a single space between them (you can switch to Browse mode, and then try it out if you want). You just need to put it into place.

Next, you need to add a line for the phone number and email address. Using the same steps as before, add a second text object below the first, with these merge fields:

```
<<Phone Number>> <<Email Address>>
```

Finally, the address information should also be in a merge field (study Figure 5-6 to see why—they all flow together in a nicely formatted line). Repeat the steps above to build a text object like this:

```
<<Street Address>, <<City>>, <<State>> <<Zip Code>>
```

Note: You can mix and match merge fields and normal text to your heart's content. When you were setting up the first and last name, you added a space between the merge fields. This time you add even more. After the street address and city merge fields, type a comma, and then a space.

If necessary, move the new text objects so they're aligned and spaced properly, using Figure 5-7 as a guide.

Matching styles

For consistency, most people like to use the same set fonts, sizes, styles, and colors throughout a database. The same goes for the color and border of graphical objects (boxes, lines, and so forth) and fields. For example, the text objects you just added may or may not be the same font, size, and color as the field labels on the People Detail layout. You could meticulously recreate every desired attribute (and visit the Menu bar a dozen times in the process) or you can let FileMaker do all the work for you by using the Format Painter, as explained in Figure 5-7.

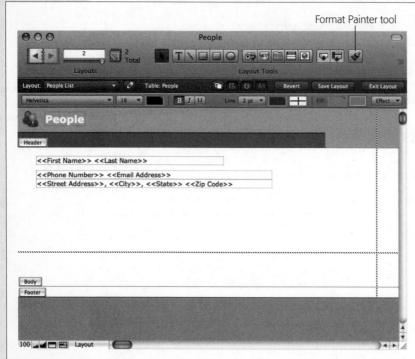

Format Painter tool

Figure 5-7:
The Format Painter makes it a cinch to transfer style from one object to another. First, select the object whose style you like. Then click the Format Painter tool. Finally, click the object to which you want to apply the style (you can switch layouts first if necessary). When you click the destination object, its styles are updated to match the first.

To style your text object, first switch to the People Detail layout, and then select one of the text labels. Then switch to the People List layout and click one of the text objects. FileMaker updates its color, font, size, and style instantly. At this point, you can choose the Format Painter tool again, and then click the next text object to style it. Repeat as necessary until all three text objects are styled.

Tip: If you plan to use a tool over and over, then, in the Status toolbar, you can double-click the tool icon. Now, FileMaker doesn't switch back to the selection tool after your next click. Instead, you can use the tool as many times as you want, and then choose the selection tool yourself when you're done.

While you're at it, make the first text object (the one with first and last name) bold so it stands out a little. When you're done, your layout should look a lot like Figure 5-8.

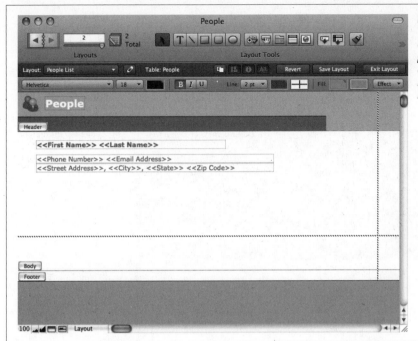

Figure 5-8:
With your three text objects for the name, phone, email, and address in place, your layout should look like this.

Adding fields to a layout

Next, you need to add the Status field to the layout. Since you won't merge this field with any other data, you can use a normal field object. FileMaker actually provides two ways to add a field. First, you can choose Insert → Field. When you do, FileMaker asks which field you want, and then drops it somewhere on the layout for you to move into place. But most people find it easier to use the Status toolbar's Field tool (Figure 5-9).

To add the status field to the layout, follow these steps:

1. **Drag the Field tool straight down.**

   As you drag, FileMaker shows a little outline of the field it'll create.

2. **Drag to where you want the field to land, and then release the mouse button.**

   When you do, you see the dialog box in Figure 5-10, letting you choose from the fields in your database.

3. **Choose the Status field.**

   This field is the one you want to add.

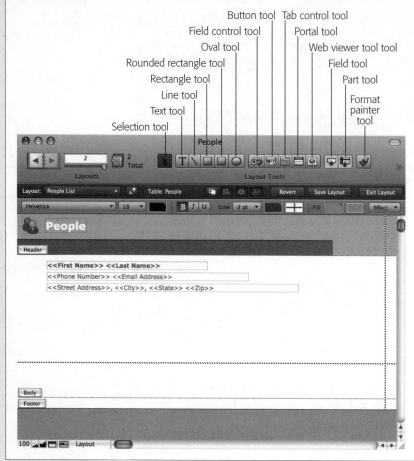

Figure 5-9:
In the Status toolbar, you can see the Field tool along with all the other Layout mode tools. The Field tool works a little differently from the others, though. Instead of clicking, you drag the field tool onto the layout. It works like a little sticky-note pad—you can peel off a new field any time, and then stick it on your layout.

Figure 5-10:
Whenever you add a field to the layout, FileMaker asks which field you want by showing you the Specify Field dialog box. Notice the "Create label" checkbox. If you turn it on, then FileMaker makes a new text object prefilled with the field name along with the field object itself.

4. **Turn off the "Create label" checkbox.**

This field is unlabeled in the finished layout. If you left "Create label" turned on, then you can easily delete the field label later.

5. **Click OK.**

The field appears on the layout.

6. **With the field still selected, choose Format → Field/Control → Behavior, and then turn off the "In Browse mode" checkbox.**

Since this list layout isn't for editing data, you don't want anyone to be able to click in the field in Browse mode.

If necessary, adjust the field formatting to it uses a reasonable font, color, size, and style.

Using symbols to show important info

Merge fields aren't the only things FileMaker can squeeze into a text object on the fly. You can also insert a handful of special *symbols*—stand-in characters that you can replace with useful information when you view your database in Browse or Preview mode. For instance, notice in Figure 5-4 how each record in the list is numbered. You can accomplish this effect with the record number symbol.

Note: FileMaker offers a host of other symbols besides the record number symbol. See the box on page 202 for full detail.

Since you're creating a *List* layout, it would be nice to show record numbers. That way, you can easily see where you are in the list at any time, even if you've scrolled down from the top. You use the record number symbol to make it happen.

To add a record number to your layout, just choose Insert → Record Number Symbol. You now have a text object that contains "@@". But if you peek at it in Browse mode, then you see that FileMaker actually puts the current record number in its place.

You can also insert symbols like this into existing text objects. Just click into the text object first, as if to type. Then when you choose the menu command, FileMaker adds the record number symbol to the existing text.

Note: The record number symbol is useful for helping you keep track of where you are in a list, but don't be lulled into thinking it helps identify a record in a reliable way. For instance, if you sort the records in a different order, then each record gets a new number since the numbers go in order. See page 311 for a way to assign a permanent ID number, or a key, to a record.

Other Symbols

On the Insert menu, FileMaker includes symbols for several special values you may want to show on a layout. You use these symbols on the layout because you don't know the information in advance, like the current date or record number. Then, when you switch to Browse mode (or Preview mode), FileMaker replaces the symbol with the up-to-the-moment correct value. You can read about the record number symbol on page 201. Here are the others:

- The **date symbol** (//) is replaced by the current date. People often include this symbol on printed reports so you can easily see when they were generated.

- The **time symbol** (::) is replaced by the current time.

- The **user name symbol** (||) is replaced by the current user's name. FileMaker takes the user name of whoever's logged into your computer. (That's two *pipe* symbols—Shift-backslash on most keyboards—typed side by side.)

- The **page number symbol** (##) is replaced by the page number in Preview mode or when you print. Otherwise, it just shows as a question mark.

The Insert menu has three related options as well, but unlike symbols, these don't get replaced by anything in Browse or Preview mode. When you use the Insert → Current Date command, for instance, FileMaker simply adds today's date to the text object in Layout mode. It shows this same date forever in either mode.

You can use the Insert menu to place symbols where you need them, but you can type them in manually faster and easier. So once you've seen that "##" makes a page number, forget about mousing around, and just type the two number signs.

Rotating objects

In the final layout shown back in Figure 5-4, the record number text actually runs up and down instead of the normal side to side. Since record numbers can get large (imagine you have over 1,000 records) it's more space efficient to tuck it along the side of the layout instead of reserving enough horizontal space for any possible number. (Plus, it looks pretty cool.)

You can easily rotate a text object, field object, graphic object, or picture on a layout. First select the object, and then choose Arrange → Rotate. FileMaker rotates the object 90 degrees clockwise. You can rotate again to get another 90 degrees, and by rotating more than once, you can turn an object upside down, or sideways in either direction. For the record number object, three rotations does the trick, causing the text to run sideways from bottom to top.

Once the object is rotated, you can resize it, style it, and slide it into place. While you're at it, you can now reduce the size of the body part so the list is nice and compact, and delete the footer part. Use Figure 5-11 as a guide.

Figure 5-11:
With a little part cleanup, and a rotated record-number-bearing text object on the far-left edge, your layout is starting to come together. Take a peek in Browse mode (be sure to switch to List view if necessary) and see how it's coming along.

Note: If, when you look in Browse mode, your record number object doesn't appear, or doesn't show up for every record, you may need to move it down a notch. If an object overlaps the header by even one tiny pixel, FileMaker assumes the whole thing belongs on the header, rather than the body part. Just switch back to Layout mode, select the object, and then press the down arrow once or twice to nudge it into place.

Decorate the layout

Just like your last layout, this layout has a few graphical embellishments that you need to drop into place:

- There's a thin line (page 177) running horizontally under the name fields.
- Another thin line runs vertically along the right edge of the record number text object.

Add these objects now. Figure 5-12 shows the final result.

Setting Layout View

Switch to Browse mode to admire your handiwork. If you're seeing only one record at a time, switch to List view (choose View → "View as List"). When you choose the blank layout template, you get complete freedom to make the layout look just the way you want. But one tradeoff is that you have to remember to tell the layout which view it's supposed to be in.

But there's nothing stopping you (or anybody using your database) from switching this layout back to Form view, or Table view, at some point in the future. If don't want anyone to see the database that way, then you can tell FileMaker you want only this layout to be seen in List view:

Figure 5-12:
Once you add two small lines, your layout starts to get a little structure. Although they're decorative, each serves a purpose. The horizontal line makes your list look neater by giving it a consistent width, since names, addresses, and phone numbers can vary in size. The vertical line runs the full height of the body part, so the end of the line on the first record touches the start of the line on the second record, and so forth. The result is a continuous line along the left edge of the layout, separating the record numbers from the records.

Vertical line   Horizontal line

1. **Switch to Layout mode, and then choose Layouts → Layout Setup.**

   Remember, Layout mode is the only place you can make changes to a layout. You work this particular piece of magic in the Layout Setup box.

2. **On the Views tab, turn off Form View and Table View.**

   You've just told FileMaker to make these two menu choices off-limits in Browse and Find modes. After all, they don't make much sense in a layout that's designed specifically to work as a list.

3. **Click OK to dismiss the dialog box.**

   Honestly, you have to tell some programs *everything*.

Now, when you switch to Browse mode and look at the View menu, "View as Form" and "View as Table" are grayed out. FileMaker doesn't let you accidentally switch your list to a useless view of the data..

Setting Anchors in List Layouts

Every good layout expects that people using the database are going to resize the window and plans accordingly, using anchors to make sure onscreen objects behave properly as the window contorts (page 168). But in List view, anchors work a little differently. In order to maximize the amount of data that can be seen in one shot, FileMaker never stretches records taller in List view. Instead, if the window gets taller, you see more records. So top and bottom anchors have no effect in List view. But left and right anchors still work as you would expect.

Part Setup Dialog Box

When you choose Layout → Part Setup, FileMaker shows you the Part Setup dialog box (see Figure 5-13). This often-ignored box isn't just a slower way to get to the Part Definition window, though. From this one screen, you can create new parts, and edit, delete, and rearrange existing parts. But, as you read on page 144, you can do most of this work more easily *without* this window, so you don't use it very often.

To add a new part, click Create. You're presented with the Part Definition dialog box, where you can decide what kind of part to create, and set various options. You can do the same thing by dragging the part tool from the Status toolbar or choosing Insert → Part.

To see the part definition for an existing part, select it in the Part Setup dialog box, and then click Change. This maneuver too has a shortcut: in Layout mode, just double-click any part tag.

To delete a part, select it, and click Delete. If the part contains any objects on the layout, then FileMaker asks you if you're sure, because when you delete a part, you delete everything on it as well. You've already deleted parts without using this window, though, by selecting the part, and then choosing Edit → Clear. But if you hate menus, then you can also just press Delete.

You can also rearrange parts using the same technique you use to order fields in the Manage Database window. Just drag the arrow icon next to a part name. But some parts (most parts, in fact) have a padlock symbol instead of an arrow icon. This symbol tells you the part is *locked* in place and you can't move it. The reason is simple: It doesn't make sense to move most parts. For example, the header is always below the title header, and above everything else. You really only need to rearrange parts when creating *subsummary reports*, which the next chapter covers.

Figure 5-13:
The Part Setup dialog box is a catchall for the options pertinent to layout parts. You'll find it especially useful for rearranging parts of your layout.

To get your List layout into shape, set the anchors as follows:

• Anchor the horizontal line on the left and right so it stretches the full width of the window.

• Anchor the three text object with merge fields on the left and right. This way, if the window gets wider, then you can see more of the address, for instance.

• Anchor the Status field on the right, but not the left. This field slides to the right as the text object gets bigger so they don't bump into each other.

If you try things out in Browse mode now, as you make the window wider, the line should always span the full width, and the Status field should stay close to the right edge.

Getting Table View to Mind Its Manners

Table view is a real boon if you want a quick and easy way to make your data look like a spreadsheet. With one command, your layout displays data in rows and columns, which you can rearrange and sort. But if you dig a little deeper, then you find that you have a lot of control over how Table view works. These controls lurk under the Layout Setup command. When you click the Views tab, you see that the Table View option has a button that leads you one dialog box deeper—into Table View Properties.

- With the **Grid** controls, you can show or hide Table view's horizontal and vertical gridlines. Try switching off the vertical gridlines to make rows more prominent. This way, you can more easily read across the data pertaining to a single record.

- The **Grid Style** option comes with two familiar pop-up menus. You can choose a new color for the grids with the color pop-up menu or apply a pattern to them from the pattern pop-up menu. A sample swatch shows you the choices you've made.

- Under **Header and Parts**, you control the header, footer, and column headers. Headers and footers anchor to the top or bottom of the screen while the records scroll through long lists. Column headers are the field names at the top of each column.

- Headers and footers are normally suppressed when a layout's in Table view. Choose **Include header part** or **Include footer part** to display those parts of the layout. (For obvious reasons, these options have no effect on a layout in which you don't have those particular parts.)

- Since the column headers tell you what information you're looking at, you don't often find a reason to turn off their display. But you can do it if you want to, by unchecking **Include column headers**.

- More often, you may want to turn off some of the column headers' other features. Stop users from resizing columns by unchecking **Resizable columns**. Turn off **Reorderable columns** to keep folks from rearranging their order on the table. That way, nobody can move the First Name field so far away from the Last Name field that the data loses its meaning. Nobody can sort records if you uncheck **Sort data when selecting column**.

- Choose **Use custom height** to set rows to a specific height, and then select one of the measurement systems and type the height you want.

Conditional Formatting

Sometimes you want the formatting (color, font, style, and so forth) of a layout object to change depending on certain criteria. For example, you might want the Status field to change color depending on its value, turning red if the person is deceased. That way you easily spot this fact whenever you look at the record.

FileMaker's conditional formatting feature lets you make database objects change when, well, conditions change. It works by letting you specify a series of criteria and the specific formatting changes that go along with them. FileMaker means *condition* in the "I'll give you a hand on one condition…" sense. As long as certain restrictions are met, the formatting applies.

Conditional Formatting of Fields

You can apply conditional formatting to any text object, button, field, or Web viewer. Follow these steps to make your status field more dynamic:

1. **On the list layout, select the Status field, and then choose Format → Conditional.**

   You see the Conditional Formatting dialog box pictured in Figure 5-14.

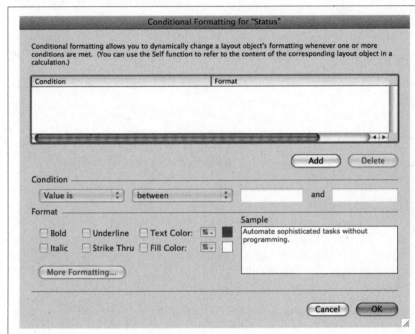

Figure 5-14:
The Conditional Formatting dialog box lets you assign formatting to a field, button, or text object that kicks in only when certain conditions are met. Simply click Add to add a new condition. Use the pop-up menus and boxes below the Condition line to tell FileMaker under what conditions the formatting should apply, and tell it what formatting you want by tweaking the options under Format.

2. **Click Add.**

   A new condition appears in the list at the top of the window. Also, the dialog box's Condition and Format sections become active (they were grayed out until now).

3. **From the first pop-up menu under Condition, make sure "Value is" is chosen.**

   You can configure your condition in two different ways. Either you place simple rules on the value of a field, or, if your needs are more complex, you use a *formula*. You'll start with the easy kind.

4. **From the second pop-up menu under Condition, choose "equal to".**

   In this case, you want the conditional formatting to apply when the Status is "Known – Dead", so you tell FileMaker that's the kind of comparison it should do.

5. **To the right of the pop-up menu, in the box, type *Known – Dead*.**

    Here's where you enter the comparison value. (If you choose a comparison type other than "equal to", then the dialog box may show you different options.)

    FileMaker adjusts the display of the dialog box so that the condition line reads like a meaningful sentence: "Value is → equal to → Known – Dead."

6. **From the Fill Color pop-up menu, choose a dark red color. Then from the Text Color pop-up menu, choose white.**

    As soon as you make a selection from either pop-up menu, FileMaker turns on the checkbox to the left of its label. This checkbox tells FileMaker you want it to go ahead and apply this style when the condition is met. If you decide you don't want to change the fill color after all, you can simply uncheck the box.

Note: You don't have to provide any formatting rules for other values in the Status field. When none of the conditions in the Conditional Formatting dialog box apply (you can add as many as you want), File-Maker leaves the object formatted as it is in Layout mode, so you don't need to add a condition for the *normal* case.

---

7. **Click OK.**

    The Conditional Formatting dialog box disappears, and your layout looks utterly unchanged. Unfortunately, you can't tell if an object has conditional formatting rules in Layout mode just by looking. You have to select the item, choose Format → Conditional again, and then see if any conditions appear in the list.

Although the layout looks unchanged, if you switch to Browse mode, then you see it works as advertised. Every person with a status of Known – Dead shows in red.

Conditional Formatting of Text Objects

You can apply conditional formatting to many kinds of layout objects—fields, text objects, buttons, and Web viewers, some of which you'll learn about later in this chapter. But typically when you format something other than a field, you need to use a formula for the condition, since those objects don't have values that change.

Note: Text objects are the exception. You can use conditional formatting rules on text objects, and they apply based on the text you type into the object. However, conditional formatting of text objects is most useful when they contain symbols (page 201) or merge fields. You can set up the text object's appearance to change when its contents change.

To demonstrate a formula-based conditional formatting rule, you'll add conditional formatting to your database in a surprising place. Take a peek at Figure 5-15 to see the problem you need to fix.

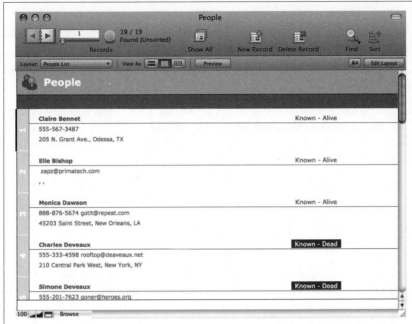

Figure 5-15:
*Take a look at the text
under Elle Bishop. You
see two extraneous
commas floating in the
middle of nowhere.
These commas separate
the address, city, and
state in the address line.
In this case, all the
address fields are empty,
so just the commas
show up.*

Most people wouldn't think of it right away, but conditional formatting can help clean up a little mess like commas between empty fields. If the address fields are empty—and that's a condition—you don't want the commas to show up. FileMaker doesn't have the power to make layout objects disappear completely, but you can turn the text white. Then, even though the commas are technically there, no one can see them. Since the formatting is applied conditionally, as soon as address information is entered for a record, the data (commas and all) appear normally.

Note: You have other ways to solve this same problem. For example, you can add a calculation field to your database that intelligently assembles the address info into a compact line. You'll learn about calculation fields in Chapter 9.

Using conditional formatting, you'll make the text color turn white when the address fields are empty. This tactic requires a relatively simple formula. Here are the steps:

1. **Select the text object containing the address merge fields, and then choose Format → Conditional.**

   The Conditional Formatting dialog box reappears.

2. **Click Add to add a new condition to the list.**

   Once again, a line appears in the list at the top of the window.

3. **Switch the first pop-up menu to "Formula is".**

   The remaining pop-up menu disappears, and a new larger box appears in its place, where you'll type your formula.

4. **In the formula box, type the following:** *IsEmpty(People::Street Address) and IsEmpty(People::City) and IsEmpty(People::State) and IsEmpty(People::Zip).*

   Don't type the period at the end. It's important to type the formula exactly, since typos may prevent the whole thing from working. This formula checks to see that all the address fields are empty. (You'll learn all you need about formulas in Chapter 9.)

5. **From the Text Color pop-up menu, choose the white color, and then click OK.**

   The Conditional Formatting dialog box goes away.

Note: If you get an error message, clear the formula box and try typing over the formula again.

Now if you switch to Browse mode, then you see that the mysterious commas have disappeared. See Figure 5-16 for proof. This technique of hiding things is surprisingly common among more advanced FileMaker developers because it helps build more data-rich layouts with less clutter.

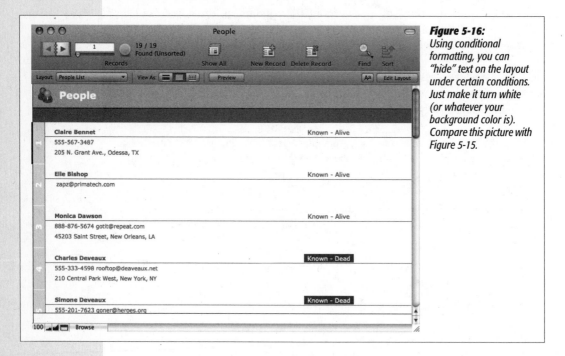

Figure 5-16:
Using conditional formatting, you can "hide" text on the layout under certain conditions. Just make it turn white (or whatever your background color is). Compare this picture with Figure 5-15.

Advanced Conditional Formatting

In both the previous examples, you added only one condition to the list in the Conditional Formatting dialog box. But it isn't a list if you can't add more than one. When you do, FileMaker looks at every condition on the list, and makes the formatting changes for each one that applies. As a result, you can easily create several different formats for several different conditions. For example, you can make numbers in your budget database turn red when you're getting behind, stay black when you're right on target, and turn green when you're beating expectations.

Two matching conditions can even have competing formatting rules. For instance, you can set the text color to something different in each rule, even though they both apply to some values. In that case, FileMaker chooses the format from the condition that comes *last* in the list. You can move these conditions around using their little arrows to influence its decision. Just put the condition that should take precedence lower in the list.

Also, in the Conditional Formatting dialog box, if you don't see the formatting choice you want, just click More Formatting, and chances are you'll find what you want. This button opens a dialog box that, like FileMaker's usual Text Format window, lets you adjust additional formatting including font, size, and a few extra styles.

Removing Conditional Formatting

If an object has conditional formatting behavior that you don't want anymore (which often happens if you duplicate one field and change it to another), then you can easily turn it off. Just select the object, choose Format → Conditional, and then delete the conditions from the list. You can Shift-click to delete them all at once, or just click the first, and then click Delete repeatedly until they're all gone.

If you spent long hours adding complex conditions and you're not quite ready to commit to losing them forever, then you can *turn them off* instead. Each condition in the list has a checkbox beside it. If you turn off a condition's checkbox, File-Maker no longer uses that condition. You can always get the condition back later by turning it back on. You can turn multiple checkboxes on or off at once as well: Just Shift-click the conditions you want to switch so they're all selected. Then turn off the checkbox beside *one* of them, and FileMaker turns all the others off as well.

Web Viewer Objects

Imagine you want to view a map of someone's address in your People database. Getting a map isn't a problem; they're readily available on the Web. Google Maps (*http://maps.google.com*) and MapQuest (*http://www.mapquest.com*) both give you free maps. Still, it's a lot of work to copy address information, change programs, find the right page, and paste the address into your Web browser for each record. Maybe you want to show the map right on the layout, instantly available at a glance. You could draw your own maps and store them in a container field, or even take screenshots right off of Google and paste them in. But that's an awful lot of work, too.

Instead, simply ask FileMaker to go get the maps from the Internet for you. Using a FileMaker Web viewer, you can get FileMaker to automatically and instantly fetch almost anything available on the Web and display it directly on the layout. FileMaker even takes care of keeping things up to date: Every time you visit a record on the layout, it checks to see if newer information is available, and automatically fetches the most up-to-date version, just like your Web browser.

You create Web viewers with the Web viewer tool. This globe-decorated tool button lives on the Status toolbar near the field tool. (You can see it in Figure 5-9.) It works like most FileMaker tools: First, in the Status toolbar, click the tool button, and then, on the layout, drag a rectangle to tell FileMaker where to put the Web viewer, and how big to make it.

Putting a Web Viewer on a Layout

Your People database could use a map on the People Detail layout. Here's how to put one there.

1. **Switch to the People Detail layout, and then (if necessary) switch to Layout mode.**

   Since a map can be large, it makes sense to put it on the Detail layout, where you have some room to work with.

2. **Make the Body part much taller by dragging its label downward.**

   The idea is to make room for the Web viewer on this otherwise crowded layout.

3. **In the Status toolbar, select the Web viewer tool, and then draw a rectangle on the page roughly the same width as the Notes field and a few inches tall.**

   As usual, you're free to tweak the exact size and position of the Web viewer any time you want, so you don't have to be perfect here. As soon as you let go of the mouse button, FileMaker shows you the Web Viewer Setup dialog box (Figure 5-17).

4. **In the "Choose a Website" list, select Google Maps (US).**

   You're telling FileMaker you want this Web viewer to show information from the Google Maps Web site. As soon as you make this selection, several entry boxes appear on the dialog box's right side.

5. **To the right of the Address entry box, click the square button, and then, from the resulting pop-up menu, choose Specify Field.**

   FileMaker pops up the standard Specify Field dialog box. Here you'll tell File-Maker which field to pull the street address from when it goes to find a map.

6. **In the Specify Field window, select Street Address, and then click OK.**

   FileMaker now knows the first piece of information it needs to find the appropriate map. Notice that the Address box now shows People::Street Address.

FileMaker's Web Browser

Is the Web viewer a modern browser? Is it standards-compliant? Can it run JavaScript, or use browser plug-ins? Should I be worried about compatibility with various pages?

FileMaker doesn't actually have a Web browser of its own lurking underneath your layout. Instead, it calls upon the services of the Web browser engine most readily available—the one that came with your computer. In Windows, FileMaker uses Internet Explorer as its underlying browser technology. In Mac OS X, it uses Safari instead. This arrangement has a few important implications:

- FileMaker is using a tried-and-true browser technology, so you know it works well with most Web pages.

It has support for all the major Web technologies, just like its real Web browser counterparts.

- If you install any plug-ins for your Web browser, FileMaker uses them as well.

- If you upgrade your operating system or Web browser, FileMaker's Web viewer gets the benefits of the upgrade as well. For example, if you install Internet Explorer 7 (or use Windows Vista), then the Web viewer gets all its page-handling capabilities. If you have Internet Explorer 6 installed instead, your Web viewers have its limitations.

Figure 5-17:
The Web Viewer Setup dialog box has a lot of options. First, from the list on the left, pick the Web site you want to show. Then fill in the appropriate boxes on the right. If you choose Custom Web Address, then, at the bottom of the window, you can use the Web Address box to type in any URL you want.

7. **Repeat step 7 for the City, State, and Zip Code boxes. In each case, pick the appropriate field.**

   As you make selections, FileMaker fills in the various boxes. The Web Address box at the bottom of the window also changes, but you don't need to concern yourself with that just yet.

8. **Click OK.**

   The Web Viewer Setup window disappears, and the Web viewer appears on the layout.

9. **Select the Web viewer and anchor it to the left, bottom, and right using the View → Object Info palette.**

   To keep the Web viewer from bumping into the expanding Notes field when the window is resized, you need to tell it to stick to the bottom of the window.

If you switch to Browse mode, then you should see the Google Maps page with a map for the current person record (Figure 5-18). You may need to make the window bigger for the map to display properly. If you fiddle with the database a bit, then you notice a few important things:

- When you switch to a new record, the Web viewer changes its contents to reflect the address information on the new record. Likewise, if you *change* the data in any of the address fields, then the map instantly updates to show the new address.

- Status information shows at the bottom of the Web viewer while the page loads.

- You're free to click links in the Web page, and the Web viewer dutifully follows your clicks and shows a new page.

- Although the Web viewer isn't a full-fledged browser (it doesn't have a Back button, for instance) you can access most typical browsing commands by right-clicking (Windows) or Control-clicking (Mac) anywhere on the Web page. In fact, the menu that appears when you do is just like the one you would see if you did the same in your real Web browser. For instance, choose Back from this menu to go to the previous page.

Web Viewer Options

FileMaker offers up a few configuration options for Web viewers in addition to the page they should load. The bottom of the Web Viewer Setup dialog box (Figure 5-18) includes four checkboxes to adjust the behavior of this particular Web viewer.

Figure 5-18:
The People database now has a Google Maps Web page showing right on the detail layout. FileMaker's Web viewer lets you embed any Web page on the layout, so you can save countless trips to your favorite Web resources. Unfortunately, Web pages tend to be big. You'll learn how to give this map more breathing room without investing in a 30-inch screen on page 217.

Allow interaction with web viewer content

When the "Allow interaction with web viewer content" option is turned on (as it is for your map), FileMaker lets you actually *use* the Web page it loads. Specifically, you can click a link on the page to navigate to a new page. You can also use shopping carts, send email messages, watch video, or use any other features on the page.

When you turn this option off, all page behavior is deactivated. A click on the page produces no more response than a click on a blank spot on the layout. You can't even scroll the page. If a page is too big to fit in the space you've given it on the layout, then FileMaker simply cuts it off.

Turn this option on when the page you're showing is just a starting point (like the login screen for your Orders Web page, or the first step in the application process). You should also leave this option on when the page is larger or its size is variable. On the other hand, you can turn "Allow interaction with Web viewer content" off when you're showing a small page that contains all the information needed.

Beyond the Built-in Sites

When you added a Google Maps page to your layout, you didn't have to figure out how Google expects to receive address information. Instead, you simply picked Google Maps from a list, and then filled in the blanks. This easy-to-integrate approach is possible because FileMaker already knows how to connect to Google Maps. FileMaker has built-in support for nine popular Web sites (you see each one listed in the Web Viewer Setup dialog box). When you pick from this list, FileMaker shows a series of entry boxes appropriate for that site. For example, with Google Maps selected, the dialog box asks for Address, City, State, Zip Code, and Country. If you pick FedEx instead, FileMaker asks for a Tracking Number. In every case, you can pick a field FileMaker should use to get the data it wants, or you can type a value instead, like *USA* for Country if all your addresses are in the United States.

But don't let FileMaker's list of companion sites trick you into thinking they're the only ones that work. You can connect a Web viewer to *any site*. At the top of the "Choose a Website" list, just choose Custom Web Address. Then, in the Web Address box at the bottom of the window, type any URL you want (or copy one from a Web page and paste it in).

Unfortunately, if you want the exact page information tied to data in the record (just like the Google Maps example), then you have to supply a calculation for the Web Address. On the bright side, you'll learn how to write calculations in Part 4.

Display content in Find mode

Normally, when you switch to Find mode, the Web viewer just goes blank. Which makes sense, since a Web viewer is usually showing a page associated with data in the current record. After all, if you go to Find mode, where you're no longer necessarily looking at a particular record, then FileMaker may not be able to tell which Web address goes in the Web viewer.

You can change this behavior, though, by turning on "Display content in Find mode". When you do, FileMaker makes its best effort to display the Web page even when you're in Find mode. For example, if you've typed a URL directly into the Web Viewer Setup dialog box, then FileMaker can continue to display the page properly no matter which mode you use (except Layout mode). If you're using a Web site that needs information from the database, then FileMaker feeds it the data from the find request instead. This behavior could come in handy if the Web page information would be helpful to a person trying to construct a find request, but usually you want to leave this option off. It can be jarring to watch a Web viewer constantly refresh itself as you enter your find criteria.

Display progress bar

Unlike everything else on your layout, Web page content isn't always immediately accessible by FileMaker. The program has to go to the Internet and pull up the page, which can take some time (just as it takes time for a page to load in your browser). If you turn on "Display progress bar" (it's on until you turn it off, in fact), then FileMaker shows a subtle progress bar at the bottom of the Web viewer (Figure 5-19).

Display status message

Another option that FileMaker automatically turns on is the "Display status message" checkbox. This option tells the Web viewer to reserve a little space along its bottom edge to show status information (Figure 5-19). Status information typically means the "Loading…" messages you see at the bottom of a Web browser window. Turn this option off if you'd rather not sacrifice precious layout space for not much more information than what the progress bar already gives you. That way, the Web viewer can use all its space on the layout for Web page content.

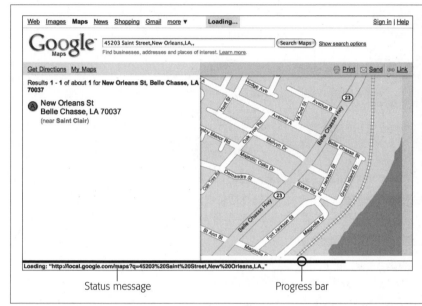

Figure 5-19:
If you turn on the right options, the Web viewer can show a progress bar and/or status message as the Web page loads. If you prefer a minimalist look, in the Web viewer setup dialog box, turn off both "Display status message" and "Display progress bar".

Status message   Progress bar

Adding Tab Controls

When a window needs to show you more information than fits comfortably on one screen, software designers resort to dividing it up onto an array of tabs. Just about every dialog box these days has a few tabs scattered across the top. For example, the Manage Database has tabs labeled Tables, Fields, and Relationships.

FileMaker windows can get overcrowded, too. The Google Maps Web viewer you just added, for example, makes your overall layout quite large, and honestly, the map page would be happier with even *more* space. Sometimes when you just can't stretch a layout any farther. Maybe some of your employees have smaller monitors and you don't want them to have to scroll to see everything on the layout. Or you may feel you've already created a beautiful layout, with perfect proportions, and stretching it to fit a big map would ruin the design you worked so hard to create. Whatever the reason, if you don't want to make a layout bigger, then you can organize lots more information by adding a tab panel (Figure 5-20). Then you can simply click a tab to see the portion of information that interests you.

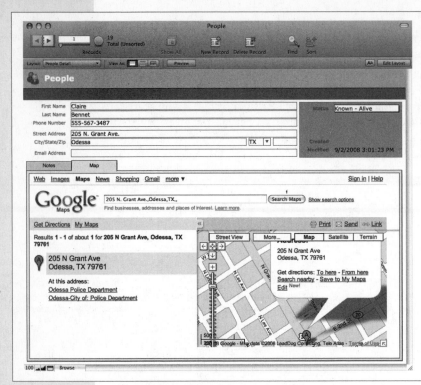

Figure 5-20:
This version of the People Detail layout has a tab for the Notes field and another for the Map. This way, you can devote the same chunk of space to both of them, and get a smaller layout (or a bigger view) at the same time.

Creating a Tab Control

The hardest part of adding a tab control is getting everything out of the way to make room for it. Here are the steps:

1. **Drag the Notes field, its label, and the Web viewer to the right so they're no longer below the other fields.**

   You need them out of the way so you can put your tab control in place and size it properly.

2. **In the Status toolbar, click the Tab Control tool (you can see it in Figure 5-9). Then, draw a large tab panel on the layout.**

   You draw a tab panel the same way you draw a rectangle—drag. It should be as wide as the set of fields above it. Since you'll be anchoring it so it grows with the window, the height isn't terribly important, but you want enough space to work in, so it should be at least a couple inches tall.

   When you finish, the Tab Control Setup dialog box (Figure 5-21) appears.

3. **In the Tab Name field, type *Notes*, and then click the Create button.**

   FileMaker adds the word Notes to the Tabs list. Repeat this step for one more tab: Map.

Figure 5-21:
The standard settings for tabs are left aligned, with rounded corners. But you can have square corners instead if you like them better. Left, center, and right justified tabs are just wide enough to enclose the names you give them. But fully justified tabs stretch out and divide the space to fill the width of the entire panel. Finally, you can control how the individual tab labels' widths, and which one is selected when you first visit the layout.

4. **When you're done, click OK to close the Tab Control Setup dialog box.**

Your new tab panel, complete with two tabs, sits highlighted in place on your layout. Notice four selection handles at each corner, and a dark box around each of the tabs. Any changes you make to the tab panel now affects both tabs.

You've just added a tab control to your layout with two tabs, which you can see labeled along the top of the control—Notes and Map. If you stop right now and switch to Browse mode, then you see that your tab control is already working. You can click tabs, and they toggle. But a tab control is pretty useless until you put something on its tabs. Switch back to Layout mode, and then continue with these steps:

1. **Click the Notes tab to make it active.**

You can tell the Notes tab is active when it's united with the gray rectangle of the tab control (the other tabs are separated from the rectangle by a dark line).

2. **Drag the Notes field into the tab.**

When you put an object (or several objects) right on top of a tab control, they go into the tab. Now, if you move the tab control, all these objects move, too. If not, your tab control may not be quite big enough. The Notes field has to be completely inside the tab control.

Note: The Notes field now operates completely within the tab. If you use the Arrange → "Send to Back" command, then the selected object goes behind other objects *on the same tab*, but not behind the tab control itself.

---

3. **Switch to the Map tab by clicking its label.**

The tabs work like normal tabs even in Layout mode. When you switch tabs, all the fields you put on the first tab disappear, leaving a new box of empty space ready to fill.

4. **Move the Web viewer into the Map tab. (You need to make it smaller to fit properly—use Figure 5-22 as a guide.)**

   Once again, make sure the object is completely within the border of the tab control.

Figure 5-22:
You need to make the Web viewer smaller to fit it in the tab control. It may seem counterproductive to make it smaller, when the whole point of adding the tab control was to make more room. But remember that the layout represents your minimum window size. Once you configure your anchors correctly, when you switch to Browse mode, the Web viewer can be as big as you want.

5. **Using the View → Object Info palette, anchor the Web viewer on the top, bottom, right, and left.**

   This way, FileMaker makes the Web viewer bigger when the window gets bigger.

6. **Select the tab control itself (by clicking any of its tabs), and then anchor it to the top, bottom, right, and left as well.**

   Since objects on a tab are *in* the tab control, they don't grow with the window unless the tab control does too. And at any rate, it makes sense for the tab control to get bigger with the window.

7. **Switch to Browse mode to test your panel.**

   Click the panels to see how the objects appear and disappear along with their panels.

Editing Tab Controls

You can edit a tab control by double-clicking it to summon the Tab Control Setup dialog box. From that box, you have many options to control the look and behavior of the tab control.

Adding, removing, and reordering tabs

In the Tab Control Setup dialog box, you can add new tabs anytime by typing a name, and then clicking Create. The new tab appears at the end of the list of tabs, and the right of the existing tabs in the control. You can also rename an existing tab: Select it in the list, enter a new name, and then click Rename.

To delete a tab you no longer need, select it in the list, and then click Delete. When you delete a tab, you delete all the objects on that tab. (FileMaker warns you of this fact first, and asks whether you're sure you know what you're doing.)

Finally, you can control the order of the tabs from left to right. FileMaker draws the tabs left to right in the order they appear in the Tabs list. Rearrange the items in the list using the arrows to the left of each name. (You've used a similar technique in FileMaker with fields, value lists, and so on.)

Default front tab

When you first switch to a layout but before you've clicked a tab, FileMaker needs to decide which tab to show automatically. You tell it what you want by choosing the appropriate tab name from the Default Front Tab pop-up menu.

Tab justification

If the total width of all your tabs is less than the width of the tab control itself, then FileMaker lets you choose where the grouping of tabs should be positioned. Figure 5-23 shows the options.

Note: If you have more tabs than can fit given the size of the tab control, then FileMaker simply doesn't show the extras. You can either force the tabs to be narrower using the Tab Width option (see below), make the tab control itself bigger, or make the tab names shorter.

Appearance

FileMaker can draw tabs with rounded or square corners. As before, this is a purely cosmetic configuration, so make your choice freely from the Appearance pop-up menu.

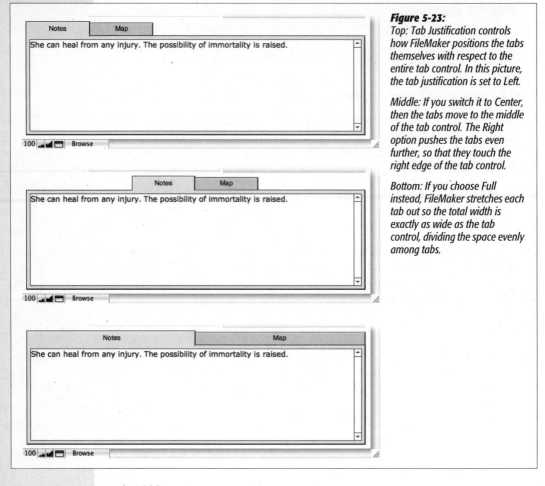

Figure 5-23:
Top: Tab Justification controls how FileMaker positions the tabs themselves with respect to the entire tab control. In this picture, the tab justification is set to Left.

Middle: If you switch it to Center, then the tabs move to the middle of the tab control. The Right option pushes the tabs even further, so that they touch the right edge of the tab control.

Bottom: If you choose Full instead, FileMaker stretches each tab out so the total width is exactly as wide as the tab control, dividing the space evenly among tabs.

Tab Width

The Tab Width pop-up menu has several choices to influence the width of the tabs:

- Choose **Label Width** if you want each tab to be just wide enough to hold its label. (From the Alignment pop-up menu, if you also choose Full, then the tabs stretch wider than their labels nonetheless.)

- **Label Width + Margin of** works a lot like Label Width, except that you can add some additional space around the label text, in that FileMaker makes the tab wider, and centers the label text within it.

- If you prefer all your tabs to be the same width, choose **Width of Widest Label**. FileMaker figures out which label is biggest, sizes its tab appropriately, and then matches that size for all the others.

- If you'd like all your tabs to be a nice consistent width, but stretch to accommodate the odd long label, choose **Minimum of.** You can enter a minimum width (75 pixels, say), and every tab uses it, unless the label is too big to fit, in which case FileMaker makes the tab wider so the label fits.

- If you want the utmost in control and uniformity, choose **Fixed Width of,** and then enter a width in the box. Every tab is exactly that width. If the label's too big, then FileMaker simply cuts it off at the end.

POWER USERS' CLINIC

Tab in a Tab

If your layouts have more doodads than the bridge of the Enterprise, take heart. You can put a tab control on another tab for even more space savings. That's right. You can put tabs inside tabs inside tabs. So long as the new control sits entirely *inside* an existing tab, it behaves just like any other object on a panel. It sits there quietly behind the scenes and doesn't make an appearance until you click its enclosing panel. Then, up the new panel pops, in all its tabbed glory.

Needless to say, the more you use the tab-within-a-tab technique, the more complex your layout becomes—and the more potentially confusing to anyone using your database. Use it sparingly.

Formatting a tab control

Out of the box, tab controls are medium gray, embossed, with a thick black border. But you can make yours striped purple with a thick yellow border instead if you want. In the Status toolbar, just use the fill and border tools to make your selections. You can customize the look of a tab control further by adjusting its fill color and pattern, and tweaking its border color, pattern, and thickness.

When you do, you probably quickly discover another unexpected reality: You can color and style each *tab* individually. The choices you make apply only to the currently selected tab. To adjust all the tabs at once, use the rubber band selection technique to select them all. (You have to rubber band around the entire tab control, not just the tab labels at the top.)

Deleting a Tab Control

If you don't want a tab control after all, just select it, and then choose Edit → Clear, or tap Delete or Backspace. FileMaker warns you that it's about to delete all unlocked objects on the tab panel as well. If that's the way you want it, click OK. If you need to keep fields or objects on the tab panels, though, click Cancel, and then move the keepers off the panel (way to the right of your layout, perhaps) for safekeeping.

Creating Layouts for Printing

You've now knocked out two good layouts—a Detail layout (Chapter 4) and a List layout (in this chapter). Layouts like these meet many typical data-base needs: You've got your Detail layout for finding and viewing individual records, and your List layout for rapidly scanning many records at once. You also want to do *reporting*, an equally important task in a typical database. A report's no different from any other layout as far as FileMaker is concerned. But Report layouts are designed from the ground up to be *printed*. Almost no database gets by without some kind of a Report layout, and most important databases have several, from straightforward lists to powerful snapshots of your data's important statistics, like sales by region or inventory by product category.

Tip: If you craft an elegant Report layout, and discover it's only printing *one* of your records (or none of them) instead of the entire found set, then you probably need to make a change in the Print dialog box. Choose File → Print, and then turn on the option called "Records being browsed". This action tells File-Maker to print all the found records. This option can be hard to find on some versions of Mac OS X. From the unnamed pop-up menu that controls which options are showing, you need to choose "FileMaker Pro".

The People database needs a reporting layout, too. In this chapter you'll create a Report layout for a simple purpose: printing a list of people. You can print a report, and then file it as a hard copy backup, take it with you on a trip, or mail it to an associate. But FileMaker's reporting powers go far beyond simple lists. The next chapter introduces FileMaker's powerful data summarization and reporting capabilities.

Note: You're going to gussy up the List layout you created in Chapter 4, making it perfect for printing. So from now on, you'll be working in the People Report layout.

Visualize the Result in Preview Mode

First, you need a rough idea of how your layout should look. This step is especially important when you create a report, since the physical constraints of a piece of paper often dictate the working space you have. When you create a Detail layout, you're free to make it large or small, tall or short, narrow or wide—whatever meets the needs of your data, and your computer's monitor. You have to live with some common restraints if you want to print your layout.

In the spirit of visualization, how about a picture? From the Preview illustration in Figure 5-24, you can get a pretty good idea of how this layout is going to come together. It has a header, a body, and a footer. The header includes a title, the date, and some column labels, and the footer has just a page number (these parts print on the top and bottom of each page). The body is the most important part: It has all the fields that show your information.

Figure 5-24:
In the steps on page 128 (Chapter 4) you created this layout. It's already a halfway decent printable layout. It's black and white to avoid wasting color ink, it fits nicely width-wise, and it includes a concise list of records. But you can improve it in several ways, as outlined in the following pages.

Note: To see your layout in Preview Mode, click the Preview button in the Layout bar, or choose View → Preview Mode.

Print Margins

Margins is the first problem you need to solve. Usually when you print from File-Maker, the page margins are set to the minimum size your printer allows. This arrangement provides the most usable space possible, but at a cost: The margins—and the printable area—change as you switch printers. For a report that may be printed on a variety of printers, all of which could have different margins, you don't want to deal with that kind of inconsistency.

Luckily, you can override this behavior, and set explicit margins. First, you need to make sure FileMaker is using units that make sense for page margins. Follow these steps to set the units and the margins:

1. **Choose Layouts → Set Rulers.**

   The Set Rulers window appears.

2. **From the Units pop-up menu, choose Inches, and then click OK.**

   You're back on your new layout, where you've just told FileMaker to use inches for just about everything. (You can opt for Centimeters if you prefer.)

3. **Choose Layouts → Layout Setup, and then click the Printing tab.**

   The printing options associated with this layout appear, as shown in Figure 5-25.

4. **Turn on the "Use fixed page margins" checkbox.**

   The Top, Bottom, Left, and Right text boxes start out grayed out. As soon as you turn on this checkbox, you can type into them.

Figure 5-25:
These settings affect the way the current layout prints. For example, you can create a layout that prints in multiple columns (imagine printing sticky labels). For now, draw your attention to the "Use fixed page margins" checkbox, which you need to turn on if you want this layout to have hard-coded (and consistent) page margins.

Note: The numbers you see in these boxes (before you type anything into them, that is) are the margins associated with the printer you're hooked up to. That's why they probably look different from what you see in Figure 5-25.

5. **In each of the Top, Bottom, Left, and Right text boxes, type *1*.**

   Don't forget to type the decimal point. Your goal is to set the margin on all sides to one inch.

6. **Click OK.**

   If your printer's driver software hogs up even more margin space, then you see a warning message, but it doesn't tell you which margin setting is too narrow. Tweak the margins until the warning no longer appears. The Layout Setup dialog box disappears, and you're looking at your layout again. If you have sharp eyes, then you notice the page width has shrunk a bit, as shown in Figure 5-26.

Tip: If you like working in pixels and don't want the bother of switching units, take heart. You can probably do the math in your head even faster. Remember, you have 72 pixels per inch: A one-inch margin would be 72 pixels, and a half-inch margin would be 36. (If you like centimeters, then figure 28 pixels per centimeter.)

Now that you've fixed the usable space on the layout, you can rearrange the fields to they fit nicely in the available width. Figure 5-26 shows how.

Figure 5-26:
The page break line (shown here) shows where your layout cuts off when printed. You can now fill up your layout any way you choose, confident that it'll all print properly on anybody's printer.

Columns

Occasionally your printed page needs to spread records across several *columns*. For example, when you print on address label sheets, the sheets you buy usually have two or three columns of labels on one page. Even when printing a List or Detail layout, if your data's narrow, then you can save paper by printing two records side by side. FileMaker has a built-in solution to just this problem: Choose Layout → Layout Setup, switch to the Printing tab, and then turn on the "Print in" checkbox. When you do, you can tell FileMaker *how* many columns you want by typing a number in the little entry box by the checkbox. When you turn on column printing for a layout, FileMaker shows you what's going on in Layout mode, as Figure 5-27 shows.

The column setting has no effect on your layout in Browse or Find modes. But if you print or switch to Preview mode, then you see the effect. Instead of repeating the Body part just vertically, FileMaker *tiles* the Body part both horizontally and vertically so that it fills the page.

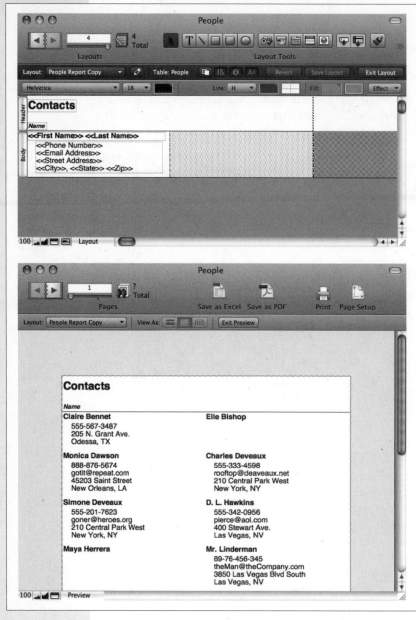

Figure 5-27:
Top: FileMaker draws a dashed line through your layout to show you where the columns land. It also covers every column but the first with a dotted pattern. This pattern is its way of saying, "Don't expect anything you put here to print." Since every column is identical, you just have to lay out the first. FileMaker repeats it for the rest.

Bottom: With the layout set to print in two columns, everything comes together in Preview mode or when you print.

Every column has to be the same width (this makes sense because every column contains the same kind of information). FileMaker automatically sets the column width so that the columns perfectly divide the page. But it bases its assumptions about the size of the page on the settings in the Print Setup (Windows) or the Page Setup (Mac OS X) dialog box at the time you turn on columns. If you later switch to a different paper size or orientation, then you probably want to resize the columns. To do so, just drag the first (leftmost) dashed line on the layout. When you finish, FileMaker makes every column the same width as the first one, with no space between them. (You can always simulate padding or a *gutter* between columns by keeping the things you add to your layout away from the column edges.)

Lastly, FileMaker gives you two choices for the way it arranges records in the columns. Choose "Across first" in the Layout Setup dialog box if you want the *second* record to be at the top of the *second* column. Choose "Down first" if it should be the second item in the *first* column. The flow arrows on the icons in the Layout Setup dialog box show how the data flows onto the printout.

Sliding Layout Objects

Suppose you want to add the Notes field to the printed report so you can use it on the road. You know enough already to get the job done. Make the body part a little taller, and then use the Field tool to add the Notes field to the layout. When you're done, your layout might look like Figure 5-28.

Figure 5-28:
Here's how you might add the Notes field to your layout. It lives below a row of data, and it's italicized to make it visually distinct from the other fields. Of course you can make it look any way you want.

If you preview this report, though, then you quickly spot a problem. Figure 5-29 shows the trouble.

Normally, a field on the layout takes up a fixed amount of space, no matter how much (or how little) data is inside. You might be tempted to try to fix this with a merge field, but that doesn't help here because no matter how tiny the text gets, the body part is still just as tall as ever. You need some way for everything on the layout to *slide up* if the Notes field isn't full. Luckily, FileMaker's Format → Set Sliding/Printing command has the answer.

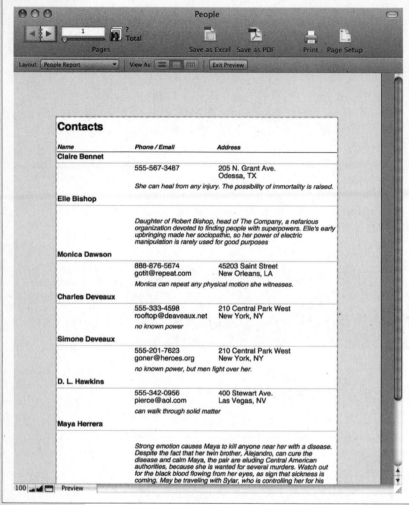

Figure 5-29:
When you preview the report, you quickly see that your nice compact printout is now very space-inefficient. The Notes field is often empty, or holds just a line of text, but FileMaker reserves lots of space for it just in case. Also, if you have lots of notes in one record, then the field may not be big enough, so the text is cut off. But if you make the field even bigger, then you just waste more space. Sliding layout objects are the solution.

When to use sliding

Usually the normal field behavior doesn't cause a problem. After all, you may *want* that empty space because you're printing onto a preprinted form, and everything needs to go in just the right spot on the page, or maybe your report design counts on consistent field sizes so things line up properly. But sometimes you can't get the effect you want without adjusting the layout based on the amount of data—usually when you're trying to tighten things up on the printed page to avoid wasted paper or excessive spacing around data.

Sliding does three things to help in this situation. First, it lets fields shrink to just the right size for their data. After a field has shrunk, any object on the layout can slide up or to the left to fill the space left behind.

Choosing the objects to slide

Object sliding in FileMaker is notoriously hard to figure out. It's a bit like that board game Go. The rules take a minute to learn but a lifetime to master. Here goes:

Sliding exists for only one reason: to compensate for changing field data. Therefore, unless you set at least one field to shrink, *nothing* on the layout moves. Unfortunately, you can't explicitly set a field to shrink. Instead, you set it to *slide*—and FileMaker makes sure it shrinks too. This seemingly simple principle is guaranteed to confuse you at least 36 times in the near future. You've been warned. Figure 5-30 shows how this field-shrinking business works.

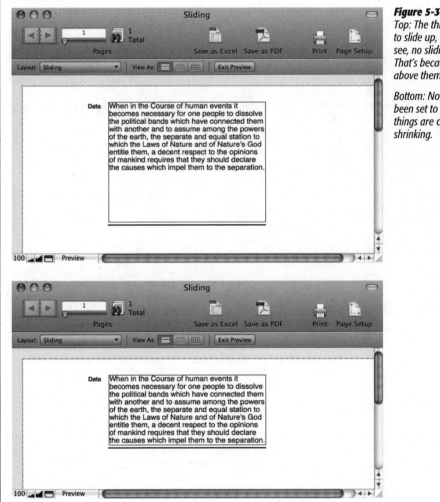

Figure 5-30:
Top: The thick black line is set to slide up, but as you can see, no sliding's going on. That's because the field above them isn't set to slide.

Bottom: Now the field has been set to slide up too, and things are clearly sliding and shrinking.

Once you've figured out which fields should shrink to fit their contents, you need to decide which objects should slide. What does that mean exactly? Normally, when you add an object to a layout, you specify exactly where it goes. But when the object is set to slide, its position is no longer fixed at an exact spot on the layout.

Instead, it moves up (or to the left) if other objects above it (or to the left of it) move or shrink.

Setting sliding options

Once you have a general idea of which elements need to slide (and which fields must shrink accordingly), you can start telling FileMaker.

FREQUENTLY ASKED QUESTION

Merge Fields vs. Sliding

Why should I bother with sliding? Isn't that what merge fields are for?

It's true that merge fields and sliding objects have some things in common. Both adjust the data shown on a layout, squeezing things together in the process. But they have some major differences:

- Merge fields work everywhere, even in Browse mode. Sliding objects, on the other hand, have no effect on Browse mode (or Find mode). Instead, they do their thing only in Preview mode and when printing.

- Any object on a layout, including pictures, can slide. You can't incorporate pictures into merge fields.

- Fields that slide act just like normal fields in Browse mode, in that you can edit the data in them. Merge fields are just text objects, and only for display.

Bearing all these differences in mind, you can easily figure out which method to use. If you have a few fields that you want to display as a single block of text, then use merge fields. If your needs are more complex (incorporating graphics, for instance), or you need to be able to edit data on the layout, then use sliding objects instead.

Also, there's absolutely nothing wrong with using both on one layout. In fact, the layout you just created could use merge fields for the name and address, along with the sliding to the Notes field. You could even tell a text object containing merge fields to slide if you want. (Phew!)

Here's how to fix up your Report layout:

1. **Select the Notes field, and then choose Format → Set Sliding/Printing.**

   The Sliding/Printing window appears.

2. **Turn on the "Sliding up based on" checkbox.**

   If you stop here, you don't quite have your problem solved. Even though the Notes field shrinks as much as possible, the Body part itself doesn't shrink, and your report still wastes paper. To solve this problem, turn on "Also reduce the size of the enclosing part".

3. **Click OK.**

   If you view your report now, things should look much better. Figure 5-31 agrees.

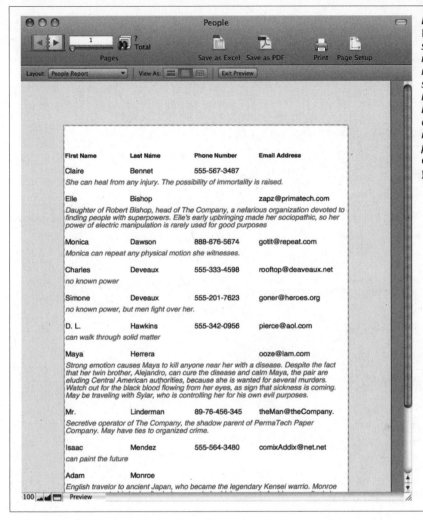

Figure 5-31:
With the Notes field set to slide up, your layout can now show long or short notes without wasting space. (In this picture, the layout arrangement has been improved from the one in Figure 5-29 to make things look more pleasing to the eye. You can do the same with your own layouts.)

Tip: Once you start adding sliding to your layout, you might have trouble keeping track of which objects do what. To ease the pain, choose View → Show → Sliding Objects. When you do, FileMaker adds little up-pointing and/or left-pointing arrows to each object that slides. Now you can see at a glance what goes where.

More Sliding/Printing options

The Sliding/Printing dialog box has several options to control just how the selected objects slide (and shrink if appropriate). In general, an object can slide left, up, or both.

If you want something to just slide left, you're in luck. Simply turn on the "Sliding left" checkbox, and you're done. When you print or preview the layout, the objects slide to the left when field data isn't long enough to fill the full width of the field.

Objects that slide up, on the other hand, need a little more thought. To start, turn on the "Sliding up based on" checkbox. When you turn this checkbox on, you make three more options available. The "All above" and "Only directly above" radio buttons are hard to explain in words. Luckily, FileMaker gives you a picture to help you understand what they mean, and so does this book. See Figure 5-32.

Figure 5-32:

Top: Everything on this layout is "above" the Do Not Contact checkbox. But for the purposes of sliding, only two count. From FileMaker's perspective, the Address field is directly above it, while the Phone field is simply above it. If the Address field and the Do Not Contact checkbox are both set to slide up, then the "All above" or "Only directly above" choice becomes important.

Middle: If you choose "All above", then the checkbox never slides because the Phone field doesn't.

Bottom: If you choose "Only directly above", then it sticks with the Address field, even if that means sliding up alongside the Phone field.

Finally, if you turn on "Also reduce the size of the enclosing part", then the part the object is on shrinks to fit its contents. This setting is a little misleading, though. For example, imagine you have two sliding objects on the Body part. One of these objects is set to reduce the Body part, while the other isn't. How can the body both reduce and not reduce at the same time?

In truth, the "Also reduce the size of the enclosing part" setting matters only for the *lowest* object on the part. If that object wants the part to reduce, then it will. If it doesn't, then the part won't. Anything you set on any other object doesn't matter. The lesson: If you're trying to get your part to reduce, then focus your attention on the bottom-most object on your layout.

Note: One more option in the Sliding/Printing dialog box is pretty self-explanatory. If you turn on "Do not print the selected objects", then every object you have selected when you open the dialog box disappears in Preview mode and when printing. This option is handy for things like navigation buttons that shouldn't show up on the printed page, or background graphics that would waste ink.

Setting Layout Order

Now that you know how to create new layouts, you'll find dozens of uses for them. Pretty soon, your pop-up menu of layouts will get lengthy. And, unless you're some kind of organizational genius, you probably won't create your layouts in exactly the order you want them to appear in the list. You can easily manage the list, though. Just choose File → Manage → Layouts. You see the dialog box in Figure 5-33.

Figure 5-33:
Drag the double-arrow to reorder the list. The checkbox in the left column lets you determine whether a layout appears in the Layout pop-up menu. When you select a layout from the list, the Layout Setup button becomes available, and you can go directly to the dialog box to rename a layout, change its views, and so on.

To make your life easier, arrange your layouts in the order of most frequent use. Since you work with your data mainly while you're viewing the People and List layouts, put them up top. Then you can move the layouts meant for printing down below, so they're grouped by function. You can make separator lines in the list to divide the groups. Just create a blank layout named – (that's a hyphen, with no extra spaces). Make as many "–" layouts as you need, and then drag them where you want them in the list. In the Layout pop-up menu, these layouts show up as divider lines.

Layout Setup

FileMaker has a few more layout options that haven't appeared in this chapter so far. These options let you control overall aspects of the layout. To see them, switch to Layout mode, and then choose Layout → Layout Setup. You see the window in Figure 5-34.

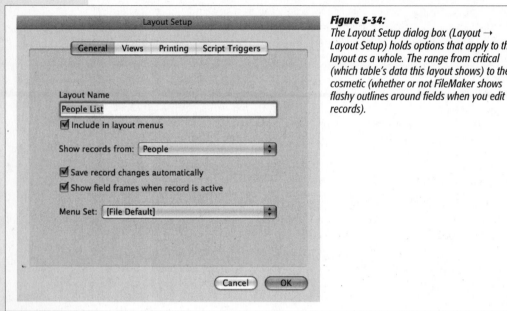

Figure 5-34:
The Layout Setup dialog box (Layout → Layout Setup) holds options that apply to the layout as a whole. The range from critical (which table's data this layout shows) to the cosmetic (whether or not FileMaker shows flashy outlines around fields when you edit records).

- The "Save record changes automatically" option is turned on with every new layout. If you turn it off instead, then FileMaker starts acting...annoying. Whenever you click out of a record after making changes on this layout, File-Maker pops up a window asking if you want to save your changes. You can opt to revert instead, and toss out all the changes you've made. You typically use this option when you're working on a small layout where you edit complex data. Normally, of course, FileMaker saves the record changes automatically with nary a word.

- When you're actively editing a record, FileMaker draws a dotted outline around enterable fields, making it immediately obvious where you can enter data because each field is outlined. But some people find this feature unsightly. Turn off "Show field frames when record is active", and FileMaker cuts it out.

- Finally, the Menu Set pop-up menu lets you pick an alternate *menu set*. You'll learn all about customizing menus in Chapter 19.

Advanced Layouts and Reports

Believe it or not, Layout mode has *even more* tricks up its sleeve. In the last couple of chapters, you've learned how to use the basic layout tools to position fields, create text labels, add graphics, and more. You've experienced stress-free layout creation with the layout assistant, and seen reports in action. You even know how to design full-fledged layouts from the ground up.

Now, you're ready to learn the more advanced layout concepts: controlling how fields look and act, and adding buttons to perform customized tasks. Finally, you'll find out how to add powerful analysis to your layouts by using summary and sub-summary parts to add groups, subtotals, and grand totals.

Value Lists

You flirted a bit with the Field/Control Setup dialog box in Chapter 4, when turning the Status field into a pop-up menu (see page 163). Field controls can be more than pop-up menus, though. The six main field styles are Edit Box, Drop-down List, Pop-up Menu, Checkbox Set, Radio Button Set, and Drop-down Calendar.

Most styles (Edit Box and Drop-down Calendar are the exceptions) let you associate a *value list* with the field. Value lists give you more efficient access to a few frequently used terms, numbers, dates, or times. Using a field control, you can then easily enter a value from the value list into the field. You tell FileMaker how you want these choices presented, by selecting one of the field control styles.

Using a value list-based field control helps in two ways. First, you can more easily enter data into your database. If folks need to put a part number into a field, for example, then they can just pick it from a list, and avoid typing it exactly. Just as important, fields formatted with a value list help ensure *consistency*. As your database grows, one of the toughest challenges you face is inconsistent data. For example, suppose you have two people entering addresses in your database. Cheryl is a fussbudget, and she *always* spells things out. Frank, on the other hand, is, ahem, keystroke efficient. He likes to abbreviate wherever possible. If all your customers are in central Arizona, you may wind up with some people in *Phoenix* and others in PHX, some in *Tucson* and others in *Tcsn*. Even worse, Frank, like most of his kind, can't even keep his own abbreviations consistent. He's got customers in *Chnd, Chndlr, Chand*, and (on a particularly bad day) *Ch*.

Even *horrendous* abbreviations may not cause a big problem to the human eye. After all, you can probably figure out where the person lives just by reading the City field. But what happens when you need to use FileMaker's find tools to find all the Chandler, AZ customers in your database? Searching for "Chandler" doesn't turn them all up. Instead, you have to try to think of all the different ways it could be abbreviated, and search for each one. If you use a field formatted with a value list, however, you can make sure that everybody enters data the same way every time.

A value list has two parts. First, you decide which items appear in your value list. In this part, you're limiting the scope of the data your users can enter in a field. Creating value lists isn't technically a task that belongs to the Field/Control Setup dialog box—you can manage them at any time, using the File → Manage → Value List dialog box. In fact, as you learned on page 114, value lists aren't used just for field entry. You can also use a value list to validate field entry or to manipulate sort order.

Creating Value Lists

Creating a value list is a breeze. In fact, if you've read this book up to this point, you've already created two (see pages 114 and 164). You can most directly create a value list when you choose File → Manage → Value Lists. FileMaker also includes a Manage Value Lists option in pop-up menus on dialog boxes throughout the program. Any time you're asked to *choose* a value list, FileMaker gives you a shortcut to the Manage Value Lists dialog box, too.

No matter how you get there, though, the Manage Value Lists dialog box looks just like the one in Figure 6-1.

Figure 6-1:
When you select a value list and click Edit, or click New to make a new value list, you see the window in Figure 6-2.

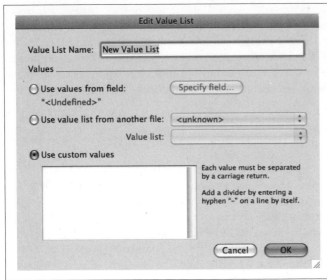

Figure 6-2:
The Edit Value List window is also where you create new lists. Start by giving it a good, descriptive name. Then choose one of the three basic value list flavors. If you have some specific ideas for what should go in the field, then create a custom value list. You can also use values from an existing field or a separate FileMaker file.

FileMaker offers three types of value lists:

- Choose **Use value from field** if you want the value list to automatically include every unique value you've typed into a particular field. You'll see an example of this shortly.

- The **Use value list from another file** is just a way to share value lists among different databases. If you choose this option, you can choose another FileMaker database, and then a value list from it. Once you make this connection, if you modify that value list, then this one reflects the change as well.

- You've already seen the **Use custom values** option in action (page 164), and it's the simplest choice. Just enter the values you want in the list, each on its own line. This value list type gives you the most control over what appears in the list, and in what order.

Values from a field

Suppose you take a trip to Spokane and fit in with the folks there like a native. Suddenly you find your list of acquaintances from that city growing vigorously. You can very easily return to the Manage Value Lists window, edit your value list, and add Spokane to the list.

But why not let FileMaker do that sort of grunt work for you instead? Rather than sit there and type a list of cities, you can ask FileMaker to build the list for you as you add new data. The program looks at what you're typing in the City field, and builds a list of every city you've ever used. When you add new records or change the city on old records, FileMaker keeps its list up to date. It even removes cities from the list if you delete a record, and that city isn't in any other record.

The key to this power is the Edit Value List window's "Use values from field" option. When you turn it on, FileMaker grays out the "Use custom values" box so you can no longer manage the list manually. Instead, you click Specify Field, and, from your database, pick a field (any text, number, date, time, or timestamp field). FileMaker then automatically keeps tabs on that field and creates a value list that always includes every unique value in the entire database.

To do this in your People database, go to the Manage Value Lists window, and then click New. Name the value list "Cities" and turn on "Use values from field". You see the "Specify Fields for Value List" dialog box (see Figure 6-3).

In this window, you see a pop-up menu labeled "Use values from first field". This pop-up menu lets you pick a table. Since you have only one table in your database right now, your choice is obvious: Choose People. FileMaker immediately lists the fields in your database; select City. When you've made the selection, click OK in the three dialog boxes you've managed to pile up to get back to your database window. If you later want to change the field your value list is based on, then return to the Edit Value List window and click Specify Field.

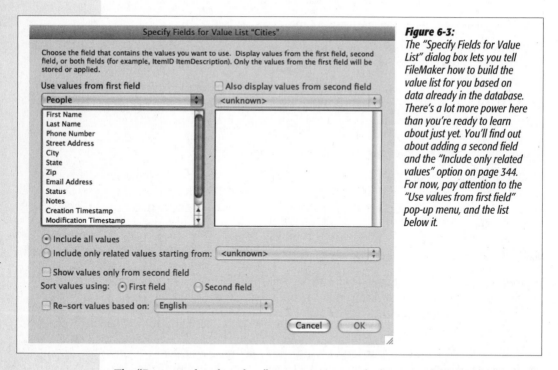

Figure 6-3:
The "Specify Fields for Value List" dialog box lets you tell FileMaker how to build the value list for you based on data already in the database. There's a lot more power here than you're ready to learn about just yet. You'll find out about adding a second field and the "Include only related values" option on page 344. For now, pay attention to the "Use values from first field" pop-up menu, and the list below it.

The "Re-sort values based on" pop-up menu at the bottom of this window lets you tell FileMaker to use sorting rules from a different language for this value list. Whatever you pick, FileMaker *always* sorts these field-based value lists alphabetically. So you no longer have a chance to put more common items first in the list, or add separators. To see the value list in action, select the City field, and then choose Format → Field/Control → Setup. Choose "Drop-down List" from the "Display as" pop-up menu, and then choose your new value list. Now, when you click into the city field, it offers an automatic list of previous cities. (You can see the settings in Figure 6-4. You'll learn more about the Drop-down List field style in the next section.)

Editing Value Lists

If your short list of approved part numbers changes, then you need a way to edit your custom value list to reflect the new company policy. Choose Manage → Value Lists, select the value list you need to change, and then click Edit.

When you're through editing a value list, just click OK. If you decide you don't want to change it after all, click Cancel instead. Either way, you wind up back in the Manage Value Lists window. Just like in the Manage Database window, if you click Cancel instead, then *everything* you've changed is tossed out. The value lists go back to the way they were before you opened Manage Value Lists. FileMaker asks you if you're sure first, since the Cancel button is precariously close to the OK button.

GEM IN THE ROUGH

Custom Sort Orders with Value Lists

Value lists play a part in so many database activities, it's a wonder they didn't call it ValueListMaker Pro. The Sort dialog box is another place value lists show up. Suppose you have a database of clothing products, each with a size: Small, Medium, Large, X-Large. If you sort these records by size, they show up in alphabetical order:

- Large
- Medium
- Small
- X-Large

Chances are, that's *not* what you want—you want them in order from smallest to largest, or largest to smallest. To arrange that, simply create a value list with custom values: each size in the proper order.

You can then tell FileMaker to sort the record by size, but to use the order of this value list instead of alphabetical order:

1. Choose Records → Sort Records. You see the Sort Records dialog box.

2. Clear any existing fields from the Sort Order list, and then add the Size field. Remember you can quickly add items to the list by double-clicking them.

3. From the Sort Order list, select Size. The radio buttons below the list are now clickable.

4. Turn on "Custom order based on value list". This option informs FileMaker to order the sizes according to a value list.

5. From the pop-up menu, select the Sizes value list. Here's where you pick which value list to use.

6. Click Move. The Size field moves to the Sort Order list. The little bar chart icon beside this field matches the "Custom order based on value list" icon.

7. Click Sort. FileMaker sorts the records according to size. This time, the records are in a good logical order.

In addition to the New and Edit buttons, this Manage Value Lists dialog box has a Duplicate button. It does just what you'd expect: creates a new value list that's an exact copy of one you already have. You can live a long, healthy life without ever using this button, because once you create a value list in FileMaker, you can use the same list over and over in a multitude of fields and databases. (But isn't it nice to know you have the option?)

The Delete button deletes the selected value list, after an appropriate warning. As usual, you can hold down the Shift (Option) key as you press Delete to skip the warning.

Advanced Field Controls

As you've seen throughout the last few chapters, FileMaker field controls can take on many forms. In this section you'll learn exactly how each of these works, and how you can configure them to get just the behavior you want. As a refresher, Figure 6-4 shows the Field/Control Setup dialog box.

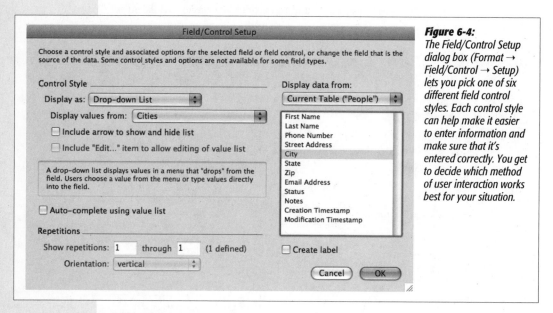

Figure 6-4:
The Field/Control Setup dialog box (Format → Field/Control → Setup) lets you pick one of six different field control styles. Each control style can help make it easier to enter information and make sure that it's entered correctly. You get to decide which method of user interaction works best for your situation.

Edit Box

Most of the fields you've used so far have been *Edit Boxes*. These fields are the click-and-type variety that normal people call a *text box*. Distinctive as always, File-Maker has its own moniker. No matter what you call it—Edit Box or text box—this sort of control isn't limited to just text. You can use an Edit Box with number fields, date fields, and so on.

When you select the Edit Box format, you have the choice of turning on the "Include vertical scroll bar" checkbox. You saw this option when you added a scroll bar to the Notes field on page 166. If you anticipate that a field will hold lots of information, a scroll bar can be a good idea, as Figure 6-5 shows.

Figure 6-5:

Figure 6-5:
Top: FileMaker fields can hold a lot of text. The Comments field here has more information than can fit in the field boundaries. Adding a scroll bar gives you a visual clue that there may be more, and makes it easy to scroll down to see it.

Middle: If you don't have a scroll bar, then when you click in the field, FileMaker increases its size to show all the text.

Bottom: When you commit the record, FileMaker shrinks the field back to its original size, leaving no clue that more text might be hiding below the fold. If you know you're expecting lots of information, you should usually add a scroll bar.

Drop-Down List

This field type *looks* just like an Edit Box. But when you click into the field, a list of available choices appears just below it (see Figure 6-6).

The items in the list come from a value list. When you pick the Drop-down List type, you get a "Display values from" pop-up menu. From this menu, choose the value list to use. You can also choose Manage Value Lists to create a new one.

Tip: If you don't apply borders to a Drop-down List, then the show/hide arrow appears only when the field is active. Add field borders (at least a right border—see page 159) to make the arrow show.

Drop Down, Pop Up, Turn On

You may wonder how a drop-down list differs from a pop-up menu. They're similar in purpose, but have three differences:

- A pop-up menu requires you to make a choice when entering data—you can't type into the field unless you specifically tell FileMaker to allow it. With a drop-down list, on the other hand, you can always dismiss the list and type directly into the field instead. When the list pops up, just click the field again to make the list go away, and then start typing. From the keyboard, press Enter (Return) to make the list go away, or press Esc to toggle the list on and off.

- Drop-down lists work just fine with *thousands* of items in them. Since the list scrolls, it doesn't much matter how long it is. Pop-up menus, by contrast, get very cumbersome with more than a dozen or so items.

- Finally, folks can make selections from a drop-down list using just the keyboard, while a pop-up menu requires a trip to the mouse. The drop-down list's keyboard ability makes it preferable in cases where speed of entry is the priority.

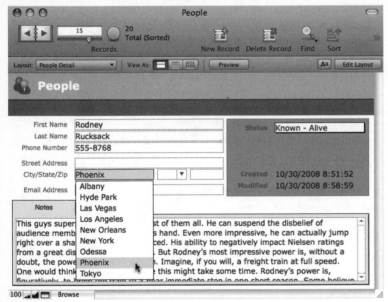

Figure 6-6:
A drop-down list like the one showing cities here gives you a scrolling list of choices to save you the trouble of typing the one you want. Just click an item in the list, and FileMaker enters it into the field. You can also use the up and down arrow keys to select an item in the list. Finally, you can type the first few letters of an item's name to select it. Once you have an item selected, press Enter (Return) to accept it.

Drop-down Lists look just like Edit Boxes until you click them or tab into the field. Then the list drops down for your data-entry pleasure. But it could get annoying to have lists flashing at you just because you happen to be tabbing through the data in a record, so FileMaker lets you stop the list waving by choosing "Include arrow to show and hide list". Now the list is a little more polite. When the field is active, the list doesn't drop down until you click the arrow. If you make a choice from the list, it disappears. Or, if you don't want to enter anything into the field after all, just click the arrow and the list goes back home.

Finally, turn on "Include 'Edit…' item to allow editing of value list" if you want your users to be able to easily modify the list of choices. When folks choose "Edit…" (always the last item in the list), the window in Figure 6-7 shows up so they can modify the value list.

Figure 6-7:
You can include an Edit item in your Drop-down List. When folks choose it, this little Edit Value List box appears. From here, they can add new items, delete items, or edit items in the list—all by typing directly in the text box. All of this assumes your value list has "Use custom values" turned on. You can't edit the items in a value list based on field values.

Pop-Up Menu

When you format a field as a Pop-up Menu, the look changes significantly, as shown in Figure 6-8. Rather than type into the field, people must click the menu and make a choice.

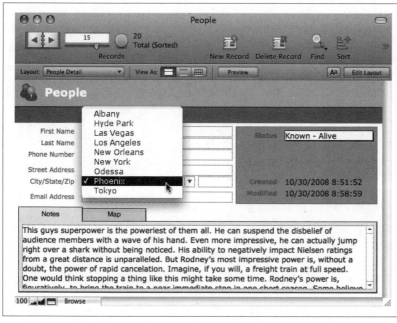

Figure 6-8:
Top: When the City field is formatted as a Pop-up Menu, it no longer looks like an ordinary field. Instead, it has a somewhat three-dimensional look.

Bottom: When you click the Pop-up Menu, the value list appears, and you have to make a choice. Unlike a Drop-down List, you can't click again and start typing.

Like Drop-down Lists, Pop-up Menus let mere mortals edit value lists, plus they up the ante by including an Other item. When people pick "Other…" from the menu, they see the window in Figure 6-9. Entering a value in this window puts it in the field but *doesn't* add it to the value list. Turn on "Include 'Other…' item to allow entry of other values" to grant this power to the masses. (See the box below for advice on the ramifications of letting people edit or bypass your carefully crafted value lists.)

Figure 6-9:
Top: If the Pop-up menu, Checkbox Set, or Radio Button Set can't cover all the bases, you can include an Other item to allow free text entry.

Bottom: Selecting "Other…" opens a dialog box with plenty of space to type into at will.

Checkbox Set

Figure 6-10 shows a field formatted as a Checkbox Set. With this format, people can simply click each item to turn it on or off. As they do, the data in the field changes to reflect the checked items.

UP TO SPEED

A Cautionary Tale

Not even the most highly paid database developer can think of everything folks might want to enter in a database, and a drop-down list with a handy edit option seems an obvious solution. But use it with caution. When some villainous or misguided soul chooses Edit, she's doing just that: editing your *value list,* and potentially defeating the purpose for which you created it. Furthermore, if other fields in your database are formatted to use the same value list, *their* list of choices changes, too, because the underlying value list itself has changed.

So remember that value-list-based fields serve *two* purposes: simplicity and consistency. If you make it easy for folks to add their own items to a value list, you're also making it easy for the value list to get inconsistent and disorganized.

Adding an Other item can undermine consistency even more, because it encourages quick-handed mousers to simply bypass the value list entirely.

If your value list's primary purpose is to gain consistency, then you should consider leaving the Edit and Other options turned off. You can always add new choices to the value list yourself at any time as the need arises.

Checkbox Sets can include the Other item, just like a pop-up menu. If someone enters a value that isn't in the value list, then FileMaker just turns on the Other checkbox to indicate the field has something more in it.

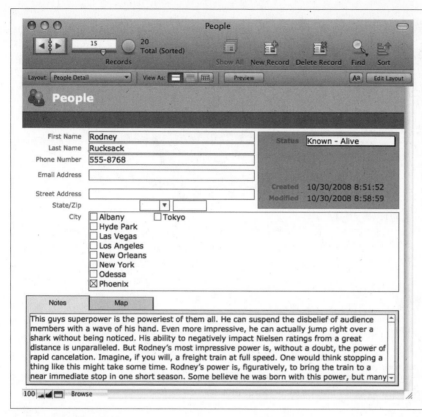

Figure 6-10:
When you format a field as a Checkbox Set, it looks like the City field shown here. FileMaker adds one checkbox for each item in the value list, and arranges them to neatly fill the boundaries of the field. You can apply borders, fills, and effects to a field like this—they affect the entire area the Checkbox Set covers.

Radio Button Set

A Radio Button Set (see Figure 6-11) works much like a Checkbox Set. The only distinction is that folks can turn on only *one* item. If they try to turn other items, FileMaker turns off items as necessary.

Warning: Some people know they can Shift-click to select multiple items in a Radio Button Set. See the box on page 256 to learn how calculations can control these people's urge to get around the system.

Just as with drop-down lists and Checkbox Sets, you can add an Other or Edit item to the Radio Button Set. (See the box above for more detail.)

Drop-Down Calendar

In FileMaker, you can easily read date fields, and easily set them up. But actually typing dates into them is notoriously tricky. If you don't get just the right combination of numbers and tiny little separators, FileMaker gets all huffy and tells you the value you've just typed isn't valid. And if somebody swipes your desk calendar, how are you supposed to know what numbers to type in the first place? FileMaker can handle both these problems. It lets you give your date fields a nifty drop-down calendar where anyone can simply point and click to enter a date.

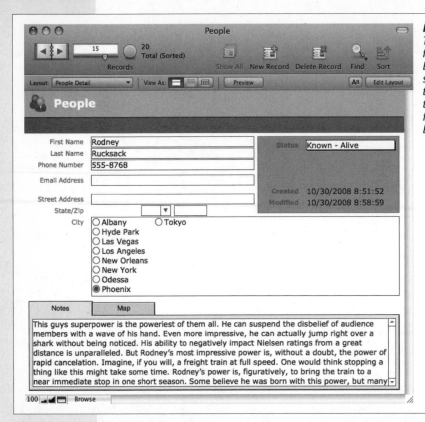

Figure 6-11:
This time the City field is formatted as a Radio Button Set. Now you can simply click the right city to set the field, making this one of the fastest field formats for mouse-based entry.

Checkboxes Behind the Scenes

The beauty of Checkbox Set fields is that they let folks click *more than one* checkbox. In other words, you can capture several values in one easy-to-use field. This method comes in handy when the things you're tracking in your database have fields like Available Sizes, Available Colors, Warehouses, or any other attribute of the *one or more* variety. But wait, you say—how can a single field hold *more* than one value?

Simple, if you're FileMaker. Just give each checkbox its own line. In other words, if you have a Checkbox Set showing colors, and you turn on Red, Green, and Blue, FileMaker actually thinks of the field like this:

```
Red
Green
Blue
```

You can show the same field on another layout—or even the same layout if you want—without the checkbox formatting. If you do, you see the selected items: one on each line. This is called a "return-separated list." If you change what's in the field without using the checkboxes, then you could end up with lines that don't match any of the value list items. In that case, the Checkbox Set turns on its Other item if it has one. (If not, the extra items simply don't show at all.)

A final note: Checkbox Sets need to be able to put several lines in the field, so they're really suitable only for *text* fields. Other field types don't support multiline values.

When you first format a field with a drop-down calendar, FileMaker doesn't give you any visual feedback letting you know a calendar's lurking there, waiting to drop down when you tab into the field. If you want to provide a visual clue, select "Include icon to show and hide calendar". Then you see a teeny, tiny calendar at the right side of your field (see Figure 6-12). Tiny as it is, the calendar icon still takes up some room, so you may have to make the field a little wider to display the entire date plus the new icon.

Note: Like the show/hide arrow on drop-down lists, the calendar icon shows up in an inactive field only if the field has a border. If you're a minimalist on the field border issue, you can format your field with only a right border to force the icon to appear.

The calendar itself is a little dynamo. To enter a date, click the Month Year display at the top, and you see a pop-up menu that lets you jump to a specific month in the current calendar year.

Figure 6-12:
The Drop-down Calendar makes entering dates a snap. It has some sweet controls, too. When the field's empty, the current date is highlighted when the field drops down. Or, if there's data in the field already, then FileMaker highlights that date when the calendar appears.

Right-click anywhere on the calendar (or Control-click on the Mac if you don't have a two-button mouse), and the pop-up menu changes to read "Go to today". The calendar closes, and plunks the current date into the field.

You can also change the month with the right and left arrows at either side. The left arrow icon moves you backward in time (careful, don't touch anything or you could change the course of human history…), and the right one moves you forward. The up and down arrow icons change the display of years. Finally, you can move the highlighted date with your keyboard's arrow keys. Tap the down arrow key a few times to see how fast time flies.

But if you get carried away playing the controls ("Is my birthday on a Friday in 2015?"), remember that the calendar's footer always displays the current date. Just click that display to enter the current date, and then click to open up the calendar again. It reorients to today's date.

Auto-Complete

Auto-Complete is a strong ally both for database designers who care about data consistency and for data entry folk who hate to type. Unlike the other Field/Control field styles, you can apply this little beauty to a regular Edit Box. Once you've turned on the option to "Auto-complete using previously entered values", the field gets ESP and tries to figure out what you want to enter. Where do these superhuman powers come from? From that old friend, the field's index.

Auto-Complete isn't a control style in and of itself; rather, you use it in conjunction with either an Edit Box or a Drop-down List (the option isn't available for other styles). But Auto-Complete behaves a little differently on Edit Boxes than it does on Drop-down Lists. The differences are discussed in the following sections.

Auto-Complete in Edit Boxes

To turn on Auto-Complete for an Edit Box field control, visit the Format → Field/Control → Setup dialog box, and then turn on "Auto-complete using previously entered values". (This checkbox only shows up when you have "Display as" set to Edit Box.)

UP TO SPEED

When Is Auto-Complete Not Useful?

With such a cool feature, one that seems to know what people want to type before *they* do, you may be tempted to add auto-complete powers to most of your fields. But there are cases when it just isn't very helpful.

Auto-Complete depends on the index to know what to show in its list. At least one field must have data for File-Maker to have any entries in the index. And indexes add a lot of size to your files, so if you index a lot of fields so that Auto-Complete works, then you may find that the file size balloons. Remember, this feature comes with all of indexing's dark sides as a tradeoff for its power (page 119).

Another weakness: When someone types a letter that's not used much—like X, J, or Z—Auto-Complete may not produce a drop-down list.

This lack of a list doesn't mean Auto-Complete is broken. It just means the index doesn't have any entries beginning with that letter. The index saves no time in such cases.

Auto-Complete works best in larger databases with lots of records. And it's usually most effective if the records have a fairly wide range of data in them. For example, if a field is going to have only a few possible values (G, PG, PG-13, R, NC-17), then a drop-down menu or a pop-up list is a better choice than an Auto-Complete Edit Box.

None of these cautions means that you shouldn't use Auto-Complete. Just be aware of its limitations, and the overhead it places on your file.

When you start typing into a field configured this way, FileMaker scans the field's index and drops down a list of matching entries. There *is no value list* in this case—it always draws from field values on other records. If you type *T*, for example, then you see a list of entries that begin with the letter T. If you type *R* next, then the list shortens to only words beginning with "TR". Once the list is short enough for you to find what you want, just click the list item to select it.

Note: The Auto-Complete list behaves just like a regular drop-down list, so if you prefer, you can high-light items with arrow keys, and then press Enter.

Auto-Complete in drop-down lists

If your field is formatted as a Drop-down List, you can make it even smarter by adding auto-complete behavior. Visit the Field/Control Setup dialog box, make sure "Display as" is set to Drop-down List, and then turn on "Auto-complete using value list". When used in conjunction with a drop-down list, Auto-Complete instead uses the values from the associated value list. In fact, in many ways, it works just like an ordinary drop-down list. Now, though, you get the automatic type-ahead behavior you've come to know and love: As you begin to type, File-Maker automatically narrows the list to include items that start with what you've entered so far. This can make your drop-down lists even faster and easier to use.

Note: When you click into an Auto-Complete drop-down list that's formatted with a show/hide arrow, the list doesn't appear until you click the arrow or pres the Esc key. If you want the list to display as soon as the field is entered, then don't select the "Include arrow to show and hide list" option.

WORKAROUND WORKSHOP

One or Many?

Strange as it sounds, pop-up menus and radio buttons both allow *multiple selections*, just like Checkbox Sets. Just hold down the Shift key while you select an item, and FileMaker dutifully turns it on without turning off the item that's already selected. Handy though it may be, however, chances are you don't want anyone to use this trick and choose more than one value—otherwise you use checkboxes to make it obvious that multiple choices are desirable.

Unfortunately, you don't have any direct way to turn off this feature. If you want to prevent people from picking too many items, you have to get creative. Here's one way of doing so:

Chapter 3 introduced you to Auto-Enter calculations (see page 109). They let you automatically change the value in a field, based on a *calculation*. You'll learn all about calculations in Part 4, so for now you just have to have some blind faith.

Here's how to limit your fields to a *single* value:

1. In the Manage Database window, select the field you want to fix, and then click Options. The Field Options dialog box appears. If it isn't already selected, click the Auto-Enter tab.

2. Turn on the "Calculated value" checkbox. The Specify Calculation dialog box appears.

3. In the big free-entry box on the bottom half of the window, type *LeftValues (Self ; 1)*. This calculation tells FileMaker you want to keep only the left-most—or *first*—value in the field.

4. Click OK. You're now back in the Field Options dialog box.

5. Turn off "Do not replace existing value (if any)", and then click OK.

You're back in your database.

Now if you try to Shift-click a second item, FileMaker immediately throws it out. In practice, it *looks* like it simply doesn't let you Shift-click.

Repetitions

On page 117, you learned about repeating fields, which let you put several values in one field, with a separate Edit Box for each one. When you put a repeating field on a layout, you get to decide how many times it shows up. Even if a field has 200 repetitions, you don't *have* to show them all on the layout. You can elect to show just the first 10. Or just the last 10. Or numbers 37 through 118.

GEM IN THE ROUGH

Tab Order and Repeating Fields

FileMaker treats each repetition of a repeating field as a separate item in the tab order. It's perfectly legal to have the *last* repetition come right after the *first*—if you're into aggravating the people using your database. But it can be a real drag to have to click each and every one of those repetitions when you set the tab order. FileMaker has a nice feature to save you the trouble.

When you click the first repetition of a repeating field (while setting tab orders), FileMaker gives it a number–and the arrow begins to flash. If you click this flashing arrow *again*, then FileMaker numbers that field's additional repetitions for you, in the logical order.

But the magic doesn't stop there: Suppose you have a series of repeating fields. The standard tab order would go *down* each column before moving to the next one, but you'd prefer to tab *across* the rows first. For example, if you're

sitting in the first Quantity field, you want to tab into the Product field, then the Price field. Then once you've completed a row, you want the next tab to take you to the next one.

FileMaker can automatically do this kind of numbering for you, too. When setting the tab order, click the first Quantity field. It gets a number and begins to flash. Now click the first Product field, and then the first Price field. The arrow by the Quantity field continues to flash. Once you've done these three clicks, click the flashing arrow again. FileMaker now numbers all your repetitions properly.

In general, you click each repeating field in the order you want them tabbed to. When you're done, click the *first* one again to let FileMaker know. FileMaker fills out each row of repetitions matching this order.

To control how repeating fields display, you use the same Field Control/Setup dialog box shown in Figure 6-4. This time, focus your attention at the bottom of this dialog box under Repetitions. Just enter the first repetition you want in the "Show repetitions" box, and the last one in the "through" box. You can't show noncontiguous repetitions here—you have to enter one beginning and one end, and FileMaker shows those and every repetition in between. But try this technique instead: Put multiple copies of the field on the layout, but specify that each copy displays a different range of repeats. You get much the same effect, as described in the box on the next page.

Note: If the "Show repetitions" and "through" options are grayed out, it probably means you didn't have a repeating field selected when you chose the Format → Field Format command.

Once you've figured out which repetitions to show, you get to pick an orientation. Your choices are Horizontal and Vertical, and Figure 6-13 makes sense of them.

Figure 6-13:
This layout shows two repeating fields, one with horizontal orientation, and one with vertical. (See the box below for further advice.) In Layout mode, FileMaker numbers each repetition in a repeating field to let you know which one it is. The first repetition shows the full field name and—if there's room—the repetition number in brackets.

POWER USERS' CLINIC

Flexible Repetitions

Suppose you *want* to show noncontiguous ranges of repeating fields. Or you need something more flexible than a straight up-and-down or side-to-side orientation. For example, your layout may be easier on the eyes if it shows the first 10 repetitions in one stack, and the next 10 in another stack right beside the first set. Or you may want to show just the even-numbered repetitions. Or perhaps you're determined to see repetition number 1, then 11 through 13, then 7 and 8, and finally number 281. No matter how capricious your desires, FileMaker's up to the job.

Here's the trick: Put the field on the layout *more than once*. Or, more correctly, put several field controls on the layout, all associated with the same field. For example, suppose you have a repeating field called Dimensions. It holds all the various measurements for a particular sprocket in your catalog. Now imagine you want to show the first 10 repetitions in a vertical stack, with the next 10 beside it.

First, add the field to the layout using the Field tool. From the Format → Field/Control → Setup dialog box, configure it to show repetitions 1 through 10 in a vertical orientation, and then click OK. Now duplicate the whole shebang. Select the copy, move it to its own plot of layout land, and then visit the Field/Control Setup dialog box once more. Configure this version of the field control to show repetitions 11 through 20. If you head back to Browse mode, then you see that you have all 20 repetitions on the layout, arranged the way you wanted.

By using various combinations of repeating field controls in various configurations, you can arrange field repetitions any way you want—even if you have to add a separate control for each repetition.

Display Data From

So far, you haven't explored the right side of the Field/Control Setup dialog box, where there lives an incredibly powerful feature—the "Display data from" option. With this powerful tool, you can change a field object on the layout so it's tied to a different field. This way, if you have a field that's already configured just the way you want, you can duplicate it (Edit → Duplicate), and then point the new copy to a different field in your table. This method is much faster than reconfiguring a fresh field object from scratch.

Borders and Repeating Fields

While you've got repeating fields on the brain, there's one more formatting choice worth talking about. You can put a border around a repeating field just like any other field. But this border goes around the entire set of fields, not each individual repetition. You wind up with what looks like one big field, and it can be a surprise when you click it and discover those repetitions. Wouldn't it be nicer if you could format those repeating fields to look like a sensible set of fields?

Nicer, yes. And possible, too. In Layout mode, just select the repeating field, and then visit the Format → Field Borders window. If you look at this dialog box with a repeating field selected, you have one additional option: "Between repeating values." When this checkbox is turned on, you get your borderline *between* each repetition, as well as around the whole thing.

Format the Number/Date/Time/Graphic

All this talk about how fields look and work is well and good, but what if you want to change how the *data* inside them looks? A price and a weight both go in a Number field, but they're different types of values and should *look* different. FileMaker provides a series of formatting options for the data inside fields, giving you loads of control over how numbers, dates, times, and pictures look.

FileMaker has a special formatting dialog box for each kind of data a field can hold: Text, Number, Date, Time, and Container. (Timestamps are just a date and a time together, so you can format both parts separately.) You've already seen one of these dialog boxes—Text Format—in Chapter 4 (see page 156). It's the thing you see when, in Layout mode, you choose Format → Text.

Below this menu command, you find four others, each of which accesses a dialog box specific to the type of information in your field.

Number Formatting

Select a number field, and then choose Format → Number to control how the number inside the field is displayed. The Number Format dialog box has a lot of options, as you can see in Figure 6-14. You can use most of these in any combination, so the possibilities are vast.

Note: As with most layout settings, if you choose this command *without* selecting a field, then FileMaker lets you edit the *default* formats. In other words, the settings you pick apply to every number field you add to the layout thereafter.

General format

If you don't tell it otherwise, FileMaker assigns the General format to any new number fields you create. Usually, this format means, "Show numbers the same

Figure 6-14:
FileMaker has four top-level number format settings: "General format", "Leave data formatted as entered", "Format as Boolean", and "Format as decimal". If you choose either of the last two, you get still more choices. If you're looking for the kind of number formatting options you're accustomed to in a spreadsheet program, then turn on "Format as decimal" and go to town. The sample at the bottom of the dialog box shows how a number looks with your settings applied.

way someone types them." But if your number has too many digits (either a very large number, or a number with lots of decimal places), then FileMaker rounds the number or uses scientific notation to shorten it.

Leave data formatted as entered

If you don't want the automatic rounding and scientific notation you get with General Format, then choose "Leave data formatted as entered" instead. File-Maker leaves your numbers alone, so they appear exactly as typed.

Format as Boolean

Sometimes you use a number field simply as a Boolean value. For instance, pretend you have a field that flags customers who get holiday cards. You could use a number field for this one, with a *1* in it if you want to send a card, and a *0* if you don't. But someone looking at the layout later could mistake all those 1s and 0s for so much computer gibberish (even if that someone is yourself).

For this reason alone, the Number Format dialog box has a choice called "Format as Boolean". With this setting, a number field shows one of two text values. The first ("Show non-zero as") shows if the number field has any non-zero value. The second ("Show zero as") shows only when the field has a zero in it. In the holiday card example, you may be tempted to turn this option on, and use Send Card and Don't Send Card as the display values. Unfortunately, FileMaker lets you enter only a maximum of *seven* characters for each display value. So you have to stick with short and sweet values, like Yes and No.

Format as decimal

The most flexible setting is called "Format as decimal". When you choose this option, you activate a host of new settings:

Fixed number of digits. Turn on "Fixed number of decimal digits" if you want to force every number to have the same number of decimal places. Of course, File-Maker also lets you say *how many* decimal places you want. If the number in the field doesn't have a decimal part, FileMaker just fills in zeros after the decimal point.

Notation and symbols. The "Use notation" checkbox lets you add currency symbols, units, or other labels to your numbers:

• Choose **Percent** to turn the number into a percent value. FileMaker automatically multiplies the number by 100, and puts a percent sign after it. That way, people can enter *.1* for 10 percent. (Entering the number this way makes math with percentages easier since you can simply multiply. After all, 10 percent of 20 is 2, not 200. You'll learn how to do math in FileMaker in Part 4.)

• Choose one of the **Currency** options to format the number as a monetary value. When you do, you can supply an appropriate currency symbol as well. The four currency options in the pop-up menu have to do with *where* the symbol is placed, as explained in Figure 6-15.

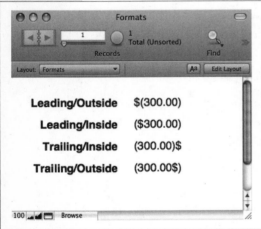

Figure 6-15:
FileMaker has four different currency options: Leading/Outside, Leading/Inside, Trailing/Outside, and Trailing/Inside. Leading and Trailing determine on which side of the number the currency symbol should live. Inside and Outside matter only for negative numbers. As this picture shows, the currency symbol goes between the negative sign and the number with the Leading/Inside option, and before the negative sign with the Leading/Outside option. FileMaker also lets you put parentheses around negative numbers if you want. In this case, you get an Inside/Outside choice for trailing currency symbols, too.

Do not display number if zero. Suppose you have a report with lots of numbers, where many of those numbers are zero. For example, a financial report that shows who owes you money (like the Aging Receivables Report in Figure 6-16) often has more zeros than anything else. All those zeros can make the report cluttered and hard to read. Turn on the "Do not display number if zero" option to make the zeros go away.

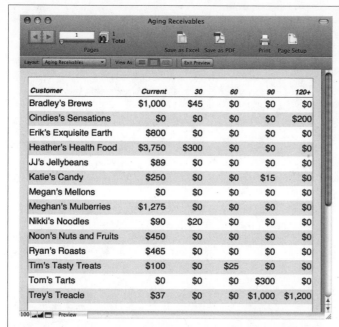

Figure 6-16:
Top: This window shows an Aging Receivables report just like you might get from your accountant. Unfortunately, with all those zeros, it's hard to see the useful information.

Bottom: Here's how the report looks when each field has its "Do not display number if zero" option turned on (in the Number Format dialog box). The zeros go away, revealing the real picture.

Separators. Numbers use special symbols to separate their parts. For example, you usually see a decimal point between the whole and fractional parts of a number, and a comma after the thousands place. FileMaker uses whatever symbols your operating system dictates for these special purposes, but you're free to override them if you want. For instance, you can use a space instead of a comma between each third digit.

WORKAROUND WORKSHOP

Currency-ish

The currency symbol is, in a sense, just an expression of *units*. It isn't at all uncommon to want to put *other* unit labels on your numbers too. But FileMaker doesn't have an option for any other variation. It seems hopelessly in love with currency.

In the "Use notation" pop-up menu, don't let the word "currency" get you down. Since you can type anything you want for the currency symbol (including multiple letters, numbers, spaces, or punctuation symbols), you're welcome to use one of the currency options for any other kind of unit too:

- From the pop-up menu, choose Currency (Trailing/Outside), and put *cm* in the Currency Symbol box. The number 3.7 now shows as "3.7 cm" automatically. Use this same technique with any unit abbreviation

you want. (Note that you need a space before the abbreviation so the label doesn't run in to the number itself.)

- If you have part numbers, serial numbers, or other meaningful codes that should display with an informative prefix, you can accomplish that too. For example, choose the Current (Leading/Outside) option, and then put *PN/* in the Currency Symbol box. Now a part number field with "17789" in it shows "PN/17789". This might be handy on a report, for example.

The Currency Symbol box accepts only up to five characters (and that includes the leading space if you need one) so it isn't perfect. But in many cases it gets the job done.

In the "Decimal separator" box, type the character you want in place of a decimal point. The box accepts only a single character. FileMaker calls the comma between every third digit a "thousands separator" and you can opt to leave them out by turning on "No thousands separator". Turn on "Use thousands separator" if you want them, and feel free to enter something other than a comma in the associated box.

Formatting negative values. The last thing you get to control with the "Format as decimal" option is the way FileMaker represents negative numbers. In the "Format as" pop-up menu, you can choose any one of six negative number formats:

- –1234 puts a negative sign before the number in the usual fashion.

- 1234– puts the sign on the *end* instead, if that's the kind of thing that makes your socks go up and down.

- For that oh-so-financial look, choose (1234) instead. It puts negative numbers in parentheses.

- <1234> is similar, but it uses angle brackets instead of parentheses.

- If you're an accountant, hold onto your hat. The **1234 CR** option makes you feel right at home when crediting those accounts.

- The last choice puts that funny triangle before negative numbers. No idea what that's all about. If you know, more power to you.

To draw more attention to a negative number, you can have FileMaker automatically color it. Turn on "Use color", and then pick a color by clicking the little icon button to its right.

Note: The "Use color" option for negative numbers may seem a little redundant considering you can get exactly the same effect using Conditional Formatting, as you learned in the last chapter. Before FileMaker Pro 9, the "Use color" option was the only way to apply a different color to negative numbers. These days, you can use whichever method you prefer.

Formatting a number's text. At the end of the day, a number is text, too, really. It's made up of numbers and symbols using some font, size, style, and color. As such, you can choose the Format → Text command with a number field selected. If you're already in the Format Number dialog box, and you want to format the text as well, then the Text Format button serves as a shortcut to the Text Format dialog box.

Note: This window has two more choices—"Numeral type" and "Use kanji separator". These options are specific to Japanese numbers and aren't covered in this book.

Date Formatting

The Date Format dialog box works a lot like its number-oriented sister. This time, though, you tell FileMaker how you want *dates* to look. This date could be the value in a date field, or the date part of a timestamp field. For example, the date at the top of a letter may look best spelled out, while the due date on a list of 25 invoices may best be served by an abbreviated numbers-only format. Figure 6-17 shows the Date Format dialog box (no surprises here: Just choose Format → Date).

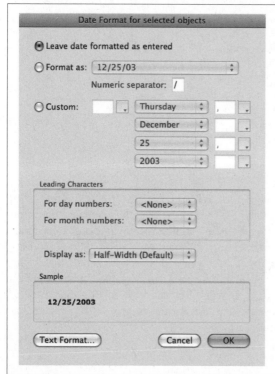

Figure 6-17:
The Date Format dialog box gives you lots of control over how dates look. You get three primary choices ("Leave data formatted as entered", "Format as", and Custom), the last two with assorted settings. And you get a sample demonstrating your choices as well.

Leave data formatted as entered

When you choose "Leave data formatted as entered", FileMaker shows the date *almost* the same way you type it. If you type a two-digit year, the program changes it to four digits. Otherwise, it leaves the data alone.

Format as

If you choose "Format as" instead, then, in its pop-up menu, you can pick from six common date formats as shown in Figure 6-18.

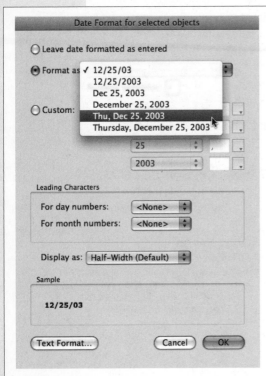

Figure 6-18:
The "Format as" pop-up menu gives you six canned date formats to pick from. If you choose either of the first two, you can pick something other than "/" to go between each number by typing it in the "Numeric separator" box (it's covered by the menu in this picture). You can also add a leading zero or a space to single-digit day and month numbers by picking from the Leading Characters area's pop-up menus.

Custom

For the ultimate in control, choose Custom. When you do, the mysterious unlabelled boxes, buttons, and pop-up menus to the right become usable. By selecting different parts of a date from the pop-up menus and adding your own text as appropriate to the boxes, you tell FileMaker exactly how you want the date formatted. You use this option when none of the "Format as" formats (Figure 6-19) are exactly right. For example, if you're in the U.S., FileMaker suggests date formats that follow typical U.S. standards (month, then day, then year). But if people in England use your database, you may want to construct a custom format in line with their expectations (day, then month, then year).

When you tell FileMaker to format a date with the Custom option, it assembles the final date value piece by piece according to your specifications. Whatever you type in the Start Text box comes first, followed by the first date value. FileMaker then adds the text from the top Between Text box. Next comes another date value and more between text. This process continues until the last text box is added to the result. By mixing and matching text and date values, you can make a date look any way you want.

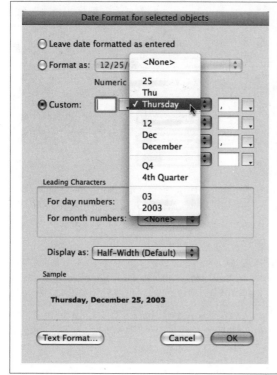

Figure 6-19:
The Custom date format options consist of a series of text boxes and four Date Value pop-up menus. You can put anything you want in the text boxes, and it appears between portions of the date. Each pop-up menu includes the same set of choices. The first three let you show the day portion of the date. You can show the day-of-month number, or the day-of-week name as an abbreviation or full name. Next, you get the same three ways to display the month. If you're so inclined, you can add a quarter to your date in two ways. Finally, you can pick between a two-digit and a four-digit year. FileMaker strings the text and date values together to produce the final result.

If you don't want to use one of the date values, from the relevant pop-up menu, choose "<none>". Likewise, to skip a between text value, clear its text box. The pop-up menu buttons to the right of each text box give you a choice of common date-related symbols for easy picking. They have a "<none>" option as well, if you want to quickly clear the associated box.

With either the "Format as" or the Custom option, in the Leading Characters area of this window, you can use the pop-up menus to tell FileMaker how to handle single-digit month and day numbers. If you want them left alone, choose "<none>". To insert a leading space, choose Space, and for a leading zero, choose Zero.

Note: The "Display as" pop-up menu applies only to Japanese dates. And if you don't recognize these choices, you probably don't need to use this pop-up menu.

International Super-Date

If people all over the world use your database, you quickly discover that date formats can lead to unending confusion. A date like 1/11/07 could mean January 11 or November 1, depending on your persuasion. To avoid all this confusion, consider a date format that strikes a nice balance between efficient display and unambiguous interpretation: 11-Jan-2007.

To get this format, select a date field, choose Format → Date, and then turn on the Custom option. Then configure it thusly:

- In the first pop-up menu, choose the number version of the day. (It's the number in the first group of options, right below "<none>".)

- In the top text box, enter a hyphen (–).

- In the second pop-up menu, choose the abbreviated month name.

- In the next text box, enter another hyphen (–).

- In the third pop-up menu, choose the year (you can use either the two- or four-digit version).

- Clear the contents of the two remaining text boxes, and then, in the last pop-up menu, choose "<none>".

Now click OK, and then switch to Browse mode. Your date field should show this svelte-yet-satisfying format.

Time Formatting

Compared to dates and numbers, formatting time values is a breeze—FileMaker gives you just a few simple choices. Figure 6-20 shows the Time Format dialog box (Format → Time).

Figure 6-20:
To have FileMaker show your time values exactly the way you type them, choose "Leave data formatted as entered". If you want to standardize the display of time values, choose "Format as" instead, and then pick your options. Unsurprisingly, the sample area shows you a sample time formatted according to your specifications.

Leave data formatted as entered

This time, "Leave data formatted as entered" really means it. The time value shows exactly as you typed it.

Format as

The only other formatting option you get with time values is "Format as" and its related options. From the "Format as" pop-up menu, choose what time information you want to include:

- **hhmmss** tells FileMaker to show hours, minutes, and seconds.

- **hhmm** says you want hours and minutes, but no seconds. If your time value has seconds, FileMaker just ignores them.

- **mmss** limits the display to just minutes and seconds. If the time value has hours, then the minutes are increased accordingly. For instance, if your field has *1:13:27* and you format it without hours, then you see *73:27*—each hour adds 60 minutes.

- **hh** gives you a field that shows just the hours. Any minutes and seconds are left off.

- **mm** tells FileMaker to show the number of minutes. Again, any hours in the time value are counted as 60 minutes, and any seconds are ignored.

- **ss** shows a time as just a number of seconds. Every minute counts as 60 seconds, and every hour as 60 minutes. They're added up along with the seconds themselves to produce the final number.

Normally time values show a colon between each number. You can change this look if you want by typing something else in the Separator box. To leave out the separator entirely, clear the box. (This method lets you make military style times: *0730*.)

Note: As with date formatting, the pop-up menu between this box and its label lets you opt for a Japanese time separator instead.

When displaying clock time, FileMaker can use 24-hour or 12-hour notation. In other words, do you want to see *14:23* or *2:23 PM?* When you choose "24 hour notation", you can add some arbitrary text before or after the value (23:00UTC, for instance). When using 12-hour notation, you get to decide what text you want to represent a.m. and p.m. by typing in the "before noon" and "after noon" boxes.

You can choose from the pop-up menu to the right of these labels to put them on either side of the time value. Like a date value, you get to tell FileMaker how to handle single-digit numbers. Again, you can leave them a single digit, add a leading space, or add a leading zero.

Timestamp Formatting

Although FileMaker has a timestamp *field* (see page 103), the Format menu doesn't have a timestamp option. Remember that timestamp fields really contain two values: a date and a time. So, you use the Format → Date command to control how the date part of a timestamp looks, and the Format → Time command for the time portion. Like time values, you can also use Format → Number to control decimal places and points in the seconds part.

In order for a timestamp field to show your settings, though, you have to format *both* the date *and* the time parts. If either is set to "Leave data formatted as entered", then the timestamp field just puts its hands over its ears and hums so it can't hear you trying to format it. Once you enter both the date and the time formats, the timestamp field straightens up and follows your formatting instructions.

You *do not* have to set the number format if you don't want to. If you don't choose a number format, FileMaker leaves the decimal part of your time values formatted as people enter them.

Tip: Timestamp formats are a little tough to read because the date and time just sort of run together with a scrawny single space separating them. Make a custom format with " at" (that's *space*-a-t) in the last placeholder, and you get "Fri, May 6, 2005 at 12:30 pm". Much better.

Graphic Formatting

In Chapter 2 you learned how to put pictures, sounds, QuickTime data, and files into container fields. Remember that with pictures and QuickTime data, File-Maker actually shows the content right on the layout. When you design that layout, you have some control over how that content is displayed (see Figure 6-21).

Figure 6-21:
With the Graphic Format dialog box, you can tell FileMaker to shrink and/or enlarge a picture to fit the field boundaries, or to crop it—showing only what fits. You also get to decide where the picture lives inside the field, or what part gets cropped. If you don't mind wildly skewed images, you can also tell FileMaker to stop keeping your pictures properly proportioned.

Note: If someone records a sound (Insert → Sound) or puts a file (Insert → File) in your container field, then you have no control over how FileMaker displays it. FileMaker automatically shows the appropriate icon and leaves it at that.

The pictures and movies you put in the field may not always be exactly the same size and dimensions as the field control itself, so FileMaker has to decide how to make things fit. Should it shrink a big picture down so it all shows, or let it get cut off on the edges? For a tiny picture, should FileMaker blow it up to use the available space, even though it may look a little blocky? For that matter, should it stretch and skew the image willy-nilly to force a fit, or leave some of the field empty? FileMaker lets you decide. When you choose Format → Graphic, you can control scale, position, and proportions.

Scale

The Scale pop-up menu lets you decide how FileMaker should handle pictures that aren't exactly the right size:

- Choose **Crop** if you want FileMaker to crop large pictures, showing only what fits. Figure 6-22 shows how this method works.

- Choose **Reduce** if you want FileMaker to shrink large pictures to fit, but leave small pictures alone. This setting is what you automatically get if you don't change it yourself.

- Choose **Enlarge** to make small pictures grow so they fit the field but are as big as possible. (The more FileMaker has to enlarge the image, the blockier it looks.) Large pictures get cropped.

- Choose **Reduce or Enlarge** if you want FileMaker to shrink big pictures and grow small ones. This setting ensures that every picture in the field (on each record) is about the same size.

Alignment

If the picture is small and hasn't been enlarged, the alignment pop-up menus control *where* in the field the picture appears. For example, choose Right from the Horizontal Alignment pop-up menu and Top from the Vertical Alignment pop-up menu to nestle the picture in the field's top-right corner.

If a picture has been reduced or enlarged so that it fills the field, it might still be smaller than the field in one dimension. In this case, the alignment pop-up menus tell FileMaker where to put the picture along this dimension. Figure 6-23 shows this process in action.

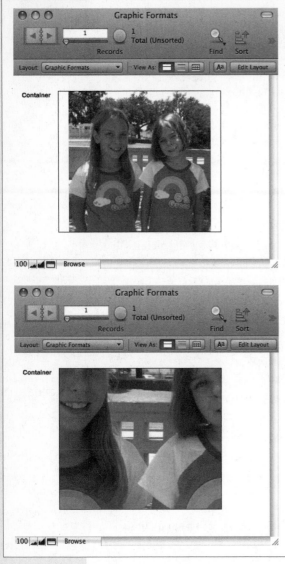

Figure 6-22:
Top: The image in this container field is too big to fit. But since the container field is formatted to reduce the image if necessary, it shrinks it down so the whole thing fits. FileMaker formats container fields this way when you first add them to the layout.

Bottom: This version shows the Crop graphic field format. FileMaker shows the image at full size, and cuts off the portion that doesn't fit.

Finally, for large images that have been cropped, alignment controls which portion of the larger image you see. If you align to the top and left, for instance, you see as much of the top-left corner of the image as possible. You can see the same cropped picture with each possible alignment in Figure 6-24.

Note: When FileMaker reduces or enlarges a picture, it keeps the picture's aspect ratio the same. In other words, a picture that's four inches by six inches may not be that *size* in the container field, but its height *is* two-thirds of its width. If you'd rather FileMaker make the picture *exactly* the size of the container field, even if it means distorting it, then turn off "Maintain original proportions".

Figure 6-23:
If a picture is smaller than the container field, or when FileMaker reduces a picture whose aspect ratio doesn't match the field, there's space left over. In these three fields, the picture's the same, but the alignment is different: Top, Center, and Bottom respectively.

Figure 6-24:
This window has three container fields, all containing an image that's too big to fit. Each field is set to crop, but with different alignments. On the left, the image is set to align Left. The center image is set to align Center. Finally, the right image is set to align Right. As you can see, FileMaker cuts off each image, but the alignment setting determines which portion of the image is visible.

Adding Buttons

The Contact Management database template described in the box on page 92 has a pretty slick system for switching between list and detail layouts. Instead of fiddling with the tiny Layout pop-up menu, you can just click tab graphics right on the screen. Each click magically transports you to a different layout.

You can easily duplicate this magic in your own databases. Just use FileMaker's Button tool, shown in Figure 6-25. But don't let the tool's name and appearance mislead you. You're not limited to the rectangular beveled buttons this tool creates. In fact, you can turn *any* object on a layout—an imported graphic or even a field—into a button. When folks click the mouse button while pointing to such an object, FileMaker highlights it so they know they're about to perform some kind of action. When they let go, something happens. You get to decide what that *something* is.

Figure 6-25:
When you're in Layout mode, you find the Button tool in the Status toolbar, right about…there. It looks like a little button being poked in the face by its big brother, or being clicked, or something.

Creating Buttons with the Button Tool

You want to add buttons to the header of your People database to switch between the detail and list layouts. You do this in Layout mode, so open the People database, switch to the People Detail layout, and then hop over to Layout mode.

To add a button, first click the Button tool, and then *draw* the button on the layout as though you were drawing a rectangle. Figure 6-26 shows you where you may want to put it.

When you release the mouse button, FileMaker immediately pops up the Button Setup dialog box (see Figure 6-27).

You want this button to switch to a different layout whenever someone clicks it, so in the action list, find "Go to Layout", and then select it (it's right under the bold-face Navigation item). When you do, the Options area shows you a pop-up menu labeled Specify. You can pick any layout in your database from this menu. For this button, choose People List.

If you're picky about such things, you can even control whether your button has square corners or slightly rounded corners. Choose, for example, the "Rounded button" option for an elegant, classy look. (If you don't make a choice, then you get square.)

Put your button here

Figure 6-26:
You can put your button anywhere you want, and make it any size you want. But if it's going to look like a button with the "Go to List" label, it should be close to the size of the button shown in this window. Also, don't forget to set the button's autoresize anchors appropriately. If you put it here, then anchor it on the top and right.

Figure 6-27:
The Button Setup dialog box shows up whenever you create a new button. You get to pick one action from the Button Action list. Most actions require a little configuration. When you pick one, its options appear in the Options area. You can come back to this box, and make changes to an existing button: Just double-click the button in Layout mode (or choose Format → Button) to open it.

Something else changes when you select a button command: The "Change to a hand cursor over button" checkbox appears below the Button Style area. By turning this option on, you tell FileMaker to use a special pointing-finger cursor whenever someone mouses over the button. (The icon is similar to the one you usually see when you point to a link in a Web browser—the universal cue that an area is clickable.)

When you're done making choices, click OK. You can now switch to Browse mode, and give your button a try.

Note: Buttons work in Browse mode and Find mode, but not in Preview mode.

While you're in a button sort of mood, add a Detail button to the top of the People List layout. This one uses the "Go to Layout" action to bounce you back to the People Detail layout.

Turning an Existing Layout Object into a Button

Buttons are handy, but they can be redundant. Often, there's already something on your layout—like a picture or even a field—that would make a perfectly good button. For example, if you've got your company's logo in the layout's top-right corner, then you can make it link to your Web site's main page. A separate button reading "Go to Home Page" would be unnecessary clutter. (Incidentally, in this case you use the Open URL button action.)

Here's another common example: When you're on the List layout, it would be handy to go back to the Detail layout for a specific person. It turns out if you put a button right on the body part of a List layout, that's exactly what happens. FileMaker notices which record you click on before switching layouts. But rather than add a button to the already full Body part on the List layout, why not turn the person's name into a link of sorts? When you click the name, FileMaker shows you details on that person.

Here's how:

1. **If necessary, switch to Layout mode, and to the List layout. Then, select the text object that holds the First Name and Last Name merge fields.**

   This is the object you want to turn into a button. You have to select it before you can work on it.

2. **Choose Format → Button Setup.**

   The Button Setup dialog box (see Figure 6-27) makes its return. This time, though, you're not making a *new* button. Instead, you're turning the selected object *into* a button.

3. **Choose the "Go to Layout" button action. When the Options area shows the Specify pop-up menu, choose People Detail.**

   This action tells the button *which* layout it should go to.

4. **Click OK.**

The window disappears and you're back on your layout. You don't see a change because you can't normally *see* if an object has been turned into a button. If you try the button now, it works fine, but it doesn't do people much good if they don't know it's there. To make it obvious that the name links to the Detail layout, why not make it *look* like a link?

Note: When you're in Layout mode, you can choose View → Show → Buttons. When this option is turned on, FileMaker outlines every button with a thick dotted line (it shows up only in Layout mode). Choose the same command again to turn it off.

---

5. **Using any of FileMaker's text formatting tools (see page 156), turn the text blue and give it an underline.**

Now your List layout looks like the one in Figure 6-28, and it works beautifully.

Figure 6-28:
Your List layout (in Browse mode) should look something like this window. When you point to a name, your mouse arrow changes to the little hand icon, and when you click, the name highlights. After the button is released, you see the Detail layout for the correct person.

If you select more than one layout object before you choose the Format → Button command, then FileMaker automatically groups the objects and turns the entire group into a single button. These objects now act like any other grouped objects: Anything you do to one in Layout mode happens to all of them. If you later *ungroup* a grouped button, then FileMaker warns you, and removes the button behavior as well.

Note: If you want four *different* buttons that do the same thing (so you can work with them individually), then you have to buttonize them one at a time.

Making a Button Not a Button

If you have a layout object that's already a button, and you don't want it to be a button anymore, you need a way to *turn off* its button-ness. It's easy but not very intuitive: Select the button, and then choose Format → Button Setup (or double-click the button). In the Button Action list (Figure 6-27), choose Do Nothing, and then click OK. Now the object isn't a button anymore.

Tip: Here's a faster way, even though it's cheating. Just click a button, and then choose the Arrange → Ungroup command (or better yet, press Ctrl+Shift+R or Shift-⌘-R). Even if the button *isn't* part of a group, FileMaker pops open a message box asking if you want to remove the buttons. Just click OK, and your object is no longer a button.

You can even remove the button action from the "real" buttons you create with the button tool. That's because, in reality, the button tool just creates a specially formatted text object, and automatically turns it into a button. If you switch it to Do Nothing, you're just left with a fancy text object. (You may want to deactivate a button when you're troubleshooting your database—or for a little April Fool's Day fun.)

POWER USERS' CLINIC

Making a Button Appear Grayed Out

Lots of programs on your computer include buttons you can't always click. FileMaker itself, for instance, doesn't let you click Delete in the Manage Database window's Fields tab if you don't have a field selected. The universally accepted look for a button that isn't quite ready to be clicked is a grayed-out label.

Accomplishing this feat is a breeze in FileMaker. Suppose you have a button that sends an email to the address in the Email Address field, logically labeled Send Email. But the label should be grayed out if there's no address in the field. How can you adjust the format of the button depending on what's in the field? FileMaker's conditional formatting (page 206) comes to the rescue again.

Since a button doesn't have a value of its own, you have to use the "Formula is" condition type, which you'll learn more about in Chapter 11. Here's a sneak peek to whet your

appetite: Select the button, and then choose Format → Conditional Formatting. Click Add to add a new condition. In the box next to the "Formula is" pop-up menu, type the following exactly as shown:

```
People::Email Address = ""
```

In this formula, People is the table, and Email Address is the field. In English, this formula says: *The Email Address field is equal to ""*. In other words, it's empty.

When this condition is true, use the settings in the Conditional Formatting dialog box to tell FileMaker to turn the button text gray. You can also lighten the background color of the button itself if you want. However you decide to make it look, you now have a button that automatically gives someone a visual clue when it doesn't apply.

Button Actions

The Button Setup window has dozens of available actions, as you can see at the left side in Figure 6-27. In the previous section, you created buttons for the "Go to Layout" action, but you have many more. As you scan through these commands, you probably notice that many of them repeat the same functions you find in FileMaker's menus. That's not just meaningless redundancy. By giving your databases buttons for lots of everyday commands, you can make FileMaker even easier to use than it already is. Design some icons (perhaps in your corporate colors), attach buttons to them, and you may find you hardly have to train your colleagues at all, because the buttons and their labels help explain what they need to do to use the database.

Here's a brief rundown on what some of these actions do.

Note: This section explains the button actions you're ready to use right now. Many available actions simply won't make sense to you until you've learned more about FileMaker. These buttons mimic the *steps* you can use when you write *scripts* to automate FileMaker procedures. (In fact, you can use *any* button action in a script.) You'll learn about scripts in detail in Part 5.

Go to Layout

"Go to Layout" is the action you used for the two buttons you created earlier in this chapter. It transports those who click it to another layout instantly. You get to pick which layout to visit.

Go to Record/Request/Page

The "Go to Record/Request/Page" action lets you switch to the next, previous, first, or last record in the found set. If you're in Find mode, then it navigates find requests instead. Despite the word "Page" in its name, it doesn't navigate pages in Preview mode because buttons don't work in Preview mode. (The reason it has this name is because you can navigate pages with a script in Preview mode. See Chapter 13 for more.)

Go to Field

Use "Go to Field" if you want a button that delivers its clickers into a specific field. You get to pick the field by clicking the Options area's Specify button. For example, you could create a button that says "Back to Square One", which places the cursor in the first field in the tab order. (If you don't pick a field, then this step goes to *no* field. In other words, it gets the user out of whatever field she's in.)

The Options area also has a "Select/perform" checkbox. For text, number, date, time, and timestamp fields, turn on this option if you also want FileMaker to select the contents of the field, so folks can just start typing to replace it. For container fields, this option tells FileMaker to *perform* the field contents. In other words, play the movie or sound, open the file, and so forth. This way, you could have a button that opens up a file (see page 87), stored in a container field. For the "Go to Field" action to work, the target field must be on the layout.

Go to Next Field and Go to Previous Field

The "Go to Next Field" and "Go to Previous Field" actions have no options at all. They simulate the Tab and Shift-Tab keystrokes, bouncing to the next or previous field in the tab order.

Note: It would be more correct to say these commands simulate whatever keystrokes you have configured to go to the next object in the Format → Field/Control → Behavior dialog box (see page 159). In fact, even if you have nothing selected here, these steps still do what they say. You don't have to fixate on the Tab key here.

Enter Browse Mode, Enter Find Mode, and Enter Preview Mode

The last three actions in the Navigation section—Enter Browse Mode, Enter Find Mode, and Enter Preview Mode—do just what you'd expect. Want a Find button on your layout? Assign it the Enter Find Mode action, and you're done.

Note: The Enter Find Mode button has a "Specify find requests" option. You can use this power-user feature to preload the find requests and save your database's searchers a little time. You'll learn how to use the complex dialog box that this button conjures on page 501.

Editing actions

FileMaker has seven editing actions, whose names are largely self-explanatory:

- Undo
- Cut
- Copy
- Paste
- Clear
- Select All
- Perform Find/Replace

The Undo action takes no options at all; it simply runs the normal Edit → Undo menu command. Select All also has no options. It works exactly like the Edit → Select All command.

Cut, Copy, Paste, and Clear all let you specify the field to act on. If you don't specify a field, then they act on the field someone's in when he clicks the button. You can also turn on "Select entire contents" for these actions if you want FileMaker to do a Select All before it cuts, copies, pastes, or clears. Again, if you don't, then it works on whatever someone has already selected.

Perform Find/Replace lets you pop up the Find/Replace dialog box. You can click Specify to preload the dialog box with your own choices. And you can turn on "Perform without dialog" if you want it to perform your user's Find/Replace choices without showing the dialog box at all.

Note: The Editing section also has an action called Set Selection. You're not ready for this one yet, but it's covered on page 532.

Field actions

In the Fields section you find several useful and familiar commands.

Insert Text lets you stick predetermined text into a field. You can tell FileMaker *which* field to put it in, or leave "Go to target field" unchecked to have it land in the currently active field. You also get a "Select entire contents" checkbox if you want the inserted text to *replace* whatever's in the field. Click the *bottom* Specify button to tell FileMaker what text to insert.

Several actions mimic the choices in the Insert menu (in Browse mode):

- Insert from Index
- Insert from Last Visited (Insert → From Last Visited Record)
- Insert Current Date
- Insert Current Time
- Insert Current User Name
- Insert Picture
- Insert QuickTime
- Insert File

For each of these, you can optionally choose the field to use, and whether or not to select everything in the field before inserting.

Finally, the Replace Field Contents action runs the Records → Replace Field Contents command. This time, you get to pick the field to replace into if you want. You can also predetermine what goes in the Replace Field Contents dialog box. If you turn on "Perform without dialog", then nobody even sees the dialog box. Instead, the replace *just happens*. You could use this action, for example, to add a Flag button to your layout. It would automatically flag every record in the found set by putting a Y in the same field on each of those records.

Record actions

Use the New Record/Request action to make a button create a new record. To duplicate the current record instead, choose Duplicate Record/Request. To delete a record, use Delete Record/Request. This action has one option: "Perform without dialog". Turn this action on if you want your button to delete the record with no warning message.

Warning: Turn off the warning message only if the people using your database are very experienced (or very trustworthy). The Undo command can't undo a deletion, so there's no going back—yet another reason for a good backup routine.

The Open Record/Request action locks the record without actually entering any fields. Chances are you *never* need to do this action from a button. Use Revert Record/Request to mimic the Records → Revert Record menu command. This one has a "Perform without dialog" option as well.

To give folks an obvious Save button, assign it to the Commit Record/Request action. This action is just like clicking out of the record. It's useful, though. If you have your layout set to show a "Do you want to save…" message whenever someone edits the record, then you can add a Save button to the layout, using this command with the "Perform without dialog" option turned on. Whenever anyone clicks the button, FileMaker saves the record straightaway without the annoying dialog box.

Found set actions

If you have certain finds that you perform a lot, you can create buttons to run them directly. Use the Perform Find, Constrain Found Set, and Extend Found Set actions to get the job done. Each action lets you specify what find requests you want them to use. See page 501 for an explanation of how to specify these requests manually.

For now, though, you can easily use them like this: First, perform the find you want the button to do (just go to Find mode, enter your criteria, and then click Find). Then add the button to the layout, and pick one of the find actions. Turn on "Specify find requests", and FileMaker shows you its complicated Specify Find Requests dialog box. But the box *already* has the requests you used last, so you can just click OK. Now your button performs the right find.

Note: You also find button actions for Extend Found Set and Constrain Found Set. These buttons are configured just like the Perform Find action, but operate like their Find mode counterparts (page 56).

The last few actions work just like their counterparts in the Records menu:

- Modify Last Find
- Show All Records
- Show Omitted Only
- Omit Record

- Omit Multiple Records (this action has two options: how many records to omit, and the now-familiar "Perform without dialog")

- Sort Records (this one also lets you predetermine the desired sort order, and avoid the dialog box if you want)

- Unsort Records

Window actions

Windows are, after all, where FileMaker displays your information, so it pays to be familiar with the button commands that control them. With these actions, you can adjust an open window so your data fits more comfortably, or even create a new window to navigate in while the first stays intact in the background.

- Use **New Window** to make a button that creates a new window. You can determine its name, size, and position, but it always shows the layout you're already on, so its usefulness is pretty limited. People more typically use it in a script (see Part 5).

- The **Select Window** action lets you switch to a different window if you know its name. Click Specify, choose Window Name, and then type in the name of the window. (The Current Window option makes sense only when scripting.)

- **Close Window** simply closes the active window. You can also supply the name of *another* window, and FileMaker closes that window instead.

- The **Scroll Window** action gives the button rudimentary control over the window's scroll bars. Choose Home to scroll to the very top. If you choose End, then a button click scrolls to the very end. Page Up and Page Down work like scroll bar clicks, moving it one screenful up or down.

  You can scroll a window while you're in a field. If you do, the field you're in may no longer be visible on the screen. The Scroll Window action's To Selection option tells FileMaker to scroll the window so that the field you're in is visible.

- Use **Show/Hide Status Toolbar** and **Show/Hide Text Ruler** to show or hide each embellishment. Your button can explicitly show or hide the item, or you can choose Toggle to have the button *switch* the setting with each click. The Show/ Hide Status Toolbar action also has a Lock checkbox. Turn this checkbox on if you want the Status toolbar control to become inactive when your button is clicked. With an inactive Status toolbar control, nobody can show or hide the Status toolbar without using your buttons.

- The **Set Zoom Level** action lets you make your own zoom buttons as well. This action also has a Lock option if you want to lock out the normal zoom control.

- **Adjust Window** lets you minimize, maximize, resize to fit, restore (to its last size), or hide the frontmost window.

• **Arrange All Windows** gives you the Tile Horizontally, Tile Vertically, Cascade, and "Bring All to Front" options from the Window menu.

• **View As** has an option for "View as Form", "View as List", and "View as Table". You can also choose Cycle to have one button that cycles through all three views.

Note: The options to lock the Status toolbar and zoom controls may seem a little odd for button actions. Why would a person ever click a button to lock herself out of something useful? Actually, you usually use these options as part of a *script* (Chapter 13). You see them here since button actions and script steps always have the same options.

Print actions

The Files section has two important actions: Print Setup and Print. These actions give you control over the File → Print and File → Print Setup or File → Page Setup commands. Optionally, you can preselect the options in each dialog box, and use the "Perform without dialog" checkbox to perform the action with no intervention. You could, for instance, have buttons that switch to landscape and portrait page layouts, and a third button to directly print the current record.

Open Menu Item actions

The Open Menu Item section gives you button access to several common dialog boxes. You can add them to a layout to save people a trip to the Menu bar, which is especially useful if they don't know where the Menu bar *is*.

• Open Edit Saved Finds

• Open Preferences

• Open File Options

• Open Manage Database

• Open Manage Data Sources

• Open Manage Scripts

• Open Manage Value Lists

• Open Find/Replace

• Open Help

• Open Remote

• Open Sharing

Exiting FileMaker

If you want a button that exits or quits FileMaker itself, then use the very last action in the list: Exit Application.

GEM IN THE ROUGH

Buttons and Tab Order

Since buttons are an important part of how people interact with your database, FileMaker makes the buttons as convenient as possible. It even lets folks operate them from the keyboard. When you set the tab order for your layout (Format → Set Tab Order), you can put buttons in the mix. If a button is in the tab order, you can tab to it in Browse mode (it gets a thick black outline), and then press the space bar to "click" the button.

While you're at it, you can put tab controls in the tab order too. Once again, the space bar switches tabs.

If you include important buttons and tabs in the tab order, then people can breeze through complex data entry tasks without separating hand and keys. They will thank you.

Summary Fields and Sub-Summary Parts

A database excels at keeping track of things—itsy bitsy teeny tiny details about hundreds, thousands, even millions of little things. But people aren't so good at dealing with all that detail (hence the invention of the database). They like to see the *big picture*. If you want to understand your customer's music tastes, then a report of 200,000 individual CD sales doesn't do you much good: The information is in there somewhere, but your feeble mind stands no chance of ferreting it out. But a report that divides that information into 25 *music genres*, each with sales totals, both in aggregate and by gender, helps you interpret all those reams of data at a glance. In other words, a well-designed report *summarizes* the data for you. FileMaker's not only fantastic at showing you information, it also excels at helping you see what it all *means*.

To get this kind of high-level analysis, you use summary fields.

Summary Fields

A summary field isn't associated with records like the other field types. Instead, summary fields gather up and process data from several records. Creating summary fields is much easier than describing what they do, as you can see from the following example.

1. **In the People database, choose File → Manage → Database.**

    You're about to add a field that counts the people in your database. This action is one of the most common ways to summarize database information.

2. **In the Manage Database window, choose the Fields tab. Then, in the Field Name box, type *Count of People*.**

A summary field, like any other, has a name. You're going to use this summary field to count the people in your database.

3. **From the Type pop-up menu, choose Summary, and then click Create.**

The "Options for Summary Field" window appears (Figure 6-29).

Figure 6-29:
The "Options for Summary Field" dialog box appears when you make a new summary field. Unlike the field types you've used so far, a summary field has options that must be set for it to be usable, so FileMaker shows you those options right away. This window also shows up if, in the Manage Database window, you select a Summary field, and then click Options.

4. **Choose the "Count of" radio button.**

A summary field can perform one of seven summary calculations. In this case, you want it to *count* things.

5. **From the Available Fields list, choose First Name.**

A summary field is always based on some other field in the database. For example, this field counts the First Name field. What does that mean? Simple: If a record has something in the First Name field, then it gets counted, but if the First Name field is blank, FileMaker skips the entire record. Since every person has a first name, this field counts every record. But beware—if you forget to type somebody's first name in a new record, then that person doesn't get included in the count.

Note: In a simple database like this one, counting the First Name field is enough to make reasonably certain that you're counting all the records. But in the real world, you want to be certain *every* customer is counted—even if the First Name field isn't filled in. You'll learn about more complex databases and their need for a field that's never empty (a primary key field) in Part 4.

---

6. **Click OK.**

   FileMaker adds the new field to the field list.

   You now have a field that helps you find out how many people are in the database. That piece of information is much more useful than it sounds; you'll be using it to find out interesting things soon.

If you squeeze this field onto the Detail layout and have a look in Browse mode, then you see something altogether unimpressive: the total number of people in the database (the Status toolbar already tells you this information).

Using Sub-Summary Parts

The real power of summary fields becomes apparent when you combine them with sub-summary parts. Instead of counting all the people in your database, you might want to count how many you have in each city, or state (or both). Perhaps you need to know how many are still living, or get counts by Zip code. Or you may want to see how your contact list breaks down by city, gender, status, and mother's maiden name (assuming you have all those fields in your database).

With the help of sub-summary parts, your humble "Count of People" summary field can tell you all this. Instead of counting all the people in the database, it can count the records in different groups, and you can define those groups based on any field value.

An example helps. Suppose you want to break your People List layout down by status, with one group for Known – Alive, one for Known – Dead, and one for Missing. You also want to see how many people fall in each group at a glance.

You already have the requisite summary field (the Count of People field you just created). Now you need a sub-summary part:

1. **Choose Insert → Part.**

   The Part Definition dialog box appears. Here's where you choose what kind of part you want (you saw it way back in Chapter 4).

2. **Turn on the "Sub-summary when sorted by" radio button.**

   The list of fields on the right side of the window becomes active. A sub-summary part is always hooked to a field.

3. **In the field list, select the Status field.**

   In this case, you're summarizing your records by status information.

4. **Click OK.**

   FileMaker asks if you want this part to summarize the records above it or below it. When you add group totals to your layout, they can appear before or after the records they summarize.

5. **Click Print Above.**

   FileMaker adds a new sub-summary part to your layout, right between the header and the body. (If you had opted for Print Below, then it would be between the body and footer instead, to make it clear it comes after the records it summarizes.)

6. **Add a text object to the new part with this for content:** *Status: <<Status>> (<<Count of People>>).*

   In other words, you want a text object that merges in the Status field and Count of People field.

7. **Style the text object as you see fit (you can use Figure 6-30 as a guide).**

   This part's up to you.

If you switch to Browse mode, then you see…nothing different. The secret to sub-summary parts is *sorting*. You *must* sort by the field on which the sub-summary part is based. In this case, you need to sort by Status.

Note: If you think about it, it makes perfect sense. How can FileMaker group all the same-status records together for you if they're all mixed up? You might think FileMaker should just sort automatically in this case, but it turns out it's advantageous that you can add more than one sub-summary part to a layout, and have them spring into action as you sort your records differently. You'll see how to do so next.

When you sort the records by the Status field, you see something like Figure 6-30.

If you scroll around, you see that each group is clearly labeled and counted.

Multiple sub-summary parts on one layout

You can do some really creative reporting by adding multiple sub-summary parts. Right now your layout groups by Status whenever you sort that way. But what if you want to group by city or state instead? No problem. Just add two more sub-summary parts. Once again, the same Count of People field you already have counts the groups appropriately, so you don't need to add more fields to the layout.

Following the same basic steps you used in the previous section to add the first sub-summary part, add two more. This time, though, attach the first to the State field and the second to the City field. In both cases, opt to "Print Above" just like you did in step 5 above. When you're done, you have three sub-summary parts stacked up in Layout mode, as you can see in Figure 6-31.

In the State sub-summary part, add a text object that says "State: <<State>> (<<Count of People>>)". In the City sub-summary part, add one with "City: <<City>> (<<Count of People>>)" instead. When you're done, your layout looks like Figure 6-32.

Figure 6-30:
The People List layout now summarizes by Status. As you can see here, a new visual separator appears between the group of Known – Alive records and the group of Known – Dead records. What's more, the Count of People field now shows the count just for the group (the "(5)" here) because it's in a sub-summary part.

Figure 6-31:
When you add more than one sub-summary part to your layout, FileMaker stacks them up in the order they were added. You can put the same summary fields in each one, and get totals appropriate to each group.

Note: If you're having trouble figuring out which sub-summary part is which, you have two options. First, you can click the part label toggle (page 179) to turn the part labels so they show a long and descriptive name. If you don't want to clutter your layout with long labels, then just double-click any part label instead. FileMaker opens the Part Setup dialog box again, and you can see which field the part is tied to.

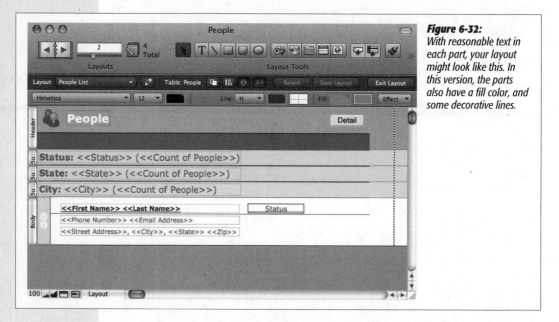

Figure 6-32:
With reasonable text in each part, your layout might look like this. In this version, the parts also have a fill color, and some decorative lines.

When you switch to Browse mode now, your list looks just like it did before, because you're still sorted by Status. When you sort by City or State, the layout instantly switches to show the groups and totals appropriately (you can see the result in Figure 6-33).

Note: If you sort by both City and State, then you see both the associated summary parts. This feature too can be handy in a complex layout (especially a report).

Leading and Trailing Grand Summaries

Sometimes you want to see the totals for the found set as a whole. For example, you may have interesting summary fields that show averages or other statistics about your data, and you want to highlight them in your layout. FileMaker calls these layout parts *grand summary* parts.

If you want a grand total *above* all the records, then add a *leading grand summary* part to the layout, and put your summary fields in it. If you use a *trailing grand summary* part instead, then the grand totals appear after the last record. You can see a leading grand summary in Figure 6-34.

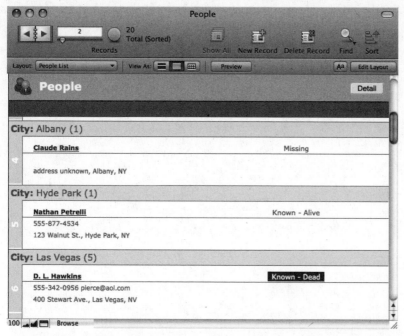

Figure 6-33:
Top: When you sort by City, the records appear in groups by city. Notice that the count of people in each city is shown in parentheses.

Bottom: Simply by changing the sort order, the layout now groups by State instead. Once again, the totals update to correctly count the new groups.

Stop That

Normally when you add a field to the database, FileMaker automatically adds it to the layout on which you just were. This feature's nice in the same way those child safety bottle lids are nice: It's probably good for kids. But big people like you find it terribly annoying.

To teach FileMaker that you're a big boy or girl now, just do this:

1. In Windows, choose Edit → Application Preferences; in Mac OS X, choose FileMaker Pro → Preferences. The Application Preferences window pops up.

2. Switch to the Layout tab. This tab is the place you set Layout mode preferences. You've already seen the Color Palette settings.

3. Turn off "Add newly defined fields to current layout".

If you someday decide to stop thinking for yourself, then you can always ask Winston to turn this setting back on.

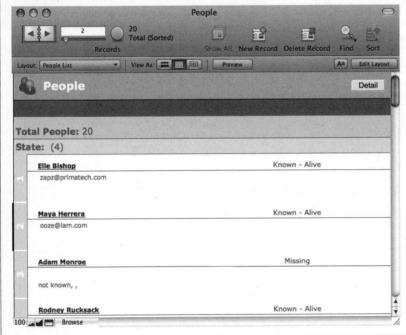

Figure 6-34:
The People List layout now has a leading grand summary part to show the overall total at the very top. If you scroll down to see more records, this total scrolls off the top of the list (unlike the header part, which never scrolls away).

Sub-Summary Parts and Printing

Although using sub-summary parts in Browse mode is powerful, they're even more at home when building printed reports. (In fact, until FileMaker Pro 10, you could use sub-summary parts only in Preview mode, and when printing. They were a reporting tool first, and came to Browse mode only recently.)

You can use sub-summary parts to build high-level reports that break the data down by multiple nested groups, and then roll up all the totals. For instance, your database of product sales may show order count, revenue, and share information. Using three sub-summary parts, you can break these down by region, then state, and finally category.

For just the highest-level analysis, you can leave the body part out of the layout entirely. When you do, FileMaker doesn't show the individual records at all. Instead, it shows just the summarized data. Figure 6-35 shows just such a layout in Layout mode.

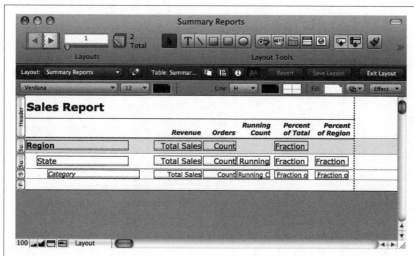

Figure 6-35:
This layout has three sub-summary parts and several summary fields. The data is intended so that when multiple sub-summary parts show at once, you can see how the groups fit together. Also notice there's no body part. This report shows only summarized data. You can see it in Preview mode in Figure 6-36.

Note: You can find the database pictured in Figure 6-35 on the Missing CD page at *http://missingmanuals.com/cds*.

Other Summary Field Types

The Summary Field dialog box's Options area offers several choices. Using these options, you can perform a lot of powerful analysis on your data. Figure 6-36 shows a sub-summary report from a hypothetical sales database. This report uses several summary field options. When defining a summary field, you need to first decide which radio button to turn on. Here's what each choice does:

Total of

Use the "Total of" option to *sum* (add) number fields. In Figure 6-36, the Revenue field is a total of the Sales Amount field. For each group (state or region), you see its total.

Figure 6-36:
This report shows summary fields in action. The Revenue column uses a "Total of" type summary field to add up sales numbers. Orders uses the Count type to show the total number of orders. The Running Count column, on the other hand, continues to count up the orders from one state to the next. Finally, two Percent fields use the "Fraction of Total" summary field type to determine how much each state contributes to its region, and how much each region contributes to the total. You'll learn about all these options on the next few pages.

When you have this option selected, a "Running total" checkbox appears below the Available Fields list. When you use a summary field on one of those magical layouts (like the one in Figure 6-36) that produces grouping—total sales by Zip code, total sales by state, and so on—you normally see just the totals for each group in the report. If you turn on "Running total", then FileMaker changes things slightly. Instead of individual totals for each group, the totals add up from group to group, much like the Balance column in your checkbook register.

Average of

Obviously, the "Average of" choice calculates the average of the values in a number field. This time, you see a "Weighted average" checkbox. When you turn it on, another field list appears (see Figure 6-37). From this list, you choose the field by which to *weight* your average.

You use a weighted average when the things you're averaging have an associated quantity. For example, suppose your database has a record for each product sale. It records which product was sold, how many were sold, and the unit price. If you want a summary field that calculates the average sale price, then you probably want to turn on the "Weighted average" checkbox. Imagine you have these sales figures:

• You sold three laptop computers for $2,500 each.

• You sold 18 more laptops for $2,200 each.

• You sold a single laptop for $2,800.

If you use a simple average, FileMaker tells you the average sale price for laptops is $2,500 ($2,500 + $2,800 + $2,200, divided by three). But that's not exactly right. You sold 18 of those laptops at just $2,200 each, but it counts only *once* in the calculation. In fact, you really sold 22 laptops in all, at three different prices. To calculate the correct average, you need to take quantities into consideration. In FileMaker, turn on the "Weighted average" checkbox, and then, in the "Weighted by" list, choose the Quantity field. Now it reports the correct average: $2,268.18.

Figure 6-37:
When you turn on the "Weighted average" checkbox, FileMaker adds a second field list—"Weighted by"—to the window, where you can pick another number field. FileMaker averages the data in the first field, and weights each record's input by the second field. If you're not a statistician, see the explanation in "Average of" on page 288.

Count of

Choose "Count of" to *count* items without totaling them. Since this option doesn't involve actual math, you can pick *any* field type, not just numbers. FileMaker counts each record in which that field isn't empty. If it's empty, then it simply doesn't contribute to the count. Choose a field that's *never* empty if you want to be sure you count *every* record. You can use this property to your advantage, though. If you want your count to reflect just the flagged records, then count the Flag field instead. In Figure 6-35, the Orders column uses this option.

This option gives you a "Running count" checkbox. It works like running total but has an option that running total doesn't offer. When you turn on "Running total", the "Restart summary for each sorted group" checkbox becomes available. This option lets you produce a column like Running Count in Figure 6-35. This column counts up with each state, keeping a running count. But it's set to restart numbering based on the Region field. Notice that the running count starts over with each new region.

Minimum and Maximum

If you want to know the *smallest* or the *largest* value in a group, use Minimum or Maximum. Both are very simple: Just pick the number field you want to look at. No checkboxes, no extra lists. You can use these to see the largest number of orders in your database, or the price of the least expensive product.

Standard Deviation of

If you're into statistics, use "Standard Deviation of". It gives you a field that calculates its namesake for the selected number field. It also has a "by population" checkbox, which is a little oddly named (it probably should be called "of population"). Turn this checkbox on if your records represent the entire population in your particular domain, and FileMaker uses the formula for the standard deviation of a population. Turn it off to calculate the standard deviation of a *sample*.

Note: If none of this makes sense to you, then rest assured you don't need to know what it means to use summary fields. But if you're cursed with a curious mind, Google *define:standard deviation* and go to town.

Fraction of Total

"Fraction of Total" is the most complex summary option. It looks at the total for the *group* you're summarizing, as well as the total for the entire database. It then reports what portion of the overall total the group represents, as a decimal number. If all your sales were in California, it shows *1*. If California accounted for only 5 percent of your sales, on the other hand, it says *.05*.

The Subtotaled checkbox that comes along with this option is also a little confusing. When you turn it on, FileMaker lets you pick another field from a list called "When sorted by". The name of this list serves to inform you that you must *sort* the record by the selected field for this summary field to work. If you don't sort the records yourself before you view the report, then the field stays empty.

Note: That problem's not as big as it may seem at first. As you learned on page 282, you have to sort records to do a lot of things with summary fields.

FileMaker looks at the selected field, figures out which records have the *same* value in them as in the current record, and calculates the fraction based only on the total of *those* records. In Figure 6-35, the "Percent of Total" column is a normal "Fraction of Total" field, while the "Percent of Region" column uses "Fraction of Total" sub-totaled by Region.

Summarizing repetitions

When you summarize a repeating field, you have another choice to make. Do you want *one* summary value that aggregates every repetition, producing a single value? If so, then choose "All together". If you want a repeating summary value that aggregates each repetition individually instead, then choose Individually.

Note: If you have sharp eyes, then you may notice that the "Summarize repetitions" radio buttons are available all the time, although they don't do anything unless you've selected a repeating field. Don't waste your time clicking them unless you're working with a repeating field. Just one of those FileMaker mysteries for the cocktail-party circuit.

Part Three: Multiple Tables and Relationships

3

Adding Multiple Tables and Relationships

In the previous chapters, you learned how to give your database all kinds of cool features and powers, but it still contains just a single table to hold your data. In the real world, one table is rarely enough. In your private investigator business, for example, you need to keep track of more than just people. You need to record the time you spend working for your customers, the invoices you send them, and the payments you receive. And you need to organize all this stuff into recognizable jobs.

You could make a separate database for each of these needs. But that's far from ideal, since you don't want to use each kind of information in isolation. You need all these different kinds of information to work in harmony, like a well-rehearsed orchestra. In database terms, what you need is a single, integrated file that keeps all your various lists, files, and records in one place, so you can arrange and rearrange them according to your needs—a *relational database*.

Relational Databases Explained

Before you dive into relational databases, you'll find it helpful to review some vocabulary. First, a *database* is a collection of tables, layouts, and other features that forms an organized system. A *table* holds information about one kind of thing, like people, orders, products, or suppliers. A *field* holds one attribute of something: the person's first or last name, the order date, the color of a product, or the supplier's address. (An *attribute* simply means an individual characteristic. For example, a bicycle might have several attributes: color, size, style, and price. In a database, each of these attributes gets its own field.)

In the previous chapters, you've created a database whose tables and fields track various attributes of people. You could repeat the process, and build any number of individual databases for organizing your time, creating invoices, and logging payments. But that approach has real problems, like the following:

- When you log some billable work, you have to type in the customer information. Then, when you create an invoice, you have to type the customer information all over again in the invoice file. When you receive a payment, you have to type it a third time in the payment file. Since the databases aren't connected in any way, they can't share that information with one another.

- Suppose you want to see how much you've billed a customer over the years. You could use the Invoices database and run a summary report by, say, the customer's name. But duplicate names, misspellings, and name changes would render the information useless. You could use the People database instead. After all, the total amount billed (or the outstanding balance) is, in some sense, an attribute of a customer. But to have that information ready when you need it, you'd have to create a field for it in the People database, and then re-add and retype the invoice total *every time you issue a new invoice to each customer*.

Even if you could live with these limitations, you'll run into trouble when you try to create the Invoices database. An invoice typically encompasses information about two different entities: the *invoice* itself, and each line item. There's simply no good way to track invoices without involving at least two tables. Your solution to all these problems? Hook multiple tables together into one big database.

Note: Database developers use the word *entity* to mean "one kind of thing." *Person* is an entity, and so is *Invoice*. Remember, though, that one thing itself isn't the entity—Bill Gates isn't an entity, and neither is Invoice #24601.

FileMaker lets you put more than one table in a database—tracking more than one kind of thing in the process. It also lets you describe how the data fits together. You can say, for example, that invoice records have attached line item records, or that each payment record is associated with a particular invoice record.

In database parlance, you create *relationships* between entities. A relationship is a connection that describes how records in each table match one another. For example, suppose you have two tables—Invoices and Line Items—as shown in Figure 7-1. The Invoice table contains information about every invoice in the database—for example, the Invoice Date, the Date Due, and the Invoice Total. The Line Items table contains information about every Invoice Line Item in the database—Product SKU, Description and Price.

To figure out which line items belong to each invoice, you need to have a relationship between the tables. Notice that each table has a field called *Invoice Number*, which you use to match the proper records from each table. By defining this relationship, you've created a mechanism to hook together an Invoice record and a line item record.

Figure 7-1:
Each box in this picture represents a table. The name of the table is on top of the box. The fields are listed inside each box. The line between the tables represents the relationship between the two tables. The line shows that the Invoice Number field in the Invoice table is connected to the Invoice Number field in the Line Items table. Later in this chapter, you'll see how FileMaker lets you use similar boxes and lines to set up relationships between the tables in your database.

Modeling Your Database

Before you create a relational database, you need to do some planning. You decide what entities you'll be tracking, which ones deserve a table, and how they relate to one another. It's easier to create the right tables and connections the first time than to go back and change them later. When you model a database, you're creating a "blueprint" to follow as you build it. The pros call this blueprint an *entity relationship* (or ER) diagram.

Choosing Entities

First, you decide what tables you need, and how they fit together. Since every table holds data about a single entity, you normally start by figuring out all the entities in your system. You probably can't list them all in one shot. Everybody forgets some that are less obvious, so start with blank paper or a word processor, and list all the things the database needs to *do*. This list will help you identify entities.

Now's the time to stretch your mind and think of every possibility. What tasks do you do every day? What do you *wish* you could do—and what information do you need to do it? What do you want your computer to show you when you sit down first thing in the morning?

When your workflow hits a wall, what piece of information would get you moving again? What questions do people keep asking you—and how could FileMaker answer them for you? The more your initial plan matches your real needs, the more quickly you can get your database up and running. You can see such a list in Figure 7-2.

With this list in hand, you can start to figure out what *entities* your database needs to track. For each item on your list, think of all the *things* it involves. Figure 7-3 shows a possible list.

Figure 7-2:
Here's a list of things your database will do. A list like this helps you start figuring out your entities and possible tables. A more complex database could have a much longer list. Some big systems start with a list several pages long.

My Database:

• Keep track of the people I do business with and the jobs I do for them

• Track my time: what I did, for whom, and for how long

• Track expenses incurred while doing work for customers

• Create invoices

• Keep track of what I'm owed, and what's been paid

Most real-world problems have lots and lots of entities, so the second step is to figure out which ones matter. You'll use a process of elimination to remove extraneous items from your list. You might eliminate items for any of four major reasons:

• **They're already covered.** The list in Figure 7-3 includes Checks and Payments. A check is really just a kind of payment, so you don't need to track checks separately in your database. Since a payment is more general than a check, you can eliminate Checks. Then, when you build your Payments table, you can add a field called Type, and put Check, Cash, or Credit Card in that field.

• **They're too specific.** Sometimes you have things in your list that aren't general enough. This list shows Airline Tickets, Hotels, and Film. But you don't really need to track the details of each of these items. Instead, you're just interested in expenses in general—what they were, how much they cost, and what job they were for. To fix this problem, think of a more general word that encompasses all three things—something like Expenses. Add that to the list, and then remove the more specific versions.

• **They're really just attributes of another entity.** Do you really need an entity called Outstanding Balances? You do need to know how much each customer still owes you, but maybe you already have that information somewhere else. A customer has an outstanding balance because one or more invoices are unpaid.

My Database:

- Keep track of the people I do business with and the jobs I do for them
  Customers, Jobs, Companies,

- Track my time: what I did, for whom, and for how long
  Tasks, Services

- Track expenses incurred while doing work for customers
  Expenses, Airline Tickets, Hotels, Film

- Create invoices
  Invoices, Line Items, Addresses

- Keep track of what I'm owed, and what's been paid
  Payments, Checks, Outstanding Balances

Figure 7-3:
You've now added some entities to your list. Don't worry too much about whether the entities you think of are good ones or not–right now you're just trying to get it all down so you don't leave anything out. You can start with all the nouns in the list–People, Time, Invoices–and try to think of nouns that cover other aspects of your work.

So to see who owes you money, you really just want to look at the balance due on any unpaid invoices. Scratch Outstanding Balances off the list. For the same reason, you can also remove Companies—they're just attributes of a customer. (For more detail, see page 303.)

Note: Just because you're crossing things off your list doesn't mean those things aren't important, or don't apply to your database. It just means they don't qualify as entities that need their own table. These things may show up as *fields* in other tables, or they may just be one *type* of a more general entity, like Check. Either way, you can still track these items in your database. See the box on page 303.

- **They're not important enough to track in your database.** Suppose your list has an item called Services. These services are the kinds of things you do for your customers: Check into a cheating spouse, find a lost dog, recover a stolen computer, or whatever. You could create a Services table in your database, and put all these kinds of services in it. But what value would it add? What kind of information are you tracking about a service? Probably just its name—which doesn't really need to be *tracked*. So, as an entity, leave out Services. Figure 7-4 shows an example of a well-edited Entities list.

Figure 7-4:
After thinking about each entity on your list, you can remove some, and possibly add some new ones. When you're through with this step, you have a pretty good list of the entities—and tables—in your database.

My Database:

* Keep track of the people I do business with and the jobs I do for them
  Customers, Jobs, ~~Companies~~

* Track my time: what I did, for whom, and for how long
  Time, ~~Services~~

* Track expenses incurred while doing work for customers
  ~~Airline Tickets, Hotels, Film~~ Expenses

* Create invoices
  Invoices, Line Items, Addresses

* Keep track of what I'm owed, and what's been paid
  Payments, ~~Checks, Outstanding Balances~~

Finding Relationships

Now that you have a list of entities, you need to figure out how they relate to one another. To get started, just pick two of your entities—Customers and Jobs, for example—and ask yourself how they go together (if you need some guidance, see the page 306). You might come up with this answer: *A customer hires me to do jobs, and a job is done for a customer*. That sentence tells you two important things:

* Customers and jobs are related.

* One customer has many jobs, but each job has only one customer.

By comparing different entities in this way, you can figure out how each relates to another, if at all. Your notes as you consider these relationships might look something like Figure 7-5.

You can easily translate most of the items on that list into database relationships. Each tells you about two entities in your list, and how they relate in each direction. You can usually translate these relationships directly into your database, as shown in Figure 7-6. That picture is one example of a diagram representing each of these relationships.

Figure 7-5:
Here's a list of relationships between entities on your list. (You may have worded things differently, or come up with some that aren't on this list.) If you follow the advice on page 306, these sentences usually exactly describe each kind of relationship.

My Database:

- A customer hires me to do jobs, and a job is for a customer.
- A customer is sent invoices, and an invoice is sent to a customer.
- A job takes time to do, and time is spent on one job.
- A job has expenses, and an expense is for one job.
- A customer is charged for expenses, and an expense is charged to a customer
- An invoice is for one job, and a job is billed on invoices.
- An invoice has line items, and a line item is on one invoice.
- A customer has an address, and an address is where a customer lives.
- An invoice is paid with payments, and a payment is applied to invoices.
…

Figure 7-6 shows you how entities like Payments, Invoices, and Customers relate to one another, but the relationship with the Time entity isn't so obvious. Is "Time" plural? For that matter, if Time is an entity, then it must be a thing, so what is a *time*? You've just discovered one of the common challenges to good relational design—choosing good names.

You added *Time* to your list of entities because you spend time working on a job. That's a little ambiguous, though, so think about what exactly you'll be putting in the database. You'll be logging the time you spend working: what you're doing, when you started, and when you finished. You could call it a *work log entry* but that's pretty cumbersome. Because this kind of entity is quite common, database types have made up a name for it—*timeslip*. A timeslip is sort of like one entry on a timesheet. It says what you were doing for one period of time.

Using this language, your relationship description becomes clearer:

• A job has timeslips, and a timeslip is for a job.

Now it's a lot more obvious: This relationship is one-to-many.

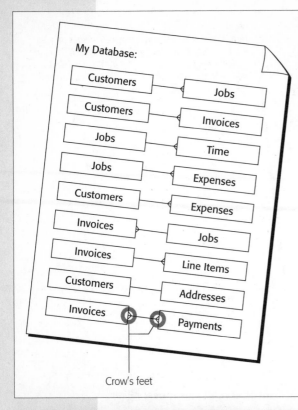

Figure 7-6:
In this picture, boxes represent entities, and the lines between them indicate relationships. The little forked end on the relationship lines (called a crow's foot) means "to-many" as in "one-to-many." If the line doesn't have a crow's foot, it's to-one. So the relationship between Payments and Invoices is many-to-many, while that between Customers and Invoices is one-to-many.

Crow's feet

Many for One and One for Many

Relationships tell FileMaker which records in two tables go together. Conceptually, relationships come in three flavors: one-to-many, many-to-many, and one-to-one.

In a one-to-many relationship, one record in the first table relates to several records in the second. For example, one invoice record has several line items, so it's a one-to-many relationship. (Likewise, several line items belong to one invoice, so you could say that line items and invoices have a many-to-one relationship. Since relationships work both ways, a one-to-many is *always* a many-to-one as well.) Figure 7-6 shows a one-to-many relationship, where one invoice has many line items.

A many-to-many relationship means something slightly different. Suppose you have a Products table and an Orders table. Each time you sell some products, you create a new order.

These tables have a many-to-many relationship: A person orders multiple products, and each product can be ordered many times.

Finally, you can have two tables locked in a one-to-one configuration. If your database holds pictures of each product you sell, then you can create a Pictures table. It would have one record for each product. But the Products record also has one record for each product. In fact, each product record is related to exactly one picture record, and vice versa.

You create any of these relationships with exactly the same steps in FileMaker. But each has its own set of considerations that affect the way you design your database. These concepts are discussed on the next page.

One-to-many relationships

Most of the relationships in your diagram are one-to-many, which is normal. One-to-many relationships outnumber all other types by a large margin in almost any system. See the box on the previous page for a description of the various types of relationships.

One-to-one relationships

Your list of entities and relationships shows a one-to-one relationship between Customers and Addresses. For the purposes of this database, one customer can certainly have one address, and vice versa. But if that's the case, are they really separate entities? In fact, Address is just an attribute of the Customer entity. That makes it a prime candidate for entity-elimination. Put the address *fields* in the Customers table instead. You might argue that despite the conflict of interest, you *could* work for two people in the same household, and would therefore have to type the same address twice in your Customers table if you didn't have an Address table. The best answer to an argument like that is: big deal. This situation doesn't arise often enough to justify a more complicated database just to eliminate duplicating one or two addresses. Even without a separate Address table, you can still separately handle all other tasks for these two clients.

On the other hand, if you're managing a high school, and it's important to know which students share a home, and which parents they belong to, then an Addresses (or more likely, a Households) entity might make sense.

Tip: If you expect to have to track several addresses for each customer, then you can create a one-to-many relationship between Customers and an Addresses entity. For the current example, though, you'll stick to a single address built right into the Customers table.

As a general rule, unless you can articulate a good reason for its existence, a one-to-one relationship is a mistake: It's just two tables where one would suffice. (For some clarification, see the box on page 309.) You'll almost always want to combine entities like people and their addresses into one table.

FREQUENTLY ASKED QUESTION

No Companies?

Why is Companies just an attribute of Customers? What if my customer is a company? Don't I need to be able to keep track of that?

Your decisions about entities depend on how you intend to use the database. In this database, you're assuming that *people* hire you. Even if they hire you on behalf of some business, you put the actual person you're working for in the database, along with the name of the company that employs her.

In a different database, you may decide companies are important enough to be in their own table. If it's important to see all the people who work for one particular company, or to keep track of lots of people from each company, then you probably want a Companies table.

Many-to-many relationships

Many-to-many relationships pose a special challenge. Normally, FileMaker knows which records are related to one another because they have something in common. For example, the Invoice table and the Line Item table each have an Invoice Number field. But you can put only *one* invoice number in a line item record. Luckily, Invoices and Line Items have a one-to-many relationship. If they had a many-to-many relationship, you'd be in trouble.

FREQUENTLY ASKED QUESTION

Only One Attribute

So, I'm supposed to eliminate Services as an entity because it has only one attribute (see page 299). Is that another rule? Should I remove all entities that have just one attribute?

Not necessarily. Sometimes an entity has only one attribute, but you still want to give it a table. For one thing, tables can help promote consistent data entry. Say your new database is going to track jobs, among other things. A job may have just one attribute—the Job Name—so you could just put the job name on each expense, time entry, and invoice. But what if you misspell the job name? Then you'll have expenses that should go together but don't, because FileMaker sees different job names. By creating a Jobs table, you have a central place to enter job names and use it as a value list. With a Jobs table, instead of typing the job name everywhere, you simply choose it from a list.

Wait—to do that, all you need is a list. Why have a table if it has just one column?

OK, wise guy. You *could* leave out the Jobs table and the job names themselves. Instead, you could just attach each expense, time log entry, or invoice to a customer. But what happens when the same customer hires you six different times? All those expenses, invoices, and entries are lumped together under that customer, and you can't track them back to the individual jobs. Sometimes a one-attribute entity exists because it gives your database greater powers of organization or categorization. (See the box on page 251 for more details—and a warning—about using a single attribute table for a value list.)

To fix things, you need to chop your many-to-many relationships in half, turning each into two separate one-to-many relationships. You always need to add a new special-purpose entity in the middle. Your database has only one unhandled many-to-many relationship: Invoices and Payments. To split it up, you need to introduce a special entity. Since it doesn't have a decent name, just call it *Invoice Payment* (as in "This record represents one invoice payment—one payment on one invoice"). Now, instead of "An invoice is paid with payments, and a payment is applied to invoices," you can say these two things:

- An invoice is paid with invoice payments, and an invoice payment is applied to one invoice.

- A payment is divided into invoice payments, and an invoice payment is part of one payment.

Figure 7-7 shows the updated diagram.

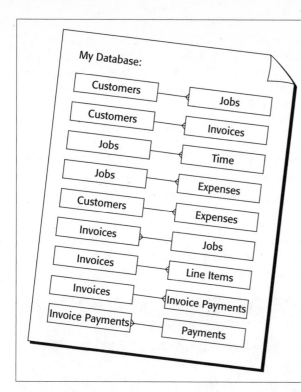

Figure 7-7:
In this updated version of the diagram, the Customers and Addresses relationship has been removed, and the Invoice Payments join entity has been added. Now you have only one-to-many relationships—perfect.

My Database:

Customers — Jobs

Customers — Invoices

Jobs — Time

Jobs — Expenses

Customers — Expenses

Invoices — Jobs

Invoices — Line Items

Invoices — Invoice Payments

Invoice Payments — Payments

Note: The diagram you're about to create isn't, in the most technical sense, a *real* ER diagram. The real kind deals with all kinds of technical details that simply don't matter in FileMaker. Nevertheless, some database big shot may chastise you for calling your beautiful picture an ER diagram. Never mind—just be glad FileMaker doesn't make you *care* about all that mumbo jumbo.

The Entity-Relationship Diagram

Now that you have a list of entities and their relationships, you're ready to assemble your master plan: the entity relationship (ER) diagram. An *ER diagram* is a picture that shows all the entities in your database, and the relationships between them. Unlike the diagram you've already drawn (in Figure 7-7), each entity appears only once in an ER diagram.

It has two purposes: to help you find relationships you missed, or relationships that don't belong, and to serve as a roadmap for your database. You'll use it when you actually create this database in FileMaker, and when you go back to make changes later. (Yes, you *will* get to use FileMaker again…pretty soon.)

Creating an ER diagram

When you assemble an entity relationship diagram, you must put all your entities and relationships together in one big picture. Your want to have each entity in the picture just *once*, and all the lines necessary to explain the various relationships.

Your ER diagram is crucial to a successful database designing experience. You almost always find ways to improve your database when you put it in a picture. When you set out to actually *build* the database, the ER diagram guides you through the process. Finally, 6 years from now, when you need to add more to your database design, the ER diagram will bring you—or your successor—up to speed on how your database fits together.

You can start by making one box for each entity you've identified. Try to place the boxes on the page so there's some open space in the middle where your lines can roam free. Then start drawing lines to represent each of the relationships you've come up with. For a simple database, you can usually get the lines in the picture without much difficulty. But creating a larger diagram without the right tools can be a real pain. If you work on paper, you end up starting half a dozen times before you get a good arrangement. If you use a typical drawing program (the drawing capabilities in Word, for example), then you spend copious hours reconnecting lines and entities, reshaping lines, and hand drawing crow's feet as you move things around. See the box below for some suggestions to solve this problem.

UP TO SPEED

Think Relational

If you're dazed and confused trying to figure out how different entities relate, you're not alone. Understanding relational database design takes practice, plain and simple. Here are some ideas to improve your thought process:

- **Don't get hung up on technicalities**. At this point in your design, you shouldn't be thinking about database tools like primary keys, foreign keys, or join tables. Those things are all *implementation details* that you can work out later. Right now, just focus on the kinds of things you're keeping track of, and how they fit together.

- **Use familiar words**. If you're trying to figure out how customers and jobs should be related, use words familiar to you, for example: "A customer hires me to do jobs," not "A Customer entity is related to a Job entity in a one-to-many configuration." As you get the hang of it, you'll discover that the simple sentences you use every day say a whole lot about relationships. For example, if a customer hires you to do *jobs* (note the plural), then you probably have a one-to-many relationship between customers and jobs.

- **Consider individual items first**. Don't think about what *customers* do. Instead, think about what *one customer* does. The answer tells you whether a single customer has many jobs, or just one job. Then turn it around. Once you've decided a customer hires you to do jobs, ask yourself what a job has to do with customers. "I do a job for a customer." This process tells you that each job is connected to just one customer. (If you didn't follow this advice, and thought, "I do *jobs* for customers," then you're not any closer to understanding the relationship.) By combining these results, you discover that a customer has many jobs, while a job has just one customer. So Customers and Jobs have a one-to-many relationship.

- **One last tip**. Don't let the word "many" hang you up. It's just a standard term to help keep things simple. (Otherwise, you could have a *one-to-quite-a-few* relationship between Jobs and Invoices, a *one-to-a-handful* relationship between Customers and Jobs, and a *usually-just-one-or-two-to-rarely-more-than-three* relationship between Payments and Invoices. Yikes!) "Many" doesn't have to mean "lots." It might mean "exactly six" or "no more than three." The relationship isn't one-to-many only when it's one-to-*exactly*-one.

When you're done, you should have a single, unified diagram with each entity showing up only once, and every relationship indicated by a line.

When you're thinking about relationships with just pairs of tables, you don't get the big picture. The ER diagram shows you how *everything* comes together, and when that happens, you often discover tangles of relationships just like those in Figure 7-8. Tangles like these aren't inherently bad; they're just usually completely unnecessary. Take the first tangled group—Expenses, Jobs, and Customers. The diagram tells you that customers have jobs, jobs have expenses, and customers have expenses.

Figure 7-8:
This diagram (created in OmniGraffle) doesn't look all that bad—except for one thing. The area labeled Rat's Nest has a lot of lines among just a few tables. Expenses, Customers, and Jobs are all interrelated—there's a relationship between Jobs and Customers, another between Customers and Expenses, and a third between Expenses and Jobs. If you look closely, the same situation exists for Customers, Jobs, and Invoices. In both cases, you have a better way.

But in point of fact, you don't need all those lines to understand all the relationships, and neither does FileMaker. It turns out that the line between Customers and Expenses is entirely superfluous. Even if it weren't there, you could still see all the expenses charged to a certain customer. Just find all that customer's *jobs* first (by following the line from Customers to Jobs). Once you've found those jobs, you can look at the expenses for each job. Since customers incur expenses only by way of jobs, you get exactly what you want. In other words, if two entities are connected by a path along relationship lines—even *through* other entities—then they're related as far as FileMaker's concerned. It can show you the expenses for a customer just as easily as it can show the jobs for that customer. Figure 7-9 illustrates this concept.

It's All About the Tools

If you plan on doing this more than once, you're best off buying a proper diagramming program. Microsoft Visio for Windows and OmniGraffle for Mac OS X are two excellent choices. These tools *understand* ER diagrams. They can hook entities together with ease, draw crow's feet on your behalf (lots of programs just don't understand crow's feet), and keep everything connected as you tinker with the arrangement.

If you give Visio a run, don't be tempted by its built-in database diagramming features—they're too complex for File-Maker work. Instead, create a basic diagram, and, from the Basic Shapes library, use Rectangles and Dynamic Connectors. With the Format → Lines command, you can put crow's feet on your lines.

Both these tools do more than you need for your ER diagrams, but the time you save is well worth the expense (about $259 for Visio and $99 for OmniGraffle). You can find free trial versions at *http://office.microsoft.com/en-us/ visio/default.aspx*, and at *www.omnigroup.com/applications/ OmniGraffle/*.

If you're an unrepentant cheapskate, here's a tip: Write the entity names on a piece of paper, and cut out each one. Then arrange them on paper, draw lines, and see how it looks. You can slide the entity scraps around a few times to find a decent arrangement, and then commit the whole thing to a clean piece of paper.

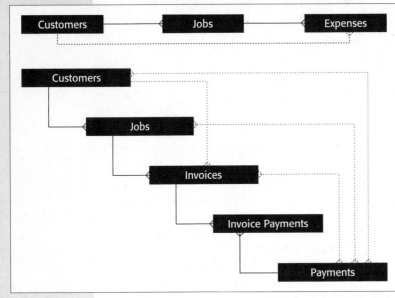

Figure 7-9:
In this picture, the solid lines represent relationships you've identified among the entities. The dotted lines show relationships you don't have to explicitly create—they're implied. As long as there's a path—any path—from one entity to another, they're related. You don't need a direct path.

When you're thinking about these implied relationships, pay attention to the crow's feet. If, when moving from one entity to another along the relationship lines, you *ever* go through a to-many relationship, then the larger implied relationship is itself to-many. This isn't just a clever trick; it's actually intuitive. If a customer has more than one job, and each job has expenses, then clearly a customer can have more than one expense.

WORKAROUND WORKSHOP

When to Go One-to-One

When two things—like people and addresses—have a one-to-one relationship, it usually means you've got an entity you don't need (as in the example in Figure 7-6). Every rule has exceptions, though. Here are some reasons you may see a one-to-one relationship in a database:

- FileMaker uses record locking to prevent two people from editing the same record at the same time. (Yes, Virginia, two people can use a database at the same time—see Chapter 18 to learn how.) Imagine you have a table of products and every time you sell something, you reduce the product's Quantity In Stock field by one. What happens if someone else is modifying the product description at the same time? FileMaker doesn't let you enter the inventory adjustment because the record is locked. Should you cancel the order? Allow the Quantity in Stock field to be wrong? Force your customer to wait while you ask your associate to get out of the record? A better solution is to put the inventory levels in a separate table. Each product has a Product record and an Inventory record, so two seemingly conflicting processes no longer lock each other out of your system.

- Sometimes you want to divide data you store about an entity among several tables. A database of stock photography might include high-resolution photographs in container fields. These photos make the database very large. By putting the photos in one table,

and the information about the photos in another, you make working with the information easier. You can back up the information to a CD, and the photographs to your high-capacity backup system. (This technique requires keeping each table in a separate file—something you'll learn about in the next chapter.)

- Imagine you have customers and employees. Employees don't place orders or make payments, and customers don't have time sheets. But they both have addresses, phone numbers, and email addresses. What's more, you like to send holiday cards to all of them every year. In a situation like this, you can create three tables: People, Customers, and Employees. The People table holds all the information that customers and employees have in common—names, addresses, and so forth. Information unique to an employee (Social Security number, hire date, and such) goes in the Employee table, and information only a customer could love (referral source, membership level, and so on) stays in the Customers table. You would have a one-to-one relationship between People and Employees, and another between People and Customers. When it comes time to send those cards, you can print envelopes right from the People table, and get customers and employees in one shot.

When you make your ER diagram, you should get rid of redundancy in your relationships. In other words, remove lines that show direct relationships when the relationship is already implied by other entities and relationships. In your diagram, you can remove the relationship between Customers and Expenses. You can also axe one between Customers and Invoices because Customers can find their Invoices by way of Jobs. With this revision, the ER diagram now looks like Figure 7-10.

Next, you need to figure out what fields your tables need to make the relationships work. But before you get to that step, take one last look over your ER diagram. Keep these points in mind as you check for errors:

- You should have no undivided many-to-many relationships.

Figure 7-10:
Here's the final ER diagram that you'll use as the roadmap for creating your database. Notice that every entity is related to at least one other entity in some way. Stray, unrelated entities are so rare in a real database system that if you see one in your diagram, then you should check to make sure everything belongs.

- If you have any one-to-one relationships, make sure you can justify them (see the box on page 309 for some ideas).

- Make sure you don't have any unnecessary entities hanging out all by themselves.

- Be certain you don't have any unnecessary lines or rats' nests.

If you discover an entity that has no relationships, you may not need it in your database at all. Read back on page 297, and see if that item might belong inside one of the other tables. Or if your diagram has two or more groups of related entities and no relationships *between* the groups, you might've forgotten to draw in a relationship, or again, you might have one or more entities that your system doesn't need. Go back and make sure you're clear on your one-to-many and many-to-many relationships.

Keys

In a diagram, you can show relationships by simply drawing a line. FileMaker, however, knows what records are related because you tell it to expect them to have some data in common. It's time to look more closely at how that works. Take, for example, the typical Invoice table and its little brother, Line Items. The Invoice table probably contains fields like Due Date, Balance Due, and Terms—all attributes of the invoice itself. Then there's the *Invoice Number* field. Unlike the other fields, it's a made-up number. It does one thing—identify an invoice—and does it very well. Without it, you and your customers might have conversations like this: "I need a refund on one of my invoices…you know, the big one…yeah, in February…right, with three items…no, the other one…." As soon as someone mentions an invoice number, though, everybody knows exactly which invoice to look at. More important, FileMaker knows which invoice it is, too.

The invoice number is good at identifying an invoice because it has three important characteristics:

- **It's unique.** No two invoices ever have the same invoice number.

- **It's unchanging.** Invoice #24601 is #24601 today and it will be tomorrow, and the next day, and the next day.

- **It's consistent.** All invoice records have an invoice number.

Since it's a unique number, if you're talking about invoice #24601, and your customer is talking about invoice #24601, there's no question that you're both referring to the same invoice. Since it's unchanging, you can go back weeks, months, or even years later and find the invoice every time. And since it's consistent, you never have lonely invoices hanging out there without an identifying number. In database terms, the invoice number is called a *key*. A key is a field whose value uniquely, unchangingly, and consistently identifies one record.

As far as FileMaker's concerned, any field you use to link one table to another is a key field. Although FileMaker doesn't differentiate between key types, the larger world of database theory has two types of keys: primary and foreign. Understanding how the two types of keys work helps you choose appropriate ones for your databases.

Choosing a good key field

Like the Invoice Number field in your database, a primary key is most often a made-up number. You can add a new field to your table, and tell FileMaker to automatically make up a unique value for it each time you create a record (using the Field Options dialog box's Serial Number option Auto-Enter tab, as shown on page 108). This kind of primary key, based on purely made-up data, is called a *surrogate key*.

Note: Unless you generate the value in your database, it's not a surrogate key, even if somebody else made it up. A surrogate key is made up *by your database*.

Occasionally, your table has a real value that meets the requirements for a key. For example, if your Product database has a field for your internal Inventory Control Number, you may be able to use that field as the primary key. If you use some real piece of data as a key, then it's called a *natural key*. Surprisingly, though, the vast majority of tables don't have a field that meets the criteria for a natural primary key. Take, for example, the Phone Number field in a contact database of people. Phone numbers are *usually* unique, and don't change *all that often*. But words like "usually" and "often" have no business in a discussion about good key fields.

In fact, in most cases the only fields that meet the requirements for a natural key are, in reality, surrogate keys from somebody else's database. For example, Social Security number is a value that everybody (in America) has, it never changes, and is always unique. It has these characteristics because it's a surrogate key made up

---

by some database at the Social Security Administration. But that's okay—FileMaker databases frequently deal with information that's generated somewhere else. Your database might contain employee numbers that come from your company's payroll system, part numbers from your supplier's catalog, or document numbers from your corporate knowledge base. All these numbers are surrogate keys in some system somewhere, but they're natural keys to you.

Primary and foreign keys

When a key field is in the same table that holds the records it identifies, it's called a *primary key*. In the Invoice table, the Invoice Number field is the primary key because the invoice number identifies an invoice record. If you put the invoice number in some other table (like, say, the Line Items table) it's not a primary key there. Instead, it's called a *foreign key*. Foreign keys identify records in other tables.

FREQUENTLY ASKED QUESTION

Going Natural

Should I try to find natural keys for the tables in my database if I can?

This question has generated an eternal debate in the broader database world. Some ivory-tower theorists are convinced that natural keys are superior to surrogate keys for two primary reasons. First, they're *meaningful:* When you look at a natural key in your own database, it means something to you. Second, if a key is also real honest-to-goodness meaningful data, then, in a relational database situation, your table always has at least one piece of good information from the table it relates to. If that happens to be the snippet you need, you save the software the trouble of going to another table and finding the right record. Thus, the theory goes, natural keys make database programs run a little faster.

But for the kinds of databases you're likely to build with FileMaker, neither of these concerns comes up very often. If a surrogate key isn't all that meaningful to the database user, just don't put it on the layout. And as for performance, the minuscule increase in speed is almost never significant enough to matter for typical databases.

And there's a much more significant argument against trying to find an acceptable natural key: It's usually impossible. You almost never have a normal piece of data in a record that meets all the criteria for a good primary key.

Even natural keys that really seem like great choices often turn out to be problematic. Suppose you work for a company that assigns an employee ID to each employee. You're building a database to keep track of employee stock options. Just like Social Security number, employee ID is a surrogate key to somebody, but it's a natural key to you. You decide to make it your primary key. Then you discover you need to track stock options for employees even if they quit, and then return to the company. When they do this, their employee IDs change, and your database can't track them properly without some inconvenient upkeep. If you had used your own surrogate key instead, you wouldn't have this problem.

The penalty for a bad key choice can be huge: anything from lost connections in your data to the need for a major overhaul of the system. By contrast, surrogate keys are easy and always work. Once you accept the fact that your database will have an extra field that serves no other purpose but to be the primary key, the choice becomes a no-brainer. Don't bother with natural keys.

But where do you *put* these foreign keys? In the Invoices database, how did you decide to put the Invoice Number field in the Line Items table? Why not create a Line Item Key field in the Line Items table, and put it in the Invoices database? Wouldn't that accomplish the same thing? At first glance, it might seem like both methods would produce an identical relationship. After all, they sure *look* the same in a picture (Figure 7-1).

Think about what a primary key means. Each value identifies one, and only one, record in the table. If you build a relationship based on a Line Item key, then each invoice can have only one line item. If it had two, you'd have two line items with the same line item ID. When you have a one-to-many relationship, you must put the foreign key in the table on the *many* side. Luckily, keeping this information straight in your head is a breeze. Since foreign keys belong on the to-many side of a relationship, just remember this rule: When you see a crow's foot on your ER diagram, you need a foreign key in the table to which it's attached. (But if you're getting confused, Figure 7-11 should clear things up.)

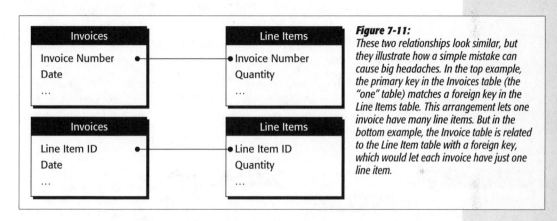

Figure 7-11:
These two relationships look similar, but they illustrate how a simple mistake can cause big headaches. In the top example, the primary key in the Invoices table (the "one" table) matches a foreign key in the Line Items table. This arrangement lets one invoice have many line items. But in the bottom example, the Invoice table is related to the Line Item table with a foreign key, which would let each invoice have just one line item.

Note: That rule bears repeating: *Whenever you see a crow's foot in your ER diagram, put a foreign key in the table it's attached to*. The key refers to whatever table is on the other end of the line. There are very few absolute hard-and-fast rules in relational database design, so cling to this singular bit of simplicity when you start to have doubts.

Later, you'll learn how to tell FileMaker to match records based on a foreign key in one table, and a primary key in another.

Join Tables

A many-to-many relationship is more complicated than its one-sided brethren. Imagine your database tracks payments from your customers. A customer could easily send a check to cover *two* invoices. On the other hand, another customer might send a check to cover just *part* of an invoice, with the promise to send another later. So an invoice can have multiple payments, and a payment can be for multiple invoices: many-to-many.

How do you build a relationship like this? If you put the Payment ID in the Invoices table, then a payment can be applied to more than one invoice (just put the same Payment ID in each invoice record). But an invoice can have only one payment, since it has just one Payment ID field. If you put the Invoice Number field in the Payments table, you get the same problem in the other direction. You may be tempted to try putting a foreign key field in *both* tables. In other words, add a Payment ID field to the Invoice table, and an Invoice Number field to the Payments table. Dig a little deeper, and you see that this has a whole *host* of problems:

- An invoice now has a field called Payment ID, but that field *doesn't* identify the payments for that invoice. To find the payments for an invoice, you have to open the Payments database, and then use the Invoice Number field. That's just plain confusing.

- Instead of one bidirectional relationship, you have two unidirectional relationships. The Payment ID in the invoice matches the Payment ID in the Payments table, but this tells you only which invoices belong to each payment. You need the other relationship (based on Invoice ID) to figure out which payments belong to each invoice. If you connect a payment to an invoice by putting the invoice number in the payment record, then you also have to put the Payment ID in the invoice record. If you forget, your data is no longer valid.

Luckily, you have a better way to accomplish a many-to-many relationship. You need something called a *join table* (see Figure 7-12). A join table doesn't usually represent a real entity. Instead, each record represents a relationship between two records in the related tables.

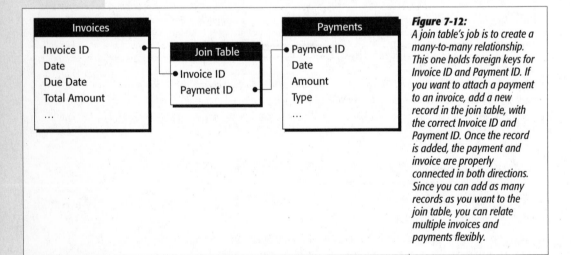

Figure 7-12:
A join table's job is to create a many-to-many relationship. This one holds foreign keys for Invoice ID and Payment ID. If you want to attach a payment to an invoice, add a new record in the join table, with the correct Invoice ID and Payment ID. Once the record is added, the payment and invoice are properly connected in both directions. Since you can add as many records as you want to the join table, you can relate multiple invoices and payments flexibly.

If it helps, think of join tables this way: Invoices and Payments both have a one-to-many relationship to the join table. So one invoice can connect to many join records, each of which connects to one payment. Likewise, one order can connect to many join records, each of which connects to one invoice. So you get many related records in both directions. A join table always contains *two* foreign keys, one from each table it's joining. If your database has many-to-many relationships, you may have to create a join table to hold just these two keys, but sometimes your database may already have a real table that can act as a join table. Figure 7-13 shows an example.

Other times, you can use a join table to hold fields that don't quite belong in any other table. Suppose you wanted to record what portion of a payment was applied to each invoice. For example, if a customer hands you a check for $100 and you have two outstanding invoices for that customer, for $80 and $30, then you may want to decide how to allocate the payment. Perhaps you apply $80 to the first invoice and $20 to the second. This dollar amount applied to each invoice can't be stored in the Invoice table because an invoice can have several payments. It can't be stored in the Payment table because you have *two* amounts and only one payment record. The best place for it is right in the join table itself.

Figure 7-13:
This database tracks orders for the products you sell. Since a product can be ordered many times, and an order can include many products, the Orders and Products tables have a many-to-many relationship. A Line Items table connects them. It records which products were on each order, but it also shows how many, and at what price. A line item is a real entity, but the Line Item table also serves as a join table.

At this point you've eliminated many-to-many relationships by adding join tables to your ER diagram, and you understand what foreign keys you need to make it all work. You're (finally) ready to actually build your database.

Creating a Relational Database

The tedious planning is finally over. Now comes the fun part—actually making the database. And believe it or not, this part will go *much* more smoothly with your plan in place. You create a relational database in three steps. First, you tell File-Maker what tables you want, and then you add the fields to each table. Finally, you add relationships. Don't be alarmed if you forget a table or miss a field: You can go back at any time and make changes—even 6 months from now when your tables are loaded with data.

Relational databases start out like any other. Go to FileMaker, and then choose File → New Database. Name your new database, pick the folder in which to save it, and then click Save.

Note: If you see the FileMaker Quick Start dialog box (the window with all the Starter Solutions) when you choose File → New, turn on "Create empty database", and then click OK. You can then name and save your new database.

Creating the Tables

When you first create a database, FileMaker shows you the Manage Database window's Field tab (you first saw this on page 95). Without your knowledge, it's already created a table for you with the same name as the database itself. FileMaker assumes you just want one table, and it's ready for you to add fields to that table.

This time, though, you *don't* want just one table, so click the Tables tab (you can see it in Figure 7-14). Your first job is to remove the table FileMaker added for you, since it doesn't match one of the entities in your ER diagram. Just select the table in the table list, and then click Delete. FileMaker asks if you're sure, and then gives you the option to "Also remove occurrences of these tables in the graph." Turn this option on, and then click Delete. (You'll learn about occurrences and the graph on page 356.)

Figure 7-14:
The Manage Database window's Tables tab lists all the tables in your database. To add a table, in the Table Name box, type its name, and then click Create. If you want to change a table's name, select it in the table list first, type the new name, and then click Change. To delete a table, select it in the list, and then click Delete. Reorder the tables in the list by dragging the double-arrow to the left of a table name. The Print button prints a list of all your tables, along with each table's fields and field types (see page 99).

Now that you've deleted the starter table, you're ready to add your own carefully planned tables. To create a table, in the Table Name field, type its name, and then click the Create button. The new table appears in the list, and its detail column tells you it's empty—0 fields, 0 records. You'll add fields after you create all your tables. Grab the ER diagram and create a table for each entity. The diagram has eight tables in all, so make sure you create all of them.

Warning: Deleting a table is a *dangerous* operation. Right now there's no risk because you're working in a brand-new database. But imagine you come to this window 2 years from now. If you accidentally delete a table, then you lose *all* the data in it. You'll also have a lot of work to do putting your relationships and layouts back together. FileMaker warns you before it lets you delete the table, but it's worth an extra measure of caution. But because there's so much potential for danger, there's one final failsafe: In the Manage Database dialog box, if you click the Cancel button, then FileMaker discards *all* your changes, including any table deletions.

Creating the Fields

With the tables in place, you're ready to add fields. Click the Manage Database window's Fields tab (see Figure 7-15). You choose which fields to add to each table the same way you learned to in Chapter 3, with one caveat: key fields. *Every* table needs a primary key. In this database, you'll be using surrogate (made-up) keys in each table.

Adding primary keys

To keep things consistent, each primary key field will match the name of the entity, with the word "ID" added to the end. For example, in the Customers table, the primary key should be called Customer ID. This technique is so common, in fact, that you can often spot the primary keys in any database by looking for the letters "ID".

You can most easily make a surrogate key in FileMaker by using a *serial number*. The process is simple:

1. **In the Manage Database dialog box, click the Fields tab, if necessary. Then, from the Table pop-up menu, select Customers.**

   You're now ready to add a field to the Customers table. You'll start with the primary key.

2. **In the Field Name text box, type *Customer ID*. In the Type pop-up menu, choose Number.**

   Key fields can be any type, but number is usually the best choice because it's the easiest to match exactly.

Warning: Although FileMaker has no trouble matching up records no matter what field type you use, when you search for a record using the Find command—or, more importantly, in a script, as you'll see in Part 4—a text-based search just isn't precise enough. For example, you may get customer ID XY13374 when you're looking for customer ID XY133. To avoid even the possibility of error, stick with a number field.

Figure 7-15:
When you have multiple tables, they all show up in the Tables pop-up menu. When you choose a table from the menu, its fields show in the field list. When you add a field, it gets added to the selected table. In the Tables tab, you can also double-click a table to jump straight to its field definitions.

3. **Click Create.**

   FileMaker adds your new field to the field list.

4. **Click Options, and make sure the Auto-Enter tab is selected, as shown in Figure 7-16.**

   To be a good primary key, this field needs a unique value on every record.

5. **Turn on the "Serial number" checkbox.**

   When you tell FileMaker to auto-enter a serial number, it automatically makes up a new unique number every time you create a record. It sets the field to a number one bigger than the *last* value it created. Since the number always grows, it never repeats.

6. **Make sure the "On creation" radio button is turned on.**

   When you make a field a serial number, you get to choose when the serial number gets entered. It can happen when you create the record, *or* when you commit it. In other words, FileMaker can automatically put the serial number in the field for you right away, when you first create the record, and most of the time, that's exactly what you want. (As you'll see on page 345, FileMaker lets you set up your layout so you can create related records automatically while editing a record; you need the serial number for that to work.)

   Alternatively, you can have FileMaker wait until you finish entering data and actually commit the record. You might choose "on commit" if, for instance, you have a complex, automated database that adds new people to your database from lists you get from other offices. You can have the database add a person record *first*, and then see if it's a duplicate before committing the record.

Figure 7-16:
The Auto-Enter options tab helps you make sure your primary keys are unique. The first number in your new table starts out with a key of "1". But if you want to display this value, say on an Invoice, you could start the serial number at 10000, or give it a prefix of Inv10001. FileMaker's smart enough to add the text prefix and still give you incremented numbers. But even if you don't want to display the number, a prefix can still be useful. For instance, if you add a CUST prefix to the primary key in the Customer table, then you can tell at a glance which table the data's from. See the box on page 320.

That way, you don't skip serial numbers. (And if you know how to do that, you probably should be the one *writing* this book.)

7. **In the "next value" text box, type *1*. Make sure the "increment by" box reads "1".**

You've just established your starting serial number, and told FileMaker how to continue. Your first customer record will have the Customer ID 1, your second will be 2, and so on.

8. **Select the "Prohibit modification of value during data entry" option.**

Since key fields provide the links between your tables, relationships would break and other database disasters could ensue if key values got changed. When you turn on this option, you prevent that unhappy fate.

Click OK to return to the Manage Database window. You'll get a chance to test that Serial Number field in a few minutes. First, though, you need to follow those steps again for each table. You can, of course, add any field to any table at any time, but here you'll create tables, then primary keys, then foreign keys, and finally other fields. It's not the quickest way, but creating a relational database requires lots of steps, and you don't want to forget anything, so an organized approach pays off.

Note: If you have FileMaker Pro Advanced, you can save time by copying and pasting. Just select the Customer ID field in the list, and then click Copy (or choose Edit → Copy). In the Table pop-up menu, switch to the next table. Now click Paste. FileMaker adds a Customer ID field to this table. You'll need to change its name, but it already has the right type and auto-enter options defined, saving you several clicks.

POWER USERS' CLINIC

Serial Text

As funny as it sounds, you can auto-enter serial numbers into text fields, and the values *themselves* can contain text. FileMaker looks at the text you've specified for "next value" and tries to find a number in it somewhere. When it comes time to generate a new value, it pulls that number out, increments it, and stuffs it back in its place.

Say your "next value" is C000LX, and "increment by" is set to 10. The first record you create gets C000LX. The second

gets C010LX, and then C020LX, and so on. When you get to C990LX, FileMaker doesn't just give up. Instead, it makes more room: C1000LX.

If your "next value" has more than one embedded number (C000LX22, for example), then FileMaker uses only the last number. Likewise, if you don't have a number at all, it simply adds one to the end.

Adding foreign keys

Adding foreign keys requires a little more thought than the primary keys, but not much—you already did the hard part by creating an ER diagram (see page 305). To decide where the foreign keys go, just look for the crow's feet —the "forked" end is where you'll add a foreign key field. Figure 7-17 offers a refresher.

Since your primary key fields are all number fields, your foreign key fields should be, too—after all, the foreign keys hold primary key values. Following the crow's feet, you come up with these foreign keys (remember that a foreign key is always just a primary key from another table):

- In the Expenses table, add a number field called Job ID.
- In the Jobs table, add a number field called Customer ID.
- In the Timeslips table, add a number field called Job ID.
- In the Line Items table, add a number field called Invoice ID.
- In the Invoices table, add a number field called Job ID.
- In the Payments table, add a number field called Invoice ID.
- In the Invoice Payments table, add two number fields: Invoice ID and Payment ID.

Note: Because these are foreign key fields, they should not be set as unique. The whole point is to allow more than one child record, so use plain number fields. In other words, don't tell FileMaker to use auto-enter serial numbers in these fields, and don't turn on the "Prohibit modification during data entry" option.

Figure 7-17:
Each crow's foot in your ER diagram indicates the need for a foreign key. Each table with a crow's foot stuck to it needs a foreign key inside it. What should the field be called? Simple: Find the other end of the line. That's the entity the foreign key points to, so name it appropriately. For example, the Line Items table needs a field called Invoice ID.

Defining the Relationships

With tables and keys, you have everything you need to create some relationships. In other words, you tell FileMaker how the tables in your database fit together by matching up keys. As usual, FileMaker manages to make a tricky task seem kind of fun. You get to work with a visual, intuitive picture of the relationships between your tables—the *relationship graph*. In the Manage Database window, click the Relationships tab, which is reproduced in Figure 7-18.

Your table occurrences (TOs) may not be in precisely the same order as Figure 7-19; they appear in the order you created them. If you want to move them around, then just drag them by the solid-colored border along the top (where the name appears). But if you click *inside* a table occurrence (where the fields are listed) and drag, then you'll discover the secret to easily creating relationships:

1. **In the Customers table occurrence, point to the Customer ID field, and then press your mouse button.**

   The field name highlights, and the mouse arrow changes shape, indicating you're about to join (relate) two tables together.

2. **Pressing the mouse button, drag the arrow over the Customer ID field in the Jobs table.**

   As you drag, FileMaker draws a line starting from the first Customer ID field. When your cursor is over the second Customer ID field, it, too, highlights. If you see tables in the way, just drag straight past them. FileMaker doesn't do anything drastic until you let go of the mouse button.

Figure 7-18:
The Manage Database window's Relationships tab is a stark departure from the other tabs. It gives you a relationship graph where you can draw your relationships. FileMaker also gives you a myriad of tiny tools, which look familiar to anyone who's used a basic drawing program, to help you lay out the graph. The boxes in the graph are called table occurrences. (There's a reason why they aren't called tables in this case; see page 356.) The scroll bar indicates that there's more to see, but if you drag the bottom right of the dialog box, you can make it as big as your screen can handle. (See the box on page 326.)

If you make a mistake and start dragging the wrong field, just point to some empty space in the graph before you let go of the mouse button. FileMaker notices that you didn't complete the connection, and doesn't create a relationship. Then you can just start over.

3. **Release the mouse button.**

Poof! You have a relationship. The Customers and Jobs table occurrences change in appearance slightly: FileMaker adds a new panel to each box, and shows the connected key fields in this space. You can see the end result in Figure 7-19.

Figure 7-19:
Here's what your first relationship looks like when you finish dragging. Notice that the line is highlighted when you've finished dragging. When a table occurrence is involved in a relationship, it has two lists of fields. The upper list shows just the fields used in relationships. The lower list shows all the table's fields.

With the technique mastered, you can now create the rest of your relationships. You can refer to your ER diagram at this point, or use this handy cheat sheet. (In these examples, the stuff before "::" is the table name, and the stuff after is the field name. You'll see this notation a lot from now on.)

- Drag Expenses::Job ID to Jobs::Job ID.

- Drag Invoices::Job ID to Jobs::Job ID.

- Drag Line Items::Invoice ID to Invoices::Invoice ID.

- Drag Invoice Payments::Invoice ID to Invoice ID.

- Drag Invoice Payments::Payment ID to Payments::Payment ID.

- Drag Timeslips::Job ID to Jobs::Job ID.

Note: It doesn't actually matter which direction you go. You can drag the Expenses::Job ID field to the Jobs::Job ID field. Or you drag the one from Jobs over to Expenses. Both ways are equally valid.

When you're done, you can spot-check your work by counting the lines in the relationship graph. Including the one between Customers and Jobs, you should have seven, and the graph should look something like the one in Figure 7-20.

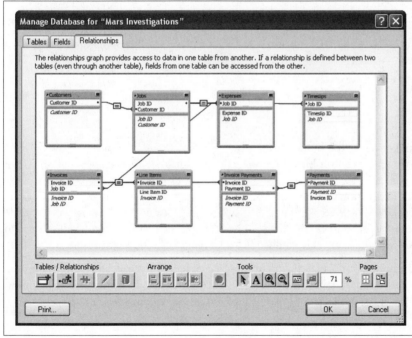

Figure 7-20:
In this zoomed-out Relationships Graph you can see all your tables. These relationships work OK, but the graph is now a little hard to read. First, there's no logical order to the tables. Even worse, there are lines running under table occurrences so it's not exactly clear what's what. You can do a little manual rearranging and fix this up.

Cleaning Up the Relationship Graph

Although this relationship graph is small and easy to understand, chances are it will grow as you power up your database by adding more tables (and even as you add new features, as you'll see through the course of the next few chapters). As it grows, your graph can easily get messy and hard to decipher. To make your graph manageable, first get rid of unnecessary information. Right now your graph shows *every* field in each table occurrence (in fact, it shows some fields *twice*, and a healthy dose of empty space, too). But you don't need to see every field here, that's what the *Fields* tab is for. Figure 7-21 shows how to reclaim the wasted space.

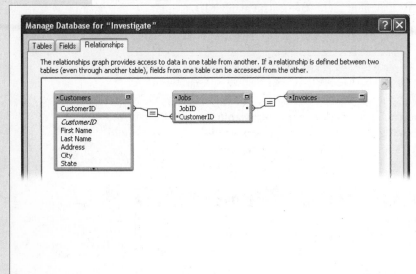

Figure 7-21:
Each table occurrence in the graph has a little button in the top-right corner. When you click it, the table occurrence changes to one of the structures shown here. The first time you click, the bottom section disappears, leaving only the fields used in relationships. Another click makes all the fields disappear. In the Customer table occurrence, a triangle at the bottom edge indicates that there are more fields than can fit. Click the triangle to scroll the field list.

To make your graph more efficient, switch every table occurrence to show only the fields used in relationships (Figure 7-21). One click for each one should do it, but if you go too far, just keep clicking, and it comes back around again a few clicks later. (The section on Selection Tools shows you more ways to manage table occurrences.) Now a lovely graph is just a few drags away: You can move the table occurrences around so they form a pleasing arrangement that you can understand more easily than the mess you had before. Figure 7-22 shows the result.

If you prefer, you can resize your table occurrences instead of closing them up.. Hover the mouse over any of a table occurrence's four edges, and the pointer changes to a doubleheaded arrow. Drag with the arrow to resize.

FREQUENTLY ASKED QUESTION

FileMaker's Sixth Sense: Crow's Feet

I haven't done anything to tell FileMaker what kind of relationships I created. How does it know where to put the crow's feet?

You never have to tell FileMaker about the types of relationships because it doesn't really matter. The work FileMaker performs to deal with a one-to-many relationship is no different from what it does for a one-to-one, so it doesn't care about the distinction.

However, it's useful to you as the database designer to know what kind of relationships you have. (It helps you decide whether an invoice should have room for one line item or a whole list of them, for example.) FileMaker tries its best to figure out where the crow's feet go, as a special

service to you. It assumes every end of every line needs a crow's foot unless it finds evidence to the contrary.

Such evidence includes:

- The field used in the relationship is a serial number.

- The field used in the relationship has the Unique validation option turned on.

A line that connects to a field that meets either of these conditions does *not* have a crow's foot. Since all your primary keys are serial numbers, FileMaker has no trouble figuring out where to leave off the crow's feet.

Figure 7-22:
You have as many ways to arrange a Relationship Graph as there are FileMaker developers. Here the graph is arranged very much like the ER diagram back in Figure 7-10. The benefit of this arrangement is that you can see how your database fits together at a glance. Plus, the table occurrences are arranged in logical groupings (Invoices, Line Items, and Payments; Customers and Jobs; Timeslips, and Expenses).

Note: If you have a stray table occurrence (named the same as the database itself) on your relationships graph, just select it, and then press Delete. It's a useless artifact from the table you deleted when you first added tables to this file. Since this table occurrence isn't part of your ER diagram, you can safely ignore FileMaker's protestations that deleting it will break things.

Selection tools

The relationship graph has a few selection tricks that make life easier. To help with selecting an entire group of connected objects, you can select just one. Then click the select tool (Figure 7-23), and choose "Select related tables 1-away". FileMaker automatically adds every table that's directly connected to this one to your current selection. You can choose this same command again to extend the selection one more notch on the graph.

If you have multiple table occurrences that have the same underlying base table (you'll learn why on page 356), then choose "Select tables with same source table" from the Select tool instead. FileMaker highlights all the table occurrences that match those you've selected.

DON'T PANIC

Lost and Found Again

You may not see table occurrences in the relationships graph for all the tables you create. Remain calm. You have all the right table occurrences; you just can't see them all at once. Chances are you just need to scroll the graph to the right. Unfortunately, it can be tricky to drag between two fields if you can't get them both on the screen at once. (You can do it, mind you. When you approach the edge of the graph while dragging, FileMaker automatically starts scrolling. It's just a little tedious.)

If you have a big enough computer screen, then you can simplify things by making the entire window bigger by dragging the bottom-right corner. If you still can't fit everything in, even when the window is as big as it can get, then you can zoom out on the window. Click the "Shrink to Fit" button (you can see all the tools mentioned in this box in Figure 7-23) and FileMaker shrinks everything so it all fits on the graph at once. In this reduced view, you can still drag relationships. When you're ready to see things full-size again, in the Zoom Level box, just type 100, and then press Tab.

(Don't press Enter or Return after changing the zoom level, or FileMaker thinks you meant to click the OK button and closes the Manage Database window. If you do close it accidentally, then just choose File → Manage Database again.)

You can zoom in on certain parts of the graph with the zoom in tool. First, click the tool (Figure 7-23), and then click anywhere in the graph. Use the zoom out tool instead if you want to zoom back out again. Unlike the zoom controls on a database window, these controls don't let you zoom in past 100 percent, but you can zoom way out—to 1 percent if you want. At that level, your tables are reduced to undifferentiated go in the corner of the graph.

When you're done zooming, be sure to choose the selection tool again so you can drag relationships or table occurrences.

Arrange the graph

The table occurrences in the graph behave like layout objects in Layout mode. You can Shift-click or rubber band several to select them all. You can even press Ctrl+A (⌘-A) to select *all* the table occurrences. Just click into empty space on the graph to deselect. Once you have some selected, you can use the arrange tools to line them up. Figure 7-23 shows them close up.

Figure 7-23:
The first group of tools helps you create and edit table occurrences. When you select more than one table occurrence, the second set, which consists of alignment tools, becomes available. The tiny triangle in the bottom-right corner shows that you can choose how the tool behaves. You have standard zoom tools, and printing tools for seeing the graph on paper.

Once you've dragged a few table occurrences around on your graph, it can look pretty sloppy. Here's how to use the tools to inflict some order on the graph:

- The **arrange vertically** tool lets you choose whether to align the left edges, centers, or right edges of any highlighted table occurrences.

- The **arrange horizontally** tool lets you align the top edges, centers, or bottom edges of the highlighted table occurrences.

- The **distribute** tool makes the space between selected table occurrences uniform. You can choose horizontal or vertical distribution.

- The **resize** tool makes short work of getting those manually resized table occurrences back in parade dress. Select some table occurrences, and then click the resize tool to tell FileMaker whether you want all the highlighted table occurrences resized to the smallest width or height, the largest width or height, or both (as in both height and width, not both smallest and largest, as cool as that would be).

Color your table occurrences

You can change the color of any selected table occurrence(s), using a standard color pop-up menu. It looks just like the one you saw on page 176 when you learned about coloring layout objects. Adding color to table occurrences doesn't affect the database's behavior at all. It's just there to help you organize your graph. (Organizing the graph becomes more important once you start to add more power to your database.)

Adding notes

You can add comments about the graph with the Note tool. Just select the tool, and then drag on the graph to create the note. The Edit Note dialog box appears (Figure 7-24). Type the text of the note and set its font, size, text, and background colors. If you want to edit a note, then double-click it, and the dialog reappears, ready to do your bidding.

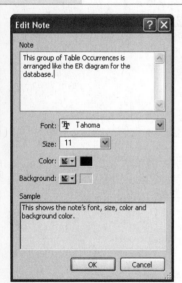

Figure 7-24:
When you use the Note tool (it looks like the text tool in Layout mode: a big letter A), FileMaker shows you the Edit Note dialog box. You can pick font, size, and color, and type any text you want. When you click OK, the note appears on the graph, and you can drag it around, resize it, or use the alignment tools much like you do your table occurrences. You can see the note itself in Figure 7-25.

Printing the graph

Last but not least, FileMaker offers some tools to help you print the graph. Since the graph is a roadmap to your tables, some people like to print it and tape it up beside the computer for quick reference while building layouts. Figure 7-26 shows how to lay out the graph so you can print without surprises.

Figure 7-25:
The Note tool lets you place floating notes anywhere on your graph. Make detailed notes about individual tables, or make them as wide as the graph, with a few words describing what kind of data is in the table occurrences directly underneath. Notes always appear under a table occurrence, so you can even put one behind a set of TOs as a visual grouping.

Figure 7-26:
Before you print, you want to see how the graph will fit on the page. First, click the Page Breaks button to show page-break lines on the graph. (If you can't see all your table occurrences clearly, zoom out as necessary.) To change paper orientation or size, click the Print Setup (Page Setup) button.

Deleting relationships

If you accidentally connect the wrong fields, or decide you don't want a relationship you already created, then you can easily delete it. Just click the relationship line itself to select it. Then click the Delete Relationship button or press the Delete key on the keyboard. (Refresh your memory about selected relationship lines with Figure 7-19.) When you select a relationship line, several things happen. The line thickens, the box in the middle changes color, and the Edit Relationship tool becomes available. Once the line is selected, you can delete it by clicking the Trash can icon, or simply pressing the Delete key.

Finishing the Field Definitions

Now that your relationships are in place, you can add the rest of the fields to your tables. Since you already know how to create fields, there's no need to bore you with the gory details. Below is a list of all the fields needed to complete this database.

Note: To save time, you can find the completed database with all fields in place on the Missing CD page at *http://missingmanuals.com/cds*. If you choose the readymade option, then you can skip ahead to page 332 and start learning how to use a relational database.

Customers table fields

Create the following fields in the Customers table:

- A text field called First Name
- A text field called Last Name
- A text field called Company Name
- A text field called Street Address
- A text field called City
- A text field called State
- A text field called Zip Code
- A text field called Phone Number
- A text field called Email Address

Jobs table fields

In the Jobs table, you need only one more field: a text field called Name. Of course, you can call this field Job Name, so that you can tell at a glance what table it comes from. But in FileMaker such redundancy is unnecessary. Almost everywhere the program shows field names, it includes the table occurrence name as well—*Jobs::Name*, for example. The exception, inexplicably, is Layout mode, where related fields look like this: *::Name*. You can always double-click a field to see where it comes from, but that gets boring after about the 79th time. To spare yourself the tedium, you have permission to change any field names listed here.

Expenses table fields

The Expenses table needs three new fields:

- A text field called Expense
- A number field called Amount
- A text field called Company Name

Timeslips table fields

Timeslips also needs three fields:

- A timestamp field called Date Time

- A number field called Duration

- A text field called Work Description

Note: You may be tempted to call the Date Time field *Date and Time* instead, but if you try to do it, File-Maker sternly warns you against putting the word "and" in a field name. You can create fields that break the naming rules, but you have to jump through hoops to use them in calculations (Chapter 9). It isn't usually worth the hassle. Pick a safe name instead.

Invoices table fields

The Invoices table is easy, too, with just three new fields:

- A date field called Date (as in the date of the invoice)

- A date field called Date Due

- A number field called Total Due

Line Items table fields

Add four new fields to the Line Items table:

- A text field called Description

- A number field called Price Each

- A number field called Quantity

- A number field called Extended Price

Payments table fields

The payments table is easy, too, with just three new fields:

- A date field called Date (as in the payment date)

- A number field called Amount

- A text field called Type

- A text field called Reference Code (this holds a check number, direct deposit transaction number, Credit Card transaction ID, or other appropriate value)

In the Manage Database window, click OK, and FileMaker shows you your database. After all that work, the result is wholly uninspiring; it looks exactly like the single-table database you already created. But take a peek at the Layouts pop-up menu (or Figure 7-27). Surprise: FileMaker has made *several* layouts for you—one for each table occurrence on your relationship graph. At this point, everything you know about using a FileMaker database still applies. The only difference is that each layout is attached to a different table.

Figure 7-27:
When your database has multiple tables, FileMaker still makes plain Jane layouts for you—it just makes more of them. Remember, you can always review Chapter 4 for advice on beautifying layouts.

Relational Databases

The essence of a relational database is its multiple tables. Now you need to learn how multiple tables affect the FileMaker concepts with which you're familiar: editing records, finding records, and building layouts.

One Table Occurrence, One Found Set

The most important thing you should understand when using a multitable database is that each layout sees the entire database from a different perspective. You'll want to do a little exploration to see this concept in action. A layout is attached to an occurrence on the graph, and that's how it sees the world. This means when you're looking at a record on the Customers layout, you're seeing a customer. If you switch to Table view (View → "View as Table"), then you see a list of customers. You don't see payments at all. To see those, you need to use the Layout pop-up menu (or choose View → "Go to Layout" → Payments) to switch to the Payments layout.

Since each table holds different data, the concept of a found set changes a little as well. When you do a find, the layout you're on determines which table FileMaker searches. Your newfound set is associated with that table occurrence, too. Just like when you had only a single table, the found set stays the same until you perform another find, or you tell FileMaker to show you all the records for that table occurrence (Records → "Show all records"). But if you switch to a different layout (one tied to a different table occurrence), your found set no longer applies.

For example, if you find the six customers from Texas, and then switch to the Expenses layout, you won't have six records in your found set anymore. Instead, you have a separate *Expenses* found set. Switch back to Customers, and you see the six Texans again. FileMaker remembers one found set for each table occurrence. It also remembers the *current record* for each table occurrence, so if you switch to a different layout, and then come back, then you're still on the same record that was active when you left that layout.

Of course, you can have more than one layout attached to the same table occurrence— Customer List and Customer Detail, for example. The found set and current record are associated with the *table occurrence*, not the layout, so a find on the Customer List layout affects the found set on the Customer Detail layout.

Note: If you want more than one found set or current record in the same table occurrence, then you can use multiple windows, just like you learned on page 40.

If you want to see two kinds of records side by side, you can create a new window (Window → New Window), and then switch one of them to a different layout.

Viewing Related Fields

Having each table occurrence completely segregated from the rest on its own layout is a good starting place, because you probably want separate lists of all your entities, but it's hardly ideal for a fully functional database. After all, if you want to view everything separately, you can create individual databases.

So think of the layouts FileMaker made for you as starting points from which you'll put those relationships to work. For starters, you'd like to show the customer name when you view a Job record. But the Job table doesn't have a Customer Name field. Instead, you'll use the fields from the Customers table, and let FileMaker find the correct *related* data using the relationships you created.

1. **In the Jobs layout, choose View → Layout Mode.**

   For a refresher course on Layout Mode, see Chapter 4.

2. **In the Status toolbar, use the Field tool and drag a new field onto the layout, somewhere below the existing fields. Or you can choose Insert → Field, if you don't mind not having as much control over where the field lands.**

   When you release the mouse button, the Specify Field dialog box appears, so you can choose the field you want.

3. **In the Specify Field dialog box, click the Table Occurrence pop-up menu (see Figure 7-28).**

   Here's where you venture into unfamiliar waters. This menu lets you pick any table occurrence on your graph.

4. **Choose Customers from the pop-up menu, and then, from the field list, select the First Name field. Click OK.**

   FileMaker adds the Customers::First Name field to the layout. It just says "::First Name" on the layout, but it does belong to the Customers table occurrence.

Note: If you forget which table occurrence a field comes from, just double-click it. The Field/Control dialog box reappears, and you can read the source table from the "Display data from" bit. Just make sure you dismiss the dialog box without making any changes. To be safe, click Cancel.

Figure 7-28:
The Specify Field window has always had a Table Occurrence pop-up menu; you've just been told to ignore it until now. This menu shows a list of all the table occurrences on the graph. FileMaker is smart enough to know which ones are related from the current layout's perspective. It breaks the list into two groups: related tables and unrelated tables. Right now you don't have any unrelated tables because the entire graph is connected in one group.

5. Change the field label FileMaker created for the new field to *Customer First Name*. Then, add the Customers::Last Name field to the layout too.

More information is better to help you remember what these fields are for.

When you're finished, switch back to Browse mode, saving your layout changes when prompted. In Browse mode, the new field doesn't look all that impressive yet. That's because you don't have any data in your database. Time to fix that.

Adding or Editing Data with Relationships

You really see the magic of relationships once you add some data and let File-Maker start making connections. Start with some customers. Open your database, and then go to the Customers layout.

1. If the status area shows there are no records, choose Records → New Record.

FileMaker creates one record for you automatically, but only in the first table you added. Unless you happened to create this table *first*, you need a new Customer record.

2. Name this customer Francis Capra by filling out the First Name and Last Name fields. Then, create a second customer record with the name Logan Echolls.

Notice that FileMaker has already filled in the Customer IDs for you—*1* and *2*. Time to add a job or two.

3. Switch to the Jobs layout, and, if necessary, create a new record. In the Name field, type *Find the Missing Cash*.

Now you have one job record, but it isn't attached to a customer yet, so the customer name fields are empty.

Note: If you try clicking in the Customer First Name field right now, then you get another surprise: File-Maker doesn't let you. It *looks* like a field, it *smells* like a field, but it doesn't *work* like a field. You're seeing the First Name field from the related Customer record, but there's no related customer record. No record, no field: no click.

4. **In the Customer ID field, type *2*, and then press Tab.**

The 2, if you recall, is the ID of the second Customer record you added. By putting 2 in this field, you tell FileMaker that's the Customer record this job record relates to. Or, in English, that's the customer for whom you're doing this job. As soon as you leave the Customer ID field, FileMaker goes to work finding the correct Customer so it can show you his name. Like magic, only better.

Note: Making different records connect by key might seem really tedious in this example. You'll learn many techniques for streamlining this process later in this chapter.

Editing Related Data

To see how editing works in a relational database, add another Job record. Using the same steps as above, name it "Find Lynn", and attach it to Customer 2 as well. It should then show the same customer name. Now try this:

1. **Change the value in the Customer First Name field on the Job layout to *Trina*.**

Now the Find Lynn job is attached to "Trina Echolls". But who's the "Find the Missing Cash" job attached to?

2. **Switch to the first Job record using the book icon in the status area.**

Drum roll…"Find the Missing Cash" is Trina Echolls', too.

3. **Switch to the Customers layout, and then switch to the first record.**

Ta da! The customer record itself *also* now says Trina Echolls.

If you don't think that's cool, you need your geek level adjusted. You can now change this customer record back to Logan Echolls. It will, of course, be corrected on the Job layout as well.

You've seen a *relational* database in action. From a Job record, you can view data from the related Customer record. You can even edit that customer data directly from the Job record. The power of a relational database is all about working directly with related data like this, instead of copying information back and forth.

Warning: While this sort of thing is cool to see in action, in practice it's usually a bad idea to edit Customer data from the Jobs layout. To protect your data so it doesn't get changed out of context, set the related field's behavior so that it can't be entered in Browse mode. Switch to Layout mode, and then choose Format → Field/Control → Behavior (page 160).

Portals

Adding the customer name field to the Job layout makes good sense because a job is attached to exactly *one* customer (it's a one-to-one relationship). But what if you want to go the other way? Suppose you put the Job::Name field on the Customers layout. How would that work since a customer can have more than one job? (In fact, Logan Echolls has *two* jobs right now.)

This question has two answers. The less interesting answer is that you can go right ahead and put that field on the Customers layout if you want. It works fine. Since FileMaker can't show two values in one field, it just shows the *first* related record—in this case, Find the Missing Cash. (You can try for yourself if you want.)

The more interesting answer is *portals*. A portal is a layout object that lets you view, edit, and even delete multiple related records. The portal shows a list of records from a related table right on the layout. It can show as many rows (records) as you want, and you can even add a scroll bar so you can scroll through lots of related records in a small space. You can also edit related field data right inside the portal. When you add a portal to your layout, you get to decide which records it shows, how they're sorted, and what the portal looks like. For example, you can add a border to your portal, or change each row's background color.

(See the box on page 340 for details on all the options available for portals.) The Customers table has a to-many relationship to Jobs, so it's a perfect candidate for a portal.

The following steps take you through an example in the Customers database:

1. **In the Customers layout, switch to Layout mode. Drag to expand the Body part a few inches.**

   The Customers layout is where you'll do a lot of data entry and management, so make plenty of room for your portal.

2. **In the Status toolbar, click the Portal tool.**

   You can see what it looks like in Figure 7-29.

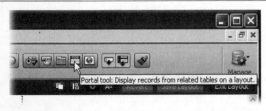

Figure 7-29:
The Portal tool is the one Layout mode tool you've never used. It works like the Shape and Button tools. Select it first, and then, on the layout, drag a rectangle. FileMaker creates a new portal inside that rectangle.

3. In the space below the Customer fields, drag a large rectangle. Don't worry too much about the size; you can always resize the portal later if you don't get it right the first time.

When you release the mouse, FileMaker displays the Portal Setup dialog box. It's displayed in Figure 7-30.

Figure 7-30:
In the Portal Setup dialog box, you can choose which table you want to show records from and how those records should be sorted. You can also decide which related records to show, and adjust the look of the portal. The last checkbox option, "Reset scroll bar when exiting record", is available only after you select "Show vertical scroll bar". This reset option, sometimes called portal pop, *can be disorienting when you have a highlighted row way down in the portal, because when you click out of the portal, it resets to show the first rows. See the box on page 340 for more info on other portal options.*

4. From the "Show related records from" pop-up menu, choose Jobs.

You're telling FileMaker to show data from the Jobs table occurrence—in this case, all the Jobs for the customer. Here's how it works: Whenever FileMaker looks at a related table occurrence (Jobs in this case), it *always* sees it from the perspective of the current layout. Working from the Customers layout, File-Maker looks at Jobs related to the customer. You could say that the Customers table is your current *context*. The idea of context is sometimes confusing, but it's important, and you'll encounter it throughout this book.

5. Turn on the "Sort portal records" checkbox. In the Sort dialog box that appears, add the Name field to the Sort Order list, and then click OK.

When FileMaker shows Job records for a customer, they're sorted alphabetically by job name.

6. Turn on "Allow deletion of portal records".

With this option turned on, you can delete records in the Jobs table right from the Customers layout, saving yourself a trip to the Layout pop-up menu.

7. Turn on "Show vertical scroll bar".

A portal has a fixed size on the layout. If you have more records than fit in the allotted space, two things can happen: It can either ignore the additional related records, or you can put a scroll bar on the portal. With a scroll bar, you can view all the related jobs, no matter how many exist.

8. **Turn on "Reset scroll bar when exiting record".**

    If you've scrolled way down in a lengthy list of related records, the first records don't show up anymore, naturally. By selecting this option, you're telling the portal to go back to the first record anytime you click out of (or exit) the portal.

9. **Click OK.**

    The "Add Fields to Portal" window takes the Portal Setup window's place. From here, you get to pick which fields from the job table should be displayed in the portal.

10. **From the Available Field list, select the Name field, and then click Move.**

    FileMaker adds Jobs::Name to the Included fields list. Click OK again.

Your layout now has a portal. It looks like the one in Figure 7-31.

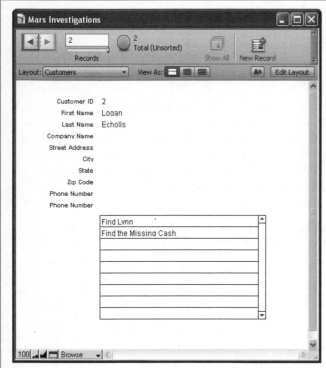

Figure 7-31:
Every portal is made up of rows. The more rows a portal shows, the more related records you can see at one time. Or you can use a scroll bar to save space. In this example, the portal row contains only a single field, but a row can have other layout objects, like buttons or graphics, inside it. In Layout mode, each portal shows what table occurrence it's associated with, and which rows it shows. You can double-click a portal to review the Portal Setup dialog box for more detail or to change the portal's settings.

Editing data through a portal

Switch to Browse mode to see your portal in action. If you look at Logan Echolls' record, then you see both his jobs listed in the portal. Like any related field, you can click into either Job Name field and edit its data. When you do, the Job record itself is updated.

You can also delete records through the portal. In the portal, click the Find Lynn row. When you do, you'll either enter the field itself or select the portal row. Figure 7-32 shows the difference.

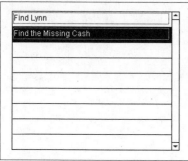

Figure 7-32:
When you click a portal row, one of two things happens. If you click into an enterable field, then you go right into that field, just as if the field were local to the layout. You would say you're on the second portal row, and in the Jobs:: Name field. If you click in a portal row outside a field, then you select the portal row instead–the entire row highlights as shown here. You're still on the second portal row, but you're not in any field this time.

When you're on a portal row, the Delete Record command takes on new meaning. If you have an entire portal row selected, FileMaker assumes you want to delete the *related* record—the one in the portal—not the so-called *master* record (the Customer record in this case). If you're in a field on the portal row when you choose the command, then FileMaker asks you instead which record you want to delete: the Master record or the Related record. Figure 7-33 shows each message.

Figure 7-33:
Top: If you select a portal row, the Delete Record command deletes the related record.

Bottom: If you're in a field on the portal row when you choose the command, you get this message instead. This time you get to pick which record is deleted. Click Master to delete the Customer record, and Related to delete the Job record.

If you're not on a portal row, the Delete Record command works exactly like it does on a layout that has no portals.

You've covered a lot of ground in this chapter. You now have a full-fledged relational database, and a good idea of how it works. But manually typing arcane customer numbers into foreign key fields and bouncing from layout to layout to add a job is not your idea of efficiency. In the next chapter you'll learn how to harness *all* the power of the FileMaker features you've learned so far: Value lists, field formats, buttons, and additional relationship options all combine to make data entry a breeze, even in a complex database with several tables.

UP TO SPEED

Portal Power

In Figure 7-30, you learned a little about how the Portal Setup dialog box works. Now it's time to dig a little deeper.

To see the settings for your portal, in Layout mode, select it, and then choose Format → Portal. (A double-click on the portal itself gets you there, too.) Portals work a lot like repeating fields. The main differences are:

- Portals work with related data, which is the way the database gods intended multiple values to be stored. In other words, portals aren't troublemakers like repeating fields.

- Portals can have a scroll bar. Got 326 items on that invoice? No problem.

- Each row in a portal can hold more than one field. In addition to the Job Name, you could show the Job Start Date if you had one. Adding objects to a portal is a breeze: In Layout mode, just drag them into the first row. When you add a field, FileMaker shows its correct value on each portal row. You can also add lines, shapes, pictures, and even buttons. You'll do some of this in the next chapter, and you'll learn how to troubleshoot when the data isn't showing up correctly.

In addition to these differences, portals have more options affecting the way they look and work. As you've already seen, you can tell FileMaker to sort the records in a portal. Whenever you view the Customers layout, for example, the job list is sorted alphabetically.

This option has no effect on the sort order of the records on the Jobs layout. It just sorts the Jobs portal in the Customers

layout. You can even put another Jobs portal on a different layout, and set it to use a different sort order.

You can also assign an "Alternate background fill" to a portal. This fill works just like its counterpart in the Part Setup dialog box. When you turn it on, every even-numbered portal row has a different background color and pattern. You can make every other row green, for example. The *odd* numbered rows have whatever background color you assign to the portal itself on the layout.

Finally, portals have the same partitioning power as repeating fields. Normally, a portal starts with the first related record (which record that is, exactly, depends on the sort order assigned to the portal). If you change the "Initial row" value, though, then the portal skips some rows. For example, if you put 5 in this text box, the portal shows rows 5 through 14 instead of records 1 through 9.

If it suits your needs, you can put the same portal on your layout more than once, and give it different initial rows. Your layout could show the first five jobs in one column, and jobs 6 through 10 in a second column, for instance. Portals also have special auto-resize powers (page 168).

If you make a portal grow vertically, you get to decide whether FileMaker *adds more rows* or just *makes each row bigger*. Here's the trick: If anything *in* the portal is anchored on the bottom, then the portal rows get bigger. Otherwise, FileMaker keeps the rows the same size, and adds more as necessary.

Advanced Relationship Techniques

FileMaker Pro 10 was built to work with related data and make it seem easy. In the last chapter you learned that related fields work just like ordinary fields. Not only can you put them on layouts, but you can use them in Find mode and the Sort dialog box too.

In this chapter you'll learn how to take advantage of FileMaker's relational capabilities. You'll learn how to create related records and make value lists from those related records. Once you have related tables, you'll want to move quickly between them. FileMaker gives you extra organizing power by letting you create multiple versions of your related tables, so you can keep your complex relationship graphs clear.

Creating Related Records

The first thing you probably noticed with the database you worked on in Chapter 7 is that getting the records to relate is a tedious affair. To add a job record, for example, you had to go to the Customers layout, copy the Customer ID, and then go to the Jobs layout, add the record, and paste in the ID. That's a pain. Since File-Maker is all about relieving the pain of working with databases, it gives you a better way—a couple of better ways, in fact. In the last chapter you learned how to use a portal to *display* related records. Here you'll learn how a portal can also *create* related records. But first, you'll learn how to create a value list to help you enter appropriate data into a key field.

Value Lists Based on Fields

You've already seen value lists based on field values—on page 114, you attached a value list to the City field to make sure users enter only valid state names. In a relational database, valid data entry is even more critical, since relationships work only when the key fields in each table match. You can use a value list in the table on the "to-many" side of a relationship to make sure that the key field in the table on the "one" side of the relationship accepts only valid key values. Good database design is all about this kind of up-front work that makes for easy data entry and consistent relationships between records. To create a value list that ensures the entry of valid Customer ID numbers in your Mars Investigations database, just follow these steps:

Tip: You can download this chapter's sample databases from the Missing CD page at *http://missingmanuals.com/cds*.

---

1. **In the Mars Investigations database, choose File → Manage → Value Lists, and then click New.**

   Name your new value list *All Customers*. Since you're likely to have lots of value lists in a finished database, descriptive names help you keep things straight.

2. **Click the "Use values from field" radio button.**

   When you click this radio button, the "Specify Fields for Value List" window appears. (You can see an example in Figure 8-1.)

3. **In the pop-up menu under "Use values from first field", choose Customers.**

   Way back in the dark ages, when you had only one table, FileMaker put that table in the pop-up menu for you. Now that you have multiple tables, you get to choose which table you want.

4. **In the list of fields, select Customer ID.**

   Customer ID is the key field that relates a Job record to a specific Customer record, so you'll use that field to make sure the information entered is accurate.

5. **Turn on the "Also display values from second field" checkbox. Then, from the right-hand field list, choose First Name.**

   To avoid having to remember Customer IDs, display another field value, so that you can more easily find the Customer ID. The second field's data won't be entered into the field, though—it's just for show.

Note: Of course, showing first *and* last name is the best way to find the right customer, but the dialog box lets you pick only one field. See page 401 for a calculation that lets you show the first and last name in one field.

---

6. **In the "Sort values using" radio button set, turn on the "Second field" option.**

After all, you probably prefer a list of customers in alphabetical order to one ordered by ID. Figure 8-1 shows the proper settings for this dialog box.

7. **Click OK in each dialog box until you're back on the Customer layout.**

Your value list is now defined, but FileMaker isn't displaying it anywhere yet. Read on to see how to apply the list to a field.

Figure 8-1:
In the "Specify Fields for Value List" window, the "Use values from field" option gives your value lists shape-shifting power: Instead of a dull list that never changes, your value lists automatically update as your data changes. So if you add a new customer, then she automatically shows up in the All Customers value list without any further work on your part. Or if you delete a customer, she doesn't appear in the value list any more.

Now that you've created the value list, you need to attach it to the Customer ID field on the Jobs layout. To do that, you need to go to the Jobs layout

1. **Switch to the Jobs layout, and then go to Layout mode. Select the Customer ID field, and then choose Format → Field/Control → Setup.**

The Field/Control Setup dialog box appears.

2. **In the "Display as" pop-up menu, choose Pop-up Menu.**

The pop-up menu looks like menu choices you see in most dialog boxes. (You could use a Drop-down List instead if you want, as discussed on page 243.)

3. **From the "Display values from" pop-up menu, choose All Customers.**

The menu displays your value lists alphabetically (but there's only one now).

4. **Click OK, and then switch back to Browse mode.**

The field's appearance changes to show that it's now a pop-up menu instead of an Edit Box.

Note: The "Show values only from second field" option is really handy when you're using the value list to enter key field values, and you don't want people to be confused by a number that might not mean much to them. They see only the value in the second field, even though the field really stores the key value.

Back in Browse mode, click the Customer ID field, and you get a list of customers to choose from. You can see it in Figure 8-2.

Figure 8-2:
Here's the Jobs layout with its new Pop-up Menu field. To attach a job to a customer, from a pop-up menu, select the CustomerID. When you do, FileMaker places the ID of the customer you choose in the Jobs::Customer ID field for you. The name appears in the pop-up menu to help you pick the right ID.

POWER USERS' CLINIC

Related Value Lists

On page 342, you saw how to make value lists that change when you add, edit, or delete records in a table. You can also decide whether the list includes values from every record in the table, or only from the related records. You start creating both types of value lists the same way: You choose a field to base the value list on, and then tell File-Maker whether you want to use values from a second field in the value list (you can even use a related field for the second value). Like regular field-based lists, you can sort the list by the first field or the second one.

But when the "Include only related values" radio button is turned on, the value list behaves differently. The list shows only the records related to the one you're sitting on. For example, you can use this option to show only a specific customer's Job IDs if you needed to choose a Job ID on an

Invoice table. For this method to work, FileMaker has to know which table occurrence you're coming *from*. In other words, if you ask for only the related Jobs, do you mean jobs related to the Customer record or to the Invoice record? It can get confusing, but in this example, you want to use the jobs that are already related to the Customer table. That way, the list's values change if you change the Invoice's Customer ID.

Careful, though: When you create a value list using related values only, the list works properly when it's attached to a field on a layout associated with the same table occurrence selected in this menu. If you try to use it on a different layout, then FileMaker doesn't know which record to start from, and the value list doesn't show the right values.

Creating Related Records Through a Portal

As a database designer, you have to think about how and where (on which layout) data gets entered. Sometimes choosing a related record's primary key from a menu doesn't make sense. The Invoices and Line Items tables illustrate this scenario. To use the pop-up menu you just created in Jobs, you have to add it to the Line Items layout. In that scenario, here's how you create an invoice:

1. Create the invoice record.

2. Go to the Line Items layout.

3. Add every line item, choosing the correct invoice ID each time.

Again, FileMaker has a better way. Portals do more than just show related records, as long as the relationship lets you *create* related records. This method's first benefit is that you don't have to leave the Invoice layout to enter all the line items you need. Second, when you create the related records without leaving the Invoice layout, FileMaker automatically adds the correct Invoice ID to each line item for you.

Preparing the relationship

When you first drag a relationship into existence in the relationships graph, it starts off pretty plain-vanilla. But you can set three special properties to make your workflow more efficient. You get to set whether a relationship lets FileMaker create or delete related records, and whether it sorts those records before it displays them. To make these changes, visit the Edit Relationship dialog box:

1. **In the Mars Investigations database, choose File → Manage → Database. If necessary, click the Relationships tab.**

   FileMaker remembers which tab you were in the last time you were here, so Relationships may already be selected.

2. **Select the relationship between Invoices and Line Items table occurrences.**

   Click the = sign in the middle of the line for an easy target.

3. **Click the Edit Relationship button (see Figure 8-3).**

   The Edit Relationship dialog box appears, as shown in Figure 8-4. (You can also double-click a relationship to open this box, saving the trip to the button.)

Note: If you're wondering why the Invoices table is on the right and the Line Items are on the left, it's because that's how you arranged those table occurrences on the graph (if your graph looks like Figure 7-22). But if you prefer seeing the "one" side of the relationship on the left with the "many" side on the right, then move your table occurrences accordingly. But see page 367 first, to see another way to arrange the graph.

Figure 8-3:
The Tables/Relationships tools (at the left) open the dialog boxes where most of the relationship work in this chapter is done. You can always back out of your mistakes…er, experiments by clicking the Trash can. The Arrange group let you arrange, align, and resize table occurrences. The Tools group shows the selection arrow, the Notes creation tool, and the zooming tools. The Pages tools show page breaks and the Page Setup dialog box. If a tool is grayed out, then you must select one or more table occurrences or other objects before you can use it.

Figure 8-4:
The Edit Relationship dialog box lets you refine your relationships. Here you see two sets of checkboxes: The set on the right pertains to the Invoices table occurrence (you can see its name above the checkboxes). The set of checkboxes on the left affects the Line Items table occurrence. In either case, you can set the relationship's automatic create, delete, and sort capabilities.

4. **In the set of checkboxes under Line Items, turn on "Allow creation of records in this table via this relationship".**

Now if you put the Line Items::Description field on the Invoices layout, File-Maker lets you type in the field even when there's no related Line Item record. When you type, FileMaker immediately creates a new Line Item record for you, *and* automatically enters the correct value in its Invoice ID field to make the two records related.

Since a relationship goes in two directions, you get to pick from the same three options for *both* table occurrences involved in a relationship. However, you rarely want to set any of these options for the "one" side of the relationship. For example, it doesn't make sense to sort a single record from the "many" side, nor do you want to delete the "one" record if you need to delete just one of the "many" records.

Tip: To help you remember which side of the relationship to set options for, think of it this way: If you need a portal to display records through that relationship, then that's the side that gets the options.

---

5. **In the checkboxes under Line Items, turn on "Delete related records in this table when a record is deleted in the other table".**

With this option turned on, if you delete an Invoice record, then FileMaker automatically deletes all the related Line Item records for you. That's exactly what you want, since a Line Item without an Invoice is meaningless—techies call it an *orphaned* record.

6. **Click OK a couple of times to dismiss the Manage Database window.**

You've edited the relationship, but you need a portal to see the results.

Note: The Edit Relationship dialog box mimics the layout you've created on your relationships graph. That is, the Line Items TO is to the left of your Invoices TO in the graph, so that's how they appear in the dialog box. If two TOs are on top of one another (vertically aligned), then the table on top appears at the left of the dialog box. The order shown in these lists has no effect on how the TOs relate to one another, but if you're having trouble reading this dialog box, close it, rearrange your graph, and reopen it.

Adding a portal to a layout

So you've edited the relationship to let FileMaker create Line Item records from the Invoices layout. Now you're ready to fix up your Invoices layout to use that edited relationship, as shown in Figure 8-5.

After you draw a portal, FileMaker shows the Portal Setup dialog box so you can specify which data to show in it. Proceed as follows:

1. **On the Invoices layout, switch to Layout mode, and then use the portal tool to draw a large rectangle. You may need to expand the Body part to make room (see page 146).**

When you let go of the mouse, the "Portal Setup" dialog box appears.

CHAPTER 8: ADVANCED RELATIONSHIP TECHNIQUES

Cascading Deletes

The "Delete related records" option can be dangerous for a couple of reasons. First, if you turn it on accidentally, then you can find yourself in an odd situation: Records keep disappearing for no apparent reason. You'll get frustrated if you don't realize how this option works.

But even if you *want* it on, keep this fact in mind: FileMaker can't bring back a record you delete. It's one thing if someone accidentally deletes a Jobs record—you just have to look up the Job Name and enter it again, being careful to give the job the same ID it had before.

It's something else entirely if you also have Delete turned on in the Jobs-to-Customers relationship, and the Customers-to-Invoices relationship, and again in the Invoices-to-Line Items

relationship. You've set up the Towering Inferno scenario called *cascading deletes*. Because now, when you delete one job record—perhaps thinking that the job is finished and you don't need the record anymore—FileMaker also obeys your "hidden" instructions and deletes the Customer record attached to that Job record, *all* the Invoices attached to the Customer, and *all* his line items, too!

Some people decide it's not worth the risk and leave the delete option off even when it *should* be on. For a better solution to the cascading deletion problem, read up on security in Part 6.

Figure 8-5:
This layout shows a portal like the one created in the steps on page 336. It needs to be wide enough to hold four fields, and tall enough to show several rows. But you don't have to get it right the first time, because you can always resize and move the portal and fields. Use this illustration to tweak your layout, or let your own design sense run wild.

2. **From the "Show related records from" pop-up menu, choose Line Items.**

   Your new Invoice record needs some Line Items, so that's the table you'll display in this portal.

3. Select "Allow deletion of portal records" and "Show vertical scroll bar", and then click OK.

The "Add Fields to Portal" window appears.

4. **Add the fields Description, Price Each, Quantity, and Extended Price to the "Included fields" list.**

Under Available fields, notice the pop-up menu. Because you selected the Line Items relationship three steps ago, FileMaker shows you fields from that table. You can rearrange the fields by dragging the arrow to the left of the field name.

5. **Click OK.**

FileMaker adds your portal to the layout, and divides the available space among the four fields. See Figure 8-5 for a better arrangement.

You don't get field headings to help you see which field is which, and you may need to tweak the relative widths of your fields, but FileMaker's done the bulk of the work for you.

Tip: In the Portal Setup dialog box, the "Alternate background fill" option lets you add color and/or a fill pattern to every other row of your portal. A subtle color really helps make it easier to read across each line. Test colors on a variety of monitors and light conditions, so you don't end up making your data harder to read instead of easier.

FREQUENTLY ASKED QUESTION

How Do I Know Where to Sort?

In the last chapter I set the sort order for a portal when I was adding it to my layout. Now you're saying I can set the sort order in the relationship. What's the difference? Does it matter?

When you set a sort order in the Edit Relationship dialog box (Figure 8-4), it applies to the relationship itself. Any time you use that relationship, the sort order applies: in portals on any layout, when showing a single related field, and when finding a set of related records (that's covered in the next section).

A portal's sort order (page 337), on the other hand, applies only to the portal itself. If you don't tell the portal to sort, then FileMaker uses the relationship's sort order (or if there isn't one, the order in which the records were created) instead.

If you know that every time you look at your related data it should be shown in a specific order, then set the relationship to sort. But if you think the related data ought to be sorted different ways in different contexts (and thus in different portals), then don't sort the relationship because you add some overhead. FileMaker has to sort the records for the relationship, then sort them a different way for your portal. (You don't see this process happening, but FileMaker's doing it behind the scenes.) So when you're planning on viewing data in lots of different orders, rely on sorted portals instead of sorted relationships.

Adding records in a portal

Now that you've edited a relationship to allow the creation of related records, and provided a portal on the Invoice layout for viewing the records, you're ready to try out some auto-creation goodness:

1. **On the Invoice layout, switch to Browse mode.**

   The portal is empty because you have no line items. You probably don't have an invoice record yet either.

2. **If necessary, create a new record.**

   Once you have a record, you see that the four fields in the portal are ready for a click. You don't have a related record yet, but FileMaker is offering you the chance to create one.

3. **Click the first (left-most) field in the portal, and then type** *Investigate Lilly's red light incident.*

   As soon as you start typing, a *second* row of fields appears in the portal. That second row is FileMaker showing you that it's ready to make another new record for you. Figure 8-6 explains.

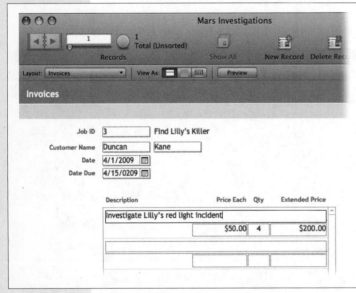

Figure 8-6:
In this example, a Job ID relates the Invoice to the proper job, and, almost as a bonus, to the proper Customer. See page 302 to find out more about how this works. Someone's just typed the first line item on the invoice. The cursor is standing at attention in the second row waiting for a new line item to be entered. As soon as you fill out any field on the first portal row, a second row appears, but FileMaker doesn't actually create another record until you type into at least one field in that new row.

You can fill out the remaining fields if you need the exercise. You can even add more line items: Just keep clicking into the last portal row. You can test the auto-deletion setting that you added in step 5 on page 347 by deleting the invoice you just created. When you do, the line item records should also go away. If you have two windows open, one showing the Invoice layout and another showing the Line Items layout, then you see this action happen live.

Note: The last portal row is *not* a new record until and unless you type something in it, and then commit the portal record. (See page 24 for a refresher on committing records.)

Of course, the Invoices to Line Items relationship isn't the only relationship in your database that can benefit from the use of portals. For an exercise in thinking like a designer, take a look at your relationships graph and think about where else you could put portals to make data viewing and record creation easier. There's no right or wrong answer. That's the beauty of FileMaker—you can use its tools to create virtually any system your business needs.

Navigating Between Related Records

With pop-up menus and auto-creating records, adding data to your new database is now a joy. But you still have to do some serious work to navigate the system. For example, if you're looking at an invoice and you want to see details about the related customer, you have to note the Customer ID, switch to the Customers layout, and then find the customer. That's two steps too many.

Simplify this process with a button (page 367) on the layout—one that uses the *Go to Related Record* command. This command (affectionately called GTRR by File-Maker gurus) does the obvious, plus a little more. It goes to the related record to be sure. But it also changes the layout appropriately, and it can find all the related records, and then sort them (if the relationship you're using has a sort specified). It can create a new window, while it's at it. That's a lot of work for one little command. If that weren't enough ways to use this little powerhouse, you can also set an option that includes the use of a found set.

Go to Related Record

Here's one way to create a button that activates the "Go to Related Record" command. In the Customers database, you already have people's names showing on a layout—just waiting to be made into buttons.

1. **Switch to the Jobs layout, and then go to Layout mode.**

   You always add buttons in Layout mode.

2. **Select the Customer Names merge fields.**

   The text looks like a link on a Web page. Since it's common knowledge that blue, underlined text is a link, you can use this graphical shortcut to "train" people to click on certain bits of text.

3. **With the text still selected, choose Format → Button Setup.**

   The Button Setup dialog box appears.

4. **From the list's Navigation section, select the "Go to Related Record" script step. When the Options section of the window appears, click its Specify button.**

   The "Go to Related Records" Options dialog box appears (Figure 8-7).

---

5. **From the "Get related record from" pop-up menu, choose Customers.**

   When you pick a table occurrence, you determine which table the button goes to. Notice that FileMaker shows you only the layouts that use the table occurrence you just selected.

6. **From the "Show record using layout" pop-up menu, choose Customers.**

   If you're going to a related record, it's usually from a different table occurrence. Your current layout can't show you related data, because it doesn't have the required fields. So you need to tell the button which layout to use.

Figure 8-7:
"Go To Related Record" options pack a powerful punch. If you turn on "Show in new window", then FileMaker leaves your current window alone and shows the related record(s) in a new window. "Show only related records" restricts the new found set to either the current record you're viewing or all the records in the new found set.

7. **Click OK, then OK again to return to your layout.**

   The button is ready to test.

Switch to Browse mode. Make sure you have a customer related to this job. If you don't, click the Customer ID field and choose one. When you assign a customer, your button works. Click the Customer's name and you're transported directly to that customer's record. Figure 8-8 shows what it looks like.

Tip: The "Use external table's layouts" option applies only when you're linking multiple *files* together. You'll learn about that later in this chapter.

GTRR with a found set

If you're looking at a customer record, then you can see all that customer's jobs because they're right there in the Jobs portal. But what if you want to see those jobs (and only those jobs) in a sorted list on the Jobs layout? It would take a bunch of steps if you had to do it manually. But the "Go to Related Record" command does all those steps for you—when you add a few new options to the mix.

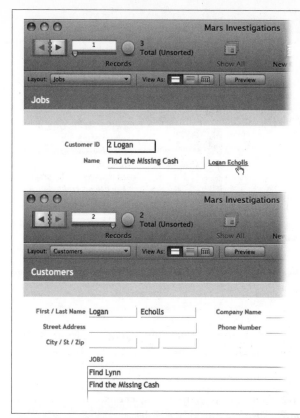

Figure 8-8:
*When you click the Customer Name (top), FileMaker
shows you that customer's record (bottom), due to the
power of the "Go to Related Record" command. Here
you can see all the records in the Customer table
because the "Show only related records" option was
not turned on. If you turn it on, you see a found set of
only one record–Logan Echoll's customer record.*

Auto-Creation Without a Portal

You don't have to have a portal to get automatic creation
of related records. Auto-creation works when you type in
any related field as long as the relationship is set up to
allow it. Suppose you have a one-to-one relationship with
one table for Bicycle Team Members and another for photos of the racers. Both tables have a Rider ID field, but only
the Riders::Rider ID field is a serial number. Finally, you tell
FileMaker to allow creation of related Photo records.

You might wind up with a database that looks like the one
shown in Figure 8-9. You have no portals in sight. (Who
needs them with just a one-to-one relationship?)

But since the relationship is set to auto-create Photo
records, you can Insert a new picture of the rider in the Picture field. FileMaker automatically creates the related
record for you.

If you don't have Auto-creation turned on, then you can't
click into the Picture field. FileMaker shows the dotted field
outline, but doesn't let you in.

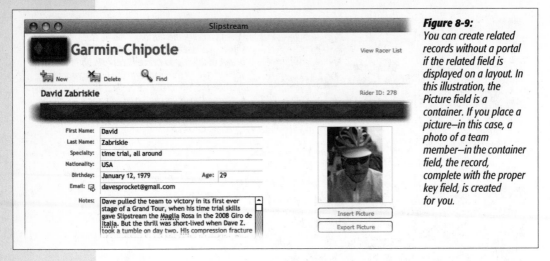

Figure 8-9:
You can create related records without a portal if the related field is displayed on a layout. In this illustration, the Picture field is a container. If you place a picture—in this case, a photo of a team member—in the container field, the record, complete with the proper key field, is created for you.

1. **On the Customers layout, switch to Layout mode, and then select the Jobs:: Name field.**

   It's the one in the jobs portal.

2. **Choose Format → Button Setup. In the Button Setup dialog box, from the list, select the "Go to Related Record" command, and then click Specify.**

   The "Go to Related Record" Options window pops up.

3. **From the "Get related record from" pop-up menu, choose Jobs. From the "Show record using layout" pop-up menu, choose Jobs.**

   You need a layout that shows you meaningful data from the Jobs table. So far, this process is just like creating a related record button without a found set. The next steps make all the difference.

4. **Turn on "Show only related records".**

   When you turn on "Show only related records", FileMaker changes the found set, showing just the related records. You land on the desired record, and you have all the other records in the found set. If the relationship has a sort order, FileMaker sorts the found set, too.

   For now, leave "Match current record only" turned on. (Selecting "Match all records in the current found set" lets you go from one found set of records to another. See the box on page 356 for more detail.)

5. **Click OK, and then OK again.**

   You're looking at your layout again.

6. **For good measure, make the Jobs::Name field blue and underlined. See page 156 for a refresher.**

   It's good to provide some kind of clue that the field is clickable.

Now you have a "Go to Related Record" button *in* a portal. Switch to Browse mode to see what happens. First, use the book icon to navigate to a customer record that has more than one related job. Click the *second* portal record. Since you're on the second row, the button takes you to the second record in your found set, not the first one. Then click the Customer name button again.

Note: If you didn't download the sample files, then you might not have any customers with multiple jobs. Just switch back to the Jobs layout and fix that: Attach a few jobs to one customer. Then go to the Customers layout again and find that customer.

As you switch back and forth, you can see another difference: The portal changes the button's context (Figure 8-10). That is, the records related in a portal are already a set, unlike the single field you made into a button in the previous tutorial. In other words, when you click the GTRR button on the Jobs layout, you expect to see only the single Customer that's related to your job. When you click the button in the Jobs portal, you get a found set of only the job records you just saw in the portal.

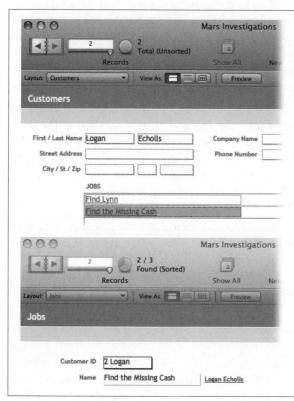

Figure 8-10:
The "Go to Related Record" command notices you're on the second portal row (top), and takes you to the second record accordingly (bottom). The Status toolbar lets you know that you're looking at a found set of two records–jobs related to Logan Echolls. To see Logan's other job, just use the book icon. You'll find going to a found set extremely useful if you use a layout that displays in List view, because you see all the related records in a list, with the specific record you clicked selected. In Part 5, you'll see how massively useful the "Go to Related Record" command is for all sorts of complex tasks.

GTRR On (Legal) Steroids

With the "Show only related records" option, you can use "Go to Related Record" to display a found set of records (from a related table) in a portal. But what if you want to do something really cool and complicated, like find a couple of invoices that don't have anything in common other than being unpaid, and somehow see the customer records in a set without performing a complicated search?

Here's how you do it: Make a button on your Invoice layout, and then give it a GTRR step that goes to the Customers table occurrence using the Customers layout.

Then, in the Options window, select "Show only related records" *and* "Match all records in current found set". Do a regular find to show Invoices from just Duncan and Logan—they're always late payers. You can omit Francis Capra, who pays as soon as he gets his invoice, thank you very much. Click the GTRR button to see a new found set in the Customer table that shows only Duncan's and Logan's records.

Apply GTRR (on steroids) liberally throughout your database, and people don't need to do as many complicated searches to find the data they're looking for.

Table Occurrences

In Chapter 7, you learned that a relationship graph doesn't really depict tables—it shows *table occurrences* (also known as *TOs*). TOs are just graphical representations of the underlying table. Because these occurrences are representations, you can make new occurrences of a table without duplicating it (and all its data). File-Maker's not trying to confuse you; it's actually helping you relate to the same table in different ways.

When you create a very simple database, you have only one table occurrence on the graph for each table, so you might be tempted to think of them as the tables themselves. But as you add new and more powerful features to your databases—and the relationships to make them work—sooner or later you'll need to graph the same table multiple times so you can keep everything straight.

Understanding Table Occurrences

Few databases can manage all their tasks without multiple occurrences of the same table. Your Mars Investigations database is no exception. Here's an example: Your database has an Expense table to record things you buy to service your customers. It also has a Line Items table to record what charges you pass along to your customers. Right now these tables are connected only by way of jobs. Figure 8-11 illustrates how your tables are currently related.

Even though there's no direct line between Expenses and Line Items, they *are* related, via Jobs, and then on to Invoices (you can read more about this concept, called Data Tunneling, on page 362). But as it is, you can't tell whether a particular Expense has been billed, or, if it has been billed, which Invoice Line Item bills it. Of course you *could* type some text into the Line Items::Description field to help

Figure 8-11:
Right now, your Relationships Graph still looks like your ER diagram. The Expenses, Timeslips, and Line Items tables are highlighted so you can see how they're connected. The only relationship between an expense (which you need to be reimbursed for) and a line item (which allows for reimbursement) is through the Jobs table, and then to the Invoices table.

you remember, but that wouldn't help FileMaker know how those two things are connected. You really need a whole new relationship—one that directly connects Expenses and Line Items. This new relationship lets you use "Go to Related Record" commands to toggle between expenses and invoices, for example. Your new relationship is "one-to-one." In other words, one Expense Line Item is related to one, and only one, Invoice Line Item.

One-to-one relationships are fairly rare birds. One example you've seen in this book is a table of bike racers and a photo of each rider, with a one-to-one relationship between each. This new one-to-one relationship—Expenses to Line Items—is even rarer, in that it connects two completely different *types* of data. It's also unusual in that it's not integral to your database's structure. Unlike the other relationships in this database, you could delete it and your system would still work just fine. This relationship exists for one purpose only: to give your database a new ability.

However, as Figure 8-12 shows, when you try to add that relationship to the existing graph, you create ambiguity in FileMaker's digital mind. Your Relationships Graph can be very complex, but you must have only one path from any table occurrence to another in the graph.

To create this new relationship and really make it work, you need three things:

• A new primary key (page 312) to hook the two tables together.

• A way to represent the new relationship in your relationship graph without throwing the whole thing into disarray. That's right—a new table occurrence.

There cannot be more than one relational path between any two tables in the graph. Another occurrence of one of the tables must be added to the graph.

Name of Occurrence: Line Items 2

Cancel   OK

Figure 8-12:
If you try to create a relationship directly between Expenses and Line Items, then FileMaker warns you that it can't be done—at least not with the existing table occurrences (TO). FileMaker tells you it needs a new occurrence of the table to resolve the ambiguity, and it even offers to make the new TO for you.

- New fields on one of your layouts (the Expenses layout in this case), to use the newly related data.

To put these new database elements into play, you need to acquire some new skills and learn new twists on some old ones. The next section covers the entire process.

Relationships with Table Occurrences

FileMaker doesn't require you to follow a set order when you create new table occurrences, relationships, and layouts. Sometimes you create a new layout thinking it's just for displaying a set of data and only later realize you need a new relationship—and a new table occurrence—to make it work. Fortunately, FileMaker makes it easy to switch modes so that you move freely from one part of the program to another, creating and arranging various bits and pieces to make your new features work. In this section, you'll create a new key field and a new table occurrence, and then add fields to a layout so you can assign invoice items to the proper expense item. The following sections take you through the process in one possible, and logical, order.

Adding a new key field to a table

Before you can hook up table. occurrences in a new way, you've got to make sure both tables have the proper key field for the new relationship. In this case, the Expenses table needs a Line Item ID. (See the box on the next page for more detail.)

In the Mars Investigations database, choose File → Manage Database, and then switch to the Fields tab and the Expenses table. Create a new number field called Line Item ID, and click OK when you're done. You'll use this new field to relate the Expenses table to Line Items.

Note: You may be tempted to create your new relationship now by dragging the new Line Item ID field to the Expenses table. In fact, you may have already tried that—and gotten a confusing error message. To figure out what you should do instead, see the box on page 363.

Putting New Keys in New Key Fields

I need to add a new key field to a table, but it's already got a lot of records in it. Since my serial numbers are created only when I create new records, am I stuck?

No, you're not. Lots of people need to "retrofit" key fields and add serial numbers after the data's already in a table. First, create a new field, and then give it the auto-enter serial number option. Put it on a layout that's tied to one of that table's table occurrences. If you have only one table occurrence for that table, so much the better—you don't have to make a choice.

Choose Records → Show All Records to make sure that all your records are in the found set. Then click in your new key field, and choose Records → Replace Field Contents. Select the "Replace with serial numbers" option. FileMaker figures that you'll have to do this stuff pretty regularly when

you're designing, so the values in the "Initial Value" and "Increment by" fields are already set correctly for this task. Select "Update serial number in Entry Options?" and then click the Replace button. FileMaker does the hard work of giving each record a unique serial number. It even updates the serial number so that the next *new* record you create has its own serial number. (See page 317 for the full story on creating key fields.)

So, in a pinch, you *can* go back and add key fields, and key field data, to tables after the fact. But it's much better practice to create a key field as the first order of business each time you add a table to your database, even if you don't think you'll be using it right away. It saves time. and annoyance later.

Adding a table occurrence

You need to make a new relationship between the Expenses TO (table occurrence) and the Line Items TO using your new Expenses::Line Items ID key field. Since you want to access line item details while you're on the Expenses layout, you'll create a new TO for the Line Items table. In general, the information you're using in a new way (the line items data, in this case) gets the new table occurrence. The Expenses table is fine as it is. (See the box on page 361 for more detail on how to make that decision.)

Figure 8-13 shows a picture of what that relationship might look like with the new Line Items TO. With the new graph in mind, here's how to create that additional TO in your Customers database.

1. **On the Relationships tab of the Manage Database dialog box, click the Add Table Occurrence button (on the bottom left).**

   You see the Specify Table dialog box shown in Figure 8-14.

2. **Select the Line Items table from the list, and then, in the Name box, enter** *Expenses_LINE ITEMS.*

   You want a descriptive name so you can pick it out of a lineup later.

3. **Click OK.**

   FileMaker adds the new table occurrence to the graph, and selects it for you.

Figure 8-13:
You can use a new table occurrence to avoid the ambiguity that arises if you could have only a single instance of each table. Two paths go from Expenses TO to the Line Items table, but because the TOs are named differently, FileMaker knows exactly which path to take to retrieve the records you need. The plain Jane Line Items TO sits below the Invoices TO to make that relationship more clear. The new Expenses_LINE ITEMS TO is below the Expenses TO, again signifying its relationship to its "parent" table. To keep things clear, arrange your own Relationship Graphs this way, too.

4. **Drag the Expenses::Line Item ID field to the Expenses Line Items::Line Item ID field.**

   FileMaker creates the relationship.

Figure 8-14:
The Specify Table box lets you tell FileMaker what table to use when you make a new table occurrence. You also get to give the new occurrence a name. When you name a new table occurrence, the goal is to help you remember the source table for the new table occurrence. The new TO's name is Expenses_LINE ITEMS. The "Expenses" part of the name tells you why you made the new TO—to help tie invoice line items to the proper expense records. "LINE ITEMS" is in all caps, so you can remember that the new TO comes from the Line Items table. Use whatever naming scheme you want, but use it consistently.

Tip: If you don't see the Line Item ID field, it may be because your table occurrences are collapsed and they show only fields used in relationships. In the upper-right corner of the TO, click the little button to expand it. Since the TO cycles through three states, you might have to click twice before you see all the fields.

Now that you have both relationships created, you can switch the table occurrences back to their just-the-key-fields modes if you want, and arrange the graph however it suits you. When you're done, click OK to dismiss the dialog box. Now it's time to add fields from your new table occurrence to the Expenses layout, because if you don't put fields on at least one layout to access the Expenses_LINE ITEMS table occurrence you just created, it won't do you a bit of good.

Deciding Which Table Needs a New Occurrence

Once you know that you need a new table occurrence, as in the Expenses_LINE ITEMS example on page 359, you face another challenge: Of which table do you make a new occurrence? To answer that question, ask yourself this one: Which table has the information I need? Here are the three possible scenarios; see which one you think makes the most sense:

- If you create a new occurrence of the Line Items table, then you're giving that table a new meaning in the relational structure of your database. You can access this new TO—Expenses_LINE ITEMS—from any table occurrence in the system. In particular, you can add Expenses_LINE ITEMS details to the Expenses layout. (You *can't* put fields from Expenses on the Line Items layout because that layout is attached to the Line Items table occurrence, not the Expenses_LINE ITEMS occurrence.)

- If you decide to create a new occurrence of the Expenses table instead, then the opposite is true: You can't view line item information from the Expenses layout, but you *can* view expense information from the Line Item layout. In this case you've given expenses a new meaning (billed expenses, perhaps).

- If you want, you can create new occurrences of *both* tables. If you do, you can see expense information from a line item *and* line item information from an expense. But unless you plan to use your data that way, you're only creating more work for yourself.

Adding fields for new table occurrences

To put your new relationship to work, switch to Layout mode, and then go to the Expenses layout. As discussed on page 358, you want to add a couple of fields so you can see invoice line items and assign them to the corresponding expenses.

Tip: Adding the fields using the Expenses_LINE ITEMS table occurrence is like adding any other fields, but make sure you're using the Expenses_LINE ITEMS table occurrence, not the original Line Items table occurrence.

Here's how to add the fields that do the trick:

1. **Drag a new field onto the layout. When the Specify Field dialog box appears, in the pop-up menu at the top, choose Expenses_LINE ITEMS.**

   The fields from the Line Items table appear (remember, this is an occurrence of the Line Items table, just like the Line Items occurrence itself).

2. **From the list, choose the Invoice ID field, and then click OK.**

   This field lets you view the Invoice ID on which this expense was billed.

3. **Add the Description, Price Each, Quantity, and Extended Price fields from the Expenses_LINE ITEMS table occurrence.**

   With these fields on the Expenses layout, you can see the details of each line item, and verify that it's the right one before moving on.

4. **Add the Expenses::Line Item ID field to the layout.**

   When you enter a valid ID into this local field, your relationship is completed, and your related data shows up on the Expense record.

Back in Browse mode, you can start entering expenses. Make some expense records and some Invoices that bill those expenses out, and then put the ID of a line item in the Line Item ID field. You may find it helpful to make a new window to view Invoices in. When you enter a valid Line Item ID, you see the associated invoice number and the details of the line item you're matching. If your fields permit data entry (page 160), then you can even edit the Invoice's Line Items right from the Expenses layout.

Managing Data with Data Tunneling

In the first part of this chapter, you learned how to manage data that's in a table only one relationship away from your source table. For example, you learned how to create line items through a portal in an invoice record. (Remember from Figure 8-13 that the Invoice table occurrence is directly connected to the Line Items table occurrence.)

But you can also manage data that's stored farther away on the relationships graph. For example, your Payments table occurrence is also related to the Expenses table occurrence way over on the other end of the graph because a continuous line of table occurrences connects them through their respective relationships (Figure 8-15). Even though they aren't directly connected, you can still work with data that's several TOs away from your current table.

Database nerds like to use the term "data tunneling" to describe how you can manage data that's multiple hops away on your relationships graph. This concept means that you don't have to navigate over to a layout based on the table where

When Dragging Doesn't Do It

When you first learned to create relationships, it was by dragging fields on the relationships graph (page 321). Since there's a clear path from the Expenses table to the Line Items table, you may have dragged the Line Item ID field to connect them—and gotten the nasty message shown in Figure 8-12.

FileMaker's not trying to be difficult. It's just letting you know that what you're trying to do doesn't work, and it's even going out of its way to suggest a solution. FileMaker's offering to create a new Line Items table occurrence for you right now. FileMaker makes this choice because you dragged *from* Expenses *to* Line Items. (If you had dragged the other way, it would be suggesting a new Expenses table occurrence instead.)

In the "Name of Occurrence" box, type *Expenses_LINE ITEMS*, and then click OK. Whenever you see this message box, you *could* click Cancel and try to figure out how your ER diagram conflicts with FileMaker's relationships graph. But it's easier to just let FileMaker create the new TO for you. A new TO may not be what you had in mind, but you can rest assured that FileMaker's doing what it needs to do to make your new relationship work.

When you click OK, FileMaker adds the new table occurrence, and creates the relationship using the key fields you dragged before you were so rudely interrupted. You just have to move it to a better place.

your data's stored to create or display it. If there's a path to the table occurrence you need on the relationship graph, then you can stay right where you are, and tell FileMaker to tunnel through your graph and bring back the data you need. In this section, you'll learn how to create layouts and arrange table occurrences to bridge the distance between you and the data you need.

Understanding Data Tunneling

Relationships like the one between expenses and line items you created in the last section are *functional*, but when you added Line Item IDs, you probably discovered that they aren't very easy to work with yet. You had to view invoices and their line item IDs to figure out which Line Item ID to add to your Expense record. A value list Line Item IDs might help, but as your database grows, so does the value list *and* the problems. First of all, your database could have *thousands* of line items. And even if it doesn't, line items don't have a very good name—their descriptions aren't unique, and their IDs aren't very meaningful.

It would be better if you could type in an Invoice ID *first*, and then choose from that invoice's Line Item IDs. A new layout (like the one shown in Figure 8-16) uses data tunneling to let you manage line item data from the Expenses table.

What you need in your data tunneling interface

The Assign Line Items layout provides a special set of tools, or an *interface*, to expedite a certain *process*. In this case, the process is matching line item records to expense records so you can track whether or not they've been billed. For the new interface to work, you need a few basic supplies. They're listed here to avoid confusion

Figure 8-15:
You can use your Relationships Graph (or the ER Diagram, if you prefer) to figure out which tables you need in your new group, and how they go together. For the new Assign Line Items to Expenses layout, you'll recreate the highlighted portion of the graph. That way, you'll have a new table occurrence Group (TOG) for the Expenses, Jobs, Invoices and Line Items table occurrences. Before you're done, the Line Item table will have two TOs within this TOG.

as you start creating them; you'll learn more about the role each item plays as you build the interface. You need:

- **A field to type in the Invoice ID.** Since this field doesn't hold information about any particular entity in your database, it's a good candidate for *global* storage. Global fields, as you remember from page 116, have the same value across every record of their table.

Note: The Assign Line Items layout needs fields to show the job name and line item description as well, but you can create them any time. In this example, you add them last (see Figure 8-16).

- **A value list that shows line items on that invoice.** Value lists based on fields come in two forms: those that show *all* records, and those that show *related* records. Since you don't want to pick from every line item in the database, you need the second type.

- **A relationship for the value list.** This relationship needs to show the line items that match the Invoice ID in the new global field.

To get these three elements to work together, you first have to revisit your relationship graph and decide which table occurrences to connect. Read on.

Note: You can download a finished copy of the database from the Missing CD page at *http://missingmanuals.com/cds*. Use the file to see how the finished process works, and as a reference as you go through the exercises that create your new layout.

Understanding Table Occurrence Groups

Since data tunneling involves relating existing table occurrences in new ways, you can easily get tangled in a mass of arrows (Figure 8-18, top). Since you can create as many

Figure 8-16:
This layout provides a nice interface for assigning line items to an expense. First, you enter an Invoice ID. Your entry changes the contents of the pop-up menu to show only the Line Item IDs from that Invoice. When you've selected a Line Item ID, you see the Description, Price Each, Quantity, and Extended Price invoiced for the Expense.

occurrences of each table as you want, FileMaker makes it easy to create an entirely *new* group of occurrences, called a *table occurrence group* (also known as a *TOG*), somewhere *else* in the graph. You can assemble and wire these together in any way that makes sense for your new interface, without complicating the existing group.

Note: Remember, table occurrences aren't tables. You can create as many groups as you like without making your database any bigger. The groups are for your convenience only, each showing you a "snapshot" of your database from a different angle.

To figure out which table occurrence you need to use to make the new layout in Figure 8-16 work, think about what you need it to do. You start by finding an expenses record on the Expenses layout, and then you need to get to the new Assign Line Items layout—via a button, perhaps. Once you're on the new layout, you choose a line item, and then FileMaker puts a value in the Line Item ID field. Everything takes place from an expense record's viewpoint.

Tip: FileMaker mavens prefer the term *context* to refer to the viewpoint of a layout. Just so you know.

Since your new layout is all about modifying an expense record, you must attach it to an occurrence of the *Expenses* table. The other tables you need are Jobs, Invoices, and Line Items. As shown in Figure 8-16, those tables already have relationships to all the other tables in your database. There's no problem in creating new relationships to the Expenses table, too—at least not for FileMaker. But if you start dragging to create those relationships, then you need a map, a GPS system, and a six-pack of aspirin to untangle all the table occurrences (see Figure 8-17 for a particularly egregious example of a graph gone wild).

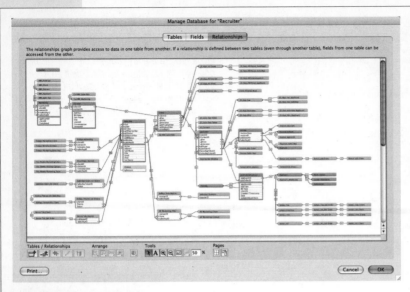

Figure 8-17:
You don't even need to be able to read the TO names in this relationships graph (top) to see how quickly good databases become the stuff of nightmares. An organization to the TOs groups processes together, but if you have to tweak this database after a long absence, then you have to walk through a lot of TOs to find the one you want to see. You can't even see the whole graph at full size, so you have to either limit yourself to a portion of the graph, or zoom so far out that you can't read the TO names and field list. And although the TOs are named reasonably well (bottom), so that similar TOs are grouped together alphabetically, the list doesn't even fit on the screen. The names, though different, are so similar that you can easily mistake one for another. See Figure 8-18 for a better way to organize your graph, and your TO menus.

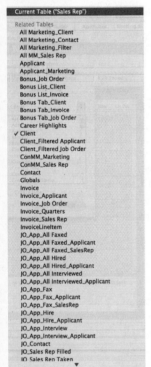

Instead, you can create new TOs for that entire group of tables, and position the new group below your other table occurrences, as shown in Figure 8-18. This graph lets you work with the two distinct "sets" of relationships separately. Since the two groups share no relationships, FileMaker can put the relevant table occurrences in the Assign Expenses group, and separate everything else in the unrelated tables group. See Figure 8-18, bottom, for details.

Note: This approach has a downside for the database developer: Since each layout is attached to a single table occurrence, if you create a new group, then you need a new layout to use it. But it's a small price to pay for the simplicity granted to the database's users.

Managing the Relationships Graph

ER diagrams are great for helping you understand which table contains the data you need. But if you carry this concept into FileMaker's relationships graph in a complex database, you can get into trouble (Figure 8-18). With only 19 tables, the graph is as neatly ordered as it can be, given that it has almost 100 TOs, but the only thing missing from this labyrinth is a hungry minotaur. The database works just fine, but when it needs troubleshooting or updating, any developer (even if that's *you*) will have a hard time figuring out what's going on.

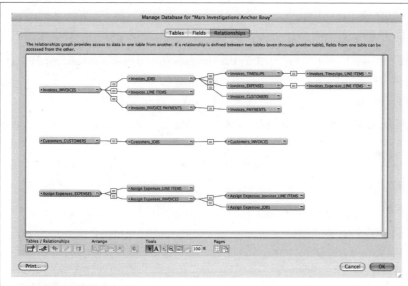

Figure 8-18:
Here's what your graph looks like if you convert the whole thing to the Anchor-Buoy model. Each new group of table occurrences (top) handles a new set of data entry and management tasks. More TOs can actually reduce the overall confusion because now they aren't lumped together in a long list, as in the Specify Field dialog box (bottom). They're grouped by Related and Unrelated Tables (note though, that this menu should really refer to "Table Occurrences" and not "Tables").

Even worse, since every table occurrence relates to every other one, the table occurrence menu is nearly useless (Figure 8-18, bottom). And the table occurrence names, though descriptive, aren't grouped consistently, so they don't help you find the TO you need. So in a database of even moderate complexity, it's better to think in terms of Anchor-Buoy table occurrence groups (Figure 8-18, top) when you're building the relationships graph. With an Anchor-Buoy graph, you create only the table occurrences you need to display specific data on each layout.

The *Anchor* is a TO at the left of the TOG, and it's the one that determines the context (page 337) of the layout. The *Bouys* are all the other TOs trailing along in its wake. (Admittedly, the nautical metaphor doesn't work completely, so some flippant folk prefer to use the term *squid* for this kind of graph management. There's a head at the left, and a lot of dangly tentacles at the other end.)

Whichever term you prefer, when you're building an Invoice layout, you'll want to display data from almost all your tables (see the top TOG in Figure 8-18). That way, when you're looking at any specific Invoice record, you can use the power of data tunneling to see:

- The job for which the invoice was created (directly from the Invoices_JOBS TO).

- All timeslips related to the job (through the Invoices_JOBS TO).

- All timeslip line items related to the timeslip (through the Invoices_JOBS TO and the Invoices_TIMESLIPS TO).

- All expenses related to the job (through the Invoices_JOBS TO).

- All expenses line items related to the job (through the Invoices_JOBS TO and the Invoices_Expenses_LINE ITEMS TO).

- The customer who is related to the job (through the Invoices_JOBS TO).

- All the line items for the invoice (directly from the Invoices_INVOICES TO).

- All invoice payment line items for the invoice (through the Invoices_INVOICE PAYMENTS TO).

The TO names (Invoices_JOBS, and so on) look geeky at first glance, but you can easily decipher their meanings. The "Invoice" part of the top group tells you what layout the TO is used on, and the part in all-caps tells you the source table for the TO. Therefore, all TOs with the "Invoice" prefix are meant to do invoice layout display work or invoice data management; the prefix indicates the context. So, if you want to display customer data on the Invoice layout (which has the context of the Invoice_INVOICE TO), then you look for the Invoice_CUSTOMER table occurrence, and place a field from it on your layout. See the page 376 for tips on managing the TOs themselves.

Note: This naming scheme is one of many out there. Many developers use a similar scheme, but abbreviate the layout names/prefix part of the TO name or the table name, so the names don't get too unwieldy. Others refuse to use spaces in their TO names, and use camel case instead (AssignExpensesINVOICE, for example). Others prefer to use underscores: AssignExpenses_INVOICE. Feel free to make up your own scheme. Just use it consistently—it's your bread-crumb trail home.

If you don't need to see a lot of data on a layout, a simpler TOG will suffice. Look at the middle TOG in Figure 8-18. It lets you find a customer record, using the Customer layout, and see customer details, all jobs performed for that customer, and all invoices for the jobs done for that customer. If you also wanted to see the individual line items for an invoice, you'd add an occurrence of the Line Items table, name it, and then put a field from the new TO on the Customer layout. The bottom TOG in Figure 8-18 shows the TOG you'll build in the next section with your new relationship graph taming skills.

Building a Data Tunneling Interface

Now that you've grasped all these concepts, it's time to start the actual construction. Start with the new global field (see the box on page 372 for more info about naming global fields). It's an easy place to begin, and logical too, since you need the global field for all the subsequent steps.

Creating a Global Field

Since the context of your interface is the Expenses table, that's where you add the field. Open the Mars Investigations database and proceed as follows:

1. **Choose File → Manage Database, and then switch to the Fields tab. From the Table pop-up menu, choose Expenses.**

   FileMaker shows the fields in the Expenses table.

2. **In the Field Name text box, enter *Global Invoice ID*, change its type to Number, and then click Create.**

   The new field appears in the field list.

3. **Click Options and then, in the Field Options dialog box, click the Storage tab.**

   FileMaker shows you the field storage options. You first saw these on page 116.

4. **Turn on "Use global storage (one value for all records)", and then click OK twice to close both dialog boxes.**

   FileMaker creates the field, and it now appears in the Field list.

You'll use this new global field as a key field in the next sections.

Creating a New Table Occurrence Group

Before you start throwing new TOs on the graph, review your goals for the new layout. Its purpose is to show you an invoice based on data you enter in a global field, and to show the job name and a list of line items related to that job.

Since the Assign Line Items layout needs the context of the Expenses table, you'll create a new Expenses TO. You also want to be able to show the line item attached to that expense, so you need a new TO for line items. Finally, you'll use the global field you created in the Expense table to hook up to another new table occurrence of the Invoice table. With these TOs, you'll be able to see and manage the following information:

- The name of the job associated with an invoice.

- The line items attached to that invoice.

A quick glance back to Figure 8-18 shows all the new table occurrences you need to create. The naming scheme helps you figure out which table each occurrence needs to come from.

The steps are simple if you take it one table at a time:

1. **If necessary, click the Manage Database window's Relationships tab.**

   You need to see your existing relationship graph.

2. **Click the Add Table Occurrence button (see Figure 8-3). When the Specify Table window appears, select the Expenses table.**

   When you create your layout later, it'll have the context (or viewpoint) of the Expenses table. Therefore, it's the Anchor in your Anchor-Buoy TOG, so it makes sense to create it first.

3. **In the "Name of Table Occurrence" box, type *Assign Expenses_EXPENSES*, and then click OK.**

   The *Assign Expenses* bit says that this new table occurrence was created especially for the process of assigning expenses. *EXPENSES* (in all caps) indicates the TO's source is the Expenses table.

   When you click OK, FileMaker adds the new table occurrence to the middle of the graph. Move it out of the way to get ready for the next steps.

4. **Add an occurrence of the Invoices table called Assign Expenses_INVOICES; an occurrence of the Line Items table called Assign Expenses_LINE ITEMS; a second occurrence of the Line Items table called Assign Expenses_Invoices_LINE ITEMS; and an occurrence of the Jobs table called Assign Expenses_JOBS.**

   You now have five new table occurrences on your graph. Since the names are so long, you might have to stretch your new TOs so you can tell them apart. See page 327 for tips on resizing TOs.

Note: When TO names are lengthy, you can often more easily just copy a TO that's already attached to the right table, and then edit its name. Or you could copy just the name from existing TO, and paste it into the name field. It's harder to read about than it is to do. Try it.

5. **Create a relationship between Assign Expenses_EXPENSES and Assign Expenses_LINE ITEMS using the Line Item ID field as keys.**

   The relationship will let you show a Line Item's detail on the layout.

Note: As a shortcut, you can copy a set of related TOs, and then rename them. When you copy related TOs, you get the relationships, too.

6. **Create another relationship, this time between Assign Expenses_EXPENSES and Assign Expenses_INVOICES, using Global Invoice ID and Invoice ID as keys.**

   The global relationship shows a little bar on the Expenses side. That's to remind you there's a global field on that side. See Figure 8-19 to complete the relationships you need between your new TOs.

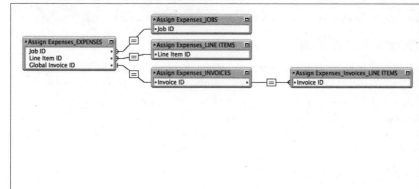

Figure 8-19:
You can start to see how this new layout works. When you put an invoice ID in the Global Invoice ID field, it matches one invoice record, which appears on a pop-up menu based on this relationship. Once you select a Line Item ID from the pop-up menu, you see related data from the invoice line items. The two relationships based on regular fields show the line item's details and the job's name.

When you create Anchor-Buoy TOGs on your own, the process probably won't be as straightforward as this exercise might lead you to believe. FileMaker is flexible enough to let you create part of a TOG, go design your layout, and then dive back into the graph to add more TOs later. In fact, real-world development is rarely as rigid as these exercises, since you often realize that you need a bit of data only while you're deep in the white hot creativity of breathing life into your database.

Now that the occurrences and relationships are in place, you can move them to a new spot on the graph where they have some breathing room. FileMaker gives you nearly infinite space down and to the right, so pick a spot that you like.

Tip: Remember, if you like things lined up nice and neat, in the relationships graph, you have Arrange tools that let you resize and align a selected group of TOs together (Figure 8-3).

One (Global) Field to Rule Them All

You know that fields set with global storage have the same value across every record in the table that holds them. Since these fields are so different from other fields, many database designers give them special names so that the fields stand out in a list. That way, they're less likely to get used inappropriately—say in a context where they don't have much meaning, or plopped down on a layout where someone can edit the values when they should stay static.

You can just preface the names of all your global fields with the word "global," like you did in the exercise on page 369.

But in the real world, people commonly just use a lower-case "g" as a prefix. With this scheme, you can name your global field "gInvoice ID" and save a few keystrokes. Plus, you look like a guru.

Some developers also use the lower-case "g" in the names of their TOs, to indicate that the relationship uses a global field as a key. It can be a handy reminder that the relationship doesn't work bidirectionally, as fields that are based on normal fields do. The relationships graph also reminds you that a global relationship isn't bidirectional, as you can see by the connector between Global Invoice ID and the regular Invoice ID fields in Figure 8-19.

Building a Global Field Layout

Now that you've finished the new table occurrence group and hooked up its relationships, you're ready to create the "Assign Line Item to Expense" layout you first saw way back in Figure 8-16. With the graph defined, this process is surprisingly simple. First, create a new, blank layout based on your Assign Expenses_EXPENSES table occurrence, and call it "Assign Line Items to Expenses". (See Chapter 4 if you need a refresher on creating layouts.) Then check out Figure 8-20 for layout suggestions.

Now add these fields to the layout:

- Assign Expenses_EXPENSES::Expense.

- Assign Expenses_EXPENSES::Global Invoice ID.

- Assign Expenses_EXPENSES::Line Item ID.

- Assign Expenses_JOB::Name.

- Assign Expenses_LINE ITEMS::Description.

Note: Remember, this layout is associated with the Assign Expenses_EXPENSES table occurrence. When you choose fields for the list above, in the Specify Field dialog box, from the top of the pop-up menu, select *Current* Table.

Figure 8-20:
*Your smallish TOG has two TOs from the Line
Items table. One is related directly to Expenses
through the Line Item ID field. The other is related
with a global field through the Invoice table and
its Invoice ID field. The one related directly
(which doesn't change if the value in your
global field changes) lets you display the
Assign Expenses_LINE ITEMS::Description field on
your layout. You'll use the global Line Items TO to
create a related-values value list in the steps on
page 374.*

POWER USERS' CLINIC

TOG Jumping

The layout in Figure 8-21 is pretty slick, but there's one problem. Suppose you're on the *Expenses* layout looking at an expense. You decide you want to assign an invoice line item to it, so you use the layout pop-up menu to switch to the "Attach Line Item to Expenses" layout. Unfortunately, when you do, you don't see the same record. That's because each table occurrence has its own current record, found set, and sort order. You're forced to find the same record again in this new context.

It turns out the "Go to Related Record" command has an unexpected power: It can transfer a found set—complete with current record and sort order—from one table occurrence to another. The "Go to Related Record" Options window has a "Get related record from" pop-up menu that shows every table occurrence in the database, not just the ones related to your current context. It shows layouts attached to *any* occurrence of the same table. In other words, when you ask to go to a record in the same table occurrence you're already viewing, you can pick the "Attach

Line Item to Expenses" layout, even though it's associated with a different occurrence of the Expenses table. If you want to get all geeky about it, you can call this technique "TOG Jumping" or "Anchor-Buoy Surfing" just like the pros do.

When you use this technique, FileMaker shows the records dictated by the relationship, but uses the layout you choose. To make the connection, add a button (page 267) to the Expenses layout that runs the "Go to Related Record" command. When you set up the button, choose the Expenses table occurrence and the "Attach Line Item to Expenses" layout. Also, make sure you turn on "Show only related records". FileMaker does all the rest of the work for you.

You can also add a button to the Attach Line Item layout that transports you *back* to the Expenses layout. This time you configure the "Go to Related Record" command to use the Assign Expenses_EXPENSES table occurrence and the Expenses layout.

Using a global pop-up field to change the display in a value list

By definition, a global field has the same value in all its tables' records. Therefore, you can change the data in a global field without affecting any of your "real" data for those records. When your global field is used in a relationship, and you change the value in the global field, the relationship changes, and so do the records related to your current record.

You use this technique to create a value list that's based on the global relationship between your new Expenses TO and the new Invoice TO. When that global relationship changes, FileMaker tunnels in the new table occurrence group from Expenses to Invoices to Line Items to get the line item that's related through the value in your global. Refer to your relationships graph (or Figure 8-19) to refresh your memory on how those TOs hook up, if this technique doesn't make sense without a visual aid.

This advanced technique is just like searching for records, without all the hassle of going to Find mode and actually performing a search. You need to make the Line Item ID field into a pop-up menu first. Here are the steps:

1. **Double-click the Line Item ID field, and then, from the "Display as" pop-up menu, choose Pop-up Menu.**

   The "Display values from" pop-up menu appears, with <unknown> displayed.

2. **From the "Display values from" pop-up menu, choose Manage Value Lists.**

   You need a new value list based on the values in the Line Item ID field from the Assign Expenses_Invoices_LINE ITEMS table occurrence you made a few pages back.

3. **Click New, and then type *Invoice Line Items* as the value list name.**

   Use a descriptive name so you can remember your thought process later on.

4. **Turn on the "Use values from field" radio button.**

   This option sets that field's data to show up in your new value list.

5. **From the Specify Fields window's drop-down list, choose Assign Expenses_Invoices_LINE ITEMS. Then click the Line Item ID field. Select "Include only related values starting from", and then, from the drop-down list, choose Assign Expenses_EXPENSES.**

   The idea is to keep your users from assigning an expense to a line item from the wrong invoice, or from assigning an invalid Line Item ID. This option tells the value list to display only line items related to the invoice that matches the value in your Global Invoice ID field. Since that field is on the Assign Expenses_EXPENSES table occurrence, that's where the value list relationship is "starting from." To understand how this works, remember the concept of context (page 337).

6. Turn on the "Also display values from second field" checkbox, and then, from the list, choose the Description field.

Since a Line Item ID isn't very meaningful by itself, you want to show the description too.

7. Turn on the "Sort by second field" radio button, and then click OK until the dialog boxes are gone.

You're back on your Attach Line Items layout, and your Line Item field is formatted with your new value list.

Switch to Browse mode, and then try out your new layout (see Figure 8-21). In the Global Invoice ID field, if you type *1* you should be able to pick a line item from the pop-up menu. When you do, the Expense Assign: Expense Line Item::Description field should show the selected line item's description. Create a few new invoices, and see how the values in the pop-up menu change when you change the value in the Global Invoice ID field.

Note: If you type an Invoice ID and see that your value list is empty (it says "<no values defined>"), then you're either using an Invoice ID that doesn't exist, or it doesn't have line items yet.

Figure 8-21:
Here's a dressed-up version of the layout you just created. It uses a mix of fields, layout objects and field controls to draw people's attention to the fields where they should enter data. And if that isn't enough, some simple instructions have been added to make it really clear what to do.

Connecting Database Files

In FileMaker, you can make two database files work together as easily as you work with multiple tables. Using the data tunneling techniques discussed in the previous section, you connect tables from another file (often called an *external database*)

Managing Table Occurrences

When you use descriptive names for your TOs, they can get pretty long. Fortunately, you can easily resize any table occurrence so its entire name is visible. No matter how the table occurrence is configured, you can drag the right or left edge to make it wider or narrower. If it's set to show all its fields, then you can also drag the top or bottom edge to change its height. A table occurrence that's too short to show all its fields has little arrow icons above and below the field list. Click these arrows to scroll through the list. (When a table occurrence is set to show just the key fields or no fields at all, its height is fixed.)

To see which table an occurrence represents, just point to the arrow icon to the left of the occurrence name. FileMaker pops up an information window that tells you everything you need to know. And if long names and pop-up tips aren't enough, then you can use the note tool (it's the tool marked with the letter "A"). Use the note as a reminder of the purpose of your new table occurrences that's more detailed than a naming prefix. Notes behave themselves, staying in the background behind all your TOs, so some designers make large notes that enclose a new TO group to visually unite them on the graph.

without the overhead of copying all that data into your file. You simply put a table occurrence from your .external file onto your relationship graph, which defines its perspective in relation to all your other tables.

For example, suppose you want to connect the People database to your new system. You'd like a portal on the Customers layout to show all the people in the People database who live in the same state as that customer. After all, you never know when one of your leads will come in handy.

Adding a Table Occurrence from Another File

Creating a cross-database relationship is as easy as adding a table occurrence. Once you have the People table on the relationships graph (in the Manage Database dialog box), it begins to act like a first-class citizen in its new environment: You can create relationships to it, attach layouts to it, and just about anything else you can do with the tables in this database. Here's how:

1. **In the Mars Investigations database, bring up the Manage Database window's Relationships tab. Click the Add Table Occurrence button.**

   The Specify Table dialog box appears.

2. **From the File pop-up menu, choose Add FileMaker Data Source.**

   A standard Open File dialog box appears—just like you see when you're opening a database. To use a table from another file, you have to add a *file reference*. A file reference is just a way to tell FileMaker where you store the external databases with which it needs to interact.

3. **Browse to the People database, select it, and then click Open.**

Use a copy of People from Chapter 1, or download a copy at *http://missingmanuals.com/cds*. The Specify Table dialog box now shows tables from the People database.

Note: File references aren't dynamic. That is, if you move the files from the location in your file reference, then you need to update the reference manually so FileMaker can find it. Just choose File → Manage File References, and then double-click the file reference to edit it.

---

4. **Select the People table, rename the new TO "Other Leads", and then click OK.**

FileMaker adds the new occurrence to the graph. As Figure 8-22 attests, you can tell at a glance that it's an occurrence of what FileMaker calls an *external* table because it shows you the table occurrence's name in italics.

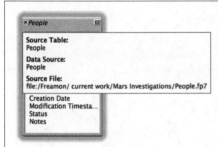

Figure 8-22:
External tables' names display in italics. To find out which database it comes from, point to the little arrow to the left of the name to show the information window. FileMaker displays the source table's name, the Data Source (or file name) and the path.

5. **In the relationship graph, drag the State field from the People table to the Customers::State field.**

Now that the People table is in the graph, you can use the table as freely as if it were a local table.

Creating a portal is a good use for the new external table, as shown in Figure 8-23.

Defining Data Sources Using a Path

Creating an External Reference is as simple as finding a file on your hard drive. Choose File → Manage → External Data Sources, and then click New to see the Edit Data Source window. Give the data source a logical name, and then click the Add File button to navigate to the file's location. If you prefer typing to pointing and clicking, you can type the path from scratch, but you must follow strict form. Acceptable form varies, based on what platform you're using and how you access the external file. You'll see examples of the acceptable File Path Formats at the bottom of the Edit Data Source dialog box.

Systems with More than One Database

Even if you're building a brand-new system from scratch, no rule says every table has to be in the same database. In fact, you have many good reasons to divide your system across multiple files. The last chapter talked about one of those reasons: You might be storing large images or other files in your database. You can keep these files in an external table so the database file itself isn't so large. Then you can back up, copy, and email the information about the images without including the images themselves.

Here are some other reasons to use more than one file:

- **You can create a database for each kind of interface you need**. For example, if you need to track sales, you can create a database with the tables you need to store the actual data: orders, line items, customers, shipments, products, and so forth. You can use this database in two ways, though: sales entry (creating and managing orders) and reporting (daily, monthly, and quarterly sales reports, trend and pro-motion analysis, and so on). To keep your system as simple as possible, you can create these separate interfaces as two distinct databases. Since they share the tables from the central sales database, the reporting data stays up-to-date as File-Maker processes new sales. But since they're in two databases, the layouts you need for order entry don't get in the way of the reporting layouts, and vice versa.

- **One company usually has many database needs**. You might have Sales, Marketing, and Engineering departments in your organization. Each of these departments has unique needs and wants a database to match them. But the Marketing department might be very interested in sales data, and the Sales department needs access to engineering information. You can create a separate database for each department, but share some tables between systems. This way you get an interface tailored to each group, but the important data is shared.

- **When you can use external table occurrences, you have a very flexible design metaphor**. A database—or file—can hold interface elements (layouts, scripts, value lists) or data (tables and fields) or both. You can construct the database in almost any way you see fit: one file for each table, all tables in one file, or tables in logical groupings; all the interface in one database, or several databases to break things up. A FileMaker file is a very flexible unit of organization: Use it as you see fit.

You can even give a file reference more than one path. When you do, FileMaker looks for the file at the first path. If it doesn't find the file, then it tries the second path. The search continues until it finds the file or tries every listed path. (If it never finds the file, then you see an error message.) Using this technique, you can have a database that opens files from different locations depending on which computer it's opened on. Or you can ask FileMaker to use your local copy of the People database if it finds one, and to use the network copy otherwise. (You'll learn about sharing databases on a network in Chapter 16.)

Figure 8-23:
You can use an external table occurrence just like you'd use a local one (top). Create a portal, and then choose the Other Leads table occurrence. Select the vertical scroll bar option, and tell the portal to sort by last name, then first name. Finally, add the First Name and Last Name fields to the portal, and you have your list of all People who live in the same state as your current Customer. In the Manage External Data Sources dialog box (bottom), you can see the names, types, and locations of all files you use for external data (here, the Other Leads file). The People file is in the same folder as the Mars Investigations file, so the path doesn't include the volume name or a long list of folders and subfolders.

Figure 8-24:
The "Use external table's layouts" option appears when you choose an External Table in a "Go To Related Record" command. Reuse work you've already done by showing data in its original form—its native layout in its source file. If you also choose the "Show in new window" option, then you can leave the found set showing in your original window while you scour the external file to mine its treasures.

Going to External Records

Now that you've got a file reference and a table occurrence from an external file, what do you do with it? You *could* create a new layout attached to the Other Leads table occurrence, and then fill it with fields from the People table. But you already have a great layout for viewing the details of a People record: the People database's Detail layout.

Once again, "Go to Related Records" comes to the rescue (see Figure 8-24). First, turn the First Name and Last Name fields on the Other Leads portal into a button that performs the "Go to Related Record" command. In the "Go to Related Record" Options window, choose the Other Leads

table occurrence. Since this occurrence is from a table in another file, the "Use external table's layout" checkbox comes to life.

When this checkbox is turned on, the "Show record using layout" pop-up menu lists layouts from the People database rather than the current database. Turn the checkbox on, and then choose the Detail layout. Don't forget to turn on "Show only related records". Now when you click a person's name, the People database pops up and shows you the correct person.

Lookups

Since you have a relationship between the Jobs and Customers tables (page 321), you don't have to enter customer information on each job record. Nor do you want to store that data in both tables. If you display the customer's name and address information on the Jobs layout, and then update the customer's data, it automatically shows on the Jobs layout. This dynamic updating of related data is the essence of a relational database. However, many times you *don't* want a piece of information to change; you want FileMaker to remember the way it was at a certain point in time. *Lookup fields* use relationships to do a sort of one-time copy-and-paste of data from one table to another. Once the looked-up data is in its new table, you can edit it, if necessary, but it doesn't change automatically if the related data changes.

Take a look at the Invoices table, for example. When you create an invoice, you attach it to a job. The job is in turn attached to a customer. When it comes time to mail the invoice, you could easily put the address fields from the Customers table occurrence on the Invoice layout, and see the customer's address. But this method is a bad idea for two reasons:

- **It doesn't allow for special circumstances.** If a customer tells you he's going to be in Majorca for a month and to please send his next invoice there, you have no way to enter an alternate address on just one invoice. You have to change the address in his customer record, send the invoice, and then change the address back.

- **It destroys relevant information.** When you *do* update the customer record with his original home address, you lose any record of where you sent the invoice. If you go back to the special-case invoice 2 years from now, it'll *look* like you sent it to his home address.

Empty Lookups

Lookup options give you some control over what happens when you don't have a matching related record. Normally, if FileMaker tries to find a related record to look up data from and it can't find one, it just leaves the lookup field alone.

That's what happens when, in the "If no exact match, then" group of radio buttons, you turn on "do not copy". Here's what the others do:

- The "copy next lower value" option looks at the closest *lower* related record. For example, if you turn it on for the Invoices::Street Address field, and there's no matching related customer, FileMaker copies the address of the customer with the next lower Customer ID alphabetically. In this case, it makes absolutely no sense.

But what if you're looking up price information based on quantity? If the customer orders 38, but you have pricing for 30 or 40, you might want to get the price for 30 items, the next lower value.

- The "copy next higher value" option works just like its similarly named counterpart. It just copies the value from the next *higher* related record instead. People don't use these two options a lot, but they sometimes come in very handy.

- The "use" option lets you specify any value you want to substitute for a missing related value. For example, if you're looking up customer age information and you don't have an age for one person, then you can tell FileMaker to use "N/A" instead.

These problems arise because invoice data is *transactional*—an invoice represents a single business transaction at one specific point in the past. But your customer record doesn't represent a single transaction with your customer: It represents an association you have with that customer. If the association changes (the customer moves and you need to store a new address), then your data should change accordingly. However, transactional data should *never* change once the transaction is complete because it must serve as a record of what happened during the transaction. Lookup fields solve the problem of saving transactional data.

While related fields automatically show new data, lookups use a semi-automatic approach. If you change a customer record, it *doesn't* affect the fields in existing Invoice records at all. But any new Invoice you create *does* get the updated data. Or if you change the Job ID on an *invoice* record, the lookup triggers again, and File-Maker fetches the new customer's data. Additionally, you can *change* the data in a field formatted with Auto-Enter Lookup at any time—for a one-time address change, for example. This semi-automatic approach to updating data turns out to be just the right thing for transactional data like address fields on invoices: When you change the *transaction* record, its fields update appropriately, but when you change *source* records (the address fields in your customer record), FileMaker leaves the transaction alone.

Creating Lookups

To create a lookup, you define a field normally but add an Auto-Enter option called *Looked-up value*. You can also add a lookup to an existing field. Simply click the field in the fields list, and then click the Options button. The following steps explain how to create a new lookup field:

1. **In the Customers database, choose File → Manage Database. On the Fields tab, from the Table pop-up menu, choose Invoices.**

   You see the fields in the Invoices table—and you're ready to add a new one. You start by adding a lookup field for the customer's street address.

2. **In the Field Name box, enter *Street Address*, and make sure the Type pop-up menu is set to Text. Click Create.**

   FileMaker adds the new field to the field list. Right now, though, it's just an ordinary field.

3. **Click the Options button. In the Field Options dialog box, click the Auto-Enter tab.**

   The Options dialog box appears. You'll create the lookup here.

4. **Turn on the "Looked-up value" checkbox.**

   The Lookup dialog box appears (Figure 8-25).

Figure 8-25:
Here's what your Lookup dialog box looks like when you're done with the steps beginning on this page In other circumstances, you might not want to copy over existing data if the related fields are blank. Imagine you have a table of currency exchange rates. If some currencies don't have data available the day you gather the rates, then those rate fields are blank. If you use a lookup to refresh exchange rates in your Products database, you don't want to wipe out any existing exchange rates. To keep last week's value, turn on the "Don't copy contents if empty" option.

5. **Make sure the "Starting with table" pop-up menu is set to Invoices.**

It almost certainly is set properly, because in this case, the context is clear. You're defining a field in the Invoices table, so that's the field's context. If you have a table on the graph multiple times, then you might have to change the "Starting with table" pop-up to reflect the context of the layout on which you'll use the newly-defined field, which influences how the lookup finds related data.

6. **From the "Lookup from related table" pop-up menu, choose Customers.**

As soon as you choose a table, the "Copy value from field" list is populated with all the fields in the Customers table. You're interested in the Street Address field's value.

7. **In the "Copy value from field" list, choose Street Address. Turn off the "Don't copy contents if empty" checkbox.**

When you turn off "Don't copy contents if empty", FileMaker dutifully copies the empty value, wiping out data in the lookup field. If you turn this option on instead, then FileMaker leaves the lookup field untouched—its value before the lookup remains in place.

8. **In the "If no exact match, then" group, turn on the "use" radio button, and leave the associated text box empty.**

If there's no customer record, the street address field should be blank. If you leave this set to "do not copy", then any existing address (for a different customer perhaps) is left in the field. (See the box on page 381 for other "If no exact match, then" options.)

You're done. Click OK thrice to back out of all the dialog boxes. Now switch to the Invoices layout, and then add the new field to it (page 199). When you choose a job from the Jobs table, the Invoices address field now looks up the appropriate address from the Customer table. If you create an invoice and give it a valid Customer ID number but no data shows up, check the Customer record to make sure you've entered addresses for your customers.

Note: You don't have to type all the addresses yourself, though. Download this database from the Missing Manuals Web site at *http://missingmanuals.com/cds*.

To finish your Invoices improvements, add lookup fields for the following customer information. Use the same options as in the steps on the previous pages, or—to save clicks—duplicate the Street Address field, change its name, and then just change the field from which it looks up. You get all the other lookup settings for free. When you're done, you can arrange your Invoices layout like the one in Figure 8-26.

• Company Name

• First Name

- Last Name

- City

- State

- Zip Code

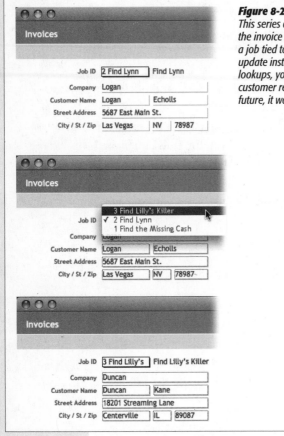

Figure 8-26:
This series of images shows your lookups in action. In the top image, the invoice is associated with Logan's job "Find Lynn". If you choose a job tied to Duncan instead (middle), then the customer fields update instantly to show his information (bottom). Since these are lookups, you can change them right here without affecting the customer record itself. And if you change a customer's address in the future, it won't affect the address on this invoice.

Using a Relookup

Normally you trigger a lookup whenever you change the data in the key field on which the relationship is based. That's why changing the Job ID field makes File-Maker look up the address information again.

Sometimes you have a reason to cause a lookup to occur *without* changing the key field. For example, suppose a new customer hires you. You do work for her for 3 months, but never receive payment—despite sending three invoices. You finally decide it's time to ask her what's up, and that's when you discover you've been sending them to the *wrong address*. You mistyped her address in the Customers layout, and now all your invoices are incorrect, too.

She agrees to pay you as soon as you mail the invoices to her correct address. You can correct her address in the Customers table, but that doesn't affect the old invoices. Luckily, you can easily fix them, too—with the Relookup Field Contents command. First, find just the three Invoices for your customer, and then click the field that normally triggers the lookup—the Job ID field in this case. Then you choose the Records → Relookup Field Contents command. You see the message shown in Figure 8-27.

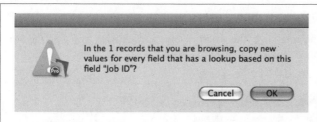

In the 1 records that you are browsing, copy new values for every field that has a lookup based on this field "Job ID"?

Cancel   OK

Figure 8-27:
When you run the Relookup Field Contents command, FileMaker shows this message. It's careful to let you know just how many records you'll be updating. That's because you can't undo this action. If you lookup new address information into old invoices accidentally, you lose historical data. If you're sure you want to proceed, then click OK.

Tip: To get into the Job ID field (it has a pop-up menu controlling it), just click it, and be sure to choose the job that's already selected. After you make your choice, the Relookup Field Contents command works as expected.

Advanced Relationships

Until now, you've created simple relationships with one rule and keys that match exactly. But you can create relationships that go far beyond those basic concepts. And even if you don't have a very complicated database, you should know how these advanced relationships work.

For example, you might have a table of Student Test Scores that contains all the tests for every kid in your school. You can view a classroom's scores on a specific test by making a relationship that matches two key fields: the Classroom ID and the Test ID. You can also find all the kids who're failing by matching every test score that's less than 70 points. Sure, you can perform a search in your Test Scores table and add some summary fields to a report to do the same tasks, but you need to perform the search again every time you want to see the data. With the techniques below, you can make this data available with just the switch of a layout or a "Go to Related Record" command (page 351).

Relationships with More than One Criterion

First, you can assign more than one rule to a relationship. For instance, you already added a relationship between Customers and People that matches based on state. Suppose you want to be more restrictive: You want to show only people who live in the same *city* and state.

It's easier than it sounds:

1. **In the Mars Investigations database, go to the Manage Database window's Relationships tab (page 322), and select the relationship line between Customers and Other Leads.**

   You can most easily select a relationship when you click the "=" box in the middle of the line (it provides a nice big target). When you select the relationship, the line gets slightly thicker, and the box gets highlighted.

2. **Click the Edit Relationship button (Figure 8-3).**

   You can also just double-click the relationship. Either way, you see the Edit Relationship dialog box, as shown in Figure 8-28.

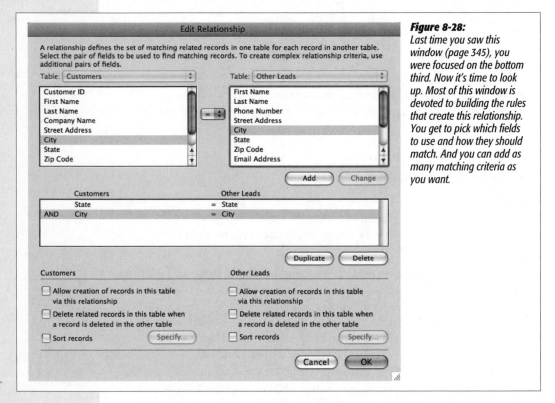

Figure 8-28:
Last time you saw this window (page 345), you were focused on the bottom third. Now it's time to look up. Most of this window is devoted to building the rules that create this relationship. You get to pick which fields to use and how they should match. And you can add as many matching criteria as you want.

3. **In the Customer table occurrence's field list, choose City.**

   The City field gets highlighted.

4. **In the Other Lead table occurrence's field list, choose City.**

   You've now described a new criterion for your rule: *Customers::City = Other Leads::City*

5. **Click the Add button.**

   FileMaker adds this criterion to the criteria list. You now have two criteria for this relationship:

   ```
   Customers::State = Other Leads::State
   AND
   Customers::City = Other Leads::City
   ```

6. **Click OK.**

   The simple relationship line now has four "ends," all of which have crow's feet.

You've just created a relationship with *two* criteria, sometimes called a *multi-key relationship* because it uses two key fields. In order for two records to relate, they must meet *both* criteria. In other words, a person must be in the same city *and* the same state as a customer to show up in his portal. Figure 8-29 shows the new relationship in the graph.

Figure 8-29:
When a relationship is based on more than one criterion—like this one between Customers and Other Leads—FileMaker forks the relationship line on each end. This fork tells you that City matches City and State matches State. The = sign in the box in the middle of the line means the data in both fields must match exactly.

If you test your Other Leads portal now, it shows only people living in the customer's city.

Other Relationship Operators

In addition to adding more rules to a relationship definition (by defining multiple criteria), you can also base relationships on different *kinds* of rules. Each relationship in your ER diagram for your database mandates that the fields on either side match exactly. This type of relationship is called an *equijoin*, in honor of the = sign that defines it. Sometimes, though, you want to relate records without an exact match. When you make a non-equijoin relationship (don't you just love technical terms?), you use FileMaker's other comparative operators

- **Equals** (=). The keys on both sides of the relationship match exactly.

- **Not Equals** (≠). All records but those with matching keys relate to one another.

- **Less Than** (<). Keys in the table on the left side of the dialog box must be less than keys in the table on the right side.

- **Less Than or Equal To** (≤). Keys in the table on the left side of the dialog box must be less than or equal to the keys on the right side of the table.

- **Greater Than** (>). Keys in the table on the left side of the dialog box must be greater than keys in the table on the right side.

- **Greater Than or Equal To** (≥). Keys in the table on the left side of the dialog box must be greater than or equal to the keys on the right side of the table.

- **Cartesian Join** (x). All records in the table on the left are related to all records in the table on the right, regardless of the value in their key fields.

As you work with your database, you might decide you need a quicker way to find invoices. You often want to see every invoice in a specified date range, and sometimes only those that are above a certain total amount due. Using relationships, you can create a new layout that makes it easy for you to see the invoices you want. You enter a start date and an end date into global fields, and a portal displays every matching invoice.

Creating the Invoice Finder

To set up your new relationship, you need to create two new global fields. Since the global fields aren't associated with any particular table, you can create a *new* table to hold them. You also need a new relationship that matches fields in the Invoices table using these global fields. This sort of job benefits from its own table occurrence group, as you saw on page 363. Call this group *Invoice Finder*.

To get the portal to show the right invoices, you need a relationship that uses your new global fields, and it'll have slightly more complicated rules than you've seen before:

```
Invoice Finder: Globals::Start Date ≤ Invoice Finder: Invoices::Date
AND
Invoice Finder: Globals::End Date ≥ Invoice Finder: Invoices::Date
```

These rules say that an invoice should match if its date is *on or after* (≥) the global start date, and if the date is *on or before* (≤) the global end date.

Below are the steps for creating a new table, defining some global fields in that new table, and then using your creations in a new table occurrence group.

You've done most of this stuff before in other tutorials, so although there are a lot of steps, they should all be pretty familiar:

1. **In the Mars Investigations database, go to the Manage Database window's Tables tab. Create a new table called Invoice Finder.**

   FileMaker adds the new table to the table list.

2. **Click the Fields tab. Then, in the Field name box, enter *gStart Date*. Make the field a Date type, and then click Create.**

   The "g" prefix reminds you that the field is a global.

Globals and Relationships

I don't get it. I thought relationships were supposed to hook different records together, but a global field isn't associated with any specific record. How come you keep using global fields to create relationships?

When you set out to design your relational database in Chapter 7, you learned how to organize your information into tables, and construct the relationships that make them work together. But relationships can do a whole lot more.

As the Invoice Finder example (page 388) and the "Assign Line Item to Expense" example (page 363) illustrate, relationships can be part of an overall interface (or layout) that performs a specific task. For example, when you use a global field in a relationship, it works just fine. Put an ID in the global field, and FileMaker makes matches to one or more records on the other side.

This kind of relationship doesn't create a permanent connection between records—rather, it just gives you temporary access to related records.

Since FileMaker doesn't index global fields, the relationship doesn't work the way you'd expect when you look in the other direction—from the normal-field context back towards the global field. In that direction, the relationship behaves like a Cartesian join (page 388), showing every record in the other table. That makes perfect sense, because every record in the other file has the same value in that global field. This behavior is not important in situations like the Invoice Finder layout, because you only care what happens from the global side of a relationship. But unlike true bidirectional relationships, where you can pull data reliably from either direction, global relationships work best in only one direction. As Figure 8-30 shows, FileMaker doesn't connect the relationship line in the graph directly to the global field. This visual cue lets you know this relationship works only from the global side to the "normal" side.

One last point: You can display data in a global field in another table *without* a relationship. Since global fields aren't associated with any record, you can view and modify them from anywhere. It's common to create a table to hold values you need to use from many different tables in a global table (say, your company's log, name, address, and other contact information), and then use those fields on printed reports. That way, if any of that data changes, you can change it in the global table, and it's immediately changed on all your reports.

Figure 8-30:
The lines on the Invoice Finder_INVOICE FINDER side of the relationship have short gaps and bars, instead of a connected line or "fork." This tells you that the relationship uses a global field on that side. It works from the global side over to the "normal" side, but not in reverse.

3. **Click the Options button. When the Field Options dialog box appears, click the Storage tab, and then turn on the "Use global storage" checkbox. Click the OK button.**

    Since this field isn't holding data about an entity, but is used to change the records that display in a portal, you need to use a global field.

4. **Repeat steps 2–3 to create another global date field called *gEnd Date*.**

    Both fields appear in the list.

5. Switch to the Relationships tab. Drag the Invoice Finder table occurrence down below your existing TOGs. Then double-click it, and change its name to Invoice Finder_INVOICE FINDER.

This new TO becomes the anchor in a new TOG, so place it near the left edge of the graph. You may also need to stretch the TO so its whole name appears.

6. Add a new occurrence of the Invoices table called Invoice Finder_INVOICES, and a new occurrence of the Jobs table called Invoice Finder_JOBS.

Since your portal shows invoices and the job associated with each invoice, you need these tables in your group as well.

7. Drag the Invoice Finder_INVOICES::Job ID field onto the Invoice Finder_ JOBS:: Job ID field to create a relationship.

When an Invoice record matches a Job, the Job Name shows in the portal.

8. Click the Add/Edit Relationship button (Figure 8-31) to open the Edit Relationship dialog box. From the left table's pop-up menu, choose Invoice Finder_INVOICE FINDER. Then, from the right table's pop-up menu, choose Invoice Finder_INVOICES.

As you select tables with the pop-up menus, their fields appear in the corresponding list.

Duplicate selected items — Edit selected items — Tables / Relationships — Add table — Create or edit relationship — Delete selected items — Print...

Figure 8-31:
The Add/Edit Relationship button comes in handy when your relationship is too complex to create using the drag-and-drop method. This tool skips the drag altogether and goes straight to the Edit Relationship dialog box, so you don't have to delete or edit the equijoin relationship that FileMaker creates when you drag. This way, you get to start with a clean slate; so clean in fact, that you start by choosing the two tables you're going to relate.

9. From the left-hand table field list, choose "gStart Date". From the Operator pop-up menu (it's between the two field lists), choose "≤".

This symbol tells FileMaker you want the field on the left to match when it's *less than or equal* to the field you select on the right side.

10. From the right-hand table field list, choose Date, and then click Add.

The Date field tells the relationship what value to compare to the sStart Date in the Invoice Finder table. In other words, you want the relationship to match only when the Start Date is *before* the Invoice Date.

Later on, you'll create a portal that uses this relationship. These criteria tells the portal to show only invoice records dated on or after the date entered in the gStart Date field.

11. **Repeat the last two steps, but this time, from the left-hand table field list, choose the "gEnd Date" field. From the right-hand table field list, choose the Date field, and from the Operator pop-up menu, choose the "≥". Finally, click Add.**

When you click Add, FileMaker adds the second criteria to the list. This part tells the portal to display records that are on or before the date in the gEnd Date field. Because FileMaker uses both relationships, you see only Invoices that have dates equal to or between the gStart Date and the gEnd Date. Compare your settings to Figure 8-32.

When you click OK to close both dialog boxes, FileMaker returns you to the graph.

Figure 8-32:
The relationship between Invoice Finder_INVOICE FINDER and Invoice Finder_ INVOICES connects two global fields to one regular. The box in the middle of the line now has an X instead of an equal sign, since you're using multiple operators in your relationship. If you want to refresh your memory on this multicriteria relationship, double-click the "X" to see the Edit Relationships dialog box.

To test your new relationship, create a new layout and show records from the Invoice Finder_INVOICE FINDER table occurrence. Add the two global fields and a portal based on the Invoice Finder_INVOICES relationship. For good measure, add script triggers (page 507) to the global fields that commit the records. When it's all done, put values in the two global fields, and the portal updates to show the matching invoices. See one possible arrangement in Figure 8-33.

Note: The Invoice Finder table has no records. You might think this lack of records would be a problem, but it isn't. However, if you're using an older version of FileMaker Pro, then you might have a problem. In some older versions, portals don't work properly when you have no records. To clear this problem up, just create a new empty record.

So what has all this work gotten you? As a designer, this technique of using global fields in a complex relationship to populate a portal has improved your understanding of relationships and tested your skill in applying that knowledge. People who use your database benefit most. Now they can see a group of invoices at a glance, without having to do a search. Next, you'll learn some techniques that you can apply to make this layout even handier. You'll learn how to create a calculation field that summarizes line items and the value of all the invoices in your portal (page 397).

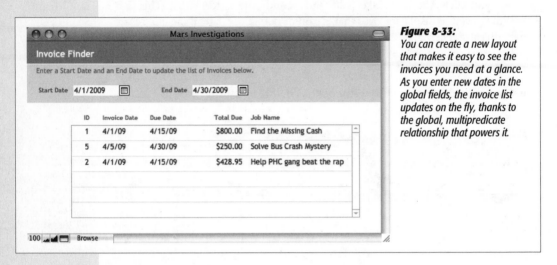

Figure 8-33:
You can create a new layout that makes it easy to see the invoices you need at a glance. As you enter new dates in the global fields, the invoice list updates on the fly, thanks to the global, multipredicate relationship that powers it.

Part Four: Calculations

4

Chapter 9: Understanding Calculations

Chapter 10: More Calculations and Data Types

Chapter 11: Advanced Calculations

Chapter 12: Extending Calculations

Understanding Calculations

When you were learned about tables, fields, and relationships in the previous few chapters, you dabbled in FileMaker's calculation dialog box. Now it's time to dive in and learn how calculations can make your database total invoices, analyze trends, calculate dates and times, and so on.

For those tasks, FileMaker provides *calculation fields* and a whole drawer full of functions that let you examine, compare, combine, and even break apart field values. Calculations aren't limited to number-crunching tasks. You can use them to find out about the computer your database is running on, track who's logged into the system, monitor their privileges, and then perform logical tests based on what you find. You'll start by learning how FileMaker handles calculations, and then you'll see how some common functions can take your database up to a new level of power.

Understanding Calculations

Way back on page 103, you saw how to create a field that's defined as a calculation. A calculation is a mathematical formula that manipulates the information in your database to give you the answers you need. For example, for a line item on an Invoice, you need to multiply the price of an item by the quantity to get an extended price. To hand that task over to FileMaker, you create a calculation field, and then write a formula that refers to the appropriate fields by name. FileMaker takes the information in the invoice fields, and does the math.

Note: The exercizes in this chapter refer to the Mars Investigations database from the Missing CD page at *http://missingmanuals.com/cds*.

FileMaker calculations can also do more than math. For starters, you can do calculations on time, date, timestamp, container, and text fields, too. (See the box on the next page for an example.) Calculation fields work just like any other File-Maker field, except that you can't type data into them. The calculations you give them determine what data they show. If you change the data a calculation refers to, you see FileMaker update the data automatically. Figure 9-1 shows where calculation fields can benefit your Invoice layout.

You can use a calculation field just like any other field: Put it on a layout, use it in Find mode, and even use it in *other* calculation fields. But as a calculation field, its value always stays up-to-date automatically.

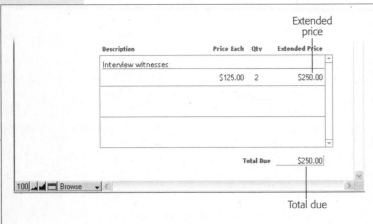

Figure 9-1:
*Without calculations, you have to manually calculate the extended price for each line item by multiplying the quantity times the price. And then, if the quantity changes, you have to visit your calculator again. But with calculation fields, the database does the math as soon as there's data in the fields the calculation refers to. Here the Extended Price field multiplies Price Each by Quantity (125 * 2 = 250). Plus, if data in either field changes, FileMaker updates the Extended Price automatically.*

Furthermore, calculations aren't limited to working inside fields. For example, you can use a calculation with the Records → Replace Field Contents command (see page 67). Instead of replacing the data in every record with the *same* value, a calculation can produce a unique value for each record. In the Manage Database dialog box, you can start using the Auto-Enter Calculation and Validation Calculation field options, making those features much more powerful. Scripts, as you'll learn in Part 5, use calculations in many of their script steps. Here are some other places you see the Specify Calculation dialog box:

- **Auto-Enter field options** let you put a calculated result in a field when someone creates a record or edits data (page 104).

- **Field Validation** uses calculations to make sure the data entered in a field conforms to rules you set up (page 109).

- **Tooltips** can use calculations to change what's displayed in the tooltip (page 752). For example, you can show a list of related data, like the number of items remaining in inventory, or the Totals of all Invoices for a specific customer.

- **Conditional Formatting** lets you apply logic to objects on a layout to change the way they look. On an invoice layout, for example, you can display the Total Due field in a bold red font *if* the invoice is more than 30 days overdue.

- **Scripts** let you use calculations to change the way script steps work. You can test conditions, create dynamic data, or even take different actions based on the results of calculations. Part 5 is where you'll learn about scripting.

- The **Data Viewer** lets you preview your calculations without making a fake field or destroying a perfectly good calculation that needs tweaking. (You need File-Maker Pro Advanced to use the Data Viewer; see page 743.)

- **Accounts & Privileges** can use calculations to limit access to tables, records, and fields. Chapter 16 tells you how to use calculations for tighter database security.

FREQUENTLY ASKED QUESTION

Text Calculations?

Aren't calculations just for numbers?

Many people see the Manage Database window's Calculation field type and assume it's for numbers. Too bad, because calculations can do all this:

- Calculations can pick apart text and put it together in different ways (on page 437, you'll use a calculation to make a Web address that links to a customer's address map). You can even modify fonts, sizes, colors, and styles (turn every occurrence of the word "FileMaker" to bold text, for instance).

- You can do math on *dates, times,* and *timestamps.* You can find out how old someone is based on his birth date, figure out how long you worked on a job, or see which payment came first.

- If you've stored a reference to a file in a *container* field, then you can use a calculation to retrieve the *path* to the original file.

You can even convert one kind of value into another when you use calculations. For example, if you have a text field that contains *12/29/2001,* then you can use a calculation to turn that date into a proper date value.

So you see, calculations can do much more than add a few numbers together.

Creating a Calculation

As your database now stands, when you add line items to an invoice, you have to type the quantity and price for each item. Then you have to multiply them together to get the extended price, and then you have to type the result. In this section, you'll learn how to tell FileMaker to do that all work for you, using a calculation that names your fields and uses computer shorthand to do the math:

1. **In the Mars Investigations database, choose File → Manage Database, and make sure you're on the Fields tab. From the Table pop-up menu, choose Line Items.**

   That's the table with your Extended Price field in it.

2. **In the field list, select the Extended Price field. From the Type pop-up menu, choose Calculation, and then click Change.**

FileMaker warns you that when it converts the field, it changes (read: deletes) any information already in the field. See Figure 9-2.

Figure 9-2:
This warning is serious. Your new calculation overwrites existing data. But even if you write a calculation, there's a way out, so long as you haven't OK'd the Manage Database dialog box. Just click its Cancel button, and you get the chance to discard all the changes you've made in the dialog box.

3. **Click OK.**

The calculation dialog box appears, as shown in Figure 9-3.

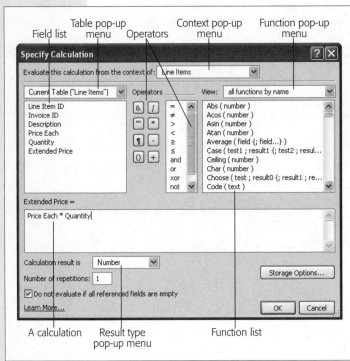

Table pop-up menu Context pop-up menu Function pop-up menu
Field list Operators

A calculation Result type pop-up menu Function list

Figure 9-3:
Any time you create or edit a calculation, you see a window just like this one. You have lots of tools here, all focused on helping you create a calculation. You'll learn how to use all these options in the rest of this chapter. And now that you recognize the Calculation dialog box, you'll start seeing it everywhere: scripts, conditional formatting, accounts & privileges, and even custom menus.

4. **In the Calculation Box, type *Price Each * Quantity*.**

You've just added a brand-new calculation that multiplies the contents of the Price Each by the contents of the Quantity field. The "*" is the same symbol you see on your computer's keypad, and it means multiply. See page 404 for details on other symbols (or operators) used for math.

Note: Although case doesn't matter, spelling and spacing do: You must match the exact name of the fields you want FileMaker to handle.

5. **In the Manage Database window, click OK, and then OK again.**

   You're back where you started.

Tip: If FileMaker complains about not being able to find a field when you click OK, check the spelling of your field names. And if you hate to type, you can double-click the fields in your field list instead of typing.

Switch to the Invoices layout, and then add a line item. You see that the Extended Price field updates *automatically* to reflect the proper price.

The Structure of a Calculation

If you accidentally mistyped or misspelled a field name in the example in the previous section, you already know that FileMaker is picky about how you create a calculation. *Syntax*—the order of elements and punctuation—is critical when you're creating calculations. So before you learn more tricks, this section outlines common calculation terms and rules of thumb.

Note: Calculations are often called *calcs* for short, or *formulas*. Although some slight differences exist between a calculation and a formula, people usually use the terms interchangeably. Sometimes, a formula is so useful or common that FileMaker defines it as a reusable formula, also known as a *function* (see page 407).

A calculation can be short and simple:

```
Pi * Diameter
```

Or it can be more complicated:

```
Case ( Shape = "Circle" ; Pi * (Diameter/2) ^ 2 ;
Shape = "Rectangle" ; ShapeLength * Width ;
)
```

Note: FileMaker doesn't let you give a field the same name as an existing function. The field containing the length of a rectangular object has the unwieldy name "ShapeLength" to avoid confusion with File-Maker's *Length()* function. The field name "Width" is fine, because there's no width function.

In fact, calculations can be *really* long and complicated if you need them to be—up to 30,000 characters. Practically speaking, the only limit on the complexity of a calculation is your patience for creating it.

Regardless of its complexity, a calculation, or formula, is made up of three different elements: *field references, constants*, and *operators*. In the first example, "Pi" is a constant, "*" is an operator, and "Diameter" is the name of a field. The second example uses a function, called a case statement. In that example, "Shape" and "Diameter" are field references, "Circle" and "2" are constants, and "=," "*," and "^" are operators.

Field references have *values* that FileMaker replaces in the formula once it goes to work. First, all the values are replaced, then the operators tell FileMaker what to do to those values, and finally, FileMaker returns a *result* in your field.

Here are some helpful definitions of terms you'll see throughout the next chapters:

• **Field References** are just what they sound like. They refer FileMaker to the data in the field you specify. Since the data inside those fields can change on each record in your database, the values that get replaced in each record can give a different result.

• **Constants** stay the same each time FileMaker does the calculation. See page 402 for details.

• **Operators** tell FileMaker what to do with the values in the calculation. See page 403 for a listing of operators and what they do.

• FileMaker has more than 180 defined **functions** that you can use as shortcuts when you create your formulas. You learn about some of the most common functions later in this chapter. Chapter 11 introduces you to more advanced functions, and in Chapter 12 you learn how FileMaker Advanced lets you create your own reusable functions, called *custom functions*.

• Each calculation has a **result**. This result is, in a sense, the "answer" to the calculation. The result of the first calculation above is the circumference of the circle. The second calculation is a little more complex: Its result is the area of a circle *or* a rectangle, depending on the value in the Shape field. (Don't worry if this calculation doesn't make sense to you now. It will before too long.)

• The result of a calculation has a **type** (just like every field has a type). The type can be any of the standard field types—text, number, date, time, timestamp, or container—or a type called *Boolean*. A Boolean value has only two possible results: yes or no. (Chapter 10 goes into more detail about calculations and data types.)

Note: Sometimes people call a Boolean value "True or False" or "One or Zero" instead. Which term you use doesn't matter much if you just remember that there is a yes-like value and a no-like value. See page 458 for more on Boolean values.

Evaluating Calculations: Now or Later

When you use a calculation, you're asking FileMaker to do something with your fields, constants, and operators and come up with a result. In technical lingo, FileMaker *evaluates* the calculation. *When* the evaluation takes place depends on *where* in your database FileMaker encounters the calculation. Sometimes FileMaker evaluates right away, as when you're calculating an Extended Price. As soon as you type in either a price or a quantity, FileMaker tries to multiply the value. But since one of the fields is empty, the Extended Price calculation has a result of zero (because any value times zero equals zero). When you provide the second value, FileMaker immediately does the math and shows you your result.

- If you create a new calculation field after you already have data in your database, then FileMaker spends some time updating the calculation as soon as you go to the Manage Database dialog box, and click OK.

You may see a progress bar if you have a slower computer and a lot of records.

- When you run the Records → Replace Field Contents command, for example, FileMaker evaluates the calculation you specify once for every record as soon as you click OK. As above, this may take a couple seconds, but it's happening just as soon as FileMaker can plow through your found set.

- Validation calculations evaluate whenever you change the field, or exit the record (you get to decide). See page 421 for more on these.

- Calculations used in scripts evaluate whenever you run the script. Part 5 of this book is all about scripts.

Using Fields in Calculations

The most exciting thing about calculations is learning all the new things you can do with the fields that hold all your data. But no matter what you do with your data, the underlying principle is simple: When you reference a field in a calculation, FileMaker takes the data stored in the field, and uses its value when it determines the calculation's result. For example, let's say a field has this calculation:

```
First Name & " " & Last Name
```

Note: See page 342 to learn how you might use this calculation.

When FileMaker performs (or *evaluates*) the calculation, it replaces the First Name and Last Name field names with the person's first and last names from a given record. The field type determines the value's type: A number field has a number value, a text field has a text value, and so forth.

Note: FileMaker uses the value *stored* in (not displayed in) a field. So if you have a number field with 3. 1415926 as the stored value, and you've formatted the field on the layout to display only two decimal places, then FileMaker uses all seven digits of the stored value to do its math. If you don't want it to use all those digits, use the *round* function (see page 431).

Using Constants in Calculations

As handy as it is to refer FileMaker to a field to find the values in your calculations, you don't want to have to store everything in fields just to use it in a calculation. When a value is going to be the same for every record, it's time to call in a constant. You simply include that value right in the calculation.

Number constants

Sales tax is one of the most common constants. If you need to add sales tax to your order, you can just type the percentage right in the calculation, since it's the same for everybody:

```
Order Total * 1.0625
```

You can enter numbers in any of the formats supported by number fields:

- 37

- .65

- 28.3

- 6.02E23

Text constants

You can also use a constant to have FileMaker plunk some text in with your results. If you want a text value instead of a number, put it in quotes:

```
Age & " years old"
```

Everything within the quote marks is a *text constant* (some people call it a *string* as in "string of characters"). Those quote marks in the calculation are very important (see the box on the next page). Suppose you have a field called First Name, and a calculation like this:

```
"This is my First Name"
```

The quote marks enclose the text that is also a field name, so the result of this calculation is always (*constantly*) "This is my First Name". FileMaker makes no connection whatsoever between the First Name field and the words "First Name" in the text, because the text is in quote marks.

Forgetting quote marks around a text string, or putting them in the wrong place, can make FileMaker whiny. If you make the following calculation:

```
"This is" my First Name
```

FileMaker shows you a warning message that says, "The specified field could not be found", when you try to click OK to close the Manage Database dialog box (Figure 9-4). The characters "my First Name" are highlighted in your calculation

so you can tell exactly which part of the calculation confuses FileMaker. Move your
quotes appropriately, and FileMaker stops telling you that it can't find your field
reference. Here's the correct answer:

```
"This is my " & First Name
```

Figure 9-4:
*When you click OK, FileMaker tries to evaluate your calculation. If it finds
any part of the text that seems like it should be a field name, but there's no
field with that name, then you see this error message. Sometimes you've
made a typing error, but sometimes the field you want is in another table.
See page 415 for more info on referring to fields in a related table.*

FREQUENTLY ASKED QUESTION

Quotes in Quotes

*You're saying that I should use quote marks to incorporate
a word or a phrase into the results of a calculation. But
what if I want to put a quote mark inside my text?*

You're out of luck. No, just kidding. Just put a backslash ("\")
in front of the quote mark, and FileMaker pretends it
doesn't exist when it analyzes your calculation. When a
quote is preceded with a backslash, you say it's escaped,
and "\" is called the escape character. When you put the
escape character in front of another character, it tells File-
Maker to ignore any special meaning that character might
have and treat it as ordinary text. It looks like this:

```
"My line was, \"There's a lady with slacks
on lying in the gutter! Who does she
belong to?"\ Can you believe that?"
```

This calculation is just one long text constant. The two quote
marks inside it are escaped.

If you're a real troublemaker, then your next question is,
"What if I want to put a real backslash *and* quote mark
inside my text constant?"

Luckily, that's easy, too. Just escape the backslash and then
escape the quote:

```
"I really want this: \\\" inside my text"
```

This calculation evaluates to:

```
I really want this: \" inside my text
```

Using Operators in Calculations

The power of calculations comes from their ability to combine various values to
come up with a new and meaningful value. Here's where *operators* come in. An
operator takes the values on either side of it (the *operands*) and *does something*
(operates) with them.

A special symbol or word stands for each operator. This calculation uses the +
(addition) operator:

```
3 + 2
```

In this case, the + operator is given 3 and 2 as operands. When the calculation
evaluates, the operator and its operands combine to produce a single value.

Operators come in three flavors:

- **Mathematical and logical operators** combine two values into one. The + operator is a good example; it takes two number values, and adds them together. Its resulting value is the sum of the two numbers.

- **Comparison operators** compare two values. For example, the = operator tells you if two values are exactly the same. This kind of operator always produces a Boolean value.

- **Parenthesis** operators are used to group parts of a calculation together. Remember your eighth grade math teacher carrying on about the "order of operations"? FileMaker remembers, too, and it uses those same rules to figure out how to evaluate calculations. If the rules don't work for you, then parentheses let you take more control.

Note: Two buttons in the Specify Calculation window's Operators section aren't really operators at all. The ¶ is a special character that tells FileMaker you want a new line in your calculation result, and the quote marks are for entering text values, as explained in the box one page 403.

Mathematical operators

A calculation's most obvious use is to do a little math. Maybe your database of products includes fields for dimensions (Length, Width, and Height), and you want to know the volume. This calculation does the trick:

```
Length * Width * Height
```

It consists of three field values and two copies of the * (multiplication) operator. The result is just what you'd get if you used a calculator to multiply the three field values together.

FileMaker includes operators for basic math:

- + for addition
- - for subtraction
- * for multiplication
- / for division
- ^ for exponentiation ("to the power of" a value)

The concatenation operator

While the mathematical operators combine numbers, the & (concatenation) operator works with text. It hooks together two text values:

```
Length & " inches"
```

If the Length field contains 36, then the result of this calculation is *36 inches*.

Tip: FileMaker can mix numeric values and text together in the same calculation. If you use a number value or field in a place where FileMaker is expecting text, then it just converts the number into text, and gets on with its business.

Comparison operators

You often need to compare two values to learn about them. For example, you may need to add an additional shipping charge if the total weight of an order is more than 20 pounds. All comparison operators result in a Boolean value (see page 458).

FileMaker can compare things in several ways:

- = tells you if two values are the same.
- ≠ or <> tells you if the two values are different.
- > tells you if the first value is bigger than the second.
- < tells you if the second value is bigger than the first.
- ≥ or >= tells you if the first value is bigger than or equal to the second.
- ≤ or <= tells you if the second value is bigger than or equal to the first.

Logical operators

The logical operators evaluate values and come up with a Boolean (Yes/No) result (page 458). Unlike the other operators, most of them are recognizable words.

- The *and* operator tells you if both values are Yes. The calculation below uses the *and* operator. It evaluates to Yes if the length is more than 3 *and* the height is more than 5.

        Length > 3 and Height > 5

- The *or* operator tells you if *either* value is Yes. The *or* calculation below evaluates to Yes if the length is more than 3 *or* the height is more than 5.

        Length > 3 or Height > 5

- The *xor* operator's function is as offbeat as its name. It stands for *exclusive or*. The *xor* operator tells you when *only one* of your two choices is Yes. Put another way, if you find yourself thinking, "I want one of two things to be true, but *not both* of them," then *xor* saves the day. For instance, you may want to track whether you've billed a customer *or* you've marked her character rating below 3. That formula looks like this:

        Invoice Sent = Yes xor Character Rating < 3

Note: If you can't think of a use for *xor*, don't worry. Most of the time when you need an "or" calculation, you can handle it with plain old *or* and not *exclusive or*.

• The last logical operator, *not*, stands alone: It works only on one value, not two like every other operator. It simply reverses the Boolean value that comes after it. So the calculation below would evaluate to Yes if the length is *not* more than 3.

```
Not Length > 3
```

Note: People usually use the comparison and logical operators with the *logical functions*. Chapter 10 covers those.

The ^ operator

The last—and probably least used—operator is the exponentiation, or ^ operator. This lets you calculate exponents:

```
Pi * Radius ^ 2
```

This calculation uses the exponentiation operator and squares the value in the Radius field.

Parentheses

FileMaker uses standard mathematical rules to decide in what order to evaluate things. The order of evaluation is exponentiation, then multiplication/division, then lastly addition/subtraction. If you need FileMaker to do part of your calculation *first*, before moving onto any other operators, put it in parentheses. The parentheses tell FileMaker to treat everything between them as a single unit.

In the calculation below, FileMaker multiplies 3 and 2 before adding 4, and gives you a result of 10.

```
4 + 3 * 2
```

Even though the + operator comes first in the calculation, FileMaker follows the order of calculation. If you want to add 4 and 3 before multiplying, you need to use parentheses:

```
(4 + 3) * 2
```

Thus, it sees that it needs to add 4+3 first, then multiply by 2, for a result of 14. You can see the value of parentheses in calculations like the one below, which calculates the interest on the sum of the balance and service charge. Without the parentheses, FileMaker would calculate the interest on only the service charge, and then add that to the balance due, with an entirely different result:

```
(Balance Due + Service Charge) * Interest Rate
```

Note: If you have trouble remembering (nay, understanding) the order of calculation, then just use parentheses when in doubt. It certainly doesn't hurt to be *too* explicit.

Functions

Values, fields, and operators alone make for a pretty powerful combination. But if you stop there, you've only scratched the surface. The meat of calculations is found in the Function list (which you saw briefly back in Figure 9-3). A *function* is simply a predefined formula, and FileMaker's list covers most common calculation purposes. If you find a function that already does what you want to do—like average all invoices over a specific time period—use it. When you add these tried-and-true formulas to your calculations, you save time and even help prevent errors.

For example, if you didn't know about functions, you could find your average with a series of fields. First, you'd need to create a calculation field to total all the invoices in your found set. Then you'd need another field to count the invoices in the set and a third one that divides the first field by the second. It would work, but it'd be clumsy and inefficient, since you've created at least two fields that you didn't really need.

Because you often need to find averages, FileMaker gives you a *function* that handles the math in a given field. All you have to do is tell FileMaker *which* field you want to average. The function takes care of figuring out the total of the found set, and how many records you have. It looks like this:

```
Average ( Line Item::Quantity )
```

The word "Average" is the function's name. "Line Item::Quantity" is a reference to a related field (see the box page 417). This field reference is called a *parameter*. Parameters tell the function how to perform its specific calculation. The *average* function has only a single parameter, but many functions have two or more.

Parameters are always enclosed in parentheses. (A few functions—most notably, Random—don't need any parameters, so you leave the parentheses off all together.) When there's more than one parameter, they're separated by a semicolon, as in the date function below:

```
Date ( Month ; Day ; Year )
```

FileMaker has more than *180* functions, divided into 16 groups, as described below. Later in this chapter, you'll learn how to use some of the more common functions. (Functions come into play in Chapter 10 and Chapter 12, as well.)

Note: FileMaker has a lengthy help file (Ctrl-? or ⌘-?) that lists each function and some sample uses. If you want to explore a function that isn't covered here, open Help, and then type in the function's name.

Text functions

Dozens of *text* functions let you work with text values. You can compare them, convert them into other types (like numbers), split them up in various ways, count the number of letters, words, or lines, change case, and replace parts of them with new text values. If you're trying to slice, mix, or examine words, look here first.

Text formatting functions

Text formatting functions let you adjust the font, size, style, and color of all or part of a text value. For instance, you could make the account balance for a customer turn red if it's over $100. See page 206 for another way to format data conditionally.

Number functions

Number functions do everything with numbers—from the mundane (rounding) to the esoteric (combinatorics). In between, you can get rid of the decimal part of a number, calculate logarithms and square roots, convert signs, generate random numbers, and perform modulo arithmetic.

Date functions

Date functions make working with dates a breeze. You can safely create date values without worrying about the computer's date settings. You can also pick date values apart (for example, get just the *month* from a date), convert day and month numbers into proper names, and work with weeks and fiscal years.

Time functions

Time functions are few: They create time values from hours, minutes, and seconds, and split times up into the same parts. You use these values most frequently when you're trying to find out how long something took. For instance, if you bill your services hourly, then you can create Start Time and Finish Time fields. Then, in a Duration field, you can subtract finish time from start time to find out how long you worked on a project.

Timestamp functions

There's only one *timestamp* function: It lets you build a timestamp value from a separate date and a time. If you're creating your own data, then you already know that FileMaker needs both a date and a time for a valid Timestamp field, and you've planned accordingly. But you may receive data from an outside source in which the date and time aren't already in a single field. No problem, just use the timestamp function.

Aggregate functions

Aggregate functions calculate statistics such as average, variance, and standard deviation. They can also count things, sum things, and find minimums and maximums. By definition, aggregate functions *gather up* multiple values, and find results based on the group as a whole. (See the box on the next page for more detail.)

Aggregate Functions

Usually when you perform a calculation on a group of records, you use an aggregate function. These functions take multiple values, and combine them in some useful way. This function helps you add up the various charges on an invoice, using fields on the Invoice layout:

```
Sum ( Subtotal ; Sales Tax ; Shipping )
```

An aggregate function can also refer to a related field. In that case, FileMaker aggregates that field's values from *every* related record:

```
Sum ( Line Items::Extended Price )
```

An aggregate function can also reference a single repeating field. Here, FileMaker combines each repetition of the field into a single value.

This special behavior for related or repeating fields works only if you use a single parameter. You can't, for example, sum two sets of related fields as one like this:

```
Sum ( Line Items::Extended Price ; Line
rItems::Shipping Charge )
```

If you refer to more than one field in a sum function, then it looks at only the *first* related value or repetition for each field. Of course, if you do want to total two related fields, you can do so by calling Sum twice and adding their results:

```
Sum ( Line Items::Extended Price ) +
Sum ( Line Items::Shipping Charge )
```

Summary functions

You have only one *summary* function—*GetSummary( )*. Its primary purpose is to let you use the value of a summary field (page 279) in your calculations. In the olden days, before FileMaker was the robust relational database it is now, the *GetSummary( )* function was the best way to sort and summarize certain kinds of data. Now that FileMaker is relational, you usually use calculations through table occurrences to do that work.

Repeating functions

Repeating functions work with repeating fields, and some of them work with *related* fields as well (see Part 4). You can make non-repeating fields and repeating fields work together properly in calculations, access specific repeating values, or get the *last* non-empty value. Since repeating fields have limited uses in these days of related tables within files, so do these functions. However, these functions have a few valid uses, as you'll learn in Chapter 11.

Financial functions

Financial functions make the MBAs in the audience feel right at home. Calculate present value, future value, net present value, and payments. Non-MBAs could calculate the cost of competing loans with these functions.

Trigonometric functions

Trigonometric functions, on the other hand, bring back terrible memories from high school math. If you're making a business-related database, don't worry; you don't even have to look at these functions. But engineers and scientists know what to do with this bunch: sine, cosine, and tangent. They can also convert between radians and degrees. And if you need to, you can get Pi out to 400 decimal places.

Logical functions

Logical functions are a powerful grouping. These functions can make *decisions* based on calculated values (if the due date is more than 3 months ago, add a late fee of 10 percent). FileMaker has functions to evaluate *other* calculations inside your calculations; functions to figure out if fields are empty or contain invalid data; performance enhancing functions to create and use variables (page 473); and functions to perform lookups inside calculations (page 469). Chapter 11 is where you learn when and how to use these big dogs of the function world.

Get functions

Get functions pull up information about the computer, user, database, or FileMaker Pro itself. They make up the largest group (70 in all). You can, for example, find out the computer's screen resolution, the current layout's name, the computer's network address, the current user's name, or the size of any database window. This list just scratches the surface, though. If you're looking for information about the current state of FileMaker, the computer, or the user, then you can probably find it with a get function.

Design functions

Design functions tell you about your database's structure. You can get a list of tables, fields, layouts, or value lists, or details about any of these items. You won't need most of these functions until you become an advanced database designer indeed. ValueListItems is one notable exception, which gives you a list of the values in a value list, separated by paragraph breaks.

Custom functions

If you have FileMaker Pro Advanced, then you can create your very own *custom* functions and have them show up on the list. Once you have them, you (or anyone you let create fields in your database) can choose them just like the built-in functions. (See Chapter 12 for details on creating and using custom functions.)

External functions

If you're not using plug-ins or FileMaker Server, then your *external* functions category is empty. If you've installed any plug-ins ("mini-programs" that add extra features to FileMaker), they probably brought along some functions for their own use. FileMaker stores them in this category. FileMaker Server also uses plug-ins, ironically to help you update your third-party plug-ins. (External plug-ins are covered on page 487.)

Expressions

Expression is a fancy name for a subsection of a calculation—one or more fields, functions, or constants, each connected with operators. When you made the first calculation in this chapter (page 397), you multiplied the contents of the field called Price Each by the contents of the field called Quantity. That's a calculation, but it's also an example of an *expression*.

An expression always reduces to a single value when you combine its individual values according to the operators. If you can't boil it down to a value, then it's not an expression. That's an important point, because it means you can use expressions as function parameters (page 407) just like any individual values—fields and constants. When used in a function, these expressions are called *sub-expressions*.

Here are some examples of expressions:

The following is a simple expression, which reduces to the value 6.

```
3 + 3
```

Below is a more complex expression. It might turn into something like "Shrute, Dwight K."

```
Last Name & ", " & First Name & " " & Middle Initial & "."
```

The following calculation is a function *and* it's an expression, because it reduces down to a single value.

```
Average(L1 * W1 * H1 ; L2 * W2 * H2 ; L3 * W3 * H3)
```

But if you look at just the stuff in parentheses, then you have this:

```
L1 * W1 * H1 ; L2 * W2 * H2 ; L3 * W3 * H3
```

That's *not* an expression because it doesn't reduce down to one value. It has three expressions in all, each separated by a semicolon. Each expression reduces to a single value—three values in all that become parameters passed to the Average function.

You can put *any valid expression* in place of a parameter in a function. In the trade, that's called *nesting* expressions. For example, you can rewrite the expression 3 + 3 like this:

```
( 1 + 1 + 1 ) + 3
```

In this case, the sub-expression (1 + 1 + 1) has replaced the original value 3. The whole thing is a new expression, and it contains one sub-expression. This idea comes in particularly handy when you work with functions. Instead of using individual fields or constants in a function, you can pass along whole expressions. You can even nest functions within other functions (see page 448).

TROUBLESHOOTING MOMENT

Think Like a Machine

If you've jumped right in and started making perfect calculations every time, then you can skip this bit of arcana. But if FileMaker throws up a warning dialog box every time you try to make a halfway complex calculation, or if the syntax seems fine, but you just aren't getting the math to work out right, then you might have to try thinking like FileMaker thinks. To understand how fields, constants, functions, and operators come together to produce a single result, you have to think very logically and in a straight line that inexorably leads to the end of a problem. When FileMaker evaluates a calculation, it looks for something it can do to simplify it—fetch a field value, perform a function, or evaluate an operator.

The calculation shown in Figure 9-5 has a function (average), several operators (* and &), a constant ("cubic inches"), and six fields (L1, W1, H1, L2, W2, H2). You might think the average function is the right place to start, because it comes first. But you quickly realize you can't compute the average until you figure out what its parameters are by performing the multiplication. The * operators multiply values on either side to produce a new value—but FileMaker needs to replace these fields with their values before it can do anything else.

In Step #1, FileMaker identifies six fields. Step #2 shows how the calculation looks once FileMaker replaces them with values.

Now the * operators are all surrounded by values, and FileMaker is ready to do some multiplication (Step #3). Step #4 shows the calculation once all the multiplication is finished.

At last, the average function has two parameters (Step #5), which is just what it needs, so FileMaker performs this function, and the new calculation looks like Step #6.

You have no more fields to replace and no more functions to perform, but there's one last operator. The & operator takes two text values and puts them together, but this & operator has a number on one side. FileMaker notices this fact in Step #7, and fixes it in Step #8. Finally, the & operator is evaluated, and Step #9 shows the calculation result.

If you apply the concepts outlined here to your problem calculations—find the answer to each step, then plod along to the next one—you can always figure out where your calculation has gone astray.

Creating a Calculation Field

The invoice line items now calculate their extended prices automatically, because you created a calculation at the beginning of the chapter to handle that. But you still have to add up the extended price of each line item, and enter the total amount due on the invoice itself. Another calculation solves this problem:

1. **In the Mars Investigations database, choose File → Manage → Databases, and then go to the Fields tab. From the Table pop-up menu, choose Invoices.**

   The field list shows all the fields in the Invoices table.

Start:	Average (L1 * W1 * H1; L2 * W2 * H2) & " cubic inches"
Step 1:	Average (L1 * W1 * H1; L2 * W2 * H2) & " cubic inches"
Step 2:	Average (3 * 5 * 4; 7 * 2 * 3) & " cubic inches"
Step 3:	Average (3 * 5 * 4; 7 * 2 * 3) & " cubic inches"
Step 4:	Average (60; 42) & " cubic inches"
Step 5:	Average (60; 42) & " cubic inches"
Step 6:	51 & " cubic inches"
Step 7:	51 & " cubic inches"
Step 8:	"51" & " cubic inches"
Step 9:	"51 cubic inches"

Figure 9-5:
Taking a complex calculation one bite at a time helps you get the results you expect. Just chip away at the parts, and check your logic at each stage to make sure you and FileMaker are in concert.

2. **In the list, select the Total Due field.**

   The Field Name, Type, and Comment at the bottom of the window update to show information about this field. It's currently a Number field.

3. **From the Type pop-up menu, choose Calculation, and then click the now high-lighted Change button. When FileMaker asks if you're sure you want to make this change, click OK.**

   The Specify Calculation dialog box pops up. (See page 396 for details on its many features.)

4. **From the "Evaluate this calculation from the context of" pop-up menu, choose Invoices.**

   The Invoices table has multiple occurrences on the graph, but since you'll be displaying the Total Due field on the Invoices layout, you want the calculation to evaluate from this context.

Note: When you manage your relationships graph using Anchor Buoy table occurrence groups, it's a lot easier to figure out the context of your calculations. You'll create most calculations in the source table for the Anchor TO, and they'll evaluate from that same context. (See page 335 to learn about context and page 367 to learn about Anchor Buoy TOGs.)

---

5. **From the View pop-up menu (above the function list), choose Aggregate Functions.**

   The function list now shows just the functions FileMaker uses to calculate various kinds of totals and averages. You're looking for the sum function.

6. **Double-click the "Sum (field {; field…})" function in the list.**

   FileMaker copies the full function example into the calculation box. To save you an extra step, it even selects everything between the parentheses (see Figure 9-6). The next thing you type or click becomes the first parameter to the function.

Tip: Anything within curly braces in a function is optional. In the sum function in step 6, you could reference several fields that all get summed up into one glorious total. But that doesn't make sense when you're trying to summarize line items on an invoice, so you're just replacing all the highlighted material with a single field reference.

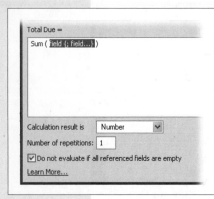

Figure 9-6:
FileMaker gives you a handy syntax reference for each function you choose from the function list. When you double-click to place the function in the calculation box, FileMaker even highlights the parameters for you, so you can start building right away. If you aren't sure what to do, click the "Learn More…" link at the bottom left of the dialog box for context-sensitive help.

7. **From the pop-up menu above the field list, choose Line items, and then, in the list of line item fields, double-click the Extended Price field.**

   FileMaker adds this field to the calculation, placing it between the parentheses that surround the parameters to the sum function. Your calculation should now read:

   ```
   Sum ( Line Items::Extended Price )
   ```

Tip: If you prefer the keyboard, you can use the Tab key to move from the Calculation box to the Field list, then the Operator list, then the Function list. Once you're in one of these lists, use the up and down arrow keys to select an item (or type the first few letters of the item's name). Finally, press the space bar to add the selected item to the Calculation box.

---

8. **From the "Calculation result is" pop-up menu, choose Number.**

   Because this field was a number type before you changed it, it's probably already set to have a Number result.

9. **Click OK in each dialog box to return to your layout.**

   If you've done everything right, the Specify Calculation window disappears. If not, check the syntax of your calculation, and then try again.

Your Total Due field should now work perfectly. Since you modified an existing field that's already on your layout, you don't need to do anything else. Every layout that shows the Line Items::Extended Price now shows the new calculated value.

Switch to the Invoices layout to try for yourself. As you edit, add, or delete Line Item records, the Invoices::Total Due field changes automatically to reflect the correct total.

Understanding the Specify Calculation Dialog Box

As you saw in the previous tutorial, whenever you create a new calculation field, FileMaker shows the Specify Calculation window (Figure 9-3). This window is loaded with options, making it seem a bit daunting—but all those buttons are there to help you. FileMaker shows you the table occurrences, fields, operators, and functions, and all you have to do is point and click to build any calculation you have in mind.

Once you learn how this box works, you can write calculations like a pro without memorizing complicated functions and/or typing out long field names. The following pages give you a guided tour of each element in the window.

Table occurrence context

Since FileMaker sees your database from the perspective of one table occurrence at a time, you have to specify which context you want the calculation to be evaluated from. The Table Occurrence pop-up menu lists every occurrence of the current table—the one you're adding a field to—on the relationship graph. All you have to do is pick the one that works for your purposes. (If your calculation doesn't reference any related data, you can skip this menu.)

Note: Anchor-Buoy relationships (page 367) make it much easier to conceptualize calculations' context, since most calculations are created in the Anchor table occurrence, looking toward the Buoys.

Field list

Since most calculations include fields, and field names are often long and hard to remember, FileMaker lets you pick field names from a list. The Table pop-up menu shows every table occurrence in the graph, with the related tables at the top, and the unrelated tables in a group below. The list below the pop-up menu shows the fields in the selected table occurrence. A calculation can refer to any related field in the database: FileMaker follows the appropriate relationships to grab the data it needs.

Note: You can use global fields from unrelated tables in your calculations. But if you try to use a regular field from an unrelated table, then you get a warning message when you try to close the Specify Calculation dialog box.

If you want to put a field in the calculation itself, just double-click its name in the list, and FileMaker does the typing for you. See step 7 on the previous page for a prime example of when *not* to type a long field name.

Note: When you double-click a field from the list of table occurrences, you create what FileMaker calls a "fully-qualified field reference", which contains the Table name, two colons, and the Field name (Invoices:: InvoiceID). Because you might have similar field names in several tables, a fully qualified name makes sure you reference the right one.

Operators

To help you remember all those operators, FileMaker shows them in the Operators area. Eight buttons represent the most common operators—just click one to insert it. Other operators appear in a scrolling list, which requires a double-click.

Function list

Some functions are so short and sweet that it's faster to type them than to hunt through this very lengthy list. Or you may come to memorize the functions you use most often. But you can't beat the Function list for convenience. It shows every function FileMaker understands, *and* all the parameters each function expects, in the right order. (See the box on page 418 for more detail.)

As usual, double-click a function to add it to the calculation. If you don't fancy an alphabetical list of every function, then you can narrow down your choices using the View pop-up menu. You can pick a specific function type, and see a list of just those functions. The pop-up menu also includes three special categories. The first, "all functions by type" reorganizes the functions in the list. You can see the effect in Figure 9-7.

Figure 9-7:
In the function list, when you choose "all functions by type", FileMaker groups the functions by their type, indents them, and then sorts them by name in each group. The type itself is shown in bold above each group. This method is the easiest way to explore the list of functions when you're not quite sure what you're looking for.

Tip: You can always switch back to "all functions by name" to see every function in one alphabetical list. This choice comes in handy when you know a function's name, but not its category.

Result type

Just as you specify field types when you create fields (page 95), you also specify result types for your calculations. You use the Result Type pop-up menu to tell FileMaker what kind of data this field holds. You can easily figure out result type. If you're using a text calculation, then your result is probably *text*. If it's a number calculation, then the result type is *number*. Surprisingly though, you can also make calculations that are *container* types (see page 454).

FREQUENTLY ASKED QUESTION

Result Type

Why do I have to tell FileMaker my calculation has a number result? I'm multiplying two numbers together, so isn't it obvious?

You're right; FileMaker can figure that out for itself. In fact, in a calculation where you're performing simple math, the field always has a number result. But the ability to set the result type for a field gives you a good measure of control.

For one thing, you and FileMaker may have different ideas about what type a result *should* be. Take this calculation, for example:

    1 & 1 * 3

Because you're mixing concatenation (&) and math (*) operators, it's not terribly obvious *what* that calculation will produce. A number? Or just a numerical text value? So FileMaker lets you say what you *want* it to produce. If it doesn't do what

you expect, then you can easily fix the calculation, but at least you don't have to wonder what type of field you have.

Furthermore, setting the type explicitly prevents FileMaker from changing it later. Imagine if a simple change to your calculation accidentally changes the result type from number to text. If you try to reference this field in a calculation or a relationship, then you get strange results. And it might take you a while to figure out that the problem is due to FileMaker calculating a text value instead of a number, rather than a mistake in your calculation.

If you've set a result type, and your calculation doesn't naturally produce the correct type, then FileMaker converts it for you before it stores the final result. Thus, you can always tell exactly what type the field is just by looking at the Result Type pop-up menu.

Calculation box

Your calculation itself goes in the Calculation box in the middle of the window (it has the field name above it as a label). You can type right into the calculation box if you're a codehead, but mere mortals usually use the field list, operators, and function list, and let FileMaker assemble their calculations for them. When you're getting started, you probably mostly point and click, but as you get more familiar with formulas and functions, you start typing more often. Most people end up using a hybrid of typing and clicking to create their calculations.

Tip: You can also copy and paste into the Calculation box. If you have a calculation in another table file that's the same or similar, you can paste, and then update it for its new home, saving yourself some typing. See the Self function on page 460. It can reduce or eliminate editing when you reuse a calculation.

The Function List

The Function list doesn't show just a list of meaningless names–it also shows an example of how to use the function. The example includes everything you need to call the function in a calculation: name, the necessary parentheses, and a placeholder for each parameter. You just need to replace the placeholders with fields, constants, functions, or expressions.

Most functions are simple, and have a simple example to match:

```
Date ( month ; day ; year )
```

This function, called Date, expects three parameters: a month, day, and year. (If you're curious, it returns a date value based on the three numbers passed to it. See Chapter 10 for more details.)

Many functions aren't quite so simple. Some functions don't have a predetermined number of parameters. The average function needs *at least* one parameter, but you can pass as many as you want. It looks like this in the Function list:

```
Average ( field {; field...} )
```

The first "field" parameter shows that you must specify at least one value. The second one is inside curly braces, meaning it's optional. And it's followed by "…" meaning you can add more copies if you want.

The case function shows up like this:

```
Case ( test1 ; result1 {; test2 ; result2
; ... ; defaultResult} )
```

This shows that you can add additional test and result parameters, and you can put a final defaultResult parameter on the end if you want.

Finally, a few functions actually accept more than one value for a single parameter. The Evaluate function is an example:

```
Evaluate ( expression {; [field1 ; field2
;...]} )
```

It always expects one parameter, called *expression* (see page 411). You can also specify a field to go with it. The brackets around the field show you that it can take two parameters, but the second can be a bracketed list of multiple values. In other words, you can call this function in three ways:

```
Evaluate ( "<some expression>" )
Evaluate ( '<some expression>" ; A Field )
Evaluate ( "<some expression>" ; [Field 1
; Field 2 ; Field 3] )
```

In the first case, it receives only one parameter. In both the second and third cases, you're passing *two* parameters. In the third case only, the second parameter is actually a list of values. Functions like this are rare, but a few exist.

Repetitions

Like any field, a calculation field can be a repeating field (see page 117). FileMaker provides this option for the rare occasion when you need to calculate repeating fields. Suppose you have a repeating field that holds five quantities, and another with five prices. You can write a calculation that multiplies the two fields, and then turn on this box. FileMaker takes care to match all the repetition numbers for you, so the third repetition of the calculation multiplies the third price and the third quantity, for instance. (You're more likely to have related tables, and use a standard single calculation to do the totals, but the option to calculate on repetitions is there if you need it.)

Do Not Evaluate If All Referenced Fields Are Empty

When you create calculation fields (like the Extended Price and Total Due fields in this chapter), you may notice a long-winded checkbox labeled "Do not evaluate if all referenced fields are empty." FileMaker always turns this option on when you first specify a calculation. Here's what it does:

Say you create a new invoice record. It's completely empty, no line items yet. If the Total Due field's "Do not evaluate if all referenced fields are empty" checkbox is turned on, that field is also completely blank, as shown in Figure 9-8. After all, there are no referenced fields (line items), so FileMaker skips the calculation, as the checkbox says.

To be perfectly accurate, however, the value of the total due isn't a blank oblivion—it's zero dollars and zero cents, or $0.00. And indeed, if you turn off the "Do not evaluate" option,

then FileMaker goes through the calculation even when the invoice's fields are empty. For a newly created invoice, File-Maker shows the correctly formatted Total Due result: $0.00. You're free to choose whichever result you prefer.

In other types of calculations, you want FileMaker to keep its paws off empty fields, though. Suppose you have a calculation like this:

```
Height & " inches"
```

If FileMaker evaluates that calculation and the Height field is empty, the result is "inches", which is pretty meaningless, and annoying to boot. In cases where something is worse than nothing, the "Do not evaluate if all referenced fields are empty" option saves you from worry.

Figure 9-8:
When you first create a record, the fields referred to in your calculations are usually empty, so your calculation results are blank, too. But is the field blank or is there a "0" in the field? The box above explains when and why it matters. As usual, FileMaker lets you control which state you get with your calculation fields.

Auto-Enter Calculations

Calculation fields are fantastic—they save time, and ensure error-free results. But they have one serious limitation: You can't *change* their values. Of course, you can adjust the calculation itself, or the fields the calculation depends on, but sometimes you need to be able to override a field's calculated value on a record-by-record basis.

For example, it would be nice if your invoice's Date Due field automatically showed a date 30 days after the date of the invoice itself. But sometimes you may want to make an invoice due earlier or later, based on special circumstances (like a holiday). If you make the Date Due field a calculation field, then you don't have this flexibility. Use a normal Date field with an *Auto-Enter calculation* (see the box on page 421).

Like all the Auto-Enter options (page 104), an Auto-Enter calculation automatically fills in a field's value, but leaves it changeable. You can get all the accuracy and time savings of a calculation field, plus the power to change your mind. Here's how to put it to use:

1. **Bring up the Manage Database window, and then switch to the now-familiar Fields tab. From the Table pop-up menu, choose Invoices.**

   The fields from the Invoices table appear.

2. **Select the Date Due field in the list, and then click Options.**

   The Field Options dialog box makes an appearance.

3. **On the Auto-Enter tab, turn on the Calculated Value checkbox.**

   The Specify Calculation window appears. It looks just like it did before, but this time you're *not* creating a calculation field. Instead, you're specifying the calculation used to determine the auto-enter value.

4. **Create the calculation Date + 30.**

   You can use any method you want to build this calculation: Click the field and operators, or type them. Notice that the calculation result is set to Date, and you don't have a pop-up menu to let you change that. Your calculation must resolve to a valid date, or FileMaker squawks at you.

5. **Click OK three times to dismiss all the dialog boxes.**

   You return to the database itself.

Now you can create a new invoice and test out your field. When you enter a date for the invoice, the Date Due field updates instantly with the date 30 days from now. Notice that you can still change the Date Due field if you want. See the box on page 421 for more on Auto-Enter calculations.

Do Not Replace Existing Value

Auto-Enter calculation fields don't act *exactly* like other calculation fields. If you *change* the invoice date, the due date doesn't update to reflect the change. Instead, it keeps its original value, as in the example on the previous page. That's normally the way Auto-Enter calculations work: It acts only when you first create a record or if the field is empty. Once the field gets a value, the calculation doesn't update it, even if the field it refers to changes.

Often, though, you *want* the calculation to change the field value every time any field used in the calculation is changed, just like a normal calculation. You can easily get this modified behavior by turning off the "Do not replace existing value of field (if any)" checkbox in the Field Options dialog box (shown in Figure 9-9). When you turn this checkbox *off*, FileMaker dutifully updates the field value whenever the calculation evaluates—in other words, when any field it uses changes.

You choose your option depending on the situation. For the Date Due field, you probably want to turn this option off. After all, if you're changing the date of an invoice, it's reasonable to assume you want to rethink the due date as well.

But suppose you have a database of products, and you use an Auto-Enter calculation to copy the distributor's product code into your internal product code field. If you then change the internal product code to something unique to you, then you probably *don't* want it to change again if you switch to a different distributor. In that case, you would leave the "Do not replace existing value (if any)" option turned on, ensuring that once you've put in your own special value, it never changes.

Figure 9-9:
Auto-Enter calculations let you protect data that's already in a field if you change the field the calculation refers to. The verbose setting here, "Do not replace existing value for field (if any)" is turned on for you. But if want an Auto-Enter calculation to update any time the field(s) it refers to changes, then uncheck this option.

Validate Data Entry with a Calculation

In Chapter 3 you were introduced to several ways to validate data entered into a field. But what if the Validation tab in the Field Options dialog box doesn't have a checkbox to meet your needs? For example, you may want to use validation on the Zip Code field in the Customers table. A valid Zip code has *either* five characters or 10 characters (in other words, it can look like this: 90210, or this: 90210-1100). The closest validation option is "Maximum number of characters"—close, but not right.

This situation is just the kind where the "Validate by calculation" option comes in handy. Your job is to create a calculation with a Boolean result. It should return True when the data is valid, and False otherwise. Here's how it works:

1. **View the field definitions for the Customers table (In File → Manage Database). Select the Zip Code field, and then click Options.**

    The Field Options dialog box pops up.

2. **Click the Validation tab, and then turn on "Validate by calculation".**

   The Specify Calculation window appears, ready for you to enter your validation calculation.

3. **From the View pop-up menu, choose "Text functions".**

   The Function list updates to show just the text functions.

4. **In the Function list, double-click "Length (text)".**

   The function appears in the Calculation box. Notice that "text" is already highlighted, ready to be replaced. The length function returns the length of a text value. You use it here to see how many characters are in the Zip Code field.

5. **In the Field list, double-click the Zip Code field.**

   FileMaker puts this field inside the parentheses, where it becomes the parameter to the length function. Now that you have a function to tell you how long the Zip code is, you need to use the comparison operator to compare it to something.

6. **Click to the right of the closing parenthesis. Then, in the Operators list, double-click "=".**

   FileMaker adds the comparison operator (=) to your calculation.

7. **After the = perator, type 5.**

   Your calculation compares the length of the Zip code to the value 5. If they're equal, then it returns True. But you also want to accept a Zip code with *10* characters.

8. **In the Operators list, double-click "or".**

   The "or" operator is added to the end of the calculation. Remember that this operator connects two Boolean values, and then returns True if *either* value is true. Next, you set up the second value.

9. **Double-click the length function again, then double-click the Zip Code function again, and then double-click the = operator.**

   This second check should also compare the length to some other value.

10. **In the Calculation box, type *10*.**

    Your calculation is complete. It should look like the one in Figure 9-10.

11. **Click OK, then OK again, and then a third time.**

    You're now back in your database and ready to test. Try giving a customer a few different Zip codes, and make sure the validation works.

Most validations occur as soon as you leave the field, even if you're just moving to another field in the record. But some validation types—including most validation calculations—don't happen until you exit the *record*.

Figure 9-10:
This calculation checks for two conditions, and it uses an "or" operator. One comparison checks to see if the length is five, while the other looks for a length of 10. If either is True, then your calculation is True as well, and FileMaker accepts the Zip code. If both conditions fail, then the calculation result is False, and FileMaker shows you an error message. See page 425 for an explanation of why in this calculation has extra spaces and paragraph returns.

```
Validation for field "Zip Code" =
Length ( Zip Code ) = 5

or

Length ( Zip Code ) = 10|

Calculation result must be Boolean
Non-zero values are true, zero and empty value
☑ Validate only if field has been modified
Learn More...
```

Tip: If you're dying to know what determines when your validation occurs, here's the skinny: If, when validating a field, FileMaker looks only at the data *in the field itself*, then it performs the validation immediately. If it has to look at data in *other fields* or *other records*, then it waits until you commit the record before validating.

FREQUENTLY ASKED QUESTION

Validate Only If Field Has Been Modified

What is the "Validate only if field has been modified" checkbox for? I don't remember seeing this in the Specify Calculation window before. For that matter, where did the Result Type pop-up menu go?

Good eye. The Specify Calculation window can show up in lots of places—when defining a calculation field, when specifying an Auto-Enter calculation, and so on—and it can change slightly in some cases.

First, the Result Type pop-up menu shows up only when you're defining a calculation field, since it can produce any data type. Since a validation calculation always has a Boolean result, there's no need to ask you here.

In place of this pop-up menu, you often see some new option specific to the calculation type—like the "Validate only if field has been modified" checkbox in Figure 9-10.

Normally when you edit a record, FileMaker validates only the fields you actually change. Any field in the record that hasn't been changed is accepted even if it violates the validation rule. This violation can happen when you have your field set to validate "Only during data entry", and the records have been set some other way—from an import (page 683) or a script (page 534). If you want to validate this field whenever you edit the record, not just when the field itself changes, then turn off this checkbox.

Replacing Data Using a Calculation

You can use calculations productively with the Records → Replace Field Contents command. This command tells FileMaker to visit every record in the found set, replacing the contents of one field with something new. When you first saw this command in Chapter 2, you entered a single value in every record. Sometimes, though, it's more useful to have FileMaker use a calculation to figure out what should go in each record.

Tip: Replace Field Contents is a huge timesaver, but since it works on a found set of records, you can't undo it. Improperly used (with a bad calculation or the wrong found set), it can be destructive. See page 743 to learn how the Data Viewer in FileMaker Pro Advanced helps you preview the results of a calculation before you make that one-way trip through the Replace Field Contents dialog box.

Imagine you attended the International Private Investigators conference in South Dakota, where you picked up 73 business cards you'd like to add to your database. Rather than type them yourself, you told your 13-year-old nephew you'd give him a gumball for each card he typed in. After the cards are tossed and the gum given, you discover he has an aversion to the Shift key—none of the names are capitalized.

You could go through all the records one by one, fixing the capitalization and regretting the cost of the gumballs. But if you use the Replace Field Contents command, you can do all your records with just one command, using a calculation. You use the Proper function, which capitalizes the first letter of each word it encounters. Here's how:

1. **From Browse mode, click the First Name field.**

   The Replace Field Contents command operates on the field you're in when you run it. So click to start in the correct field first.

2. **Choose Records → Replace Field Contents. In the Replace Field Contents window, select the "Replace with calculated result" radio button.**

   As soon as you make this choice, your old friend the Specify Calculation window appears.

3. **From the View pop-up menu, choose "Text functions" (above the function list).**

   The list updates to show only text functions.

4. **Double-click "Proper (text)" in the function list.**

   FileMaker inserts the proper function in the calculation box. Since it has only one parameter, it's already selected. You just have to tell it what text to perform its magic on.

5. **In the field list, double-click the First Name field.**

   FileMaker inserts *First Name* as the parameter for the proper function.

6. **Click OK to close the Specify Calculation dialog box. Then, in the Replace Field Contents window, click Replace.**

   Notice—and beware—that the Cancel button in this dialog box is automatically highlighted. If you hit Enter too quickly, or accidentally click Cancel, then you have to start all over, because the dialog box doesn't remember your calculation. It's worth taking an extra second to make sure you're clicking the appropriate button.

If you have a lot of records, then you see a progress dialog box. Normally, though, the replacement happens so quickly that you don't even notice.

Tip: FileMaker has two other functions for changing case: Upper and Lower. It probably goes without saying that Upper converts all the text to uppercase, and Lower converts it to lowercase.

Comments

Everything you can put in a calculation has some kind of value—unless it's a *comment*. Comments are chunks of text whose sole purpose is to help guide you through long calculations. Professional database developers, like all good programmers, provide lots of comments for the benefit of people who might work on the computer code months or years later. Once you have a few sets of parentheses or nested function calls, you may have trouble understanding even your *own* FileMaker calculation when you have to go back and make changes. When it evaluates the calculation, FileMaker ignores all comments completely—it's as if they weren't there. (But you'll be glad they are.)

Note: You may have noticed that this book shows some extras spaces and paragraph returns that FileMaker doesn't throw into your functions automatically. These spaces are for ease of reading, and lots of developers type them into their calculations. Like comments, FileMaker ignores those spaces, as long as all the other syntax is correct.

You can use two different styles for your comments. First, any text that comes after two consecutive slash marks (//) is considered a comment. This kind of comment goes all the way to the end of the line:

```
// this is a comment
3.14 * Diameter // and so is this
```

A comment is also any text that comes between the symbols /* and */. This symbol pair comes in handy in two places. It saves typing if you need to type a long comment across multiple lines:

```
/* this is a comment that runs across multiple
lines. To make life easier, you can use the second
comment style */
```

Also, this comment style lets you add comments *within* a line:

```
3 /*sprocket size*/ * 10 /*sprocket count*/ * 57 /*tooth count*/
```

In addition to comments, you can—and should—use white space to make your calculations easier to read. Calculations don't have to be strung together in one long line, even though that's the way FileMaker does it in the Specify Calculation dialog box. Press the Return key or space bar to add space anywhere, except in a field name, function name, text constant, or number. Comments and white space can make a world of difference. Here's a long calculation that doesn't use either:

```
Let([DaysToAdd=Case(DayOfWeek(theDate)=1;1;DayOfWeek(theDate)=2;0;DayOfWeek(t
heDate)=3;-1;DayOfWeek(theDate)=4;-2;DayOfWeek(theDate)=5;-
3;DayOfWeek(theDate)=6;-4;-
5)];Date(Month(theDate);Day(theDate)+DaysToAdd;Year(theDate)))
```

The calculation works just fine, but it's a nightmare to read and worse to edit. Here's the same calculation, written with a comment and helpful spaces:

```
/*Figure out what day it is, and then add or subtract the
proper number to the DayOfWeek value to identify This Monday.*/

Let ( [ DaysToAdd =
Case (
DayOfWeek ( theDate) = 1; 1; // Sunday
DayOfWeek ( theDate) = 2; 0; // Monday
DayOfWeek ( theDate) = 3; -1; // Tuesday
DayOfWeek ( theDate) = 4; -2;  // Wednesday
DayOfWeek ( theDate) = 5; -3; // Thursday
DayOfWeek ( theDate) = 6; -4; // Friday
-5) ] ; // Saturday
Date ( Month ( theDate ); Day ( theDate ) + DaysToAdd; Year ( theDate ))
)
```

Sure, it takes up a bit more space, but this way, you can much more easily pick apart the pieces to figure out what the calculation does. In the next chapter, you'll learn about the functions used in this calc.

More Calculations and Data Types

The last chapter introduced the terminology and concepts behind FileMaker's calculations. You learned how to create them using the Specify Calculation dialog box's tools. The sheer length of the functions list shows how big a role functions play in good calculation construction. FileMaker divides that long list into types so you can more easily find the one you need, and because the types usually share some common traits that that make using them easier. In this chapter, you'll learn about the most common functions for the various data types—text, number, date, time, timestamp, and container—and when to use them. To test a calculation, just create a brand new calculation field, and then start building it using the techniques you've learned so far. If it doesn't work the way you expect, or if you don't need it after your experiment is done, then just delete the field.

Note: Download a copy of the database used in this chapter from the Missing CD page at *http://missingmanuals.com*.

Number Crunching Calculations

Although they don't come first in the function list, number functions are the most obvious application of calculations, so they're a logical place to start. Plus, many concepts you'll learn for number functions apply to other functions as well.

Number Operators

Operators, along with fields, constants, and functions, are one of the basic building blocks of a calculation. FileMaker has five operators that specifically apply to numerical calculations, the same five that you probably already know:

- + is for addition
- – is for subtraction
- * is for multiplication
- / is for division
- ^ is for exponentiation ("to the power of")

Page 403 explains how to use these operators in detail, but here's a quick example. Say you're an event planner and you always plan for 10 percent above the expected number of attendees. Use this calculation to find your fudge factor:

```
Confirmed Attendees * 1.1
```

Number Function Types

Since you have so many number functions, the Function list breaks them up into smaller groups with descriptive names. You can easily find the group you need (or skim by them without looking, if you might be traumatized by accidentally seeing a sine or cosine function). The function groups you use with your numeric data are:

- Number functions
- Aggregate functions
- Financial functions
- Trigonometric functions

Note: This book doesn't cover the financial and trigonometric functions, which have highly specialized uses. If you need to use these brawny functions, you probably have the mental muscle to decipher the technical terms in FileMaker's Help file, where you'll find them explained.

Using Number Functions

As you saw on page 407, most functions expect one or more parameters. Number functions' parameters must be number values, and all the number functions return a number result. In the next sections, you'll see examples of several of the most commonly used number functions. These examples are from the Number and Aggregate groups, but you might find them more easily if you sort your function list alphabetically.

Abs()

Abs is short for Absolute, and it returns the absolute value of a number, which is the positive value of the number or zero. For example, you might have a series of readings from a brainwave scan that range from negative to positive, but you just need to know how far each value is from zero. You could add an *Abs( )* function to each field to find out. This calculation returns 343.7634:

```
Abs ( -343.7634 )
```

This calculation returns 4:

```
Abs ( 2 * 42 / -21 )
```

Average()

The Average function can work with one or more: constant values, regular fields, repeating fields, all related fields in a relationship, or just the first related field. For example, if you store a series of student test scores in several related tables, then you can use an *Average( )* function to round them all up. This calculation returns 10:

```
Average ( 3 ; 6 ; 21 )
```

When you use fields instead of numbers, FileMaker uses the values from those fields. This calculation returns the average of all tests in the related table:

```
Average ( Tests::Score )
```

This calculation returns the average for all the first related test records:

```
Average ( AIMS::Score ; Reading::Score ; Math::Score )
```

Count()

The *Count( )* function counts all non-blank values in a field, whether it's a repeating field, all related fields, or several non-repeating fields. Because it's possible to have a record that doesn't have a value in a particular field, it's usually more accurate to count a related field that is guaranteed to have a value, like the table's ID field. This way, you can easily count related values, like the number of invoices for a customer or tests taken by a student. This calculation returns the number of Invoices in the related table:

```
Count ( Invoice::InvoiceID )
```

This calculation returns the total number of changes you record for an employee's status:

```
Count ( NameChanges ; DeptChanges ; LicenseChanges )
```

Floor( ) and Ceiling( )

The *Floor( )* function is like a supercharged rounding function. It rounds any value down to the next lowest integer. It just takes a single parameter, so you can use a number, an expression, or a field reference. This calculation returns 3:

```
Floor ( 3.1416 )
```

Watch what happens with a negative number. This calculation returns –4:

```
Floor ( -3.1416 )
```

It can be awkward to show values of multiple decimal places for prices, so you can use ceiling to get a whole dollar figure instead, like so:

```
Floor ( Tax * Extended Price )
```

The *Ceiling( )* function is a close relative of *Floor( )*, but it rounds a number up to the next highest integer. So, this calculation returns 4:

```
Ceiling ( 3.1416 )
```

And this calculation returns -3:

```
Ceiling ( -3.1416 )
```

To figure out how to charge your customers the actual price you spent on fuel (32. 987), plus a 10% surcharge (1.1), but without the weird decimal places, use this calculation for a result of 37:

```
Ceiling ( FuelExpense * 1.1 )
```

List( )

This aggregate function works with numbers, but is even more useful on text. *List( )* gathers up all the values you specify, and then returns them in a *return-separated list*. That is, each value appears on a line by itself, and each line has a paragraph symbol after it. So for this calculation:

```
List ( Line Items:: Description )
```

You might get:

```
35mm Film
IGB USB Flash Drive
Bento v2
```

Use *List( )* to suck related data, repeating fields or a series of nonrepeating fields into a single text block for easy display, reporting, or manipulation. You could display the results of a *List( )* in a Tooltip, which you'll learn about on page 752. Or, if you need to grab a list of related IDs, *List( )* is your go-to function.

Round()

The *Round( )* function rounds a value to the number of places you set. It takes two parameters: number and precision. So if you set the precision to 3, this calculation returns 3.142:

```
Round ( 3.1416 ; 3 )
```

Tip: You might be tempted to simply use number formatting on a field to display a value to a specific number of decimal places. But remember, that method changes only what you see on a layout. If you perform math on that field, then FileMaker uses the real value (with all its decimal glory) in the calculation. But when you use the Round function, you're actually changing the value in field, and any calculations acting on that field use that *new* value.

SetPrecision()

Some calculations demand a high degree of precision, like those that track radioactive isotopes or other scientific data with lots of places following the decimal point. The *SetPrecision( )* function extends FileMaker's default precision of 16 decimal places, up to a maximum of 400. To get more than 16 decimals places, add a *SetPrecision( )* function to the calculation that produces the value that requires precision. You can use *SetPrecision( )* with all other numeric functions, except trigonometric functions, which don't accept this extended precision (see Figure 10-1).

Figure 10-1:
The first item in this window shows how FileMaker normally evaluates the value of pi. In the second, the SetPrecision function shows 21 decimal places. The third item shows 42 decimal places. You can see the formula on the left, and the result on the right. (This window is the Data Viewer, which you'll learn more about on page 743.)

The *SetPrecision( )* function requires two parameters: expression and precision. The first parameter is a number, or any expression that results in a number. The second is the number of decimal places you want to see.

Note: The *SetPrecision()* function affects your calculation's result, but not necessarily the way FileMaker displays it. To save space on your layout, you can use Number formatting on the field to show only a few decimal places until you click the field, when you see the real, stored value.

The *Max()* and *Min()* Functions

Often, you need to know either the highest or lowest value in a series. The *Max()* function and its twin sister, *Min()*, fulfill these needs, and you find them in the function list's aggregate functions category. Like all the aggregate functions, these functions expect at least one parameter, and are glad to get more. Every parameter should be a number. Your parameters can be:

- Constant data

- Fields within a record

- Repeating fields

- All related fields

- The first related record of from multiple tables

The max function looks at every number referenced, and returns whichever is largest. *Min()*, on the other hand, returns the smallest value.

For example, look at this calculation:

```
Max ( 10 ; 3 ; 72 ; 19 ; 1 )
```

Its result is 72, since that's the largest parameter.

If you have a repeating field called Distances that holds the distances from your office to each Krispy Kreme store in your city, then you can use this calculation to find the closest sugar fix:

```
Min ( Distances )
```

The same is true for *related* fields too. This calculation finds the most expensive line item on an invoice:

```
Max ( Line Items::Price )
```

With both repeating fields and related fields, you pass just one field to the min or max function, but FileMaker considers *all* the values in that field. If the field is a repeating field, then FileMaker considers every repetition. If it's a related field, then its value from every related record is considered. But you can refer to multiple related tables, too. If you have several tables of updates, each with a date the update was done, then you can find the most recent update this way:

```
Min ( Name::Update ; License::Update ;
      Department::Update )
```

Going Beyond Basic Calculations

In the last chapter you created two very simple calculation fields using numbers: Extended Price and Invoice Total. But those calculations were very simple. Now, you build on those basic concepts, and use some of the number functions you've just learned to make a set of calculations that fit an upcoming sales promotion.

Preparing the Data

You've decided to start reselling personal security products to your customers. To help keep track of things, you need to add a Products table to your database. The table should have these fields:

- A text field called SKU

- A text field called Description

- A number field called Cost

- A number field called Price

Note: See page 316 for advice on creating tables.

Once you've created this new table, FileMaker automatically creates a layout—Products. Switch to that layout now and create a few product records. To help drive sales to your larger clients, you want to implement a volume discount scheme; they should get a 5 percent discount if they buy enough. But some of the products you sell don't have enough mark-up to justify these discounts. You want to be sure the discount never reduces your mark-up below 20 percent.

First, you add a line to your marketing materials: "Volume discounts not available for all products." You can make this line as small as humanly possible, and hide it way down in the corner. Next, you need to fix your database so it tells you the discount price for each product.

Building the Calculation Fields

To implement this discount scheme, take what you need to know, and translate it into calculation terms.

- First, calculate 95 percent of the price (a 5 percent discount):

    ```
    Price * .95
    ```

- Second, you also know the cost (in the Cost field) and you can figure out the lowest price by adding 20 percent to this cost:

    ```
    Cost * 1.2
    ```

- Finally, the discounted price is either the calculated discount price, *or* the cost + 20-percent price, whichever is *greater*. Put another way, you want the *maximum* of these two values:

    ```
    Max ( Price * .95 ; Cost * 1.2 )
    ```

Using the *Max()* function, the previous calculation results in either the discounted price, or the minimum price, whichever is greater (see the box on the next page). That result is *almost* perfect. But suppose you have a product whose *normal* price is less than 20 percent above cost (hey, it's a competitive market). If you use the *Max()* calculation as it is now, then the new discounted price is *more* than the normal price. You need to go back and add to your calculation so that it takes the regular price into account, and uses *that price* if it's lower than the calculated discount. Read on to learn how to think through this calculation quandary.

Constructing the Calculation

When calculations start to get complicated like this discount price example, imagine that you have a field that contains the value you already want. You can use this pretend field in your new calculation, and then, when you're all finished, put the old calculation in place of the pretend field. In this case, just pretend you have a field called Calculated Discount that holds the discount price. With that imaginary field in mind, you can fix your problem with this calculation:

```
Min ( Calculated Discount ; Price)
```

The result of this calculation is either the calculated discount or the regular price, if it's lower. Now, just put the old calculation in place of the words "Calculated Discount" (since the old calculation *results in the calculated discount*):

```
Min ( Max ( Price * .95 ; Cost * 1.2 ) ; Price)
```

The entire *Max( )* function, complete with its two parameters, is now the *Min( )* function's first parameter. You might think it looks a little confusing at first, but with practice you become accustomed to looking at functions-inside-functions like this.

If it helps, you can add white space and comments to clarify the calculation, Figure 10-2 shows.

Figure 10-2:
You may find it hard to write nested calculations, and hard to read them if you need to come back later and tweak them. In this case, though, the calculation is formatted with copious white space and plenty of comments. Chances are you understand this version better than the one shown in the text above.

To use the calculation, just create a new calculation field (call it *Discounted Price*) with the calculation above. It automatically adjusts, and shows you an appropriate discounted price.

If you want to test a complicated calculation, spot-check a few records where you know the result. Sometimes the math is so complex that you just have to work it out on paper and enter dummy records to check the calculation. Usually, if a calculation isn't working, you can figure out how to fix it when you compare your math to the value in the field.

Text Calculations

Although most people think of functions for doing dry stuff like math in a spreadsheet, you can also use functions in your database's text fields. Just as you can add and subtract numbers with number functions, you can use text functions to slice and dice the words in your database. For example, you might receive data from an outside source that needs major cleanup before you can use it. This data has people's first and last names in the same field; it's even got entire email messages crammed

Repeating Fields for Multiple Results

What if one discount price isn't enough? Suppose you want to give your customers 5 percent off on orders of five or more, 10 percent off on orders of 10 or more, 15 percent off on orders of 15 or more, and so on. You could create more calculation fields with slight variations on the calculations you've already specified:

- Discounted Price for 10:

```
Min ( Max ( Price * .90 ; Cost * 1.2 ) ;
Price)
```

- Discounted Price for 15:

```
Min ( Max ( Price * .85 ; Cost * 1.2 ) ;
Price )
```

If you want seven price breaks, then you have to create seven fields. And if you want to change the calculation slightly (for example, to give an additional 2 percent discount per break instead of 5 percent), then you have to change every single field's calculation.

This example is one of those cases where repeating fields come in handy. When you create a repeating calculation field, you have only one calculation, but you get multiple results. With only one calculation, though, FileMaker doesn't show you an obvious way to provide different discount rates. The secret ingredient is the *Get (CalculationRepetitionNumber)* function. It returns the repetition number being calculated at the moment. For example, when FileMaker goes to calculate the *third* value in your repeating field, this function returns 3.

With this function in mind, you can devise a single calculation that uses different discount rates depending on the repetition number:

```
Min (
 Max(
  Price[1] * (1 -
  Get(CalculationRepetitionNumber) * .05);
  Cost[1] * 1.2
  ) ;
 Price[1]
 )
```

In this calculation, you replace the constant discount rate by the expression:

```
(1 - Get(CalculationRepetitionNumber) *
.05)
```

You also need to add [1] to the end of each mention of the Price and Cost fields since they aren't repeating fields (this step tells FileMaker to grab the *first* repetition–the only one with anything in it).

If you test this calculation with a few numbers, then you see it results in an extra 5 percent discount for each subsequent repetition. Once you've created a field like this, a lot of things become really easy:

- To add *more* price breaks, just change the number of repetitions in the Specify Calculation dialog box:

  Going from seven breaks to 20 is a 5-second change.

- To change the discount rates for *every* break, just change one number–the .5–and you affect every calculated value.

into a field—address, subject, and body—when all you need is the email address. You can equip a temporary database with fields and text calculations to *parse* (think of it as sifting) the data into the form your better-designed database expects.

Note: Fixing data with parsing calculations is called a *calculated replace,* since you use the Replace dialog box to enter the calculation. Since Replace works on the found set of records, you do a find first, to isolate just the records that have the problem you're fixing, and then (and only then) do a calculated Replace Field Contents that fixes the error.

The Concatenation Operator

In contrast to the wide variety of mathematical operators for working with numbers, only one pertains specifically to text—the *concatenation* operator. Represented by the & sign (ampersand), it strings bits of text together. (When you need to chop and divide your text in order to parse it, you use a function instead of an operator, as described on page 438.)

To use this operator, put it between units of text, as in the expression below:

```
"This is a " & "test"
```

The result of this calculation is *This is a test*.

The concatenation operator lets you combine text from two different fields, and make them work better together. For example, when you set up the jobs layout in your database in Chapter 8, you had to compromise. On the value list for the Customer pop-up menu (page 342), you could pick only *one* field to show along with the ID value. That example used the First Name field, but the full name would make the menu more useful. That's where concatenation comes in.

Create a new calculation field in the Customers table called *Full Name*. Set the result type to Text, and then create this calculation:

```
Last Name & ", " & First Name "
```

Some results might be "Trout, Kilgore" or "Pilgrim, Billy". Note that the calculation includes a comma and the appropriate spaces for separating data between your fields. Now you can modify the All Customers value list to use the Full Name field instead of First Name. Figure 10-3 shows the result.

Figure 10-3:
When you switch the value list to use the new calculated Full Name field, your pop-up menu can show your Customer's full name instead of just the first name. People often use calculations to combine multiple field values for display purposes.

Text Functions

It's surprising to database newcomers, but text requires nearly as much manipulation as numbers do. That's because data frequently comes from another source, like Excel or Access. If you're lucky, the data is already in the form you need. Often though, you have to massage the data to get it divided up to match your tables, fields, and field types. Sometimes, as with the Full Name calculation in the previous section, you just want to make the data display better. To know how to solve your problem, you need to know about text function types.

Advanced Web Viewer URLs

In Chapter 5 you learned about the Web viewer, a full-featured Web browser you can stick right on a layout. Web Viewers come configured to visit some canned Web sites. But if you want to go beyond the basics, then you have to code your own custom URL, and that almost always requires calculations. The concatenation operator (&) will take your Web viewer expertise to the next level.

In the Web Viewer Setup dialog box (page 211), in the "Choose a Web Site" list, click the first item: Custom Web Address. On the right side of the window, the configuration options disappear.

Click the Specify button, which brings up the Specify Calculation dialog box, pre-filled with a highlighted calculation. Delete it, because you'll be making a custom URL that matches the one in your browser. Find the parts based on changing data, and then convert them to a calculation. Here are a few ways to make a calculated URL:

- Your easiest solution: Store a Web address in your database. Suppose you have a Home Page field in your Company database that holds the URL for a company's home page. Use this simple calculation to display the home page in your Web viewer:

    `"http://" & Company::Home Page`

- If you look up a stock symbol on Yahoo Finance, then the address box in your browser shows something like this:

    `http://finance.yahoo.com/q?s=AAPL`

In this case, the URL shows stock information for Apple, whose stock symbol is *AAPL*. To make the Web viewer show the correct page for any symbol in your database, use this calculation (which assumes you have a field called Stock Symbol):

`http://finance.yahoo.com/q?s=" & Company::Stock Symbol`

- Finally, suppose you use the Basecamp project management system (*http://basecamphq.com*), and you want to show the project overview page in your FileMaker billing database. Basecamp's URL looks like this:

    `https://myaccount.com/projects/12345/project/log`

    If you look closely, then you come to the conclusion that the "12345" bit is a unique identifier for the project. Everything else looks pretty generic. So you can store just that identifier in your FileMaker database, and use this calculation to show any project in a Web viewer:

    `"https://myaccount.com/projects/" & Project::Basecamp ID & "/project/log"`

Using the power of calculations, you can integrate just about any Web content into your layout. You're no longer limited to the list of sites FileMaker provides.

Text function types

FileMaker's text-handling functions come in two flavors: *text* and *text formatting*. Text functions handle tasks like finding whether a particular string of characters occurs in a field, or changing all instances of specific characters within a field, or counting text length. Text functions can break up text in three ways: by *characters*, *words*, or *values*. When FileMaker does the dividing, it gives you three ways to decide which parts you want: *left*, *middle*, or *right*.

Text formatting functions change the way your text looks, like making a part of the text in a field bold and red. These functions are a lot more flexible than just making a field bold and red on your layout, because you can tell the calculation to search *inside* the field, find just the characters "Propane Sale!", and make them red, but leave all the surrounding text untouched.

POWER USERS' CLINIC

A Calculation in a Button

On page 267, you learned how to create buttons on a layout and program them to perform all kinds of database duties at a click. The only problem is, the more features you give your database, the more buttons you have to make. And some of the folks using your database need a completely different assortment of buttons. Fortunately, most button commands have one or more options you can set with a calculation. The calculation can adjust what the button does based on field data, user information, the current date or time, and so forth.

Suppose you have two different layouts to view the people in your People database. One's for the people who are *customers,* and the other's for *employees.* In Chapter 5, you added a button to the list layout of a database that takes you to the detail layout. You might think with two different detail layouts you would need two buttons. But you can summon the power of calculations to make one button do double duty.

If you take a peek at the options for the "Go to Layout" button action, then you see that in addition to all the layouts in your database, the pop-up menu includes two options you haven't used before: "Layout Name by calculation" and "Layout Number by calculation".

If you pick either of these options, FileMaker presents the Specify Calculation dialog box. You simply write a calculation that evaluates to the correct layout name (or number if that's your persuasion), and FileMaker goes to the right one. For example:

```
If ( Person::Type = "Customer", "Customer
Detail", "Employee Detail" )
```

Character functions

Parsing by character comes in handy when you have data in a predictable format, and you need to access pieces of it. You can use functions to grab the first three digits of a Social Security number, the last four digits of a credit card number, or the style code buried inside a product number.

FileMaker can work with individual characters inside a text value. The first letter in a text value is number 1, the second is number 2, and so on. Then you can ask for the first few characters, or the last few, or just the fifth, sixth, and seventh.

Note: Every letter, number, punctuation mark, space, tab, carriage return, or other symbol counts as a character.

- The **Left( )** function returns only the leftmost letters of a text value. You *pass* (that is, tell) the calculation the actual text value to parse, and the number of letters you want. For example, to get a person's initials, you can use a calculation like this:

  ```
  Left ( First Name ; 1 ) & Left ( Last Name ; 1 )
  ```

  To get the first three digits of a Social Security number, you can use this calculation:

  ```
  Left ( SSN ; 3 )
  ```

- The **Right( )** function does the same thing but starts from the other end of the text value. If you want to record the last four digits of someone's credit card number, then you can do it like this:

  ```
  Right ( Credit Card Number ; 4 )
  ```

- If the information you want isn't on either end, you may need to use the **Middle( )** function instead. This function expects *three* parameters. Just as when using left and right, the first parameter is the text value FileMaker's inspecting. The second parameter is the starting position. Finally, you tell FileMaker how many characters you want.

  For example, suppose you have a product database that uses a special coding system for each item. The code "SH-112-M" indicates shirt style 112, medium size. To pull out just the style number (that 112 in the middle of the product code), you want your calculation to grab three characters from the Product Number field, starting with the fourth character.

  ```
  Middle ( Product Number ; 4 ; 3 )
  ```

Tip: Use the Right function to pad a number with leading zeroes (or any other character. For example, the calculation *Right ("0000" & InvoiceID ; 5)* puts two zeroes in front of InvoiceID #789, only one in front of #6789, but none at all in front of #56789.

Word functions

FileMaker also understands the concept of words. With word functions, you don't have to bother dealing with every single character.

In FileMaker's mind, a *word* is any stretch of letters, numbers, or periods that doesn't have any other spaces or punctuation in it. Most of the time, this definition means FileMaker does exactly what you expect: It sees the real words in the text. For example, each of the following is one word:

- FileMaker

- ABC123

- This.is.a.word

Any sequence of other characters isn't part of a word at all. Each of these has two words:

- FileMaker Pro
- ABC 123
- A-Test
- Two *** Words

Note: If your text value doesn't have normal words (like a long URL, for example), then you may have to pay special attention to the letters-numbers-periods rule to get the results you expect.

Along the same lines as the character functions, FileMaker has three word-oriented functions called *LeftWords( )*, *RightWords( )*, and *MiddleWords( )*. Each takes two parameters: the text value to examine, and a number to tell FileMaker which words you're interested in. You can use a word function to parse a person's first and middle names if you ever get a file with all three names unceremoniously dumped into a single field.

- **LeftWords( )** returns all the text before the end of the specified word. For instance, this function:

      LeftWords (Preamble ; 3)

  might return *We the People*. But if Preamble contained "This *** Is *** a *** Test," it would return *This *** Is *** A* instead. In other words, it doesn't just return the words. It returns *everything* before the end of the third word.

- Likewise, **RightWords( )** returns everything *after* the specified word's *beginning*, counting from the end. This calculation:

      RightWords (Revelations ; 1)

  returns *Amen*.

- What would *LeftWords( )* and *RightWords( )* be without **MiddleWords( )**? You can probably guess how this function works: You pass in a text value, a starting word, and the number of words to return. It then returns everything from the beginning of the starting word through the end of the finishing word. The following calculation shows how it works; it returns "or not" because they're the third and fourth words.

      MiddleWords ("To be, or not to be" ; 3 ; 2)

Text editing functions

FileMaker includes dozens of text functions, but a few of them are worth special mention because you see them throughout the rest of this section, and because they're so useful for cleaning up messy data.

FREQUENTLY ASKED QUESTION

The Middle Way

It looks like you can tell the Middle( ) *function to isolate characters anywhere in a text field, just by telling it which characters to count. So why do we need* Left( ) *and* Right( ) *functions when you can do the same thing with* Middle( )?

As the example on this page suggests, the *Middle( )* function indeed provides all the power you need to pick text values apart character by character. For example, instead of:

```
Left ( Model Number ; 3 )
```

You could do this:

```
Middle ( Model Number ; 1 ; 3 )
```

It gets a little tougher to mimic the *Right()* function, but it's possible.

In *lots* of places, one function can do the same thing as another (or a few others).

For example, you can use *Left( )* and *Right( )* instead of *Middle( )* if you want. This calculation:

```
Middle ( Product Number ; 4 ; 3 )
```

can be rewritten like this:

```
Right ( Left ( Product Number ; 7 ) ; 3 )
```

The good news is, there's no *right answer*. Shorter is usually better, if only because you can often read it more easily. But if a few extra keystrokes make the calculation easier to understand, then they're usually worth it.

- The **Substitute**( ) function performs a find-and-replace within a text value. For example, if you want to turn all the Xs to Os in your love letter (maybe you felt like you were coming on too strong), then you can do this:

```
Substitute ( Love Letter ; "X" ; "O" )
```

Substitute( ) is one of a few FileMaker functions that support a special *bracketed syntax*. You can perform *several* replacements on a piece of text with one substitute function. Each pair in brackets represents one search value and its replacement value. Here's how to remove all the vowels from a field:

```
Substitute ( My Field ; ["a" ; ""] ; ["e" ; ""] ; ["i" ; ""] ; ["o" ; ""] ;
["u" ; ""] )
```

Note: This example shows another nice fact about the substitute function: You can use it to *remove* something. Just replace it with empty quotes: *""*.

- While the substitute function can be used to change or remove what you specify, **Filter**( ) can remove everything you *don't* specify. For example, suppose you want to strip any non-numeric characters from a credit card number. You can *try* to think of all the possible things a person might type in a Credit Card Number field (good luck!), or you can use the filter function instead:

```
Filter ( Credit Card Number ; "0123456789" )
```

This calculation tells FileMaker to return the contents of the Credit Card Number field with everything except the numerals removed. In other words, simply put the characters you'd like to *keep* in the second parameter.

- The **PatternCount( )** function tells you how many of a specific character string exist in the text. The function needs to know what you're searching, and what to look for. Consider:

```
PatternCount ( Ten Commandments ; "shalt" )
```

In this case, the calculation returns 10. If the pattern doesn't occur in the text, then the calc returns a 0.

- The **Trim**() function cleans up after those data entry folks who can't stop typing extra spaces before and after the important stuff. Just tell the function what to look at. From the calculation below, you get the string "Anyway" placed in your field.

```
Trim ( "Anyway   " )
```

Text value functions

If a field holds more than one chunk of text, with a paragraph symbol putting each chunk on its own line, then it's very much like a value list (page 237). The data inside the list is called *return-separated values*. Text value functions let you grab individual lines from a value list. And since you can so easily grab a particular line from a value list, you'll often use a related function, called *List( )*, to put your data *into* a list to make it easier to grab. See page 430.

Here's a simple example to show how parsing a value list works. Suppose you have a field called Colors with a list of data like this:

- Red
- Green
- Blue
- Orange
- Yellow

Since this field contains five values, this *LeftValues( )* formula returns "Red" and "Green".

```
LeftValues ( Colors ; 2 )
```

Use the *GetValue( )* function when you need to parse just one value from a list. The value you need has to be in a predictable place in the list, as in the whole-email-slammed-into-one-field example at the beginning of this section. Say the email comes to you like this:

- Email From
- Email To
- Subject
- Body

You could grab the Email To address with this function:

```
GetValue ( Email ; 2 )
```

You can figure out how many values in a list with *ValueCount( )*. Just tell File-Maker which value list to count. The text parameter can refer to one or more fields or to static text. For example, this function returns 2:

```
ValueCount ( "Tom Cruise¶Keith Urban" )
```

Tip: Notice that the value list doesn't need a paragraph symbol after the last value to return the proper count. So if you're building a return separated list in order to grab data from it, then don't have worry about that last symbol.

FilterValues( ) works like its plain cousin *Filter( )*. You specify the text, and then the values you want to allow. For example, the following function returns

Nicole

Katie

```
FilterValues ( "Mimi¶Nicole¶Katie ; "Katie¶Nicole" )
```

FileMaker has *RightValues( )* and *MiddleValues( )* functions, too. See the box on page 441 for ideas on how to use them.

WORKAROUND WORKSHOP

When Data Doesn't Comply

Sometimes the text you need to break up doesn't come in pieces that FileMaker automatically recognizes, like characters or words. For example, suppose you have a file path:

```
C:\My Documents\Product Shots\Tools\Large
    Hammer.jpg
```

You need to get the name of the file (Large Hammer.jpg) and its parent folder (Tools). Unfortunately, this text value isn't divided into characters, words, or values. It's divided into *path components*, each with a backslash in between.

When you're faced with something like this, your best bet is to make it look like something FileMaker *can* deal with. If you can turn every backslash into a new line symbol (¶), then you can simply use the RightValues function to pull out the last value. In other words:

```
Substitute ( File Path ; "\ " ; "¶" )
```

The result of this expression is the list of path components, each on its own line:

```
C:
My Documents
Product Shots
Tools
Large Hammer.jpg
```

To get just the file name, you can do this:

```
RightValues ( Substitute ( File Path ; "\
    " ; "¶" ) ; 1 )
```

Unless your data already contains multiple lines, you can always use the substitute function to turn any kind of delimited list into a list of values. Bear in mind, though, that the substitute function is *case-sensitive*. You can read more about case sensitivity on page 467.

Text counting functions

You can also work with text by counting its individual parts. FileMaker has three related functions for finding out *how much* text your fields contain:

- The **Length**( ) function returns the length of a text value by counting characters.

- The **WordCount**( ) function tells you how many words are in a text value.

- Using the **ValueCount**( ) function, you can find out how many lines a field has.

These functions become powerhouses in combination with the various left, right, and middle functions. When the fields you're parsing contain varying amounts of text, you can have FileMaker count each one so you don't have to. For example, you might have a Parts Number field that contains parts numbers of varying length. Always, though, the last character is one you don't want. To return all but the last character in a field, use this calculation:

```
Left ( My Field ; Length ( My Field ) - 1 )
```

It uses the left function to grab characters from the field, and the length function (minus one) to find out how many to get. Just change the number on the end to chop off any number of junk characters from the end of a field. You're welcome.

POWER USERS' CLINIC

Outsmarting the Smarties

LeftValues( ) and *RightValues( )* are helpful when you need to pull some items from a return-separated list. But they're also helpful when you want to protect your database from people who know a few workarounds. Say you have a sales promotion going, where your best customers get to pick one free premium from a list of four items. So you've set up a field with a value list and a set of radio buttons. Everybody knows that you can choose only one item from a radio button set, right? Apparently not, because you've got some salespeople who know they can beat the system by Shift-clicking to select multiple radio buttons. (Those folks read page 247.)

You just have to add an Auto-Enter calculated value to your Premiums field. Make sure you uncheck the "Do not replace existing value (if any)" option. Here's how the calculation goes:

```
RightValues (Premiums ; 1 )
```

Now your savvy salespeople can wear out their Shift keys, but they still can't select more than one item in the premium field, because your calculation holds the field to a single value.

You can even add smarts to a Checkbox Set with a similar technique. Make this calculation:

```
LeftValues( Premiums ; 2 )
```

People using the program can't select more than two checkboxes. FileMaker knows the first two items they selected, and just keeps putting those same two back into the field, no matter how many checkboxes the salespeople try to select. For another twist, change the calculation to:

```
RightValues ( Premiums ; 2 )
```

Now FileMaker remembers the last two items selected, and very cleverly deselects the oldest value, so that the field always contains the last two items selected from the Checkbox Set.

Text Formatting Functions

Normally when you see data in a calculation field, it's displayed in the format (font, size, style, color, and so on) you applied in Layout mode. Every character in the field shares the same format, unless you want to manually search through all your records selecting the words "Limited Time Only" in your Promotion Notes field, so you can make that bold and red every time it appears. Not only does that method waste your precious time (especially if you're on salary), it also plays havoc with your design when you try to print the field.

FileMaker's text formatting functions let you specify exactly what bit of text you want in 18-point, boldfaced, red Verdana. And you don't have to visit a single record in person. You just write a calculation and FileMaker does the drudgework for you, without tampering with the real data.

FileMaker has six text formatting functions, as described below.

Note: Since that big heading clearly reads "*Text* Formatting Functions," any reasonable person would assume that this formatting applies only to text. Luckily, the unreasonable people rule the world. You can apply text formatting to any data type.

TextColor( ) and RGB( )

The *TextColor( )* function takes two parameters: some text, and a color. It returns the text you send it in the right color. Like many computer programs, FileMaker thinks of colors in RGB code, which defines all colors as combinations of red, green, and blue as expressed by numerical values. The second parameter to the *TextColor( )* function is (almost) always the RGB function (and FileMaker automatically adds it when you add *TextColor( )* to your formula).

This function returns a color based on three parameters: red, green, and blue. For example, if you want to change the Full Name field to show the first name in bright red, and the last name in bright blue, you use this calculation:

```
TextColor ( First Name ; RGB ( 255 ; 0 ; 0 ) )
& " " &
TextColor ( Last Name ; RGB ( 0 ; 0 ; 255 ) )
```

Note: For a crash course in RGB code—including how to avoid using it—see the box on page 446.

TextFont( )

To change the font in a calculation result, use the *TextFont( )* function. You just pass it the text you want to format, and the name of the font to use. FileMaker returns the same text with the font applied:

```
TextFont ( "Dewey Defeats Truman!" ; "Times New Roman" )
```

Color My World (with 16M Colors)

FileMaker has a basic conflict over color. After all, it's a computer program that works with data, which comes in a limited number of types, like text value, number, date, and time. So what kind of data type is a *color*? The explanation isn't very, er, colorful. FileMaker understands 16,777,216 distinct colors, each subtly different from the one before, and numbered from 0 to 16,777,215. Unfortunately, *learning* all those colors by number is beyond the reach of even the most bored developer. So FileMaker uses a standard (albeit entirely unintuitive) method of specifying a color as a mixture of component colors—red, green, and blue—with varying intensities.

Each parameter to the RGB function is a number, from 0 to 255. The number says how intense—or bright—the component color should be. A zero in the first parameter means red doesn't enter into the equation at all. The number 255 means FileMaker should crank the red component to the max. The RGB function returns a number, identifying one of those 16-odd million choices. To make it doubly confusing for anyone who doesn't have a degree in computer programming or television repair, the RGB system deals with red, green, and blue as sources of *light*, not the more intuitive red-yellow-blue primary colors of paints and pigments.

When colored lights mix (like those little pixels on a monitor), red and green make…yellow. In other words, to FileMaker and other RGB experts, it makes perfect sense to see bright yellow as the following:

```
RGB (255 ; 255 ; 0)
```

So what's a person to do? Don't use RGB codes. Find some other tools.

If you use Mac OS X, you have just such a tool in the Utilities folder (in your Applications folder). It's called Digital Color Meter. Launch the application, and then, from the pop-up menu in its window choose RGB As Actual Value, 8-bit. Now the little blue numbers show proper red (R), green (G), and blue (B) values for any color you point to on your screen. For example, in the status area (in Layout mode), pop open the Fill Color menu, and then point to any of the colors there to see the RGB equivalent.

On Microsoft Windows, you can see RGB colors in the standard color picker window. Just go to Layout mode, and then, in the status area, click the Fill Color button. Choose Other Color. When you click a color, you see the red, green, and blue values listed in the window's bottom-right corner.

TextFont( ) also has a third optional parameter called fontScript. Most people can simply ignore this option. It tells FileMaker which *character set* you're interested in, and to select an appropriate font. (The character set determines which languages the font can be used for.) FileMaker accepts the following fontScript values:

- Roman

- Greek

- Cyrillic

- CentralEuropean

- ShiftJIS

- TraditionalChinese

- SimplifiedChinese

- OEM

• Symbol

• Other

Note: Unlike the font name, which is simply a text value, the script value shouldn't be in quotes. It's not a text value. Instead, you must specify one of the above values exactly, with no quotes.

If FileMaker can't find the specific font you've asked for, then it selects another font in the specified script, so if you're on an English-based system and need to select a Chinese font, this parameter can help. (If you don't specify a script, File-Maker automatically uses the default script on your computer. That's why you rarely have to worry about it—you automatically get what you probably want.)

TextSize()

The *TextSize( )* function is simple in every case. Just pass some text, and the point size you'd like (just like the sizes in the Format → Size menu in Browse mode). FileMaker returns the resized text.

TextStyleAdd() and TextStyleRemove()

Changing text *styles* (bold, italic, and so on) is a little more complicated. After all, a piece of text can have only *one* color, *one* font, or *one* size, but it can be bold, italic, and underlined all at the same time. With text styles, you don't just swap one style for another; you need to do things like take italic text and add bold formatting or even take bold-titlecase-strikethrough text and un-strikethrough it, leaving everything else in place.

To solve these problems, FileMaker gives you *two* functions for dealing with style: *TextStyleAdd( )* and *TextStyleRemove( )*. You use the first to add a style to a piece of text:

```
"Do it with " & TextStyleAdd ( "style" ; Italic )
```

Likewise, the *TextStyleRemove( )* function removes the specified style from the text.

```
TextStyleRemove ( My Text Field ; Italic )
```

The text style parameter goes in the calculation without quotes, just like the examples above. You can use any and every text style in FileMaker: Plain, Bold, Italic, Underline, Condense, Extend, Strikethrough, SmallCaps, Superscript, Subscript, Uppercase, Lowercase, Titlecase, WordUnderline, and DoubleUnderline. And then there's AllStyles. When you use the AllStyles parameter, it adds (or removes) *all* existing styles.

With these two functions and all these style options, you can do any kind of fancy formatting footwork imaginable. Here are some guidelines:

• When you add a style to some text using *TextStyleAdd( )*, it doesn't change any style that you've already applied. The new style's simply layered over the existing styles.

- Plain style's the notable exception to the above point. Adding Plain style effectively *removes* any other styling. This style comes in handy when you need to remove a mess of styling and apply something simpler. Say your fields contain the words "Past Due", styled in uppercase, bold, italic, and double underlined, and you decide that modest italics would work just fine. Nesting the *TextStyleAdd( )* function with the Plain parameter does the trick:

```
TextStyleAdd ( TextStyleAdd ( "past due" ; Plain ) ; Italic )
```

Note: As you may suspect, using *TextStyleRemove( )* with the AllStyles parameter does the exact same thing as *TextStyleAdd( )* with Plain. They both remove existing styling, but as you can see above, when you add Plain, you can write neater expressions.

- When you add more than one style parameter, FileMaker applies them all to the text. You can use nesting, as shown in the previous point, or simply stack them up with + signs:

```
TextStyleAdd ( "WARNING" ; Bold+Italic )
```

- If you take a bit of text that was formatted with a text formatting function, and then send it to another calculation as a parameter, then the formatting goes along with the text. With the substitute function, for example, you can format text that hasn't even been typed yet. If you add this function to a text field into which people can type letters to customers, then it changes every occurrence of "for a limited time" to bold italics.

```
Substitute ( Letter ; "for a limited time" ; TextStyleAdd ( "for a limited
time" ; Bold+Italic )
```

Date and Time Calculations

Before you start writing date and time calculations, you need to know how FileMaker keeps track of dates and times. FileMaker internally stores any date or time value as a single number that uniquely identifies every day and time of that day. Then, when it needs to display a date or time, it converts the number to a value people recognize, like "11/7/2009" or "10:23 AM". As with other numbers that it stores one way and displays another, FileMaker does the math on the stored value, and then converts it for your convenience. Here's how FileMaker keeps track of time:

- It stores a *date* as the number of days since the beginning of the year 1 A. D.

- It stores a *time* as the number of seconds since midnight.

- It stores a *timestamp* as the number of seconds since midnight at the beginning of the year 1 A. D. (a really big number).

This secret to date and time storage isn't just a technicality. It actually tells you a lot about how you can use dates and times in calculations. For example, without this knowledge, you could spend ages trying to write a calculation that gives you the first day of the month following the date an invoice is due. But it's actually pretty simple:

```
Date ( Month ( Invoice Due Date ) + 1 ; 1 ; Year ( Invoice Due Date ) )
```

To break it down, you're just adding 1 to the month in question, and then looking for the first day of that month. This section tells you what you need to know to analyze this calculation, and then use its lessons in your database.

Math with Dates and Times

Because FileMaker looks at dates and times as numbers, you're free to use them right along with other numbers and operators in all kinds of mathematical functions. By adding, subtracting, multiplying, and dividing dates, times, timestamps, and numbers, you can come up with meaningful results.

Dates

You can use the information in your database's date fields to have FileMaker figure out due dates, anniversaries, and so on. You can use date fields and numbers interchangeably. FileMaker's smart enough to figure out that you want to add whole days to the date value it's storing. Here are some general principles:

- To get a date in the future or past, add or subtract the number of days. For example, if your policy is that payments are due 10 days after invoices are presented, then, in your Date Due field, use this calculation:

```
Invoice Date + 10
```

- Of course, you aren't limited to adding constant numbers to dates. You can add a number field to a date field just as easily. If your video rental database holds the checkout date and the rental duration, you can find the due date with this calculation:

```
Checkout Date + Rental Duration
```

- To get the number of days between two dates, subtract them.

  Suppose your registration database holds arrival and departure dates. You can find the duration of the stay (in days) using this calculation:

```
Departure Date - Arrival Date
```

Note: When you're adding a number to a date, the result is a brand-new date, and you should set the result type of your calculation accordingly. On the other hand, if you're subtracting two dates, the result is a number—the number of days between the two dates. In this case, set your calculation to return a number result.

From Numbers to Times

If you can treat dates and times like numbers, it makes sense that you can go the other way, too. Suppose you have a field called Race Time that holds each athlete's race time as a number of seconds. If you'd rather view this time in the Hours:Minutes:Seconds (or Minutes:Seconds) format, then you can easily use a calculation to convert it to a time value:

```
GetAsTime(Race Time)
```

When you pass it a number value, the *GetAsTime( )* function converts that number into the equivalent time. (If you view the field on a layout, then you can use the time formatting options to display hours, minutes, and seconds in just about any way you want, as shown on page 262.) The *GetAsTime( )* function has another purpose: It can convert *text values* into times. If someone puts "3:37:03" into a text field, you can use *GetAsTime( )* to convert that text into a valid time value.

FileMaker has *GetAsDate( )* and *GetAsTimestamp( )* functions, too, which work just the same.

Times

Although FileMaker's internal clock counts time as the number of seconds since midnight, a time value doesn't always have to be a time of day. Depending on the field format (page 262), a time value can be a time of day, like 2:30 p.m., or a *time* (as in duration, like 3 hours, 27 minutes).

Note: FileMaker is savvy to the concept that time passes, but not all programs are. For instance, if you're exporting data to Excel, then you should first convert time fields containing durations to plain old number fields.

In both cases, times have a numeric value, in hours:minutes:seconds format. When considered a time of day, 14:30:05 represents 5 seconds after 2:30 p.m., but if you look at it as a duration, it represents 14 hours, 30 minutes, and 5 seconds. If the time has fractional seconds (a decimal point), then the numerical value does too.

You can record how long your 5-year-old takes to find her shoes (34:26:18), or how long she takes to find the Halloween candy (00:00:02.13).

The key to doing math with any kind of time value is to remember you're always adding and subtracting amounts of *seconds*. Here are the guidelines:

• To get a time in the future or past, add or subtract a number of seconds or a time value. If you know when a student finished her exam, and you know how long the exam took in minutes (1 minute = 60 seconds), then you can figure out when she started:

```
Finish Time - ( Exam Duration * 60 )
```

• To get the number of seconds between two times, subtract one from the other. Your Test Reporting database stores start and finish times for each exam. To find the duration, use this calculation:

```
Finish Time - Start Time
```

To get a time of day value in the future or past, add or subtract the number of seconds or a time value. Suppose you have a database of movie show times for your theater business. You use a timestamp field to record the date and time when each showing starts. You also use a time field to keep track of each movie's length. Now you need to know when each movie *ends*:

```
Showtime + Duration
```

Note: If you store the date and time the movie starts in separate date and time fields, then the movie time calculation is much more difficult. Suppose a movie starts at 11:30 p.m., and runs for 2 hours. Adding these together, you get 25:30, a perfectly valid time value, but not a valid *time of day*. When you add to time values, they don't "roll over" after midnight. Timestamps, on the other hand, work as expected: You get 1:30 a.m. on the next day.

• You can subtract one timestamp value from another. The result will be given in seconds, so you'll have to more math on the result to get minutes or hours. For example, you use timestamps to record the start and finish times for a job. To find out how long the job took, in minutes, use this calculation:

```
(Finish Time Stamp-Start Time Stamp) / 60
```

• To increase or decrease a time duration value, add or subtract the number of seconds, or another time duration. Say you have a related Songs table with a Song Lengths field to hold the length of each song on a CD. This calculation tells you how long the entire CD is:

```
Sum ( Songs::Song Lengths )
```

• To double, triple, halve, or otherwise scale a time duration, multiply or divide it by a number.

If chilling your microbrew always takes twice as long as cooking, then you can determine the chilling time with this calculation:

```
Cooking Time * 2
```

Parsing Dates and Times

Just as you can parse bits of text from text fields, FileMaker lets you pull out parts of a date or time value. For example, you can keep track of all your employees' birthdays in a normal date field, but when you're trying to get statistical data from the year they were born, you're not concerned about the month or date part of that value. You have six functions at your disposal to pick those individual components from a date, time, or timestamp value. They are: *Year( )*, *Month( )*, *Day( )*, *Hours( )*, *Minutes( )*, *Seconds( )*.

With a date value, you can use *Year( )*, *Month( )*, and *Day( )*. If you have a time, *Hours( )*, *Minutes( )*, and *Seconds( )* apply. You can use all six functions with a timestamp value.

These functions all have the same form. Each takes a single parameter—the value—and returns a numerical result. For example, the day function returns the day portion of a date. This calculation returns 27:

```
Day ( "7/27/2009")
```

Tip: Just because FileMaker thinks of dates as numbers, you're not limited to using them that way. See the box below to see how to use parts of a date as text.

Name the Day (or Month)

Even when you're using the month number to group your data, you may prefer to see months by *name*. For example, if you produce a report of sales by month, you probably want the groupings labeled January, February, March, and so on, instead of 1, 2, and 3. You can use the *MonthName( )* function to get this effect:

```
MonthName ( Invoice Date )
```

You can still sort all your invoices by the date field to get them in order, but you use your new *MonthName( )* value to display in the subsummary part. See page 281 on "Creating a sub-summary part" for a refresher on using sub-summary parts in reports.

Sometimes you need to see the day name (like Monday, Tuesday, or Wednesday). The *DayName( )* function does just that. To get its numerical equivalent, use *DayOfWeek( )* instead, which returns 1 for Sunday, 2 for Monday, and so forth.

Calculations that Create Dates and Times

Almost every database in existence has fields that create date and time values—otherwise, folks would still sit around pecking out business forms with a typewriter, an adding machine, and a wall calendar. It sounds quaint, but there was one advantage—the human brain. Without even being aware of it, people do incredibly complex math every time they glance at a paper calendar or analog clock. When the boss said, "I want these invoices to go out two days before the end of next month," a human clerk knew exactly what to do.

When you work with dates and times in FileMaker, sometimes you can get away with simple math as in the previous section, plugging date and time values into basic calculations. But how do you tell a computer to put "two days before the end of next month" in the Invoice Date field? FileMaker provides three functions to assist the translation:

- The **Date**( ) function accepts three parameters—Month, Day, and Year—and returns the appropriate date value. For example, to put a date value of June 21, 2009 in a calculation, you use the date function like this:

```
Date ( 6 ; 21 ; 2009 )
```

- The **Time**( ) function wants three parameters as well, this time Hours, Minutes, and Seconds. It returns the time value. (The Seconds parameter can have a decimal point if necessary.) For example, you can construct the time value "8:00 p.m." like this:

```
Time ( 20 ; 0 ; 0 )
```

Note: For time-of-day values, the time function doesn't let you specify a.m. or p.m., so you have to use 24-hour notation.

- The **Timestamp**( ) function takes just two parameters: Date and Time. It combines the two into a single timestamp value. It shows June 10, 2009 at 8:30 p.m. like this:

```
Timestamp ( Date ( 6 ; 10 ; 2009 ) ; Time ( 20 ; 30 ; 0 ) )
```

In this example, you use all three functions: the date function to produce the correct date value, the time function for the time value, and the timestamp function to put them together.

FREQUENTLY ASKED QUESTION

Do I Have to Use Functions?

Why can't I just put "1/10/2006" in my calculation, just like I'd put it in a date field?

Because "1/10/2006" is a text value, not a date value. When you're entering data in a date field, FileMaker knows it's a date field, and is nice enough to convert text like this into a date for you. In a calculation, though, FileMaker may not know you want a date, so it treats what you put in as text instead.

You can use the *GetAsDate( )* function to convert text values like this into dates:

```
GetAsDate ( "1/10/2006" )
```

But even this method isn't advisable. Remember that dates are interpreted depending on how you've configured your computer. On one computer, this calculation could produce the date value June 10, 2009, while on another machine it might result in October 5 instead. In other words, you have no safe way to ensure you get the date you really want when you use *GetAsDate( )* with a text value, unless you're using text the user supplied.

The date function always expects the month, then the day, then the year. Computer settings don't affect it. So the *Date( )* function is the safest way to record dates in calculations.

The secret powers of Date()

Although FileMaker doesn't look at calendars the way people do, that's not all bad. You see a calendar in absolute terms: April 30 belongs to April, May 1 belongs to May, and that's that. FileMaker, however, thinks of dates in relative terms and sees no such limitations. You can use this flexibility to your advantage in calculations—big time. You can give seemingly illogical parameters to the Date () function, and have FileMaker produce a valid date anyway.

For example, this calculation actually produces a valid date:

```
Date ( 7 ; 0 ; 2009 )
```

You might expect a nonsense result—July 0, 2009. But FileMaker looks at the same code and says, "No problem. Zero comes before 1, so you must mean the day that comes before July 1." And so it returns June 30, 2009.

These same smarts apply to the month as well:

```
Date ( 15 ; 11 ; 2009 )
```

That calculation produces March 11, *2010*. In other words, 3 months into the next year, since 15 is 3 months more than 1 year.

This behavior comes in super handy when you're trying to fiddle with dates in calculations. Suppose you have order records, each one with an order date. You bill on the last day of the month in which the order was placed, so your calculation needs to figure out that date, which could be 28, 30, or 31, depending on the month, or even 29 if it's February in a leap year. That calculation would take an entire page in this book. But here's a much easier approach: Instead of calculating which day each month ends, use the fact that the *last* day of *this* month is always the day *before* the *first* day of *next* month. To start with, you can calculate next month like this:

```
Month ( Order Date ) + 1
```

So the date of the first day of next month is:

```
Date ( Month(Order Date) + 1 ; 1 ; Year(Order Date) )
```

To get the day before, just subtract one from the whole thing:

```
Date (
    Month(Order Date) + 1;     // the _next_ month
    1;                   //the _first_ day
    Year(Order Date)     // the same year
)- 1                    // subtract 1 to get the day before
```

It may look a little confusing at first, but it's much shorter than a page. And it works perfectly every month of every year.

Containers in Calculations

Although it isn't a typical calculation data type, you can do a few interesting things with container fields in calculations. You don't have the same vast options you do with other types. It would be great if you could subtract Cousin Clem.jpg from Family Reunion.jpg to get the scoundrel out of the picture, but alas, the technology's not quite there yet. Nevertheless, FileMaker doesn't leave containers entirely out in the cold when it comes to calculations.

Calculations with Pictures, Sounds, Movies, and Files

When you create a calculation field, you can set its result type to Container. You can't *create* container data in a calculation, but you *can* refer to other container fields. When you do, the picture, sound, movie, or file in the referenced container field shows in the new calculation field.

You can, for example, make a calculation field that shows the contents of one container field when you're in Browse mode, and another in Preview mode. This field lets you use low-resolution images when you view on the screen, and higher resolutions when you view in print. (You'll learn to do that in the next chapter, when you learn about calculations with that kind of decision-making ability.)

You may also want to use container fields in a calculated replace. Suppose you have a found set of 30 records that don't have a low-resolution image. You have to have something in that field, so you decide to take the hi-resolution image for those few records and plunk them down in the low-resolution image field. Choose Records → Replace Field Contents, and then perform this calculated replace:

```
Graphics::High Resolution Image
```

The entire calculation consists of a reference to a field of that name in the Graphics table. The calculation does the grunt work of copying the high-resolution image into the low-resolution field in each record.

Calculations with References

If a container field holds a reference to a picture, movie, sound, or file, instead of the object itself (page 85), then you can do even more. When you treat such a field as *text*, FileMaker gives you some information about the referenced file.

If you have a field called Product Shot that holds a reference to a photograph file, then you can use this calculation:

```
GetAsText ( Product Shot )
```

This calculation's result looks like this:

```
size:266,309
image:../../../../../ quilt pix/batik squares.jpg
imagemac:/Macintosh HD/current work/ quilt pix/batik squares.jpg
```

FileMaker tells you the size (width and height in pixels) and location of the file (if this weren't a picture, then you wouldn't see the "size:" line).

You can use this calculation to help you keep track of a set of images that the whole company needs to use. You really need two container fields for this purpose. One holds the graphic itself, or a low-resolution copy, if you don't want the file size to balloon. Then, when you place the graphic as a reference in the second container field, the calculation stores the graphic's original location. The calculation's not dynamic, however, so the path serves as a reference of where the file *should* be, not where it really is. Company policy about putting things back where you found them has to reinforce your good data practices.

Advanced Calculations

In the previous two chapters, you learned how calculations can make your databases work harder for you. But the functions you've learned so far can't make your databases work much *smarter*. For example, what if you want to add a five-percent delinquency charge to invoices over a month old? You could create a special "past due balance" field on a special layout that you use only when you've searched for late invoices, but that's just extra complexity to create and maintain, if the late fee rules change. On the other hand, if you create a calculation that makes a *decision* based on current data, you can let the database itself can figure out when to apply late fees, and it works for every invoice, not just the late ones. This chapter shows you how to give your calculations that brainpower by using logical functions and other advanced techniques.

Note: Download a copy of this chapter's sample file at *http://missingmanuals.com/cds*.

Conditional Formatting Formulas

A database's whole purpose is to let you more easily find and use information. Using conditional formatting, you can make important data more visible on your layouts, so you can more easily see what you need to know with a quick glance. For example, when your collections department has to call your client's accounting department, they can more easily find information they need if you make the Due Date and Total Due fields turn bold and bright red if the invoice hasn't been paid.

Back on page 206, you learned how to use conditional formatting to change the way fields or text objects display data. You dipped your toe into the power of the Condition pop-up menu (Figure 11-1) by choosing "Formula is", and then typing a simple calculation. Now it's time to learn more about *Boolean* functions, and a specific function used by conditional formatting called *Self( )*.

Note: You can use Boolean logic and the *Self( )* function in most places where you find the Specify Calculation dialog box. But since you're already grounded in conditional formatting, you'll use it to examine the principles. From there, you can apply the concepts elsewhere.

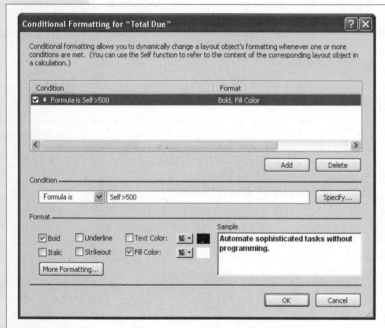

Figure 11-1:
You can learn a lot about conditional formatting, and calculations in general, by setting conditions using the "Value is" pop-up menu, and then switching the menu to "Formula is". FileMaker converts the setting to a bona fide calculation, in which you see heavy use of the Self( ) function (page 460). Here the Total Due field is set to display in Bold with a light gray fill when the field's value is greater than 500. The Self( ) function lets you apply the same formula and formatting to many different fields at one time, because the formula doesn't reference the field by name.

Understanding Boolean Functions

The result of any conditional formatting calculation must be a Boolean value. But Boolean isn't a choice in the "Calculation Result is" pop-up menu. Instead, you write an equation that produces a Boolean result: They're either "true" or "false," "yes" or "no," "not empty" or "empty." The Boolean world has no shades of gray, no "maybe," and no glasses that are half full.

For example, these statements are true, as most any modern schoolchild can tell you:

$4 > 3$

$6 * 6 = 36$

$E = mc^2$

In Boolean terms, they are "True." So are the values:

```
1
True
T
Yes
Y
```

If you turn a Boolean loose on these statements, then they evaluate as "False."

```
0
False
F
f
No
N
n
Blank or ""
```

That last item in the list can make things a little murky. Typing the word *Blank* in a field doesn't make it evaluate as false; *leaving* it blank does. And that's what the "" (empty quote marks) mean. For example, in a record for 2008 Presidential Election, even the value of "hardly any" in the "Voter Turnout" field means "True" to a Boolean statement. If the entry isn't "0" or "False" or another item in the list above, then all the Boolean cares about is whether there's a value in the field. You've already used this fact to your advantage on page 272 when you used a calculation to format the text of an Email button as gray if the Email Address field was empty:

```
Customers::Email Address = ""
```

This calculation is explicit about what it's looking for. It checks the contents of the Email Address field for blank contents. The statement evaluates to "True" when the field is blank, and to "False" when there's data in the field.

Note: Just remember that the Boolean calculation isn't checking the validity of the email address. You can write a calculation that tests the email address for its essential parts (under the PatternCount function) or use a plug-in (page 487) to send an email and actually test the address.

Even though it's more explicit to add the equal sign and the empty quote marks, it isn't necessary because "empty" means "False" in the Boolean world. Plus, some developers don't like the inverted logic required when you check for the presence of nothing in a field. That's why you often see Booleans written more simply, like so:

```
Customers::Email Address
```

Unlike the first example, this calculation evaluates to "True" when the field contains data, and to "False" when it's empty. But you can reinvert the logic by putting a "not" in front of a calculation:

```
not Customers::Email Address
```

This syntax means that the result is "True" when the field is empty, and "False" when the field contains data.

So is one method better than another? Probably not. But when you look at other developers' calculations, you may see all these forms, so it helps to know how they work. If you're the only developer working on your files, then you're free to use the construction that makes most sense to you. But when you develop in a team, you might want to develop a standard for constructing your Boolean calculations. In either case, it's a good idea to comment your Boolean calculations, so those who follow you can save time trying to retrace your logic.

Separating Formatting from Data

Why would a math major like me use lowly, layout-based conditional formatting when I can make a whole bunch of very cool, very complicated calculations using text formatting functions?

It's true that conditional formatting doesn't give you a whole bunch of new options that you didn't already have in text formatting functions. However, you do get a giant leap closer to something that's been difficult to do in FileMaker—separating the presentation layer from the data layer of your file.

In programmer-speak, the *presentation layer* is anything having to do with showing your data. It's the layout, and all the stuff you put on a layout to make your data easy to understand. Even the fact that you can move fields around in relation to one another is part of FileMaker's sophisticated presentation layer. Boldface fields, portals, buttons, and Web viewers are presentation tools, as well. Custom menus (page 753) and tooltips (page 752), which help you help your users work with their data, are also forms of presentation.

The *data layer* is just what it sounds like—the tables and fields (or rows and columns) of actual information. Most calculations also fall onto the data layer. For example, when you multiply the Quantity and Price Each fields together, using a calculation in the Extended Price field, that's data.

So is adding a five percent surcharge to late payments. Adding another five percent 30 days later, when those deadbeats have come up with more excuses, is still data.

But when you use number formatting to display the results of any of those calculations with dollar signs, commas, and decimal places, then that's presentation-layer territory. And if you use a text function to display the late penalty in red, boldface at 18 points, then you're treading in the presentation layer, even if you use a sophisticated calculation to see if the penalty is due before you apply the format.

Furthermore, when you rely solely on calculations for formatting, you've got to add more *complexity* to your calculations to *simplify* some layouts. Say you use a text formatting function to display unpaid invoice totals in red after 30 days. The field *always* displays the red text, even if that's not the purpose of the layout. For example, if the marketing department needs a list of invoices over $500 to decide who gets special offers, the red invoice amounts make no sense—and may violate customers' privacy. But if you separate presentation and data using conditional formatting, you can apply the format on a layout-by-layout basis. So all in all, it makes life easier down the road if you confine your use of calculations to mathematical operations *on* your data and use conditional formatting to handle the display *of* your data.

Using the *Self()* Function

You got a peek at the *Self()* function back in Figure 11-1. The *Self()* function simply returns the contents of the object to which it's applied. Without a *Self()* function, you have to write a calculation that refers to the Total Due field, and then uses a Text Formatting function. Then to use it on another field, you copy and paste, but you have to change the field reference so that the formula works in its new location. But that's just too much work, so FileMaker's engineers created the *Self( )* function to make calculations portable—that is, you don't need to retrofit them if you move them from one field or object to another.

Here's one example of how it works. The five volunteer data entry folks keeping up with your theater group's subscription and donor list are expressing their artistic temperaments by using different formats for phone numbers. So when you print out the contact list, you've got (800) 555-1212, 800-555-1212, 800.555.1212, 555-1212, and every other variation under the sun.

FileMaker's Auto-Enter calculations can help you transform self-expression into standard formats. To straighten things out, you could add this calculation to your Phone field:

```
"(" & // start with an open paren sign
Left ( Filter ( Phone ; "0123456789" ) ; 3 ) & // grab the area code
") " & // finish the area code with a close paren and a space
Middle ( Filter ( Phone; "0123456789" ) ; 4 ; 3 ) & // grab the exchange
"-" & // give me a hyphen
Middle ( Filter ( Phone ; "0123456789" ) ; 7 ; 4 ) // the last four digits
```

This calculation takes the data entered into the Phone field, and imposes its own order onto the data. As the comments show, one part of the phone number format is assembled from each line of this nested calculation.

Note: This formula uses several techniques covered in Chapter 10: The *Filter( )* function (page 441); *Left( )*, *Middle( )*, and *Right( )* functions (page 439); and nested functions (page 448). Also, the Phone field in the sample database at *http://missingmanuals.com/cds* shows you the *Self( )* version of the formula in action.

This calculation solves the problem for one Phone field, but what if all your records contain three Phone fields? Plus, you've got three Phone fields in your Employees and Vendors tables, too. To transfer this calculation, you have to paste it into each field's Auto-Enter calculation dialog box, select each instance of "Phone", and then change it to "Mobile" or "Work Phone" so the calculation can work properly in each new context. Don't you have *real* work to do?

With the *Self( )* function, which takes no parameter, and therefore doesn't need its own set of parentheses, you can write the calculation this way instead:

```
"(" &
Left ( Filter ( Self ; "0123456789" ) ; 3 ) &
") " &
Middle ( Filter ( Self; "0123456789" ) ; 4 ; 3 ) &
"-" &
Middle ( Filter ( Self ; "0123456789" ) ; 7 ; 4 )
```

The *Self( )* function knows that it's referring to the field it's in, so you can copy and paste this function until the digital cows come home, and you never have to edit it for its new context. Good as it is, this calculation still has a couple of loopholes. See the box on page 475 for another way to clean up stray data entry in a Phone field.

Using Storage Options

When you defined calculation fields in Chapter 10, you may have wondered about the Specify Calculation dialog box's Storage Options button (Figure 11-2). You learned about indexing and other storage options back in Chapter 3 (see page 116). When you use similar options in your calculations, you exercise more control over the information with which your functions work.

Figure 11-2:
In the Specify Calculation dialog box, when you click the Storage Options button, you can set global storage and indexing options, just like any other field type. You also get a choice you haven't seen before: "Do not store calculation results". With this option, you can make your calculations save information as a kind of snapshot or use the most up-to-date information as your database changes. This example shows the storage options for the Invoice::Total Due field, which isn't stored because you want FileMaker to update if you add, delete or edit any line item on the invoice. Notice though, that you can't index unstored calculations. So finds are a little slower, and you can't use an unstored calculation as a key field (page 310).

Stored and Unstored Calculation Fields

Normally, a calculation field holds a value just like any other field. *You* can't edit the value, because FileMaker creates it for you from the calculation. When you use this field on a layout, for example, FileMaker simply displays its results. Depending on whether you turn on the "Do not store calculation result" option in Figure 11-2, FileMaker either grabs saved (stored) results from a table or calculates the value *on the fly* whenever necessary. For example, when you have an unstored calculation field on a layout, FileMaker recalculates the value as soon as you switch to the layout. In fact, whenever an unstored field is showing onscreen, FileMaker updates it automatically any time something causes its value to change.

At the same time, whenever the data in a field changes, FileMaker also works behind the scenes, finding all the *stored* calculation fields that depend on the changed field, and *recalculates* them (even if they're aren't on your current layout), storing the new value in the field. Whether it's stored or unstored, a calculation field usually changes because a field used in the calculation has changed, as you'll see next. Understanding *when* fields recalculate and how dependencies work can help you avoid future mistakes.

Note: When you use a field in a calculation, you can say the calculation depends on the field (or, in other words, it has a dependency on the field).

Field dependencies

Take a look at the example in Figure 11-3 to see how FileMaker knows when to recalculate fields. Calculation fields often use other calculation fields in complex arrangements, as this hierarchy of field dependencies illustrates.

Figure 11-3:
This picture shows a series of interdependent fields. The Full Name field is a calculation field that uses First Name and Last Name. The Full Address field uses Full Name (and some others not shown here). The fields in gray are unstored calculation fields. Collection Letter uses Account Balance and Full Address. Account Balance in turn uses Balance Due. Since an account can have several invoices, each with a balance due, Account Balance actually uses several balance due values—one from each related invoice.

First Name and Last Name are the only editable fields in Figure 11-3. But they aren't the only fields that can change. When someone edits a Customer's name, FileMaker sees that it needs to recalculate Full Name, which in turn triggers a recalculation of the Full Address value. The recalculation trickles down through all the dependent fields as soon as someone makes the change, and then exits the First Name field.

By contrast, since Collection Letter is an *unstored field and it's not shown on this layout*, FileMaker *doesn't* recalculate it right away. (It doesn't need to recalculate since you aren't displaying the value anywhere on the current layout.) Instead, the program waits until someone brings up the field onscreen, and *then* it runs the calculation on the current data, and displays the result.

That recalculates the Collection Letter value as FileMaker grabs the stored value for the Full Address field. But it also needs the Account Balance, which is not stored. So *that* field is recalculated first. That calculation requires the new Balance Due on each invoice in turn, and then they're added up to get an Account Balance. Finally, the database has the values it needs to show you the Collection Letter.

Happily, FileMaker keeps track of these dependencies internally, so when you use *unstored* calculations, it pulls the necessary data down through the hierarchy of dependencies when your edits call for it. But if you understand how dependencies work, you can make good decisions about when to store data.

Deciding when to store

When you first create a calculation field, FileMaker makes it a stored field automatically, *if possible*. Some field values aren't eligible for storage:

- If a field depends on any other unstored fields
- If a field depends on any global fields
- If a field depends on any related fields
- If a field depends on any summary fields

If your calculation meets any of these criteria, then FileMaker automatically turns on the "Do not store calculation results—recalculate when needed" option for you, and it doesn't let you turn it off. Otherwise, FileMaker automatically stores the field.

- An unstored field has to be recalculated every time it appears onscreen, in a layout, or in a report. All that recalculation can slow your database down, especially if the unstored field is part of a summary field or a calculation that aggregates many records. So it's best to store a field unless you need a freshly calculated value every time you see that data.

- If you perform a find based on an unstored calculation field, then FileMaker has to go through all your records one by one, calculating each one as it goes. The result is a slow search process. If you plan on searching a field, then store it. (For more detail, see the box on the next page.)

Even if FileMaker can store a certain value, you may not always want it to. Here are some reasons you might turn *on* that "Do not store" box:

- Stored fields automatically recalculate as needed when *other fields* change. But FileMaker has no such automatic behavior for other kinds of information. For example, when you use the *Get(CurrentDate)* function in a calculation, FileMaker doesn't recalculate it when the date changes. In general, when you use any of the Get functions (page 410), you usually want to make your field unstored to "get" the most up-to-date information.

• A stored field takes up space on disk, while an unstored field doesn't. FileMaker 10 files can hold 8 terabytes of data, so space isn't a major consideration for most people. But if you're into slim and trim files, then you can save space by making calculations unstored.

• Lots of stored calculation fields can really slow down *record creation*. That's usually not a big deal, but if you often import data (Chapter 17) or use a script to regularly create lots of records, then you can speed things up by reducing the number of stored calculations.

Tip: Obviously, you have some gray area here. When in doubt, store the field. You can always make it unstored later. Choose File → Manage Database, select your field from the list, click Options, and then Storage Options to find the "Do not store calculation results–recalculate as needed" option.

FREQUENTLY ASKED QUESTION

I Want to Store My Field

What if I want to search on a field that FileMaker won't let me store?

Just because you can't store a field doesn't mean you don't wish you could. For example, in your Invoices layout, you probably do want to be able to search for invoices with a balance due. But since that field uses related data, it's not storable.

The good news is, you don't have to store a field in order to search it; the search is just a little slower. You don't notice the slowdown until you've amassed *lots* of invoice records. Sadly, there's no easy way to speed it up.

One remedy is to change the way people work with your database. You have to make your Invoice Detail layout *read only*—meaning people can't change data on the invoice directly (see page 641). Instead, they use a special layout and a script to make invoice changes.

When they're finished, your script can calculate the balance due and update a number field on the invoice appropriately. This way, the Balance Due field is a normal, nonrelated field, eligible for indexing and quick searches.

Also, remember that FileMaker can't search a field based on related data very quickly, but it can search the related data *itself* with lightning speed. For example, to find an invoice that has payments applied to it, don't search the Amount Paid field in the invoice. Instead, search for invoices where Payments::Amount is greater than zero. That search turns up every invoice with a related payment record that's not negative. You get exactly what you want, and FileMaker can carry it out using indexed fields.

Indexing calculations

Unless they're global fields or unstored fields, you can set indexing for calculation fields just like any other field, as discussed on page 462. The available options and their effects depend on the result type of the calculation: text, number, date, or time.

Global Calculation Fields

A calculation field can use *global storage* (page 116) just like most other fields. When you turn on "Use global storage" (Figure 11-2), FileMaker calculates just one value for the entire table, rather than a value for each record. If your calculation uses other global fields—and *no* other fields—then it works just as you expect. That is, when you modify one of the global fields it depends on, FileMaker automatically recalculates its value.

If the calculation uses nonglobal fields, on the other hand, things get a little tricky. Whenever you change one of the fields referenced in the calculation, FileMaker recalculates the global calculation field using the values from the current record. For example, if you turn on "Use global storage" for your Full Name field, then it shows the name of the person you're looking at when you dismiss the Define Database window. If you were on the first record, that's whose name you see in the field, just as expected. But as you flip through the records, you see that first person's name on every record. You're changing records, but with global storage, the Full Name value stays the same. That's because nothing it depends on has changed.

Now imagine you switch to the *last* record. If you then change the First Name field, Full Name recalculates. This new value displays the first and last name from the last record, since FileMaker re-evaluates the calculation in its entirety.

This behavior may seem kind of odd, but it has a really cool use. If you need to track the data in the last record you *changed*—maybe you need an informal audit of which record just got changed while you're scanning through other records—throw a global calculation field on your data entry layout. Then, no matter which record you're looking at, you see the value of the last *edited* record in that field.

Logical Functions

The logical function group is diverse and powerful. You get functions for making decisions (called *conditional functions*), learning about field values, and even evaluating calculations *inside* other calculations. This section covers all those possibilities. Along the way, you learn how to define and use *variables*, which act as placeholders while complex calculations go through their many steps.

Note: Though you learned about it at the beginning of this chapter, you find the *Self( )* function (page 460) in the functions list, under the Logical functions heading.

Conditional Functions

This chapter began by posing an interesting challenge: You have a calculation field in the Invoices table called Total Due. It calculates the total amount due on an invoice by subtracting the sum of all payments from the total amount of the invoice. Can you modify the Total Due calculation to add a five-percent penalty when an invoice is past due?

The answer lies in the three conditional functions. Each one lets you specify more than one possible result. The functions require one or more parameters—called *conditions* or *conditional expressions*—that tell them what result to pick. The conditional functions—*If( )*, *Case( )*, and *Choose( )*—differ in how many possible results they support, and what kind of conditions they expect.

The If( ) function

The first and most common conditional function is simply called *If( )*. The *If( )* function is the basic unit of decision making in FileMaker calculations. It's the ticket when you have to decide between two choices, based on some criteria.

It looks like this:

```
If ( Condition ; True Result ; False Result )
```

When you use the *If( )* function, FileMaker evaluates the condition looking for a Boolean result (True or False). If the condition has a True value, the function returns its second parameter (True result). If the condition is False, though, then it returns the False result instead. Here's an example:

```
If ( First Name = "Dominique" ; "Free" ; "$299.00" )
```

For example, this calculation returns Free if the First Name field matches "Dominique." If it *doesn't* match, then it returns $299.00 instead. (See the box below for more details.)

FREQUENTLY ASKED QUESTION

Matching Text Values

What do you mean by "First Name field matches 'Dominique'?" What constitutes a match?

When you use the = operator with text values, FileMaker compares the two values on each side, letter by letter. If every letter, number, space, punctuation and so on matches, then you get a True result. But the comparison isn't case-sensitive. In other words, this expression has a True result:

```
"TEXT" = "text"
```

If this function is too forgiving for your needs, then you can use the *Exact()* function instead.

Exact takes two text parameters, compares them, and returns True if they match exactly—including case. This expression has a False result:

```
Exact ( "TEXT" ; "text" )
```

It's perfectly legal to use the Exact function (or any other function, field, or expression) as the first parameter of the *If( )* function, like this:

```
If ( Exact ( First Name ; "Dominique" ) ;
   "Free" ; "$299.00" )
```

This version of the calculation returns "$299.00" if the First Name field contains "dominique", since the case on the letter D doesn't match.

The Case( ) function

Sometimes you need to pick from more than just two choices. Luckily, the *If( )* function has a cousin named *Case( )* that simply excels at such problems. For example, suppose you want to show one of these four messages on the top of your layout:

- Good Morning
- Good Afternoon
- Good Evening
- Go To Bed

FileMaker chooses a message based on the time of day. The *If( )* function doesn't work very well for this problem because *If( )*allows only one condition and two possible results. You *can* nest *If( )* statements one inside the other, so that the False result is really another *If( )* statement. But nested *If( )* functions are really hard to read and even harder to tweak, so if you find that your business rules require a change in your calculation, you may rue the day you decided to use 12 nested *If( )* functions to decide which discount your customers should get.

The *Case( )* function has this form:

```
Case ( test1 ; result1 ; {test2 ; result2 ; ... ; defaultResult } )
```

You can add as many parameters as you want, in pairs, to represent a condition and the result to be returned if that condition is True. Since the conditions and results are sequential and not nested, you can easily read a *Case( )*statement, no matter how many conditions you pile on. You can even add an optional parameter after the last result. This parameter represents the *default* result—the one File-Maker uses if none of the conditions were true.

Note: Since the *Case( )* function accepts several conditions, more than one condition can be true at the same time. If so, FileMaker chooses the *first* True condition when it picks a result.

To implement the greeting message, a calculation using the *Case( )* function might look like this:

```
Case (
    Get ( CurrentTime ) > Time ( 4 ; 0 ; 0 ) and Get ( CurrentTime ) < Time (
    12 ; 0 ; 0 ) ;
    "Good Morning" ;

    Get ( CurrentTime ) > Time ( 12 ; 0 ; 0 ) and Get ( CurrentTime ) < Time (
    18 ; 0 ; 0 ) ;
    "Good Afternoon" ;
```

```
Get ( CurrentTime ) > Time ( 18 ; 0 ; 0 ) and Get ( CurrentTime ) < Time (
22 ; 0 ; 0 ) ;
"Good Evening" ;

"Go To Bed"
)
```

In this calculation, the *Case( )* function checks first to see if the current time is between 4:00 a.m. and 12:00 p.m. If it is, then the "Good Morning" value is returned. If not, it then checks whether the time is between 12:00 p.m. and 6:00 p.m., which would produce the "Good Afternoon" message. Again, if not, it checks to see if it's between 6:00 p.m. and 10:00 p.m. If so, the user sees "Good Evening".

You don't need to specify a condition for the last result—"Go To Bed"—because if all the previous conditions are false, then it *must* be time for bed. In other words, if it *isn't* the morning, and it *isn't* the afternoon, and it *isn't* the evening, then it must be late at night. (If you need further help deciphering the above calculation, then see the box on page 470. On the other hand, if you're so far ahead that you can see a better way to do it, then see the box on page 472.)

The Choose( ) *function*

The *Choose( )* function is sort of the forgotten third member of the conditional trio. People don't immediately grasp how to use it—so they don't. But if you think of it as a value list with the choices coded into a calculation, then you see how the *Choose( )* function can turn an awfully ugly *Case( )* function into a specimen of neatness.

It looks like this:

```
Choose ( Condition ; Result Zero ; Result One ; Result Two ... )
```

Unlike the other conditional functions, *Choose( )* doesn't expect a Boolean expression for its condition. Instead, it looks for a *number*. The number tells it which of the results to choose: If the Condition is zero, then the function returns Result Zero; if it's one, then it returns Result One; and so on.

Imagine you have a Student table, and one of its fields is called GPA. This field holds the student's current grade point average, as a number. You'd like to turn this number into a letter grade on the printed report.

Many FileMaker developers would immediately jump to the *Case( )* function to solve this problem. They'd do something like this:

```
Case (
GPA < 0.5; "F";
GPA < 1.5; "D";
GPA < 2.5; "C";
GPA < 3.5; "B";
"A"
)
```

While this calculation gets the job done, you can do it more succinctly with the *Choose( )* function:

```
Choose (Round(GPA; 0); "F"; "D"; "C"; "B"; "A" )
```

First, you turn the GPA value into an integer (using the *Round( )* function on page 431), so the *Choose( )* function can use it. When the GPA is 3.2, FileMaker rounds it to 3, and selects the result that represents the number 3: "B." (Remember that the first result is for *zero*, so number three is actually the *fourth* result parameter. For more detail, see the box on page 473.)

UP TO SPEED

A Complex Case

The *Case( )* function on page 468 expresses a familiar concept—do Plan A in one case, do Plan B in a different case, and so on. But you might not immediately know how you get from that simple idea to the more complicated calculations shown in this chapter. Here's how it breaks down:

Remember that semicolons separate the parameters you pass to a function. So the first parameter is *all* of this:

```
Get(CurrentTime) > Time(4;0;0) and
Get(CurrentTime) < Time(12;0;0)
```

That whole expression forms the first condition. Remember that the *and* operator works on two Boolean values. It returns a True result if the values on each side are *both true*.

So really, you can split this condition in two. First, this expression must be true:

```
Get(CurrentTime) > Time(4;0;0)
```

If that expression is true, then FileMaker checks to see if this expression is true, too:

```
Get(CurrentTime) < Time(12;0;0)
```

These sub-expressions are much simpler. Each has the same form, comparing the current time to a time you construct with the Time function. The first makes sure it's after 4:00 a.m. The second makes sure it's *before* 12:00 p.m. The other two conditions in the calculation are exactly the same—except they look at different times.

Constructing a Conditional Calculation

Now that you've seen the three conditional functions, it's time to take a stab at that calculation way back from the beginning of this chapter: Add a five-percent penalty when the due date has passed.

When you're trying to come up with a logical calculation, think about what information FileMaker needs to make the decision, and what action you want FileMaker to take after it decides. Then consider how best to do that using your database's existing fields and structure. First, decide which conditional function to use.

Total Due calculation #1: Using the If( ) function

Most people's first thought would be to use the *If( )* function, since the calculation needs to check *if* one condition is true:

• Is the value of the Date Due field earlier than today's date?

The calculation then takes the result of the *If( )* function, and returns one of two possible results:

- If it's *true* that the due date has passed, then add five percent (.05) of the Total Due to the value in Total Due.

- If it's *not true* that the due date has passed, then display the Total Due normally.

In plainer English, the *If( )* condition checks to see if the due date has passed. If so, it adds five percent to the Total Due amount; if not, it returns the Total Due amount.

The full calculation might look like the following:

```
If (  // Test

Get ( CurrentDate ) > Date Due
   and // Calculate the total due here to make sure it's not zero
Sum ( Line Items::Extended Price ) > Total Paid ;

// True Result
   Sum ( Line Items::Extended Price ) + ( Sum ( Line Items::Extended Price )
   * .05 ) ;

   // False Result Display the Total Due normally
      Sum ( Line Items::Extended Price )
)
```

To put this calculation to work in your sample database, delete the calculation currently in the field definition for Total Due, and then type in this one. When the due date has passed, the value in your newly smarter Total Due field changes reflects a late payment penalty.

Note: Since the Total Due field already calculates the due balance, you may be tempted to create a *new* field that calculates five percent of every invoice, and then only adds that value in if the invoice is past due. But that would clutter your database with a superfluous field. Also, it's far better to have all your math in one place in case your business rules change.

Total Due calculation #2: Using the Case( ) function

Lots of people like the *Case( )* function so much that they always use it, even in places where the *If( )* function is perfectly competent. You might choose to use *Case( )* if there's any chance you'll want to add some conditions to the statement later on. Instead of editing an *If( )* expression later, you can save time by using *Case( )* from the start.

Clever Case Conditions

If you were one of those students who handed in homework early and always sat in the front row, you may be jumping up and down in your chair right now, waving your hand in the air. What you're *dying* to say is, "I can make that *Case( )* function simpler!" Well, you're probably right. In fact, this calculation does the same job:

```
Case (
  Get(CurrentTime) <= Time(4;0;0) or
  Get(CurrentTime) > Time(22;0;0);
  "Go To Bed";

  Get(CurrentTime) < Time(12;0;0);
  "Good Morning";

  Get(CurrentTime) < Time(18;0;0);
  "Good Afternoon";

  "Good Evening"
  )
```

This version takes advantage of the fact that the *Case( )* function returns the result associated with the *first* True condition. FileMaker looks at the first condition, which checks to see if it's before 4:00 a.m. or after 10:00 p.m. If either's true (note the "or" operator), then the function returns *Go To Bed*.

If both *aren't* true, then FileMaker moves on to the second condition, which asks if it's earlier than 12:00 p.m. If so, it returns *Good Morning*. (What if it's 3 in the morning? That *is* earlier than 12:00 p.m., but you don't see "Good Morning" because FileMaker never gets this far. If it's 3:00 a.m., then the search for truth stops after the first condition.)

If it still hasn't found a true condition, then FileMaker moves on to the next: Is it before 6:00 p.m.? Again, the structure of the case statement *implies* that it must be after noon at this point since any time before noon would've been caught in the previous conditions. So this condition is *really* looking for a time between noon and 6, even though it doesn't say so in so many words.

If you're comfortable with this kind of logic, then you can save yourself some clicks and a little typing. (Technically you also make a more efficient calculation, but unless you're using the abacus version of FileMaker, you don't see a speed increase.)

Many people, on the other hand, find a calculation like this one utterly confusing. In that case, just use the longer version, and find something else in your life to brag about.

The same calculation using *Case( )* (and minus the helpful comments) looks like this:

```
Case (
    Get ( CurrentDate ) > Date Due and Sum ( Line Items::Extended Price ) >
    Total Paid ;
    Sum ( Line Items::Extended Price ) + ( Sum ( Line Items::Extended Price )
    * .05 )
    Sum ( Line Items::Extended Price )
)
```

Note: With a single condition and default result, the syntax for *If( )* and *Case( )* are the same. So if you do need to change an *If( )* statement to *Case( )* later, then simply change the word "If" to "Case", and add the conditions.

This calculation works as advertised, but it has a couple weak points. First, it has to calculate the total amount due *three times*. That makes for thrice as many chances to introduce typos and thrice as many places to edit the *Sum (Line Items::Extended Price)* expression if you change the calculation later.

Second, Total Paid is an unstored calculation based on the sum of related records. That's one of the slowest things you can ask a calculation to do. It may not matter much in this database, but in a more complicated situation, a calculation like this could slow FileMaker to a crawl.

In the next section, you'll learn how FileMaker helps you write leaner calculations that are easier to read—and quicker for FileMaker to work through.

FREQUENTLY ASKED QUESTION

No Zero

The Choose() *function insists that the first parameter should be for a zero condition. What if I don't want zero? My condition values start with 1.*

You're in a common predicament. Luckily, you have two equally easy ways to get what you want from the *Choose()* function. Perhaps the most obvious is to simply add a dummy zero result:

```
Choose ( Door ; "" ; "European Vacation" ;
"New Car" ; "Wah Wah Wah" )
```

In this calculation, there's no Door number zero, so you just stick "" in the spot where the zero result belongs. You could just as well put "Death by Boredom" there, since it never gets chosen anyway. Just make sure you put a set of empty quotes there, so your first real result is in the number-one spot.

If you just don't like having that dummy result in your calculation, then you can take this approach instead:

```
Choose ( Door-1 ; "European Vacation" ;
"New Car" ; "Wah Wah Wah" )
```

This version simply subtracts one from the Door number. Now Door number one gets the zero result, and Door number two gets the one result. This approach becomes more appealing when your choices begin with an even higher number:

```
Choose ( Year - 2000 ; "Dragon" ; "Snake";
"Horse" ; "Sheep" )
```

Since this calculation uses the year as the condition, it would be a real drag to enter 2000 dummy values. Instead, you just subtract enough to get your sequence to start with zero.

The *Let( )* Function and Variables

The *Let( )* function creates a temporary holder for a value, called a *variable*, which can be plugged into a calculation over and over again. You'll do a little more work upfront to set up a variable, but that effort pays off with faster calculations that are easier to read, edit, and troubleshoot.

Defining Calculation Variables

In a *Let( )* function, you define a value and give it a name, and then use that name as often as you need throughout the calculation. In this case, you can calculate the amount due once, and then store the result in a variable called Amount Due.

The *Let( )* function is unique among functions because it controls the way you write your calculation, not the result. Here's an example:

```
Let ( [ L = 5 ; W = 10 ; H = 3 ] ; L * W * H )
```

Like the *Substitute( )* function described on page 441, *Let( )* uses bracketed notation. It really takes just two parameters. The first is a list of variable definitions. Each variable gets a name and a value using this format:

```
Name = Value
```

Note: FileMaker uses the terms "var" for Name and "expression" for Value in its help files. The terms mean the same things, but "var" and "expression" sound much more impressive.

If you have more than one variable to define (as in the example above), put a semicolon between each one, and then put them all between a pair of square brackets. You can use any calculation expression as the value.

In fact, the expression that determines the value of a variable can even use other variables defined earlier. For example, the next calculation is perfectly legal. Its Hours variable has a value of 240: 24 times the value of the Days variable:

```
Let (
  [ Days = 10 ;
    Hours = 24 * Days ;
    Minutes = 60 * Hours ];

  Minutes & " Minutes"
  )
```

The second parameter can be any calculation expression. This parameter is special because you can use any of the variables you've defined inside the expression, just like fields. The first example above has three defined variables (L, W, and H); the expression then multiplies them together.

When FileMaker evaluates the *Let( )* function, it determines the value of each variable just once, and then plugs this value into the expression every time that variable is used. The result of a *Let( )* function is simply the result of its expression.

Total Due calculation #3: Using the Let() function

Your Total Due calculation can use the *Let( )* function to solve all its problems. Just put the Amount Due in a variable, and use it throughout the calculation:

```
Let ( AmountDue = Sum ( Line Items::Extended Price ) ;
  If (
    Get(CurrentDate) > Date Due and AmountDue > 0;
      AmountDue + ( AmountDue * .05 );
    AmountDue
  )
)
```

This version of the calculation is simpler, easier to change, and more efficient. You can't beat that.

Field Formatting Calculations

Now that you understand most of FileMaker's calculation power features, you're ready to see something really powerful. To clean up phone number data when it's entered, just add an Auto-Enter calculation to the Phone Number field. This calculation, which consolidates a lot of techniques you've covered in this section, does the trick:

```
Let(
 cleanPhone = Filter ( Self; "0123456789"
 ) ;

 Case (
  Length( Self ) = 10 ;

  "(" & Left ( cleanPhone ; 3 ) & ") " &
  Middle ( cleanPhone ; 4 ; 3 ) &
  "-" &
```

```
  Right ( cleanPhone ; 4 ) ;

   Self
  )
 )
```

First, the calculation uses the Filter function to remove any non-numeric characters from the entered phone number, and puts the result in a variable called "cleanPhone". Then, if cleanPhone has exactly 10 digits, the calculation breaks it apart according to the format you want. Otherwise, it just returns the phone number the way the person entered it.

To make the calculation work properly, in the Field Options dialog box, be sure you turn off "Do not replace existing value (if any)".

The Life of a Variable

Most variables last only as long as it takes FileMaker to work through the calculation, and then they're gone. These variables are called *local variables* because they aren't valid outside the *Let( )* function that calls them into existence. But you can also create a special variable called a *global variable*, which lives beyond your calculation. Read on to see when to use each type.

Local variables

The variables you've written so far have all been local variables. Now it's time to learn that local variables having shockingly short memories.

Local variables can lose their values even before a calculation is finished. If you write:

```
Let ( AmountDue = Sum ( Line Items::Extended Price ) ;
 If (
   Get(CurrentDate) > Date Due and AmountDue > Total Paid;
    AmountDue + ( AmountDue * .05 );
   AmountDue
 )
) & If ( AmountDue < 0 ; "CR" ; "" )
```

The calculation tries to use the Amount Due variable after the end parenthesis in the *Let( )* function. Anything that happens after that in the calculation is outside the *Let( )* function's *scope*, so when you try to close the Specify Calculation dialog box on this calculation, FileMaker complains that it doesn't know what that last Amount Due is supposed to be. Here's one way to rewrite that calculation using a local variable:

```
Let ( AmountDue = Sum ( Line Items::Extended Price ) ;
 Case (
 Get ( CurrentDate ) > Date Due and AmountDue > Total Paid;
     AmountDue + ( AmountDue * .05 ) ;
     AmountDue < 0 ; "CR" ; ""
     )
 )
```

In this example, you're including the last test condition within the scope of the *Let( )* function, and you've switched to a *Case( )* function, so that you don't have to read a set of nested *If( )* functions.

If you want the local variables you set inside calculations to follow the same naming conventions as variables you set in scripts (see Chapter 15), then prefix their names with "$". In that case, you'd write the calculation you just saw like this:

```
Let ( $AmountDue = Sum ( Line Items::Extended Price ) ;
 Case (
 Get ( CurrentDate ) > Date Due and $AmountDue > 0;
     $AmountDue + ( $AmountDue * .05 ) ;
     $AmountDue < 0 ; "CR" ; ""
     )
 )
```

Note: When you create a variable with a "$" prefix in a calculation that runs during a script, you extend its lifespan beyond the *Let( )* function. In this case, the variable's scope is now the script. See page 591 for more information on how variables work in scripts.

Notice that you have to include the prefix in the *Let( )* function, *and* in the formula that follows it.

Global variables

But just as FileMaker gives you global fields, it also gives you *global variables*. Unlike local variables, global variables hold their results after the *Let( )* function is finished. To create a global variable, add a "$$" prefix to its name. Here's the same calculation rewritten with a global variable:

```
Let (
 $$AmountDue = Sum ( Line Items::Extended Price ) ;
 Case (
```

```
   Get ( CurrentDate ) > Date Due and $$Amount Due > 0;
   $$AmountDue + ( $$AmountDue * .05 ) ;
   $$AmountDue < 0 ; "CR" ; ""
 )
 )
```

The $$ prefix is the only difference you can see in the calculation. But the practical difference is vast: Global variable values remain until you change them (through another calculation or through a script), or until you close the file.

Note: As with local variables, scope changes if global variables are created within scripts. FileMaker Pro Advanced's Data Viewer (page 743) eliminates guesswork by letting you check the contents of variables, whether you create them in calculation fields or from scripts.

You could run a script that checks to see if a payment was made within 10 days of the invoice date, and if it was, apply a one-percent discount to the $$Amount Due field. Sure, you can do something similar with a straightforward calculation field, but in that case, it gets a little trickier to apply the discount to some of the records, but not to others. With a script, you can find the records you want to give a spur of the moment discount, run the script on that found set, and you're done.

Nesting *Let( )* Functions

As with other functions, you can nest *Let( )* functions inside each other. In fact, you can define a variable once, and then *redefine* it inside a nested *Let( )* function. The variable's value changes while inside the nested *Let( )* function, and then changes back when it ends. By the same token, you can define a variable with the same name as a *field*, and FileMaker uses the variable's value while inside the *Let( )* function.

Here's a very simple example of a *Let( )* function *inside* another *Let( )* function:

```
Let ( X = 3 ; // only X is defined here
 Let ( Y = 4 ; // X and Y are both defined here
  X * Y
 )
 // Only X is defined here too
 )
```

You can also use the *Let( )* function more than once in a single calculation without nesting:

```
Let ( X = 3; Y = 4 ; X * Y ) &
Let ( units = "inches" ; " " & units )
```

Extending Calculations

As you've seen in the past three chapters, FileMaker's calculation functions can do everything from text processing to financial analysis. Since calculations show up in so many different places in FileMaker, you might want to use the *same* calculation more than once. It would be a shame to have to type it in every time—and then make changes in several places the next time you need to modify it. Or maybe you need a function or a feature that doesn't exist in FileMaker.

For these situations and more, FileMaker provides *two* ways to extend the calculation system. The first, called *custom functions*, lets you design your own calculation functions. You can then use these functions in any calculation in the same File-Maker file.

The second way is more complex, and thus more powerful. You (or someone you hire) can create a FileMaker *plug-in* in a programming language like C++. The plug-in also adds new functions to FileMaker's Specify Calculation window. The difference is that those functions can do *anything* a programmer wants them to do.

Note: To *create* custom functions *or* plug-ins, you need FileMaker Pro Advanced, a special version of FileMaker that has extra tools for developers. (Find out more in Chapter 19.) Once you've created a custom function or plug-in, though, it can be *used* in any version of FileMaker. Read on to find out more.

Custom Functions

You may create a custom function for many reasons. First, you might find yourself using the same calculation in many different places throughout your file, like when your business rules change. To update that calculation, you have to find and edit it in every place you use it. But if you use a custom function instead, you have to edit only the function's parameters, and you're done. Second, custom functions can actually simplify complex calculations, by combining FileMaker's regular functions—or even other custom functions—into a neater calculation you can easily to ready and troubleshoot. Finally, custom functions can be *recursive*, which means they repeat the same task over and over until a specific condition is met (page 484).

You create custom functions using the Manage Custom Functions dialog box (Figure 12-1). Custom functions have to follow the same syntax as FileMaker's regular functions. That is, they require a name and zero or more parameters. That might sound odd, that a custom function might take no parameters; it's unusual, but possible. Most custom functions have at least one parameter.

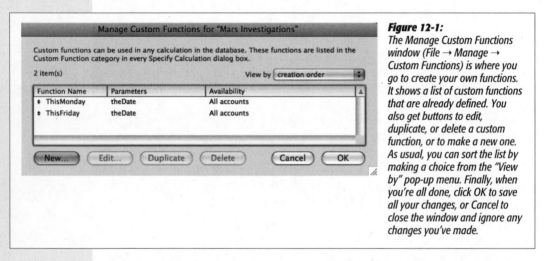

Figure 12-1:
The Manage Custom Functions window (File → Manage → Custom Functions) is where you go to create your own functions. It shows a list of custom functions that are already defined. You also get buttons to edit, duplicate, or delete a custom function, or to make a new one. As usual, you can sort the list by making a choice from the "View by" pop-up menu. Finally, when you're all done, click OK to save all your changes, or Cancel to close the window and ignore any changes you've made.

Rules for custom function names and their parameters are similar to the rules for naming tables and fields. Function and parameter names can't:

- Contain $+ - * / \wedge \& = \neq < > \leq \geq (, :) [] : \$ \}$

- Contain AND, OR, XOR, NOT

- Begin with a digit or period

- Have the same name as another function, parameter or keyword

If you violate any of these rules, FileMaker shows a warning dialog box. Unlike the slight leeway you get with table and field names, the program doesn't let you finish creating your custom function until you comply. You're safest if you stick with alphanumeric characters.

Once you've created them, you can see Custom Functions in a special category of the Specify Calculation dialog box's functions list (Figure 12-2).

Figure 12-2:
Unless you say otherwise, all custom functions appear in the functions list of each Specify Calculation dialog box. Here you see the list arranged as "all functions by type". The section labels are lighter gray than the functions themselves. You can see the two custom functions from Figure 12-1 listed in alphabetical order. Just below them are the plug-in functions for a free plug-in that lets FileMaker Pro download updates from FileMaker Server. You'll learn more about plug-ins on page 487.

Note: The next few exercises require FileMaker Pro Advanced if you want to create custom functions. Download a 30-day trial at *http://www.filemaker.com/products/fmpa/*. But you can see the custom functions for this chapter in FileMaker Pro, if you download the finished sample file for this chapter from the Missing CD page at *http://missingmanuals.com*.

Defining a Custom Function

To get started, you'll add a new function that can calculate the circumference of a circle. Since a circumference is derived by multiplying the circle's diameter by Pi, it makes sense to use the words "circumference" and "diameter" in your function. That way, your formula will be easy for other people to use later.

Note: You may not actually need to calculate circumferences in your own databases much, but this example illustrates important concepts common to creating any custom function. Plus, it's easier to type than most real world examples. See this chapter's sample file for other examples.

1. **In FileMaker Pro Advanced, choose File → Manage → Custom Functions.**

   You see the window shown in Figure 12-1. If you've never created your own function before, the list is blank—but not for long.

2. **Click the New button.**

   The Edit Custom Function window appears. You can see it in Figure 12-3.

3. **In the Function Name box, type *Circumference*.**

   You've just given your function a name, which you'll call upon later when you want to *use* this function in calculations.

4. **In the Function Parameters box, type *diameter*, and then click the Add Parameter button (Figure 12-3).**

   FileMaker moves "diameter" into the parameter list.

Note: When you add more than one parameter to the Function Parameters list, you can use the arrow icon by each item to move it up or down in the list. The order here is important: It determines the order in which you want the parameters to pass to the function (page 407).

---

5. **From the View pop-up menu (above the function list), choose "Trigonometric functions".**

   The function list changes to show just the relevant options.

6. **In the function list, double-click the *Pi( )* function, and then click the * operator button (or type *).**

   The function calculation area now reads *Pi **.

7. **Finally, in the parameter list, double-click "diameter".**

   FileMaker adds the word *diameter* to the end of the calculation, like so: *Pi * diameter*.

Figure 12-3:
The Edit Custom Function window is where you actually create the function. It looks a lot like the Specify Calculation dialog box you've seen so much of lately. But instead of fields, it has a list of function parameters (which is empty right now). Aside from this distinction, you should be in familiar territory here.

Note: The default setting in the Availability options lets anyone who accesses your database see and use the custom function in her own calculations. If you choose "Only accounts assigned full access privileges", then the function still works for everybody, but only superusers (page 634) can see the function in the functions list.

When you're done, click OK, and then OK again to close the Edit Custom Function and Manage Custom Functions dialog boxes. The database has a brand-new function called Circumference. To use the Circumference function, create a calculation field that uses it, and point the parameter to a field that contains a diameter value.

UP TO SPEED

Using Custom Functions

You can use custom functions just like any of FileMaker's built-in functions. When you're in the Specify Calculation dialog box, choose Custom Functions from the View popup menu to access the functions you've made. (When you create a custom function, you're adding it to the FileMaker file you're working in. It isn't available in other files unless you add it to them as well.)

Just like other functions, custom functions can also use *other* custom functions to do their job.

For example, if you want to add a new function that calculates the surface area of a cylinder, then it can take two parameters (diameter and height) and use your custom Circumference function, like so:

```
Circumference(diameter) * Height
```

With this in mind, you can create functions that build upon one another—to keep each one simple, or to provide different but related capabilities.

Editing Custom Functions

You probably feel like a pro at the Manage Custom Functions window already, since it works a lot like other FileMaker dialog boxes. But even you could end up with a custom function that needs adjustment or repair. To edit an existing custom function, either double-click its name, or select it from the list, and then click Edit. In the Edit Custom Function window (Figure 12-3), you can modify the definition of a function as follows:

• To change its name, in the Function Name box, just type a new name.

• You can add new parameters, just like you added the "diameter" parameter in the Circumference function. If you no longer need a function parameter, select it, and then click the Delete Parameter button.

• To change a parameter's name, you must first select it in the parameter list. When you do, FileMaker puts the parameter in the Parameter Name box, where you can edit it. When you're done, click the Edit Parameter button to apply your change to the one in the list.

• You can reorder parameters by dragging them up or down in the list.

- If you click Duplicate, then FileMaker makes an exact copy of the selected function. That way, you can use a custom function as a starting point for creating a new one

- If you don't need a function anymore, select it, and then click Delete.

Note: Be careful adding, reordering, or deleting parameters for an existing function. If the function is being used in a calculation somewhere, then that calculation breaks because it no longer passes the right parameters back to the function. On the other hand, it's safe to *rename* a function or its parameters—FileMaker fixes any existing calculations when you do.

Recursion

As described in the box on page 483, you can create custom functions that call other custom functions, creating whole strings of mathematical wizardry that perform to your exact specifications. Even more interesting, a custom function can *use itself*, a technique known as *recursion*. With recursion, you can create calculations that repeat a process over and over again until they reach a result—called *iterative calculations*.

Note: Recursion is a notoriously complicated topic, and many *very* capable FileMaker developers are stymied by it. Fortunately, recursion is rarely the only solution to a given problem, so you can certainly get by without it. For example, consider using a script instead.

Imagine you need a function that removes duplicate lines from a list. For example, if a field contains a list of colors, then you want a new list with each *unique* color name, even if it appears in the original list several times. You can't do that with a normal calculation, because you just don't know how many words you need to pull out. A recursive function solves the problem by repeating its work until it takes care of all items (colors).

While the concept of a recursive function is simple, creating one can be tricky. To implement a recursive function, you're best off tackling the calculation in three distinct steps. First, solve the initial problem; second, call that first formula over and over again (that's the recursive part); and third, tell the formula how to stop.

Note: If you're having trouble getting through the following recursion example on your own, you can download a sample database from the Missing CD page at *http://missingmanuals.com*.

Step 1: Solve the first case

Rather than think about how to solve the entire problem, just figure out how to deal with the *first* line in the list. If you have a field called Values, for example, and you want to make sure the *first* line appears only once in the list, you can use this calculation:

```
LeftValues ( values ; 1 ) & Substitute ( values ; LeftValues ( values; 1 ) ;
"" )
```

Suppose the Values field contains:

```
Red
Green
Orange
Red
Orange
Yellow
```

The Substitute part of this expression does the lion's share of the work, so start with that to figure out how the formula works. The Substitute function sees that "Red" is the first item in the Values field and takes it out of the field everywhere it occurs. If Substitute were the whole shooting match, then "Red" would disappear entirely from the Values field. But the *LeftValues (values ; 1) &* piece of the expression also notices that "Red" is the first item in the Values field, and it puts "Red" back at the top of the list. When both are put together (using &), the result is the first item in the list, then the rest of the list with the Red is removed. Here's the result you see if you make a calculation field with the formula on the previous page:

```
Red
Green
Orange
Orange
Yellow
```

Now you're ready to move on to the rest of the function, where you call the same action over and over again—and things start to get interesting.

Step 2: Assume your function already works, and use it

You're ready to take the *recursion leap of faith*. A recursive function, by definition, calls itself. So at some point, it depends on its own resources to work. But when you're *writing* the recursive custom function, it obviously doesn't work yet. You'll be at a total impasse if you don't *assume* it already works, and just get on with writing.

So since you're writing a new custom function called *RemoveDuplicates( )*, write its syntax as if you already have a function called *RemoveDuplicates( )* that does what you want. If such a function did exist, you could use it in the above calculation like this:

```
LeftValues ( values ; 1 ) & RemoveDuplicates ( Substitute ( values ;
LeftValues ( values ; 1 ); "" ) )
```

This new version works a lot like the last one. It first pulls the first item from the list, and then adds it to the result. It also removes duplicates of the first item rfom the rest of the list (using *Substitute( )*). But instead of adding that to the result, it sends the entire remaining list through *RemoveDuplicates( )*. If you assume *RemoveDuplicates( )* already works, then it removes duplicates from the rest of the list. You take care of the *first* line using your calculation skills. Then you rely on the function itself to take care of all the rest. Notice that the new list that's passed to

RemoveDuplicates( ) starts with the *second line* of the original list. So when the function runs again, the second line becomes the first, and the function takes care of it. Unfortunately, this process goes on forever, which is probably not exactly what you want.

Step 3: Find a stopping point

You now have two of the three critical components of a recursive function: You're manually doing the *first* part of the job, and you're telling recursion to do the rest. If you leave the function like this, though, you're in trouble. If *RemoveDuplicates( )* calls *RemoveDuplicates( )*, which in turn calls *RemoveDuplicates( )* (ad infinitum), then you have a problem: This function just keeps going forever.

Note: When you work on recursive functions, you inevitably create such *loops* accidentally. When you do, you see FileMaker think for several seconds, and then give up and return *invalid* (a question mark). If FileMaker seems to be hung, give it some time; it gives up eventually.

To avoid ending up in a loop, you need to figure out when to *stop* calling *RemoveDuplicates( )*. Think about what happens after this function calls itself several times. Each time it's called with a slightly smaller list than the time before (because the first item—along with any copies of it—has been removed). Eventually it's going to get called with just one item (or zero items). When that happens, you no longer need the services of *RemoveDuplicates( )*. Instead, you can just return that last word by itself since it obviously has no duplicates. You use an *If( )* function to help the recursion figure out when to stop. The final function looks like this (with comments added):

```
// Start the result with the first item in the list
LeftValues ( values ; 1 ) &

// If there are more items in List...
If ( ValueCount ( values ) > 1;
// ...then remove duplicates from the remaining items
RemoveDuplicates ( Substitute ( values ; LeftValues ( values ; 1); "") );
// ...otherwise we're done
""

)
```

Now you just have to create the *RemoveDuplicates( )* custom function. *RemoveDuplicates( )* needs one parameter, which is the values from which you're sifting duplicates. A descriptive name, like "values," helps you remember what this parameter does. Finally, create a calculation field using your new custom function, and create a reference to the field containing the list of duplicated values.

Figure 12-4 illustrates an example of a recursive calculation calling the *RemoveDuplicates( )* custom function to remove all duplicate colors it finds in the list. (It takes four iterations to remove all the duplicates and return a unique instance of each item in the list, in the order in which they occur.)

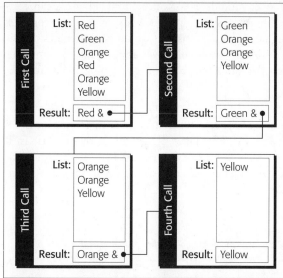

Figure 12-4:
In the top-left corner, the box shows how RemoveDuplicates( ) is first called. It receives a list of colors as its one parameter. It returns the first item in the list, and the result of the second call. This time, though, Red has been removed from the list. The second call returns Green and the results of the third call. This progresses until the fourth call, when the script passes a single item to RemoveDuplicates( ). This time RemoveDuplicates( ) simply returns the item without calling itself again. When it returns, the third call has all it needs, so it returns as well. This process goes back up the chain until the first call is reached, and the final result is returned. If you join up the results of each call, then you see the correct list.

WORKAROUND WORKSHOP

The Point of No Return

RemoveDuplicates( ) works great for finding unique values in a list, so long as the last item in the list has a ¶ (paragraph return) following it. If it doesn't, then the function gets confused and may leave the last line in even if it's a duplicate. You can adjust for lists that don't have a trailing ¶ by adjusting your calculation field slightly:

```
RemoveDuplicates ( values & "¶" )
```

You could also modify the custom function itself to guard against this possibility. Doing so makes the formula more complex, but here it is in case you want a challenge:

```
Let (
    [cleanList = if ( Right ( values, 1
"¶", values, values & "¶" );
    first = LeftValues ( cleanList, 1

first &
if ( ValueCount(cleanList) > 1;
    RemoveDuplicates(cleanList);
    ""

)
)
```

Plug-Ins

Some things just can't be done (or can't be done *well*) using calculations and custom functions. When you run into this situation, you may consider looking into *plug-ins*, tiny applications that live inside FileMaker to help it do specific tasks that it can't do on its own.

Many plug-ins focus on doing certain things: processing credit card transactions; creating charts; or interacting with special devices like cameras, bar code readers, and so on. Although plug-ins work through calculation functions, scripts (which the next section covers) generally control them.

Some plug-ins, though, are perfect candidates for calculations. Plug-ins can convert, resize, and otherwise modify images in container fields, or perform complex mathematical, scientific, or financial calculations that would be difficult or inefficient in a calculation. Although this book doesn't cover any specific plug-ins, this section shows you how to access the functions provided by any plug-in you install.

Installing Plug-ins

A plug-in comes in a file bearing a special FileMaker plug-in icon (shown in Figure 12-5). In order to use plug-ins, FileMaker needs to *load* them—that is, it has to put the plug-in code into its own memory. Every time you launch the program, it searches for plug-ins in a folder called Extensions, which is inside its own folder, and loads all that it finds.

AutoUpdate.fmplugin

Figure 12-5:
FileMaker plug-ins come in many varieties—with many names—but they all look like this. (Some plug-ins have a .fmx filename extension, some have .fmplugin, and some have no extension at all.) Your job is to put the file where FileMaker can find it.

Installing a plug-in is thus a simple matter of making sure it's in the right folder:

- On Windows, it's typically C: → Program Files → FileMaker → FileMaker Pro 10 → Extensions.

- On Mac OS X, it's usually Applications → FileMaker Pro 10 → Extensions.

Note: If you're using FileMaker Pro Advanced, then the FileMaker folder is called FileMaker Pro 9 Advanced, not FileMaker Pro 10.

Once you've found the folder, just drag the plug-in file into it, and then restart FileMaker. You don't see anything on your screen to let you know it worked. To see which plug-ins FileMaker has actually loaded, you need to visit the application preferences (FileMaker Pro → Preferences on Mac OS X, Edit → Preferences on Windows). In the Preferences window, click the Plug-ins tab, or look to Figure 12-6.

Once you've installed plug-ins, you can use their functions from the Specify Calculation dialog box's External functions section of the list (page 481). For details on how to use these functions, consult their developer's manuals or Web sites. In most cases, you'll use Set Field script steps (page 534) to put calculation results into global fields you create specifically for your plug-in.

Old and New Plug-ins

You actually have two kinds of plug-ins for FileMaker: older FileMaker 4-style plug-ins and newer FileMaker 7+-style plug-ins. FileMaker 10 works with *both* types of plug-ins, but ask your plug-in provider which type you're getting, since the FileMaker 4 plug-ins have limited abilities:

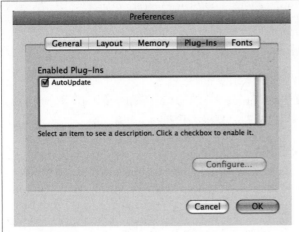

Figure 12-6:
In FileMaker's Preferences dialog box, The Plug-ins tab shows you all the plug-ins you've installed. Disable a plug-in by turning off the checkbox by its name. If a plug-in requires any configuration, select it in the list, and then click Configure. When you have a plug-in selected, you see a description of it below the list.

- The functions provided by FileMaker 4 plug-ins always expect *one* parameter. Even if the function doesn't need a parameter, you have to pass "", which is just an empty parameter. If the function really needs more, consult the documentation that came with the plug-in to find out how to accommodate it.

- This single parameter's type is *always* text in a FileMaker 4 plug-in's function. If you want to pass a date, time, timestamp, or number, then you have to convert it to text first, using *GetAsText( )*.

Newer FileMaker plug-ins give you a lot more options. Functions can have as many parameters as their creator cares to give them. They can also deal with all data types, including pictures, movies, and files stored in container fields. Thankfully, these days almost all available FileMaker plug-ins use the new capabilities.

Finding Plug-ins

Most FileMaker developers lack the know-how to build their own plug-ins. Although you can hire a programmer to make one to your specifications, you can often find one on the market that already does what you want. You can find a comprehensive list of available plug-ins on FileMaker's Web site. Just choose Products → "Made for FileMaker". Then, on the right side of the page, look for the Plug-ins link.

You can also visit the more prolific FileMaker plug-in vendors' Web sites:

- 24U Software (*http://www.24usoftware.com*)

- 360Works (*http://www.360works.com*)

- CNS Plug-ins (*http://www.cnsplug-ins.com*)

- FMNEXUS (*http://fmnexus.com*)

- New Millennium Communications (*http://www.nmci.com*)

- Productive Computing (*http://www.productivecomputing.com*)

- Qutic Development (*http://www.qutic.com*)

- Troi Automatisering (*http://www.troi.com*)

New vendors come up with great products all the time so if you don't see what you want, then head over to Google and get your search on.

Creating Your Own Plug-ins

If you're feeling adventurous (or have helpful programmer friends), you can create your own plug-ins. To do that, you first need FileMaker Advanced (it's the only version of FileMaker that includes the *Plug-in Software Development Kit* or SDK). You also need a C++ development environment. In Windows, you're best off with Visual C++ or Visual Studio.NET. On Mac OS X, you can use XCode (it's included with the Developer Tools that came with your computer, although you have to install it yourself from the CD). Plug-in SDK includes sample projects for each of these environments—and sample plug-in code—to get you started.

Part Five: Scripting

5

Understanding Scripts

Calculation fields let you tell FileMaker how to automatically update and validate the *data* in your database. But *working with the database* is still a manual affair. If you often need to print a summarized report, then you have to perform a find, sort the records, switch layouts, print, and then switch back to the original layout manually. Once you've done it 27 times, you start wishing you could click a button and have the report print itself. Well, you can: Just tell FileMaker the same series of steps you've been doing over and over again, and attach the list to a button (page 267). That's the essence of scripting.

A *script* is a series of steps bundled together. When a script runs, FileMaker carries out all the steps on your behalf, one after the other. You can create a script to automate almost any routine task, and then give it a name so you can easily call it up and repeat the steps later with just a click or two.

You can run a script by selecting it from the Scripts menu. But more typically, you put a button on a layout somewhere, and have FileMaker run your script when someone clicks the button. You can even use *script triggers* to make scripts run automatically in response to what someone does. For instance, you can make a script run every time someone goes to a particular layout, clicks into a certain field, or selects a tab panel in a tab control. Using the "Install OnTimer Script" script step, you can make a script run periodically or at a certain point in the future. Finally, you can run scripts on a schedule using FileMaker Server (see Chapter 18) to perform automated imports, send notifications, clean up data, and so on. Scripting is FileMaker's real power feature, and you get lots of ways to take advantage of it.

Scripts can be simple—just the same five steps you'd go through if you printed a report manually. Or they can be much more complicated—and handle tricky or tedious tasks you wouldn't want to do manually. Advanced scripts can even incorporate calculations to do different things in different situations by making simple decisions based on the data in your database, the current time or date, or any other condition you want to test.

Note: If you've worked with other scripting environments—like Visual Basic for Applications, AppleScript, or JavaScript—then FileMaker's scripting commands are pleasantly familiar.

Your First Script

To get a feel for how scripting works, you'll create a really simple script. Suppose you want to find all invoices with a balance due, and view them in a sorted list. The following pages show how to go about preparing your database, planning, creating, and polishing the script, and finishing off with a way to run it.

Preparing the Database

FileMaker is flexible enough to let you create fields and layouts on the fly, at the same time as you write a script, but you can more easily focus on the script if you create all the supporting material you need before you even open ScriptMaker. In particular, for this script to work, you need an Invoice List layout. Since you haven't made one yet, you must do so before you can start scripting.

Your list layout should include the Invoice ID, Job Name, Date, Date Due, and Balance Due fields. As for look, feel free to express your creativity. Figure 13-1 shows one possibility.

Figure 13-1:
To follow along in this chapter, you need an Invoice List layout like this one. You can build one yourself, or just grab the database from the Missing CD page at http://missingmanuals.com.

Note: For help building a List layout, see Chapter 5.

Planning Your Script

Before you dive in and create the script, you should review what you want it to do. A script is just a series of steps that FileMaker repeats for you. When you're planning a script, it often helps to manually work through the process the script should do first, so you can see whether it works. This trial run helps you clarify the steps you're scripting. Plus, some scripts are easier to write if you do the steps manually beforehand, since dialog boxes retain their settings until you change them. For example, if your script needs to sort records, the dialog box already has the settings you need when you're actually creating the script.

So go through the steps necessary to find the balance due, and take notes. You probably end up with something like the following:

- **Switch to the Invoice List layout.** This layout has the fields the script needs to create the invoice list. It's also going to display the final list, so you want to make sure the script runs in this layout.

- **Choose View → Find Mode.** The script needs to *find* all invoices with a balance due. Scripts can't click a button or even choose a menu command, but you know you need a script step that puts FileMaker into Find mode.

- **In the Total Due field, enter ">0", and then press Enter.** This step tells File-Maker what to find, and puts it into action. When the script runs this step, FileMaker performs the find and shows the correct records, just as if you'd performed the find yourself.

Note: If none of your invoices has a balance due, just click Cancel when the error message pops up, and then choose Records → Show All Records so you can do the next step. Jot down that your script needs to account for this message box if it pops up when someone runs your script. In Chapter 15 you'll learn how to make your script account for errors like these.

- **Choose Records → Sort, and then sort the records ascending by Date Due.** You should now see your final list, properly sorted.

Now that you know all the steps involved, you're ready to get acquainted with ScriptMaker. A script is just a series of steps, and FileMaker shows it to you that way. Figure 13-2 shows a complete script to do the steps in this section. Even if you know nothing about scripting, you can probably look at it and get a general idea of what it does. You'll learn the specifics of each step as you work through the next three chapters.

Creating Your Script

You create, edit, run, and delete scripts in FileMaker using ScriptMaker. It's the first item in the Scripts menu, and it's available from any mode, except while a script is running. When you choose this command, you see the window shown in Figure 13-3. Your window may not have scripts in it yet, but otherwise, it's the same.

Figure 13-2:
This script tells FileMaker to switch to the Invoice List layout, go to Find mode, put a find criteria in the Total Due field, perform the find, and sort the found records. It may not use exactly the words you would expect, but you can tell at a glance roughly what it does.

Now it's time to build the script. First, tell FileMaker to repeat each of the steps you went through when you planned the script. Here's how:

1. **Choose Scripts → Manage Scripts, or choose File → Manage → Scripts. When the Manage Scripts window appears, click New.**

   The Edit Script window appears (Figure 13-4). Make sure to click the New button, and not the pop-up menu. You'll learn how and when to use the pop-up menu later.

Figure 13-3:
The Manage Scripts window, more affectionately known as ScriptMaker, is a blank canvas—in a file with no scripts. Scripts appear in the list as you create them. Tools along the bottom let you create and manage your scripts. The New pop-up menu lets you create folders to organize your scripts. Separators show up as hyphens in the script list, and as menu separators in the Scripts menu. You'll learn more about these options in the next sections.

2. **In the Script Name box, type *Find Unpaid Invoices*.**

   Your script's name is important. It's how you'll identify it when you want to run it later.

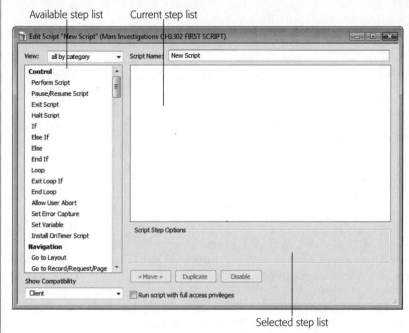

Available step list   Current step list

Figure 13-4:
In the Edit Script window, you build your script by choosing steps from the Available Script Steps list, and use the Move button to add them to your script. Or double-click a step to move it. Once moved, you can configure script steps using buttons, checkboxes, and radio buttons that appear in the Script Step Options area.

Selected step list

3. **A little more than halfway down the list on the left, just below the Navigation headline, choose the "Go to Layout" step, and then click the Move button.**

   The Move button doesn't become available until you've clicked a script step. When you click Move, FileMaker adds a "Go to Layout" step to the list of current steps. This step is already selected, so you can quickly make changes to its settings.

Note: You can double-click a step in the list to avoid the trip to the Move button. When the script step list is active, you can type the first part of a step's name to scroll to it, and then press the space bar to add it. If the script step list isn't active, then use the Tab key to move between the script step list, the current steps list, and the Script Name box.

---

4. **From the Specify pop-up menu (in the Script Step Options area), choose Invoice List.**

   You want FileMaker to go to this layout when the script runs. Now your script has just one step, or line. If you run it as is, then it simply takes you to the Invoice List layout. (If you're *already* on the Invoice List layout, then it doesn't do anything.)

5. **From the View pop-up menu (top-left corner), choose "all by name" to sort the script steps alphabetically, and then double-click Enter Find Mode.**

   FileMaker adds a second line to your script. The Script Step Options area now has new options (those that make sense with the Enter Find Mode step). Notice that the Pause option at the left side of the Script Step Options area is turned *on*.

6. **Turn off the Pause option.**

   Turning off this option tells the script not to wait for user input when it's run. (You'll learn more about pausing a script on page 554.)

7. **Add a Set Field script step to the script.**

   Use the scroll bar to skip down to the steps that start with "s," and then double-click Set Field, or click it, and then click Move.

   The Set Field step lets you put (or set) data in a field. You can use Set Field in Browse or Find mode. In Browse mode, it enters data; in Find mode, it specifies find requests. Since this Set Field step comes right after an Enter Find Mode step, you're specifying a find request for the invoices.

8. **In the Script Step Options area, turn on "Specify target field".**

   You can save a step by clicking the top Specify button. Here you tell FileMaker *which* field to set. As soon as you turn on this option, FileMaker shows a slightly different Specify Field window (Figure 13-5).

Note: If you *don't* turn on the Specify target field option, then the Set Field step modifies whichever field happens to be active when the step is carried out.

Figure 13-5:
This Specify Field dialog box looks almost exactly like the one you've seen in Layout mode. The only difference is the Repetition box at the bottom. If you select a repeating field (page 117), then you can use this box to tell FileMaker which repetition to set.

9. **In the field list, select Total Due, and then click OK.**

The Set Field step in your script (Figure 13-6) shows the option you've selected. In the Script Step Options area, click the bottom Specify button (the one beside "Calculated result").

FileMaker shows you the Specify Calculation dialog box, the same one you used to build calculation fields in the previous chapters. Here you'll use a calculation to tell FileMaker what to put in the Invoices::Total Due field. Remember, you're in Find mode when this script runs, so the Set Field step tells FileMaker what records you want to find.

10. **In the Calculation box, type ">0" (including the quotes), and then click OK.**

This bit of computerese sets the Invoices::Total Due field to the appropriate value for finding unpaid invoices. FileMaker now shows the calculation beside the Set Field step as well. (Spoken out loud, this step reads, "Set the Invoices:: TotalDue field to greater than zero.")

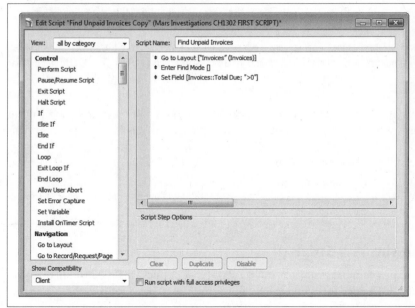

Figure 13-6:
FileMaker shows your script steps in the order they're performed. If a step has any options, then they're displayed in brackets after the step name. In this example, the Invoices::Total Due field is modified by the Set Field step.

11. **Add the Perform Find script step to your script.**

Don't specify any options. This step carries out the find operation. It's the equivalent of clicking Find or pressing Enter if you were doing it yourself.

12. **Add the Sort Records script step to your script. Then, in the Script Step Options area, select "Perform without dialog".**

This action tells FileMaker you want the script to go ahead and sort, instead of opening the Sort dialog box every time it runs. That way, the sort is the same every time you run the script.

13. **Turn on the "Specify sort order" checkbox.**

    If you went through the script-planning phase, as described in "Planning Your Script" on page 495, the Sort dialog box is already configured properly. When you add a Sort Records step to your script, FileMaker configures it to match the *last* sort you performed. If you skipped the dry run, then set the dialog box to sort by Date Due, in ascending order.

14. **In the Sort Records window, click OK.**

    Unlike some other script steps, Sort Records doesn't show its settings. It just says Restore. But if you forget, you can always click the Specify dialog box, and then check it out.

15. **Click the Edit Script window's Close button, and then click the Save button.**

    The Edit Script window has no Save button, but when you close it, you always see a warning dialog box that lets you save your scripts.

16. **Click the Perform button.**

    It's the one with a green triangle at the bottom right. FileMaker runs your script.

Note: FileMaker has lots of script steps, each designed to meet a certain set of needs. In this chapter, you'll learn some basic scripting concepts, and see a few useful scripts in action. The next chapter explains the most common script steps in detail.

You should see the correct list of invoices, or—oops!—a message telling you no records were found, if you don't have any unpaid invoices in your database right now. In the next section, you'll refine your script to help deal with these message boxes if they pop up when someone runs the script. (See the box on page 504.)

Note: You can adapt the basic structure of this script for a host of purposes. Just edit the script's find or sort criteria, and specify a different layout.

Improving Your Script

On the preceding pages, you created a script that mimics what you would do to get an unpaid invoice list, step by step. But ScriptMaker has a lot of options to make writing scripts fast and easy. Often, a script can get the results you want with *fewer* steps than it would take to do it yourself. For example, to see your unpaid invoice list, the steps boil down to the following:

• Switch to the Invoice List layout.

• Find the right invoices.

• Sort the records.

This version has just *three* steps instead of five because it assumes you can "find the right invoices" in one step. Luckily, ScriptMaker's Perform Find script step *really can* find what you want in one step. Here's how to revise your script to use the simpler form:

1. **Choose Scripts → ScriptMaker. In the Manage Scripts window, select the Find Unpaid Invoices script, and then click Edit.**

   Or you can double-click the script instead. In the Edit Script window, the Find Unpaid Invoices script pops up.

2. **Select the second and third steps in your script (Enter Find Mode and Set Field).**

   You can select both by clicking Enter Find Mode in your script, and then Shift-clicking Set Field.

Note: You should select the steps in your script (in the window on the right), not the steps in the available script steps list (on window's left side).

---

3. **Click the Clear button.**

   FileMaker removes the two selected steps from the script. It now has two steps that look a lot like the simplified process on the previous page. Also notice that the Perform Find step is already highlighted, since FileMaker automatically selects the *next* step when you clear one or more steps from the script.

4. **In the Script Step Options area, select the "Specify find requests" checkbox.**

   The Specify Find Requests dialog box (Figure 13-7) appears, and, like the Sort script step in the previous tutorial, it's already set with the find you did when you planned your script. Since that's exactly what you want, you don't need to do anything in the Specify Find Requests window. But if you skipped the recommended planning work on page 495, then you have to set your find request manually now, as described in steps 5–7. If, on the other hand, you followed instructions, then you can skip to step 8.

Figure 13-7:
This window shows find requests that are built into the Perform Find step. You can add or edit the find requests directly here. Doing your editing here is usually easier than adding Set Field steps like you did the first time 'round.

5. **Click New.**

The Edit Find Request dialog box appears. You can see it described on page 65, and in Figure 13-8.

Figure 13-8:
You construct a find request in this dialog box. The list at the top shows all the fields that have criteria in the request. From the list on the left, you can pick a field, and then put something in the Criteria box to set that field in the find request. From the top list, you can also select criteria, and then edit them (click Change when you're done) or click Remove to remove them. Everything you do in this window is just like typing into fields in a single request in Find mode.

6. **In the "Find records when" pop-up menu, choose Invoices, if necessary, and then scroll through the list until you see the Total Due field. Click to select it.**

The Balance Due field is highlighted so you can remember which field you're telling FileMaker to search.

7. **Type *>0* in the Criteria list box, and then click OK.**

Your search is entered at the top of the dialog box, in the Action box. (You wouldn't have all this trouble if you'd followed directions.)

8. **Click OK until you're back in the Edit Script window.**

The Perform Find script step now has options set (Figure 13-9). Notice that the Edit Script window has a * (or star) at the end of its name. That tells you you've made changes to the script that haven't been saved. Whenever you close an Edit Script window that has a star, FileMaker asks if you want to save changes to your script.

9. **Close the Edit Script window, and then, in the dialog box that follows, click the Save button.**

Or choose Scripts → Save Script, or press Ctrl+S (Windows) or ⌘-S (Mac). Either way, the Edit Script window stays open, but the script is saved. You can use this command to save a script midstream while you're working on it.

Figure 13-9:
Your finished script should look like this. It wasn't too hard to improve, and it's very easy to understand. The * at the end of the window's name tells you that the script's changes haven't been saved.

Note: The Scripts menu also has a Save All Scripts command and a Revert script command. These commands have no keyboard shortcuts, but you don't have to click the Close box on an Edit Script window to handle your save/revert chores.

---

10. **Click the Perform button.**

The Manage Scripts window stays open, and your database window comes forward to show you the results of your script. Later in this chapter (page 510), you'll learn more about ScriptMaker's windows and how they work.

This new, simpler script does everything the first script did. It's simpler because you didn't have to script all the steps involved in performing a find: Enter Find Mode; Set Field; Perform Find. Instead, you let FileMaker do all that in one Perform Find step. You'll find that you can reduce *many* of FileMaker's common multistep operations to a single step in ScriptMaker.

The Importance of the Layout

In a script, the active layout is very important, since it's what determines the script's *context*. Context is critical when you do things like delete records. If you write a script that simply deletes a record, without checking for context, then it deletes the current record from whatever layout someone happens to be on. That record may not be the right one at all. You could end up deleting a record from the Customer table instead of the single invoice record you meant to delete!

UP TO SPEED

To Be Continued

If your database has no unpaid invoices when you run the Find Unpaid Invoices script, then you see a message indicating that no records were found. The message is the same as the one you see if you perform the find manually, with one exception: This time you get a Continue button.

Since FileMaker was running a script when the error occurred, it gives you the choice to cancel the script (in other words, stop in the middle and return control to the user) or continue the script (keep going and pretend nothing went wrong). In this case, Cancel and Continue do the same thing since the error happened on the *last* step in the script.

If you don't want the database user to make this choice, then you can tell FileMaker to *capture* the errors as they happen, and let you deal with them inside the script. You'll learn about this process on page 593.

Take the script you've created in this chapter, for example. Before it does anything else, your Find Unpaid Invoices script goes to the Invoice List layout—but what would happen if you left that step out? Figure 13-8 shows the options ScriptMaker gives you for the Perform Find script step. See if you can spot what's *missing*.

You can see that Perform Find—like every other script step—makes absolutely no mention of which table it should act upon. Just because you're asking it to "Find records when Invoices::Invoice ID > 0" doesn't mean you're looking for *invoice* records. You could be looking for customers whose attached invoices have a balance due. Or you could be looking for any line items on an unpaid invoice. FileMaker can tell what you're looking for only by the context of the layout you're on. That's why the first step in the script goes to the Invoice List layout. That layout is attached to the Invoices table occurrence. This tells FileMaker which records to look through (those in the Invoices table) and from what perspective to resolve relationships (the Invoices table occurrence on the relationship graph).

When to Switch

Now that you've dutifully absorbed the lesson in the previous paragraphs, don't get lured into the idea that you *always* have to switch to a layout for your script to work. The fact that a script can do something useful from more than one context can be a good thing. In general, you have three choices when you write a script, and here are some guidelines on when to use each:

- **Switch to a layout associated with the table you want to work with.** The "Go to Layout" script step makes sense when you're showing certain results (like the Find Unpaid Invoices script) or when your script always makes sense, but only from one particular context. If necessary, you can then switch *back* to the original layout at the end of the script ("Go to Layout" has an Original Layout option).

- **Don't include a "Go to Layout" script step at all.** Just let the script go about its business, whatever the context. If you use this approach, then you have to make sure the script works and makes sense from any perspective. For instance, a script could switch to Preview mode, resize the window to show the whole page, and then ask someone if he'd like to print. This script can run on nearly any layout and still do something useful: print. See the box on page below for one example of context independent scripting.

- **Prevent the script from running on the wrong layout.** As you'll see on page 555, you can make it so a script doesn't run at all if it's not designed to work properly on the current layout. This alternative is your best bet when switching layouts within the script isn't feasible. For example, suppose you have a Refund Invoice script that carries out the steps necessary to pay someone back. Using "Go to Layout" to switch to the Invoices layout would ensure the right layout, but not the right *invoice*. It's best if this script runs only when someone's *already* open to the Invoices layout—presumably looking at the invoice she wants to refund.

Note: When a script can do damage to your database if it's run from the wrong layout, use the failsafe of the third option even if you're the only person who uses your database. If your mouse hand slips when you're insufficiently caffeinated, then the script can show you an error message rather than running at the wrong time.

POWER USERS' CLINIC

Context Independence

You may be wondering why the Send Email to Customer script you created on page 513 doesn't go to the Customers layout first. After all, doesn't it only make sense from this context? Actually, this script is a perfect candidate for *context independence*. If you run this script from the Jobs layout, it creates a new email message addressed to the *related customer*. The same holds true from the Invoice layout. In fact, you can run this script from *any* layout, and get a useful result: FileMaker finds the related customer record, and addresses the message to her.

But what if you have more than one related customer record? If you just run the script from the Scripts menu, FileMaker automatically selects the *first* related customer based on the active record on the current layout. Remember, the Send Email to Customer script is set to send only one email, even though the Send Mail script step lets you send multiple

emails to all customers in a found set. If the relationship to Customers is sorted in the Relationships tab of Manage Databases, then it's the customer that sorts to the top. Otherwise, you get the oldest customer record.

But if your layout has a portal of related customers, then you can put a button inside the portal row. Then, when you click this button, the script automatically addresses the email to the appropriate related customer, even if he's not the customer in the first related record.

The point is, you can put a button just about anywhere and tell it to run this script. FileMaker does something a little different depending on where the button is. So this example is one of those scripts that you *don't* want to associate with a specific layout.

Running Scripts

At this point you're probably starting to see how scripts can be really useful in your database. The fact is, most large database systems are *loaded* with scripts that do all kinds of things. But the only way you've seen to run a script is pretty tedious: Chose Scripts → ScriptMaker, select the script, and then click Perform. That's lots of clicks to run a script that's supposed to *save* you time! Thankfully, you have a few *other*, more convenient, ways to run scripts, and you can set them up when you first create a script.

The Scripts Menu

You can show some or all your scripts right in the Scripts menu. If you have a script (or two) to which you want quick access from *anywhere*, then it makes sense to put it in the Scripts menu. That way, anyone can run it by simply choosing it from the menu. FileMaker even has keyboard shortcuts for the first 10 scripts in the Scripts menu: Ctrl+1 (⌘-1) through Ctrl+9 (⌘-9) for the first nine, and Ctrl+0 (⌘-0) for number 10. Figure 13-10 shows how to assign a script to this menu in the Manage Scripts dialog box.

Note: If 10 scripts in a list isn't your idea of a highly organized command center, take heart. In Chapter 19 you'll learn how to completely customize the menus in your database. You can add an item to any menu, name it whatever you want, assign a keyboard shortcut, and then have it run a script. You can remove the menus you don't want, add new items to existing menus, or even add entirely new menus. And you can completely customize the keyboard shortcuts to your liking.

Figure 13-10:
Top: In the Manage Scripts window, every script has a checkbox by its name. If you turn on this box, then the script appears in the Scripts menu, and you can run it simply by selecting its name.

Bottom: Here's the Scripts menu that results from the settings above. On page 510 you'll learn how to make the folders shown here.

Buttons

As you learned in Chapter 6, you can add buttons to any layout—or turn existing fields, labels, pictures, and so forth into clickable buttons. At the time, you used simple single-action buttons, like a button that switches layouts. If you revisit the Specify Button dialog box now, then you see the list of button commands is almost exactly like the list of available script steps. A button is, in some sense, just a one-line script.

But sometimes you want a button to do more. With almost no effort, you can get a button to run any script. Just assign the Perform Script action to the button. When you do, you can pick from among the scripts in your database. Then, when you click the button, the script runs. Figure 13-11 shows how to set up a button this way.

Buttons are an exceptionally handy way to run scripts. The button is easy to see and understand, and it's just one click away. And best of all, since buttons are on layouts, you can put just the right commands in just the right places, preventing anyone from running the wrong script, since you wouldn't put a button where it doesn't make sense.

Script Triggers

You don't have to wait for someone to click a button to make a script run. Using *script triggers*, you can tell FileMaker to automatically run a script whenever someone performs a particular action. You can apply a script trigger to a layout or an individual layout object. For instance, you might run a script when someone first switches to a particular layout. Or trigger a script when she tabs into a field. You can set up triggers in all these circumstances:

- When you view, commit, or revert a record.

- When you press a key on the keyboard when you're on a particular layout.

- When you switch to a particular layout.

- When you switch to or from Browse, Find, or Preview modes.

- When you enter an object. For instance, when you click or tab into a field, or highlight a tab panel or button with the Tab key.

- When you press a key on the keyboard while in a field, or while a button or tab is selected.

- When you change the contents of a field in any way.

- When you switch from one tab panel to another.

- When you leave a field or tab away from a button or tab panel.

- When you leave a field after you've made changes to it (in other words, when FileMaker has to save changes to the field).

You'll learn how to use script triggers in the next chapter.

Figure 13-11:
Left: When you create a button, you can choose the Perform Script action. In this case, the button has already been configured to run the Show Unpaid Invoices script, which you can see in the second line of text at the top of the window.

Right: When you click Specify, this window appears. From here, you can pick any script in your database, and then click OK.

Opening and Closing Scripts

The *opening* and *closing* scripts are a lot like script triggers, but FileMaker doesn't call them that. You can configure a script run when the database is opened or closed. The opening script runs when you first open the file. You can use this script if you want to be greeted with the list of unpaid invoices first thing every morning. The closing script runs when you close the *last window* for an open file. This option is a little less common, but it has its uses: If you want to make sure other related files close whenever the main file closes (even if they have open windows), then you can write a script to close them all whenever you close the main file.

To make the selection, you need to visit the File Options dialog box (File → File Options). In the File Options window, make sure the Open/Close tab is selected. In this window, you first turn on one of the "Perform script" checkboxes (there's one under "When opening this file" and another under "When closing this file"). Then you can select one of your scripts from the associated pop-up menu. Figure 13-12 shows the result.

Figure 13-12:
The Open/Close tab of the File Options window (File → File Options) lets you tell FileMaker what to do when someone opens or closes a file. Most of this window is devoted to the things that happen when a file opens. Only the last checkbox (under "When closing this file") has to do with which script should run when the file closes.

Timer Scripts

Finally, using the Install OnTimer Script script step, you can tell FileMaker to run a particular script periodically. For instance, you might set up a special computer that runs a script every 10 minutes to grab order information from your Web site.

Or perhaps when someone switches to a sensitive layout, you want a timer to automatically switch to some place more innocuous after 5 minutes, in case he walks away from the computer.

Timer scripts are notoriously tricky, so be prepared to experiment and test thoroughly. Timer scripts are definitely not for the faint of heart. The process of setting one up, however, is simple. Just write a script that uses the "Install OnTimer Script" script step. When you configure this step, you specify a script, and then provide an interval, which is how often the script runs. You express the interval as a number of seconds using a calculation.

Organizing Your Scripts

Most mature databases end up with dozens, or even hundreds, of scripts that make life a lot easier for the folks who use it. But developers don't usually have the luxury of creating scripts in an order that makes sense for display in the Manage Scripts window. That's why FileMaker gives you a suite of tools you can use to organize your scripts.

Creating Script Folders

In Figure 13-13, you can see the Manage Scripts window from a database with a lot of scripts. The window looks a little like a window on your operating system, where documents are organized in folders. FileMaker lets you create folders for organizing your scripts that same way. Not only can you give a new folder a descriptive name, but also, like folders on your desktop, you can collapse them, so you don't have to scan a lengthy list of scripts to find those under Reports.

Figure 13-13:
When your database has lots of scripts, like this one, organization becomes critical. Here, the scripts are arranged in a logical order, and grouped into folders, as described in the steps starting on the next page.

Script folders make the Manage Scripts window nice and tidy, but they also organize the Scripts menu. Any scripts inside a folder appear in a hierarchical (or pop-out) menu when you click the Scripts menu.

To see how all this works, you need to create a few extra scripts in your sample file. Just select your Find Unpaid Invoices script, and then, in the Manage Scripts window, click the Duplicate button a few times.

1. **In the Manage Scripts window, select the top script in your list, and then, at the right edge of the New button, click the little arrow (see Figure 13-14).**

   The New item pop-up menu appears.

Figure 13-14:
In the Manage Scripts window, the New button makes a new script. But if you click the little arrow, then you get a list of additional choices. You can make a new folder instead, or add a separator to the script list.

2. **Choose New Folder.**

   The Edit Group dialog box appears.

3. **In the Folder Name box, type** *Reports.*

   Just like everything else in FileMaker, a descriptive name helps you figure out what's what. "Reports" is a little arbitrary, since this exercise is theoretical, but it's still a good habit to use descriptive names.

4. **Click OK.**

   The Reports folder appears as the second item in your list. A new group always appears below any selected item in the list.

5. **Drag the double arrow to the left of a script to move it into the Reports folder.**

   The motion can be a little twitchy until you get used to it. Drag straight up or down to move a script to a new position in the list. But drag toward the *right* to move a script into a group. If the new group is directly above the scripts you're moving, then it's easiest to move the first script under the group right, and then move each successive one right, also.

Move a few scripts into the Reports group to get the hang of the technique. When you have some scripts in the new group, to the left of the group name, click the gray triangle to collapse it. A second click opens the group again. Finally, click the Scripts menu to see how script groups work there.

Creating Menu Separators

Groups help you when you're plowing through a list of scripts trying to find the one you need to tweak. But you can also help people who use your database by giving them menu separators. It's a good idea to use them to organize sets of scripts that do different things. To create a menu separator, click to select the script that's just *above* where you want the separator to appear, and then, from the New item pop-up menu, choose New Separator. If a separator isn't where you want it, then you can drag it into place.

You can also use the Duplicate button to copy a whole bunch of separators with just a few clicks. Each new separator appears just below the original; just drag them into place.

A separator is really just an empty script whose name is "–", so if you're so inclined, you can make one manually. In Figure 13-15, you can see how a separator looks in a menu. It's the gray line under ScriptMaker.

Figure 13-15:
In the Manage Scripts window, separators just show up as scripts named "–" but everywhere else, they turn into proper visual separators. Here, in the window you use to pick a script for a button, the separator is right under Make Some Coffee.

Branching and Looping in Scripts

Now that you have a basic foundation in what scripts do and how you can run them, it's time to see some of ScriptMaker's more powerful features. The script you created at the beginning of this chapter was the simplest kind: It goes through a series of steps from start to finish every time. Sometimes your script needs more smarts. You can add steps to the script that cause it to take different actions depending on the situation (called *branching*), or make it do the same thing over and over again (called *looping*).

Branching with If, Else If, Else, and End If

If you're comfortable with the *If( )* and *Case( )* functions in calculations (see page 467), then you'll feel right at home with this topic. You've noticed that you often look someone up in the Customers layout, copy his email address, and then go to your mail program to send him an email. You'd like to add a button to the Customers layout that creates the email directly, saving you all the trouble of copying, switching, and pasting.

You can use FileMaker's Send Mail script step, which is just like the File → Send Mail command, to accomplish this task. First, create the script:

1. **Choose Scripts → ScriptMaker, and then, in the Manage Scripts dialog box, click New.**

   The Edit Script window pops up.

2. **In the Script Name box, type *Send Email to Customer*.**

   When you want to *run* this script, from the Scripts menu, you choose this name.

3. **In the list of available script steps, select Send Mail, and then click Move.**

   FileMaker adds the script step to the script.

Note: The Send Mail script step is near the bottom of the list, under Miscellaneous. If you don't like looking through this long list, then from the View pop-up menu, choose Miscellaneous to see just the steps in this category. Whenever you're *not* sure which category holds the step you want, from the menu, choose "all by name", to see every step in alphabetical order.

---

4. **In the Script Step Options area, turn on the "Perform without dialog" checkbox.**

   This action tells FileMaker you *don't* want a window that lets you enter or edit the Send Mail Options dialog box when the script runs. In this case, you just want it to do its work as you specify in the script step.

5. **Click Specify.**

   The Send Mail Options window (Figure 13-16) appears. In this window, you configure all the options you want for the email FileMaker will send. (See the box on page 515 for more details about these options.)

6. **To the right of the To field, click the pop-up menu, and then choose Specify Field Name.**

   You now see a Specify Field dialog box. Here, you *tell* FileMaker where to find your customer's email address. Make sure "One email using data from the current record" is selected or you could get some dicey results, like sending an email about a customer's recent invoice to all the customers who happen to have records in your found set.

Figure 13-16:
The Send Mail Options appears when you configure the Send Mail script step in FileMaker. Here, you can type an ordinary email address directly in the To, CC, or BCC boxes, and enter a Subject, and Message. Or, click the triangle by any box and pick a field or enter a calculation instead. That way, you can send email to the person in the database, or fill the message with details from the current record.

7. **Switch to the Customers table, if necessary, and then choose the Email address field. Click OK.**

   FileMaker closes the Specify Field window, and shows you the Send Mail Options window again. Now, though, in the To field, it shows your Email Address field reference. You can also add field references or calculations for CC, BCC, Subject, or even the body of your email message in those fields. This dialog box even lets you choose a file to attach to your email. But for now, just leave all these options blank.

   You now see your single-line script in the Edit Script dialog box again, with the Send Mail options [No dialog; To Customers::Email Address] listed as a reference.

Tip: Turn on the "Multiple emails (one for each record in found set)" option to use this script step to send email to more than one person at a time. But remember, use this option for good, never for evil. You'd never send spam emails, would you?

---

8. **Close the Edit Script window, and then click the Save button.**

   You don't have to close the Edit Script window to save your script. Choose Scripts → Save Script, or press Ctrl+S (Windows) or ⌘-S (Mac).

Two Ways to Send

The first option in the Send Mail Options window (see Figure 13-16) is "Send via", and it gives you two options, letting you either use or bypass the email program on your computer.

- Choose E-mail Client to send the message using your email program. If you turn on "Perform without dialog" for the Send Mail script step, then the message goes directly into your mail program's outbox, and that program sends it the next time the send/receive mail process runs (which is automatic in most mail programs). If you leave "Perform without dialog" off, then the message goes into the Drafts folder instead. FileMaker also opens it up and switches to your mail program. This way, you get a chance to double-check the message and edit it as needed before you send it.

- Choose SMTP Server to send the message through your mail server. In other words, you're asking File-Maker to bypass your email program, and go straight to the network post office. You have to put in information about your mail server, including its network address and any user name and password it requires. This configuration has no "Perform without dialog" option, so you can't edit the message before FileMaker sends it off, and it doesn't show up in your sent mail folder.

Under most circumstances, you're probably best off sticking with the E-mail Client option. You can use it more easily (because you don't need to put in mail server settings). It's also more flexible since you can edit the message. Finally, you get a record of the emails you've sent from your sent mail folder.

But sometimes the E-mail Client option isn't a good choice. Sometimes you have a script that runs on the FileMaker Server (you'll learn about that in Chapter 18) or on a shared computer that has no email client. In a case like that, you're better off going straight to the server so you don't have to set up and manage a mail program.

Also, when you use the SMTP Server option, you get to specify the from name and address. If the message comes from your email client, then it comes from you. But what if you're sending shipment notifications for your company? You may want the messages to come from *orders@mycompany.com*, or some other shared address instead. In a case like this, you can use the SMTP Server option, and everybody in the office can send email from the same account through FileMaker.

Finally, if you're sending lots of email, it can be faster and more reliable to send messages directly to the mail server (after all, its job is to send lots of email).

As a general rule, it's fine to use the E-mail Client option unless you need for the increased power (and hassle) of the SMTP Server option.

At this point you have a working script. If you run it, it indeed creates a new email addressed to the current customer. But what happens if you *don't* have an email address for this customer? If the Customers::Email Address field is *empty*, then your script tries to send an email without a valid address to your email program, which complains mightily. Fortunately, you can head off this problem at the pass. If the Email Address field is empty, then you'd rather have your script tell you about it, and skip the Send Mail step entirely. The If step is the tool for this job, so add it as follows:

1. **In the Edit Script dialog box, add the If step to your script.**

   FileMaker adds this step *after* the Send Mail step. It also adds a third step: End If. You can't have an If without an End If, so you get both automatically.

Note: If you accidentally delete the End If step from your script, then FileMaker shows an error message when you try to save the script. To fix the error, you need to add the End If step back to your script, and then drag it to its proper place.

2. **Using the double-pointed arrow to the left of the If step, drag the step up above the Send Mail step.**

    By rearranging the steps in your script, you're telling FileMaker what order they should run in. (A script doesn't work as intended if you've got a step above something that needs to happen *first*.) Your script should look like Figure 13-17.

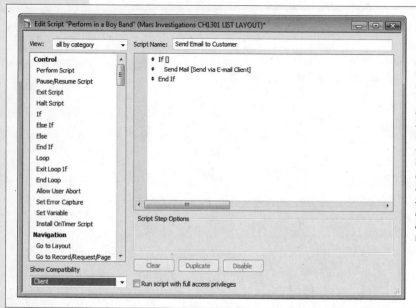

Figure 13-17:
To prevent FileMaker from making an email message when the customer has no email address, you need to wrap the Send Mail step inside an If block as shown here. Next, in step 4 below, you'll put a condition in that If step to tell FileMaker when the message should be sent. Notice that the Send Mail step is now indented. Every step inside an If block gets indented this way.

3. **Select the If step and, in the Script Step Options area, click Specify.**

    FileMaker shows you a standard Specify Calculation dialog box. You use a calculation to define the *condition* of this If step. If the calculation evaluates to True, then FileMaker does the steps after the If. If the calculation evaluates to False, then FileMaker skips to the End If, and continues running the script from there.

4. **In the calculation box, type *Not IsEmpty(Customers::Email Address)*, and then click OK.**

    This calculation evaluates to *True,* and sends your customer an email only if the Email Address field isn't empty. See the box on page 519 for details on how this calculation makes these decisions.

Your script now checks to see if the Email Address field has something in it before running off to create the email message. But what happens when you run the script and the Email Address field is empty? Right now, nothing at all. FileMaker evaluates the If condition, sees that it's False, and skips to the End If. There's nothing after the End If, so the script just stops and your user waits in suspense, until he finally realizes that the requested email message simply isn't coming and investigates the problem on his own—or chucks his computer out the window.

In the interest of preventing property damage, it's better for your script to tell him *why* nothing's happening. For example, you can have your script show a message box saying, "You can't email this customer, since there's no email address on file", or whatever. You can get exactly what you want with the Else step:

1. **In your script, select the Send Mail script step.**

   When you add a *new* step, FileMaker inserts it after the selected step. You want the Else step to go right after the Send Mail step, so you select that step first.

2. **Add the Else step to the script.**

   FileMaker inserts an Else step between Send Mail and End If.

Note: Don't click the Else If step by mistake. You want the step called just Else. If you added the wrong step, select it, click Clear, and try, try again.

---

3. **Right after the Else step, add the Show Custom Dialog script step to the script.**

   This step is also under Miscellaneous. Its job is to pop up a dialog box for someone. You get to decide what the box says, which buttons it includes, and which fields—if any—it should show.

4. **In the Script Step Options area, click the Specify button.**

   The "Show Custom Dialog" Options window appears (Figure 13-18).

5. **In the Title box, type *No Email Address*.**

   Whatever you type in this box appears in the title bar along the top of your custom dialog box. Punctuation marks like commas and periods look odd in title bars, but you're welcome to include them.

6. **In the Message box, type *You can't email this customer because there's no email address on file*.**

   This tells FileMaker what to put *inside* the dialog box.

7. **From the Button 2 box, select and delete the word Cancel.**

   A custom dialog box can have up to three buttons. In this case, you want only one: an OK button. (If you don't type anything in the Button 2 and Button 3 boxes, then those buttons don't show up.)

Figure 13-18:
The Show Custom Dialog script step lets you provide feedback, like why an email script isn't behaving as expected. You can give your dialog box a title, a message, and up to three buttons for people to click. You can also add input fields to the dialog box by visiting the Input Fields tab. You'll learn about these on page 580.

8. **Click OK.**

Your script should now look like the one shown in Figure 13-19.

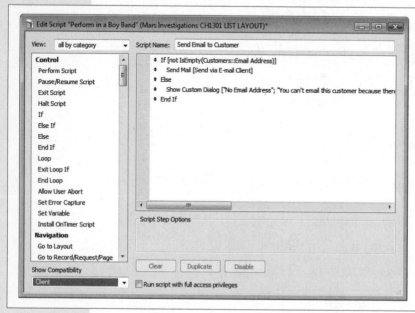

Figure 13-19:
The finished Send Email to Customer script looks like this. If you read it like a book, it says, "If the email address field is not empty, Send Mail. Otherwise show an error message to the person." The If/Else/End If steps create two branches in the script: one when the email address field is full, and one when it's empty.

Now return to your database, and then try your script out: Select a customer without an email address (enter Find mode, in the Email address field, type *>0*, and then click the Omit button), and choose Scripts → "Send Email to Customer". If you look at a customer record with an email address, then the script creates a message in your mail program, ready for you to fill out. If the email address field is empty, then you see an error message instead. You can create a button for this script, and then add it to the Customers layout for the ultimate in convenience.

UP TO SPEED

Not What?

FileMaker lets you create calculations that involve layers of Boolean logic. In the script you wrote on page 516, the If script step runs the indented steps only when the whole calculation evaluates to True. To figure out when that happens, you have to deconstruct the calculation itself.

By itself, the *IsEmpty()* function returns True when the value you pass to it is completely empty—in other words, when the Email Address field is empty:

```
IsEmpty ( Customers::Email Address )
```

But that action doesn't help you because you want the email sent only when there *is* data in the email field. If you have no email address entered, then the calculation above returns True, and causes the Send Email step to run. If the email address field is filled in, on the other hand, then the calculation's result is False, and FileMaker skips the Send Mail step.

This behavior is exactly the opposite of what you want. To flip the result of the calculation around, you use the Not operator. It looks at the Boolean value to its right, and turns a True to a False, or a False to a True. Here's the calculation you need:

```
Not IsEmpty ( Customers::Email Address )
```

You can easily tell if you've got the right construction by reading the If step like a sentence: "If not is empty Email Address." It may not be grammatical perfection, but it does get the logic right.

If this kind of logic makes your head spin, then you have another option. Just switch your steps around. Put the Send Mail step after Else, and the Show Custom Dialog after If. Then you can use a more straightforward formula:

```
IsEmpty ( Customers::Email Address)
```

Testing Multiple Conditions

If you have more than one condition to consider, you can use the Else If script step. It works a lot like the *Case()* function in a calculation. You could have a script like this, for instance:

```
If [ Get ( CurrentTime ) < Time ( 12 ; 0; 0 ) ]
  Show Custom Dialog [ "Good Morning!" ]
Else If [ Get ( CurrentTime ) < Time ( 18 ; 0 ; 0 ) ]
  Show Custom Dialog [ "Good Afternoon!" ]
Else
  Show Custom Dialog [ "Good Evening!" ]
End If
```

When this script runs, it tests each condition in turn, deciding which custom dialog box to show someone, based on the actual current time. If the current time is before noon, she sees a "Good morning" message, and the script jumps to the end (the End If script step) without needing to test the second condition.

If it isn't before noon, the script does a second test to see if it's before 6 p.m. If it is, the user sees a "Good Afternoon" message, and the script jumps to the end. But if both tests fail, no third condition is tested, and the Else just shows the "Good Evening" message, like a default condition in a Case statement. However, you can add other Else Ifs to test other conditions.

You can add as many Else If steps as you want, but they must come between the If and End If steps. Each Else If can test a different condition. If you have an Else step, it should come after the If and every Else If, but before the End If. You can think of the Else condition as the default condition in a *Case( )* or an *If( )* statement when you write a calculation.

Tip: For a really cool way to tell which of the conditions in your scripts are evaluating as True and which ones evaluate as False, see the section on the Script Debugger (page 736).

Looping

Sometimes you want to do the same thing over and over again, until you reach some kind of end point. For example, people often write a script that does something to every record in the found set, one after another. This script is called a *looping script*. You make a script *loop through records* using the Loop script step.

Like the If step, the Loop step has a necessary partner called End Loop. When you put script steps between Loop and End Loop, FileMaker simply repeats them over and over, forever.

So how does a script like this end? Simple: You tell FileMaker to *exit the loop* at the right time. FileMaker has three ways to exit a loop:

- The Go To Record/Request step has an "Exit after last" option when you go to the next or previous record. That way, you can easily loop through all the records in the found set, exiting the loop when you get to the last one.

- The Exit Loop If script step lets you provide a condition formula (just like If). If the condition evaluates to True, then FileMaker immediately skips to the first step after End Loop.

- The Exit Script and Halt Script steps both end a script immediately, even if you're in a loop.

For example, a simple looping script might look like this:

```
Loop
 # Do some stuff
 Exit Loop If [ // some condition ]
End Loop
```

Using what you've learned in this chapter and about calculations in Part 4, you can easily build a script like this. For "some condition," just use a calculation that describes the condition when the loop should stop repeating itself.

Using Go to Record/Request/Page to exit a loop

If you've used loops in other programs, you may think you have to devise some kind of test to figure out when you've reached the last record in your found set. You may be tempted to write a loop like this:

```
Loop
  # Your script's work goes here.
  Go to Record/Request/Page [ Next ]
  Exit Loop If [ Get ( FoundCount ) = Get (RecordNumber) ]
End Loop
# Your script's work goes here. Again!
```

This script starts with a loop that does your task on the current record, and then moves to the next record (just as if you'd clicked the book icon's right-hand page). If the number of the record you're now on *equals* the current found count, then FileMaker exits the loop. But this approach has a problem. The Exit Loop If step exits when you *first* reach the last record. Structuring a loop so it does the right thing can be tricky. Instead, in the "Go to Record/Request/Page" step, just turn on the "Exit after last" option. Now your loop looks like Figure 13-20—clean and simple.

Figure 13-20:
The "Exit after last" option for the "Go to Related Record/Request/ Page" step has the power to break out of a loop just after processing the last record in the found set.

Script Triggers

Scripts are all about saving you (and your users) time. And what could be less time consuming that something you don't have to do at all? As you learned earlier in this chapter, script triggers let you tell FileMaker to run a script automatically in response to something that already happens when people use your database. You'll get a brief introduction to each of FileMaker's trigger options here. Then, throughout the next chapters, you'll use these triggers in key places to make your database come alive.

Script triggers come in two flavors. *Layout triggers* apply to the layout as a whole. These triggers include actions like loading or committing a record, switching layouts, or pressing a key on the keyboard. *Object triggers* are tied to a single layout object (like a field, portal, tab control, or web viewer). These triggers fire when you interact with that object in some way, like editing the data in a field, or switching to a different tab panel.

Layout Triggers

The layout triggers are configured in the Layout Setup dialog box (Layout → Layout Setup), in the Script Triggers tab. You can see this window in Figure 13-21.

Figure 13-21:
The Layout Setup dialog box has a Script Triggers tab. From here, you can turn on various triggers, pick which scripts run, and choose which modes the triggers apply to. You can turn on as many triggers as you want, but each trigger can have only one script. If you need to do more than one thing for a trigger, just bundle them together in one script, and then run it.

You can understand the layout triggers easier than their object counterparts. Each is explained next.

OnRecordLoad

The OnRecordLoad trigger fires when a record is *loaded*. In other words, when you first visit a layout, switch to a new record, make a new record, or perform a find, a record is loaded. You'll use this trigger in the next chapter to automatically sort a set of records.

OnRecordCommit

When you commit a record, the *OnRecordCommit* trigger fires. It doesn't matter how you commit the record (by clicking out of the record, switching layouts, or running a script, for instance). In every case, if this trigger is turned on, then the script runs.

Note: This trigger (among others) is cancelable. In other words, the script that runs can cancel the commit operation if it wants to, by returning a False value (you'll learn about returning values from scripts on page 583). If you cancel the commit, then you don't leave the record, and FileMaker doesn't save your changes. You can use this power to force the person using the database to make some kind of change to a record before saving, or require some kind of extra confirmation.

OnRecordRevert

In the rare case that someone reverts a record (using the Records → Revert Record command, or the equivalent script step), the OnRecordRevert trigger kicks in. Once again, you can cancel the revert if you want.

OnLayoutKeystroke

The *OnLayoutKeystroke* trigger fires every time a key is pressed. Obviously, any script you trigger should be quick, because it can be called very frequently. You can use the *Get (TriggerKeystroke)* and *Get (TriggerModifierKeys)* functions to find out which key was pressed.

You can also cancel keystrokes. So if you want to stop allowing the letter L in your database, you can. Truthfully, though, keystroke triggers are not for beginners. People can press *lots* of different keys. Your script needs to be fast, and it takes a lot of knowledge to figure out which keys were pressed. For instance, this trigger fires even if someone presses an arrow key, or the Ctrl or ⌘ key, or a function key. You'll get a course in keystroke triggers in on page 622.

Note: One exception is Ctrl or ⌘ key combinations. These *don't* fire keystroke triggers. If you want to configure keyboard shortcuts like this, then use custom menus (Chapter 19).

OnLayoutLoad

When you switch to a layout, the *OnLayoutLoad* trigger fires. You can do some initial tab setup, or sort the records, or even bounce to a different layout if you want. OnLayoutLoad is one of the bread-and-butter triggers for an advanced database that aims to streamline people's workflows.

OnModeEnter and OnModeExit

The *OnModeEnter* trigger fires when you switch *to* a mode. For instance, if you switch to Find mode, then the OnModeEnter trigger fires when you get there.

By contrast, the *OnModeExit* trigger fires when you *leave* a mode. If you use both triggers, then OnModeExit fires first, before you leave the current mode. Then OnModeEnter fires after the switch. The distinction between these two is subtle but important. First, a script triggered by OnModeEnter runs once you're in the new mode. So it can look at the current mode (using the *Get(WindowMode)* function), and act accordingly.

On the other hand, OnModeExit is cancelable. So if you choose, you can refuse to let someone leave the current mode.

Object Triggers

To configure an object's triggers, on the layout, first select the object, and then choose Format → Set Script Triggers. The resulting window looks familiar (Figure 13-22).

Figure 13-22:
The Format → Set Script Triggers menu command lets you configure triggers for the selected layout object. The list of triggers is smaller than for layouts, but since so many object types exist, it can be harder to make sense of them. Read on to get the full scoop.

Before you look at each type, bear this in mind: You can apply triggers only to fields, tab controls, portals, buttons, and Web viewers. You can't put a trigger on a text label, line, shape, or picture.

OnObjectEnter

The *OnObjectEnter* trigger, generally speaking, fires when you *enter* an object. Usually you use this trigger with a field. It fires when you enter the field, whether by clicking, tabbing, or script.

If you set an OnObjectEnter trigger on a button or tab control, then it fires if you put the object in the tab order, and then tab to it (causing it to get a black outline). If you use the mouse to click a button or tab, then the OnObjectEnter trigger *doesn't* fire.

For portals, the trigger fires whenever you go to a new row. For instance, if you click into a field on the portal, then the trigger fires. If you click a second field on the same row, then it *doesn't* fire again. But if you click a field on a *different* row, then it fires again. This way you can track someone as she switches from row to row.

For a Web viewer, the trigger fires if you click into the Web page, or tab into a field on the page.

OnObjectKeystroke

Once you're entered an object, it becomes the target for keystrokes. If you press a key on the keyboard, the object's OnObjectKeystroke trigger fires. For fields, the script runs repeatedly as you type or arrow around in the field. It also fires when you press the Tab key or Enter key to leave the field. For buttons and tab controls, you have to tab into the object for it to receive keystrokes. Portals and Web viewers never receive keystrokes, so this trigger never fires if you assign it to one of them.

Finally, the keystroke trigger is cancelable, which lets you, for instance, prevent entry of certain characters in a field. You'll see an example of this on page 622.

OnObjectModify

The *OnObjectModify* trigger also varies from object to object. For a field, it fires anytime something in the field changes *while you're in the field*. For instance, if you type into the field, then the trigger fires each time you add or delete a character. But it *doesn't* fire if you just use the arrow keys to move around in the field, or if you press Tab or Enter to leave the field. It also fires once each time you cut or paste in the field.

Warning: The OnObjectModify trigger doesn't fire if you modify the field without entering it. For instance, if a script runs the Set Field script step while you're on the layout, then the field changes but the trigger doesn't fire. Likewise, if you drag text from one field into another, then you're in the field you drag from, which doesn't change. The field you drag to changes, but you're not in that field. So no OnObject-Modify triggers fire in this case.

If you attach this trigger to a tab control, then it fires whenever you switch tabs. OnObjectModify never fires with buttons, portals, and Web viewers.

OnObjectSave

While OnObjectModify fires as you modify a field, *OnObjectSave* fires only after you change the field value *and leave the field*. With this trigger, you can modify the field repeatedly without interruption. Then, when you're done and you leave the field by tabbing, pressing Enter, clicking in another field, or by any other means, the trigger fires.

This trigger fires only if you actually make a change. If you click in a field, and then immediately leave, nothing changed, so nothing is saved, and the trigger doesn't run. Once again, this trigger is cancelable. If your script returns False, then it forces the user back into the field.

This trigger applies only to fields.

OnObjectExit

The *OnObjectExit* trigger is exactly the opposite of OnObjectEnter. It fires when you leave an object. For fields, this means tabbing away, committing the record, and so forth. For buttons and tab controls, it means tabbing away. For portals, it fires when you leave a portal row in any way. Finally, for Web viewers, it fires when you had previously clicked or tabbed into the page, and you then click away.

Many actions can trigger an exit from a field, portal, or Web viewer. For instance, you might leave the layout, close the window, or quit FileMaker. In every case, the trigger fires, and in every case, if the script returns False, then the action is canceled. So you can even stop folks from closing the window before they attend to the demands of your trigger.

A Simple Script Trigger

To illustrate how script triggers work, you can try the simplest version: Run a script when you switch to a layout. A prime candidate is your Find Unpaid Invoices script. Currently, you run this script when you want to see the unpaid invoice list. Instead, you can make it run automatically when you switch to the List layout. Setting it up is a breeze:

1. **Switch to your Invoice List layout, and then go to Layout mode.**

   You're creating a layout trigger (that fires when you switch to the Invoice List layout), so you need to be on the right layout.

2. **Choose Layout → Layout Setup, and then switch to the Script Triggers tab.**

   This tab is where you configure triggers for the layout. You can see it in Figure 13-21.

3. **In the list, turn on the OnLayoutLoad checkbox.**

   The Specify Script window immediately appears.

4. **Select your Find Unpaid Invoices script, and then click OK.**

   In the list, the OnLayoutLoad trigger is now turned on, and, in the Script column, the Find Unpaid Invoices script shows.

5. **Turn on the Browse and Preview checkboxes, and turn off the Find checkbox.**

   This script really makes sense only in Browse mode and Preview mode, so you want it to trigger only in those cases.

6. **Click OK.**

   Now your trigger is installed, and ready to test.

To test things properly, go to the Invoices layout, and then choose Records → Show All Records. Then switch to the Invoice List layout. If all goes well, File-Maker should automatically find only the unpaid invoices, and sort them for you.

Now that you're on the List layout, you can find again if you want to see different records, or sort in a different way. The trigger fires only when you come to the layout from somewhere else.

You'll see many other script trigger examples as you work through the next two chapters. Script triggers are possibly FileMaker's most powerful and complex feature. A simple trigger like this can be a real timesaver, and for the adventuresome, more advanced trigger scenarios can produce very powerful results.

Exploring Script Steps

Now that you know how to create scripts (you did read the previous chapter, didn't you?), it's time to expand your repertoire. FileMaker has a script step for just about everything you can do from the menus and Status toolbar. You can use any combination of these steps with script techniques like looping, branching, custom dialog boxes, and more to automate just about anything FileMaker can do. Major areas of scripting include working with field data and records, finding, sorting, working with windows and files, and printing. This chapter is a compendium of steps—and boatloads of scripting possibilities.

Go to Layout

The "Go to Layout" script step was introduced in the last chapter. Its purpose is simple: Change layouts. It works just like making a choice from the Layout bar's Layout pop-up menu, except that the script can go to *any* layout (even if it doesn't show in the menu).

"Go to Layout" has just one option, a pop-up menu labeled Specify. In addition to every layout in your database, this menu also has three special choices:

- The **original layout** option causes FileMaker to switch to the layout someone was on when the script started. After all, you can run lots of scripts anywhere, especially if they're on the Script menu. Since scripts often change layouts as they run, this option makes sure folks end up back where they started.

• The **Layout Name by calculation** option lets you specify a typical FileMaker calculation. The result of the calculation must be text, and it should exactly match the *name* of one of the layouts in the database. When the script runs, FileMaker evaluates the calculation, and then switches to the layout with the correct name.

• The **Layout Number by calculation** option is similar. You specify a calculation with a *number* result. FileMaker numbers every layout sequentially, in the order in which it's listed in Layout mode. The result of the calculation determines which layout to visit by number.

Note: Layout numbers don't necessarily correspond to their positions in the Layout pop-up menu. Remember that not all layouts show in this list, and you can reorder them manually. To find out a layout's number reliably, switch to Layout mode first. Then go to the layout, and, in the Status toolbar, look at the Layout box. It shows which layout number you're on.

See the box below to learn when to use "Go to Layout" with Layout Name and when to use Layout Number.

FREQUENTLY ASKED QUESTION

Specifying a Layout

There are three ways to tell the "Go to Layout" step which layout to visit. Which one should I use?

The easiest way is to choose the layout directly from the Specify pop-up menu. When the script runs, FileMaker goes to your chosen layout, period (that is, unless somebody deletes the layout).

The other two options—specifying a layout by name or number—are trickier, for a couple of reasons. First, they're a pain: You have to write a calculation when you could just pick from a menu. Second, both calculation methods have soft underbellies. If you specify a layout name using a calculation, and later rename the layout, even just by adding an accidental space somewhere in the name, then the script can't find the layout any more. If you use the layout number, and then add or delete a layout, or rearrange your layout list (page 235), then the script goes to the wrong layout.

Still, these options give you greater flexibility. For example, if you use "Go to Layout" and specify by Layout Name, then you can use script parameters to name any layout in your database. With this technique, you can create a single navigation script, and use it in all sorts of routine database tasks.

If you want to create a scripted process that's like a wizard or an assistant in some programs, then the Layout Number is a godsend. Create the layouts that control your process, and make one Next button that you copy onto each layout. The button gets a "Go to Layout" script step, specifying a Layout Number that's one more than the current layout number *(Get(LayoutNumber) + 1)*. Now, no matter how you rearrange the layouts, the button always takes people to the next one in the Set Layout Order list—and you've used only one script step.

Scripting for Fields

Most people using FileMaker spend *a lot* of their time working with field data, so it's no surprise that script steps devoted to fields abound. You can put someone in a specific field, select field text, and even play sounds and movies from container fields. You can perform a find and replace operation, run the Replace Field Contents command, and export field contents to a file. Finally, you get more than 10 ways to put data into a field.

Navigating Fields

FileMaker offers a couple of ways to field-hop—pressing Tab to move to the next field in order, or just clicking the desired field. It has script steps that mimic both techniques.

Go to Field

The simplest field navigation script step is called "Go to Field". It's really a two-purpose step, with two checkboxes to prove it. In its simplest form, you turn on the "Go to target field" checkbox and pick the field you want to go to. When the script runs, FileMaker puts folks in the specified field (provided it's on the layout).

Note: When you use "Go to Field" in a script, FileMaker dutifully ignores the field behavior specified on the layout, and puts people right into the field, even if they normally couldn't click into it. You can use this fact to create a field that people can get to only by using your script.

The step also has a checkbox called "Select/perform". When this option is turned on, the script either *selects* the contents of the field it goes to or *does* what's in the field—if possible. For example, if the step goes to a *container* field that holds a sound or a movie, FileMaker *plays* the contents instead. If the container field holds a *reference* to a picture or a file, FileMaker *opens* the correct file, using the appropriate program.

The mildly weird thing about "Go to Field" is you can turn on "Select/perform" and *turn off* "Go to target field". With the options set this way, "Go to Field" doesn't go to a field at all. Instead, it simply selects or performs the contents of the field you happen to be in when the script runs.

Go to Next Field and Go to Previous Field

To mimic the process of tabbing through fields, FileMaker has two more script steps. The first, called "Go to Next Field", just tabs to the next field in the tab order. You probably already figured out that "Go to Previous Field" goes to the *previous* field in the tab order. These steps don't have a "Select/perform" option—they just go to the field.

Tip: To get the effect of "Select/perform", use "Go to Next Field" or "Go to Previous Field" to get to the field you want, and then use "Go to Field" to select/perform it. When you add the "Go to Field" step, don't turn on "Go to target field", and it acts on the field you're already in.

Editing Commands

FileMaker has all the classic commands in its Edit menu: Undo, Cut, Copy, Paste, and Clear. It also has a script step for each of these commands. The Undo step is the simplest. It has no options at all, and has exactly the same effect as choosing Edit → Undo. You rarely want to undo something you just scripted, so you rarely use this script step. It's quite handy, though, if you use custom menus (page 753) to control people's access to certain menu commands.

Cut, Copy, and Clear are slightly more complicated, with two options each. The first, "Select entire contents", lets you decide which part of a field's value gets cut, copied, or cleared. If you turn this option on, then FileMaker selects the entire field before acting. If this option's turned off, then FileMaker cuts/copies/clears whatever happens to be selected in the field. (But see page 533 to learn why you should rarely use these commands.) You also get a "Go to target field" option, through which the script can tell FileMaker *which field* to act on. If it's not turned on, then it uses the *current field*—the one someone's in when the step runs.

The Paste step is the most complicated of these four. In addition to specifying the field you want, and whether or not to select everything in the field before pasting, you get an option to "Paste without style". When you turn this option on, FileMaker pastes the text on the clipboard, but throws away any style information. If you're in Windows, you get a fourth option: "Link if available". If the data on the clipboard comes from a source that supports object linking, then FileMaker embeds the linked object. Changes to the original data show up in FileMaker. Turn this option off if you want the script to just paste a *copy* of the data.

Selecting Text

FileMaker has two script steps to help you select text. The first, called Select All, selects everything in the current field, just like the Edit → Select All command. If you need more control, then use Set Selection instead. This step has two options. First, you can specify a target field so that FileMaker operates on the current field. The step also has a separate Specify button (below the one associated with "Go to target field") that brings up the Specify Set Selection window (Figure 14-1).

Figure 14-1:
This window lets you tell FileMaker exactly what text you want the script to select. You can type numbers directly in the Start Position and End Position boxes, or click either Specify button to bring up the Specify Calculation dialog box.

If you imagine the text in your field as a string of letters, numbers, spaces, and punctuation, then you can pretend each of these is numbered. For instance, the word "Missing" has letters numbered one through seven. You first tell FileMaker where the selection should *start* by putting the number of the first character in the Start Position box. Next, you put the number of the *last* character in the End Position box. When the step runs, FileMaker selects these two characters and everything in between.

POWER USERS' CLINIC

Positioning the Insertion Point

You can use the Set Selection script step to put the insertion point anywhere in a field, too. The trick is to make sure *nothing* gets selected. When you specify a Start Position and an End Position, FileMaker selects the characters at each position, plus anything in between. If these two numbers are the same, then FileMaker selects just one character.

But what if the End Position comes *before* the Start Position? When you set the End Position one number lower than the Start Position, FileMaker doesn't select anything. Instead, it puts the little flashing insertion point right before the Start Position. Using this technique, you can get your script to put someone anywhere you want inside a field, say at the beginning of a Notes field, so she can just start typing, without needing to move the cursor.

Editing Field Data

Editing field data is such an important part of FileMaker that it gives you more than 10 ways to put stuff in fields with a script step. In the last chapter, you learned that the scripted process for finding records could actually be shorter and more efficient than the manual process. Editing field data via scripts is also different from manually editing data, and the following sections cover those differences.

The first thing to understand is that, except for Set Field and "Set Field by Name", the steps in this section *work only if the field is on the current layout*. This property is no problem for scripts you use to structure someone's data entry, but it can be a roadblock in other cases. Suppose you have a script that sets a "Paid in Full" flag on an invoice. You want this script to work no matter what layout you're on (as long as it's one that shows invoice records), and whether or not the field is on that layout. In that case, you need to understand the Set Field script step (and sometimes its power-user partner, "Set Field by Name").

Avoiding Cut, Copy, and Paste

Your first inclination might be to use Cut, Copy, and Paste in a script to move data from one field to another, and it does work. You can, for example, have a script copy the Customer ID field, and then go to the Invoices layout, create a new invoice, and paste it into the Customer ID field there.

But most developers don't use this approach for two reasons. First, many developers consider people's clipboards to be sacred ground. They argue you should *never* change what's on the clipboard unless someone asks you to. So it would be OK to have a Copy button by the Address fields, for example, that copies the address to the clipboard because the person would know exactly what's going into the clipboard. But what if he manually copies a long product description to the clipboard, and then runs the "Create Invoice for Customer" script? He then tries to paste the description in the invoice line item, only to find that the description's gone, replaced by the Customer ID for some odd reason. To keep from frustrating him (or yourself), you should generally avoid Cut and Copy.

Also, these steps don't work if the field isn't on the layout. People often show the customer's *name* on an invoice, but not his *ID*. But if you delete the Customer ID field from the Invoices layout, then any scripts that use Cut, Copy or Paste and the Customer ID field break. That's where Set Field steps in to save the day.

Set Field

Set Field is the one field-editing power step that doesn't care a whit about what fields are on the layout. This step replaces the contents of a field with the result of a calculation. Its two options let you specify the field to set, and the calculation to use. The calculation result must be the same type as the field you've specified. For text, date, time, and timestamp fields, Set Field is usually the step of choice: It's flexible and reliable, no matter what's on the layout.

Tip: As with many other FileMaker processes, be aware of context when you use a Set Field script step. You can edit data through a relationship using Set Field, but make absolutely certain the context is what you intend. If you aren't careful, you can edit data in the wrong record.

Like many of the steps you've seen so far, you don't have to specify a field at all. In this case, Set Field changes the field you're in *at the moment the step runs*. (The current-field method works only with text results; otherwise, you have to specify the field so FileMaker knows what type you have in mind.)

Insert Calculated Result

Set Field's one weakness is that it *always* overwrites a field completely (but see the tip below). Another step, Insert Calculated Result, lets a script put data in a field while keeping the data that's already there. It has three options. First you can specify a target field. You can also choose "Select entire contents" in the field first (in which case it overwrites the entire field, just like Set Field). Finally, you get to specify the calculation. Here are some variations on these options:

- If you *don't* turn on the "Select entire contents" option, then FileMaker inserts the calculation result *after* whatever's already in the field.

• If you *don't* specify a field at all, and you *don't* turn on "Select entire contents", then FileMaker inserts the result of the calculation into the current field. If you select data when the script step runs, then the calculation result overwrites whatever's highlighted. Otherwise, the text goes in wherever the insertion point happens to be, just as though you'd typed it from the keyboard.

Tip: You can use Set Field to append results to existing data: Just include the field's data in the calculation. If you want to add "Esquire" to the end of the customer's last name (in the Last Name field), then just use this calculation in your Set Field step:

    Last Name & ", Esquire"

Inserting other values

FileMaker has six other *Insert* script steps that work like Insert Calculated Result. Each step lets you specify a target field, and select the field contents if you want. They differ only in what gets inserted:

• **Insert Text** lets you specify any static text value and add it to the field verbatim. Use this step if you know ahead of time what you want your script to put in the field, and don't need to calculate it.

• **Insert from Index** makes your script show the same View Index window just like choosing Insert → From Index in Browse or Find mode. Someone picks a value from the list, and FileMaker inserts it into the field. This option's especially valuable in Find mode, both to keep people from having to type a value (and possibly making a typo) *and* to make sure the search always finds records, since if a value's in the index, then it's in a record somewhere.

• **Insert from Last Visited** is an interesting step. It grabs the value from the *same* field on the *last visited* record, and inserts it. This step is particularly useful on data entry layouts. Imagine, for example, you have to enter 300–person records from 15 different companies. You could use this step to create a button that pops in the *last* company you typed into the Company Name field, rather than type it over again.

Note: You can't just take a peek at a record and call it visited, though. The record must be entered or opened (page 24). An Open Record/Request script step helps ensure you get the record you intend.

• **Insert Current Date** and **Insert Current Time** do just as they say. Unfortunately, no Insert Current Timestamp step exists; use Insert Calculated Result and the *Get (CurrentTimeStamp)* function instead.

• **Insert Current User Name** puts the user name of the person using FileMaker into the field. Your operating system normally determines this user name, but you can easily change it from FileMaker's Preferences' General Tab.

See the box on page 537 for advice on when to use Set Field and when to use an Insert step.

Putting data in container fields

In Part 4, you learned that calculations can work with container data. Set Field and Insert Calculated Result are no exception: You can use either of them to move pictures, movies, sounds, and files from one container field to another. You can also use Cut, Copy, and Paste to work with container fields, provided you're willing to live with the caveats for intruding on someone's clipboard described on page 533.

But FileMaker has special commands in the Insert menu to get container data into your database in the first place, and these commands have script step equivalents:

- **Insert Picture** lets you specify the file to insert, and whether you want to "Store only a reference" (see page 84 for a refresher on references). If you don't specify a file, then FileMaker asks people to pick one when the step runs.

Note: The dialog box someone sees when he's asked to pick a picture file includes the "Store only a reference" checkbox, regardless of how you set this option on the script step itself. In a sense, your choice in the script becomes a *suggestion* to him: It determines how the checkbox is set when the dialog box pops up. He's free to change it.

Insert QuickTime has only one option: the file you want to insert. Again, if no file is selected, people get to pick one when the script runs. Since QuickTime files are *always* stored as a reference, you don't get that choice this time.

- **Insert File** has the most options of all. Of course, you get to pick the file to be inserted. You also get a "Store only a reference" checkbox. This time, though, you also get a "Go to target field" checkbox. You can use it to tell FileMaker which field to put the file in.

Insert Picture and Insert QuickTime don't have an option to tell FileMaker *which field to use*, which probably seems odd. They're designed to put things in the current container field someone clicks before the script runs. If you want more control, just use "Go to Field" first, specifying the appropriate field, and then use Insert Picture or Insert QuickTime to insert into that field.

Set Field by Name

Every once in a while, you need an extra jolt of flexibility. Suppose your script sets one of any number of possible fields, and which one varies from one running of the script to the next. For instance, imagine you have a script that puts a measurement into any one of 24 different fields in a database of statistical recordings, one for each hourly sample (with a new record for each day). When your script goes to put the data in the right place, you might feel like you're going to need a giant If/Else If block with 24 cases, and 24 nearly identical Set Field steps.

For unusual circumstances like this one, FileMaker has a script step called "Set Field by Name". This step works just like the regular Set Field step, but instead of selecting the target field from a list, you use a calculation to produce the target field

Set Field vs. Insert

FileMaker's field editing script steps have a lot of overlap (page 534). For example, Set Field with no target field does exactly the same thing as Insert Calculated Result with no target field and the "Select entire contents" checkbox turned on. And you can use Insert Calculated Result with the appropriate calculation to do the same thing as Insert Date, Insert Time, Insert Text, and Insert Current User Name. In general, it doesn't matter one bit which one you use.

But you should think twice about using the Insert script steps with a target field specified *and* the "Select entire contents" checkbox turned on. With both options set, these script steps simply overwrite the value in some field—exactly what Set Field does.

Since these steps need the field on the layout, though, they're more *fragile:* The script can break if you make changes to a layout. You'll probably save yourself a headache tomorrow if you just use Set Field today.

Of course, if you're inserting *into* a field (without "Select entire contents" turned on), then you *must* use an Insert step. Luckily, with settings like this one, a step makes sense only if someone's already in the field—and thus the field's obviously on the layout.

Finally, you can't accomplish some of the Insert steps from a calculation. Specifically, you can't access the last visited record or the View Index dialog box from a Set Field step.

name. For instance, imagine your 24 fields are called "Measurement 1" through "Measurement 24". You could use a formula like this for your target field:

```
"Measurement " & Hour(Get(CurrentTime))
```

This formula produces the name of the field for each given hour, so a single "Set Field by Name" step can replace all those If conditions.

"Set Field by Name" has a down side, though: If you rename a field, the step stops working. To combat this problem, you have a special function called *GetFieldName( )*. This function gives you the name (as a text value) of the field you pass to it. That might sound a little loopy, but consider a formula like this:

```
Choose(
    Hour(Get(CurrentTime)) - 1;
    GetFieldName ( Measurements::Measurement 1 )
    GetFieldName ( Measurements::Measurement 2 )
    GetFieldName ( Measurements::Measurement 3 )
    GetFieldName ( Measurements::Measurement 4 )
    GetFieldName ( Measurements::Measurement 5 )
    GetFieldName ( Measurements::Measurement 6 )
    GetFieldName ( Measurements::Measurement 7 )
    GetFieldName ( Measurements::Measurement 8 )
    GetFieldName ( Measurements::Measurement 9 )
    GetFieldName ( Measurements::Measurement 10 )
    GetFieldName ( Measurements::Measurement 11 )
    GetFieldName ( Measurements::Measurement 12 )
    GetFieldName ( Measurements::Measurement 13 )
    GetFieldName ( Measurements::Measurement 14 )
```

```
        GetFieldName ( Measurements::Measurement 15 )
        GetFieldName ( Measurements::Measurement 16 )
        GetFieldName ( Measurements::Measurement 17 )
        GetFieldName ( Measurements::Measurement 18 )
        GetFieldName ( Measurements::Measurement 19 )
        GetFieldName ( Measurements::Measurement 20 )
        GetFieldName ( Measurements::Measurement 21 )
        GetFieldName ( Measurements::Measurement 22 )
        GetFieldName ( Measurements::Measurement 23 )
        GetFieldName ( Measurements::Measurement 24 )
    )
```

This formula considers the current time, then returns the correct field name for the hour. But since it uses *GetFieldName( )*, it returns the right name even if you rename a field. And as a formula to the "Set Field by Name" function, it is still lots shorter and easier to manage than those 24 If steps. For instance, suppose you want to change what goes into the measurement field. With "Set Field by Name", you have one place to change. With 24 separate Set Field steps, you'd have to fix things in all 24 places.

"Set Field by Name" is a rare bird, and it can be hard to grasp. If you need it, you really need it, but you probably never will.

A Field Script in Action

Suppose you decide to add a Notes field to the Customer table in your database. You use this field to hold any arbitrary information you think is important about the customer. Unfortunately, you soon realize this field is a little *too* unorganized. You have no idea if the note that says, "Customer already paid" is from last Tuesday or last year. You need a consistent way to keep track of *who* left a note, and *when*. You decide everybody should record this information along with any notes they leave. To make things even easier, you want to be sure people add *new* notes *above* older notes. Thus, when a customer record has been around for a while, the Notes field looks something like this:

```
--- 12/11/07 @ 3:30 PM by Jim ---
Called the customer, confirmed both orders were received. Placed a copy of
the order in Jello, along with Dwight's stapler, in the top drawer of his
desk.

--- 12/01/07 @ 1:25 PM by Dwight ---
Customer called saying he never got his order. I checked and we have no
record of shipment because some people are so lax! I'm shipping again.

--- 11/28/07 @ 4:58 PM by Jim ---
Order came in really close to quittin' time. I'll finish the paperwork
Monday.
```

In this example, you create a script that "forces" all added comments into that format. This script adds a separator line with the date and time (plus a couple blank lines) and leaves the insertion point under the separator. You also create a button next to the Notes field that runs this script. People just have to click and type.

Note: Like almost every problem you ever solve with a script, you can do this process in *about* 24,601 ways. One way's described below, and another in the box on page 541 You may prefer a different way, and that's OK.

Before you start creating your script, think about what you need to do in sequence. Here's a breakdown:

- Put the insertion point at the start (top) of the Notes field.

- Insert two blank lines—to create some space before the previous comment.

- Put the insertion point back at the start, and add the separator line with the date and time.

- At that point, the script ends and someone can start typing.

Your next mission is to translate these plain English steps into ScriptMaker steps, which you'll do in the next section.

Building the script

If your Customers table doesn't already have a Notes field, create one before you write the script. Then proceed as follows:

1. **Choose Scripts → ScriptMaker. Create a new script called** *Add Note Separator.*

   Develop the habit of giving your scripts descriptive names so you can remember what you want them to do.

2. **Add a Set Selection script step to the script.**

   You can find this step under Editing in the list, or, from the View pop-up menu, you can choose "all by name" to see an alphabetical list. When you add the step, it appears in your script.

3. **Turn on the "Go to target field" checkbox. If necessary, from the table pop-up menu, choose Customers, choose the Notes field, and then click OK.**

   The Set Field step in your script updates to show the target field.

4. **In the Script Step Options area, click the second Specify button.**

   It's not labeled, but it's *below* the first Specify button. When you click it, the Specify Set Selection window appears.

5. **In both boxes (Start Position and End Position), type *0* (zero).**

   Zero in both boxes tells FileMaker you want the insertion point right at the start of the field, and you don't want any text selected.

6. **Add an Insert Text step to the script, and then turn off the "Select entire contents" option.**

You don't want the two blank lines you're about to insert to replace everything in the field.

7. **Click the bottom Specify button.**

A window called simply Specify appears (Figure 14-2).

Figure 14-2:
The Specify dialog for Insert Text seems puzzling, because you don't have any options to click. You just type the exact text you want the script step to insert. Note that this box isn't a calculation dialog box. It lets you insert only literal text. Use Insert Calculated Result if you need to insert dynamic text with a script step.

8. **In the Specify window, add two empty lines (press Return or Enter twice), and then click OK.**

That's the regular Enter key, not the one in the numerical keypad: In this dialog box, that key just clicks the OK button. Anyway, after pressing it twice, you don't see the returns you've typed in the dialog box, but, in the Insert Text script step, you do see two blank spaces inside quotes. Those returns tell File-Maker to add two blank lines to the top of the Notes field.

9. **Select the Set Selection step at the top of the script, and then, at the bottom of the window, click the Duplicate button.**

FileMaker adds a second copy of the Set Selection step, right below the first.

10. **Drag either Set Selection step to the bottom of the script.**

Mouse junkies can use Ctrl+down arrow (⌘-down arrow) to move script steps.

Your script now has Set Selection, then Insert Text, and then Set Selection again.

11. **Add the Insert Calculated Result step to the script, and then turn off the "Select entire contents" option.**

Make sure the step lands *after* the last Set Selection script. If it doesn't, move it there. Turning off the selection option ensures that the calculation goes in at the insertion point (which is at the beginning of the field now).

12. **To the right of "Calculated result", click the Specify button, and then, in the Specify Calculation window, enter this calculation:**

```
"--- " & Get(CurrentDate) & " @ " & Get(CurrentTime) & " by " &
Get(UserName) & " ---¶"
```

You can use any method you want to enter the calculation, as long as it does the same thing as this one.

13. **Save the script.**

Your new script is ready to test.

Now you just need to add the Notes field to the Customers layout, and a button by it that runs the new script. When you click the button, FileMaker adds the separator to the field, and puts the insertion point in place. People can now type notes that are nicely organized and separated.

Other Steps That Work with Fields

Lots of times, you want to be able to write scripts that work on multiple records. You may need to change values across a found set of records, or you may want to let FileMaker handle the serial numbering of all the records in a table. The next script steps let you manage data in lots of records without lots of hassle.

Perform Find/Replace

The Perform Find/Replace script step brings all the power of the Find/Replace command (page 68) to your scripts. You can include the find parameters in the script step, or create a calculation to determine the parameters on the fly, as shown in Figure 14-3.

GEM IN THE ROUGH

Fewer Steps, Bigger Calculations

You can easily create the Add Note Separator script described on page 538, but it has one weakness: It uses four steps where two could accomplish the same thing. A more concise approach would be to first put the separator and a few blank lines at the top of the Notes field, and *then* use the Set Selection script step to put the insertion point after the separator. The drawback here is that you have much more complex calculations to write. The choice is yours.

In the Insert Calculated Results step, you need a calculation that builds the separator line, adds two blank lines after it, and finally adds the *old* contents of the Notes field to the end:

```
"--- " & Get(CurrentDate) & " @ " &
Get(CurrentTime) & " by " & Get(UserName)
& " ---¶¶¶" & Customers::Notes
```

To keep the contents of your field from being duplicated, make sure you leave the "Select entire contents" option on this time.

Now you need to get the insertion point in place after the first line, using the Set Selection script step. Use the same technique as before: Set Selection with an End Position that's *smaller* than the Start Position. FileMaker puts the insertion point *before* the character at the Start Position. Since you want it *after* the end of the first line, you need to find the first new line symbol, add *1* to it, and put *that* in the Start Position. Here's the calculation that does the trick:

```
Position ( Customers::Notes, "¶", 1, 1 )
+ 1
```

Put this same calculation, but without the last *+1*, into the End Position field, and you're ready to test your script. You can use this script with or without the "Go to Target Field" option, as described in step 3 on page 539.

Figure 14-3:
The window behind the Specify button on a Perform Find/Replace script step looks a lot like the normal Find/Replace window. But this version has a new pop-up menu (called Perform) and a couple of new Specify buttons that let you specify calculated values for what you're looking for and what you want to replace the found results with.

When you use this step, from the Perform pop-up menu, you pick which action you want to perform. Your choices are Find Next, Replace and Find, Replace, and Replace All (these correspond with the buttons you use to dismiss the normal Find/Replace dialog box). The "Find what" and "Replace with" boxes each has a Specify button by it. If you know exactly what you're looking for, then you can type it right in these boxes. If you click Specify, then you get to use a calculation to set these values instead.

For example, say your Notes field is such a smashing success, you find some customers have *pages* of notes—and it's becoming a problem to find what you want. You'd like a quick way to search the material in the Notes fields. The script is simple. It just needs to go to the Notes field, and then use the Perform Find/Replace script step. You need a field to type the search value into, which you could create one before starting in on your script, but in real life you probably don't think that far ahead. FileMaker lets you easily create fields without leaving the warmth and protection of ScriptMaker, as you'll see in the following steps.

Here's how to make the script. Call it *Search Notes Field*:

1. **Add "Go to Field" as your first script step. Set it to go to the Customers::Notes field.**

   First things first: You want to make sure the script searches the correct field.

2. **Add the Perform Find/Replace step to the script, and turn on the "Perform without dialog" option. Click the Specify button.**

   You see the Perform Find/Replace Options window.

3. **Make sure the Perform pop-up menu is set to Find Next, and then, to the right of the "Find what" box, click the Specify button.**

   The Specify Calculation window appears.

4. **From the pop-up menu above the field list, choose Manage Database.**

   It makes sense for this field to use global storage, and since it doesn't really belong to a customer, you add a new table for it as well. You can do that right here in the Manage Database window.

Note: Scripts often make use of global fields, so FileMaker lets you create a quick table to hold them without cluttering or interfering with your relationship graph (see page 321).

---

5. **Click the Tables tab, and then add a new table called Globals.**

   This table holds global fields that aren't tied to specific tables. You don't need a relationship to a table to grab the value from a global field, so a table like this makes them very easy to find. If you're working in the file you used back in Chapter 8, then you may already have a table for your globals. If so, add your new global fields there.

6. **Click the Fields tab, and, from the Table pop-up menu, select Globals. Add a new text field called Note Search Value, and then set it to use global storage. Click OK.**

   You now have the only field your script needs. See page 116 for more information on global storage fields.

7. **Double-click the Globals::Note Search Value field to add it to your calculation. Click OK.**

   This calculation tells FileMaker where to look when it runs the Perform Find/Replace step—whatever's in the new field, in this case. Clicking OK when you're done returns you to the Perform Find/Replace Options window.

8. **In the Direction pop-up menu, choose All.**

   This options tells FileMaker to look through the entire Notes field.

9. **Turn on the "Current record/request" and "Current field" radio buttons. Click OK until you're back in your database.**

   You don't want the search to spill into different fields or records. These options restrict it to just the record someone's viewing. Since the script first goes to the Notes field, FileMaker searches only that field.

To finish the job, add the new global field and a Find button, formatted with your new script, to the Customers layout. Then type a value into the search field, and click your script button to test your new script.

Replace Field Contents and Relookup Field Contents

It's probably no surprise that you can execute the Replace Field Contents and Relookup Field Contents commands from a script. These steps let you specify a field to act upon. If you *don't* specify a field, then they act on the current field. You

---

A Reusable Notes Separator Script

The mark of a FileMaker power-scripter is someone always on the lookout for the opportunity to write *one* script that can be used in *several* places. After all, who wants to spend his life writing scripts? The fact is, you're probably so happy with your new Notes field and its separator script that you want to use it in other places—on a Job, an Invoice, a Payment, and so forth.

It would be much nicer if the Add Note Separator script could add a note separator (and place the insertion point) in *any* field you wanted. You could then tell people to click the Notes field before running the script.

The only thing tying your script to the Customers::Notes field is the "Go to target field" checkbox on the Set Selection steps. If you edit the script and turn this option off for *both* Set Selection steps, then it works on whatever field is active when the script runs.

If you don't like to have to click the field before running the script, then you can fix it in two ways, but both require information you haven't learned yet. See page 592 for a continuation of this technique.

also get the typical "Perform without dialog" checkbox. When you turn this checkbox on, the action happens immediately when the step runs. If you leave this option off with the Replace Field Contents step, then people see the typical Replace Field Contents dialog box (with all the settings you specified in the script). With the Relookup Field Contents step, they just see a confirmation message first, asking if they really want to perform the relookup operation.

Set Next Serial Value

The Set Next Serial Value script step is invaluable—in the rare cases when anyone actually uses it. It's a one-trick pony: If a field auto-enters a serial number, then this step changes the "next value" stored in the Field Options dialog box. In other words, if you want to start your customer ID values over again, then you can use Set Next Serial Value to do it from a script. (See the box above for an example.)

Warning: Use extreme care when you change a field that's used as a key in a relationship. You risk leaving related records orphaned if you don't change their key fields, too. See the box on page 621 for a script that helps you change key fields without losing related records (or your sanity).

The step has two options. First, you can specify the field to update. As usual, if you don't specify a field, then it works on the current field. You tell FileMaker what to set the "next value" to by entering a calculation.

Working with Records

You can get only so far with your scripts by working with field values. Eventually you need to deal with more than one *record*. Thankfully, FileMaker has script steps for creating, duplicating, and deleting records; navigating among existing records;

and even managing the process of opening and editing a record, and saving (committing) or reverting the changes. You can also work directly with portal rows on the current layout—and the records they represent.

Creating, Duplicating, and Deleting Records

New Record/Request and Duplicate Record/Request have no options, and do exactly what you'd expect. The first script step creates a new record, just like the Records → New Record menu command. The second duplicates the current record. In either case, the *new* record becomes the current record, just like when you do it manually. You use these steps most often on buttons, when you're taking away menu commands from people and providing them with buttons that appear only on the layouts where you want people to be able to create records.

POWER USERS' CLINIC

Why Set Next Serial Value

The Set Next Serial Value script step may seem odd to you. After all, if you want to set the next serial value for a field, you can just do it yourself from the Manage Database window. But this step can come in very handy in some situations.

Imagine you're in the auto parts business and you have 200 stores around the country. Each office has its own copy of your database, which gets updated periodically. The main office sends a new empty database to each store with all the latest enhancements, and the folks at each store have to *import* all the data from their old databases into the new one (you'll learn about importing and exporting data in Chapter 17).

Now suppose this database includes an Orders table with an Order ID field. After the old orders have been imported, the database may have orders with IDs from one to 1000. But since no *new* records have been created yet, the Order ID field still has a "next value" of *1*. The store's first thousand orders use IDs that are *already used by other records*. That's a big no-no.

The solution's obvious: You need to fix the "next value" on the Order ID field after the import's finished. To save the store manager the trouble, you can put a script in the database to fix this glitch for her. (In fact, you can make a script that does *all* the work of importing old data and fixing next serial values in every table.)

Note: Duplicating a record from a script step works just like doing it manually—that is, the script duplicates the static values in the record, too. If calculations depend on those static values, they also get duplicated, but they change if you edit the static values later. Some Auto-Enter calculations, like serial numbers, are *not* duplicated, but recalculated at the time the duplicate record is created.

The Delete Record/Request script step deletes the current record. If you turn on its "Perform without dialog" option, then the delete happens with no warning. When this option is turned off, the manager sees the same "Are you sure" message box he'd see when deleting a record manually.

Note: Each of these three script steps also works for *find requests* when a script runs in Find mode.

Navigating Among Records

You have two ways to change to a different record. You can move to it with the "Go to Record/Request/Page" script step, which works a lot like the Status toolbar's book icon. Or you can switch to a related record, or a set of related records, using the "Go to Related Record" script step.

Go to Record/Request/Page

FileMaker has one script that handles changing *records, find requests, and pages*. This may seem strange at first, but it makes sense because it's exactly how the Status toolbar's book icon works: If you're in Browse mode, then the step goes to a different record. If you're in Find mode, then it switches find requests instead. Finally, if you're in Preview mode, then it flips through pages.

Note: You can't run scripts when in Layout mode, and a script *can't* go to Layout mode, so it doesn't apply here.

The "Go to Record/Request/Page" step has just one option. You get to pick *which* record, request, or page to go to from a simple list:

• First

• Last

• Previous

• Next

• By Calculation

When you lock people out of the usual interface and control everything they do through the script (see the box on page 569), the First, Last, Previous, and Next options let you provide your own customized replacement for the Status toolbar and book icon. For example: Make four buttons and arrange them in a horizontal line (like those on a tape recorder or CD player). Give each button a "Go to Record" step, and then set them up in the following order, so they mimic the tape recorder concept:

• Leftmost button – "Go to Record/Request/Page" [First]

• Second button – "Go to Record/Request/Page" [Previous]

• Third button – "Go to Record/Request/Page" [Next]

• Rightmost button – "Go to Record/Request/Page" [Last]

This visual concept is so common that people are likely to know how the buttons work without any instructions. But you can add a tooltip (page 752) to each button if you want to provide that extra boost.

Another common but more advanced use of this step is to provide a way for a looping script to end. When you choose the Next or Previous option, a new checkbox appears in the Script Step Options area, called "Exit after last". When it's turned on, FileMaker knows to exit the loop after it's finished with the last record (when you choose "Go to Record" [next]) or after the first record (when you choose "Go to Record" [previous]). (When to exit a loop is no small matter, as page 613 explains.)

When you choose By Calculation, you get the chance to specify a calculation with a number result. FileMaker goes to exactly that record, request, or page. You could use this option if the record number's in a field, or if you want to skip ahead 25 records each time the script is run, for example. This technique is more useful than it sounds. For example, it's an ideal way to show records in a list using Instant Web Publishing (IWP), which you'll learn about in Chapter 18. In IWP, FileMaker limits the list to 25 records at a time, so you have to give your Web users some way to see the next patch of records.

Go to Related Record

You were first introduced to this power step when learning about relationships (see page 351). It can go to a different record, found set, layout, window, and even file—all in one step. This step's job is simple: It takes you to a related record. But carrying out that job *isn't* so simple. When you click the Specify button, you get a wealth of choices, as shown in Figure 14-4. To go to a related record, you need to tell FileMaker which related table occurrence you're interested in, by selecting it from the "Get related record from" pop-up menu. For example, if you're on the Customer layout, and you want to see a related invoice, then, from the menu, you should choose Invoices.

Figure 14-4:
This window's the same one you saw when you attached a "Go to Related Record" script step to a button back on page 352. But inside a script you wield a whole new level of power when you tie this command to other processes, like printing a report from a found set that changes based on whichever record someone's on when running the script.

With this done, FileMaker can find the right record. But how should it *show it to you?* If you're visiting related records, chances are you can't view them directly on the current layout (since the layout is associated with the wrong table occurrence). So a "Go to Related Record" command almost always involves changing layouts. From the "Show record using layout" pop-up menu, you pick the layout you want.

At first you may be surprised by the menu choices. It shows all the layouts associated with the table occurrence in the first pop-up menu, as you might expect. But it *also* shows layouts associated with any *other* occurrence of the same table. FileMaker uses the specified table occurrence to find the right related record, and the specified layout to show it to you. You can show an invoice record from any layout that shows records from the Invoices table, no matter what *occurrence* it uses.

If the table occurrence you picked in the first menu is an occurrence of a table from a *different* file, then you can turn on "Use external table's layout" to see layouts in the file the table comes from. When you use this option from a button, FileMaker switches to a window for the other file instead of showing records in the current window. If you use this option in a script, though, then you need to add a Select Window script step (page 565) if you want the external file's window to be active.

If you want a *new* window (whether you're using an external table or not), then turn on the "Show in new window" checkbox. When you do, you see the New Window Options dialog box, which is explained alongside the New Window script step on page 564.

Finally, you get to decide how to deal with the found set when the script step finishes. See the box below to help you decide when each option makes sense.

- If you don't turn on "Show only related records", then FileMaker goes to the related table, but you see all the records in the related table, not just those that are children of the formerly active record. The first related record is active in your new found set. So, from the Customer layout, GTRR without "Show only related records" shows all your invoices, and the active record is the first one for the customer that you're viewing when the GTRR script step runs.

- If you turn on "Show only related records" and "Match current record only", then FileMaker returns a found set of only those records that match the active parent record. The customer invoice GTRR set, as described above, shows you a found set of just the invoices for the customer record that was active when the script step ran. The first related record would be the active one.

- Choosing "Show only related records" and "Match all records in current found set", is most useful when you have a found set selected before the GTRR script step runs. In this scenario, FileMaker shows a new found set in which all the records are related to at least one of the records in the old found set. So, in the Customers layout, you've found your two highest volume customers. Use GTRR, matching all records in the current found set to find all the invoices related to either of these two customers. The first record that's related to the customer record that's active when the GTRR script step runs is the active record in the new found set.

FREQUENTLY ASKED QUESTION

To Show or Not to Show

How do I decide when to turn on "Show only related records" and when to leave it off?

The "Show only related records" option is useful when you use Go to Related Record as a navigational aid for your users, or when you really want all the related records, not just one. For example, if someone clicks a button on the Invoice portal, it makes good sense to show not just the invoice he clicked, but also the other related invoices. Then he can just use the book icon to flip through the rest of the records. Likewise, if your script is going to loop through all the related invoices to do its job, then you want to show just the right records before starting the loop.

The tradeoff is performance. When you turn this option off, FileMaker simply shows the record. It doesn't worry about the found set or the sort order. With the option turned on, though, FileMaker has to find the correct records first, and then show the one you asked for. If your relationship is sorted, then FileMaker even sorts the records for you. This sorting takes more time. If your script just needs to visit a specific related record, do something to it, and then come right back, you can leave this option turned off to make your script run more quickly.

Opening, Reverting, and Committing Records

When you use your database in Browse mode, FileMaker does a lot of things automatically. When you start typing in a field, it locks the record. When you exit the record—click outside any field or press Enter—it commits the record. When you use a script, though, you're not really clicking fields and pressing Enter. So how does FileMaker know when to lock a record and when to commit? You have to tell it, by including the appropriate script steps: Open Record/Request, Revert Record/Request, and Commit Record/Request.

Open Record/Request

The Open Record/Request step tells FileMaker you're about to start editing a record. If the record is already open, then it does nothing—that is, it doesn't automatically commit the record first. It just locks the record if it isn't locked already. But if the record is already open (by you, via another window, or by someone else), then you get a record-locking error. (See page 593 to see how you can check for errors while a script is running.)

Commit Record/Request

Whether you've used the Open Record/Request step or just let FileMaker lock the record for you, you can explicitly commit the record with the Commit Record/Request step. It has two options:

- The "Skip data entry validation" option tells FileMaker to commit the record even if it violates field validation. This option works only when you turn on the "Only during data entry" radio button in the Validation options for the field. If you've set the validation to happen "Always", then the script *can't* get around it.

- When the "Perform without dialog" option is turned off, and, in the Layouts → Layout Setup window's General tab, you turn *off* "Save record changes automatically", FileMaker shows the message in Figure 14-5 when the step runs.

Figure 14-5:
If the layout is set not to save record changes (page 236), and you don't turn on the "Perform without dialog" checkbox, then you see this warning when the Commit Record/Request step runs. Click Save to commit the record. If you click Don't Save, then FileMaker reverts the record instead. The Cancel button leaves the record open and locked.

Note: You know how to handle dialog boxes when they come up, but they often confuse other people. Most database designers try to avoid requiring people to interact with FileMaker's normal dialog boxes while scripts are running, especially when people could make a choice that circumvents the purpose of the carefully crafted script.

Revert Record/Request

The Revert Record/Request step has only one option: "Perform without dialog". When this option is turned off, someone sees a confirmation message. Otherwise, FileMaker reverts the record immediately when the script runs.

You can understand these script steps relatively easily to understand, but *when* to use them is hard to figure out. Here are some things to keep in mind when you're trying to decide when you need to open or commit a record in a script:

- When you use a script step that *inserts* data into a field (and leaves someone in the field), then FileMaker locks the record when the step runs, but doesn't commit the change. You can then do *more* work with fields if you want. FileMaker commits the record later, when she exits the record.

- If your script changes to a different layout, switches to Find or Preview mode, or closes the window, then FileMaker automatically commits the record if needed.

- If you use a script step that modifies several records—Replace Field Contents, for example—FileMaker commits the records in batches as it goes. When it's finished, every record that was modified has been committed.

- If you perform a series of Set Field steps in a script, and you are *not* in the record when the script runs, then FileMaker locks the record and makes the field changes. When the script is done, you're not in the record (no field is active), but the record's still locked and uncommitted. In other words, you can use the Records → Revert Record command to revert all the changes made by the script, which probably isn't what you want. Add a Commit Records/Requests script step at the *end* of the script to avoid losing the data your script enters.

- If your script changes some records and includes a step to revert them if something goes wrong, then you should probably make sure to commit any changes someone was making before your script changes anything. That way, the script doesn't undo any of her work. Thus, put a Commit Records/Requests step at the *beginning* of your script.

And if you're still not sure if your script really needs an Open or Commit step, go ahead and open the record at the beginning of your script and commit it at the end. Sure, it takes a nanosecond or two extra to run a couple of steps that may not be strictly necessary. But what's a nanosecond on the grand scale of time when your data may be at risk?

Why Open a Record?

Why would I ever use the Open Record/Request step? Doesn't FileMaker automatically lock a record as soon as my script starts editing it?

For simple scripts, this step is almost always unnecessary. FileMaker does, indeed, do the right thing. But as you'll learn in Chapter 18, you can set up your FileMaker database so multiple people can use it at the same time, each on her own computer. When you set up FileMaker this way, lots of interesting things can start happening.

For example, a record can change while you're looking at it. Suppose a new area code is added in your area, and you write a script that looks at the phone number and decides, based on its exchange code, whether or not to change the area code. The script might look like this:

```
If [ "Exchange Code = 555 or Exchange Code
= 377" ]
    Set Field [ Area Code, "602"]
End If
```

You probably find this hard to believe, but technically, someone could change the Exchange Code field after the If step runs but before the Set Field happens. (Remember that other people are editing records on other computers, so they're free to make changes while the script is running on your computer.) If this scenario happens, you end up assigning the customer an incorrect phone number.

To fix this, you need to lock the record before you start looking at it:

```
Open Record/Request
If [ "Exchange Code = 555 or Exchange Code
= 377" ]
    Set Field [ Area Code, "602"]
    Commit Record/Request [No Dialog]
Else
    Revert Record/Request [No Dialog]
End If
```

Now, somebody else can't edit the Exchange Code field because the record is locked. In general, if many people use your database, then you should open a record before you start looking at it in a script.

This script reverts the record when it didn't make any changes. FileMaker does this reverting for two reasons. First, committing a record means saving the data, and that's unnecessary here. Second, suppose a field has had validation turned on since this record was created. It's possible that this unmodified record has now-invalid data. If you try to commit this data back, then you get a validation error. Reverting avoids this error since nothing's being saved. Moral of the story: Try to commit a record *only* when necessary.

Copying Records

FileMaker has two record-related script steps that do something you can't easily do manually in Browse mode: Copy an entire record to the clipboard. One version copies just the current record, while the other copies every record in the found set at once.

Copy Record/Request

The first, called Copy Record/Request, copies data from *every* field on the layout, and puts it on the clipboard. FileMaker puts a tab character between each field value.

If any field has *more* than one line, FileMaker converts the new line character into a funny character called a *vertical tab*. Some programs, like Microsoft Word, convert these characters back into new lines when you paste in a copied record. Figure 14-6 shows the result of pasting a customer record into Text Edit. In that example, the new line character is an "ā;" and the data's strung into one long line. Your mileage may vary.

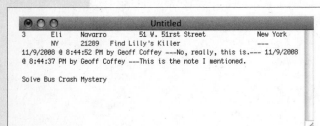

Figure 14-6:
This picture shows what you get when you copy a customer record, and then paste it into a word processor that's not great at rendering vertical tabs. Everything's all smushed together, but it's sometimes easier to copy/paste it all in one shot than to copy each field value individually.

Note: As usual with FileMaker, you have more than one way to get things done. See page 677 for two other ways to export data. Remember, using a scripted Copy, Cut, or Paste command violates your sacred trust not to mess with the contents of someone's clipboard unless he knows it's happening.

Copy All Records/Requests

While Copy Record/Request copies the entire *current* record, its brother—Copy All Records/Requests—copies *every* record in the found set. Each individual record is added to the clipboard in the same format as the Copy Record/Request command produces, and FileMaker puts one record on each line.

Suppose, for example, you want to get all the Invoice IDs for a particular customer, and put them in an email to a coworker. Or perhaps you're compiling a list of all the Zip codes in Phoenix where you have customers. Using Copy All Records/ Requests, you can do this job with ease.

The trick is to create a *new* layout that has only one field on it. For example, make a new layout with just the Invoice ID field, or just the Zip Code field. Write a script that switches to this layout, and then run the Copy All Records/Requests command to get a simple list of values on the clipboard.

Working with Portals

FileMaker has a script step specifically designed to go to a certain portal row. Why would you want to do that? First, when you use the "Go to Field" script step to target a field in a portal, it goes to the *first* portal row, which may not have anything to do with what someone needs at that point. If you want to put people in the field on a *different* row, you need to go to that row first.

When you use data from a related field, or put data in a related field, and you have *multiple* related records, FileMaker grabs the value from the *first* record. If you want to tell FileMaker to work with a different related record instead, then use a portal, and go to the right row. See the box below for tips (and a warning) on working with portals.

GEM IN THE ROUGH

Beware the Portal

Technically, you can do all kinds of things through a portal using a script—but it's not always wise. For example, if you want to discount every line item on an invoice by 10 percent, then you can write a looping script. It starts by visiting the first portal row, and then applying the invoice. Then it can go to each additional row, applying the discount as it goes. In each pass through the loop, you're modifying the Line Items::Price field; the active portal row determines which line item is changed. Unfortunately, the active portal row is too transient to rely upon. A script can do all kinds of things that make FileMaker forget which portal row you're on (change modes, change layouts, go to another field, commit or revert the record, and so forth).

If you accidentally do confuse FileMaker like this at some point inside your loop, then you end up looping forever because you never reach the end of the portal.

It's much safer to find the appropriate records, and work with them directly. You can get the same effect by using the "Go to Related Records" script step to find all the line item records, and then looping through the records directly with "Go to Record/Request/Page", avoiding the perils of the portal.

Go to Portal Row

The "Go to Portal Row" script step works a lot like the "Go to Record/Request/Page" step. You can go to the First, Last, Previous, or Next portal row, or specify the row *number* with a calculation. It even has an "Exit after last" option to help when looping through portal rows.

This step includes an option you can use to make what's happening onscreen a little more obvious to people: "Select entire contents". When you turn this checkbox on, FileMaker highlights the whole portal row. Otherwise, it goes to the portal row without highlighting it onscreen. (After all, you don't always want people to see what's going on.)

One setting you *don't* find with "Go to Portal Row" is *which portal to use*. The guidelines below are how FileMaker knows which portal you have in mind:

• If the current layout only has one portal, then FileMaker uses it automatically.

• If the layout has more than one portal, then it assumes you want the portal that's currently active.

Note: In general, a portal is active whenever a person (or a script) puts the cursor in one of its fields. If you aren't sure what someone will be doing before your script runs, then throw in a "Go to Field" script step, just to be safe.

Finding Records

FileMaker has three nearly identical script steps to handle the grunt work of finding records. You can let people tell the script what to find, you can decide what the script finds (a *hard-coded* find), or you can script a dynamic find using calculations.

Deciding which one to use depends on whether people know what they're looking for—or how much work you want to save them. The upcoming sections go into this topic in detail. You'll also see a find script in action, and learn how to make a script pause and wait for information.

Performing People's Find Requests

The first, Perform Find, is the equivalent of a visit to Find mode, followed by a click of the Requests → Perform Find menu command. Perform Find's single option lets you specify what find requests to use, but, surprisingly, you can skip it entirely. If you *don't* turn this option on, then Perform Find assumes you're already in Find mode with one or more requests, and works just like the Requests → Perform Find menu command (and the Status toolbar's Find button). It looks for records that match the already defined find requests. All the matching records become the new found set.

But where do those find requests *come from*? Either someone creates them, or your script does. For example, many developers like to add special "Find" layouts to their databases. These layouts can show just the right fields, along with helpful text, to make things easier for people. Figure 14-7 shows a Find layout for the Customers table.

Next, you'll write a script that goes to the Find layout and puts someone in Find mode. The script then *pauses*, giving her a chance to enter find requests. When she's done, she clicks a button to *resume* the script, which performs the find, and then switches back to the Customers layout.

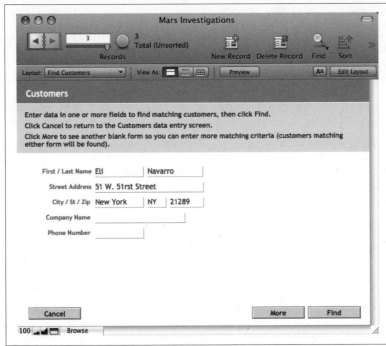

Figure 14-7:
This layout is designed specifically for Find mode. Two sets of instructions help people figure out what to do. The Find button resumes your script. The More button runs a New Record/Request script step. Since this layout is for Find mode only, make sure someone's in Find mode when she gets here, and take her to a different layout when she's done. You need a script like the one in the steps that start below.

Note: The finished file for this chapter has the layout created for you. Download it at *http://missingmanuals.com/cds.*

To set this process up yourself, first create a Find Customers layout like the one shown in Figure 14-7. Then visit the Manage Scripts window, click New, and name the script appropriately. Follow these steps to create the script itself:

1. **Add the "Go to Layout" script step, targeting the Find Customers layout.**

   You want to make sure the person's in the right context—the new Find Customers layout—before the script enters Find mode.

2. **Add the Enter Find Mode script step to the script.**

   The step already has its Pause option turned on and its "Specify find requests" option turned off. That's just what you want. This step switches to Find mode *and* pauses the script.

Note: If you want to start someone off with some basic criteria, you can specify them right in the Enter Find Mode step. FileMaker doesn't perform the find now. It just puts her in Find mode and creates the requests you specify. She's then free to *modify* or *delete* them as necessary.

---

3. **Add the Perform Find script step to the script.**

Once the script continues, you assume she has added the necessary find requests, so you're ready to use the Perform Find step with no find requests specified. (Be careful not to choose the Perform Find/*Replace* script step, which doesn't work in this script.)

4. **Add another "Go to Layout" script step to the script. This time, pick the Customers layout.**

This step takes her back to the Customers layout once FileMaker finds the correct records.

To complete your layout, on the Find Customers layout, create a Find button. You don't even have to write a script for this button. Since the person's always in the middle of a paused script when she sees this layout, just set the button with a Resume Script action. If you're feeling adventuresome, you can also create a More button with a New Record/Request script step.

Finally, the Cancel button should run a new script that simply switches back to the Customers layout, and then uses the Enter Browse Mode step to go back to Browse mode. Since your user will click this button in the middle of a paused script, you need to think about what will happen. She will go back to the Customers layout in Browse mode, but she'll still be in the middle of a paused script. That's a recipe for confusion the next time she presses Enter.

When you assign a script to a button, you get to decide what happens to any running script, as you can see in Figure 14-8.

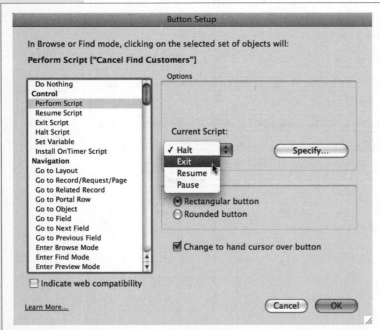

Figure 14-8:
When a button runs a script, FileMaker knows a paused script may already be running. This pop-up menu lets you decide what should happen to it. Choose Halt or Exit to have the running script immediately stop, and the new script take over (on page 583, you'll learn about the subtle difference between these two). If you choose Resume, the button's script runs, and then the paused script resumes. If you choose Pause, then the paused script stays paused while the new script runs.

In this case, set the Current Script pop-up to Exit so the paused script is stopped. That way, when someone clicks Cancel, she gets back to a normal state.

Tip: It's probably a good idea to hide the Find Customers layout from the Layouts pop-up menu so people don't accidentally switch to it without running your script. In the Layout Setup dialog box, turn off the "Include in layouts menu" checkbox (page 134).

Triggering a Find script

Once you have your scripts and layout in place, you only need to decide how people will run it. You could put a Find button on the Customers layout. But what happens if people try to find another way (like the Mode pop-up on the bottom of the window, or the View → Find Mode menu command, or a keyboard shortcut, or the Status toolbar's Find button—yikes!).

In a case like this, rather than track down all the ways a person might get to Find mode and try to deal with them proactively, why not get reactive instead? It would be best if your script could simply kick in when you switch to Find mode, no matter how you do it.

Script triggers to the rescue again (page 507). Among FileMaker's many triggers is OnModeEnter, which runs whenever you enter a mode on a particular layout. You get to decide which modes you care about, and which script to run. Setting it up is a snap.

1. **Switch to Layout mode, and then go to the Customers layout.**

   Script triggers are always associated with a particular layout or object, so you need to get to the layout in question first.

2. **Choose Layout → Layout Setup, and then switch to the Script Triggers tab.**

   You see the list of layout-oriented script triggers FileMaker supports.

3. **Scroll down the list, and then select OnModeEnter.**

   The list is two lines too short to show every trigger, so you have to scroll just a touch to find the one you want. Once you select it, the bottom portion of the window shows you information about this trigger.

4. **Click Select, and then choose the Find Customers script you just created.**

   The Select button shows the same Select Script window you see when you're setting up buttons.

5. **Turn off the Browse and Preview checkboxes (and leave the Find checkbox turned on).**

   The OnModeEnter trigger normally fires when you first go to any mode (except Layout mode, which is script-averse). In this case, you want the trigger to fire only when you enter Find mode. When you're done, the window looks like Figure 14-9.

Figure 14-9:
Here's how your OnModeEnter trigger looks once you've configured it. To recap, whenever someone enters Find mode on this layout, the Find Customers script runs automatically.

When you're done, OK the Layout Setup dialog box, save your layout, and then switch to Browse mode. Now, switch to Find mode using any of the 427 available methods and bask in the glory of script triggers, as FileMaker automatically starts your stylish find process.

Static Find Requests

With the script you created on the previous few pages, people can search for just about anything they want, by entering find requests. More often than not, you *don't* want to make people enter the find requests manually. After all, the whole point of a script is to have FileMaker do things so people don't have to. If you know ahead of time exactly what you want the script to find, use the Perform Find step all by itself: Just turn on the "Specify find requests" option, and put those requests right in the dialog box; the search options stay the same each time the script runs. When you specify find requests in a script, you see the window shown in Figure 14-10.

This window is pretty straightforward. To add a new find request, click New. To edit an existing request, select it first, and then click Edit. You can also delete or duplicate the selected step using the Delete and Duplicate buttons. Using the Specify Find Requests and Edit Find Request windows (Figure 14-11), you can tell the Perform Find step to do any find you can do from Find mode.

POWER USERS' CLINIC

Pausing a Script

Normally when you run a script, FileMaker performs its steps one by one as fast as it can. When they're all finished, the script's done. But sometimes a script should pause, usually to wait for someone to do something (like enter Find criteria) or to show the user something (like a Preview mode for a report). The Pause/Resume Script step, and some other steps (like Enter Find Mode) can pause the script automatically when their Pause options are turned on. When FileMaker gets to a step like this, it stops executing the script, but remembers where it left off. Later, the script continues, starting with the next step in line. While a script is paused, you're free to edit records, switch modes, change layouts, and so forth. You *can't* open the Manage Database, Manage Value Lists, Manage Custom Functions, or Manage Scripts windows, though, until the script finishes running.

While a script is paused, FileMaker adds two new buttons to the Status toolbar. The Continue button causes the script to continue immediately (pressing the Enter key does the same

thing). The Cancel button tells FileMaker you don't want to run the rest of the script. Your script stops, and you get back full control of the program.

If you want to, you can tell FileMaker how long to pause by clicking the Script Step Options area's Specify button when the Pause/Resume Script step is selected. The dialog box that appears has two choices: Indefinitely and For Duration. If you choose For Duration, you get to enter the number of seconds you want the script to pause, or you can click *another* Specify button to use a calculation to set the number of seconds. If you have set the script to pause for a specific duration, then you can still do things with your database while the script is paused, including click the Continue or Cancel buttons.

With a name like "Pause/Resume Script" you'd think this step can also *resume* a paused script. But then again, if the script is paused, then how can the step possibly execute? Don't be fooled: This step can only pause.

Figure 14-10:
When you add a new find request or edit an existing one, you see this dialog box. It's just a more structured way to type data in fields in Find mode. Instead of using your layouts, you use this window, which gives you direct access to every field in the database (the Fields list) and lets you easily see exactly what fields are being used in the Criteria list.

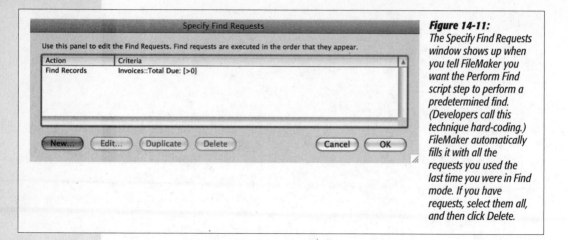

Figure 14-11:
The Specify Find Requests window shows up when you tell FileMaker you want the Perform Find script step to perform a predetermined find. (Developers call this technique hard-coding.) FileMaker automatically fills it with all the requests you used the last time you were in Find mode. If you have requests, select them all, and then click Delete.

Tip: The Edit Find Requests dialog box is confusing until you get used to it. But there's a way you can learn how it translates requests into its own particular syntax. Perform a find manually, and then write a test script with a Perform Find script step. FileMaker sets the dialog box with the criteria for the search you just did.

To create a find request, from the "Find records when" list, select a field (if it's a repeating field, then you can specify the repetition number in the Repetition box), and then, in the Criteria box, enter text. The Insert Symbol button gives you quick access to the same symbols you see in the Status toolbar in Find mode, and the Criteria box accepts all the standard symbols. Once you've finished entering the criteria, click Add to add it to the Criteria list.

• To edit an existing item in the criteria list, select it. When you do, FileMaker automatically selects the matching field in the Field list and puts the criterion in the Criteria box. You can then make any changes necessary, and click Change.

• To remove a criterion from the list entirely, select it, and then click Remove.

• Finally, you get to choose whether this request should be used to *find* matching records, or to *omit* them (see page 54). To turn this into an omitting find request, from the Action pop-up menu, choose Omit Records.

• When you've finished adding criteria, click OK. Just like Find mode, you can add more find requests if you want. In the Specify Find Requests window, just click the New button a second time. When you're all finished adding requests, click OK again.

Dynamic Find Requests

As dependable as static finds are, you may not always be able to predict what someone wants to find. Or the criteria for finding the same thing over and over can change, like when you're searching in a date field. For example, suppose you want to find all the invoices created a week ago. You can easily do so in Find mode: Just put the date from a week ago in the Invoices::Date field. But what you put in that field *changes every day*. For example, if today is November 7, and you create a script to find invoices from a week ago, then you could attach this request to the Perform Find step:

```
Invoices::Date = "10/31/2008"
```

Unfortunately, as soon as November 8 rolls around, this script *won't* find week-old invoices. It always finds invoices from October 31, 2008. When you're faced with a situation like this, you do have an option: Make the script build the find request the same way you would in Find mode. In other words, tell your script to go to Find mode, have *it* put the right date in the field, and then perform the find. You can use the Set Field script step to put the date in the Invoices::Date field since it conveniently lets you use a calculation to determine the actual date.

The script would look like the one in Figure 14-12.

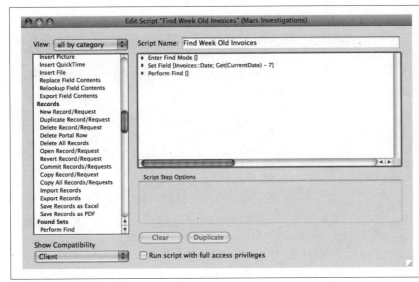

Figure 14-12:
This script builds the find request itself since it needs to use a calculation to determine the proper date to search for. Notice that the second step uses the calculation Get(CurrentDate) – 7 to determine the date a week ago. The Perform Find step has no requests specified, so FileMaker uses the one the script created. This kind of find script, which changes as your data changes, is called a dynamic find.

Tip: If your find request can be handled using the *symbols* supported by Find mode (page 52), then you can use Perform Find all by itself. For instance, to find invoices created today, tell Perform Find to find records with Invoices::Date = //. Since "//" stands for "today's date," it works on any day.

Constraining and Extending the Found Set

You may have already noticed that Perform Find doesn't have an option for the Requests → Constrain Found Set and Requests → Extend Found Set commands. That's because each of these is a separate script step. It makes sense, really, because to constrain or extend a find, you have to *have* a find first. In other words, this process always takes two separate steps to complete.

The Extend Found Set and Constrain Found Set script step options work *exactly* like Perform Find. Everything you just learned about Perform Find still applies: You can hard-code the find requests, pause the script, and then let the user enter them, or build them in the script.

Omitting Records

The Omit Record script step lives a dual life. If you're in Browse mode when it runs, it simply omits the current record from the found set. If you're in Find mode, on the other hand, in the Status toolbar, it turns on the Omit checkbox.

Omit Multiple Records works only in Browse mode and does the same thing as the Records → Omit Multiple command. As usual, you can specify the number of records to omit in the script, either as a number or a calculation. You also get a "Perform without dialog" option so you can decide whether or not people get to enter the number of records to omit.

Finally, the Show Omitted Only script step has the same effect as the Records → Show Omitted Only menu command.

GEM IN THE ROUGH

Mix and Match

You have three basic options when performing a find in a script: You can let someone enter the find requests, hard-code the requests right in the Perform Find step, or build the requests bit by bit using script steps. But these choices aren't mutually exclusive: You can mix and match techniques.

For example, suppose you need a relatively complex set of find requests that, for the most part, never change, but one value in one field on just one request needs to be based on the current date. It would be tedious to have to add dozens of Set Field and New Record/Request steps to your script when all but one use a hard-coded value.

Other times, it would be nice to let people specify the find requests, but add a little more to it when they're done. You can start on the Enter Find Mode script step, by turning on the "Specify find requests" option. This step tells FileMaker to go to Find mode *and* load it up with the requests you specify in a Specify Find Requests dialog box.

Once you're in Find mode, though, you're free to use Set Field, New Record/Request, and "Go to Record/Request" to modify the prefab requests to your heart's content. Just go to the right request, and use Set Field to work the dynamic date value into it.

Suppose you want to let people search for invoices. You create a Find Invoices layout and a script just like the one for Find Customers. But this time, you want to restrict people to invoices created only in the last year. Before the Perform Find step, you can add these two steps:

```
New Record/Request
Omit
Set Field [Invoices::Date; "..." &
Get(CurrentDate) - 365]
```

Now the script finds just what someone asks for, but omits records more than 365 days old. You've used the script to add a new request to the ones she created. What's more, she doesn't even know you've controlled her find.

Modify Last Find

The simplest find-related script step is Modify Last Find. It has exactly the same effect as the Records → Modify Last Find command: It puts you in Find mode with the same requests you created the *last* time you were in Find mode.

Sorting Records

After all that fuss about finding records, the sorting script steps are refreshingly simple. Only two of them exist, and you already know how to use both. The Sort Records script step behaves in a now-familiar way. All by itself, it brings up the Sort dialog box when the script runs. If you turn on its "Specify sort order" option, then you can preload the sort dialog box with a specific sort order. Finally, turn on the "Perform without dialog" option to sort the records without bothering anyone with a dialog box at all.

If the records are already sorted, then you can *unsort* them from a script. For instance, you might sort records for a report, but you want to return them to their unsorted order when the report is finished so people don't get confused. Just use the Unsort Records script step. It does its job with no options.

Sorting Records Automatically

Sometimes you have a sort order that's so darn handy you want FileMaker to do it every time, without being asked. For example, it might make sense to always sort your customers by name. After all, if you don't sort, you get them in the order they were created, which is often completely irrelevant. Write a script that sorts the way you want (using a simple one-line script with the Sort Records step). Then call upon the OnRecordLoad trigger. This trigger fires whenever a new record is loaded. (And you can still sort the records a different way any time you need to.)

That may seem like overkill—why not just use OnLayoutLoad instead? But if you do a find while on this layout, the results come back unsorted. You want this layout to automatically sort when you first come by and when you find new records. The OnRecordLoad trigger fires whenever a new record is loaded, which always happens after a find. True, it happens when you switch records too, but File-Maker's smart enough to know it doesn't need to sort an already sorted list, so this doesn't cause an appreciable slowdown.

On the Customers layout, switch to Layout mode, and then choose View → Layout Setup. On the Script Triggers tab, turn on the OnRecordLoad trigger and point it to your sort script. This time, turn the trigger on for both Browse and Preview modes (Figure 14-13). Now whenever you visit the Customers layout, you find your data pre-sorted. If you sort manually, then your new sort order sticks until you leave the layout and come back, or sort manually again.

Figure 14-13:
This trigger configuration causes the Customers records to pre-sort (by running the Sort Customers script) whenever you visit the layout.

Working with Windows

Scripts give you complete control over the database windows on the screen. You can create new windows, close existing windows, bring any window to the front, and move or resize any window. (Why would a script need to monkey with someone's onscreen windows? See the box on page 567 for some ideas.)

Creating Windows

To make a new window on the screen, you use the New Window script step. With this step selected in your script, in ScriptMaker's Script Step Options area, you see a Specify button. Clicking this button brings up the "New Window" Options dialog box, pictured in Figure 14-14.

The first box—Window Name—gives your script control over the name of the window. (Window name is something you can control *only* from a script. When you create the window from the Window menu, FileMaker assigns it a name for you.) You can also tell FileMaker how big the window should be (Height and Width), and where to put the window on the screen ("Distance from top" and "Distance from left").

Here are some tips on using the "New Window" Options dialog box:

- If you leave any of the values blank, FileMaker uses the same value from the *current* window (it adds a number to the end of the window name so the new name is different). For example, if the current window is called "My Database" and you run the New Window script step without specifying a name, then the new window's name is "My Database – 2."

Figure 14-14:
The "New Window" Options dialog box lets your script open and close windows, and move them around the screen. You can use it to make annoying coworkers think they have poltergeists in their PCs, or just make windows behave properly when your scripts run. See the box on page 567 for advice.

- If you also don't specify a size and position, FileMaker puts it right over the top of the current window (with the same size and position).

Tip: To avoid confusing people, it's usually best to offset the new window at least a little so they can see new windows on top of their old ones.

- You can set each value directly by typing in the box in the New Window Options dialog box, or set them from a calculation by clicking the Specify button by any box. See the box on page 567 for more detail.

Bringing a Window to the Front

In ScriptMaker parlance, you bring a window to the front by *selecting* it. As such, you use the Select Window script step. It has one option, which lets you specify a window by name, or select the current window, as shown in Figure 14-15. You also use the Select Window script step to show a hidden window and bring it to the front.

Figure 14-15:
This window appears when you click the Specify button with a Select Window script step selected. From here, you can specify the Current Window, or choose Window Name, and then put the name of the window you want in the box. As usual, you can use a calculation to determine the window name as well.

Note: Usually, the current window is already in the front, and you don't have to worry about this step. But when you run scripts that involve more than one database, as you'll learn in Chapter 15, you may need this step to bring forward the current window from *another file*.

Closing a Window

The Close Window script step has the same options as Select Window. You tell FileMaker which window to close: the current window, or one you specify by name.

Moving and Resizing Existing Windows

FileMaker has three ways to move and resize a window. You can opt for one of its canned window maneuvers, or you can set the exact pixel size and location of the window just like you can with the New Window step. You can also *hide* the current window.

Adjust Window

The Adjust Window script step always operates on the current window, and it gives you just five simple choices:

- Choose **Resize to Fit**, and FileMaker makes the window exactly the right size to fit its contents.

- Choose **Maximize** to make the window as large as possible.

- Choose **Minimize** to shrink the window to a little bar (Windows) or a Dock icon (Mac OS X).

- Choose **Restore** to switch the window back to the *last* size it was, just before it was most recently resized.

- Choose **Hide** to hide the window (just like the Window → Hide Window command).

Note: The Maximize options have slightly different behavior on Mac OS X and Windows. For example, when you maximize a window in Windows, and then select a different window, the second window also gets maximized. On Mac OS X, the second window keeps its original size. Also, a maximized window on Mac OS X fills as much of the screen as possible. On Windows, it fills FileMaker's outer application window, whatever size it may be, and you can't adjust the application window from a script.

Arrange All Windows

The Arrange All Windows script step is the equivalent of the four window arrangement options in the Window menu. You can tile windows horizontally or vertically, or cascade them (see page 41). On Mac OS X, you can also bring all FileMaker windows to the front.

Window Size and Position Calculations

The fact that you can set a new window's size and position using a calculation may seem a little strange. After all, do you really need a bigger window for someone named Bill? Do you want your windows in a different place on Thursdays?

In fact, though, you can do a lot of interesting things with window size and position calculations. FileMaker provides a handful of functions that let you find out about the size and position of the current window, and of the computer screen, and use that information in calculations:

- The *Get (WindowHeight)* function, for instance, returns the height of the current window, in screen pixels (the little dots on your screen). Its brother, *Get (WindowContentHeight)* returns the height of just the window's content area; that is, the area inside the title bar, scroll bars, and Status toolbar. The *Get (WindowHeight)* and *Get (WindowContentHeight)* functions are similar.

- *Get (WindowTop)* and *Get (WindowLeft)* functions tell you where the window is on the screen. The first returns the distance from the top of the window to the top of the screen. The second tells you the distance from the window's left edge to the screen's left side. Both distances are measured in pixels.

- The *Get (WindowDesktopHeight)* and *Get (WindowDesktopWidth)* functions tell you how much desktop space you have. On Windows, it's the area of FileMaker's main application window. On Mac OS X, it's the size of the desktop.

- Finally, *Get (ScreenHeight)* and *Get (ScreenWidth)* tell you how big the screen is. (If you have more than one screen, then they tell you about the screen the current window is on.)

By combining these functions in creative ways, you can make your scripts smart about how they size and position windows. For example, to make the new window appear slightly offset from the current window, use these settings:

- Distance from top: *Get (WindowTop) + 20*

- Distance from left: *Get (WindowLeft) + 20*

If you're paranoid, and you want to make sure the new window never hangs off the bottom of the screen, use this calculation for the "Distance from top" value:

```
Let (
    [Limit = Get(WindowDesktopHeight) -
Get(WindowHeight);
    Offset = Get(WindowTop) + 20;
    Best = Min(Limit; Offset)];

    Best
)
```

Similarly, you can use the "Distance from left" value to make sure it doesn't hang off the screen's right edge. Just substitute WindowDesktopWidth, WindowWidth, and WindowLeft for WindowDesktopHeight, WindowHeight, and WindowTop.

Move/Resize Window

For the ultimate in window control, call upon the Move/Resize Window script step. It can move and/or resize any window with pixel-perfect precision. Its Specify button shows the dialog box in Figure 14-16, where you can choose the window's size and position. As with New Window, you can leave any of the size or position values empty. When you do, FileMaker leaves that part of the window's size or position alone. For example, if you specify a new value for Width but leave Height blank, FileMaker makes the window wider or narrower, but its height doesn't change.

Note: Move/Resize Window also selects the window it acts on, which always brings the window to the front, and, if it's a hidden window, shows it.

Other Window-Related Script Steps

FileMaker has a handful of other window-related script steps, listed below. These steps come in handy if you need to exert more control over what people see (not to imply that you're a control freak or anything).

- **Freeze Window** tells FileMaker to stop showing changes in the window while the script runs. For example, if your script is looping through all the records in the found set, then you normally see each record on the screen as it runs. If you add a Freeze Window script step before the loop, then people see only the first record while it runs. When the script is finished, FileMaker updates the window again. Looping scripts that have to visit lots of records run decidedly faster when the window's frozen.

Figure 14-16:
The Move/Resize Window settings look like a combination of the Select Window settings and the New Window settings. First, you pick which window you want to work on (Current Window, or a window selected by name). You then specify the new size and position for the window.

- **Refresh Window** forces FileMaker to update what's inside the window when it normally wouldn't. This action can be because you previously ran the Freeze Window step, or because FileMaker's simply being conservative. If you want to make sure someone sees a particular record or field value on the screen while a script is running, then add a Refresh Window step after making the change.

- **Scroll Window** lets you simulate a vertical scroll bar click in a window. You can scroll to the Home (top) or End of a window, or move up or down one screenful. You also get a To Selection option, which scrolls the window so that the selected record and field value both show. You'll design most of your windows so that scrolling isn't necessary, which means you may never need this step.

- **Show/Hide Status toolbar** lets you decide if people should see the Status toolbar. You can explicitly show or hide the Status toolbar, or ask that it be *toggled* (shown if it's hidden, and hidden if it's showing). You can also turn on the Lock option to prevent people from manually changing the Status toolbar. For example, if you never want anyone to see the Status toolbar at all, then hide and lock it in the script that runs when your database opens. Then the Status toolbar is locked, and its toggle icon and menu command are grayed out. More commonly, though, the Status toolbar's turned off and locked during a process, such as a scripted find. You don't want people using the Cancel button during a Pause step to cancel a script, and then end up dumped on a layout that you meant them to see only while a script is running. If you hide the Status toolbar, though, then you should provide a button that cancels the process, in case people change their minds. That way, they don't have to go all the way through a process if they get an urgent phone call and need to do something different from the script's agenda.

- **Show/Hide Text Ruler** can toggle, show, or hide, the Text Ruler. Unlike Show/Hide Status Toolbar, this step doesn't have a Lock option. Someone can always override your setting, so this step is rarely worth the trouble.

- **Set Window Title** lets you change any window's name. You can specify the current window, or any window name, as well as the window's new name. FileMaker normally names a window with the file's name, but you can tailor each window to a person. Write a script that runs when the file is opened, and use the Set Window Title script step with this calculation: *Get (FileName) & " " & Get (AccountName)*. See page 649 to learn about Account Names.

- **Set Zoom Level** sets the window zoom level, just like the zoom controls in the window's bottom-left corner. You can pick a specific zoom level, or choose to zoom in or out to the next level. Again, you get a Lock option. If you set the zoom level and turn on the Lock checkbox, then people can't manually change the zoom level.

- **View** As is in the Windows section of the script step list, but it isn't really a window-related step. It changes the view option for the current *layout*. You can pick Form view, List view, or Table view. You also get a choice called Cycle that tells FileMaker to switch to the *next* view setting in the list. If you really want to control how people see your database, use Layout → Layout Setting (View Tab) to turn off the views you don't want them seeing. You can then let folks override those settings with this script step.

Working with Files

In the Script Step list, the Files section contains some of the *least often used* script steps in all of FileMaker. But if you work in a school, say, the day may come when you need to automate the process of formatting files or saving backup copies for every student in a class. You can also script the process of converting older databases to FileMaker .fp7 format and recovering damaged databases, but these processes are sensitive, and usually better handled manually.

Controlling the Interface

If you want to pull out all the stops, you can use a combination of layouts, custom menus (page 753), tooltips (page 752), and scripting to almost completely take over control of your database. You can hide and lock the Status toolbar, and then give people buttons to go to the next, previous, first, and last records. You can make it so that when you click a customer on the list layout, a new detail window pops up named after that particular customer. You can even make your script so smart that it selects an existing detail window for the customer if one exists, and makes a new one otherwise.

In this way, you give people the impression that each customer has his own window, and you make comparing customers side by side a breeze.

This kind of high-level window management takes a fair amount of work, so most people stick with the normal every-layout-in-one-window approach and let people create windows as needed. Your approach depends entirely on how much time you want to spend writing scripts and how important the multiple-window interface is to you.

Opening and Closing Files

The Open File script step lets you open another FileMaker file. You can pick any of your existing file references (see page 376) or create a new file reference if necessary. When the step runs, the specified file opens and appears in a new window. If the file has a script set to run when it opens, it runs.

If you want the file to open, but you don't want to see a window on the screen, then turn on the "Open hidden" option for this step. The file opens, but it's listed in the Window menu's Show Window submenu, with its name in parentheses.

The Close File script step closes any open file. When you add the step, you get to pick any file reference or add a new one. You can also choose Current File to close the file the script is in. If the file is open when the script runs, then all its windows close, and its closing script runs.

Note: In general, FileMaker is very smart about when to open and close files. It opens a file when it needs to and closes it again when it no longer needs it. You usually don't need to open and close files from a script, but there's one important exception: when the file has an opening script that should run before someone can see the file. If you jump directly to a related record in another file, then FileMaker bypasses the opening script, so use an Open File script step to ensure that the open script runs.

Save a Copy As

If you need to make a copy of an open database, use the "Save a Copy As" script step. It works just like the File → "Save a Copy As" command. When you're working on a set of files and want to back them up without a lot of manual muss and fuss, just add a "Save a Copy As" script to each one. Then, from your main file, call that script in each file, and you've made a backup with one script.

Note: This script step (or menu command, for that matter) doesn't work on files shared using FileMaker Server. See page 724 to learn how to create automatic backups.

Other File-Related Script Steps

The rest of the file-related script steps are almost never used, but that doesn't mean *you* won't find a good reason to use them.

- **Convert File** lets you convert an older FileMaker database to a FileMaker 7 database. Since this process requires so much preparation and manual checking, you have very little reason to do this from a script.

- **Set User System Formats** toggles the Use System Formats file option on or off. When you first create a database, FileMaker remembers how your system expects dates, times, and numbers to be formatted. If someone opens the file on a computer with different settings (usually a different language), then File-Maker has to decide if it should use the original format settings for the file, or those specified by the new system. You usually set this choice in the Edit → File Options window.

- **Recover File** runs FileMaker's automatic file repair process on a selected database. Recovering a file is a rare thing in general since FileMaker is careful to avoid damaging databases even when your computer crashes. It's even more rare, and even inadvisable, to do this on the same database so often you'd need a script to do it for you.

Printing

Printing typically involves two specific commands on Windows or Mac OS X: File → Print Setup or File → Page Setup and File → Print. ScriptMaker sees it this way, too.

You use the Print Setup script step to set the options in the Print Setup or Page Setup dialog box. Turn on "Specify print setup" or "Specify page setup" to see the standard dialog box. You can pick the option you want to associate with the script step. When the script runs, FileMaker restores these same options. You can also turn on a "Perform without dialog" checkbox. When this option is off, a person sees—and gets a chance to configure—the dialog box when the script runs. If you just want to set the options without user intervention, turn on "Perform without dialog".

The Print script step works very similarly. You can specify which printer to use, the number of pages, and so forth or let people make the choice. Either way, when the step runs, FileMaker prints. Remember, though, you get to control which records are printed. In the Print dialog box, if you select "Records being browsed", "Current record", or "Blank record, showing fields", FileMaker remembers this setting along with all the other options. So be sure you make the right choice for people.

Note: Many of the options you can set in the Print dialog box are specific to a particular printer model. For example, some printers let you pick color or black-and-white printing or have settings for different kinds of paper. If someone uses your database and script on a different printer, then these options don't work.

Other Script Steps

You've now seen most of the often-used script steps (and a few of the not-so-often used ones). You'll see even more as they come up in the next few chapters. The rest of this chapter covers a few oddball steps that don't seem to fit in anywhere.

Open URL

You first saw the Open URL script step as a button command when learning about text calculations. When FileMaker runs this step, it asks your computer's operating system to open the URL you specify. Most often the URL is a Web address (HTTP), but it can be any URL type your computer supports, including FTP, MAILTO, SSH, and even FMP7 (to open a file on a network server). As usual, you can specify the URL or let someone else do it, and you can use a calculation if needed.

Dial Phone

The Dial Phone script step tells your modem to dial the telephone using a phone number you provide. You can use a calculation to specify the phone number, or enter it directly.

Note: This script step doesn't exist on Mac OS X.

Set Web Viewer

Web viewers are pretty cool on their own, but the Set Web Viewer script step (Figure 14-17) can make your FileMaker layouts look even more like a Web browser. With this flexible script step, you can make a series of buttons:

- **Reset** sets the Web viewer back to the Web address that's specified in its Web Viewer Setup dialog box.

- **Reload** gets you a fresh copy of the Web page you're currently viewing.

- **Go Forward** lets you move forward through your Web page history.

- **Go Back** lets you move backwards through the Web pages you've been browsing.

- **Go to URL...** lets you specify any new Web address via the Specify Calculation dialog box.

But to use this script step, you have to refer to your Web viewer by name. Check out the screencast at *http://missingmanuals.com* for a refresher on naming layout objects using the Info palette. One cool thing about referring to a Web viewer by name is that you can display more than one Web viewer on a layout and choose which one your scripts affect.

Figure 14-17:
This Set Web Viewer dialog box is set to work on a Web viewer with the prosaic name of "viewer." When you select the "Go to URL…" option, you see the same Set Web Viewer dialog box that comes free with every Web viewer.

Execute SQL

If you need to manipulate data in an ODBC data source, like Oracle, SQL, or MySQL, then this script step is at your service (Figure 14-18). Unlike many other script steps, this one requires some prior setup. You'll need an OBDC driver installed on any computer that runs an Execute SQL script. Each driver is a bit different, so use the drivers' documentation for installation and setting up data sources. Finally, if you don't write SQL queries, then you need help from someone who does, to make sure you get to the data you want. See page 666 to learn how you can use SQL data almost as easily as native FileMaker data.

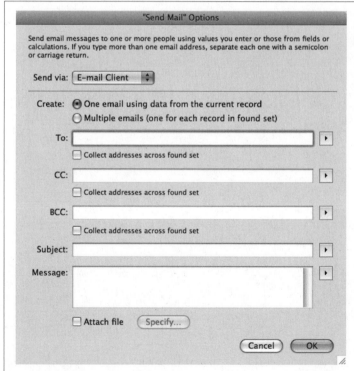

Figure 14-18:
This picture shows the Specify SQL dialog box in its unvarnished state. Once you prepare your computer, and select an ODBC Data Source, the source name shows up beside the top Specify button. Then, you can use the Calculations dialog box to assemble a query, or just type directly in the SQL text field.

Flush Cache to Disk

Any time changes are made to a record, FileMaker records those changes in your computer's memory first, and writes the change to the hard drive later—when it gets some free time. If you want to *force* the changes to be written to disk immediately, then you can run the "Flush Cache to Disk" script step. For instance, you might add this script step after a script that creates a new customer order. That way, if your computer crashes while you're busily taking orders, then you lose only the last order you were working on.

Exit Application

Last but not least, you can have a script exit or quit the FileMaker application on your behalf. Of course, this causes every open window and file to be closed as well. People usually use this when they have just one database, and they never use File-Maker unless they're in that database. They add the Exit Application step to the very end of their database's closing script so that when they close the last database window, FileMaker goes away, too. (Of course *you* find FileMaker so useful you *never* want to close it, right?)

Advanced Scripting

Being familiar with FileMaker's lengthy list of script steps, which you saw in the previous chapters, is a great foundation, but putting together a workable script takes practice. Although some scripts are simple five-line affairs, sometimes a script requires a lot of forethought, planning, and organization. FileMaker gives you tools to help you write scripts and troubleshoot them when they aren't working. Plus, you can organize and document your work as you go. In this chapter you'll pull these concepts together to learn how to write and manage complex scripts.

Commenting Scripts

When you look at a script someone else created—or you created a long time ago—you can't always tell what the script does. To help keep things clear, add comments to your script. You add each comment using a Comment script step. This step has just one option: the text of the comment itself. The Comment step is special for two reasons. First, it doesn't *do* anything. Second, it appears in bold when you view your script in the Edit Script window. You can see a commented script in Figure 15-1.

Use comments to document anything important about the script. Here are some things you may want to include in a comment or set of comments:

- What the script does and why to use it

- Who wrote the script

- The date the script was written

- The date, if any, the script was last edited

- Who edited the script

- Anything special about how or when the script should be run, like whether only some database users can run it, or if the script requires parameters to do its work (see page 586).

Documenting scripts is standard operating procedure among programmers for a couple reasons. First, if something's wrong with the script, or it needs to be changed, you've got extra information that could help. You know exactly what the script should do, plus you have a list of people who've worked on it and can give you background or pointers. Second, the date can help identify whether a particular business rule was in effect that made certain parts of a script necessary. If you see that script is really old, you may decide to rewrite it with some of FileMaker's newer features. Comments don't take up much space or slow down your scripts, so commenting scripts as you create them saves you time later.

Figure 15-1:
Here's the Send Email script you worked with in Chapter 14, with comments added. The first comment lets you know what the script is supposed to do. The second and third comments tell you who created the script, and when. The fourth comment is blank and serves just to make a little space. The two comments inside the script explain what the script does at critical junctures. Comment lines appear in bold and with a # symbol in front.

Note: There's another way you can indicate what your scripts are doing: Put comments in any embedded calculations. When a script has an *If( )* statement that uses a complex calculation for its condition, you can put comments in the calculation itself (page 575).

Communicating with Database Users

Sometimes a script needs to tell people something—"There are no records to include in this report"—or ask a question—"How many copies of the report do you want?" The Show Custom Dialog script step lets you write a message and display it in a dialog box. Calling it a "Custom" dialog box may be a bit too generous—you don't have much say in how it looks—but you can at least give information to people using your database, and ask them simple questions.

When you add the Show Custom Dialog step to your script and click its Specify button, you see the window shown in Figure 15-2. The Show Custom Dialog script step has three basic purposes. First, it can display a simple message. In a script that finds all overdue invoices, for example, you can have a message that says, "No invoices are overdue" if FileMaker finds nothing.

Figure 15-2:
The Show Custom Dialog Options window has two tabs. Here you see what's under the General tab: Title, Message, and the buttons. In its most basic form, a custom dialog box shows a message with one, two, or three buttons. Figure 15-3 shows the dialog box that results from these settings.

Second, you can create a dialog box that asks a simple question. Say you have a script that posts a customer payment. Before launching into the process, your custom dialog box can ask, "Are you sure you want to post a payment?," and include Post Payment and Cancel buttons for feedback. Finally, you can use this script step when you need to ask for some information, not just click a button. For example, a script that runs a sales report might start by asking what date range to report on. Here's how to create all three types.

Showing a Simple Message

In its simplest form, the Show Custom Dialog script step just delivers a message to whoever's using the database. Figure 15-2 shows how to configure a box like this. You can see the final result in Figure 15-3.

Figure 15-3:
A custom dialog box, like this one, has a title, a message, and a single button—exactly what you need to get a message across to folks using your database. The title appears along the top of the dialog box, the message in the middle, and the button at the bottom. The first button (called Default Button in the Show Custom Dialog Options window) is the one that people can "click" by pressing Enter or Return—or, if they insist, by clicking with the mouse.

You can generate the title and message from a calculation to make it more dynamic. For instance, if someone wants to see all open invoices for a particular client, but there aren't any, you can show a calculated custom message that says, "Nathan Petrelli's account is paid in full," instead of something equally true but less helpful, like "No records were found."

To use a custom dialog box like this in a script, simply place the Show Custom Dialog step wherever you want in your script. When the dialog box pops up, your script waits for someone to click the button, and then continues with the next step.

Asking a Simple Question

To ask a simple question (with either two or three possible responses), just add more buttons to the dialog box by filling in the Button 2 and Button 3 boxes in the Show Custom Dialog Options window. You can see this process in action in Figure 15-4.

When a dialog box like this appears, your script waits for a click of one of its buttons, and then continues. Although FileMaker knows whether button 1, 2, or 3 got clicked, you have to add logic to your script to tell the program what to *do* in each case. For that, you use the *Get (LastMessageChoice)* function and If statements based on its results. (The function returns *1* for the default button, 2 for Button 2, and 3 for Button 3.) The script in Figure 15-5 uses *Get (LastMessageChoice)* to take action only if someone clicks the Post button in the custom dialog box. Nothing happens if she clicks the Default button, or hits Enter.

Note: To make the script shown in Figure 15-5 carry extra weight, you can put the invoice's balance due amount in your new payment record. There are a few ways to move data between tables, and you'll learn about them later in this chapter.

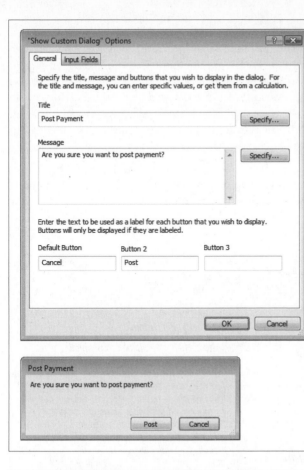

Figure 15-4:

Top: This custom dialog box asks a question and offers two choices—Cancel and Post.

Bottom: Notice that Cancel is automatically highlighted (bottom), which acts as a safety device, since people often reflexively hit the Return or Enter key when they see a dialog box. By making Cancel the default button in this way, you can prevent potentially destructive processes when people fail to read instructions.

Figure 15-5:

This script asks a question, then an If statement with a Get (LastMessageChoice) function decides what to do. If someone clicks Post, then function result is 2, and the script goes to the Payment layout and creates a new record. If he clicks the Default button, or hits Enter, nothing happens.

Asking a More Complex Question

If you need user input that goes beyond two or three simple choices, you can venture into the second tab—Input Fields—in the Show Custom Dialog script step (Figure 15-6). The Show Custom Dialog Options window's Input Fields tab lets you add fields to your custom dialog box. To add a field to a custom dialog box, in the Input Fields tab, turn on one of the "Show input field" checkboxes. When you do, FileMaker shows a Specify Field dialog box, in which you can pick the field to use. (If you want to change the field later, click the Specify button.)

You can also give the field a label, like "Start Date" and "End Date" in Figure 15-6 (top). A label can be the result of a calculation. Finally, if you turn on "Use password character" for an input field, the field works like a typical Password box: It shows * or • instead of the letters you type, so someone watching over your shoulder can't see what you're entering.

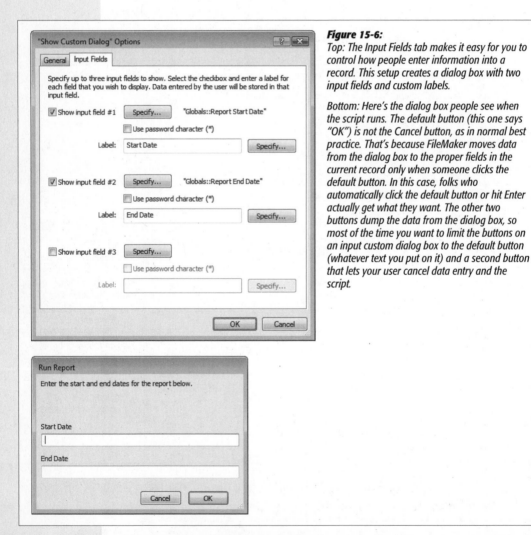

Figure 15-6:
Top: The Input Fields tab makes it easy for you to control how people enter information into a record. This setup creates a dialog box with two input fields and custom labels.

Bottom: Here's the dialog box people see when the script runs. The default button (this one says "OK") is not the Cancel button, as in normal best practice. That's because FileMaker moves data from the dialog box to the proper fields in the current record only when someone clicks the default button. In this case, folks who automatically click the default button or hit Enter actually get what they want. The other two buttons dump the data from the dialog box, so most of the time you want to limit the buttons on an input custom dialog box to the default button (whatever text you put on it) and a second button that lets your user cancel data entry and the script.

The fields you add to a custom dialog box have some limitations, including the ones listed below. (For other alternatives, see the box on page 581.)

- As far as data entry goes, Show Custom Dialog can have only free-entry fields like those shown in Figure 15-6. You can't use radio buttons, checkboxes, or pop-up menus. You also have no control over the size of the field, so you can't specify, say, short fields for dates or tall fields for lots of text.

- "Data-entry only" validation doesn't apply to fields in custom dialog boxes. If you use a dialog box to gather data for a record, either use the Always option in the field validation, or check the validity of the data in your script (page 513).

- You must use the OK button as the default when you're using input fields in a custom dialog box or FileMaker won't enter the data into a record. Consequently, you have to trust people to read the dialog box before they type information into it.

WORKAROUND WORKSHOP

Truly Custom Dialog Boxes

If the window that the Show Custom Dialog script step creates (Figure 15-4) doesn't meet your needs, all is not lost. You have two options: For professional-level needs (resizable dialog boxes with text you can control with a calculation, progress bars, and multiple input fields), you can get a third-party plug-in made for the task. See page 487 for more information on how to use plug-ins and where to find them. But for light duty, you can get a similar effect by assembling your own dialog box from a window, a layout, and a script.

First, you need a layout that shows what you want. You can use text objects on the layout to show messages, field controls to gather input, and layout buttons. Once you've got the layout just the way you like it, you need a script to show it.

To get the effect of a typical dialog box, you must do a few things. First, you want the new layout to appear in its own window. It probably shouldn't have the status area showing. And while the window is up, your users shouldn't be able to switch to a different window. Here's how to do all these things in a script:

- Use the New Window script step to make a new window. Then use Show/Hide Status Area to hide and lock the status area, and Adjust Window with the 'Resize to Fit' option to make the new window just the right size.

- To keep the window frontmost, pause the script once the window is showing. When a script is paused, people can't switch windows. For added assurance, add the Allow User Abort script step with the Off option before you pause the script. This step prevents people from doing anything that would cancel the script.

- If someone presses Enter, FileMaker continues the script, so make one of the buttons look like a default button, and have the script take its action when it continues. To handle other buttons, you can have them set a variable (see page 591) and resume the script. The script can then check the variable when it continues to see what action it should take.

- After the pause script step, take any steps you need to deal with the user's input, and then close the window with the Close Window script step.

This layout-based approach has some drawbacks—most notably, it lacks the convenient default Cancel button of FileMaker's built-in custom dialog boxes. If you want this behavior in a layout-based box, you have to take special measures to avoid losing valuable information if someone clicks the wrong button. For instance, you could put entered data into global fields, and then move the entered data into the real fields only when the script continues.

Organizing Complex Scripts

Sometimes you need a script that does a lot. At the end of this chapter, you'll build a script that generates an invoice for a selected job. As you'll see, this process involves many steps across several tables. To do all this work in one long script can be cumbersome, especially when several levels of If and Loop steps get mixed up with each other.

In other situations, you may need two or more scripts that do similar things. In fact, sometimes, entire sections of two scripts are identical with only minor differences. You may have a script that finds unpaid invoices so it can print a statement, and another that finds unpaid invoices to send email payment reminders.

If you build these two scripts independently, you have two problems. First, you have to write all the "find the unpaid invoices" stuff twice, which is a waste of time. More importantly, next month when you realize you need to exclude voided invoices from the list, you have to make the change in *both* places. A database that's been growing for years can be a real bear to manage if the same general business logic is implemented over and over in dozens of different scripts.

You can make your work easier and less error-prone by dividing your scripts into smaller parts. That way, you can break up a complex script into simpler scripts that each do part of the job. Also, you can make one script that finds unpaid invoices and use it in another script that prints a statement and/or sends an email payment reminder. Writing scripts in small pieces that you can then reuse in other scripts is called *modular scripting*.

The Perform Script Script Step

The key to modular scripting is the Perform Script script step. It lets one script run another script—a *subscript*. When you add the Perform Script step to your script, you get only one option: a Specify button. Figure 15-7 shows how to use the Specify Script dialog box to tell your script which subscript you want to run and what file to find it in.

When one script runs another, it waits for the subscript to finish before continuing. Imagine you have a script called Find Unpaid Invoices, and you want to make a new script to print statements for all your customers. The Print Statements script might start off by performing the Find Unpaid Invoices script. Once that's done, the main script can sort and print the invoices.

When you perform a script from another file, FileMaker uses that file's frontmost window (which is behind the user's window). If it doesn't have any windows, FileMaker automatically creates one. In either case, you're in a unique scripting situation: The window you're working with in your script isn't the one in front. Here's where the Current Window option in the Select Window script step comes in handy.

Figure 15-7:
The Specify Script Options dialog box is where you tell the Perform Script step what script to run. You can pick any file you have a reference to from the File pop-up menu (or choose Add File Reference to add a reference to another file). The script list shows every script in the selected file, complete with its groups and separators. Just select the script you want and click OK. See page 586 for details on script parameters.

Halt Script and Exit Script

Normally a script ends when its last step runs. But you can force a script to end early if you want to. FileMaker actually has *two* script steps that end a script prematurely: Exit Script and Halt Script. These two steps do exactly the same thing if you run a script yourself directly. But if the current script was run by *another script*—via the Perform Script step—then they do different things. The Exit Script step tells FileMaker to stop the current script and continue the script that ran it. Halt Script, on the other hand, causes *all* script execution to stop immediately, no matter how the current script was started. (To learn more about these ominously powerful steps and when to use them, see page 586.)

Exit Script (Result)

Exit Script also has a powerful option that Halt Script doesn't have: a script result (see Figure 15-8). With a script result, you can tie all the power of the calculation dialog box to Exit Script. Then your main script can check the script result and decide how to proceed based on the results of the test. For example, you don't want to bother going through a sort and print process if your script doesn't find any invoices. An Exit Script step at the end of Find Unpaid Invoices will help the Print Invoices script figure out whether it should sort and print. Here's how to add an Exit Script step to an existing script:

1. **In the Manage Scripts window, double-click the Find Unpaid Invoices script.**

   The Edit Script window opens. The Exit Script step is always added to your subscript.

2. **Double-click the Exit Script step.**

The step is added to your list. If necessary, move it to the bottom of the list. (You don't want the script stopping before all the work is done.)

3. **Click the Specify button.**

The Specify Calculation dialog box appears.

4. **In the View pop-up list, choose the *Get (FoundCount)* function.**

The function appears in the calculation field, so the script will record the number of unpaid records it finds.

5. **Choose Scripts → Save Script.**

You want to keep your work, don't you?

Exit Script Result doesn't do much on its own. You also need to test those results in the main script. Use an If test, with a *Get (Script Result)* function to see if any records were found that should be sorted and printed. See Figure 15-8 for a script that calls Find Unpaid Invoices and then checks its results.

Figure 15-8:
The Print Unpaid Invoices script calls the subscript you to which you've just added an Exit Script step. Next, a couple of comments help you remember what's going on in the subscript, so you don't have to go over there to figure it out. Then, an If test checks the results of the subscript to see whether it should sort and print invoices. If no invoices need to be printed, a dialog box tells the user what's happening, (or in this case, what's not happening).

Organizing scripts that use Halt or Exit Script

The Halt Script and Exit Script steps are useful exit strategies when you want to abort a script's execution because some problem has come up. But more often than not, you're better off without them. Take, for example, the two scripts shown in Figure 15-9.

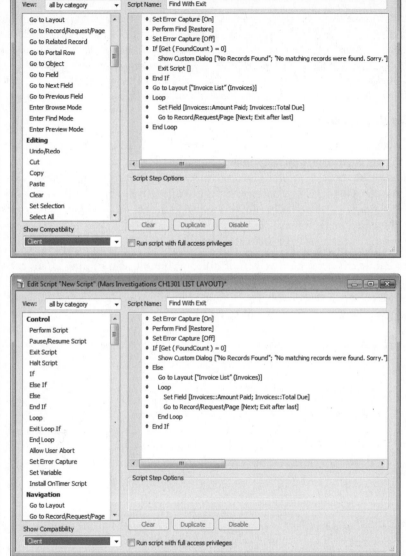

Figure 15-9:
Top: This script performs a find. Then, if it finds no records, it shows a custom dialog box and exits the script.

Bottom: This version does the same thing, but doesn't exit the script if no records are found. Instead, it puts all the remaining script steps in the Else section of the condition. The result is the same—the extra steps run only if the script finds some records—but the bottom script always ends after the last step. The top script, on the other hand, can end in two different places, depending on what it finds.

Suppose you revisit this process later and want to add some more steps to the end that should happen *last*, every time the script runs—not just when records are found. If your script looks like the one on top, you have a problem. You either have to add your new steps to the script *twice* (once before the Exit Script, and again at the end of the script), or reorganize the entire script to support the changes. But the script on the bottom is easy to fix: Just add the new steps to the end. In general, if a script ends in more than one place, it will come back to bite you later.

You're much better off organizing your script so it always reaches the same ending place.

Note: Halt Script has an even bigger downside. Since scripts can run other scripts, and most databases grow and change over time, you never know for sure if the script you're writing today is going to be run by another script some day in the future. It's rarely acceptable to run another script that could halt before reaching its normal end. It gives your new script no opportunity to recover if something goes wrong, so use Halt Script sparingly.

Script Parameters

When you call a script using the Perform Script step or attach the script to a button, the Specify Script window shows a box labeled "Optional script parameter." You can type a static value in the box, or you can click Edit to create a dynamic calculation that FileMaker evaluates when the script starts to run. FileMaker stores the value, and you can check it anywhere inside the script. You can then branch the script based on the value of the parameter.

As shown later in Figure 15-10, you might make a script that can sort the records in three different ways. That way, four different buttons can run the same script, with different results. The script parameter that's attached to each button tells the script which sort order to use. Then, your script uses the *Get (ScriptParameter)* function to check the value stored when the script is run.

Note: Script parameters don't automatically pass on to subscripts. If the subscript needs to know what's in your main script's parameters, luckily you don't have to resort to any funky workarounds. Just use *Get (ScriptParameter)* as the subscript's optional parameter.

Suppose you want buttons to sort your Customer records by Name, City and State, or Zip Code. By using script parameters, you can get the job done with just one script. Each button passes a different parameter to the script, which then takes the appropriate action. Before you can create the buttons, you need to create the script they'll run:

1. **Create a new script called Sort Customers.**

   This script will handle a few common sorts. (See page 494 for a refresher on creating scripts.)

2. **Add the If step to the script.**

   FileMaker adds two new lines—If and End If—to your script.

3. **Click the Specify button. From the View pop-up menu, choose "Get functions".**

   The function list now shows all the *Get( )* functions.

4. **Find *Get (Script Parameter)* in the list and add it to your calculation.**

   From the View menu, choose "Get functions", and then scroll through the alphabetical list. The *Get (ScriptParameter)* function returns the parameter value that was specified when this script was called. If the parameter was a calculation, it returns the *result* of the calculation, which is now in the calculation box.

5. **In the calculation box, after *Get (ScriptParameter)*, type = *"Name"*, and then click OK.**

   You're back in the Edit Script window, where the If step shows your calculation. Your calculation should look like this: *Get (ScriptParameter) = "Name"*. Its result is *true* if the parameter sent to this script is "Name", and *false* otherwise.

6. **Add the Sort Records script step to the script, and then turn on "Perform without dialog".**

   Insert it after the If step and before the End If step. (If yours is somewhere else, move it between these two steps.)

Note: FileMaker inserts new script steps just below any highlighted step. If no script step is highlighted, then the new script step lands at the end of your script.

---

7. **Turn on the "Specify sort order" checkbox, add the Last Name field, and then the First Name field to the Sort Order list. Then click OK.**

   You've written your first test. The rest of the script will be variations on this theme.

8. **Add the Else If script step to the script.**

   You want Else If to come after the Sort Records step and before the End If step. (If it doesn't land there, move it.)

9. **Click Specify. In the Specify Calculation box, type *Get (ScriptParameter) = "City and State"*, and then click OK.**

   You're setting up a new test, this time checking to see if "City and State" is the script parameter. If it is, then you want a Sort step following this parameter to sort by—you guessed it—city and state.

Note: Sometimes, it's quicker to copy one If test, and then paste and edit it in the Else If steps.

---

10. **Add another copy of the Sort Records script step to the script. Turn on "Perform without dialog." Set the sort order to State, then City, and then click OK.**

    Your second test, and what to do if that test is true, is now complete.

Note: Another shortcut is to select the Else If and its Sort, and then use the Duplicate button to make copies of both steps. Then, edit the Else If test and the Sort order.

11. **Add one more copy of the Else If script step, this time with *Get (ScriptParameter)* = "*Zip Code*" as the calculation.**

    If the first two tests fail, your script makes this third test.

12. **Add another Sort Record step, this time set to sort by the Zip Code field. Then click OK until you're back in the database.**

    Your finished script should look something like Figure 15-10.

Figure 15-10:
Your finished sort script should look like this example. It has three branches (one for each of the possible sort orders). Now you just need to add buttons on the Customer layout to run this script.

Note: When you're making a series of tests like the ones in this script, it's more efficient to put the condition that most often tests as true at the top. That way, the script doesn't have to test conditions that usually fail.

Now it's time to add buttons to the Customers layout to make it easy for people to run the script. You need three buttons, one for each sort in the script you just wrote.

1. **Add a new button to the Customers layout.**

    Use the Button tool (the one that looks like a finger pushing a button). FileMaker shows you the Specify Button dialog box.

2. **Choose the Perform Script button command, and then click Specify. In the "Specify Script" Options list, select Sort Customers.**

You created this script on page 586.

3. **In the "Optional script parameter" box, type *Name*, and then click OK until you're back on the Customers layout.**

The first test of the Sort Customers script (*Get (ScriptParameter) = "Name"*) is true when people run it by clicking this button. Back on the layout, your button awaits its new name.

Note: If you check the text in the Optional script parameter box, you see that FileMaker put double quotes around "Name" for you. That's because it considers "Name" a text constant. If you like to be thorough, you can type the quote marks yourself, or you can rest easy knowing FileMaker will do it for you.

---

4. **Name the button *Sort by Name*.**

You now have one button on your layout. Test it. It always sorts by name.

Time to work on the second button. To do so, you can save time by starting from a copy of the one you already have.

1. **Duplicate the Sort by Name button and double-click the new copy. In the dialog box's Options section, click the Specify button.**

The Specify Script Options window pops up.

2. **Change the "Optional script parameter" box so it contains City and State.**

Type carefully, since you're telling the script to exactly match what's in the Else If statement. Case doesn't matter, but spacing does. The second test of the Sort Customers script (*Get (ScriptParameter) = "City and State"*) is true when the users run it by clicking this button.

3. **Click OK until you're back on the Customers layout and can rename your button.**

Now you have two appropriately named buttons, and you can switch the sort order back and forth by clicking each button in turn.

To add the third button, follow steps 1 through 3 again. This time, set the parameter to "Zip Code," and name the button *Sort by Zip Code*.

Note: You don't have to write the script first, and then create your buttons. Lots of developers prefer to create buttons first, complete with the appropriate parameters, and then write scripts later. The order doesn't matter. Just make sure both tasks get done and that the parameters set on your buttons match up with the tests in the script.

These three buttons each call the same script, but the script parameters attached to each button allow the script to do double, even triple duty. To make this script even more flexible, you can keep adding Else If and Sort steps, and then make a button with a script parameter that matches each new test. See the box on page 592 for a way to use script parameters to extend the flexibility of the Add Note Separator script you wrote back on page 539.

See the box on page 592 ... back on page 539.

POWER USERS' CLINIC

Indirection

Script parameters let you more easily write multi-purpose scripts—scripts that you can use under many different circumstances. You can almost imagine you're writing your own script steps. You can call a script, and pass it a little parameter info whenever you need its behavior in whatever script you're writing.

In fact, this sort of scripting is exactly how expert FileMaker developers work. They're constantly augmenting FileMaker to make their everyday programming tasks easy and accurate.

When you're ready to take your FileMaker skills to the next level, you need to learn *indirection*—referring to things (generally fields) indirectly to make your scripts more reusable. For instance, a script that finds a record by ID might need to put the search value in a different field depending on what table it's searching. Or a script that time-stamps a record using a special formula may target a different field depending on the parameter passed to it.

So you can use indirection, FileMaker offers a special script step called Set Field by Name. To understand how it works, start by taking a look at the normal Set Field script step, which lets you specify a field to receive the result of a calculated value. For example, you might set the Zip Code field to a known value, for instance, or set the Balance Due field to the sum of costs minus the sum of payments.

By contrast, the Set Field by Name step lets you specify two calculations. The second determines the value to store, just like Set Field. But the first evaluates to the name of the field you want to set. In other words, if the result of the calculation is "Customers::First Name" then the step stores its value in the First Name field. Later, the formula might return "Customers::Last Name" instead, in which case it changes the *Last* Name field. If you put a field in this calculation, you don't set that field, you set the field name in that field. For example, you can use this formula:

```
Get(LayoutTableName) & "::First Name"
```

This formula makes the Set Field by Name step target the First Name field in the table associated with the current layout. So if you have a Customers table, and an Employees table, you can make this step work in both places.

You can also fetch a field value indirectly using the *GetField( )* function:

```
GetField ( Get(LayoutTableName) & "::First
Name" )
```

This formula gets the value from a field whose name is passed to it.

Finally, the *GetFieldName( )* function helps you get at field names reliably. For instance, suppose you have a script that finds records with today's date in any field you specify. You can pass the field name in the script parameter, and then use **Set Field by Name** to put today's date into the specified field.

But this approach is inherently unsafe. Since you're passing the field name around in a calculation text value, FileMaker doesn't see it as a proper field reference. Later, if you rename a field, your scripts may not work because you're passing the old field name. To solve this problem, use *GetFieldName( )*:

```
GetFieldName(Invoices::Modification
Timestamp)
```

This formula returns the text value "Invoices::Modification Timestamp," which may seem pointless. But since the field name isn't in quotes, if you ever rename the field, FileMaker corrects the formula for you, and your script keeps working properly. If you ever want to pass the name of a field as a script parameter (or otherwise refer to a field's name directly in a calculation), use *GetFieldName( )* to protect against name changes.

Script Variables

Global fields are great for storing a value that's not tied to a specific record in a table. Script variables are similar; use them when you need to store a value for your script to use, usually when you're testing a condition. But variables are better than globals in one important way: You don't have to add a field to a table to use them. Instead, variables are created as a script is running, and can vanish again when the script is finished, leaving no impact on your data's structure. (See page 473 for a refresher on using calculations to create variables.) Figure 15-11 shows you how to create a variable.

POWER USERS' CLINIC

Passing Multiple Parameters

A script can have only one parameter, and its result type is always text. But the parameter itself can be multiple values, if you're willing to use your calculation skills. To pass multiple parameters, string your values together with a separator character, and then pull them apart again in the script.

For example, if you want a script to have a pair of static values, you could type this text as the script parameter:

```
Molly¶Walker
```

Since the separator is the "¶", each value is on its own "line," and that makes it easy to grab the bits you need using the *GetValue( )* function. A calculation to pull "Molly" out from the script parameter would look like this:

```
GetValue ( Get ( ScriptParameter ) ; 1 )
```

Here's how to assemble a set of dynamic values into one script parameter:

```
Customer::First Name & "¶" & Customer::
LastName & "¶" & Customer::Phone & "¶" &
Customer::Email
```

The *GetValue( )* function above can pull apart the pieces of your multivalue parameter.

Figure 15-11:
*The "Set Variable" Options dialog box is full of useful information. First you create a variable by giving it a name. Since you can use variables inside calculations, their naming rules are similar to those of field names. Basically, you don't want to use any characters like a comma, +, -, *, or any other symbol that has a mathematical meaning and confuses the calculation that uses your variable. See page 596 for a tutorial using a variable.*

The Set Script Variable script step has three options:

- **Name.** Choose a short, descriptive name. All script variable names require a $ prefix. If you forget to type the prefix, ScriptMaker adds it for you. But get in the habit of typing the prefix, since it determines how long the value in the variable is available. A single $ means the variable is local and lasts only while your script is running. If you set a local variable, and then perform a subscript, the local variable isn't sent to that subscript. But if you need a global variable (the value persists through subscripts and even after all scripts have finished running), prefix the variable's name with $$. Global variables are cleared when you close the file.

- **Value.** The value you want to store in the variable. Values can be static text or the dynamic result of a calculation.

- **Repetition.** Repetitions are optional. You can make a variable store multiple values, similar to the way a repeating field stores multiple values. Most of the time, though, you don't set a repetition.

Since you can pass the value in a local variable with either a script result or a script parameter, there is rarely a reason to use a global variable. Programmers consider global variables sloppy housekeeping, because once the script finishes running, variables just lay around your database full of values that don't have meaning outside a script.

Warning: Global variables are potential security risks, since the Data Viewer (page 743) in FileMaker Pro Advanced will reveal their values to anybody who knows their names and has enough privileges to run scripts. If security is a big consideration at your business, make sure you don't leave sensitive data laying around in global variables by resetting their values to "0" or "" when the script is done. In practice, though, it's usually a lot easier, and cleaner, to use only local variables and rest assured that FileMaker is cleaning up after you.

UP TO SPEED

Note Separators Revisited

In the previous chapter, you learned how to make the Add Note Separator script work with any field (see page 544). The only drawback is that you have to click the field you want to work with before running the script. With script parameters, though, you can easily fix this problem. Just add a series of If and Else If script steps to the top of the script. Each one checks for one of the Notes field types (Invoice, Job, Customer, and so on) in the script parameter.

For instance, if the script parameter is "Invoice," then the script should use the "Go to Field" script step to go to the Invoices::Notes field first.

With these conditions in place, you just need to pass the right parameter from your Add Notes button. Just add tests to check the script parameter, and then use an appropriate "Go to Field" script step, depending on which button the user clicks. Use the script you wrote back on page 586 to see how to do this kind of branching.

Now if you want to add a new Notes field, you just need to add an Else If and a "Go to Field" step to this script. If you want to change the way the note separators look, you can change it in one place and the change applies to every Notes field in the database.

Handling Errors

As discussed on page 504, when an error occurs during a script (a Perform Find finds no records, for instance), FileMaker shows an error message almost like the one it would if you were doing the steps manually. The one difference is a button called Continue, as Figure 15-12 explains.

If someone clicks a Cancel button in an error message, the script stops immediately, and leaves him wherever the script was when it stopped. If he clicks Continue instead, FileMaker ignores the error and moves on with the script. In the Perform Find example, for instance, the script continues with no records in the found set. Some errors (like the one in Figure 15-12) gives this user a third choice. If he clicks Modify Find, for instance, FileMaker takes him to Find mode on the current layout and pauses the script.

Figure 15-12:
Here's the warning you see if FileMaker can't find records that match your request if you search within a script. When an error occurs during a script, FileMaker gives the user all the normal choices he'd usually see in a warning dialog box, plus the option to ignore the error and continue the script. In this case, the Continue button is added to the normal mix.

Sometimes this error-handling approach is just fine. If the script is simple and everyone using it knows a little about FileMaker, it isn't too big a problem. But often, you need more control:

- If your system is complex—or your database's users inexperienced with File-Maker—all sorts of confusion can result. First, the error message may make absolutely no sense to the person reading it. The message complains, for instance, about not finding any records. But the person reading it thinks, "I just wanted to create a new invoice for this job. Who said anything about finding records?" Even worse, if she clicks Cancel, she could wind up just about anywhere: some layout in some window on some record. It could be a layout (like the Line Items layout) that she's never even seen before.

- If an error happens in the middle of a larger multistep process, it might be really important that the script know about it and deal with it appropriately. But it's the *user*, not the *script*, that decides whether to continue or cancel. You may want to make sure the script *always* continues, so it can get on with important work.

Luckily, you can opt for more control over error handling if you want it. File-Maker gives you three functions for finding and dealing with errors that may occur when scripts run.

The Set Error Capture Script Step

The Set Error Capture script step lets you turn on *error capture*. That way, instead of displaying potentially confusing error messages to your database's users, File-Maker keeps track of error information (*captures* it) so you can pull it into your script and handle it there. Although error capturing is a great feature, it's not part of FileMaker's normal behavior. You have to activate it by adding the Set Error Capture step to your script, and choosing the On option. At any time in the script, you can turn it back off again by using the step a second time and switching the option off.

If a script turns error capture on, and then uses the Perform Script step to run another script, the second script also runs with error capture on. In other words, the error capture setting sticks around as long as scripts call other scripts. But as soon as script execution stops for good, FileMaker turns off error capture. Understanding this behavior helps you determine when you need an error capture script step and when it would just be redundant. Figure 15-13 shows a script that turns on error capture before performing a find, then turns it back off when it's done.

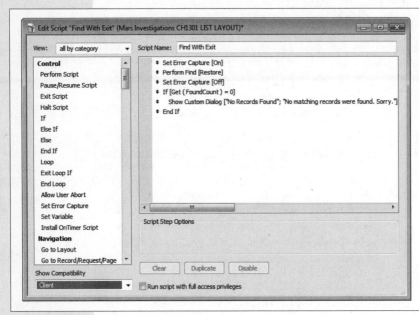

Figure 15-13:
This script turns error capture on, and then performs a find. That way, if the find fails, the script doesn't produce an error message. Instead, the script checks for no found records (in the If step), and displays a more helpful, customized error message.

As discussed in the box on page 595, you can just turn error capture on so that your script ignores any and all errors—but that's not good script writing. The best way to use Set Error Capture is hand-in-hand with the *Get (LastError)* function, described next, to achieve error-free results.

The *Get (LastError)* Function

When error capture is on, FileMaker doesn't just *ignore* the errors. Rather, it remembers which error occurred and gives you the chance to ask about it if you're interested. The script in Figure 15-13, for example, *isn't* interested. It doesn't ask if an error occurred at all. Instead, it just checks to see if the find worked by counting the records in the found set.

But sometimes you can use such error information within your script, much like any other value, to trigger other script steps. To check an error, use the *Get (LastError)* function to find out what happened. This function returns an *error code*, which is always a number. If there was no error in the previous step, *Get (LastError)* returns a zero. In other words, it doesn't return the number of the last error that

WORD TO THE WISE

Keep It Off

Using Set Error Capture to eliminate those pesky dialog boxes sounds so cool, you may be tempted to turn it on at the start of every script. You can't anticipate every error, but at least you can keep FileMaker from casting doubt on your database skills by throwing error messages in people's faces. But if all your script does is turn on error capture, and then never checks to see which errors are happening, you're not doing your database's users—or yourself—any favors.

If odd error messages pop up, people may let you know about it (perhaps via cell phone while you're trying to relax on the beach), giving you a chance to figure out the problem and improve your script. With error capture turned on, a script might seem to be working because no warning dialog box shows up, but really, something's gone kablooie and

occurred. Instead, it returns the error number for the last step that ran. You wouldn't, therefore, put a *comment* step before the step that checks the last error, since the comment step itself always sets the last error back to zero. The same goes for End If and even Set Error Capture [Off].

In FileMaker, just about everything that could possibly go wrong has its own error number. This feature gives you a lot of flexibility, but it also makes it a real pain to figure out which errors you should check for. A complete list of error numbers is found in Appendix B. Luckily, most of these errors are pretty obscure, and chances are you'll never have to worry about them. Here's a list of the more common error numbers you may actually be interested in:

error capture suppresses the dialog box that would have explained what happened.

You have little hope of figuring out what went wrong—especially if no one realizes there's been a problem until long after the script has run.

Usually, you find errors when you're developing your scripts, and you can use a custom dialog box (page 577) or error capture to deal with them. Don't turn error capture on unless you've already anticipated an error and figured out how your script can handle it; then turn it off again. That way, *unanticipated* errors don't get swept under the rug. In general, you should have just a few steps between Set Error Capture [On] and Set Error Capture [Off].

- **Error 9, 200–217, 723–725:** Assorted security-related errors (see Chapter 16).

- **Error 112:** Window is missing (you get this error if you try to select, close, or move/resize a window that doesn't exist).

- **Error 301:** Record is in use by another user (you get this error when you try to modify a record that is locked in another window or by another user).

- **Error 400:** Find criteria are empty (if you let users enter find criteria during a script, the Perform Script step gets this error if they don't enter anything).

- **Error 401:** No records match this request (this is the actual error that happens when no records are found; most people choose to check *Get (FoundCount)* instead since it's easier to understand).

- **Errors 500–507:** Assorted field validation errors (you get these errors when you try to modify a field in a way that violates its validation setting and it is set to "always" validate).

- **Errors 718 and 719:** XML processing errors (see Chapter 17).

- **Errors 1200–1219:** Calculation-related errors (you see these errors in conjunction with the EvaluationError and Evaluate functions).

- **Errors 1400–1413:** Assorted ODBC errors (see Chapter 17).

Tip: To capture an error by number, try this: Turn on error capture before the step that's producing the error, and then add a Show Custom Dialog step right after the offending step. Set the dialog box to show *Get (LastError)*. When you run the script, instead of the error message you've been seeing, you'll see a custom dialog box with the real error number. You can then modify the script to handle this particular number. But it's even easier to use FileMaker Pro Advanced, which has a script debugger (see page 736). It automatically shows you error numbers as they occur—no need to write junk steps into your scripts that you just have to strip out again.

The Allow User Abort Script Step

One more script step has ramifications when dealing with errors: Allow User Abort. This step lets you turn off a user's ability to cancel the script. Allow User Abort has only two options: on and off. Its normal state is to be turned on, unless you specifically turn it off with the script step. Like Set Error Capture, when you turn user abort off or back on within a script, the setting carries through any sub-scripts called by the main script. Allow User Abort always turns back on again when the script finishes running.

If you turn user abort off, but leave error capture on, the Cancel button in error messages is removed, so the person is forced to continue the script. Turning off user abort also prevents the user from pressing Escape (Windows) or ⌘-period (Mac) to cancel a running script. Finally, if the script pauses, he doesn't get a Cancel button in the status area. Instead, the only choice is to continue.

Note: When a script turns off user abort and pauses, the database user also can't switch to a different window, close the window, or quit FileMaker.

Putting a Complex Script Together

Building a complicated script takes time and planning. Because scripting gives you so much flexibility, you can write a script that applies your business rules to your database in any number of ways. Your job is to find a *good* way.

In this section, you'll make a script that generates an invoice for a job. You want to gather all the unbilled expenses and timeslips for the job, and then add appropriate line items for them to the invoice. To make a script like this, you need to cover all your bases:

- **Planning**. Before you even start writing the script, you must decide what upon a general approach. Outline all the things your script will do, and in what order. This process usually evolves from the general to the specific. The most specific version is the script itself, where you tell FileMaker *exactly* what to do.

- **Exceptions**. What kinds of things can go wrong? Think about how you'll check for, and prevent those problems.

- **Efficiency**. Are you doing the same things several places in the script? Are there other reasons to break your script into multiple smaller scripts?

Note: The rest of this chapter is one long exercise. Here, you'll get a chance to put some theoretical concept into practical use. Since each section builds on the one before it, this complex script is best digested if you work straight through from here to the end—without skipping parts or jumping around.

Planning the Script

Planning a big script is usually an iterative process. You start by outlining the steps the script will take in very general terms. You then go in and fill in more and more detail with each pass. When you're done adding detail, you know exactly what steps your script will use. Using the invoicing script as an example, you'll see how FileMaker gives you the tools to plan and execute your new script.

You can do this planning on paper, or in a word processor, or with any other tool you choose. But one good place you may *not* think of is ScriptMaker itself. Since the planning process involves a series of steps, and since it naturally produces the finished script when it's done, ScriptMaker is an ideal candidate. Just start with comments explaining each general step. You can then replace a comment line with some real script steps, and perhaps more comments. You never get lost or forget essential parts of the process because you always have a comment to tell you exactly what you still need to add, and exactly where it should go. When you're done, you've got the script is written and commented for posterity.

For this script, begin your planning by creating the script shown in Figure 15-14.

Considering Exceptions

Many people forget one of the most critical steps in script writing—planning for exceptions. The old saw, "A stitch in time saves nine," truly applies. Spend a few minutes thinking ahead to what might go wrong and planning how to prevent problems. These minutes can save you hours of troubleshooting and repair work on your data later.

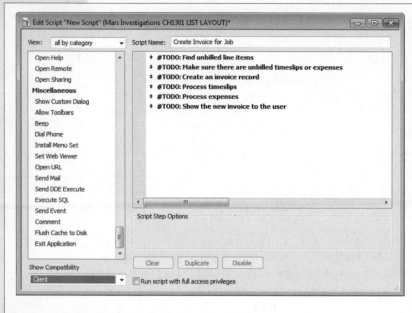

Figure 15-14:
This first rough-cut of your script doesn't do anything yet. Instead, it's just a series of comments that map out, at the most general level, what the script is going to do. You'll add more and more details as you go. Since these comments are just placeholders for real steps and comments yet to come, each one starts with the word TODO. You're welcome to use any marker you want, as long as you can easily tell these placeholder comments apart from the real comments you'll add later.

Look at what your script is supposed to do and try to think of reasonable *exceptions*—situations where your script might not be able to do its job. Thinking of exceptions is important for two reasons:

- **If your script always assumes ideal circumstances, it can wreak havoc if your assumptions are wrong when it runs**. The last thing you need is a wild script running amok in your data, changing and deleting the wrong things.

- **If a script gets halfway through its job, and then discovers that it can't continue, you may be left with half-finished work**. It's usually best to look for the problems up front, so the script can simply refuse to run if it won't be able to finish. (For more detail, see the box on page 600.)

For example, the Invoice creation script may run into two potential problems:

- **How does the script know which job to create an invoice for?** This problem is easy to solve: Make the script available only through a button on the Job layout. That way, people can run the script only from the right context. In other words, the script always runs on the job record the user is looking at. Make a comment at the top of your script that reminds you how the script is run.

- **What if the job has no timeslips or expenses that haven't been billed?** You wind up with an invoice that has no line items, and you don't want to send *that* to your customer. You can go ahead and create the invoice, and then delete it if it's empty. But this approach uses up an invoice number, and it means your script has to go through all the work of creating an invoice only to throw it away when it's done. Instead, have script check first to be sure there's something to bill. Then, it can display an informative message and skip all the hard work when there's nothing to bill.

Figure 15-15 shows how to edit your script to take these two problems into account.

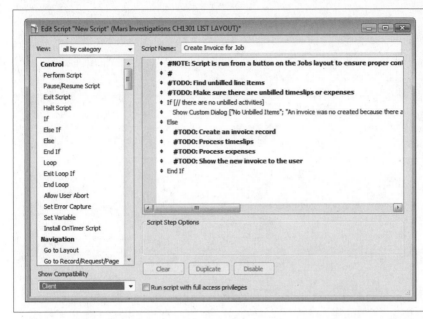

Figure 15-15:
Your first pass at editing the script shows where you'll put the test that determines whether an invoice needs to be created. And since you want to show the user a message if no invoice is made, add the Show Custom Dialog script step to the If part of the test.

- **The If step doesn't need a fully realized test yet.** Put a commented calculation (page 575) as your test for now, just to remind yourself what needs to be tested. You can put the real test in later.

- **Add feedback by putting a custom dialog step in the *true* part of the If step.** If you don't give feedback here, the person using the database may become confused, since nothing happens when he clicks the button to create an invoice for the job. The dialog box should explain why FileMaker isn't producing an invoice.

- **Add an Else step.** Since you don't want to create an invoice if there aren't any billable items for the job, put the last three TODO items in an Else step. The End If for this test should be just above the final End If in the script.

Creating Subscripts

Now that you've figured out how to solve problems your script might encounter, you've come to a fork in the road. You can write a script containing all the necessary steps, but it'll be long and hard to follow. For example, the End If steps at the end of the script will be a long way from their If and Else counterparts, making it hard to figure out where they belong. Alternatively, you may decide to break this script into smaller, more manageable pieces.

The Problem with Problems

Although detecting problems up front is usually best, it isn't always possible. Sometimes you can't find out about problems until your script has run partway through.

Most database systems handle this problem with something called a *transaction*, a chunk of work that's held in limbo until you tell the database to make it permanent. In a nutshell, you open a transaction, and you then can do anything you want, but your changes don't get saved until you commit the record. If you decide you don't want the changes after all, you can undo the transaction.

FileMaker uses this transaction concept under the hood to handle record changes, but unfortunately you have no easy way to tap into the transaction system from a script. Here's why: When you first enter a record—using the Open Record/Request script step, for instance—FileMaker begins a transaction for you. When you exit the record—Commit Record/Request—FileMaker commits the transaction, writing all changes to the database. If you revert the record instead—Revert Record/Request—FileMaker essentially rolls back the transaction, leaving the database untouched. Just remember that each transaction is linked to a record. For example, you can't begin a transaction, then make changes to five different customer records and eleven invoices, and then roll back all those changes.

But if you create, edit, or delete records in *portal rows* while you're still in the record, all your changes happen in one transaction.

Try this exercise in the Customers file to explore how the transaction works. Have two windows open—one showing the Invoice layout and the other showing line items. Create a new invoice record and add a few line items. Notice that FileMaker creates the new line item records when you add items to the Line Item portal on the Invoice layout. Being very careful not to commit the record (that is, don't hit the Enter key or click anywhere outside the fields onto your layout), choose Records → Revert Record. The parent invoice record disappears, *and* all the child line items disappear, too. You've just witnessed FileMaker's version of transactions.

Knowing this, you can use the Open Record/Request script step on an invoice record, and then make changes to dozens of line items. Then if your script detects a problem, you can revert the invoice record, and toss out all your line item changes as well. If you absolutely, positively must have control over your transactions, arrange your scripts so they do everything through relationships from one single record.

When you're trying to decide whether to write one long script or several shorter ones, you might consider a few other things. If you have several small scripts, you can run any one of them individually. This method gives you the chance to try out parts of the script to see if they work properly. Also, since you can pass parameters to scripts when you run them, using subscripts to do some jobs often saves you the trouble later on, since you can pass errors, or script results (page 583), via script parameters (page 586). But in the end, either approach is perfectly valid. Some people really like short, simple scripts, even if it means more of them and more opening and closing of the Edit Script window. Others find this multiple-script song and dance far worse than a script that needs a little scrolling.

For this example, you'll be creating subscripts. Figure 15-16 shows a repeat of your script-in-progress with places for subscripts clearly identified. Each of these scripts is relatively short and easy to understand, but you'll have *five* scripts in all. (See the box on page 604 for some tips for breaking up long scripts into subscripts.)

Creating subscript placeholders

You can use the comment steps you wrote earlier to figure out what subscripts you'll need. Then you can create placeholders for them by putting Perform Script steps underneath the appropriate comments. Figure 15-16 shows your edited script.

Figure 15-16:
Each empty Perform Script step marks a place for a subscript you'll create later. The first script finds the unbilled expenses and timeslips; the second creates the new invoice record that's related to the job; the third loops through all the timeslips and add the necessary line items; the fourth adds line items for all the expenses.

The "Create Invoice for Job" script performs four subscripts at the right time to pull everything together. Even though the script doesn't do much work at this point, you have a good roadmap for the rest of the script-writing process. If you get lost or interrupted, your main skeleton script contains everything you need to pick up right where you left off.

Creating skeleton subscripts

Next, you'll create all the subscripts you need—but that doesn't mean writing them all yet. You just need to create scripts in the Manage Scripts window and make some placeholder comments to remind you what they should do.

Start by adding a new script called Find Unbilled Activity. You can see the Find Unbilled Activity script in its planning stage form in Figure 15-17.

Note: Since the script you're building actually consists of several connected scripts, you can use a folder to keep things organized. Just click the little triangle by the New button in the Manage Scripts window, and choose Folder, and then give your folder a nice name like "Create Invoices." Now you can keep the main script and all its helper scripts in a tidy package.

Figure 15-17:
You'll create the Find Unbilled Activity subscript first. Since a subscript is just another script, approach it like you did the "Create Invoice for Job" script: Start with a plan. You'll come back later and implement the actual script steps.

The Process Expenses and Process Timeslips scripts are almost exactly the same. The context is different, because the data is in different tables and the data each script moves is different. But the process you'll use to find and process totals is very similar, so your comments notes can be the same for now. You'll create the custom pieces for each script in later exercises. Create the two subscripts shown in Figure 15-18 now.

Finally, you'll create the comments for the Create Invoice Record subscript. Like the others, it switches to the proper layout, and then gets on with its work. This script makes a new invoice record, then switches back to the original layout and sends script results back to the main script (Figure 15-19).

Note: Now that all your skeleton subscripts are finished, you can go back to your main script and change each empty Perform Script step to specify its proper subscript. But if you hook up each subscript as you finish it, the main script serves as a To Do list. You can tell at a glance which scripts you've done and which ones still need attention.

Finishing the Subscripts

You've created a series of subscripts that have placeholder comments to remind you what process the script will perform. Now it's time to finish your subscripts and turn them into working scripts by replacing those comments with real script steps.

Figure 15-18:
*The comments for these
two scripts are almost
identical. In the tutorials
on the following pages,
you'll create each
subscript independently,
and you'll see the details
in which they vary from
one another. But as you
gain experience, you
may find it quicker to
create one script and test
it thoroughly to make
sure your logic is sound.
Then, when the first
script works perfectly,
you can copy it, and
change the script steps
as appropriate.*

The Find Unbilled Activity subscript

Before you leap into finishing this script, a short refresher about what you're trying to accomplish is in order. This subscript is the first step in the "Create Invoice
for Job" master script. As the name says, it finds unbilled activity by searching the
Timeslips and Expenses tables for items related to this job. It runs when a user
clicks a button on the Job layout. You'll use a script parameter to send a Job ID to
the script, so it can find the right items.

Figure 15-19:
*Here's the skeleton
Create Invoice Record
script. Since nothing
actually happens in your
comments, and you
aren't running them until
they're done, you won't
mess anything up by
writing your subscripts in
a different order than
they'll be performed from
the main script.*

The Right Way to Create Subscripts

When you think about ways to break your script into smaller pieces, you should be thinking about tasks. It makes good sense to create a smaller script to do one of the *tasks* needed in the larger script. It doesn't make sense to simply take a long script and break it in two, so that the last step in the first script simply performs the second script. Breaking scripts up that way has all the disadvantages of multiple scripts (more windows to work in, more scripts to scroll through) and none of the advantages (neither script is particularly simple or self-contained, and neither can be run individually for testing purposes). Also, as you look for places to use subscripts, look for opportunities for reuse. In other words, look for things the script has to do more than once in two different places. It almost always makes sense to use a subscript in this situation.

In almost every case, the right way to subdivide a script is to create one master script that starts *and* finishes the process. The "Create Invoice for Job" script does just that. It starts by finding unbilled line items, and finishes by showing the invoice. Along the way, it relies on other simple scripts to get the whole job done.

There's no problem with a subscript having subscripts of its own. In fact, subscripts often do. But you should structure the entire set of scripts so that the top-level script implements the highest-level logic and behavior of the entire script itself. Each subscript should, in turn, do some particular task from start to finish. If the task is particularly complex, then the subscript itself might implement only the highest level of logic, calling on more subscripts to handle parts of the task. Since scripts are named by the mini-task they carry out, they provide helpful overviews of what's going on. When you complete the "Create Invoice for Job" script, even though it's somewhat complex, you can easily follow its structure. The script almost reads like a book, describing exactly what it's doing.

The first TODO item inside the script is a cinch: Just use the "Go to Layout" script step to switch to the appropriate layout. Next, for the current job, you need to find expenses that don't have a line item ID. You'll use a combination of Enter Find [Restore], Set Field with the Job ID (from your script's parameter), and Perform Find, to make sure you don't get items that have already been billed. Then, the script will count the found items so it can send that value back to the main script. Finally, you'll do the same thing for the Timeslips table.

1. **In ScriptMaker, double-click the Find Unbilled Activity script to edit it. Add the "Go to Layout" script step to the script.**

   If necessary, drag the "Go to Layout" step just below your first comment. Remember, if a script step is selected, any new step you create lands just below it.

2. **From the "Go to Layout" Script Step Options area's Specify pop-up menu, choose Expenses. Select the first TODO comment, and then add an Enter Find Mode script step. Turn off the Pause checkbox and turn on the "Specify find requests" option.**

   The Enter Find Mode script step lands below your comment, and then the Specify Find Requests dialog box opens.

3. **If any requests are showing in the list, click Delete until they're all gone. Click the New button.**

   The Edit Find Request window appears.

4. **From the "Find records when" pop-up menu, choose Expenses, and then click the Line Item ID field.**

   The selected field is now highlighted.

5. **Click the Insert Symbol button and choose "== match entire field" from the resulting menu. Click the Add button. Then click OK, and click OK again to get back to your script.**

   FileMaker puts "==" in the Criteria box. If you prefer, you can just type "==". Two equal signs, used alone, tell FileMaker you want records where the Line Item ID field matches *nothing*. These are all your expenses that haven't been billed.

6. **Add the Set Field script step to the script, and then turn on the "Specify target field" checkbox. Select the Expenses::Job ID field and click OK.**

   The step should appear after the Enter Find Mode step. If it doesn't, move it there now. Make sure you get the right Job ID field: You need to pick the Expenses table from the pop-up menu first.

7. **Click the Specify button to the right of "Calculated result." In the calculation box, type "==" & Get (ScriptParameter). Click OK.**

   This calculation puts the Job ID (from the script parameter) into the field, with "==" before it, telling FileMaker you want to find records that match this ID exactly. Together with the find request above, the script finds unbilled activity for the current job.

8. **Add the Set Error Capture script step to the script and make sure its "On" option is selected.**

   You're about to perform a find, and you don't want the database user to see an error message if there are no unbilled expenses.

9. **Add the Perform Find script step to the script.**

   The script step belongs below the Set Error Capture step. Make sure you don't select Perform Find/Replace by accident.

10. **Add another copy of the Set Error Capture step to the script, this time with the "Off" option selected.**

    You can select the existing Set Error Capture step, then click the duplicate button, then drag the new step into place, and set the option to "Off." Once the Perform Find step is finished, you want FileMaker to stop capturing error messages.

11. **Add a Set Variable script step below Set Error Capture [Off]. Name the variable *$unbilledItems*. Set its value to *Get (FoundCount)*. Save the script.**

    Remember, you want to make sure you have unbilled items for this job before you create an invoice. By grabbing this value now, and passing it to the main script later on, the main script will have the information it needs to decide whether to create an invoice.

    Your script should now look like the one in Figure 15-20.

Figure 15-20:
The Find Unbilled Activity script is half done. You've got helpful comments, plus the steps to find unbilled line items that should be billed to the job for which you're creating an invoice.

You can refine your script further by removing the "TODO" from your first two comments, so you can see that they're now explanations of what should be happening, instead of reminders of what you still need to do.

Copying and editing existing script steps

Since the timeslips half of the script is almost a duplication of what you did in the last tutorial, you could repeat all those steps above and you'd be done. But it's a lot faster to duplicate those steps, and then make a few changes so that your duplicated steps operate on the Timeslips table, not on the Expenses table. Here's how:

1. **Click the "Go to Layout" top line in the script. With the Shift key held down, click the Set Variable step, and then click Duplicate.**

   FileMaker creates an exact copy of all the selected steps. They all wind up below the first set.

2. **Select the next step—"Go to Layout"—and, from the Script Step Options area's pop-up menu, choose Timeslips.**

   This time you want to work with Timeslips records, so you need to go to the Timeslips layout.

3. **Double-click the next step: Enter Find Mode. Double-click the find request in the list. Select the only criterion in the list. From the "Find records when" pop-up menu, choose Timeslips, and, in the field list, select Line Item ID. Finally, click Change.**

   You're changing the find request so that it searches for empty Line Item IDs in the Timeslips table instead of in Expenses. The line in the criteria list changes to show *Timeslips::Line Item ID* instead of *Expenses::Line Item ID*.

4. **Click OK, and then OK again.**

   These two clicks close the Edit Find Request and Specify Find Requests windows, respectively. You're back in the script.

5. **Double-click the next Set Field step, and then change the targeted field to Timeslips:: Job ID instead of Expenses::Job ID.**

   Your Calculated result is just fine and so are the Set Error Capture and Perform Find steps, so you skip ahead to the last step.

6. **Select the next Set Variable step (the last non-comment step), and click the Specify button. Change the value calculation to read: *$unbilledItems + Get (FoundCount)*. Then click OK.**

   This time you don't want to *replace* the value in the script variable, so this calculation simply adds your new count to it.

7. **Remove the "TODO:" from the first two comments.**

When you're getting started writing complex scripts, more comments are better. As you get more experience, you may prefer to have fewer comments.

8. **After the last comment, add a "Go to Layout" step and set it to go to** *original layout*.

Once the script is done finding things, it needs to return to the layout it started on so the script that ran this one won't be surprised by a layout change. It's usually best when a subscript puts things back the way they were when it started.

9. **Add an Exit Script step at the end of the script. Click the Specify button, and then type** *$unbilleditems* **in the calculation box. Don't forget to save your script.**

You're telling the subscript to pass the value in the $unbilledItems variable back to the main script.

Whew! Finally, the Find Unbilled Activity script is finished. It should look just like the one in Figure 15-21. When you're done looking, click the OK button.

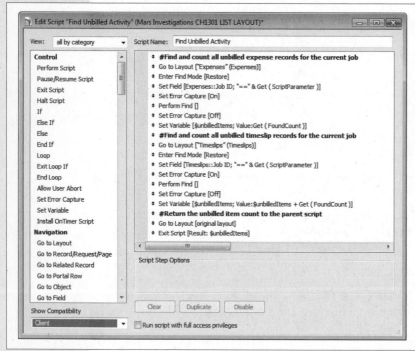

Figure 15-21:
Here's the completed "Find Unbilled Activity" subscript. It finds and counts the expenses, and then the timeslips. This serves two purposes in the final process: The $unbilled items variable helps the "Create Invoice for Job" script decide whether it should create an invoice or not, and FileMaker uses the found sets later to create line items.

Adding a Script Parameter to a Perform Script Step

You already know you can set a script parameter for a button as it runs a script. You can also set a script parameter when you run a script with a Perform Script step. Back when you started creating the Find Unbilled Activity script, you learned that it needs to find all the activity for the *current* job, using that job's ID. Since the "Create Invoice for Job" script is performing this script from the Jobs layout, it can put the Job ID in a script parameter so it'll be available when subscripts move to other contexts.

Also, now that you know what the subscript is doing to check for unbilled activity (it's returning a count), you can grab the subscript's result and finish the If step with the proper test.

1. **In ScriptMaker, double-click the "Create Invoice for Job" script to edit it. Select the first Perform Script [<unknown>] step.**

   The Script Step Options area shows a Specify button.

2. **Click Specify. Select the Find Unbilled Activity script. In the "Optional script parameter" box, type Jobs::Job ID.**

   If you don't like typing field names, click Edit instead and add the field in the Specify Calculation window. Then close the Specify Calculation window by clicking OK.

3. **Add a Set Variable step below the first Perform Script set. Name the variable *$unbilledItems*, and set its value to *Get (ScriptResult)*.**

   This step completes the job of passing the variable's value from the subscript up to the main script.

4. **Double-click the If test to edit it. Set its calculation to *$unbilledItems = 0*.**

   This tells the script to test the count of found items made by the subscript.

5. **Save your script.**

   Now the script can find and count unbilled activities for the current job and then perform a test on the count so it can decide whether to create an invoice, or tell the user that no invoice is necessary (Figure 15-22).

The Create Invoice Record subscript

The Create Invoice Record script needs to switch to the Invoices layout, create a new record, attach it to the job (by filling in its Job ID field), grab the new Invoice's ID, and then switch back to the original layout. And like the last subscript, this one needs the Job ID in its script parameter, when you hook it up.

Figure 15-22:
The main script now has one completed subscript with a script parameter. It also tests the subscript's results and branches based on the value it finds. The remaining TODO comments and Perform Script [<unknown>] steps give you a perfect roadmap of the work ahead.

Since you're used to removing the "TODO:" part of your existing comments and placing the appropriate script steps just below them, the remaining tutorials in this chapter will skip those instructions for simplicity's sake. Now you're ready to polish off the Create Invoice Record script itself:

1. **Double-click the Create Invoice Record script in ScriptMaker to edit it.**

   You're ready to add the real steps.

2. **Add the "Go to Layout" script step to the very top of the script. From the Specify pop-up menu, choose Invoices.**

   You can't add an invoice record from the Jobs layout, so you're switching to a layout attached to the Invoices table first.

3. **Select the first comment and add the New Record/Request step to the script.**

   The step appears after the second comment.

4. **Add the Set Field step to the script. The target field is the Invoices::Job ID field in the list, and the calculated result is *Get (ScriptParameter)*.**

   You're matching the new invoice to the Job ID that was set as the script's parameter way back when the script began running.

5. **Add a Set Variable script step after the Set Field. Name the variable *$invoiceId*, and set its value to Invoices::InvoiceID.**

   You're grabbing the new invoice's ID, so you can put it in the line item records later. You have to grab it now, before you return to the script's original context.

6. **Add the "Go to Layout" step to the script.**

Subscripts should always return the database to its previous state, so the main script doesn't get confused about its context.

7. **Add an Exit Script step at the end of your script. Its result is *$invoiceId*. Save the subscript.**

Since you set the new invoice's ID in a local variable, you'll pass it back to the main script with a script result.

8. **In the "Create Invoice for Job" script, set the first Perform Script step under the Else to run the Create Invoice Record subscript, with a script parameter of Jobs::Job ID.**

You're passing the Job ID to the subscript, so it knows which job it's creating an invoice for.

9. **Add a Set Variable script step below Perform Script ["Create Invoice Record"; Parameter: Jobs::Job ID]. Name the variable *$invoiceId*, and set its value to *Get (ScriptResult)*. Save the script.**

The subscript will pass the ID for the invoice it's just created back to the main script so it can create related line items in the next subscripts.

You can see the finished Create Invoice Record subscript in Figure 15-23. Now that your script creates a new invoice, you're ready to write the subscripts that create its line items.

Figure 15-23:
The finished Create Invoice Record subscript has almost as many comments as it has working script steps, yet its task is relatively simple. It makes a new invoice record for a specific job. But even if you understand the process perfectly, it's good to leave comments intact. Someone else who doesn't have your experience may take over the database some day, and your comments will serve as a tutorial.

Testing Multiple Conditions Redux

Back on page 586, you learned how to write a script that tested multiple conditions. Now that you're familiar with setting variables, it's time to learn how to take a more advanced approach to the same problem. Instead of calling three different custom dialog boxes that are each hard-coded, you can set your message in a *local variable*, and then call a single custom dialog box that changes based on which condition tested as true.

Why go to all that trouble? It's certainly not because File-Maker gives you a limited number of Show Custom Dialog boxes and makes you ration their use.

The rationale behind this exercise is to give you a taste of the software engineer's approach to FileMaker's variables. By thinking in terms of storing data that doesn't need to last inside a local variable (which itself has a very short shelf-life), instead of as an option in a dialog box, you're well on the way to solving more advanced problems as they arise. And if you've come from another programming background, you'll be glad to see that FileMaker handles variable storage like some of the big toys in the programming world.

Here's how it looks:

```
If [ Get(CurrentTime) > Time(4; 0 ; 0) and
Get(CurrentTime) < Time(12 ; 0 ; 0) ]
    Set Variable [ $customMessage ; Value:
"Good morning!" ]
Else If [ Get(CurrentTime) > Time(12 ;
0 ; 0) and Get(CurrentTime) < Time(18 ; 0
; 0)
]
    Set Variable [ $customMessage ; Value:
"Good afternoon!" ]
Else
    Set Variable [ $customMessage ; Value:
"Go to bed" ]
End If
Show Custom Dialog [ Title: "Greetings" ;
Message: $customMessage ; Buttons:
"Thanks" ]
```

The Process Timeslips subscript

Now you'll tackle the subscript that processes your unbilled timeslips. This script creates a line item record and then moves a lot of data around. First the script puts the Line Item ID into an unbilled timeslip, so it's related to the line item record and won't be found next time you run the script." (Remember, your Find Unbilled Activity script looks for all timeslip and expense records that don't have a Line Item ID.) Then the script grabs the time worked from the record, so the data can be put into the new line item record. Finally it'll loop through the found set of unbilled timeslips and grab the time worked from each record, until it's done.

Some steps in these scripts are variations on what you've been doing—switching layouts, doing If tests, creating records, and setting data into records from variables. You'll get them out of the way so you can concentrate on the harder part—processing the data in the found set. To get started, replace your first few TODO items with appropriate steps, per Figure 15-24.

- **Creating a looping script.** As you learned back in Chapter 13, you can use a loop to run a set of script steps over and over again. But there's more to a loop than just cramming steps between a loop and an end loop pair. Most times, you have to do a little prep work to get the database ready to enter the loop. And you must always have a way for the loop to stop. In this case, since you're working on a found set of records, you'll use a "Go to Record" step that exits after the last record (see page 547).

Figure 15-24:
The Process Timeslips subscript goes to the Timeslips layout to see if the earlier subscript found any records. If there are records in the found count, the script switches to the Line Items layout and makes a new record with the Invoice ID that is passed via the subscript's parameter. Finally, it puts the new line item's ID in a variable so that you can put the ID into each timeslip record.

Here's what to do:

1. **Add a "Go to Layout" step below the Set Variable step. Specify Timeslips for the target layout.**

   The script was just on the Line Items layout, so you need to make sure the loop will happen in the proper context.

2. **Add a "Go to Record/Request/Page" step below "Go to Layout"**

   You want to make sure your loop starts with the first record in your found set.

3. **Add a Set Variable step below "Go to Record." Name the variable *$totalHours*, and set its value to 0.**

   This variable helps the script add up hours as it loops through the found set of timeslip records.

4. **Add a Loop step below the Set Variable step.**

   ScriptMaker also gives you a matching End Loop step. The next few script steps will go between this pair.

5. Add a Set Field step as the first step of your loop. The target field is Timeslips::
Line Item ID, and the calculated result is *$LineItemId*.

When you put a Line Item ID into a timeslip record, you're relating the Line
Item and Timeslips table. Now you can look at any timeslip record and see any
line item related to it, and you can look at a line item record and see any
timeslip related to it. You'll use this relationship later on to move dates without
switching layouts.

6. Add a Set Variable step below the Set Field step. Name the variable *$totalHours*,
and set its value to *$totalHours + Timeslips::Duration*.

The script will add the hours worked on each timeslip record to the value that's
already in the variable. On the first record, the variable will have 0 in it, so the
result of the first calculation will be the same as the duration. But every time the
loop runs again, the value in the variable will increment by the amount in the
current record.

7. Add a "Go to Records/Request/Page" step after the Set Variable. Specify Next
in the pop-up menu, and select the "Exit after last" option.

Now the script goes to the next record in the found set. It exits the loop automatically after it performs the looped steps on the last record. The rest of your
script steps will go after the End Loop step.

8. Add a "Go to Layout" step below the End Loop step. Set it to go to the Line
Items layout.

You're putting the data you gathered into your new line item record, so make
sure you're back on the Line Item layout.

9. Add a Set Field step next. Set the target field to Line Items::Price Each, and set
the calculated result to *20*.

This step tells the line item record how much money to charge for each hour
worked. When you get your private investigator's license, you can change this
calculation to reflect your new status, and it won't change any old invoices.

10. Add a second Set Field step below the first one. Set the target field to Line
Items::Quantity, and set the calculated result to *$totalHours*.

This step tells the line item record how many hours were worked on the job.

11. Add a third Set Field step below the second one. Set the target field to Line
Items::Description, and set the calculated result to Labor. Edit your TODO
items and save the script.

Your time line items are labeled with static text describing the charge, and your
looping script is finished.

Your finished script should look like the top picture in Figure 15-25. Then take a
gander at the box on page 617 to see some other ways you might've handled the
problems presented in this script.

Figure 15-25:
Here's how your finished Process Timeslips script would look if you deleted all your comments. Keep your comments intact if it'll help you remember what the script is doing, or if somebody else might need to figure out what the script is doing. Remember, comments don't take up computer processing power, but they can help you save brain processing power, since you don't have to reinvent the wheel months down the road if your business rules change and you have to adapt your script to the new paradigm.

The Process Expenses subscript

You'll apply lessons learned in the Process Timeslips subscript to this script, but there are some important differences. First, although this example assumes your business rules say that all labor is combined into one line item per invoice, you'll create a line item record for each expense in the found set. So the steps that create a new line item will fall inside this script's loop. Second, you're gathering more bits of data for each expense, so the steps that set data into Line Item fields are different from what you did for Timeslips. But the overall process is still very similar. Here's what to do:

1. **Add a "Go to Layout" step to the top of your script. Set the target layout to Expenses.**

   You need to be on a layout tied to the Expenses table so you can check to see if any records need to be processed.

2. **Add an If test and set its calculation to *Get (FoundCount) > 0*.**

   You don't want to go to any trouble if there are no expenses for the current job.

3. **Add a "Go to Record/Request/Page" step between the If and End If steps. Set the "Go to Record" option to First.**

   You want to make sure the loop begins with the first record in the found set so nothing gets missed.

4. **Add a Loop step below the "Go to Record" step.**

   You'll also get an End Loop step. Most of the rest of your script's steps will go between the Loop and End Loop steps.

5. **Add a Set Variable step as the first step in the loop. Name the variable *$description*, and set its value to Expenses::Expense.**

   You're grabbing data to put into the new line item record you'll be creating later in this script. The remaining steps should be set in the order you see below.

6. **Add a Set Variable step. Name the variable *$amount*, and set its value to Expenses::Amount.**

   You're grabbing more data.

7. **Add a "Go to Layout" step. Set it to go to the Line Items layout.**

   The context has to be right to create your new record.

8. **Add a New Record/Request step.**

   It doesn't have any options.

9. **Add a Set Field step. The target field is Line Items::Invoice ID and the calculated result is *Get (ScriptParameter)*.**

   You'll need to remember to set this script's parameter when you hook it up to the main script later.

10. **Add a Set Field step. The target field is Line Items::Description and the calculated result is *"Expense:" & $description*.**

    You want the calculation to set the static text Expense: into the field, and then add the contents of your $description variable, so be sure to include text quotes around the text part of the calculation.

11. **Add a Set Field step. The target field is Line Items::Price Each and the calculated result is *$amount*.**

    The amount is how much you spent.

12. **Add a Set Field step. The target field is Line Items::Quantity and the calculated result is 1.**

    Don't include the quotes this time, since 1 is a number. You need the value so your Extended Price can perform its math properly.

Other Right Ways

Back when you were planning your complex script, you saw that there's no single right way to accomplish a particular task. Your job is to find a *good way*. To be sure, there are best practices—tried and true methods that scripters rely on—but if your script does what you need it to do, and your users can't find a way to make it break, then you've got a winner. Still, it pays to have a variety of tools in your scripting toolbox. Here are some things you can do differently in the Process Timeslips subscript.

- **You don't have to go to a layout to move data.** If you have a relationship between two records in your script, you can use the relationship to "push" data into the right record. In this case, you'd have to make a special table occurrence (page 321) for this purpose, but it would be worth doing if something happened to change the active line item record during your script. Remember, you *can* use a "Go to Layout" script step in Process Timeslips and trust it to find the new line item record you've just made, because your script doesn't do anything to change the active record. But sometimes your script needs to change the active record. Pushing data is just the thing in that situation.

- **You can push more data through a relationship.** The subscript increments a variable with the amount of time spent working on a job for each record in the found set. But if the relationship is valid when you enter the loop, you could just increment the Timeslip::Duration value in the line item record directly. That way, you can save the $totalHours variable if you want.

- **You can create the relationship and push no data at all.** You can use a Sum calculation (page 409) in the Line Item table to add up related line items' Duration fields. It means creating a new field in Line Items, but it would be dynamic, unlike the Set Field step, which produces a static value. That is, if you run the "Create Invoice for Job" script, and then find out that the Duration amount on a timeslip record is wrong, then you can't just change the timeslip and expect it to update on the line item. (If your business rules require one line item for each expense, as covered on page 597 then this calculation won't fit the bill.)

- **Local variables don't have to be initialized.** In this chapter, you set the subscript's $totalHours variable to 0 before you entered the loop that increments its value. In other words, by setting its value to 0 before you add any data to it, you *initialized* the variable. Initializing the variable is considered a best practice for working on complex scripts. It's perfectly possible to use the same variable for different parts of a lengthy script, but if you do, you can get unexpected results if the variable already has some other value in it. So initializing a variable (resetting it to 0) heads off problems before they occur. But, if you're sure the script won't ever create or set a variable with the same name, you can save a Set Variable script step by not initializing the variable before you put data in it.

13. **Add a Set Variable step. Name the variable $lineitemID, and set its value to LineItems::Line Item ID.**

You're grabbing the Line Item ID now so you can put it into the expense record next. This step creates the relationship between the Line Item and Expenses tables, and it insures that the next time you run the script, this same expense record won't be found again.

14. Add a "Go to Layout" step. Set it to go to the Expenses layout.

The script will return to the expense record it started the loop on.

15. Add a "Go to Record/Request/Page" step. Specify Next in the pop-up menu, and select the "Exit after last" option.

This step makes sure you're working through the found set, and can get out of the loop after the script has worked on the last record.

16. Add a "Go to Layout" step at the end of your script. Set it to go to "original layout." Edit your TODO comments, move them into place, and save the script.

You always want a subscript that changes context to return to the settings it started with.

Compare your script with Figure 15-26.

Figure 15-26:
The finished Process Expenses script looks like this example. It includes suggestions for revised comments, if you're the type who likes to keep them to remind yourself what you were thinking when you wrote a complicated script.

Finishing the main script

As your last bit of housekeeping, you'll need to hook up your *Perform Script [<unknown>]* steps and set their parameters.

1. Open the "Create Invoice for Job" script, and then double-click the unfinished Perform Script below the TODO: Process timeslips comment.

   The Specify Script Options dialog box opens.

2. Choose the Process Timeslips script, and set its script parameter to *$invoiceId*.

   The subscript uses this value to relate its new line item to the proper invoice record.

3. Double-click the last unfinished Perform Script step, and then choose the Process Expenses script. Set its script parameter to $invoiceID.

   This subscript needs the same value, and for the same purpose as the one above.

4. Add a "Go to Layout" step before the End If step. Set it to go to the Invoices layout.

   You want the database user to see the fruits of your labor, don't you?

Compare your finished script with Figure 15-27.

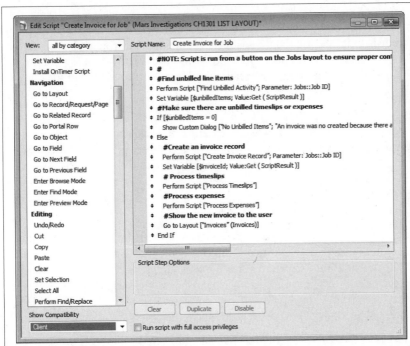

Figure 15-27:
You're finished! If there are too many comments for your taste, delete any you find extraneous; the script doesn't need them to work. And after all, a well-named subscript— like Create Invoice Record or Process Timeslips—doesn't need many comments, since its name explains what it does. But the top comment, about context, may be important for troubleshooting later. If problems arise, or if you need to tweak the script later because your business rules have changed, you can skim this main script to remind yourself how it works before you dive in and make changes.

Testing Scripts

To test your script, first go to a job record that has unbilled timeslips and expenses (or create a new job record, plus new unbilled timeslips and expenses, if necessary). Once you're on the job record, run the "Create Invoice for Job" script. To make your testing as much like the conditions your users will see, create a button for running the script.

In a flash, you should see a new invoice, properly assigned to the customer and containing line items for each unbilled item. You may be a little miffed that it took you *hours* to build the script, and FileMaker runs the whole thing in seconds. Cheer up, though; think how much time it will save you *in the future.*

Note: If the script doesn't work, you have a few options. First, check your data to make sure you have appropriate timeslips and expenses for the script to work on. Second, you can surf over to *http://missingmanual.com/cds* and compare your scripts to the ones in this chapter's finished file. But if you have FileMaker Pro Advanced, you should also read about the Debug Scripts and Data Viewer tools in Chapter 19. These gems can make hunting down script problems a breeze. Few serious scripters work for long without the debugger and Data Viewer.

In this exercise, you walked through a lengthy task where the steps and outcome were known. Out there on the mean streets of development, you won't always have a road map. Still, the concepts you learned when you started thinking in terms of planning, execption handling, and efficiency will get you out of a lot of sticky script situations.

When you're first scripting, or if you're attempting to do something that you aren't quite sure will work, following a similar approach will serve you well. In addition to creating your scripts in comment and subscript form, you can break scripting down even further. Create a few script steps, and then test them to make sure they behave as you expect. If they don't work properly, tweak them until they do. Then add a few more script steps and test again. If a new problem arises, you know it's in the new steps you've just added.

Finally, don't forget that the state of your database can influence what happens when you test a script. For example, a button on the Jobs layout insures that your users can run only the "Create Invoice for Jobs" script from the proper context. But in the heat of testing, you might accidentally run the script from ScriptMaker while you're on the wrong layout. If you do, your script parameter won't be set properly, and all kinds of havoc will be loosed in the script.

As you gain experience, you'll find that planning, finding exceptions, and subscripting will become second nature. You'll start envisioning scripts of increasing complexity, and soon you'll be making them your own way, without following a rigid plan.

Referential Integrity

By now, it's ingrained in your developer's brain that rela-tionships work because there's a match between key fields in the related tables. But what if you absolutely, positively *have* to change the value in a key field? You know it'll wreak havoc with your related records, because as soon as you change the value in the "one" side of the relationship, all the "to-many" records are no longer related to their parent records (or to any other record). In other words, they're orphaned.

If you changed the value in key fields manually, it'd be fairly easy to figure out how to keep this from happening. You use the existing relationship to find the child records, change their keys, and only then, go back to the parent record and change its key. The record family is reunited and everybody's happy.

Here's a script that handles that grunt work for you:

```
Allow User Abort [ Off ]
Go to Layout [ "Customers" (Customers) ]
Set Variable [ $newID; Value:Customers::
NewCustomerID ]
Go to Related Record [Show only related
records ; From table: "Jobs"; Using
layout:
"Jobs"
(Jobs) ]
```

```
Loop
        Set Field [ Jobs::Customer ID;
$newID ]
        Go to Record/Request/Page [ Next;
Exit after last ]
End Loop
Go to Layout [ "Customers" (Customers) ]
Set Field [ Customers::Customer ID; $newID
]
```

There's still some brainwork that this script doesn't handle, like making sure your NewCustomerID value is unique before you try to use it. If you're changing your key field value, it's probably not a surrogate key, so you'll have to know how your business policy creates and insures unique key values, and then apply that logic to your script. And you need to ensure that each related record is unlocked and available for your script to change. (See the box on page 43 for the scoop on record locking.) Only you can decide whether changing a key field is something you want to hand over to your users or if you'll manage this task your-self. Whichever way you go, this skeleton script will get you started.

Advanced Script Triggers

Back in Chapter 13, you got an intro to using *timers* with the Install OnTimer Script step. This step lets you schedule a script to run repeatedly. In this chapter, you'll get the full Install OnTimer story, and learn how the OnKeystroke trigger lets you respond to every keystroke your user makes.

Note: These are power-user triggers that require a lot of expertise to use properly. They give you a lot of power, but they're more complex than the script steps you've seen so far. Approach them once you've got some experience under your belt.

Install OnTimer Script

The Install OnTimer Script step has two options. First, you specify the script you want to run (along with an optional script paramter). Then you specify the "Inter-val seconds." For instance, you can schedule your Find Unpaid Invoices script with an interval of 10 seconds. If you then run the script with the Install OnTimer Script step, your Find Unpaid Invoices script runs every 10 seconds forever.

Of course *forever* is a long time. How do you stop a timer like this? There are two ways:

- Timers are associated with the window that was active when the timer was installed. If this window closes, the timer stops running. So you can close the database window to stop its timer.

- A window can only have one timer running. If you install a new timer in the same window, it *replaces* the one you last installed. So if you run the Install OnTimer Script step with no script specified, then you effectively turn off the timer entirely. This way, you can keep the window open, but stop its timer.

Tip: Timers can be trouble (after all, if you accidentally schedule a complicated script to run every second, it can be difficult to do anything else, including unschedule it). While you're still working out the kinks in your timer-based process, make a second window to work in. That way, if you accidentally get a timer running you can't stop, you can just close the window, then make a new window and start testing again.

Here are some situations where a timer might come in handy:

- You have a series of informational layouts you want to display on a wall-mounted screen (like shop operation information or information for customers standing in line). Using a timer, you can automatically switch between the set of layouts periodically, so your big screen shows one set of info for 30 seconds, then another, then back to the first.

- Your editing process is time sensitive. For example, say you have lots of people working in your database, and a shared Notes field that everyone edits periodically. To keep someone from staying in the notes field too long, install a timer when she switches switch to the edit layout. It can switch back to the read-only layout after a few minutes in case she walks away from her computer.

- You want to set up a computer to run periodic tasks. Maybe you have to import order information from your company's web server every 10 minutes, or you want to send shipment notifications every hour. You can install FileMaker on a computer, and schedule a timer to run the appropriate scripts periodically, with no intervention from anyone.

You'll see an example of a timer in action in the next section.

Keystroke Triggers

The Keystroke trigger is probably the most complex FileMaker scripting technique. The concept is actually very simple: A script runs whenever someone presses a key.

You can set up a keystroke trigger either on the layout, or on a particular layout *object*:

To configure a keystroke trigger for the layout, visit the Triggers tab of the Layout Setup dialog box (Layout → Layout Setup). While your user is on that layout, a trigger on the layout fires with every keypress. You can use a trigger like this to add direct keyboard navigation (for example, pressing C to switch to the Contacts tab, using the arrow keys to switch between records, and so on). This kind of trigger is also useful if you want to cancel keystrokes layout-wide. For instance, you can prevent the entry of punctuation into any field, or (if you're so inclined) keep the arrow keys from working.

To use an object keystroke trigger, you configure it for a specific layout object. So select the object in Layout mode, and then choose Format → Set Script Triggers. In this case, you're looking for the OnObjectKeystroke trigger. This time, the trigger fires only if the object has keyboard focus when the key is pressed. Most often, you apply the trigger to fields, where you can limit which keys your users can press, jump to the next field when they press the space bar, or some other specialized field-level action.

Detecting which keys were pressed

Suppose you have a report you show in Preview mode. As a convenience to the people using the database, you want the up and down arrow keys to jump to the previous and next page respectively. It's a perfect job for a keystroke trigger.

Note: If you want Ctrl or ⌘ key shortcuts for your database, you should use custom menus, not keystroke triggers. See page 743 for details.

First, figure out how you want to identify the arrow keys in your script. When FileMaker calls your script from a keystroke trigger, it remembers which key the person pressed. The script asks FileMaker about that key using the *Get (TriggerKeystroke)* function. For instance, if he presses the "a" key, then *Get (TriggerKeystroke)* returns "a" to the script. If he presses "A" (using the Shift key) the script gets a capital "A" instead.

Tip: If you care about uppercase vs. lowercase in your script, you can use the Exact function. This function compares two values, and returns *true* only if they are exactly the same, including case. So instead of this:

If (Get (TriggerKeystroke) = "a"; "Yes", "No")

You can do this:

If (Exact (Get(TriggerKeystroke), "a"); "Yes", "No")

The first example results in "Yes" if the user presses "A" or "a", while the second gives you "Yes" only if she types a lowercase "a."

But the fun doesn't stop there. After all, how do you check *Get (TriggerKeystroke)* for an arrow key? You can't very well put an arrow key in quotes in FileMaker's Specify Calculation window. In fact, keystroke triggers can handle all sort of keys you can't put in a string, like the Delete key, the function keys, the Escape key, and so on. To handle these special cases, FileMaker assignes every trigger-friendly key on the keyboard a special numerical code. You can then use the Code function in conjunction with *Get (TriggerKeystroke)* to figure out what key was pressed. For instance, this calculation identifies the Up arrow key:

```
Code ( Get(TriggerKeystroke) ) = 29
```

The numeral 29, it turns out, is the magic code for the Up arrow key. These codes are seemingly random, but you can find them all in the FileMaker online help (search for "Code") or right here:

- Backspace: 8
- Tab: 9
- Enter: 10
- Return: 13
- Escape: 27
- Left Arrow: 28
- Up Arrow: 29
- Right Arrow: 30
- Down Arrow: 31
- Space: 32
- Forward Delete: 127

There's one more wrinkle to keystroke detection. What if someone presses Shift plus the up arrow key? To give you insight into this possibility, FileMaker has one more keystroke function: *Get (TriggerModifierKeys)*. This function, plus a little math, tells you which of the modifier keys was pressed. Once again, special codes represent each key:

- Shift: 1
- Caps Lock: 2
- Ctrl (Control): 4
- Alt (Windows) or Option (Mac OS X): 8

This list is special, though, because you could conceivably have *several* modifier keys pressed at the same time. What should FileMaker return if someone presses Shift and Control? Would you believe 5?

FileMaker takes the value for each key from this list and adds them up. Each value is a power of two, which happens to be just enough separation that every possible combination produces a unique number. Luckily, you never have to work backwards and figure out, say, that 5 means Shift and Control in your script. Instead, simply decide what key combination you want to trigger something in your script—Alt and Shift, say. When you write the script, add them up yourself: 8 + 1 = 9. Then you can do a check like this:

```
Get(TriggerModifierKeys) = 9
```

Since you know ahead of time the exact combination you're looking for, the check is simple.

Note: By the way, the *Code( )* function has an alter ego called *Char( )*. Given a code (or series of codes) this function returns the original character equivalents. This function is far less useful than *Code( )* (which is commonly used for keystroke triggers). Use it, for instance, if you need to force a tab character into a calculation–*Char(9)*–or something equally esoteric.

Creating a simple keystroke trigger

Armed with all that information, you're ready to write your page navigation trigger. As with any trigger, you need to write the script first. This script navigates to the previous or next page, depending on which key someone presses. You can see such a script in Figure 15-28.

Figure 15-28:
This script is ideally suited for a keystroke trigger. It checks for the key that was pressed (it's looking for the Up and Down arrow keys) and navigates records appropriately. In both cases, it exits with a result of False, since the arrow keys already do something in Preview mode: they scroll the page up or down a bit. By returning False, the script tells FileMaker to skip the normal behavior.

Once you've written the script, you need to set up the keystroke trigger:

1. **Switch to the Invoices layout, and then go to Layout mode.**

   As usual, you set up triggers in Layout mode.

2. **Choose Layout → Layout Setup, then switch to the Script Triggers tab.**

   This tab is where you set up layout-wide triggers. Since this keystroke trigger should fire in Preview mode, when no specific object has focus, it should be set on the layout itself.

3. **Turn on the OnLayoutKeystroke checkbox.**

   The Specify Script Options window appears. Here's where you tell FileMaker which script to run.

4. **Choose the Navigate Pages script (Figure 15-28), and then click OK.**

   You're now back in the Layout Setup dialog box.

5. **Turn off the Browse checkbox and turn on the Preview checkbox.**

   You get to tell FileMaker which modes your trigger should run in. In this case, you only want the trigger to run in Preview mode.

6. **Click OK, save your layout, and switch to Preview mode.**

   Now you're ready to test your trigger.

Press the Up and Down arrow keys. If you look closely, you see FileMaker is switching from one page to the next as you do.

Setting up a keystroke filter

Keystroke triggers also let you limit what folks can type into a field. Way back in Chapter 3, you learned how to use validation to show an error message if someone types something inappropriate into a field. That's fine as far as it goes, but in some cases you want to be a little more proactive. Keystroke triggers give you that power.

For example, you might want to limit your Zip Code field to five numbers. You can do so easily enough with validation, but the person won't get a message until after he's entered the wrong stuff. You might want something a little more immediate: If he tries to type too much or the wrong things into the Zip Code field, you can make your database refuse the entry and go *beep!*

To do so, you want your script to double-check *each* key he presses, and cancel any invalid keystrokes. Writing a keystroke trigger like this takes special care. First of all, you must decide what makes a keystroke invalid. In the Zip Code case:

- If the keystroke isn't a number (0 through 9) then cancel it.
- If the field already has five digits in it, then cancel any keystroke.

With this in mind, your script consists of two If statements. First you check for non-number keys with a formula like this one:

```
Get ( TriggerKeystroke ) ≠ 0 and
Get ( TriggerKeystroke ) ≠ 1 and
Get ( TriggerKeystroke ) ≠ 2 and
Get ( TriggerKeystroke ) ≠ 3 and
Get ( TriggerKeystroke ) ≠ 4 and
Get ( TriggerKeystroke ) ≠ 5 and
Get ( TriggerKeystroke ) ≠ 6 and
Get ( TriggerKeystroke ) ≠ 7 and
Get ( TriggerKeystroke ) ≠ 8 and
Get ( TriggerKeystroke ) ≠ 9 and
```

Inside this If, you add a beep (using the cleverly named Beep script step) and then exit the script with a result of False. Your user hears *beep!*, and the key he pressed—the *wrong* key—doesn't show up in the Zip Code field.

Your second If statement checks for *excess* keystrokes. It has a simple calculation:

```
Length ( Invoices::Zip Code ) ≥ 5 and Get ( ActiveSelectionSize ) = 0
```

Once again, inside this If statement, you beep and exit with a False result. You can see this script in Figure 15-29.

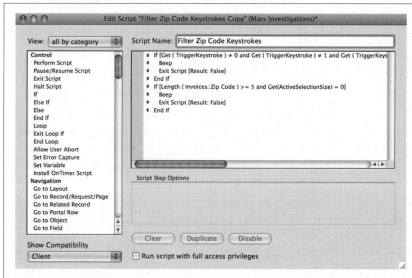

Figure 15-29:
You may write a script like this one if you want to filter keystrokes for the Zip Code field. (You can see the calculation formulas for each If step above.) Unfortunately, this script doesn't work very well, since keystroke triggers fire for almost every key. Therefore, this script has the nasty side effect of blocking the arrow keys, the Delete key, and even the Enter and Tab keys.

A quick test reveals that the script in Figure 15-29 is a little too aggressive. Since it cancels every keystroke that isn't a number, it doesn't let folks use the Delete key to clear an accidental entry. It blocks the Enter, Tab, and arrow keys so they can't exit the field easily. In the end, you have a field that can't be edited.

Luckily, the fix is fairly easy. If you refer back to the list of special key codes on page 627, you see that most of the special navigation keys have codes less than 31. The notable exception is the rare-but-handy Forward Delete. So instead of adding a special case for each and every key, you can allow all the special keys in one block with a simple formula. Just wrap your entire script in a new If step with this formula:

```
Code ( Get(TriggerKeystroke) ) > 32 or Code ( Get(TriggerKeystroke) ) ≠ 127
```

As luck would have it, this tactic is perfectly safe because every normal key (letters, numbers, space, and punctuation) has code 32 or above. You can see your new and improved script in Figure 15-30.

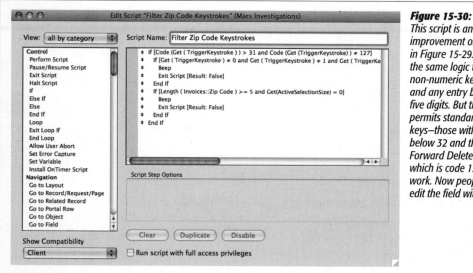

Figure 15-30:
This script is an improvement on the one in Figure 15-29. It uses the same logic to reject non-numeric keystrokes, and any entry beyond five digits. But this time, it permits standard editing keys—those with a code below 32 and the Forward Delete key, which is code 127—to work. Now people can edit the field with ease.

To finish up, just select the Zip Code field, choose Format → Set Script Triggers and assign this script to the OnObjectKeystroke trigger. You might be tempted to assign the trigger for both Find and Browse mode, but remember that you might want to find for a range of zip codes (46077…90201) or use a wildcard in your zip-code search (852*). So you're probably best off applying this trigger only in Browse mode.

Once you set up the trigger, you should get exactly the desired effect. If someone types any text or punctuation into the Zip Code field, FileMaker beeps, and nothing appears in the field. But if she types a number key, it goes right in. And once there are five numbers in the field, it rejects any additional entry.

Part Six:
Security and
Integration

6

Adding Security

FileMaker's all about easy access to information. But that's a double-edged sword. As it stands now, every person who uses your database has unrestricted access. Of course, you can take all the usual precautions (give your computer a password, install virus protection software, lock your door, and so on). But eventually, you'll probably want to let other people work in your database, and that brings up all kinds of security challenges. Mike in Accounting is free to rename all your scripts if he so desires. And Kelly in Sales can delete all those "old" order records that are getting in her way. Fortunately, FileMaker has features of its own that give you a finer level of control, so you can let selected people use your database to the fullest, while keeping important information out of harm's way.

You may be tempted to think you don't have to worry about security. But the best time to think about protecting your data is *before* you have a problem. If you wait until your database grows big and complex before considering security, then it'll take you longer to build in later.

How Security Works

FileMaker's security system has two levels of control: *who* can get into your database in the first place and *what* they can do once they're there. You determine who gets access to your database by setting up *user accounts*, and you control what each person can do by assigning *privilege sets* to each account.

Who Gets Access

FileMaker understands that different individuals access your database. The *who* part of security is important for several reasons. For instance, Malcolm and Lois each need access to the database, but their manager Craig doesn't. When you give each user of your database an individual account, you can keep track of who's using the file. Plus, if Lois leaves the company, then you can keep her from accessing the database. Likewise, when Lois's replacement is hired, you can give him access, too.

You control access by creating an account for each person who uses the database. Each account has a user name and a password. Users have to type an Account name and Password when they open the file. If they don't know the right combination, then they can't get in.

Note: When FileMaker asks for an account name and password, propeller-heads say it's *authenticating* the user. In other words, it's making sure the user's for real. This book, for the most part, dispenses with this jargon, but you may run across the term elsewhere. Just so you know.

POWER USERS' CLINIC

Spying by Script

When you've set up database accounts, FileMaker remembers the account name of whoever's currently signed in. You can write a script to find out who it is with the *Get (AccountName)* function. For example, if you want to record the account name in a Notes field when someone runs a particularly important script, then you could include a script step like this:

```
Set Field [Notes::Notes & Get(AccountName)
&"ran the script on" & Get
(CurrentDate) & "at" & Get
  (CurrentTime)]
```

Then every time the script runs, FileMaker looks up the name and password of whoever's using the file at the moment, and puts the person's account name and the date and time in the Notes field.

FileMaker also knows the name of the privilege set used when someone logs in. The *Get (PrivilegeSetName)* function tells you which one it is.

What They Can Do

But who gets into your database is only half the story. You also control *what* they can do. You decide which layouts they can see, and which scripts they can run. You can even choose to let them see only certain records. Each bit of access is called a privilege. Every person is unique, but you probably don't need to grant each person a unique set of privileges. For example, you may have one privilege set for Accounting and another for Sales. People with the Accounting privilege set can run reports, but they can't enter new orders. People with the Sales privilege set can enter and edit data, but they can't run reports. You can make as many—or as few—privilege sets as you need. And you can give 50 accounts the same privilege set, or make a privilege set just for one account.

Note: Usually, you create privilege sets *first*, and then add accounts for each user. When you add an account, you must pick a privilege set to control the account access. But FileMaker's flexible: If you start to create an account, but don't yet have an appropriate privilege set, then you can create one right then and there, before you save the account.

Privilege Sets

When you're creating privilege sets, there's a big temptation to give people too much power. The more folks can do on their own, the less often they'll come bugging you, right? Unfortunately, this attitude invites trouble. For instance, if your database holds credit card numbers along with order records, and your Order Entry privilege set lets users export data, you may one day find yourself the subject of an FBI investigation. To be on the safe side, if you aren't *sure* someone needs a privilege, then don't give it to him.

This rule has a practical component as well. If someone has access to a feature he shouldn't have, then he's very unlikely to complain. He probably doesn't even notice, and neither do you until someone abuses it. However, if you lock someone out of a capability he needs, you can bet you'll hear about it right away. You can easily add the needed power when it comes up. In other words, if your privilege sets start out too restrictive, then they'll naturally grow to the right level of power over time based on user feedback. FileMaker mimics this approach by creating each new privilege set without any privileges at all. Your job is to add each privilege a user might need.

You do all the work of creating and maintaining accounts and privilege sets in the Manage Accounts & Privileges window (Figure 16-1). You can get there by way of the File → Manage → Accounts & Privileges command.

Figure 16-1:
The [Guest] and Admin accounts are added for you when you first create a new database. The checkbox to the left of Admin tells you that it's the only one that's currently active.

Understanding Privilege Sets

Every FileMaker database has three built-in privilege sets: [Full Access], [Data Entry Only], and [Read-Only Access].You can only make a few minor edits to these sets. The brackets make it easy to pick them out of a list with your custom sets. You can see the Privilege Sets tab in Figure 16-2.

Figure 16-2:
The Privilege Sets tab of the Manage Accounts & Privileges dialog box lists all the privilege sets in your database. Each privilege set has a name (in the Privilege Set column) and a description. The list also shows you all the accounts assigned each privilege set. Out of the box, only the [Full Access] privilege set is being used–by the Admin account.

The built-in privilege sets

The standard privilege sets cover three very common access levels, and you're welcome to use them if you want, but you have to live with the way they work out of the box, because FileMaker doesn't let you edit them.

- Although you probably didn't realize it, you've been using the **Full Access** privilege set all along. As the name says, it gives you full access to the file with absolutely no restrictions.

- The **Data Entry Only** privilege set is much less powerful. Accounts assigned to this privilege set can't create or modify tables, field definitions, scripts, or layouts. But they can add, edit, and delete records in any table, print, change their own password and export data.

- The least powerful built-in privilege set is **Read-Only Access**. Not only does it prevent all developer activities, but it also prevents modification of the data. Accounts with this privilege set can't create, edit, or delete records. They can *view, print or export* the data that's already there, and change their passwords.

Custom privilege sets

Those built-in privilege sets provide basic security, but they don't give you a full range of possibilities. Using just FileMaker's default privilege sets, you can't give Malcolm full control of some tables, but let him just enter data in others. In developer's lingo, you don't get a lot of *granularity*.

Note: Think of granularity as a medium for sculpture. If you're building a statue from boulders, then you can't create delicate details like the nose or eyelashes. If you're building with grains of sand (get it?), then you can work at a much finer level. Similarly, granularity in security lets you control specific access to your database.

In FileMaker, you can exercise precise, granular control over security by creating your own privilege sets, and assigning them to certain people or groups.

When you create a new privilege set, it starts out with absolutely no privileges. In other words, accounts attached to this set—if left alone—can't do *anything* in the database. You have to turn on exactly the privileges you think the user should have.

To save time, you could duplicate the [Data Entry Only] or [Read-Only Access] privilege set, and then add or remove privileges as necessary. This way is usually a little faster, but it does open up the possibility that you'll accidentally leave something turned on that shouldn't be allowed.

Note: You can't duplicate the [Full Access] privilege set. This is FileMaker's way of encouraging you to really think about the privileges you assign, and it should encourage you to give users the least access possible for them to do their jobs. If you want a privilege set that grants *almost* full access, then you have to build it up by hand.

Understanding Individual Privileges

Since FileMaker has a privilege for almost every single thing you can do, you have *lots* of them. To help you navigate the maze of privileges, the Edit Privilege sets dialog box (Figure 16-3) is divided into three primary sections:

- In the **Data Access and Design** section, you control access to the data via records and layouts. You also decide what kinds of developer operations the user can perform. For example, can she create new layouts? Or edit your scripts? Create value lists? Numerous dialog boxes and dozens of options live behind the pop-up menus in this section.

- **Other Privileges** includes a block of simple checkboxes controlling access to assorted database-wide features like printing, exporting, and password restrictions.

- The **Extended Privileges** section shows a scrolling list of checkboxes. For the most part, FileMaker adds these to control how you share your data, but you can also add your own custom extended privileges.

You'll learn more about each of these sections in the following pages.

Other privileges

With just a set of checkboxes to turn options on or off, the Other Privileges area is the easiest section, so it's a good place to start. Here's where you select basic File-Maker features:

- **Allow printing.** Turn this option on, and the user can print layouts. If it's off, then the Print menu command is grayed out, and the Print script step fails.

Figure 16-3:
When you create a new privilege set, you see FileMaker's granularity of control in action. Notice how many things aren't turned on, or say "All no access". You set each privilege one by one, until you've built up a set that's appropriate for the kind of user you have in mind—in this case, a Project Manager.

- **Allow exporting**. This option lets people access the Export Records command. Again, if it's off, the menu command is grayed out, and the Export Records script step doesn't work.

Tip: *Even if you turn a privilege off, a script that's set to run with full access privileges can work around the restriction (page 657).*

- **Manage Extended Privileges**. Normally, only accounts with full access can manage security settings. Extended privileges are the exception. You'll learn more in a later section, but if this option's turned on, then people can assign extended privileges to different privilege sets themselves.

- **Allow user to override data validation warnings**. This option is a companion to the "Allow user to override during data entry" option in the Field Options dialog box (page 111), which you can turn on if you want to let people ignore the error message that's displayed if they enter invalid data in the field. But when this privilege is *not* selected, people can't override the errors even when the field options say they should be able to. In other words, this privilege trumps that field option.

- **Disconnect user from FileMaker Server when idle**. This isn't actually a privilege. It's more of an *un-privilege*, and it's turned on when you create a new privilege set. When it's on, people are kicked out of a shared database if they don't use it for a while (you get to decide how long when you configure FileMaker Server). Turn it *off* if you want to give these people the power to stay connected right through their lunch breaks.

• **Allow user to modify their own password.** FileMaker lets you implement some typical password management features. First, you get to decide if someone can change his account password at all. If you want to give him this power, then turn this option on. Once it's on, you can choose "Must be changed every", and then enter a number of days to force him to change his password periodically. You can also enforce a minimum password length.

Note: You probably want to turn this option off if people *share* accounts in the same database. If you have just one account for each group, for instance, then you don't want one wisenheimer changing the password on everybody else just for laughs.

• **Available menu commands.** A brand-new privilege set gets full access to the menu bar. Of course most menu commands are grayed out unless you turn on the corresponding privileges. If you don't want people running menu commands willy-nilly, then you can change the "Available menu commands" pop-up menu. Choose "Editing only" to give these people access only to the Edit menu and basic formatting commands. Choose "None" to turn off every menu command that affects the current database.

Creating a privilege set

You start adding security to your database by creating a privilege set in your Mars Investigations database for Project Managers. PMs set up jobs and create invoices for those jobs, so you'll design a privilege set with appropriate privileges. Since so many steps are involved, this exercise spans several sections.

1. **On the Manage Accounts & Privileges dialog box's Privilege Sets tab, click New.**

   The Edit Privilege Set dialog box (Figure 16-3) appears.

2. **In the Privilege Set Name box, type *Project Manager*, and in the Description box, type *create and edit jobs, create new invoices*.**

   If the privilege set name matches the department name or personnel role, it's a lot easier to apply it later on when you're creating accounts. Use the description to help you remember the basic rules for the set.

3. **Select these checkboxes:**

   • Allow printing

   • Allow user to override data validation warnings.

   • Disconnect user from FileMaker server when idle

   • Allow user to modify their own password

4. **Set the "Available menu commands" pop-up menu to "Editing only".**

   People can't get into trouble exploring if they can't even open dialog boxes that are above their pay grades.

That's it for the Other Privileges part of the dialog box. But if you leave the Project Manager privilege set with these settings, people can't do anything very useful. Next, you'll look at the section where all the granularity is hiding so you can start adding real privileges to the list.

Note: You may have noticed there's no checkbox for "Allow user to manage the database", or "Allow user to create tables". Only accounts with full access can open the Manage Database window and use its features. The same goes for the Accounts & Privileges window's Accounts and Privilege Sets tabs.

Data Access and Design Privileges

The Edit Privilege Set dialog box's "Data Access and Design" section is where you control access to your specific database elements. Records, Layouts, Value Lists, and Scripts each have pop-up menus where you'll set those privileges. Right now, the Project Manager privilege set doesn't allow access to any of these. To start adding privileges, click the Records pop-up menu. Figure 16-4 shows all your choices.

Figure 16-4:
Here you see the Records pop-up menu in the Edit Privilege Set window. Like privilege sets themselves, you get a few canned choices, the default no access option and a custom privileges dialog box. Often, one of the canned choices work just fine, but for the utmost control—like letting people see only the records they've created themselves—you have to dive into custom privileges.

Record privileges. If the three built-in privilege sets form the first level of granularity in the security system, then the options in this pop-up menu are part of the *second* level. Without much fuss, you can pick one of the accurately named prebuilt options:

- **Create, edit, and delete in all tables** is the level you're accustomed to. People can do anything they want with the records—including delete them all.

- **Create and edit in all tables** is almost as good. It just prevents people from *deleting* records.

- **View only in all tables** is for the browsers. They can *see* anything they want, but they can't *change* anything.

- If, for some reason, you want to give somebody access to your *database* but not your *data*, then keep **All no access** selected.

Each of these options applies to *every* record in *every* table. But you may want to let some people "Create, edit, and delete" only in *some* tables, and let them "View only" in others. For instance, you can let part-timers create new customer records, but not tamper with the Expenses table. For that kind of control, choose "Custom privilege" (Figure 16-5).

Figure 16-5:
Now you're starting to see some real granularity. The Custom Record Privileges window lets you control view, edit, create, and delete privileges on each individual table. You can also control exactly which fields people have access to by choosing options from the Field Access pop-up menu.

To modify privileges for a particular table, you first have to select it. But don't waste time: You can select *several* tables if you want to, and then modify the settings for all of them at once. FileMaker even gives you a Select All button so you can easily make a change to *every* table.

For the Project Manager privilege set, you want to give *at least* View access to every table. PMs should be able to create, edit and delete records in the Customers, Jobs, Expenses, and Timeslips tables.

1. **From the Records pop-up list, choose Custom Privileges, and then click Select All.**

   FileMaker selects every table in the list. You can apply the same privilege to them all at one time.

2. **From the View pop-up menu, choose Yes.**

   In every table's View column, the word "yes" appears. Accounts with the Project Manager privilege set can see data in every table in the file.

3. **From the Field Access pop-up menu, choose "all".**

   The word "all" appears in the Field Access column. Now project managers can see the contents of every field in all the tables.

4. **Click in the list to deselect the group. Click the Customers table, and then press Shift and click Timeslips.**

   Shift-clicking, select a continuous range of items in a list. You can select a non-contiguous list by Ctrl-click (⌘-click).

5. With all four tables selected, from the Edit pop-up menu, the Create pop-up menu, and the Delete pop-up menu, choose "yes".

Your settings should match Figure 16-5.

Tip: The list starts out sorted into creation order. Clicking the column headings in the Custom Record Privileges dialog box re-sorts the list. The striped triangle above the vertical scroll bar switches the sort between ascending and descending order.

Creating record-level access

Invoice privileges are a little more complicated. You want project managers to be able to "create invoices," but invoices involve multiple tables and processes, which you have to translate into a set of privileges. They need to create invoice records, of course, but they also need to be able to create line item records. And once they've added items to an invoice, they should also be able to edit those items. You decide, however, that they *shouldn't* be able to edit items on invoices from last year. In fact, they probably shouldn't change any invoice that isn't dated today. You can handle even a complicated security requirement like this easily in FileMaker: Just add a simple calculation to the mix. (See Part 4 for a refresher on calculations.)

To limit access to individual records, FileMaker lets you use a calculation to decide which ones people can edit. This calculation gives you tremendous control over the security system. You can use data from the record itself, information about the current date, time, or account name, and even global field or global variable values. Your calculation must return a Boolean result: True if the record should be editable, and False if it shouldn't.

Here are the steps to set up the invoice privileges described above:

1. In the Custom Record Privileges dialog box, select just the Invoices table. Then, from the Create pop-up menu, choose Yes.

   FileMaker puts "yes" in the Create column, meaning that managers with this privilege set can create invoice records. From here on, things get more complicated.

2. From the Edit pop-up menu, choose Limited.

   You don't want the person to be able to edit *any* invoice record. Instead, you're giving her *limited* edit privileges. Your old friend, the Specify Calculation dialog box, appears.

3. In the calculation box, enter *Date ≥ Get (CurrentDate)*.

   This calculation returns a true result when the invoice date is on or after the current date. It's false for invoices dated before today, so FileMaker lets project managers edit today's invoices or those with a future date.

Note: This security calculation has a significant weakness: Someone can simply change the date on his computer, and bypass the restriction. Luckily, in most cases, a secured multiuser database is shared with FileMaker Server (Chapter 18). When that's the case, you can use a more robust calculation: *Date ≥ GetAsDate (Get (CurrentHostTimestamp))*. The *Get (CurrentHostTimestamp)* function gets the date and time from the server computer. Since you, or your IT folks, control this computer, ordinary people can't fiddle with its clock.

4. **Select the entire calculation, choose Edit → Copy, and then click OK to close the calculation box.**

   You've copied the calculation so that you can paste it into another privilege calculation. The word "limited..." shows in the Edit column for Invoices.

5. **From the Delete pop-up menu, choose Limited.**

   The Specify Calculation dialog box returns. This time, you're going to limit the managers' ability to delete invoice records. The rule is the same: They can delete only *new* invoices.

6. **Choose Edit → Paste to use the calculation from step 3 here.**

   FileMaker adds the calculation to the calculation box. Click OK when you're done.

7. **Repeat the above steps for the Line Items table. In this case, though, you want to let managers edit or delete line items when the invoice they're attached to contains today's date. So use the following in steps 3 and 6:**

   ```
   Invoices::Date ≥ Get ( CurrentDate )
   ```

   Project managers at your company have no business creating or editing payments or products, so you can leave Edit, Create, and Delete set to "no" for Invoice Payments, Payments, and Products.

Note: FileMaker shows a "–" instead of the word "no" when you turn off a privilege. The dashes make the denied privileges easier to spot when you're looking at a long list.

Field-level access. The Payments table has a field for Credit Card Number. This type of information falls into the *need-to-know* category: Unless someone *needs* it to do his job, he has no business seeing it. Even though project managers can view payment records, you can still control access to individual *fields* in that table. You're about to exercise field-level granularity:

1. **Select the Payments table, and then, from the Field Access pop-up menu, choose Limited.**

   The Custom Field Privileges window appears (Figure 16-6). FileMaker offers three field-level privileges: *modifiable* means people can see *and* edit the field data; *view only* means they can see the information in the field, but can't change it; and *no access* means they can't even see it.

Figure 16-6:
The Custom Field Privileges window lets you control access to individual fields. Select the fields you want to change, and then select one of the Privilege radio buttons. FileMaker dutifully changes every selected field accordingly. Click Select All to quickly select every field.

2. **Select the Credit Card Number field, and then select the "no access" radio button.**

   And indeed, the words "no access" appear in the Privilege column for the selected fields. Click OK.

Note: Even though the other fields in this list say "modifiable", the entire record isn't editable for this privilege set, so people can't change field data. The table-level security settings trump those at the field level.

The Invoice Finder table has only global fields, so it doesn't need records at all. But you still have to turn on the Edit privilege so the managers can change values in the globals. Select it, and then, from the Edit pop-up menu, choose "yes". When you're finished, your Custom Record Privileges dialog box should look like the one in Figure 16-7.

When you're done looking, click OK to close this dialog box. Because you just made a set of complex choices, FileMaker sums up everything you just did by displaying "Custom privileges" in the Records pop-up menu in the Data Access and Design section of the Edit Privilege Set dialog box. To review or edit the record-level or field-level access you've set, in the pop-up menu, click "Custom privileges" again.

Layout privileges. If you've been following along in this section, you've given Project Managers access to data that lets them do their jobs. But if you stop now, then they still can't get very far. They don't have access to any *layouts* yet, and without layouts, a FileMaker database isn't of much use. If someone were to open the database with this privilege set now, she'd see something like Figure 16-8.

Figure 16-7:
Project managers have wide-open access to some tables, limited access to others, and view-only access to a few. Notice that if you create a new table, then PMs can view data in all its fields, but they can't edit, create or delete records. If that's not what you want, you must edit this privilege when your database changes. See the box on page 644 for more info.

Figure 16-8:
When people try to view a layout they don't have access to, this blank screen is what they see. FileMaker tries hard to avoid this situation, though; it removes layouts the user can't access from the Layouts pop-up menu. But your scripts can still put them somewhere the user doesn't belong. And in this case, they don't have access to any layout, so FileMaker doesn't have much choice.

FileMaker uses layouts to display your file's data, which means you need to add layout access to your privilege sets. To give people all-important access to the various database layouts, use the Edit Privilege Set window's Layouts pop-up menu:

- **All modifiable** means people can use *and* edit every layout. (Here, "edit" means "add fields, delete portals, resize parts, and the whole nine yards.")

- **All view only** gives people access to every layout, but doesn't let them change any.

- **All no access** prevents *any* layouts from showing, as shown in Figure 16-8.

The final option—Custom Privilege—lets you exercise the greatest control over access to specific layouts. Since layouts are a vehicle for the other database items *on* the layout, you have two distinct layers of privilege.

- **Layout.** These privileges control people's ability to view or edit the layout itself. They're basically the same as the All layout privileges described above, but they apply only to the selected layout. Choose *modifiable* if you want to let people edit the layout (enter Layout mode, and then move fields and things around), *view only* if you want them to only see it, and *no access* if you want them to see that gray screen that prompts tech support calls in Figure 16-8 instead.

- **Records via this layout.** Use this option to determine whether or not people should be able to see or edit data in fields on a particular layout. If you make records from the Customer layout "view only", then you can still edit them from the Customer List layout.

Note: If you want to prevent editing of customer data altogether, it makes more sense to use the record-level privileges instead. The "Records via this layout" setting is available just in case you want to restrict editing from one particular layout, even though the data in the table can be edited elsewhere.

UP TO SPEED

Any New Anything

Both the table list in the Custom Record Privileges window and the field list in the Custom Field Privileges window have an unusual last item: [Any New Table] and [Any New Field]. These items don't really exist in your database. Instead, when you set privileges for them, you're telling FileMaker how this privilege set should treat any new items added later.

Most FileMaker databases are living creatures that grow and adapt constantly. You might add new fields, layouts, scripts, and even tables at any time, so it would be foolhardy to give everybody access to any and every new item. Instead, you're more secure assuming that no one gets access to anything new until you set the new privileges specifically. To implement this more strict security rule, turn off all privileges for the [Any New...] items. In fact, File-Maker already has "any new" turned off whenever you make a new privilege set.

Figure 16-9 shows the Custom Layout Privileges dialog box. This window has something else that didn't exist on the Custom Record Privileges dialog box: The "Allow creation of new layouts" checkbox lets you decide if these people can create their own new layouts. In fact, you can let people who can't even add or edit data create layouts. For example, you might have a whole class of people—the Accounting Department, say—who shouldn't be editing customer records or adding product information, but who need to create monthly and annual reports (read: layouts) *from* that data.

Figure 16-9:
The Custom Layout Privileges window looks a lot like its records counterpart. You get a list of layouts and some privilege choices. Fortunately, you have fewer things to do here, and thus fewer things to learn. As usual, select the layout (or layouts) first, and then make changes.

In the current example, you want Project Managers to be able to use any layout (and edit records through them). But you also want them to be able to create their own layouts in case they need to do some custom reporting. These new layouts should, of course, be editable.

1. **If you're looking at the Custom Layout Privileges window, click OK to dismiss it and return to the Edit Privilege Set dialog box. Then, from the Layouts popup menu, choose "All view only".**

   You really intend to make custom privilege settings, but when you first visit the Custom Layout Privileges dialog box, everything is turned off. Since you want most options on, save your wrist by choosing "All view only". and FileMaker turns them all on for you. In the next step, you'll just turn a few options off.

2. **From the Layouts pop-up menu, choose "Custom privileges".**

   The Custom Layout Privileges window reappears. This time, though, every layout is set to "view only" with "modifiable" records.

3. **Turn on "Allow creation of new layout", and then, in the layout list, select the [Any New Layout] item.**

   You may have to scroll down to see it, as it's always at the bottom of the list.

4. **Under Layout, turn on the "modifiable" radio button.**

   Turning this setting on tells FileMaker you want new layouts to be modifiable. Click OK when you're done.

If you try to click OK without making new layouts modifiable, then FileMaker complains that it doesn't make sense to let someone make a new layout she can't edit. Now, anybody with the Project Manager privilege set can edit any new layouts she creates.

Value list privileges. Value lists may not seem as critical a security choice as records and layouts, but since value lists help people enter consistent data, you want to pay attention to these choices. If you put a pop-up menu on a field to limit data input, but then you give those same people the ability to modify the value list underlying the pop-up menu, then they have a way to circumvent your control.

You can see the Custom Value List Privileges window in Figure 16-10. This window lets you assign any of three privileges to each value list: modifiable, view only, or no access. You can also let somebody create new value lists with an "Allow creation of new value lists" checkbox, and set the privileges to be assigned to any new value lists.

You can control access to value lists in much the same way you manage record and layout privileges. And like record and layout privileges, you have three canned choices in the pop-up menu, plus Custom privileges:

- **All modifiable** means people can use and edit every value list.

- **All view** lets people only see and select from your value lists, but not change them.

- **All no access** prevents people from seeing value lists at all.

- **Custom privileges** gives you a dialog box where you can create your own set of privileges.

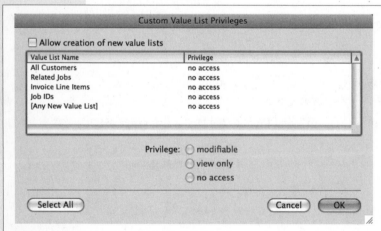

Figure 16-10:
The Custom Value List Privileges window is even simpler than the Custom Layout Privileges version. It works just like the others: Select a value list or two, and then choose a privilege.

In the business rules you're applying to your database, project managers should have view-only access to all value lists, so, from the Value Lists pop-up menu, choose "All view only".

Note: If you select all value lists in the dialog box, and then make them "view only" there, then your settings say "Custom privileges", which may be confusing down the road.

The Value List access you assign to a privilege set overrides layout designs. That is, even if you set up a pop-up menu with the option of "Include 'Edit...' item to allow editing of value list", then people with the Project Manager's privilege set can't edit values in the list.

Script privileges. The final option under "Data Access and Design" lets you control access to your scripts. As with layouts, you can have a class of people who can create new scripts, but can't edit data. If it's the accountants mentioned in the example on page 632 they need to write scripts to run the reports on the layouts you're letting them create. You could also create a privilege set that lets people at one level run most scripts, but doesn't let them run certain scripts that do destructive activities like deleting sets of records. You could save those scripts for higher-level people instead. Figure 16-11 shows the control choices you have.

Figure 16-11:
The Folder column refers to the organizer folders you can create in the Manage Script window (page 496). The Notes column tells you when a script is set to "Run with full access privileges". You'll learn about this later in this chapter.

Again, the pop-up menu gives you three canned choices and a custom option:

- **All modifiable** means people can run *and* edit any script.

- **All executable only** lets folks *run* scripts, but not edit them.

- **All no access** keeps people from running any scripts at all.

- **Custom Privileges** brings up the now-familiar Custom Privileges dialog box.

For the Project Managers set, from the Scripts pop-up menu, choose "All executable only". With this change, you've finished creating your privilege set. Your window should look just like Figure 16-12.

Figure 16-12:
When your privilege set is finished, it looks like this. You have so much detail there that you can't see all your settings in one screen, but the "…" in the Records and Layouts pop-up menus lets you know there's more detail to be seen if you need it. Just choose the appropriate pop-up menu if you need to review or edit.

To save your new privilege set, click OK. FileMaker adds Project Manager to the list of privilege sets in the Manage Accounts & Privileges window (Figure 16-1).

Note: When you give an element—a record, field, layout, value list, or script—the "no access" setting, it literally disappears from the user's view. Scripts disappear from the Scripts menu, layouts from the Layouts pop-up menu, fields from sort dialog boxes, and records from lists and portals. People aren't tempted to run a script or go to a layout to which they don't have access.

Editing a privilege set

If you need to make changes to a privilege set later (maybe you've added new fields, layouts or scripts to the database, and you have to make sure all your privilege sets give each group its proper access), just come back to this window, select the privilege set you need form the list, and then click Edit. You see the Edit Privilege Set window again, and you're free to change anything you want.

You can't edit FileMaker's built-in privilege sets. If you want to change one, duplicate it first, and then change the duplicate. Remember, though, that you can't duplicate [Full Access].

Managing Accounts

At the start of this chapter, you learned that FileMaker security has two facets: *who* can get in and *what* they can do. So far, you've created a privilege set called Project Manager, which handles the *what* part of the security equation. But a privilege set has no effect until you tell FileMaker who gets those privileges. You handle the *who* part by assigning a privilege set to an account. As you can see in the Manage Accounts & Privileges window's Privilege Sets tab, your new privilege set has no "Active accounts" assigned to it. This section covers creating and managing accounts.

Note: You can have privilege sets that don't have active accounts, but you can't create an account without assigning a privilege set to it, which is why most developers start out by creating privilege sets before they create accounts. But if you start creating an account first, and then realize you need a custom privilege set for it, that's OK. Just choose "New Privilege Set…" and then create it on the fly.

The Manage Accounts & Privileges window's Accounts tab (Figure 16-13) shows you all the accounts in your database. You never knew it, but all this time you've been using an account called Admin. FileMaker added this account when you first created your database so you'd have full access to the file without a password. Unfortunately, so does the rest of the FileMaking world. So your first job is to give the Admin account a proper password.

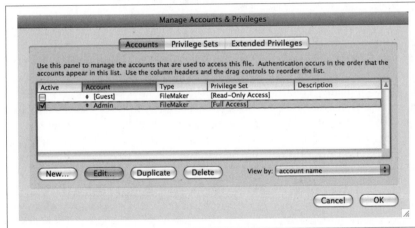

Figure 16-13:
The Accounts tab works a lot like the Privilege Sets tab. Click New to make a new account, or select an existing account, and then click Edit to change it. You can also duplicate or delete the selected account. Every account has an Active checkbox, an Account name, a type, an assigned privilege set, and an optional description.

To assign a password to the Admin account, in the Manage Accounts & Privileges window's Accounts tab, select it from the list, and then click Edit (or double-click the Admin account). The Edit Account window appears (Figure 16-14). In the Password field, type any password. Passwords can take any mix of alphanumeric characters and uppercase and lowercase characters you like. Click OK when you're done. Now that you've assigned a password to the Admin account, the next time you open this file, FileMaker asks you for an account name and password.

Tip: Account names aren't case-sensitive, but passwords are. If the Account Name or the password includes spaces, then make sure you type them precisely or you can't log in. FileMaker gives you five chances to log in, and then it stops showing you the login dialog box. But you aren't blocked permanently. You can try again right away.

Figure 16-14:
After creating a privilege set, the Edit Account window is refreshingly simple. It's even simpler when you consider that you can completely ignore the "Account is authenticated via" pop-up menu for now. You get to edit the account name and password, make an account inactive (when an account is inactive, FileMaker doesn't let users log in), assign a privilege set, and edit the description.

If you want, you can change the name of the Admin account, too. You don't have to have an account called Admin. On the other hand, you're required to have an account with full access. If you try to dismiss this dialog box without one, then FileMaker complains. Finally, in the Manage Accounts & Privileges window, whenever you click OK, FileMaker wants to make sure you know an account name and password with full access, so it asks you to enter them. If you don't get it right, then FileMaker doesn't let you save your changes. This password box is the final layer of protection from losing your file forever, because once you forget a password, you have no way to retrieve it.

Warning: Make sure you don't forget your Full Access password. FileMaker uses industry-standard and ultra-secure techniques to manage passwords, you simply have no way to bypass them. FileMaker, Inc. may be willing to change the password in the file, but the process takes several weeks and is not guaranteed.

If you forget a more restricted password, on the other hand, then the fix is simple. Just open the database with a Full Access password, visit the Manage Accounts & Privileges dialog box, and then change the forgotten password.

Adding a New Account

You can add a new account almost as easily as you can edit an existing one. Since it's so easy to add accounts, there's no reason not to follow best security practices and give everyone an individual account, complete with a unique name and password combination. You can even give people more than one account. For example, you can designate some people as super-users who mostly do data entry and editing but sometimes need to create layouts. As much as you trust them, you just want to make sure they don't inadvertently damage layouts and scripts while they're doing other work. So you require them to log in with higher-level access when switching from data entry to tasks that require more care, like database design. (See page 660 for more detail on re-login.)

FREQUENTLY ASKED QUESTION

Automatic Login

If I've been using the Admin account all this time, how come FileMaker never asked me to log in? Does it just skip the authentication dialog box when some account has no password?

Actually, FileMaker's been logging in for you. Every new database is set up to log in automatically using the Admin account and a blank password. Once you give the Admin account a password for a given database, automatic login stops. But you can set your database to log in with any account automatically, or you can turn off automatic login entirely, a much more secure option.

The setting is behind the File → File Options command. When you choose this command, you see the File Options

dialog box. Turn off the "Log in using" checkbox to stop the automatic login process. Or, you can type a different account and/or password in the appropriate box to log in a different way. Finally, you can have FileMaker automatically log into the file using the guest account (see the box on page 652).

If you set your file to automatically log in with an account that doesn't have full access, including the guest account, then you can't come back to this window to turn it off. You may think you've just locked yourself out of your file completely, but you haven't. If you hold down the Shift key (Option key on a Mac) while a file opens, then FileMaker asks you for an account name and password even if the file's set to automatically log in.

To create a new account, click New. In the Edit Account window, give the account a name and a password, and assign a privilege set. If you don't see a suitable privilege set, from the Privilege Set pop-up menu, choose New Privilege Set. You can also edit the selected privilege set by clicking Edit.

If you let each person manage his or her own password, then you can turn on "User must change password on next login". When you turn this option on, you can create an account for someone with a generic password, and then email the account information to her, with instructions to create a more secure and secret password when she first opens the database.

Note: If your colleague forgets his password, you can't retrieve it for him because FileMaker masks it as soon as you click OK in the Edit Account dialog box. You can *change* his password, though, so long as you have an account with full access to the file.

You can also make an account inactive. When you do, FileMaker keeps the account—and all its information—in the Accounts list, but it doesn't let people open the database using that account. You can make an account inactive if someone leaves the company for an extended period of time, but plans to return. You can easily reactivate the account when you need to. You can also use this option to create accounts for new employees before they start.

Create a new account with the name and password of your choosing. Assign it to the Project Manager privilege set, and then close and reopen the file. When prompted, enter the new account name and password. Now experiment. Try modifying or deleting old invoices, or editing product records. You should see your new security settings in action. When you're done, close the file again, and then open it one more time. This time use the Admin account to log in.

External Authentication

If you work for an organization that uses Windows Active Directory or Open Directory in Mac OS X, then you can take advantage of the fact that your coworkers *already* log in to their computers each morning. Since everybody already has a company-wide user name and password, you can use *external authentication*, which tells FileMaker to hand off the chore of identifying people. This setup has two advantages. First, you can save yourself the trouble of creating scads of accounts in all your database files. And when your IT department creates a new user, or removes someone who's left the company, access to FileMaker is automatically adjusted as well. Additionally, on Windows your users can take advantage of Single Sign-on: They don't have to enter a password to access FileMaker if they already logged in to their computer with their own user names and passwords.

Note: On Mac OS X, the system-wide Keychain handles automatic login for FileMaker just like every other program. You don't need to use external authentication to speed past the password dialog box. Just click "Add to keychain" the first time you log in instead.

Since these external accounts aren't actually stored in FileMaker, you don't need to add the accounts themselves to your database. Instead, you tell FileMaker which *groups* in the external system should be granted access. For example, if your Windows Active Directory already has a group for Accounting and another for Customer Service, you can tell FileMaker what privileges people in each of these groups have.

If you don't have appropriate groups in the external system, then you can have the system administrator add a new group (or several new groups) just for you. You can then assign a privilege set to each group that should be given access, and the system administrator assigns individual people to each group.

To assign a privilege set to an external group, you create a single account in File-Maker. But instead of entering a user name and password, from the "Account is authenticated via" pop-up menu, choose External Server. The Account Name and Password boxes disappear, and a new Group Name box appears instead. Just type the name of the Active Directory or Open Directory group in this box.

You can set up external authentication in two ways, but both require a working directory server and FileMaker Server (see Chapter 18):

- **Local accounts on your FileMaker server.** You can manage account names and passwords on the server itself, and have them apply to every database. This method saves you the trouble of creating individual FileMaker accounts in every file.

- **Domain accounts.** FileMaker Server communicates with the directory server on your company's network to authenticate users. This approach centralizes account management *and* lets people log in with the same account names and passwords they use for every other computer system on your network.

Both methods require coordination with your IT department. Consult it (or the documentation for your directory server) for more information on setting up and maintaining external authentication.

Note: You're free to use a mixture of normal FileMaker accounts and external authentication accounts. In fact, you *must* have at least one full access FileMaker account in every file. If you need to extend access to someone who's not in the directory server, then you can add a FileMaker account for that person, too. People from the directory server can log in, and so can this special person.

Extended Privileges

Extended privileges come in two flavors. A set of default extended privileges lets you determine how people interact with shared databases. These privileges control how your database works with other FileMaker products (primarily FileMaker Server), so they're covered in Chapter 18. You can also create custom extended privileges of your own. Each extended privilege can be turned on or off for each privilege set you define.

These custom extended privileges don't actually add any capability on their own. Instead, using scripts, you can check to see whether the active privilege set has an extended privilege before you let anyone do anything important or irreversible. To use this feature fully, write your scripts with extended privileges in mind. Then, when you need to temporarily give extra power to a particular privilege set, in the Edit Privilege Set window, you just turn on a checkbox, and all your scripts do the right thing. The next section takes you through one example.

Creating an Extended Privilege

Suppose you've decided to let project managers delete records directly, and you give them that power in their privilege set. When other people try to delete a customer record, you want FileMaker to *flag* the record instead, so that a manager can find and delete the flagged records later. To automate the process, you write a Delete script, using the *Get (PrivilegeSetName)* function to check whether the person's a manager before deleting the records.

Here's how to set up the extended privileges so you can use them in the script. Open the Manage Accounts & Privileges window, click the Extended Privileges tab, and then click New. You see the Edit Extended Privilege window on your screen. It's also in Figure 16-15. This extended privilege controls a person's ability to directly delete customer records, so put "Delete customer records directly" in the Description box. For the keyword, enter *delcust* as an abbreviation. While you're here, turn on the checkbox next to [Full Access]. For now, only those people with full access can delete customer records. When you're done, click OK.

Figure 16-15:
The Edit Extended Privilege window lets you give your extended privilege a keyword and a description. The description should say what the extended privilege is for. The keyword can be anything you want; it's what you'll look for in your scripts, so once you start using an extended privilege, you probably don't want to change its keyword. You can also tell FileMaker which privilege sets have this extended privilege turned on by clicking the Access list's checkboxes.

Checking for an Extended Privilege

Now you need to write your script. You'll use the *Get (ExtendedPrivileges)* function to ask FileMaker for the list of extended privileges turned on for the active privilege set. The script checks to see if this list includes "delcust", and takes the appropriate action. While creating this script, you need to add a new text field called Delete Flag to the Customers table. You can see the finished script in Figure 16-16.

Try out your script by running it from the Customers layout. Assuming you're working in the Admin account, the script should delete the customer record, since you have the [Full Access] privilege set. Then close the database and open it again. This time, log in as someone assigned the Project Manager privilege set. Project Manager *doesn't* have the "delcust" extended privilege turned on, so when you run the script this time, it sets the Delete Flag field instead of deleting the record.

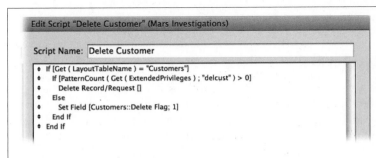

Figure 16-16:
This script first checks to make sure you're on a layout associated with the Customers table occurrence. If not, it refuses to run. If you're on the right layout, then it checks your extended privileges to see if you have the "delcust" privilege turned on. If you do, then it deletes the record. If you don't, then it sets the Delete Flag field instead.

Assigning Extended Privileges

To give project managers the ability to delete customers directly, which is the whole point of the script you just wrote, you have two options: First, you can edit the Project Manager privilege set itself. The Edit Privilege Set window has a list of extended privileges in the bottom-left corner where you can control which extended privileges are turned on (see Figure 16-17). To give project managers the power to delete customer records, just turn on the checkbox next to "Directly delete customer records". If you're adding it only to a privilege set, then editing the privilege set itself is the easiest way to turn on an extended privilege.

If you have a few privilege sets that need the same extended privilege, there's an alternate method: Go to the Manage Accounts & Privileges window's Extended Privileges tab, and then edit the "delcust" extended privilege instead. This way, you see all the Privilege Sets in a list. In the Edit Extended Privilege window, you can turn the extended privilege off or on for any privilege set by clicking the checkboxes in the list of privilege sets.

To test the "delcust" extended privilege, turn it on for the Project Manager privilege set, and then close the database. Then open it, log in as a project manager, and run the Delete Customer script. This time it deletes the customer right away. (See page 660 to see how the re-login script step can make testing security settings easier.)

Figure 16-17:
The list of extended privileges in the Edit Privilege Set window shows every extended privilege in the database, each with a checkbox beside it. If you turn one of these checkboxes on, then you're giving this privilege set access to everything controlled by that extended privilege.

Scripts and Security

Security and script writing intersect in two areas. First, you need to take into account the level of access people have, and whether or not your scripts override some or all of their privileges. (The previous section describes one way of doing so with extended privileges.) Second, FileMaker lets you automate some of the security features described earlier in this chapter with scripting. ScriptMaker has a handful of steps dedicated to security-related tasks, and this section shows you how to use them.

Detecting Privileges in a Script

The first way to handle security in your scripts is to deal with it directly. In the last section you learned how to check for extended privileges and take appropriate actions. If you want, then you can check for specific privilege sets, or even specific account names.

- To check the privilege set, use the **Get (PrivilegeSetName)** function. It returns the name of the privilege set assigned to the current user. Bear in mind that if you change the name of a privilege set, then you have to modify any scripts that use this function.

- If you must restrict an action to a particular account, then use **Get (AccountName)** instead. As you probably expect, it returns the name of the account with which the user logged in. The same warning applies here: Beware of renamed accounts.

Note: *If someone logged in with external authentication, then Get (AccountName) gives you her real account name in the external directory server.*

• Finally, FileMaker has one more tempting function: **Get (UserName)**. This function normally returns the user name from the computer's operating system (the name you use to log into the computer itself). If you use shared accounts in FileMaker, then you may want to use the user name to find out who's actually doing something. Bear in mind, though, that most people can change their user name settings to anything they want, so it isn't useful for security-related purposes.

You can easily use these functions, but they have some drawbacks. Chances are that, at some point in the future, you'll need to change the account names, privilege sets, or users that can do certain things. Every time you do, you have to check and probably edit all your scripts.

Furthermore, the *Get (UserName)* function has a *severe* limitation: Anybody can change it at any time. If someone does, then all scripts referencing the old name fail, at least as a security device. Here's why: In FileMaker's Preferences window, under the General tab, FileMaker lets anyone type in any name he wants. This characteristic means it's *easy* for someone to pretend to be someone else. If you want to secure a scripted process, then the extended privilege feature described on page 653 is safer and lets you much more easily update accounts and privilege sets.

Handling Security Errors

If your script tries to do something the person isn't allowed to do, then FileMaker shows the error message in Figure 16-18. If you turn error capture on in your script, then this error doesn't show on the screen. Instead, you can use the *Get (LastError)* function to check for an error (see page 594). That way, you can have the script display a custom message box, email you the name of the misbehaving person, or take some other action. The most common security-related error is number 200: "Record Access is Denied." (If you're interested in learning more about error codes, check out the resources in Appendix B.)

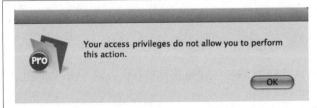

Figure 16-18:
When someone tries something your security setup doesn't allow, he sees this message–even if it's a script that's breaking the rules. Unfortunately, FileMaker doesn't tell him–or you–what the script is trying to do.

Running Scripts with Full Access Privileges

Sometimes you *want* the script to do its duty even though the user doesn't have the necessary privileges. For example, you may want to remove an accountant's ability to delete invoice records since she's not supposed to delete any orders. But you may still want to let her run a script that finds old completed invoices, exports them to an archive, and then deletes them. Since this script is careful to delete only invoices that are ready to go, the accountant can safely run it when necessary.

For those kinds of circumstances, FileMaker lets you specify when a script should run with full access privileges for *anyone*. In other words, the script overrides the normal restrictions you set up in the user's privilege set. At the bottom of the Edit Script dialog box, just turn on the "Run script with full access privileges" option. With this option turned on, the script dutifully deletes the invoices even though the accountant running it isn't allowed to delete records in the Invoice or Line Item tables with her account's privilege set.

Even when you set a script to run with full access privileges in this way, you can still prevent some folks from running it by switching it to "no access" in the Custom Script Privileges window for a privilege set (page 647). You can also make the script check for an extended privilege, and take appropriate actions for different people.

Managing Security with Scripts

ScriptMaker's Edit Script window (Figure 13-2) has an entire section called Accounts. It includes six steps that give you some control over the security system from your scripts. All these steps require full access privileges to work. If you don't manage a lot of accounts in your database, then you might not find much use for these steps. But if you have a large organization, or one that has lots of turnover—like a school system that's constantly adding new teachers or graduating a whole class of students who no longer need access to databases for class work—these script steps can save tons of time and effort.

Add Account

FileMaker lets you add new accounts to a database from a script—and for good reason. If you build a system that uses several databases, and you can't use external authentication, then the Add Account step is your best friend. Instead of adding each account to all your files manually, try this: Write a script that asks for the account name and password with a custom dialog box, and stores them in global fields. Then use scripts in each file to add the same account to every file at once. When you're all done, be sure to clear the password from the global field to protect it from prying eyes.

Or, if you have to populate your brand-new file with a huge number of people when you're first installing your database, then you save tons of time creating accounts if you have an electronic list of user names and passwords. Import them (page 683) into a table, and then use a looping script to create hundreds of accounts in a few seconds.

Tip: The Add Account step lets you specify the account name and password using calculations, but you have to select a specific privilege set for all users in the loop. If you want to script the creation of accounts with different privilege sets, use the If/Else If steps and several copies of the Add Account step, each with a different privilege set selected.

Delete Account

If you're going to create accounts with a script, why not delete them, too? The Delete Account script needs only an account name—and you can supply it with a calculation. With this script, you can build the other half of your multifile account management system.

Warning: If you write a script that adds or deletes accounts, then pay special attention to its security settings. You can all too easily give a database the tightest security FileMaker allows, and then leave a gaping security hole through a script. Customize privilege sets so that only you (or a trusted few) can run it, and *don't* put it on the Scripts menu.

Reset Account Password

If lots of people use your database, then forgotten passwords will undoubtedly become your worst nightmare. You could spend all day changing passwords for people. Why not write a script that can reset a password to something generic, and then email it to the person? If you set the script to run with full access privileges, then you can even delegate password resetting to someone else. The Reset Account Password step needs an account name and a new password to do its job.

Change Password

You'll probably use this script step only in cases where you're creating a special interface that lets people who don't have full access privileges manage security. For example, you may have someone on staff who should be able to manage accounts, but you don't want him to have full access privileges. So you can build a special layout (or two), and write scripts that run with full access privileges to manage all your security tasks. That way, you can even do special workarounds like allowing some members of a privilege set to change their passwords without giving this power to each of them. To do so, you usually need a user's table with a field that controls who can and can't run your Change Password script.

Enable Account

Once you've created a bunch of new accounts using the Add Account step, the Enable Account step lets you turn them on and off at will. That way, you can create accounts for, say, an entire class of students, and later turn on accounts for those who've arrived on campus. This step does the same thing as *make active* and *make inactive* in the Edit Accounts dialog box, and it works only when there's a valid account name that matches your script settings.

Re-Login

The most exciting step in the Accounts section is Re-Login. It provides a function that doesn't exist anywhere else in FileMaker. It lets you switch to a different account without closing the file, which gives you almost superhuman ability to test security settings. Instead of opening and closing the files until your mouse button wears out, just run a Re-Login script. Add steps in the script that set global fields on pertinent layouts to *Get (AccountName)* and *Get (PrivilegeSet)* so you can keep track of what you're testing as you re-login over and over. To get the most realistic testing conditions, make sure your Re-login script calls any script that runs when your file opens.

You can also use Re-Login when someone inevitably calls you to his desk to show you a problem in the database. Just re-login as an account with full access, and then you can poke around and find out what's happening *on his computer*. When you re-login, you're not just saving time by not closing and reopening the file. You can actually work in the same window, on the same record, with the same found set and sort order without all the trouble of recreating the situation back at your desk. Again, since you can re-login only from a script, consider adding a Re-Login script to the Scripts menu in every database you create.

Sharing Data with Other Systems

Building a big database can make you feel like a slave to your computer, but the point of a database is to let you manage information more efficiently. Nothing illustrates this point better than FileMaker's ability to pull data into your database from various sources, and dump it back out again in assorted ways.

If you have data in almost any kind of program—spreadsheets full of figures, lists of names and phone numbers, electronic orders in XML, folders full of pictures or text documents—FileMaker can *import* it directly into your database. If your data is already in FileMaker, then you can *export* it to lists, other databases, XML, or almost any other format imaginable. FileMaker takes a wonderfully flexible approach: It lets you handle simple imports and exports with just a click or two, and provides the features to tackle the most complex cases as well—if you (or some hired help) are willing to do the necessary work.

If your company uses one of the vast corporate databases—Oracle, Microsoft SQL Server, or MySQL—FileMaker Pro 10 can integrate directly with them, bringing its powerful (and easy) developer tools to bear on their complex-yet-oh-so-speedy data. You can put your corporate SQL data right on the FileMaker layout, perform FileMaker finds, write scripts, and even add calculation fields, all without writing a single line of SQL code.

Sharing Your Data with Others

Most database systems don't live in a vacuum. Chances are your information is important to someone else, or important to you some*where* else. You may want to transfer job information to your Accounting software, or send the sales report to your associate across town. Luckily, FileMaker provides options for getting the data out of your database in all kinds of forms.

Save/Send Records As

If your data is destined for a person (rather than some other computer program), then you want a format that's easy to look at and to work with on almost any computer. FileMaker lets you save your data in two ubiquitous formats: an Excel spreadsheet and a PDF document. Choose Excel if you want to be able to work with the data (perform analysis, combine it with other data, create graphs, and so forth). But if you want the output to look just like it looks in FileMaker, and you don't need it to be editable, then a PDF is the perfect choice.

Saving as Microsoft Excel

If people need to work with the data you send them, but they aren't lucky enough to have FileMaker, you can create an Excel file for them. (And presumably, if they're working with data, they have either Excel or a program that can open Excel spreadsheets.) Just choose File → Save/Send Records As → Excel. When you do, FileMaker shows the window in Figure 17-1.

Figure 17-1:
The Save Records As Excel window lets you tell FileMaker where to save the spreadsheet file. It also gives you the option of automatically opening the file you're creating, so you don't have to go rummaging around your hard drive looking for it.

The Save pop-up menu lets you choose whether you want to save all the "Records being browsed" (that is, the found set) or just the "Current Record." Turn on "Automatically open file" if you want to see the spreadsheet as soon as FileMaker finishes saving it. When you do, FileMaker automatically launches Excel and shows you the spreadsheet. You also have the option to "Create email with file as attachment," so it's easy to check your work and create a quick email with the data your boss just asked you to email her. Once you save, FileMaker creates a new email message in your email program, attaches the spreadsheet, and opens the message so you can add recipients, a subject, and any message you want.

If you click Options, you can set up some basic details for your new Excel file. For example, you can choose whether you want your FileMaker field names to appear in the first row of the spreadsheet. You can also type in a worksheet name and a title, subject, and author (each of which appear in the spreadsheet in the appropriate places).

Saving as Portable Document Format (PDF)

Just about anybody with a computer can view PDF files. With PDF, you get to choose exactly how the data looks, since this format preserves your beautifully crafted layouts. With FileMaker's layout tools, your keen design sense, and the "Save/Send Record as PDF" command, you could use email to distribute invoices, product catalogs, sales brochures, or annual reports. You can even send vision-impaired people a file their software can read aloud. Even if all you need to do is send people data they can see but can't change, then a PDF file is just what the software engineer ordered.

Note: The most common PDF viewer, Adobe Reader, is a free download at *http://www.adobe.com/products/acrobat/readstep2.html*. Mac OS X also comes preloaded with its own PDF viewer, called Preview.

The basic choices are the same as for Excel. You choose between sending just the current record or the whole found set. You can have the file opened in a PDF viewer or attached to a new, blank email just as soon as FileMaker's created it. But behind the Options button you find a much richer set of choices. There are three tabs—Document (Figure 17-2), Security (Figure 17-3), and Initial View (Figure 17-4). Starting with the Document tab, you can set:

- **Title.** This title isn't the name you give the file in the dialog box. It's an additional title that becomes part of the properties of the document. Most, but not all, PDF viewer programs let you see a file's properties.

- **Subject.** This document property helps you tell a series of similar documents apart from each other.

- **Author.** This document property is usually your name, but may also be the name of your company or department. Again, it helps you organize a bunch of similar files.

Figure 17-2:
The PDF Options dialog box shows up when you choose File → Save/Send Records As → PDF, and then click Options. The Document tab lets you add information to the PDF document. The first four options become part of the document's properties, as described in the note below.

- **Keywords.** Some file management programs can search these keywords to locate documents.

- **Compatibility.** Choose from "Acrobat 5 and later" or "Acrobat 6 and later." Choose the lower number if you think your recipient might not have the latest and greatest PDF viewer.

- **Number pages from.** You can make a different numbering system than the one you have in FileMaker.

- **Include.** You can set a limited page-number range with these options, so that only a part of the found set is included in the PDF file. You may have to go to Preview mode in FileMaker first, though, to help you set the page range properly.

Note: You can see the PDF file's Title, Subject, and Author in Adobe Acrobat's PDF viewer's Document Properties Summary window. In Mac OS X's Preview program, choose Tools → Get Info instead.

In the Security Tab (Figure 17-3), you can decide how much access you give your recipients when they receive your file. You can choose:

- **Require password to open the file.** Click the checkbox to turn this option on, and then enter a password. This checkbox is useful if you're selling a catalog and provide passwords only to people who've paid to receive it. Then, of course, there's the standard use; you just don't want every Malcolm, Reese, and Dewey poking around in your PDF files.

Figure 17-3:
The Security tab lets you lock down your PDF file if you need to prevent inappropriate use. Some older PDF reading programs may not recognize all these options. If someone's PDF reader doesn't have security features, it can't open the PDF file at all, so your data is still safe.

- **Require password to control printing, editing and security**. Click the checkbox to turn this option on and enter a password. You might want your PDF freely distributed, but not so freely used. If so, don't require a password to open the file, but lock it down so nobody without a password can use the material without your permission. With this option checked, a whole raft of new options becomes available. You can set:

  — **Printing**. Choose from Not Permitted, Low Resolution (150 dpi), or High Resolution. These options would protect photographic or other artwork images that you want to send in a catalog but don't want people to reprint freely. You also may want someone to *see* your document onscreen, but not print it and risk having it fall into the wrong hands.

  — **Editing**. Although PDF files are generally considered view-only, with the right software, they can actually be edited. If you don't want to allow this (or want to restrict what can be done), choose options from this pop-up menu. For example, if you're sending a contract for review, and you want to be sure no new clauses are snuck in while it's away, you can choose **Not permitted**.

  — **Enable copy of text, images and other content**. With this option checked, recipients can copy and paste material from your PDF file.

  — **Allow text to be read by screen reading software**. This option lets people with vision or reading problems have their screen reading programs read your document out loud.

The final tab in the PDF Options window is probably the one you'll use the least. But if you like to control which PDF viewer options are visible when your recipient first opens your PDF file, then Initial View (Figure 17-4) is the panel for you:

Figure 17-4:
You get to decide what the user sees when she first opens the PDF containing your database info. Once again, not all these options work in older versions of PDF software, so consider your settings here a suggestion.

- **Show.** Your choices include **Page Only** (just the FileMaker layout, with no extra tools or panels), **Bookmarks Panel and Page**, or **Pages Panel and Page** to offer viewers some navigation options.

- **Page Layout.** Control the way the PDF viewer displays multipage documents. If you choose *Default*, your recipients' preferred view remains in force. But you can also specify **Single Page**, **Continuous**, or **Magnification**.

Note: These Initial View options may or may not actually take effect, depending on what program and what version of that program the PDF is opened with.

External SQL Sources

If you don't know MySQL from MySpace, and have no interest in taking your humble FileMaker skills to the hard-core level of IT professionals, then feel free to skip right past this section. But if have to cross between these worlds or need to bring the power and capability of industrial-grade database servers into your systems, FileMaker's new *External SQL Sources* (or ESS) feature will seem like magic.

In a nutshell, you point your FileMaker database in the general direction of an Oracle, Microsoft SQL Server, or MySQL (pronounced "my sequel") database (heretofore referred to as a SQL database). FileMaker then takes in information about that database, learning all it needs to know to make those normally complicated systems almost as easy to use as FileMaker. You can create table occurrences in your relationship graph that are actually references to the tables in the SQL database. You can draw relationship lines between SQL tables, or even between your FileMaker tables and the SQL tables. You can create a layout based on a SQL table, drop a few fields on the layout, and then jump to Find mode, where FileMaker searches the real honest-to-goodness SQL data and shows you a found set of records.

With few exceptions, a SQL table works just like any other FileMaker table. But instead of storing the data on your hard drive, the SQL database stores and manages the data. You don't need to know a lick of SQL programming to work with it. When you add a record using the Records → New Record command, FileMaker sends the right secret code that adds the record to the SQL database. Just type in a field and press Enter, and FileMaker updates the SQL database. It doesn't get more seamless this.

Setting Up ODBC

Before you can take advantage of ESS, you need to set up a few things. This business of getting things installed and configured is the hardest part—and it's not FileMaker's fault.

The SQL database server

First of all, you need a SQL database. To integrate as seamlessly as it does, File-Maker needs to know exactly which database you're using:

• Microsoft SQL Server 2005

• Microsoft SQL Server 2000

• Oracle 10g

• Oracle 9g

• MySQL 5.0 Community Edition

If your SQL database isn't in this list, you have to upgrade or migrate to one that is. Trying to make a different type of database work is futile—just ask someone who's tried. Luckily, this list represents recent versions of three very popular database systems. If you don't have a SQL database, but you want to get one, you need to research which is best for you. But if you just want to experiment, start with MySQL. For most purposes (including real commercial use), it's completely free. To get MySQL for Mac OS X or Windows, visit *http://www.mysql.com* and look for the MySQL Community Server link.

The rest of this section assumes you have a working SQL database server, and that you have access to at least one database on that server.

Installing the ODBC driver

In order for FileMaker to communicate with the SQL database, you need an ODBC driver. This software acts as the bridge between programs on your computer and the SQL database server software. The driver is specific to your database server. If you're using Oracle, you need an Oracle ODBC driver, for instance. If you use Microsoft Windows, this step is usually a breeze. Each of the supported SQL databases has an ODBC driver provided by the manufacturer. Just visit their Web site and find out how to get the driver you need.

Note: If you're not sure what you need, try searching the Web for *microsoft sql server odbc driver download*. The first site listed is probably the download page you need. (Substitute *oracle* or *mysql* for microsoft sql server, as appropriate.)

Mac OS X users aren't so lucky. The big database developers don't provide free ODBC drivers for the Mac. Instead, head over to *http://www.actualtechnologies.com*, and purchase the right driver (they're cheap and work beautifully). FileMaker, Inc. worked directly with Actual to ensure maximum compatibility, and they provide the drivers of choice. (For MySQL, choose the driver called *ODBC Driver for Open Source Databases*.)

Once you've acquired the correct driver, install it on your computer. After you've installed the driver, you have to configure it.

Configuring the data source

Your computer's operating system has the ODBC system built in. You use a special program on your computer to tell it which SQL databases you want to work with. The configuration process is entirely different on Mac OS X and Windows, so go directly to the section that applies to you.

Configuring data sources on Windows. You configure your Windows machine for ODBC in the Control Panel (Start → Control Panel). The control panel looks a little different in various Windows versions:

- On Windows Vista, you may see a category called "System and Maintenance." Open this category, and click Administrative Tools at the bottom of the list. If you don't see "System and Maintenance", look for Administrative Tools in the Control Panel window and open it.

- On Windows XP, you may see a category called "Performance and Maintenance". Open this category and click Administrative Tools. If you don't have "Performance and Maintenance", look for Administrative Tools right in the Control Panel window and open it.

Assuming you've found the Administrative Tools window, look inside it and open Data Sources (ODBC). You should see something on your screen that looks like Figure 17-5.

In this window, you add a *DSN (data source name)* for each SQL database you want FileMaker to work with. A DSN can be one of two flavors: A *System* DSN is available to everyone who uses your computer; and a *User* DSN is available only to the person who created it. FileMaker works only with the System DSN variety, so to get started, switch to the System DSN tab. Unfortunately, you may not have permission to define these computer-wide data sources on your work computer. If Windows doesn't let you add a system DSN, contact your system administrator.

Figure 17-5:
The ODBC Data Source Administrator on Windows lets you configure the SQL databases your computer has access to. The acronym DSN stands for Data Source Name, since you name each data source you define here, and then refer to it by name in FileMaker.

Once you're on the System DSN tab, click Add. Windows shows you a list of available ODBC drivers. Select the appropriate one and click Finish. (Don't get too excited by the label on this button; you're nowhere near finished.)

Note: You may get a little confused by the list of available drivers on Windows. First, you may see many drivers whose names are apparently in a foreign language. Just scroll right past them. Also, you may be tempted to select the driver called SQL Server. After all, every database FileMaker works with could legitimately be called a SQL database server. But this driver is specifically for *Microsoft* SQL Server. If you use one of the other database systems, keep looking.

From this point forward, configuration works a lot like Mac OS X. Skip ahead to "Finishing ODBC data source configuration" below.

Configuring data sources on Mac OS X. On Mac OS X, you configure ODBC data sources using an application called ODBC Administrator. You can find this program in your Applications → Utilities folder. When you launch the program, you see the window in Figure 17-6.

When you open ODBC Administrator, first click the padlock icon in the bottom-left corner to unlock it. Then click the System DSN tab. (FileMaker works only with system-wide data sources.) Next, click Add. A sheet slides down showing a list of ODBC drivers installed on your computer. Select the one you want, and then click OK.

At this point, the exact configuration will vary based on the driver you're using.

Finishing ODBC data source configuration. The exact setup procedure varies with each ODBC driver, but a few things remain constant:

- On Mac OS X, even though you're in the System DSN tab, you have the option of creating either a *user* or a *system* DSN. Make sure you choose *system*.

Figure 17-6:
The ODBC Administrator on Mac OS X lets you create ODBC data sources. You need to log in to your computer as an administrator to create the kind of data source FileMaker needs. You also may need to click the padlock icon in the bottom-left corner of this window before you can make changes.

- Give the data source any name you like. You'll use this name later when you connect FileMaker to the database. But bear in mind if you *change* a name here, you'll have to update every FileMaker database that uses it or the connections will break.

- The description is not important. Leave it blank, or leave a note for yourself.

- You need to know the address (IP address or host name) of the database server, as well as a user name and password. You also need to know the name of the database you're connecting to (not Oracle or MySQL, but the name of the actual database on the server, like Products or Financial).

- Your driver may ask lots of questions, but you can usually accept the pre-entered answers for most of them. If you're not sure, talk to your database administrator. If you don't have a database administrator, make friends with one.

- On the last page of the setup process, you get a chance to test data source. Click this button—it tells you whether all the info you just entered is correct. Better to find out now than when FileMaker gets confused later on.

Once you're finished, you see your data source listed in the System DSN tab of your ODBC configuration program. Go ahead and close the window. Your configuration work is finished.

Connecting FileMaker to a SQL Data Source

Suppose you've decided to harness the power of the Web to grow your private investigation business. You hired a hotshot programmer to build you a sweet little Web site that's sure to put you at the top of the Google search results. Even better, visitors to your Web site can fill out an inquiry form asking for your help. The programmer set up the site so the form submissions go directly into a MySQL database. Now you want to work with that data in FileMaker.

WORKAROUND WORKSHOP

The Case of the Missing Driver

A bug in the MySQL ODBC driver installer can leave your ODBC system in a confused state where it stops showing new ODBC drivers you've installed (even non-MySQL drivers). If you installed your driver but it isn't in the list, don't beat yourself up. You didn't do anything wrong.

The fix requires a trip to the RegEdit program, where non-technical folks rarely dare to tread. Luckily, the steps are straightforward. Just follow them exactly, and you'll be fine. If you're worried, show this page to your nerdiest friend (or anyone under 20) and ask for help.

1. Run the RegEdit program.

2. On Windows Vista, click the Start button and, in the search panel, type *regedit*. Then click regedit.exe at the top of the Start menu. On Windows XP, click Start → Run, type *regedit* in the box that pops up, and then click OK.

3. Choose File → Export and save your current registry someplace safe.

4. On the off chance you mess up here, you can restore your old settings by running RegEdit again and using the File → Import command.

5. In the folder list on the left side of the window, click the plus signs to expand each of these folders in succession: HKEY_LOCAL_MACHINE, SOFTWARE, ODBC, and ODBCINST.INI.

6. The Windows registry works like a hierarchy of folders, and you're digging your way down to the thing you need to change.

7. Select the ODBC Drivers folder inside ODBCINST.INI.

8. RegEdit fills the list on the right with what looks a lot like the list of ODBC drivers.

At this point, you need to look for the problem. At the top of the list on the right side, you see an entry called "(Default)" (with parentheses and all). In the Data column for that line, it should say "(value not set)." If the top row of the data column is empty, or has a pair of quotation marks, then you're a victim of the bug. Just select the "(Default)" item and press the Delete key on your keyboard. The words "(value not set)" should appear where they weren't before.

Close RegEdit and, if prompted, agree to save the changes. Now exit the Data Sources control panel and open it again. You should see your driver.

You've acquired all the necessary information from the programmer, and configured an ODBC data source. Your next step is to tell your FileMaker database about the SQL database:

1. **Open the FileMaker database you've been building, or download a copy from** *http://www.missingmanuals.com/cds.* **Then choose File → Manage → External Data Sources.**

   Here's where you tell your database about other places it can find data. You used this same window to connect one FileMaker database to another (see page 377). This time, though, you're going to connect to a non-FileMaker database.

2. **Click New.**

   FileMaker shows you the Edit Data Source window.

3. **In the Name box, type** *Web Leads.*

   You can name the data source anything you want. This name will show up when you're choosing tables to add to the Relationship graph.

4. **Click the ODBC radio button below the Name box.**

FileMaker revamps the dialog box so it looks like the one in Figure 17-7.

5. **Click Specify.**

You see a list of all the system ODBC data sources defined on your computer.

6. **Choose the data source you want to connect to, and then click OK.**

FileMaker puts the data source name in the box next to DSN.

At this point you have a decision to make. When someone opens this database, how it logs into the remote database? You have three options here:

- Turn on "Prompt user for username and password" if you want people to enter the login information when FileMaker makes the connection. This option means everyone has to log in to the SQL database every time they open the FileMaker database (in addition to any password they need to open the FileMaker file).

- Turn on "Specify username and password (applies to all users)" if you want File-Maker to automatically log in to the SQL database on everyone's behalf. When you do, you can enter a calculation to determine either value, so you can hard code a text value, automatically use the current user's FileMaker account name (with the *Get (AccountName)* function) or any other mechanism you need.

- If you're using Microsoft Windows and Microsoft SQL Server, you can turn on "Use Windows Authentication (Single Sign-on)." This option lets FileMaker automatically connect to the SQL database using the Windows user name and password. Your database administrator has to configure the Windows accounts properly for this setup to work (you can find details in the FileMaker help by searching for "ODBC Single Sign-on"). Also, you have to get the Service Principal Name (SPN) from your database administrator.

Note: You may be wondering why you have to enter a user name and password here at all, since you already typed them in when you created the ODBC data source. It turns out the ODBC system just really wants that information so it can test your data source and ease configuration. It doesn't actually *use* that login info when you open the database.

In this case, turn on "Specify user name and password (applies to all users)," and type the user name and password for your SQL database. Click OK to tell File-Maker you're done. Click OK again in the Manage External Data Sources window to get back to your database.

Adding SQL Tables to a FileMaker Database

Your database now has a pipeline to the tables in a SQL data source. But you haven't told it what to do with those tables yet. Your next stop is the Relationships tab of the Manage Database window, where you can fold the SQL database tables into your overall system.

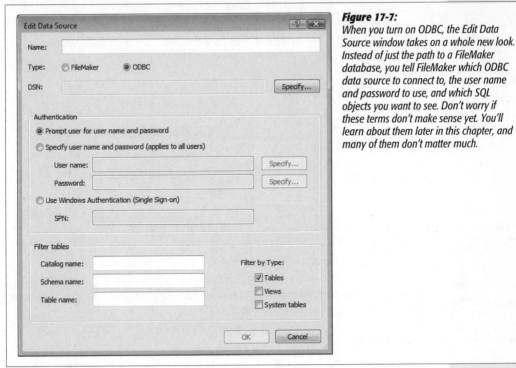

Figure 17-7:
When you turn on ODBC, the Edit Data Source window takes on a whole new look. Instead of just the path to a FileMaker database, you tell FileMaker which ODBC data source to connect to, the user name and password to use, and which SQL objects you want to see. Don't worry if these terms don't make sense yet. You'll learn about them later in this chapter, and many of them don't matter much.

Choose File → Manage → Database, and switch to the Relationships tab. Then click the Add Table button, just as though you were adding a normal FileMaker table occurrence. But this time, when the Specify Table window pops up (Figure 17-8), click the Data Source pop-up menu and choose Web Leads (or the name of *your* SQL data source).

The list below the pop-up menu changes to show all the available tables in the SQL database. Choose the table you're interested in, adjust the table name as necessary (in the Name box at the bottom of the window), and then click OK.

Creating relationships

When you're viewing a record from the Web Leads table, you might want File-Maker to show you if that person is already in your Customers table. To make this possible, you need some kind of connection between Customers and Web Leads. When you add a table from an external data source, FileMaker puts a table occurrence right on the relationship graph, so making the connection is easy. The table occurrence looks, smells, and functions just like a FileMaker table. For example, it would make sense to connect it to the Customers table by Email Address, since they both have that information in common. Just drag the email_address field from the Web Leads table to the Email Address field in the Customers table. File-Maker now knows how they relate.

Figure 17-8:
Once you've worked through the complexity of ODBC configuration, adding a table from a SQL database to your FileMaker relationship graph works exactly the way you'd expect: simple.

You're free to relate tables in any combination you want: Connect a FileMaker table to a SQL table, or connect two SQL tables together. Connect a SQL table to a FileMaker table, which then connects to another SQL table. You can even connect tables from two *different* SQL databases.

Shadow tables

If you switch to the Tables tab in the Manage Database window, you may see something unexpected. FileMaker includes every SQL table you've added to your graph in the Tables list (in stark contrast to tables from other FileMaker databases, which never show in the Tables tab).

Note: No matter how many *table occurrences* you create for a particular SQL table, the underlying table is listed only once. Also, SQL tables are always shown in italics so they're easy to spot.

The italicized entry in the Tables tab is called a *shadow table*. In other words, it isn't the table. Rather, it's a representation of the real table. It reflects information about the real table, and even lets you add a little FileMaker magic to an otherwise bare bit of computer science.

If you double-click the table (or switch to the Fields tab and select the table from the Table pop-up menu), you'll see the fields (sometimes called *columns* by non-FileMaker database folks) from the SQL table listed in italics as well. You can do certain things to these italicized fields:

- You **can't** rename a field or change its type. That sort of thing is controlled on the SQL database side of things.

- You **can** add a field comment if you want.

Advanced ODBC Data Source Options

At the bottom of the Edit Data Source window, you see a section labeled "Filter tables" (Figure 17-7). These settings are entirely optional, but may prove very useful if you are connecting to a complex database system. These settings tell FileMaker which tables you consider important, and which ones it can safely ignore. Doing so means you don't have to look at very long lists as you build your database, and helps FileMaker keep things running as quickly as possible.

Database terminology is inconsistent from one system to another. The "Filter tables" section gives you three empty boxes to fill in, some with mysterious names. Here's how it shakes out:

- If you use Oracle, the Catalog box is irrelevant: leave it empty. In the Schema box, you can enter a user name. When you do, FileMaker will only look at tables owned by that user.

- If you use Microsoft SQL Server, you can put the name of a particular database in the Catalog box to limit FileMaker to only tables in that database. If you use schemas, or collections of tables and views, you can also restrict FileMaker to just one schema.

- If you use MySQL, the Catalog box has no bearing on things, so you can leave it empty. If you want to see only tables for a particular user, enter the user name in the Schema box.

- Whatever your database, if you care only about one particular table, enter its name in the Table Name box. FileMaker will then show that table alone.

To the right of these three boxes, FileMaker offers three checkboxes. In the world of SQL databases, there are two or three *different* things that all act like tables.

- **Tables** are real honest-to-goodness tables, a lot like their FileMaker counterpart.

- **Views** are sort of like smart folders in iTunes or your mail program: They show portions of one or more tables based on criteria defined on the database server. If you're accessing a complex database, and you need read-only access to a specific portion, you might consider asking your database administrator to create a view that includes just the data you need. This will make things simpler for you down the road.

- **System tables** are tables the database system creates itself for various purposes. (MySQL doesn't have this kind of table, so don't fret about it if you're a MySQL user.)

Your job is to turn on the checkbox for each type you want FileMaker to show. You can also turn off all three checkboxes, and FileMaker will show everything it can.

If you don't know what any of this means, try leaving every box blank, and turning on Tables and Views. If FileMaker takes a long time showing tables to pick from, if the table you want is not in the list, or if you feel like you're seeing loads of tables you don't want to see, consult your database administrator for help.

- You **can** click Options and set Auto-Enter and Validation options for the field. Remember, though, that the rules you set here apply only when you add or edit records *in FileMaker*. Other systems that interact with the database are restricted only by settings in the SQL database.

- You **can** delete a field. You're not actually deleting the field from the SQL table. Rather, deleting a field tells FileMaker you simply don't want to see that field in FileMaker anymore. (You can always get it back later by clicking the Sync button, as explained on page 676.)

SQL databases tend to be more restrictive about acceptable values than FileMaker itself. For instance, a text field in a SQL database usually has a maximum size that is relatively small, compared to FileMaker's 2 GB field limit. If you select a field, click the Options button, and visit the Validation tab, then you'll see that the "Maximum number of characters" option is turned on, and you can't turn it off. Right by the checkbox, FileMaker also shows how many characters the field can hold.

Perhaps most important, you can *add new fields* to the shadow table. Specifically, you can add unstored or global calculation fields and summary fields. Neither of these field types work with SQL databases, but both are super important to File-Maker developers. By adding them to the shadow table, you can treat the SQL tables a little more like normal FileMaker tables. For example, you can add summary fields so you can do complex reporting on the SQL data, or add a calculation field to show a subtotal on a FileMaker layout.

Note: Remember, the fields you add to the shadow table aren't in the real table. They live only in FileMaker.

Finally, if the underlying SQL table changes in some way (perhaps the database administrator added a new column you're particularly interested in seeing), click Sync at the top of the window. This button tells FileMaker to go back to the SQL database and find out if any columns have been added, removed, or adjusted.

Syncing has nothing to do with the *data* in the database, though. FileMaker always interacts with the SQL database directly to show up-to-the-moment data as you perform searches or make changes. The Sync button synchronizes only the field definitions from the SQL table.

Using SQL Tables

There's no secret to using a SQL table—it works just like any other FileMaker table. You can create a new layout to show records from the SQL table. You can view those records in list view, form view, or table view. You can write scripts that loop through SQL records, or use the "Go to Related Record" script step to find the records associated with a particular customer.

Everything you know about FileMaker still applies. But keep a few points in mind as you develop your database around SQL tables:

- You can configure access to a SQL table using privilege sets just like any other FileMaker table. But a privilege set can't overrule the underlying SQL database. If the user name and password you're using to connect to the SQL database don't provide permission to delete records, FileMaker can't delete them, no matter how hard you try. FileMaker does its best to give meaningful error messages in such situations.

- Speaking of error messages, since SQL databases are more restrictive than File-Maker, you may see error messages in places you wouldn't normally expect. For example, a Name field might be limited to 30 characters. If you try to enter more than that, FileMaker lets you, but you can't then commit the record. It would be nice if FileMaker simply stopped you from typing too many letters, but it doesn't. It's up to you to go back and delete enough to make it happy.

- FileMaker does some powerful computing magic to make these SQL tables work. So if you have a large amount of data in your SQL table, FileMaker can take a long time to show you data. Be patient and grateful for FileMaker's efforts.

- FileMaker may have trouble performing some finds efficiently. If you include only fields from one table in your find request, then it should move quickly. But if you search in related fields, and there are thousands of matches in the related table, FileMaker can take a very long time to sort things out. If you find that SQL tables aren't performing well, and you can't simplify your find requests, consider enlisting the help of a SQL expert (or learning it yourself). You may be able to offload some of the heavy lifting to the SQL database server, where ready access to the data makes things faster. For example, a complex find in FileMaker could be converted to a SQL view that is super-snappy. This same advice applies to large summary reports. If you're dealing with lots of records, it may be faster to let the SQL database server calculate the subtotals and averages for FileMaker.

You can use ESS to get direct access to enterprise data, interact with the back end of your Web site, or even replace chunks of FileMaker data with a set of tables that's more open to other applications. This powerful feature may need a little setup and some new expertise, but if you have big needs, it can be an incredibly powerful option.

Exporting Data

The Save/Send Records As options (page 662) make good sense when you just want to send FileMaker data to an associate. But sometimes your recipient is a computer. You may send your customer information to a mailing house to be printed on postcards, or load it into QuickBooks. In cases like this, you *export* the data.

When you export data, FileMaker needs to know *what* data to export. You tell it with the Export dialog box (Figure 17-9). The Table pop-up menu shows you what FileMaker considers the *current table*—in this case, Customers. Below it, the field list shows every field in the current layout for that table. But click the pop-up menu, and you can choose Current Table, which shows you all the fields in the current table, instead of just the fields on the layout. You're also welcome to pick other tables from the pop-up menu and see their fields. When you choose fields from other tables, you're still exporting Customer records. If you include fields from other tables, FileMaker gets the values from the first record related to each customer record.

Figure 17-9:
When FileMaker exports the data, it includes each field in this list in the export file. The order of the fields in this list determines their order in the export file, and you can change it by dragging fields up or down in the list. To add every field in the field list to the field export order list, click Move All. Likewise, to remove all fields from the export order, click Clear All.

To choose a field for export, select it and click Move. FileMaker adds the field to the "Field export order" list, but doesn't actually move it there. Rather, the field stays in the list because you may want to export the same field *twice* in the same export file. Imagine, for example, you're creating an export file that needs the billing address info in the first four fields and the shipping address info in the next four fields. Since your database has only one set of address fields, you can export them twice so the resulting file has the right number of fields. (Unfortunately, you can't ask FileMaker to export a blank field. If you often export to a format that needs fields you don't have, and leaving them blank is OK, just export an empty global field in each one's place.)

Note: If a field isn't on the current layout, it doesn't show up in the export field list, so if you're wasting time scrolling through fields that you don't need, switch to a simpler layout from the same table. But if you can't find a field that you *know* is in the table, use the pop-up menu to choose Current Table. That way, you'll get a list of all the fields in the table, regardless of which ones are on the current layout.

At the bottom of the window, the Character Set pop-up menu lets you tell File-Maker how to *encode* characters in the export file so the receiving computer can read them properly. For instance, if you're using Mac OS X and you know the person receiving the export file is using Windows, it probably makes sense to choose the Windows (ANSI) choice. Unfortunately, the conversion from Macintosh to Windows or Windows to Mac is imperfect, so some less common characters may be switched out for others in the output file. Unicode is the best choice, assuming your recipient can accept it, because it can handle *all* the characters you may have in your database (even foreign language characters like Chinese and Korean).

Finally, the checkbox called "Apply current layout's data formatting to exported data" is a little misleading. It has nothing to do with font, size, style, or color. Rather, when you turn this option on, FileMaker formats numbers, dates, times, and timestamps according to the formatting options for each field on the layout: number of decimal places, date formats, and so forth. If you leave this option off, FileMaker exports the data exactly as it was originally entered.

Note: The "Group by" list lets you summarize data as you export it. You'll learn how this feature works on page 680.

The following steps take you through a typical database export. You've hired a printing company to print, address, and mail personalized cards to all your customers at holiday time. To do the job, the card company needs a list of names and addresses. Instead of typing all your customer info by hand, you can produce the list by exporting it from your database in the appropriate format. Often, plain text is fine, so that's what this example uses.

1. **Switch to the Customers layout.**

   Like many FileMaker features, the Export command is layout-based—that is, it decides which table to export (and from which table occurrence to find related data) by looking at the current layout. To export customer records, you need to be on a layout associated with the Customers table.

2. **Choose Records → Show All Records.**

   If this command is grayed out, then all records are already showing. Otherwise, take this step to ensure that you export *every* customer.

3. **Choose File → Export Records. If the command isn't available, you're probably in Find mode, so switch to Browse mode.**

   You can also export from Layout and Preview modes, too, should the need arise. The "Export Records to File" dialog box appears. It looks a lot like a normal Save dialog box, except that it has a pop-up menu at the bottom called *Type.*

4. **Name the file *Holiday Card List.txt*, and choose any location you want.**

   When FileMaker exports data, it creates a new file and puts the data in it. You use this window to tell FileMaker what to call the file and where to put it.

5. **From the Type pop-up menu, choose Comma-Separated Text, and then click Save.**

   You'll learn what each of these types means in the next section. The "Specify Field Order for Export" window appears (Figure 17-9).

6. **While pressing Ctrl (⌘), select these fields in the field list: First Name, Last Name, Company Name, Street Address, City, State, and Zip Code. Then click Move.**

   FileMaker adds the highlighted fields to the field export order list.

Note: If you want to export most of your fields, but not quite all of them, it may be faster to click the Move All button, and then clear the few you don't want from the Field export order list.

7. **Click Export.**

FileMaker creates the file and returns you to your database.

So what just happened? If you open the Holiday Card List file you just created, you see names, company names, and addresses from your customers file. Dig a little deeper and you notice:

- Each *record* is on its own line. If the program you're viewing the file in wraps lines, it might look like a record goes across two or more lines, but there's a return character at the *end* of each record, and nowhere else.

- Each field value is in quotes, and there are commas between them.

These factors are important because this file conforms to a *standard*. Other programs—including the program used by the card printing company—that recognize the Comma-Separated Text format can read this file and grab the data.

Grouped Exports

You may have noticed the "Group by" list in the "Specify Field Order for Export" dialog box. Under normal circumstances, you see "(Unsorted)" in this list. But if you sort the records in the found set *before* choosing the Export Records command, you see instead a list of the fields in your sort order, each with a checkbox by its name. You can see this in action in Figure 17-10.

Figure 17-10:
When your data is sorted, FileMaker shows the sort fields in the "Group by" list. By turning on one or more of these checkboxes, you tell FileMaker you want to group the data in the export file.

If you opt to group the data, you get just one record in the export file for each *unique* value in the "group by" field. For example, if you export 300 people records, grouped by state, you get one record for each state. If you include *summary* fields in your export list, FileMaker summarizes all the records represented by each group. You can see, for example, how many people you have in each state.

You're free to select as many fields as you want in the "group by" list. If you select more than one, you get a hierarchical list of records, similar to a sub-summary report (Chapter 6). For example, if you sort first by state, then by city, and turn on the checkbox next to both fields in the "group by" list, you get a list of states, and below each state, you see one record for each city in that state. Again, summary fields included in your export show proper totals for both the state as a whole, and each city.

Export formats

When exporting data, you always create a file, but you get to decide what *format* the file should be in. In the previous example, you exported your data to a Comma-Separated Text file. This example is one of the many file formats File-Maker can produce when it exports. Most formats exist simply because computer software has put forth a lot of standards in the last 50 years, and FileMaker wants to be as flexible as possible. Some formats do have unique advantages, though.

The first question you need to ask is, "Where is the data going?" Your export format choice almost always depends on what the person you're sending it to needs. Each is explained below:

- **Tab-Separated Text** and **Comma-Separated Text** are very common formats for database data. They put each record on its own line. With tab-separated text, you get a tab between each field value, while comma-separated text has quotes around field values, and commas between them. Almost every program in the world that can import data supports one of these formats. If you're not sure, try Tab-Separated Text first—it's the most common.

Note: Sometimes the Comma-Separated Text format is called *Comma-Separated Values* in other programs. They're the same thing.

- The **Merge** format is just like Comma-Separated Text format, with one difference: The first line of the file shows individual field names. The advantage is that when you import this file in another program, you can see what each field is called, making it easier to get the right data. Unfortunately, most programs don't expect this extra line, and treat it as another record. People most often use this format for mail merge in word processing programs.

- If you want to put the data on a Web page, use **HTML Table**. The resulting file isn't suitable for importing into another program, but it can be displayed nicely in a Web browser. You can also open the file, copy the HTML table from inside it, and paste it into another Web page.

Where's My Style?

Most of FileMaker's export formats are *text based*. In other words, what gets produced is just a normal, plain text file. The structure of this file determines which format it is, but you can open them all in Notepad or TextEdit and read them directly. A side effect of this reality is that none of them support *styles*. In other words, if you go to great lengths to change the first names in all your records so the font matches the customer's personality, you can kiss your hard work goodbye when you export.

In addition to the font, you lose the size, style, and color of the text. The notable exception to this rule is the FileMaker Pro format. Since this export format creates another FileMaker Pro database, all the formatting you painstakingly put in place is preserved.

If you *must* have text styles in your exported data, there is an option, but it ain't pretty. FileMaker has two calculation functions designed to aid this process: *GetAsCSS( )* and *GetAsSVG( )*.

Each function takes a single text parameter and returns a snippet of ordinary text with style information embedded using special *tags*. *GetAsCSS( )* produces text that can be put on a Web page. When viewed in a Web browser, the text takes on its original fonts, sizes, styles, and colors. *GetAsSVG( )* works the same way, but uses a different tagging scheme: the one used in the SVG, or Scalable Vector Graphics format.

To take advantage of these functions, you need to create a calculation field with a formula something like this:

```
GetAsCSS ( First Name )
```

You then export *this* field instead of the First Name field. If you do this with the HTML Table export format, you get properly formatted text on your Web page. More realistically, you'd use these along with the XML format and a special XSLT style sheet that produces a Web page or an SVG image. You'll learn more about this option at the end of this chapter.

- The **FileMaker Pro** format is your best choice if your data is destined to go back into FileMaker some day, or if you just want to view and work with the exported data directly. When you choose this format, FileMaker creates a brand new database with just one table and only the fields you choose to export. This format is the only one that preserves font, style, size, and color in field data (see the box on page 682) and one of the few that supports repeating fields (see page 117).

Note: Usually, if you just want to export records from one FileMaker file to another, you don't have to export them first. Just go to the database where you want the data to end up and import them directly (page 683). Of course, if one database is in South Africa and the other is in Tibet, then by all means export them first.

- For the ultimate in flexibility, choose **XML**—the un-format. When you export XML, you get to apply something called an XSLT style sheet. An XSLT style sheet is a document written in a programming language all its own that tells FileMaker exactly how the exported data looks. If you need to produce an export format that FileMaker doesn't support directly, XSLT is the way to do it. But be forewarned: XSLT is *not* in the same league as FileMaker itself, ease-of-use-wise. You may need some hired help. (XSLT is introduced briefly on page 695.)

Tip: Although it applies to one *field value* and not a set of records, don't forget about the Edit → Export Field Contents command. This command lets you export the data in the current field to a file. It exports text, number, date, time, and timestamp fields to a plain text file. Container fields create a file whose type is appropriate for the data in the field.

- Last but not least, you can choose one of the **Excel** options to create a bona fide spreadsheet. To ensure that most people can use the spreadsheet, choose "Excel 95–2004 Workbook," which creates an .xls file that works in just about any version of Excel. If you know your recipients have the most recent Excel version, using the new .xslx format, choose "Excel Workbook" instead. When you choose either format, FileMaker opens an extra dialog box, which lets you put FileMaker's field names in the first row of your new spreadsheet. You can even give your Excel file a worksheet Name, document Title, Subject, and Author if you so desire.

Regardless of which format you choose, the "Export Records to File" dialog box has two options that let you determine what happens to the file after FileMaker creates it. Choose "Automatically open file" to avoid hunting down the file on your hard drive and launching it yourself. And "Create email with file as attachment" does just what it promises: opens your email program and creates a new message with your fresh new document attached. To share your data, you just need to supply the email address, add a subject line, and click Send.

Importing Data

Sometimes, the data you need is already somewhere else, and you need to get it into FileMaker. Before you start lamenting your lackluster words-per-minute typing skills, consider doing an *import*. Chances are FileMaker can load the data directly into its tables with just a little help from you to tell it where things go.

FileMaker can handle the most common data types—and quite a few lesser-known ones—by a straightforward process. You tell FileMaker which file contains your incoming data, and then show it how you want to match the incoming data (the source) with the fields in your file (the target). This procedure is called *field mapping*, and it's the only time-consuming part of any import. See Figure 17-11 for a preview of the Import Field Mapping dialog box.

This window lists all the fields in the source file on the left, and the fields in your table on the right. FileMaker will transfer the data, field by field and record by record, into your database. The first field in the Source Fields list goes into the first field in the Target Fields list.

Unfortunately, FileMaker can't always tell which fields match. You might be importing records from a system that uses different field names, for example. How is FileMaker supposed to know that *t_fname* is the First Name field in your old contact manager software? Worse still, many data formats have no field names, so all you have to work with is the data itself.

Figure 17-11:
Use this dialog box to tell FileMaker what data to import and where to put it. In the top-left corner of the window, FileMaker tells you where this data is coming from (in this case, a file called People.fp7). To the right, you see where the data's going (the Customers table). The arrows down the middle show you what data will go where. Creation Date, for instance, has no arrow, so FileMaker won't import it.

Using the Import Field Mapping dialog box, your job is to tell FileMaker which source fields match with each of the target fields. The concept is simple, but the procedure can be a real drag. First of all, you can't rearrange the fields in the Source Fields list at all. They match the order in which they appear in the file you're importing and that's that. So instead, you move the target fields up or down so they line up next to the appropriate source fields. (You move them just like you do fields and tables in the Manage Database window—by dragging the little arrows.)

If you don't have many fields, this process is quick and painless. If you have lots of fields, it can be tough for a few reasons:

• Since the whole point of this operation is to put the target field list in a very particular order, you can't simply sort the list by name whenever you're having trouble finding a field. If you're looking for First Name in a long list, there's no way to find it short of looking through the list field by field. If this process proves overwhelming, here's a trick: Click Manage Database, and in the familiar Manage Database window it summons, rename the field with a whole lot of X's at the end of its name. When you close the Manage Database window, the field in question will stand out from the list.

• As you drag fields up and down, if you have to drag beyond the visible list (because your destination has scrolled past the top or bottom), FileMaker sometimes scrolls the list by so quickly while you drag that you easily overshoot your destination, repeatedly. To avoid this runaround, don't drag. Instead, click the field you want to move to select it. Then hold down the Control (⌘) key, and use the up or down arrow keys to move the field. As long as you hold the appropriate modified key down, you can move the field up or down as far as you want by repeatedly pressing the arrow keys. This more controlled method may go a little slower, but it makes it easy to hit the right spot.

FREQUENTLY ASKED QUESTION

Making It Fit

A lot of FileMaker's Export formats use special characters for important things. For instance, the Tab-Separated Text format uses a return character to separate records. What happens if I have a return character in my field?

Good question! Special characters are one of those problems with no ideal solution. But FileMaker does the best it can within the limitations of each export file type. For a file to be called Tab-Separated Text, for example, you simply can't have return characters inside records. It's just against the rules. In this particular case, FileMaker turns the return character into something else, called a *vertical tab*, which is a standard but rarely-used character left over from when computers had green screens. Presumably, you don't have any of these in your fields (you can't type them, so it is a pretty safe bet you don't), so it's easy enough to turn vertical tab characters back into return characters when you open the file in another program. In fact, that's exactly what happens when you *import* a Tab-Separated Text file into FileMaker.

Another character of concern is the quote mark. If you have these in your fields, and you export a Comma-Separated Text file, FileMaker has to do something with them so they don't interfere with the quotes around field values. In this case, FileMaker turns your quote mark into two quote marks together.

That doesn't sound like a solution, but it is. If you assume any quote mark that is immediately followed by a second one is really just data, and not the end quote mark for a field value, you can figure out which is which in the export file. Most programs that support Comma-Separated Text understand this convention. (You might think commas would also be a problem with Comma-Separated Text, but they're not. Since every field value is in quotes, commas are OK. Only the commas between quoted values are considered field separators.)

The HTML and XML formats have all kinds of special characters, but each has a special *entity* form that's used if they're supposed to be treated as ordinary data. FileMaker converts any such characters appropriately, and every program that processes these formats understands the conventions.

Finally, FileMaker has a data-structure concept that most formats simply don't understand: repeating fields. The idea that one field could hold several values is foreign to most database programs. When you export repeating fields, FileMaker pulls another freaky character out of its hat: the Group Separator, which is used to separate each value. Thankfully, this action is almost never a problem because you generally don't export repeating field data to a file that needs to be read by a program that doesn't understand repeating fields. One last note: The FileMaker Pro export format *does* directly support repeating fields.

- Finally, if you accidentally drop a field in the wrong spot, the field you're moving changes places with the one you dropped it on top of. If the one you replaced was already in the right spot, it is now far away, and you have to reposition it once you correctly place the first field. In other words, an accidental drop leaves *two* fields in the wrong place. The only solution to this problem is to be careful (and use the keyboard trick from the previous paragraph to minimize mistakes).

Sometimes you don't care about some of the fields in your source file (maybe it includes a Fax Number for each customer, and you don't need that particular value). Between each source and destination field, you see one of two symbols: an arrow or a line. The arrow means FileMaker plans to import the data on the left side into the field on the right. A line tells FileMaker to ignore this particular piece of data in the import file. Click an arrow to change it to a line, or vice versa. Just make sure there's a line next to the field or fields you don't want to import. (You sometimes see *other* symbols between fields, but they show up only when you change the Import Action setting. You'll learn about that on page 668.)

Note: If you forget what the importing icons mean, never fear. The Import Field Mapping window has a legend at the bottom right.

UP TO SPEED

Mapping Out Your Options

FileMaker's smart, but when it comes to something as picayune as deciding which field to put where, there's no substitute for human input. As you can see in Figure 17-11, the Import Field Mapping dialog box looks a trifle crowded, but every tool, button, and gizmo has saved a life (or a career, anyway).

For example, your input data source may or may not include field names. If it doesn't, the Source Fields list shows you the first record in the import file instead. Or, even if your data already has named fields, you may *want* to see some of the data being imported so you can see what's really in that field called Q1GPFnw. Either way, FileMaker lets you check as many records as you wish before you import by providing arrow buttons below the list. As you click, FileMaker replaces items in the source field list with data from the next (right) or previous (left) record. When field names are included, you see them as the *first* record. Occasionally, the format you're importing doesn't accommodate field names, but the import file has them anyway, as the first record. When this happens, turn on "Don't import first record" so FileMaker doesn't treat that record as data.

The "Arrange by" pop-up menu lets you bulk-reorder the target fields in the list. Most choices are obvious (alphabetical by field name, and by field type), but others aren't so clear. If you choose "matching names," FileMaker tries to match fields up by matching their names. If your input file has the same field names as your database, this option sets the right order for you. The "last order" choice restores the field order you used the last time you imported data. Choose "creation order" to see the fields in the order in which you created them. Finally, if you manually drag the fields in the list, FileMaker switches to the "custom import order" choice. If you decide to try one of the other arrangements, you can get back to the order you were working on by choosing "custom import order" yourself.

Finally, just like the export dialog box, this window lets you specify a character set (page 678). This time, though, you don't decide what you *want* it to be. Rather, you need to tell FileMaker what it *is*. If you're lucky, this pop-up menu is grayed out, meaning FileMaker was able to figure out the encoding itself. Otherwise, you need to make sure you make the right choice so special characters in the import file come through intact. You'll choose either Windows (ANSI) or Macintosh 99 percent of the time. And for typical data (letters, numbers, and basic punctuation), the choice is largely irrelevant.

For the sake of illustration, here's the simple rundown on how importing works:

1. **Choose File → Import Records → File.**

   FileMaker can import data from all kinds of sources. In this case, you're telling it you want to import records from a *file*. When you choose this command, the standard Open File dialog box appears.

2. **Choose the file you want to import, and then click Open.**

   The Import Field Mapping dialog box pops up.

3. **Drag the fields in the target field list so they line up properly with the input data.**

   As you drag, you can ignore the arrows completely. You can fix them once you've got the fields in the right order.

Note: If your data source has a field that doesn't match any existing field in your target table, and you decide you want to import that field anyway, just click the Manage Database button to create a new field, and then return to your field mapping. See page 690 for how to handle an entire *table* that's missing.

---

4. **Click the arrows or lines between fields until each matching field has an arrow, and each remaining field has a line.**

   This part is the most time-consuming. Just take it slow and be glad you don't have to type all this data.

5. **Make sure the "Add new records" radio button (in the Import Action area) is turned on.**

   This action tells FileMaker you want a new record created in the Customers table for each record in the import file. (The Import Field Mapping dialog box has more features, but you don't need them right now. See page 688 for full detail.)

6. **Click Import. When the Import Options dialog box appears (Figure 17-12), turn on "Perform auto-enter options while importing".**

   You want to make sure the new customers have valid customer IDs, and those come from Auto-Enter serial numbers.

Figure 17-12:
If you have any Auto-Enter fields, or you're importing repeating fields, you see this window after clicking Import. Turn off "Perform auto-enter options while importing" if you don't want FileMaker to auto-enter data in your records as they're created. When importing repeating fields, you usually want to choose "Keeping them in the original record." If you don't, FileMaker makes a new record for each repetition that has data in it.

Note: If you import into a field that has Auto-Enter options set, and you tell FileMaker to perform Auto-Enter options when importing, you might wonder *which* value will wind up in the field: the auto-entered data or the imported data. In almost every case, the imported data wins. The one exception: If a field is set to auto-enter a looked-up value, FileMaker performs the lookup and thus overrides the imported value.

When you're done, click Import. After a very short delay, the Import Records Summary dialog box appears (Figure 17-13). Click OK to make it go away.

Figure 17-13:
This window appears after FileMaker completes the import operation. It tells you important information about your import, including how many records were imported. Sometimes problems can occur during import (for instance, some data in the import file may violate your field validation settings). When this happens, FileMaker may skip certain fields or whole records. This window also tells you when that happens (although it doesn't tell you which fields or records were skipped).

After the import's complete, FileMaker shows you a found set of just the records it imported. But don't reach for the Show All Records command yet: The fact that it's a found set is your safety net. If something goes wrong with your import (the wrong records came through, field mapping doesn't look right, or whatever), just delete the found set and start over. You can scan through the data and make sure you got what you wanted and that the data went into the fields you intended. You can also take this opportunity to perform other actions (like use the Replace Field Contents command) on every imported record.

Importing Over Existing Data

When you import data into a file that already has some records in it, the Import Action section of the Import Field Mapping dialog box (page 684) gives you three ways to specify how you want to deal with that existing data. Normally, it starts out with the "Add new records" setting turned on, meaning that FileMaker simply adds imported records to your database. Sometimes, though, you want to update existing records instead. For example, suppose your database holds shipping rates for every state you ship to. When your freight company updates its rates, it sends you a new file with one record for each state, and the new rates in a Rate field. If you add these records to your database, you end up with *two* records for each state, which is probably not what you want. So FileMaker gives you two other choices that let you update records as you import.

Update existing records in found set

To avoid creating duplicate records as in the shipping rates example, you can turn on "Update existing records in found set" and map just the Rate field to the appropriate field in your table. When you import, FileMaker takes the rate from the first record in the import file and puts it in the first record in the found set. It then copies the second rate into the second record. This process continues until it has imported every rate.

If your import file has more records than the found set, FileMaker simply skips the extra records. If you'd rather import *all* the records (adding new records once all those in the found set have been updated), turn on "Add remaining data as new records."

Warning: This import action is useful only if you're certain the records in the import file are in the *same order* as those in the export file. If they're not, FileMaker updates the wrong records, leaving you with incorrect data. If you aren't positive the records are in the right order, use "Update matching records in found set" instead.

Update matching records in found set

"Update matching records in found set" works much the same way. When you import with this action, FileMaker updates data in existing records by copying it from the import file. This time, though, you get to tell FileMaker how to figure out which records in the import file match each record in the found set. You tell FileMaker this by specifying one or more *matching fields*, as described in Figure 17-14.

Figure 17-14:
When you turn on "Update matching records in found set" FileMaker lets you use a new symbol between source and target fields. In this picture, the Customer ID field has an "=" symbol beside it. This symbol tells FileMaker to match records based on ID. In other words, when it imports the first record, it finds a record in the found set with the same ID. FileMaker then updates that record's data based on the import file. If FileMaker doesn't find a match, it skips the import record. It's safest to use a key field for import matching.

To get the new symbol in the field mapping list, just click the spot between fields. FileMaker now toggles between the three possible symbols: Import, Don't import, and Match. (If you forget what each symbol means, the Field Mapping area in the window reminds you.) Again, if you'd rather have FileMaker import every record in the import file, adding new records when no match is found, turn on "Add remaining data as new records."

Creating Tables on Import

All the importing you've learned about so far assumes that your tables and fields are already created. In other words, your target table is already in place when you choose your source file. But when you're doing a big conversion job (say, upgrading from 15 over-extended Excel spreadsheets to a smooth-running FileMaker dream system), it'll take you quite some time to create all those tables and fields. And even though you have access to the Manage Database dialog box while you're importing, this process isn't quick or easy when you've got hundreds of fields coming in from dozens of files. FileMaker's already thought of that, and offers to handle the tedious work of table and field creation for you.

Choose Import → File and select a data source. In the Import Field Mapping window, there's a handy pop-up menu called Target. Click it, and you see the current table (remember that's based on the layout that was active when you chose the Import command), all your other tables (grayed out, so you can't choose them), and a very useful command, New Table (Data Source). The stuff in parentheses is the name of your data source and the name FileMaker gives the new table it creates for you. (If you already have a table with the same name as your data source, FileMaker appends a number to the end of the new table's name.)

Choose New Table, and then click Import. FileMaker creates a table and an appropriate set of fields for you, and then populates the new fields with data. You also get a simple form layout for your new table and a table occurrence on your relationships graph. You can treat this table just like one you created yourself. For example, you can start creating relationships to hook it up to other table occurrences.

Note: See page 734 to see how FileMaker Pro Advanced lets you import tables and fields *without* the data that normally comes with them.

When you let FileMaker create fields for you, it does its best to create the field types you want. For instance, if the data source is a FileMaker file, your new fields match the old file's field names and field types. But if the source is a plain text file with no formatting information to go by, FileMaker doesn't have any names to go by, so the new fields become text fields and get the prosaic names of f1, f2, f3, and so on. In either case, check the fields in your new table to make sure you get the names and field types you want. You have to manually create any calculations you need.

Creating a New Database from an Import File

If you have a file full of data, and you want to build a brand new database around it, FileMaker has an even simpler option than creating a database and importing the data. Just choose File → Open and select the file you want to convert. You can also use drag and drop: On Windows, drag it to the open FileMaker Pro window. FileMaker promptly converts the file to a database for you. On the Mac, drag a file onto the FileMaker icon.

Note: If you can't see the file you want in the Open dialog box, or it is grayed out, change the option in the "Files of Type" (Windows) or "Show" (Mac) pop-up list. If your file is one of the formats FileMaker supports, you can select it once you identify its type.

If FileMaker finds data with a first row that looks like field names, it asks whether you want to use those when FileMaker creates fields. If it can't find anything that looks like field names, you get those old standbys, f1, f2, f3. In addition to a single table and the appropriate number of fields (complete with data, of course), you get two very plain layouts. One is a generic form layout, showing one record at a time, and the other is a simple columnar list.

Converting Older FileMaker Files

Use this same process (the Open file command) if you're converting files from very old versions of FileMaker (FileMaker 3, 4, 5, 5.5, or 6) to the more capable format used by FileMaker 7, 8, 8.5, and 9. FileMaker does its best to carry all the data, scripts, layouts, and so forth from the old file into the modern era. But if the original file was complex, you'll almost certainly have some work to do to get things up to snuff. Converting old files is a huge topic, and most people find that conversion requires a certain amount of retrofitting, either to make scripts and other things that break during conversion whole again or to take full advantage of the .fp7 multiple-table-per-file power. (FileMaker offers two excellent white papers on this subject for download at *http://www.filemaker.com/support/whitepapers.html*. Look under Migration Topics.)

Import Data Sources

You've learned about the most common importing task—when your data's coming in from a single file. But you have other needs and FileMaker's got other choices. File → Import is an entire submenu, with commands to suit even the most demanding database manager. From there, you get to pick where the data should come from (the data source), and you get several choices.

File

The File → Import → File command shows an Open File dialog box. Select any file that matches one of the export formats explained earlier in this chapter. You see your old friend, the Import Field Mapping dialog box (Figure 17-11). Match your source to your target, and away you go.

You can also use a similar command when you have to move data from one table to another within the same file. Go to your target layout and choose File → Import Records → File. In the dialog box, choose the database you're in, and you see the Import Field Mapping dialog box. Select the table that's your data source from the Source pop-up menu and you're ready to go.

Folder

Using this command, you can pick any folder, and FileMaker imports the contents of each appropriate file in that folder. It creates *one* record for each file it imports, and puts the file into the field you specify. In other words, if you have a folder full of letters you've written, you can import them into a Letters database using this command. The complete text of each letter would go in a field, with one record per letter. (Remember, though, that FileMaker only supports pictures, movies, and plain text files when importing. If your letters are in Microsoft Word format, for example, you're out of luck.)

Choosing File → Import → Folder summons the "Folder of Files Import Options" dialog box shown in Figure 17-15.

Figure 17-15:
This window is what you see when you choose the File → Import → Folder command. In the top part of the window, you get to choose which folder to import (click Specify). In the bottom half, you decide what kind of files you're interested in.

Normally, FileMaker finds only files directly inside the folder you pick; it ignores any other folders contained inside. You have to turn on "Include all enclosed folders" to make FileMaker look inside those folders, too. With this option turned on, it digs as deep as necessary to find every file.

Once you've picked a folder, you get to decide what kind of files to import. You have only two choices: "Picture and movie files" and "Text files." In the first case, FileMaker ignores every file that isn't a supported picture or movie type. You choose whether the files themselves are inserted in the container field or just references to them. If you choose the "Text files" option instead, it seeks out only plain text files.

Importing a folder of pictures or movies

When you choose the "Pictures and movie files" option and click Continue, you may be in for a bit of a wait. Depending on the number of files FileMaker has to look through, you may see a progress dialog box for as long as several minutes. When the import is complete, you see the now-familiar Import Field Mapping dialog box. But the list of source fields looks entirely unfamiliar—in a good way.

As outlined in Figure 17-16, FileMaker translates the file information into logical field types, perfect for database use.

Figure 17-16:
When you import a folder full of pictures, FileMaker practically reads your mind. It not only lets you dump the picture into a container field, but it also offers you the chance to put the file name and full path into text fields. Best of all, FileMaker can shrink the picture down to a thumbnail and put that into a container field, too, which saves space by reducing size and resolution. The thumbnails appear even when the original images aren't available (if a network drive is unavailable, for instance).

Importing a folder of text files

When you choose to import text files, you still get an Import Field Mapping dialog box. This time, the source field list includes Text Content, File Name, and File Path. Each expects to be imported into a text field.

Digital Camera

If you're using Mac OS X, the File → Import Records menu has a Digital Camera option. Unfortunately, this option relies on a feature unique to Mac OS X, so you can't import directly from a camera on Windows. You have to download the images to your computer first, and then import them. (There's a workaround if you can set up your camera to show up as a USB disk on Windows. In that case, use the Import → Folder command to import images directly from the camera.)

When you first plug your camera into your Mac, chances are iPhoto launches and prepares to import the images. To avoid any potential confusion, quit iPhoto first (or be careful not to click iPhoto's Import button while FileMaker's working with the camera).

Note: If you import from your camera to FileMaker a lot, you can tell iPhoto to get out of the way: Just launch Image Capture (in your Applications folders) and in its Preferences → Camera tab, select File-Maker. If you use iPhoto sometimes and FileMaker others, choose No Application in the pop-up menu instead. That way, you get to decide what program each time.

With the camera connected, choose File → Import Records → Digital Camera. The verbosely titled FileMaker Pro Advanced Photo Import Options dialog box appears (Figure 17-17).

Figure 17-17:
This dialog box appears when you import from a digital camera in Mac OS X. The device pop-up menu lets you pick which camera to import from (on the off chance you have several connected). You also get to decide which images to import, where to put them (more on these options in a moment), and whether or not you want to store just references to the pictures.

If you want to import *everything* on the camera, turn on "All images." But if you just want, for example, the last five shots you took, turn on the last radio button— "The last [blank] images"—and put the right number in its box. Finally, you can choose "Some images," and click Specify to see a list of image thumbnails to choose from.

Even if you want to import all the images, the "Some images" choice can come in handy. It's the only place you can *rotate* the images before you import them. There's no direct way to rotate an image once it's in the container field. You have to export it, rotate it in another program, and then insert it again.

Even if you're importing the images directly into FileMaker (rather than just a reference), it still puts them in the folder you specify in the "Download to" pop-up menu. If you want to, you can simply delete them when you're done. (If you're storing references, though, the folder you pick becomes very important. If you import the pictures and then move them to a different folder, the references are wrong, and the pictures don't display in FileMaker.)

When you're through making choices, click Continue. The Import Field Mapping window that appears next is loaded with source fields this time. FileMaker lets you import loads of image data along with the pictures, including dimensions, resolution, shot date and time, and all that photographer-speak stuff you see when you accidentally put your camera in advanced mode.

At this point, you're in familiar territory. Just match up the fields and click Import. Be prepared for a wait as it takes FileMaker longer to import full-color digital pictures than, say, Zip codes.

XML Data Source

Because there are so many programs and data formats out there, the World Wide Web Consortium (W3C) created the XML format to make data exchange more predictable. FileMaker uses a special subset of XML's code, called FMPXML-RESULT, to facilitate import. If your data source was created by another FileMaker Pro database, it already uses FMPXMLRESULT, and you can import that data straight up, no chaser. But if the XML document doesn't use FileMaker's Document Type Definition (DTD), you'll need an Extensible Stylesheet Language (XSLT) document to tell FileMaker how to make the XML file work with FileMaker. In fact, with the help of XSLT style sheets, FileMaker can import *any* XML file in any form. An XSLT style sheet converts the XML you're importing into FMPXMLRESULT.

Note: You can learn to write your own XSLT style sheets, and thereby turn FileMaker's XML into just about anything, from specialized XML your accounting software uses, to an HTML Web page, to a standard RSS news feed. XML and XSLT are complex languages and this book can't cover them in full. If you're ready for a challenge, check out the book *Learning XSLT* by Michael Fitzgerald (O'Reilly). You can also find dozens of premade style sheets on FileMaker's Web site at *http://www.filemaker.com*.

To import XML data, choose File → Import Records → XML Data Source. When you do, you'll see the window in Figure 17-18. Here, you tell FileMaker where to get the XML data, and optionally what XSLT style sheet to apply. (If you don't apply a style sheet, FileMaker assumes the data is already in its special FMPXML-RESULT format.)

Figure 17-18:
When you import from an XML data source, FileMaker first asks you where to get the data from, and how to process it. You can instruct FileMaker to look in any XML file on your computer, or to fetch the XML data from a Web server (see the box on the page 697).

Unlike the typical import command, when you import XML data, you don't actually have to have a *file* to import from. This window also lets you specify an "HTTP request," which is just a fancy way of saying "Web page." Type the URL of a Web page here, and FileMaker goes out over the Internet, grabs the page, and pulls it down for you. Believe it or not, a lot of XML data is available hot off the Web like this. Likewise, you can choose to fetch the XSLT template from the Web as well.

When you're finished choosing XML and XSL options, click Continue. FileMaker processes the XML and XSLT (which may take a few minutes), and then shows you the Import Field Mapping dialog box. From there, you can proceed like any import, as described earlier in this chapter.

XML export

When you export to XML, FileMaker exports the data in the FMPXMLRESULT format, and then applies the style sheet. You create the style sheet to translate this XML into the appropriate format for your intended recipient. You have slightly more flexibility when exporting than when importing: XSLT can translate only XML documents, but it can *produce* any text-based format. So although you can import only XML files, you can export just about anything.

Bento Data Source

If you use Mac OS X and have Bento (see the box on page 5), you can import data directly from your Bento libraries into a FileMaker database. Just choose File → Import Records → Bento Data Source. When you do, the window in Figure 17-19 appears.

Once you select the appropriate library (and optionally a collection), click Continue to see the standard FileMaker Import Records window. From here, you can match up fields and configure options, just like any other data source.

XML and HTTP

Sometimes the XML data you want to import is in a file on your computer. But a big part of the XML data source feature's power is that FileMaker can also get XML data from other computers using *HTTP*, or Hypertext Transport Protocol. You probably recognize this acronym because it usually sits in front of Web addresses (as in *http://missingmanuals. com*). HTTP is the way Web browsers talk to Web sites, but it's used for a lot more than that. Often, companies make important information available on HTTP servers in XML format. It's this kind of information that FileMaker wants to let you tap into:

Many news-oriented Web sites make headlines and article excerpts available in XML formats called RSS or Atom. Using the XML Data Source feature in FileMaker, you could import news directly into your FileMaker database.

You can grab current or historical exchange rates from various sources to perform accurate currency conversions in FileMaker.

Some shippers let you track packages by downloading XML data. You can build package tracking right into FileMaker Pro.

FileMaker's XML import does have two significant limitations. First, it can't access data that's available only over a secure connection (in other words, it doesn't support HTTP over SSL, or HTTPS). If the data you need to access is available only in this form, you need to find another way.

Second, some XML data sources need information passed to them as *post arguments*—the equivalent of form fields on some Web pages. FileMaker can't send post arguments with the URL. Luckily, most data sources let you pass this information as part of the URL instead. Refer to the documentation for your data source for details.

Figure 17-19:
The Bento Data Source import option lets you take information from any of your Bento libraries. Just choose the library you want from the left-hand list. If that library has collections, they appear in the list on the right. There's also an Entire Library option.

Note: Bento automatically turns your Mac OS X Address Book, Calendars, and To Do lists into libraries in which you can link up to your own data in various ways. While this tool doesn't have nearly the power of FileMaker Pro, its ability to seamlessly integrate with your existing data is compelling. And since you can easily import from Bento to FileMaker, you can use it as a conduit to get address, calendar, and to-do info into your FileMaker databases too. For $49, it's the easiest and least expensive way to import this info into FileMaker.

ODBC Data Sources

The last import data source is called ODBC. This data source is a popular standard to let programs access information stored in database systems. For instance, if your company has an Oracle, Sybase, or Microsoft SQL Server database to manage orders, you can extract data directly from that database and import it into your FileMaker Pro database (perhaps you want to make your own reports with FileMaker).

Note: Although you can *import* data from other big database systems, FileMaker also offers a much more powerful means to interact with some of them: External SQL Sources, or ESS (page 666), which lets you work directly with data from Oracle, Microsoft SQL Server, and MySQL in FileMaker. ESS is often a simpler and more powerful choice unless you're just after a one-shot copy of the data.

ODBC is the most complex import data source to set up. It's a two-step process:

- First, you need to install an **ODBC driver** for the kind of database you're connecting to. For example, if your corporate database is in Oracle, you need an ODBC driver for Oracle. These drivers are platform specific, and most vendors supply only drivers for Microsoft Windows. If you're using Mac OS X, you can buy high-quality FileMaker-compatible drivers from Actual Technologies at *http://www.actualtechnologies.com/filemaker.php*. (When you visit their site, make sure you get the version that is appropriate for the number of simultaneous users you will have.)

- Next, you need to set up an **ODBC data source**. FileMaker doesn't connect to the database directly. Rather, it uses a data source that's been specified in the ODBC system on your computer. So you have to set up that data source first. In Microsoft Windows, you do this setting up in the ODBC control panel. In Mac OS X, you use the ODBC Administrator application in your Utilities folder.

Once you have a driver installed and a data source set up, you can use the File → Import Records → ODBC Data Source command. When you do, you see the Select ODBC Data Source window (Figure 17-20).

Figure 17-20:
When you tell FileMaker you want to import from an ODBC data source, it first asks you which source to use. This window shows every data source you've created in your ODBC system. You just highlight the one you want and click Continue.

When you click Continue in this window, you probably need to enter a user name and password for the database you're connecting to. You need to get this information from the database administrator, unless you created it in the ODBC software yourself.

Next, FileMaker shows the SQL Query Builder dialog box (Figure 17-21). When you extract data from *most* databases (FileMaker being the notable exception), you have to use a special programming language called Structured Query Language, or SQL (often pronounced *sequel*). Writing an SQL *query* (or program) is a complicated affair. Luckily, in most cases, FileMaker can do it for you—you just make the right choices. (For more detail, see the box on page 700.)

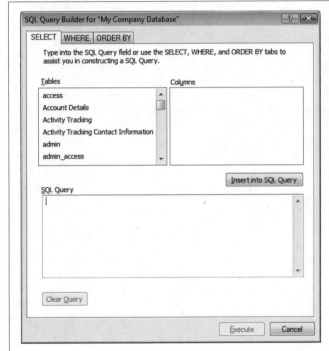

Figure 17-21:
In the SQL Query Builder dialog box's SELECT tab, the Tables list shows every table available from the database you're connecting to. When you select a table, FileMaker lists all its fields (called columns in most database systems) in the Columns list. Select a field and click "Insert into SQL Query" to include that field in the data you're importing. If you're a SQL pro, you can simply type in the SQL Query box instead.

When you're all finished building your query, click Execute. FileMaker performs the query, gathers the data from the data source, and shows the same Import Field Mapping dialog box you always see when importing data. If you find yourself doing a lot of ODBC imports, you may be well served by a good book on SQL.

Although the query builder supports only a little SQL, you can use any SQL commands supported by your database server if you type the query directly. And SQL can do *a lot*.

Importing and Exporting in a Script

Like almost everything else in FileMaker, you can completely control the import and export process from a script. You use the *Import Records* and *Export Records* scripts, which you can find in the Records section of the script steps list. You also find script steps for "Save Records as Excel" and "Save Records as PDF", with similar options.

POWER USERS' CLINIC

SQL Queries

To make use of FileMaker's query builder, you need to know just a little bit about SQL. A SQL query is made up of *clauses*, each of which influences the results you receive from the database server. Although SQL understands several clauses, the query builder window supports just three of them: SELECT, WHERE, and ORDER BY. The window has a tab for each of these.

The SELECT clause is where you tell the database what *fields* you want to import. You can include fields from more than one table if necessary. A SELECT clause alone imports every record in the table. If you include fields from more than one table, you get a result that may surprise you: Every record from each file is mixed in every possible combination. In other words, you import lots of records (multiply the record counts from each table to figure out how many).

The WHERE clause's job is to control which *records* get imported and how the tables are related. To specify certain records, you build find criteria into the WHERE clause. First, select a table and column from the pop-up menus. Then select something from the Operator pop-up menu. You can match this field with a value you type yourself (turn on the Value radio button) or with another field (turn on the Column radio button). Either way, enter or select the correct value. Finally, select either the And radio button or the Or radio button and turn on Not if you want to *omit* the matching records. When you're finished defining the criteria, click "Insert into SQL Query."

Relationships in SQL are probably the most confusing. SQL databases don't have a relationship graph like FileMaker, so the database doesn't know how things relate to one another at all. Each time you build a query, it's your job to tell it how to relate records from one table to those in another. You do this job by matching field values in each table in the WHERE clause.

For instance, you might pick the Customer ID field from the Customers table, the "=" operator, and the Customer ID field from the Orders table. When you add criteria like this to your WHERE clause, you've told the database how Order and Customer records relate. You can add as many criteria in this way as you need.

The last tab is called ORDER BY. This clause lets you specify a sort order for your data. It works just like FileMaker's normal Sort dialog box: Just add the fields to the Order By list, selecting Ascending or Descending as appropriate. When you've given it the order you want, click "Insert into SQL Query" again.

As you do these things, FileMaker builds the actual query in the SQL Query box at the bottom of the window so you can see how it comes together. If you feel adventurous, you can manually change this query at any time.

Save Records Script Steps

To automate the creation of Excel spreadsheets, use the "Save Records as Excel" script step. Not surprisingly, there's a "Save Records as PDF" script step as well. Each of these lets you specify all the options the standard menu commands offer, so you can completely automate the process.

As an added bonus, the "Save Records as PDF" script step includes one option you don't get when you run the command manually: an "Append to existing PDF" checkbox. When you turn this option on, if the file you're saving already exists, FileMaker adds the new pages to the end of the existing file. This scheme makes it possible to lump together several reports, or data from several different layouts into one complete PDF package for printing or distribution.

The Import Records Script Step

This script step has three options. First, you get to specify the data source to import from. Your choices match those in the File → Import Records menu: File, Folder, Digital Camera (Mac OS X only), XML Data, and ODBC Data. Which ever option you choose, FileMaker asks you for more information (*which* file to import, or *which* ODBC data source to use, for instance). When specifying a file, you get the standard path list dialog box. In other words, you can specify several paths if you want; FileMaker imports the first one it finds. (If you don't specify a source, your users have to do it as they run the script, in a potentially confusing series of dialog boxes. Since you're presumably providing a script to make things easier for people, it's best to store source files in a safe place and have the script escort your users to them.)

Once you've specified the source, you can turn on "Specify import order" to record the import field mapping, and other import options. Finally, you can turn on "Perform without dialog" if you want FileMaker to import the data directly, with no input from your users. If you leave this option off, FileMaker displays the Import Field Mapping dialog box when the script runs, so folks can make changes to any field mapping you specified.

The Export Records Script Step

The Export Records script step offers similar options. You can specify the output file and export order, and you can choose "Perform without dialog" if you don't want your users to see the export dialog box.

When you specify the output file, you may be surprised to see an Output File Path list. In other words, FileMaker lets you specify *more than one file*. This choice doesn't mean FileMaker exports more than one file, though. Instead, it exports to the first file path that is *valid*. If the first path in the list includes a folder name that doesn't exist, for example, FileMaker skips it and tries the next one.

Sharing Your Database

You've now got a solid foundation for building even the most complex database systems in FileMaker Pro. But your databases have so far been limited to just one user: you. Only the smallest small business, though, has only one person. Most databases are *multiuser databases*, used by lots of people, all at the same time. You can easily set up any FileMaker database for lots of people to use; you simply turn on a checkbox or two. In this chapter, you'll learn about those settings, plus some of the things you can expect from FileMaker when you're sharing databases.

Before you dive in and start changing settings, consider where you're going to keep the shared file and how other people's computers connect to it. You can choose from three types of sharing:, FileMaker Network, Internet Sharing, and FileMaker Server.

- **FileMaker Network**. This type of file sharing is also called *peer-to-peer*—that is, you don't use a server or any special software. You just use your ordinary computers to share files. Peer-to-peer sharing is limited to nine users at once. If more than nine people need to use the database at the same time, use FileMaker Server.

- **Internet Sharing**. Internet sharing has its own set of benefits and tradeoffs. On the plus side, people who need access to your files don't need a copy of File-Maker. All they need is an Internet connection and a recent-model browser. On the downside, not everything you can do in FileMaker translates to the Web, so you may have to live with fewer features. FileMaker uses a type of Internet sharing called **Instant Web Publishing (IWP)**. It translates your layouts to Web language according to settings you specify.

- **FileMaker Server** is the Big Daddy of FileMaker database sharing. FileMaker Server offers protection for your files in case of a crash, automated backups, and tremendous speed and stability boosts over peer-to-peer sharing. It also lets 250 (that's right, *two hundred and fifty*) people use the database all at once.

Note: Another type of Internet sharing, called *Custom Web Publishing,* offers more features than IWP. Using XML/XSLT or PHP, you can build incredibly powerful Web-based databases. With add-on software, you can even use other web technologies like Ruby on Rails (*http://www.sixfriedrice.com/wp/products/rfm*) or Lasso (*http://www.lassosoft.com*). But these technologies have steep learning curves—plus, they're beyond the scope of this book.

FileMaker Network Sharing

You can most easily share your data with *FileMaker Network Sharing*. If you already have a network in your office, and a few copies of FileMaker, then you're ready to share your database. First, you put all your databases on one computer. Then open those files, change a few settings in each file, and call that computer the *host*. Each computer that opens those files is called a *guest*, since it opens the same databases that are on the host. Up to nine guests can connect to one host.

Once you're set up, all nine people can work in the database at the same time, adding, editing, and deleting records, performing finds, printing, and running scripts. No two people can work in the same *record* at the same time, though. Once you're sharing files, you need to revisit the topic of record locking. See the box on page 711 for a refresher.

Note: You can do more than just browse data in a shared database. If your privilege set lets you, you can add or modify tables and fields, manage relationships, work in Layout mode, and even write scripts. When you do, the same one-at-a-time concept applies: Only one person can edit a particular script or layout at a time, and only one person can use the Manage → Database window. As soon as one person saves the layout or script or closes the Manage Database window, then someone else is free to hop in.

Setting Up a Host Computer

To set up the host, open the databases you want to share on one computer, and then choose Edit → Sharing → FileMaker Network. Either way, you see the File-Maker Network Settings dialog box: command central for all file sharing. From the list at left, choose the database you're setting up (if it's not there, make sure the file's open). Then, as described in Figure 18-1, turn sharing on.

Once you've turned on network sharing for the host computer, you need to tell FileMaker which databases to share. The dialog box shows a list of each open database (if you don't see the one you want, click OK, open the database, and then choose File → Sharing → FileMaker Network again). You must turn on network access for at least one privilege set in each file you want to share. First, from the "Currently open files" list, select a database. Then choose one of the following three settings to control who gets access to the file:

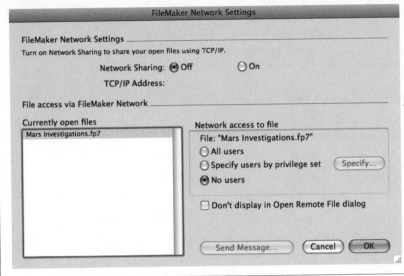

Figure 18-1:
The FileMaker Network Settings dialog box lets you set up your database host. The first step is to turn on the Network Sharing option by clicking the On radio button. When you do, FileMaker shows the computer's TCP/IP address, if it's connected to the network. (If you don't see a valid TCP/IP address, then you may have network problems.)

- **All Users** means that anybody on your network with a copy of FileMaker and a valid account can get in, so long as only nine people are on at a time.

- **Specify users by privilege set.** When you choose this option, you see a dialog box listing all your privilege sets (see page 633). Click the checkbox to the left of each privilege set that should have access to the file.

- **No users.** If a file needs to be open on the host, but you don't want it shared, choose this option.

When you make changes to these settings, FileMaker is actually making changes to the privilege sets in the selected file. When you turn on "All users", FileMaker simply turns on the "Access via FileMaker Network" extended privilege for every privilege set. Likewise, if you choose "No users", it turns this extended privilege off for every set. When you specify people by privilege set, you get to decide which privilege sets have this extended privilege turned on. If you prefer, you can make these changes manually in the Extended Privileges tab of the Manage Accounts & Privileges window (File → Manage → Accounts & Privileges). Look for the [fmapp] extended privilege if you're setting access manually (page 653).

Note: You can control the access settings for each file even if you don't turn on network sharing. The settings you make to a file stick with that file even when you move it to another computer, so you can use this window to set the sharing options for a file *before* you send it to the host computer.

When a database is shared this way, you use the File → Open Remote command to open it from another computer (you'll learn how to do so in the next section). FileMaker then shows every available shared database. If you don't want this database to show up, then turn on the "Don't display in Open Remote File dialog" checkbox.

Why would you share a database, and then make it invisible? Suppose you have a database system that's made up of several files, but you want people to open only a specific one (because only one file has an interface and the others just hold data, for example). You want only that main file visible in the Open dialog box, so nobody opens the wrong one. However, you still need to *share* the other files.

Opening a Shared File

If you just shared your database so a colleague can access it, the easiest way to get him connected is to send him a link to your database. Just choose File → Send Link, and FileMaker creates an email in your email program with a clickable link to the database. (The recipient needs FileMaker installed for the link to work.)

But FileMaker has a more direct route to opening shared files, too. Launch FileMaker Pro on another computer on the network, and then follow these steps:

1. **Choose File → Open Remote.**

   If you're already looking at the Open File dialog box, click the Remote button instead. Either way, you see the Open Remote File dialog box (Figure 18-2).

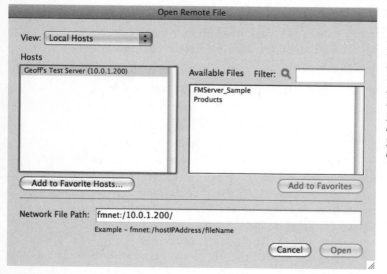

Figure 18-2:
The Open Remote File dialog box lets you find files that are shared on the network. This box lists all the hosts it can find in the Hosts list. Select a host to see all the available files in the list to the right. If you like the typing thing, then in the Network File Path box, you can enter exactly what FileMaker needs.

2. **From the Hosts list, select the appropriate host.**

   The shared files show in the Available Files list. (If the host computer you're looking for isn't listed, see the next page for advice.)

3. **Select the file you want to open from the Available Files list, and then click Open.**

   If you've added accounts to the file, FileMaker asks you for an account name and password. When you give it what it needs, the database opens.

Note: When a database opens from a host, in the window title bar, FileMaker puts the host name in parentheses to help you keep things straight. If you don't like seeing host names in your window's title bars, then use the Set Window Title step to change that name in a script that runs when the file is opened (page 569).

The Open Remote File Dialog Box

The Open Remote File dialog box (File → Open Remote) has even more tricks up its sleeve, mostly geared towards folks with a lot of databases. If you're perfectly happy with the previous instructions, then you have permission to skip this section.

Choosing a host computer

When opening a remote file, you first choose the host computer. Above the Hosts list, the View pop-up menu offers three choices:

- Choose **Local Hosts**, and FileMaker searches your local network and lists any host computers it finds. This view is usually the easiest way to share files in the office (or house or wherever all your computers are in one place). You can see each computer's name and IP address.

  Unfortunately, the Local Hosts option has a few weaknesses. First, it can be a little slow, which may drive you crazy if you can't stand to waste a single second. Worse, sometimes FileMaker can't find the host you want, usually because the guest computer and the host computer aren't on the same network (you might have a host computer at the office, and need to access it from home, for instance).

- If Local Hosts doesn't do the trick, from the View pop-up menu, choose **Favorite Hosts** instead. When you do, FileMaker doesn't show anything in the Hosts list at first. Click the Add button to summon the Edit Favorite Host dialog box, and then type the host computer's information, as shown in Figure 18-3.

  When you're done setting up the favorite host, click Save. FileMaker now shows the computer in the Hosts list. Now, whenever you visit the Open Remote File dialog box, FileMaker has Favorite Hosts preselected, with all your favorites instantly available.

  Of course, you can change a favorite at any time (just select it, and then click Edit) or remove it from the list when you don't need it anymore (select it, and then click Remove).

Note: When you add a host to your favorites, FileMaker also shows it in the Quick Start dialog box (page 4). Click the Open Database icon in that window, and, in the box on the left, you see your host listed.

- The **Hosts Listed by LDAP** option is for the big guys. If you have a lot of FileMaker servers, and you don't want end users to have to manage their Favorites list manually, you can set up an LDAP server with available host information. Refer to the FileMaker Server documentation for details on this uncommon option.

Figure 18-3:
In the Favorite Hosts list, when you add (or edit) a host, FileMaker shows this window. In the first box, type the host computer's address. You can use the IP address, or, if the computer has a name (like filemaker.mycompany.com), then you can type that instead. Next, in the Favorite Host's Name box, give it any descriptive name you want. Normally FileMaker shows every visible database from a host. You can enter specific database names if you want, though (if you routinely use just one database from a host with dozens, say). Just turn on "Show only these files", and then, in the big box below it, type one name on each line.

Choosing a file

Once you've made your host selection, you get to choose the file you want to open. Typically, each shared file is listed in the Available Files list on the window's right side, and you can just double-click one to open it (or select it, and then click Open).

If the Available Files list has *lots* of databases, then you can find the one you want by typing in the Filter box. FileMaker reduces the list to show each file whose name contains the letter or phrase you enter. For example, if you type *mars*, then you probably see only the Mars Investigations file.

If you find yourself opening the same files often (a pretty common thing), select a file, and then click "Add to Favorites". When you do, FileMaker adds this file to the Quick Start dialog box's list of favorite files (see the box on page 94).

Finally, on some occasions you may need to open a file that doesn't show in the list. For example, you might have an ancillary file that you've configured to share but not show in the Open Remote dialog box. That setup is fine for your users, who never need to open this file directly. But you, O wise developer, may need to open the file to look under the hood.

1. **From the Hosts list, select the host computer, if you haven't already.**

   In addition to showing files from the host, FileMaker adds the host's address to the Network File Path box at the bottom of the window. For example, if you select a host with the address 192.168.1.10, then FileMaker puts *fmnet:/192.168.1.10/* in the box.

2. **Add your database name to the end of the network file path (after the "/").**

Since the file you want doesn't show in the list, you have to type its name directly. You're actually creating a FileMaker network file path, which File-Maker will use to open the file for you.

3. **Click Open.**

If you typed the name correctly, then FileMaker opens the file.

If you get an error, check to make sure you spelled the file name correctly, and that the file really *is* shared and open on the host computer.

Note: You don't need to put the ".fp7" in the network file path. FileMaker knows you're looking for a FileMaker database.

Sharing over the Internet

FileMaker Network Sharing is the easiest way to share your database. Folks simply open the file, and it works *exactly* like a file on their hard drives. The catch is that they need a copy of FileMaker Pro on whatever computer they're using to connect. (Of course, when you consider how cool FileMaker Pro is, you're probably doing them a favor.) If you want to open up your database to people who don't have FileMaker—and you're willing to live with a less elegant interface—you can use Instant Web Publishing. This feature turns your computer into its own Web server. Like magic, it turns all your layouts into Web pages, and lets anybody with an up-to-date Web browser search, sort, and edit your data directly.

Turning on Web Sharing

Enabling Instant Web Publishing (IWP for short) is just as easy as turning on File-Maker Network Sharing. First, choose File → Sharing → Instant Web Publishing, and then click On. Once IWP starts up, FileMaker shows you the URL by which people access your databases. (You also get to pick a language for your Web pages. This action doesn't translate the information in your database, though. Instead, it controls what language all of FileMaker's built-in buttons, labels, and links use in the Web browser.)

Advanced Web Publishing Options

The Advanced Web Publishing Options window lets you configure FileMaker's built-in Web server. You get to pick a *port* (more on that next) and restrict access to only certain computers, among other settings. In the Instant Web Publishing window, clicking Advanced Options opens the dialog box (Figure 18-4).

Network servers set up shop at a *TCP/IP Port Number*, and once you turn on IWP, your computer is a network server, too. The usual Web publishing port is 80 and, if you have no other Web services running on your computer, that's the one you'll usually use. But if you do need to set up your Web server with multiple services, then you can change FileMaker's port number to avoid a conflict. As you can see in the figure above, FileMaker has registered its very own port number just for Web publishing (591). If you stick with port 591, chances are no other program's using it, and you'll avoid conflicts even if you need to add other services later on. When you assign any port other than 80, FileMaker automatically adds the port number to the URL it displays in the Instant Web Publishing dialog box, as a reminder of the link your browser uses to connect to your site.

Advanced Web Publishing Options	
Guest Access	
TCP/IP Port Number: [8080]	Maximum number of connections: 5
☐ Accessible only from these IP addresses:	
Use a "," to separate multiple addresses.	
Logging options:	
File: application.log	File: access.log
☑ Script errors	☑ Web activity
☑ Web publishing errors	
Session management:	
Set web publishing to disconnect users who have been inactive for the specified period. The time limit may be set from 1–60 minutes.	
Disconnect inactive accounts: [15] minutes	
	(Cancel) (OK)

Figure 18-4:
In the Advanced Web Options dialog box, you get to decide which information FileMaker records in log files (you can refer to these files if you have problems or you're curious who's using the database). Also, you can tell FileMaker to forget about people who haven't clicked the Web page for a while by setting the "Disconnect inactive accounts" value.

Note: When you use port 80, links to your site don't need to include the port number, but if you're using any other port number, then you have to make sure they do. In a URL, the port number comes right after the server name, with a colon in front, like this: *http://mycomputer:591/.*

If you don't want just anybody trying to connect to your databases, then you can turn on "Accessible only from these IP addresses". You then have to list the network address of each computer you want to allow (with commas in between). If you have a large intranet, you don't have to type dozens of IP addresses, though. You can specify a range of addresses using an asterisk. For example, 192.168.15.* lets everyone whose IP address matches the first three sets of numbers access the file.

While IWP is running, it can keep track of activity and errors. FileMaker keeps this information in log files in its Web Logs folder. The "Web activity" log records each time someone interacts with the database. The log includes the person's network address, and the URL she requested. The "Script errors" log records errors in your FileMaker scripts. The "Web publishing errors" log holds other errors that occur in IWP, like invalid requests and missing databases. You can use these logs to see if you need to fix your scripts, or to see who's been using the databases and what problems they've encountered. If you use IWP a lot, these logs can get large. Turn any or all of them off to keep FileMaker from recording this information.

UP TO SPEED

Record Locking Revisited

Back in Chapter 2, you learned about *record locking*. When you start editing a record, FileMaker locks it, so it can't be changed in another window until you commit it in the first. At the time, this scenario probably seemed like a pretty obscure situation: How often do you try to edit the same record in two different windows? But when several people start sharing the same database, record locking takes on a whole new meaning. Now, when you start editing a record, *nobody else* can edit it. If you type a few lines in the Notes field, and then go home sick without clicking out of the record, you keep it locked all day.

When you try to edit a locked record, FileMaker warns you with a message box. It tells you the record's locked, and *who* has it locked (including the user name on his computer, *and* the account name with which he's logged in).

If you'd like to politely ask him to get out of the record, click Send Message. You see the "Send Message to Conflicting Users" window. Enter any message you want, and then click OK. A window pops up on his screen with your message.

While record locking can be a minor annoyance to the user, it can be a real problem for the database developer. If you've

designed all your scripts with the mistaken notion that you can *always* edit *any* record you want, then you might get an unpleasant surprise the first time a script tries to modify a locked record.

Even worse, sometimes you build a process that simply doesn't work for multiple users. For example, suppose you expect people to flag a series of records, and then run a script that does something to all the ones they flagged. If the script *finds* the flagged records and loops through them, then FileMaker gets utterly confused when two people try to use the same script at once. The script sees everyone's marked flags, unless you take special care to make each person's flag unique. It's anybody's guess how your poor records will wind up. In this example, you could mitigate the problem by entering the person's account name in the flag field. The script could then find just that person's flagged records.

In general, you should think about how the script you write works if a record can't be edited, or if several people are using it at the same time. Or, to avoid the issue altogether, make it so only one person can use certain scripts, and use privilege sets to keep everybody else away from them.

Web browsers don't work exactly like FileMaker itself. Someone has to explicitly log out to tell FileMaker he's disconnecting. If he doesn't—for example, if he just quits his browser or goes to a different Web site—FileMaker doesn't know he's left your site. To keep people from tying up connections forever, FileMaker automatically disconnects anyone who hasn't requested a page in a while. You get to decide how long "a while" is. A smaller setting (like 15 minutes) ensures that people don't hold connections long if they forget to log out. But if they spend more than 15 minutes looking at a single record (reading a long Notes field, for instance), then they're disconnected even though they're still using the database. If you have situations like this one, set the "Disconnect inactive accounts" value to something larger (the maximum is 60 minutes).

Configuring file access

Just like FileMaker Network Sharing, you get to decide which files are shared by IWP, and which privilege sets have Web access. In fact, the settings are identical: Select an open file, and then choose the appropriate access level. Finally, you manage IWP access using the [fmiwp] extended privilege.

Connecting from a Web Browser

Not all Web browsers are created equal. They aren't all good at showing you Web sites that use Cascading Style Sheets (CSS). And since FileMaker translates your layouts into CSS when you share them via IWP, you must have a browser that understands CSS to use databases on the Web, like one of the following:

- Microsoft Internet Explorer 6.0 or higher in Windows

- Safari 1.2 or higher in Mac OS X 10.3

- Safari 2.0 or higher in Mac OS X 10.4, 10.5 or Windows

- Firefox 1.0 or higher in Mac or Windows

To connect to the database from a Web browser, you need to know the URL in the Instant Web Publishing dialog box. In your Web browser's Location box, type this URL. The resulting Web page looks like the one in Figure 18-5.

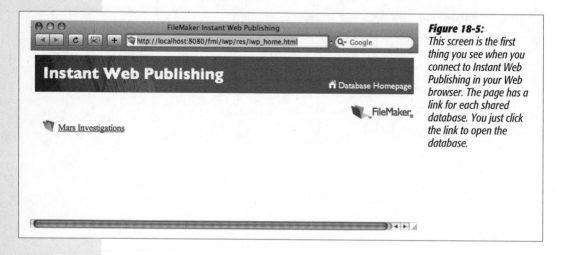

Figure 18-5:
This screen is the first thing you see when you connect to Instant Web Publishing in your Web browser. The page has a link for each shared database. You just click the link to open the database.

When you click a database link on the Web page, FileMaker asks you to log into the database—even if you haven't set up accounts on your database. If you've created accounts, then enter a valid account name and password. Otherwise, enter *Admin* for the user name, and leave the password box blank. After you log in, you see what probably looks a *lot* like your real database displayed right inside the Web page (Figure 18-6).

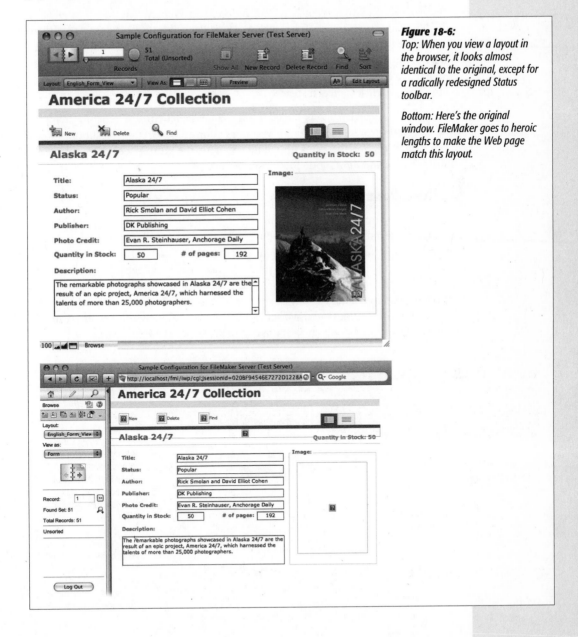

Figure 18-6:
Top: When you view a layout in the browser, it looks almost identical to the original, except for a radically redesigned Status toolbar.

Bottom: Here's the original window. FileMaker goes to heroic lengths to make the Web page match this layout.

The most noticeable difference is the Status toolbar: It's bigger and has more options, as Figure 18-6 attests. When you view your data in List view or Table view, the Web page shows only a few records at a time. To see more, click the pages in the book icon, or type a record number in the Current Record box, and then click the "Go to Record" button in the Status Toolbar. Since you're working on the Web, you *must* click this button to reload the page with the desired record.

The process of editing records is also different in IWP. When you first click an editable field (or, in the toolbar, click the Edit Record button), FileMaker reloads the page in editable form. The Status toolbar also changes: Submit and Cancel buttons appear, while all other tools become unavailable. After you've made changes, you have to click Submit or FileMaker doesn't save them. If you don't want to keep your changes, click Cancel instead.

The Status toolbar has icons for common database activities. The icons change if you switch to Browse mode, and if you hold your mouse arrow over a button for a few seconds, then a label pops up telling you what the button does. You can see the Browse mode and Find mode toolbars in Figure 18-7.

Custom Home Page

The IWP home page, shown in Figure 18-5, gets the job done, but it's not likely to match your corporate identity. And some people find it a bit confusing, since it doesn't provide them with a lot of clues about what your IWP database does. But you can make a Custom Home Page to replace it. First, take the HTML file you want to use for the home page and name it *iwp_home.html*. Then put it in FileMaker's Web folder. On Windows, you find it at Program Files → FileMaker → FileMaker Pro → Web. On Mac OS X, it's at Applications → FileMaker Pro 9.0 → Web. If FileMaker sees a file with this name, then it automatically shows it instead of the normal IWP home page.

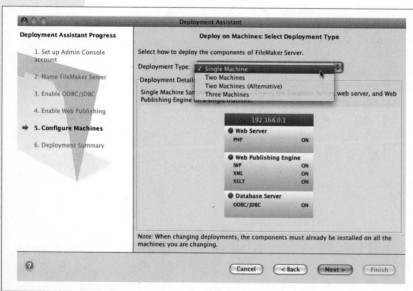

Figure 18-7:
Since FileMaker can't control the menu bar in your Web browser, it has to cram everything it thinks you'll ever need into the Status toolbar. Almost everything here has an exact counterpart in FileMaker Pro itself. Notable exceptions: the Home icon (in the top-right corner), which returns you to the list of shared databases, and Log Out, which tells FileMaker you're done using the connection.

Of course, you'll want to include links to your databases on this page. Direct links to an IWP database look like this:

```
/fmi/iwp/cgi?-db=Database Name&-startsession
```

Just replace "Database Name" with your database's name.

FileMaker Server

Using FileMaker Pro on an ordinary desktop computer to host your files is easy and decidedly inexpensive, but it has some pretty severe drawbacks. First, it can handle no more than nine guests at once. If you have more, you have to find a better way. You find some less obvious problems as well, including the following:

- If somebody's working on the host computer, chances are she's doing more than just FileMaker. The more you do on a computer, the more likely it is to crash—especially after you contract the next email virus. The host in a peer-to-peer setup can sometimes be unstable. You probably don't want your database server interrupting your office workflow. But more serious than that, databases that crash often are likely to get corrupted. And that's not safe for your data.

- FileMaker Pro is designed for *using* databases, not hosting them. It does an admirable hosting job, but it simply wasn't built for speed or large numbers of simultaneous users.

- As you remember from Chapter 1, you should close databases before you back them up. But if they're open on a host computer, you have to disconnect all the guests before closing the files. This necessity makes midday backups a little inconvenient.

The answer to all these problems—and more—is FileMaker Server. It's a special piece of software designed for one thing: turning a dedicated computer into a lean, mean, and *stable* database host. When FileMaker Server hosts your databases, you can have *250* guests connected at once. Since it runs on a dedicated server, it tends to be much more stable (and you can put it in the closet, where nobody will pull the plug or close the files accidentally). From a performance perspective, you *can't* launch FileMaker Server and use the database directly. In fact, it has no windows, menus, or dialog boxes at all (it has an administration tool through which you can monitor the server and make changes to it, though). Instead, it's a true *server* (sometimes called a *service* or a *daemon*), designed specifically to share data over the network. Finally, it's loaded with special server-only features, including an automatic backup feature that can safely back up files while people are connected.

So what's the catch? Money. FileMaker Server costs $999, while another copy of FileMaker Pro is only $299. Don't be fooled, though. This cash is money well spent if your database is at all important to your business.

Note: FileMaker Server comes in two flavors: *FileMaker Server* and *FileMaker Server Advanced*. Both do a fine job with FileMaker Network Sharing, but only the Advanced version does those *other* kinds of sharing—Instant Web Publishing. (Regular Server can do Custom Web Publishing too, if that's your need. But you need Advanced for ODBC and JDBC support.) If you're not sure you need Advanced just yet, don't sweat it. You can buy FileMaker Server today, and then trade it up to Advanced later if the need arises. This book doesn't cover the Advanced version. If you're interested in getting into big-time Web publishing, check out the resources in Appendix A.

File Compatibility

As you learned back near the beginning of this book, the file extension for database files created with version 7, 8, 9 and 10 is "fp7". Therefore, you can do a fair amount of version mixing between FileMaker Server, FileMaker Developer, and FileMaker Pro, and still get good results. You can develop files on FileMaker Pro Advanced 8, put them on a FileMaker 10 Server, and then let people with FileMaker Pro 7 share them. You can mix and match versions 7–10 at will.

Note: The files open just fine across versions. However, some features, like Tab controls, script variables, conditional formatting, script triggers, and External SQL Sources (ESS) don't work properly in version 7 or 8, so take care how you mix versions if you're using these recent additions.

However, files prior to version 7 have to be converted before you can use them with any FileMaker product that's version 7 or above. But those good folks at FileMaker, Inc. have been careful to provide support for conversion. FileMaker Pro 10 can convert files from as far back as FileMaker 3. You *can* convert even older versions, but it's tricky. You have to find someone with FileMaker 5 first, and use it to convert older files to the .fp5 format. Once the files have been updated, FileMaker Pro 10 can take over and get you up to .fp7-land.

POWER USERS' CLINIC

Global Fields and Multiple Users

When many people share a single database, you might be worried about global fields. If one person changes a global field, does it change for *everybody*? In a word, "No." FileMaker keeps global field information on the *guest* computer. If you change what's in the global field, it has no effect on what's in that global field for other people.

This characteristic is, in general, a very good thing. But it does have an annoying side effect. Since everyone has his own globals, you *can't* change them for other people even when you want to. If you open a shared database, change a global, and then close it, you lose your changes. The next time you open the database, the globals have the same values as the *host* computer.

If you're using peer-to-peer sharing, then you can change the globals on the host directly to make them stick. Since FileMaker Server has no real interface, you can't directly modify the initial value for a global field. You have to close the files on the server, move them to another computer, open them with FileMaker Pro, make the change, and then copy them back to the server. In other words, it's a pain.

If you have globals you often need to change permanently in a multiuser system, then it's often easier to simply set them from a script that runs when the database opens. Then you're sure they have the right value, and you can always modify the script if you want to change the starting value while the databases are still hosted.

If you have files to convert, be sure to check out two excellent documents on migration: "Migration foundations and methodologies" and "How to migrate existing solutions". Look for them in the Migration Topics section at *http://www.filemaker.com/support/whitepapers.html*.

Installing FileMaker Server

If you decide a FileMaker Server is the right thing for your database, then your first step is to install the software. (Although you may want to buy a good server computer first. See page 730 for some guidelines.) FileMaker Server (in both its standard and Advanced versions) includes an installer program that takes care of the basic complexities of configuration for you. When you run the installer (and after you accept the terms of the license agreement), FileMaker asks you a simple question, as shown in Figure 18-8.

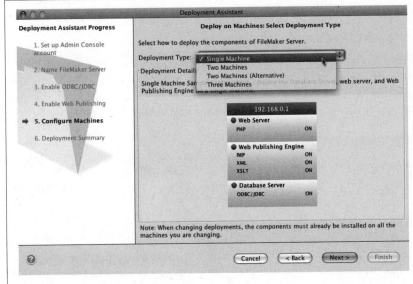

Figure 18-8:
When you install FileMaker Server, the first question you have to answer is what type of installation you want. Choose Single Machine if you want to install all server components on one computer. If you're going to use two servers (one Web server and one database server, for example) then choose the second option. You should also choose Multiple Machines if you're installing FileMaker Server Advanced but you don't want all the Web components just yet.

If your database will be heavily used (by dozens or even a couple hundred people) and you plan on using the Web publishing capabilities of FileMaker heavily, then it probably makes sense to install different portions of the server setup on different machines. Three configurations are typical:

- **FileMaker Server and Web Server.** Install FileMaker Server and the Web Publishing Engine on one computer, and use an ordinary Web server computer as the "front end" for your Web publishing. This configuration works well if you already have a Web server in your organization, and you want to add some FileMaker based Web content. You can keep all the FileMaker parts together in one place, with minimal impact on the Web server computer.

- **Web Server and Database Server.** Install FileMaker Server on one computer, and the Web Publishing Engine on another. The database server handles all your pure data serving needs. The Web Server handles both ordinary Web pages and the FileMaker Web publishing system.

- **Web Server, Web Publishing Engine, and Database Server.** Install the FileMaker Server on one computer, the Web Publishing Engine on another, and use a third as a Web server. In this configuration, the load of the Web Publishing Engine doesn't interfere with ordinary Web server tasks, and doesn't slow down the File-Maker Server. This configuration is generally the fastest for maximum load.

Note: If you aren't using FileMaker Server Advanced or you don't need plan on doing any Web publishing, then your decision is simple. Just do a Single Machine installation on the server computer, and you're done.

If you plan on using any of these multicomputer configurations, choose Multiple Machines when asked about Installation Type, and then click Next.

Single Machine installation

If you opted for a Single Machine installation, you're almost done. Just click Next and (if necessary) key in your software license code. The installer program then goes to work installing all the various parts and pieces. When it's finished, skip past the next section to Configuring Your Server to finish the installation process.

Two Machine installation

If you want to install on two machines, you get two options: Choose "Two Machines" for the most typical configuration, with the database server on one machine, and all the Web components on the second.

Sometimes, though, you don't want to (or more typically aren't allowed to) install the Web Publishing Engine on your company's Web server. If that's the case, choose "Two Machines (Alternate)." In this configuration, the first machine—which has the database server and Web publishing engine—does all the heavy lifting. The Web server has only a small connecter. You'll usually use this first "Two Machines" option if you have complete control over both server computers.

Configuring your server

Once the installer has finished putting software on your computer, it asks if you want to start the Deployment Assistant. This step is necessary since otherwise, the software sits dormant on your computer. Click Continue.

When you first start the Deployment Assistant, it can take several minutes. File-Maker has to start up its server software, download the configuration tools to your computer, and start up the admin application. But if you exercise some patience, then you eventually see the first screen of the Deployment Assistant, as shown in Figure 18-9.

Figure 18-9:
The Deployment Assistant is divided into several steps. Once you reach the last step, your server is ready to go. Luckily, most of these steps are simple.

In the first screen, you're asked to set up an "admin console account." When you interact with your FileMaker Server in the future, you'll use the Admin Console application. It can tweak configuration settings, install new databases, perform backups, and more. And it can do all this from any computer on the network. To prevent unauthorized people from working with your server, you set up an account (with a name and password) for authorized administrators.

Just enter the User Name and Password you want to use. You have to type the password twice so FileMaker can be sure you didn't mistype it. Then click Next, and the next page (Figure 18-10) asks you to name your server.

Figure 18-10:
In the Name FileMaker Server section, you give your FileMaker Server a friendly name (which people see in the Open Remote dialog box). You can also add a description, which shows up on the Admin Console page. Use this to remind you (or your administrators) where the server computer is, what it's used for, or anything else useful. Finally, you can record contact information in case an administrator ever needs to talk to you about the server.

Everything on this screen is optional except the Server Name. Fill out the parts you think will be useful, and then click Next.

The next page simply asks if you want to use ODBC/JDBC with your server. This option has nothing to do with ESS, ODBC Import, or the Execute SQL script step: You're *always* free to use these features. Instead, this setting controls whether *other* programs can talk to FileMaker using ODBC or JDBC. If you don't need this ability, keep this option turned off. (You can always turn it on later.)

Finally, FileMaker asks if you want to enable Web publishing. If this is just a plain-vanilla FileMaker Server for FileMaker users only, then turn this option off. Otherwise, turn it on.

When you're through, FileMaker shows one more page, with a summary of your various settings (Figure 18-11).

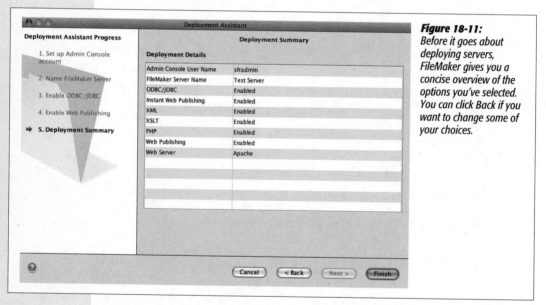

Figure 18-11:
Before it goes about deploying servers, FileMaker gives you a concise overview of the options you've selected. You can click Back if you want to change some of your choices.

When you're confident you have the server set up the way you want, click Finish. The assistant then configures all the parts of your server, and launches the Admin Console for you.

Administering FileMaker Server

Once you have a server installed and configured, you can administer it at any time using the Admin Console. On the computer you performed the installation, you see a shortcut on your desktop that takes you to the FileMaker Server Admin Console Start Page (Figure 18-12). But you can visit this page from *any computer on your network* so you don't have to leave your desk to work with your server. If this is the first time you've accessed this page on your computer, then you have to type the URL directly. It looks like this:

```
http://myserver:16000/
```

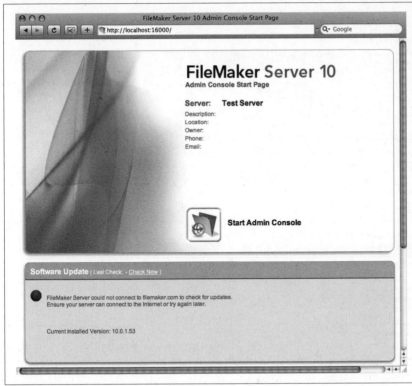

Figure 18-12:
The FileMaker Server Admin Console Start Page is a one-stop shop for server information. At the top, you see information about the server itself, including its name, description, and administrator contact information. The page tells you if an update is available for your FileMaker Server software (bottom). You can't see it in this picture, but if you scroll down, you also get links to online server documentation and useful tools.

In other words, use the name of your server, followed by ":16000". This URL tells your browser to access FileMaker Server's start page directly.

From the start page, you can launch the Admin Console itself. Just click the icon next to Start Admin Console. Again, the first time you use the Admin Console (Figure 18-13), it takes a few minutes to configure the software on your computer. (Later, when you come back to the Admin Console, it'll be faster.)

The sidebar in the Admin Console includes several important sections:

- **Clients.** All the people who are connected to your server. Generally, they're folks who have one of your shared databases open, or are using Instant Web Publishing. You can see their FileMaker account name, the type of connection they have, their computers' network address, and even which version of FileMaker they're using. You can also send them a message, or disconnect them from the server. To do so, first select someone in the list, then pick from the Actions pop-up menu, and click Perform Action.

- **Databases.** A list of databases being shared with this server. You can see which databases are being shared, and in what ways. And just like with Clients, you can select a database and perform any of several actions.

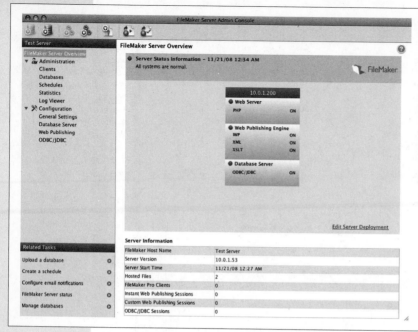

Figure 18-13:
The Admin Console is a vast application. The bar along the left side of the window lets you switch between the various sections. At the bottom of this bar, you can click links to perform important tasks. For example, you probably want to install a database on your server. To do that, click "Upload a database".

- **Schedules.** Gives you high level information about scheduled tasks on your server. You can schedule three different things on FileMaker Server: backups, scripts, and messages. Backups are the most important, and you'll see how to create a backup schedule on page 724.

- **Statistics.** Tells you about your server. The myriad numbers presented on this screen give your (or FileMaker's tech support staff) information about how much load your server encounters, and how it's performing.

- **General Settings.** Includes all the configuration options you set when you set up your server, plus some additional options. Here, you can rename your server (in the Server Information tab), tell the server to email you important information periodically (in the Email Notifications tab), change the administrator password (in the Admin Console tab) and decide if the server should start automatically when the computer boots (in the Auto Start tab).

- **Database Server.** Shows configuration options specific to the database server portion of FileMaker Server. In addition to numerous parameters like how many people can connect to the server and how many databases can be installed, you can also decide where database backups are stored.

- **Web Publishing and ODBC/JDBC** let you configure these optional portions of the FileMaker Server.

Below this list of console screens, the Admin Console has a list of common tasks. You'll probably visit each of these when you first set up your server.

Installing a Database

When you first install your server, it's like a well of untapped potential. Although the server is ready to go, you don't have any *databases* installed. Your first job is to install at least one shared database so you can take advantage of FileMaker Server's high performance capabilities:

1. **In the Admin Console sidebar, click Databases.**

   FileMaker shows you the Databases section of the admin console, including an Actions pop-up menu.

2. **From the Actions pop-up menu, choose Upload, and then click Perform Action.**

   The Upload Database Assistant appears (Figure 18-14).

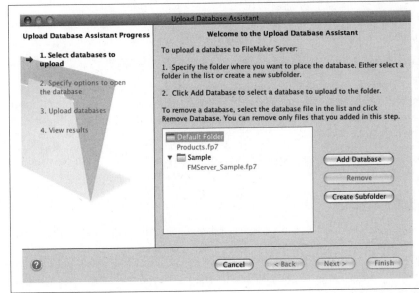

Figure 18-14:
The Upload Database Assistant makes it a breeze to install databases on your FileMaker server. You just pick the database(s) from your computer, and decide where they should go. The assistant takes care of copying them to the server, and installing them in the appropriate place.

3. **Click Create Subfolder and, in the box that pops up, type *My Database System*, and then click OK.**

   FileMaker Server organizes shared databases in folders. This step is entirely optional, but if your database system has several files, or you want to share different database systems, it's helpful to keep related databases together in one folder.

4. **Click Add Database.**

   You see a standard Open File dialog box. Here's where you pick the file you want to share.

5. **Navigate to the file you want to share, select it, and then click Open.**

Make sure the database isn't already open in FileMaker Pro before you try to upload it. When you've made your choice, FileMaker adds it to the list in the assistant window. If you have other databases to share, select a folder, and then click Add Database again.

6. **Click Next.**

FileMaker inspects your files to be sure they're ready to share, and then asks if you want to open the files once they're uploaded. (A file can be opened and closed on the server just like on your own computer. An open file is shared and ready to be opened by other people. A closed file is on the server, but people can't access it.)

7. **Leave "Automatically open databases after upload" turned on, and then click Next.**

The Upload Assistant uploads the databases (it shows a progress bar as they're copied), and then reports that the "Upload has completed successfully".

8. **Click Next.**

The Upload Assistant shows you the status of each uploaded file. Generally, each file indicates "File uploaded successfully and opened". This means your database is shared and ready to be accessed in FileMaker Pro using the File → Open Remote dialog box.

When you're done uploading, click Finish. You return to the Admin Console window, where, in the Databases section, you can see your database.

Scheduling a backup

One of a true FileMaker Server's primary advantages is the ability to perform database backups easily. You can't overestimate the importance of this step. Some day your server will crash, perhaps because a hard drive fails, or the power goes out, or for any of a dozen other reasons. When this happens, your best course of action is to take your lumps, restore from backup, and re-enter any missing data. The more often you back up, the less difficult it is to do that.

If you want, you can configure FileMaker Server to back up to a location different from the main hard drive on your server computer. It makes good sense, for example, to back up on a second hard drive. This way if the main hard drive fails, then you don't lose your database *and* your backup.

But you should also make offline backups that are stored in a remote location. This protects against the "office burns down" type scenarios, where all the computers and drives in your office are lost. FileMaker's automated backup gets the files cleanly copied to a drive of your choice, but it's up to you to copy those backups to tape, CD, DVD, or over the network so they're stored offsite.

To configure the backup location, in the Admin Console sidebar, choose Database Server. Then switch to the Default Folders tab. At the bottom of this window, you see the backup folder location (Figure 18-15).

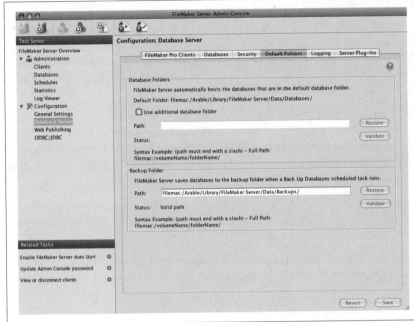

Figure 18-15:
On the Default Folders tab, you tell FileMaker where you want to store backup files. You can enter any valid path on your computer (following the syntax example). Your best bet is a path on a hard drive other than the one on which your databases are stored.

In the Path box, type the full path to the folder where you want backups stored. The path must start with filewin: (Windows) or filemac: (Mac OS X), and end with a slash. When you're done typing, click Validate, and FileMaker tells you if your path is valid.

Once you've set the backup location, you're ready to schedule the backup. Like many things in FileMaker, you can do it the easy way if your needs are basic, or you can peek under the hood and make numerous configuration choices to get exactly what you want. A backup schedule runs periodically (you control how often), and backs up certain files (you control which ones). Each time FileMaker makes a backup, it puts the files in a folder with the date and time in its name so you can easily tell how old the backup file is. You also configure the schedule to keep a certain number of copies. For instance, if you choose to keep three copies, then FileMaker automatically keeps three complete backups. When the schedule runs again, it deletes the oldest and makes one more new one.

FileMaker Server includes three handy built-in schedules. If you want the most basic backup (every file, every night, keeping a week's worth of copies), then you don't have to do anything. FileMaker Server comes preconfigured to run just such a backup automatically. (You can see it in the Admin Console's Schedules section, labeled Daily.)

If you want more frequent backups, turn off Daily, and turn on Hourly instead (you turn on a schedule using the checkbox by its name). This version keeps eight copies of your database, one for each hour from 8:00 a.m. to 5:00 p.m. Alternately, you can turn on Weekly if you just want backups every week (in this configuration, it keeps four copies).

It often makes sense to turn all these schedules on. That way, you get hourly backups for the current day, daily backups for the last week, and weekly backups for a month, which is a nice balance of frequent recent copies and a few old copies in case of catastrophe (imagine, for instance, you accidentally delete hundreds of older records, and don't notice for a week).

If you want to modify any of the built-in backups, in the left-side bar, just click Schedules, and then double-click any schedule. FileMaker walks you through a step-by-step configuration. You can, for instance, switch the hourly backups to run from 7:00 a.m. instead of 8:00 a.m., or tell the weekly backup to keep eight copies instead of four.

If you need a more advanced setup (maybe you want to do a special backup that your offsite backup system picks up every Friday at midnight), then you can make as many new schedules as you want.

1. **From the Actions pop-up window at the top of the screen, choose "Create a Schedule", and then click Perform Action.**

   The Schedule Assistant window (Figure 18-16) appears.

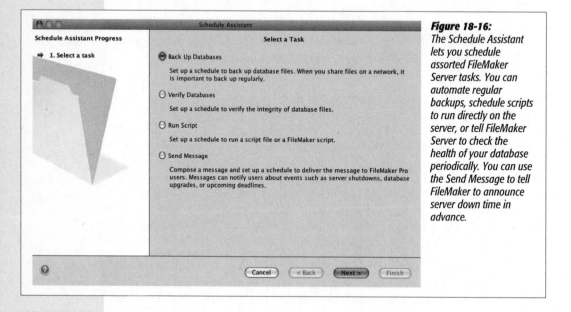

Figure 18-16:
The Schedule Assistant lets you schedule assorted FileMaker Server tasks. You can automate regular backups, schedule scripts to run directly on the server, or tell FileMaker Server to check the health of your database periodically. You can use the Send Message to tell FileMaker to announce server down time in advance.

2. **Make sure "Back up Databases" is selected, and then click Next.**

The Schedule Assistant asks what kind of schedule you want. You can choose one of the canned schedule types listed earlier in this chapter (Hourly, Daily, or Weekly) to use as a starting point, or you can start with a clean slate by choosing Custom.

3. **Turn on Custom, and then click Next.**

The assistant now asks which databases you want to back up. You can choose to back up all your databases, just those in a particular folder, or a single selected database.

Note: If you need to back up a specific collection of databases, you can put them into a folder in your database folder on the server computer. If that isn't an option (maybe they're already in different folders for other schedules), then you need to make a schedule for each one.

---

4. **Leave All Databases turned on, and then click Next.**

The screen changes to show still more options (Figure 18-17).

Figure 18-17:
This step in the Schedule Assistant lets you choose where to store the backup, how many copies FileMaker Server should keep, and whether or not the backup file should be verified. By "verified," FileMaker means it checks the structure of the database file to be sure it has a clean bill of health. This process can detect a file problem early, but it takes a little processing time on your server, so you might choose to perform this step only once per day, rather than with every backup.

5. **In the Backup Folder, enter the full path to the folder on your server where you want the backup stored.**

In this hypothetical example, you might have your offsite backup system configured to copy every file from a certain folder every Friday at midnight, so you would send the backup to that folder.

6. In the "Maximum number of backups to keep" box, enter *1*.

You only want one to keep one weekly copy of the database in this example, since the files will be copied by your offsite backup system.

7. Click Next.

The assistant now asks you when the backup should run. This screen has a lot of options (Figure 18-18).

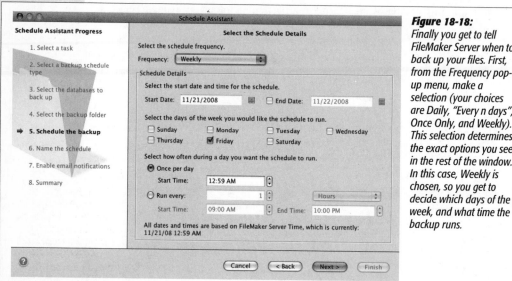

Figure 18-18:
Finally you get to tell FileMaker Server when to back up your files. First, from the Frequency pop-up menu, make a selection (your choices are Daily, "Every n days", Once Only, and Weekly). This selection determines the exact options you see in the rest of the window. In this case, Weekly is chosen, so you get to decide which days of the week, and what time the backup runs.

8. From the Frequency pop-up menu, choose Weekly.

The rest of the window changes to match Figure 18-18.

9. Turn off every checkbox under "Select the days of the week you would like the schedule to run"—except Friday.

You've now told the assistant you want this backup to run only on Friday.

10. Turn on "Once per day", and then, in the associated box, type *11:00 PM*.

This setting tells FileMaker Server to back up the file at 11:00 p.m. That way, the backup is finished in time for the offsite backup script at midnight. (For most databases, the backup takes just a few seconds, but this time can stretch if your database is very large or your server is very busy. You should test your backups to see how long they take, and leave a little extra time just in case.)

11. Click Next.

The assistant asks you to name your schedule. This step just helps you identify it among a potentially long list of schedules you've created.

12. **In the Schedule Name box, type *Friday Night Offsite*, and then click Finish.**

The Next button is grayed out at this point because you're at the last step, so Finish is the button for you. The assistant creates your new schedule, and then closes, leaving you back at the list of schedules.

In most cases, the built-in backup schedules are sufficient, but should the need arise, FileMaker's scheduling system is almost infinitely configurable.

Testing Your Server

You can test your FileMaker Server's various components at any time to be sure they're configured correctly and working. To do so, first go to the FileMaker Server Admin Console Start Page (page 720). On this page, under Troubleshooting, click the FileMaker Server 10 Technology Tests link. You can see the page in Figure 18-19.

From this page, each section tells you if the particular sharing technology is turned on and working. You can click the link in each section to go to a test page or database. The test pages use the appropriate technology to load data from a database, so if they display successfully, then you can be confident your server is ready to publish your content.

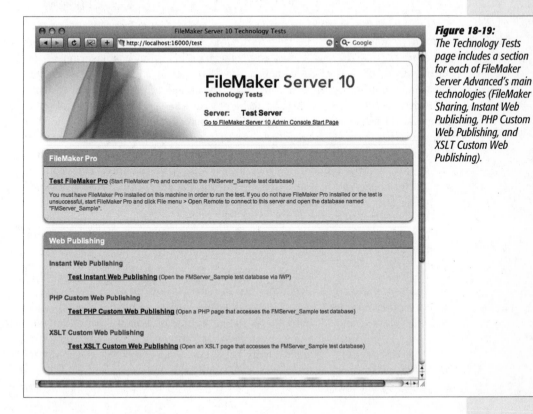

Figure 18-19:
The Technology Tests page includes a section for each of FileMaker Server Advanced's main technologies (FileMaker Sharing, Instant Web Publishing, PHP Custom Web Publishing, and XSLT Custom Web Publishing).

Server Hardware

While you're spending money, why not get a better *computer*, too? If you have lots of users or lots of data (or both), your database server needs all the power you can give it. After all, FileMaker Server performs finds, edits records, sorts, imports, exports, and otherwise constantly busies itself with the work of *every user*.

The most important thing you can do to make FileMaker Server faster is give it faster access to the data on the disk. At the very least, this increased speed means you should *never* store the files on a file server. Instead, they should always be on a hard drive in the host computer. If you still find things aren't as fast as you'd like them, your best upgrade is often a faster disk system—something called a RAID, or Redundant Array of Inexpensive Disks. You can ignore the "Redundant" part and the "Inexpensive" part, though. A RAID is an *array* of hard disks. By putting several disks together, you can get faster access to your data than you would with just one disk. As important, you can get *more reliable* access as well, since the same data can be stored in more than one place in case a disk drive fails, as outlined in the box on the next page.

In addition to a fast disk system, you should consider adding plenty of RAM to the host computer. The least important component is the CPU speed itself (but that's not to say it doesn't matter; don't expect a fast server with a 500 MHz processor).

If you find all this terribly confusing, be comforted by the fact that most major computer companies sell specially configured server computers. Let them know you're setting up a database server, and you can probably buy a fantastic host computer with RAID, lots of RAM, and a fast CPU—all in one box. For all but the most basic multiuser purposes, you absolutely should consider a dedicated computer designed by the manufacturer to be used as a server. Dell, Apple, and many others have specific server-class computers. It may *seem* like one of their desktop computers has the same specs as the servers for less money, but appearances can be deceiving. Server computers may have the same processors, amount of memory, and hard drive space, but they generally use upgraded versions of key components. Everything from the hard drive to the fan that keeps things cool is designed for much more intensive use than a normal desktop computer. Consider the cost of a good server computer part of your FileMaker installation, or you'll regret it down the road when you experience poor performance, poor reliability, or (worst of all) loss of data.

Finally, no matter how reliable your server computer is, if the power goes out, it will crash. And a crashed server can lead to database corruption and a lot of lost time. To protect against this, consider purchasing an *Uninterruptible Power Supply*, or UPS. You plug one of these battery backup devices into the wall, and then plug the computer into it. If the power goes out, the battery automatically kicks in to keep the server running. Higher-quality UPS devices can even signal the computer to safely shut down when the power is out and the battery runs low, eliminating the possibility of a crash.

RAID Overview

RAID is just a generic term for any assemblage of several disks that look, to the computer, like just one disk. But the devil is in the details. It turns out there are several different *kinds* of RAID out there, and each serves a different purpose.

If speed is all you care about, there's something called *striping*. With striping, the data's spread across all disks so that when FileMaker Server reads or writes, it can usually do it to every disk at once. In general, a four-disk array with striping can shuffle data four times faster than just one disk. The trouble with striping is that every doubling of performance also produces a halving of reliability. In other words, if you expect one drive to fail sometime in the next four years, then one of the drives in your array will fail in the next year, on average. Since the data is spread across the disks, when one disk fails, you can permanently lose data (sometimes all of it).

On the other end of the spectrum is *mirroring*. This model gives you *maximum reliability*, but with no speed benefit. In a mirrored array, every piece of data is written to every drive at the same time. If one drive fails, the system can simply switch to another drive without losing any data. But you often need more performance than a mirrored array can give.

Unless you're certain you know what you're doing, you should never use just striping. The idea of maximum performance can be appealing, but data integrity and reliability are paramount. Generally, the best bet is a combination of mirroring and striping. Ideally, you create a few mirrored sets of disks, and then connect these sets into a striped super-set. If you use RAID, you should look for a system that lets you set up this kind of *striping over mirroring* configuration for the maximum in reliability and performance. You get to decide how much reliability you want (by picking the number of disks in each mirrored set) and how much speed you want (by choosing the number of mirrored sets to create).

Another type of RAID (called RAID 5) gives you a performance boost and redundancy with fewer disks. It does this through magic only a computer scientist would appreciate. RAID 5 tends to be cheaper than the mirroring and striping systems because you can buy fewer hard drives. But RAID 5 gives you a performance boost only for reading data. Writing data to the drive is actually slower than a normal disk. You're better off spending a little more money to get a mirrored and striped system.

Applying Developer Utilities

FileMaker Pro takes you from your first simple database all the way into power user territory. It lets you create complex relational databases with ease, design virtually any layout imaginable, and add features of your own invention with buttons and scripts. With it, you can create any database you may need for a small business or organization. Once you have more than a handful of people using your database, you may eventually outgrow even FileMaker Pro's abilities, and need to buy another FileMaker product. In Chapter 18, for example, you can see how File-Maker Server lets more than five users work in a database at once—something FileMaker Pro simply can't handle. FileMaker offers another upgrade, called File-Maker Pro Advanced. This version doesn't make your database run better, or accept more people, or hold more data. Rather, with Advanced, you can be a more productive database *developer*.

For a couple hundred dollars more ($299 for Pro vs. $499 for Advanced), you get a whole raft of developer tools to make your life easier and your databases better. If you find yourself troubleshooting long, complex scripts, then Script Debugger may save your sanity and your valuable time. The analysis tools are indispensable if you're in a consultant role, working on databases that other people created. And most File-Maker developers have longed for an easy way to keep their more adventuresome users away from potentially destructive menu commands (including but not limited to Delete All Records). Finally, a new feature called Custom Menus gives them—and you—the godlike power to determine which commands are available to people who use a database. If you spend a good portion of your time building FileMaker databases, then FileMaker Pro Advanced is an extra $200 well spent.

Copying and Pasting Database Structure

Since a large percentage of a database designer's work is fairly repetitive, FileMaker Pro Advanced provides some tools that let you take shortcuts through the tedious process of creating tables, fields, and scripts. By copying work you've already done, you can spend less time defining fields or recreating complex scripts, and more time doing the creative work of designing a database. You can import tables and fields without copying data between tables in the same file and between different files.

FileMaker also provides Copy and Paste buttons in several major dialog boxes so you can reuse fields in the Manage Database window, scripts and script steps in Script Maker, and even entire tables or groups of table occurrences. (You need full access privileges in both the source file and the target file to import or copy and paste elements from file to file.)

Importing Tables and Fields

If you have a handful of tables in one file that would also be useful in another, then you can *import* the table and field information. Importing tables doesn't copy the data inside them. Rather, it copies the tables' design and structure, with all their fields, including their names, types, comments, calculations, and so on. Start by choosing File → Manage Database, and then clicking the Table tab. Click Import, and then locate the file that contains the table you want to copy.

Next, tell FileMaker which specific tables to import in the dialog box shown in Figure 19-1. When FileMaker Pro Advanced has finished importing the tables and fields, it displays a dialog box similar to the one you see when you import data. You see a summary of how many tables and fields were created during the import.

Figure 19-1:
You see a simple list of all tables in the source file from which you've chosen to import tables. Turn on the checkbox by all the tables you want to import. You don't get to specify which fields are imported—they all come in. So if you don't need a few, delete them when the import's finished.

Note: When FileMaker Pro Advanced builds your new tables and fields, it saves a record of its progress in a log file. If you see an error in the summary window, click the Open Log File button to see what went wrong. Things might go wrong if you have calculation fields that reference table occurrences that don't exist yet, for example. When this happens, FileMaker puts the calculation in comments so you can reconstitute it later once you've added table occurrences.

Copying and Pasting Tables

If you prefer, you can copy and paste tables in the Manage Database dialog box instead of using the Import button. In the Tables tab, just select a table, and then click the Copy button. If you want an exact copy in the same file (since your new table will contain common fields like ID, Creation Date, and so on), then just click Paste. Alternatively, you can dismiss the Manage Database window, go to a different file, bring up its Tables tab, and paste the table there. As usual, you can use the Shift key to select several items next to each other in the table list. Use the Ctrl (⌘) key to select tables that aren't right next to each other.

Warning: When you copy a table into another database, it may include calculation fields that FileMaker can't successfully copy. For example, a calculation may reference a table occurrence that doesn't exist in the new file. In such cases, FileMaker keeps the field, but puts the entire calculation in comments (like /* this */). Be sure to check all calculation fields after pasting.

Copying and Pasting Fields

If you have complex calculations that you want to reuse in another table within the same file, or in a different file, then, on the Manage Database dialog box's Fields tab, use the Copy and Paste buttons. Just like with tables, select one or more fields, and then click Copy. Then open the table where you want to create the new fields, and finally click Paste to do the deed.

When you copy *calculation* fields, your results may vary depending on whether you also copy the fields it references. It usually saves time to plan ahead and make sure the field references already exist in the target table before you copy and paste. But you can always paste the calculation fields and clean up the references later, especially if you intend to use different field names anyway. Here are some general rules:

- If fields matching the references in your copied calculation don't exist in the target table, then FileMaker pastes the calculation as a comment (*/*Amount * Quantity*/*), since it can't find matching fields in the new table. Simply edit the calculations with the new field references, and then click OK.

- To save yourself some editing work, *first* paste into the target table (or create) fields with names that match the ones in the calculation you're transferring. Then, when you paste the calculation, FileMaker resolves the field references automatically.

- If the field references are local (that is, they refer to other fields within the same table), then you can copy the fields referenced in the calculation *and* the calculation field at the same time. When you paste the set of fields, FileMaker resolves the field references automatically, and you have nothing to edit.

- If you're copying a calculation field that contains a fully qualified field reference (containing both a table name and a field name, like Expenses::Job ID), then the calculation again transfers just fine, assuming a table occurrence exists with the same name in the target file.

Copying Scripts and Script Steps

In the Manage Scripts dialog box, you can use the Import button to import whole scripts from other files, but if you have FileMaker Pro Advanced, you can avoid that cumbersome process. Simply open the file that contains the scripts you want to copy, and then, in the Manage Scripts dialog box, use the Copy and Paste buttons. Copy the scripts you want to reuse, then open the Manage Scripts dialog box in the *target* file, and finally click Paste. Check all pasted scripts to see if any field, layout, or other reference needs to be pointed to another element in its new location. Copying or importing scripts works best when you need the whole script, and all the elements referenced in your script are already in place, so that no script steps break on the way in.

You can also copy script steps individually or in chunks. In the Edit Script dialog box, select just the script steps you want, and then click Copy. Then you either create a new script or open the script that needs your copied steps. Highlight the script step just above where you want the next steps to land, and then click Paste. Your recycled steps appear in your script. Fix any broken references as needed.

You don't even have to move to a new script to find Copy and Paste useful. Sometimes it's faster to copy and paste a series of steps, and then edit them so they work slightly differently, than to type them from scratch. Sure, you can use the Duplicate button, but then you have to move each step down into place one by one. With Copy and Paste, you get to place the new steps right where you want them.

Script Debugger

When you write a script using FileMaker Pro, your testing and troubleshooting routine is pretty simple. You perform the script and wait to see what happens at the end. In a simple script, like one that prints a report, you can easily enough see what went wrong, and fix it: Your script just went to the wrong layout, perhaps. But when you're creating a complex script that sets variables and works with different sets of records that you can't verify before the next script step whizzes past, it's devilishly hard to figure out where your script veers off course. Even simple scripts can go wrong in puzzling ways that you can't detect by reading over your steps.

That's where Script Debugger comes in. When you run scripts with Script Debugger turned on, FileMaker performs scripts at human speed, so you can see exactly what's happening, each step of the way.

Note: To run Script Debugger, it's best to be logged into the file with a password that has script editing privileges (see page 647). But if you need to figure out how a script runs for lesser accounts, then you can log in as someone else, and then use the Authenticate/Deauthenticate button (see page 739).

To see the Script Debugger, choose Tools → Script Debugger. When you do, the Script Debugger window appears on the screen (Figure 19-2). Left to its own devices, the Script Debugger window doesn't do much. It consists of a couple of blocks of empty space, and several buttons you can't click.

But it shows its true colors when you run a script. As soon as you do, it swings in to action. It shows the name of the script you're running near the top, and the complete contents of that script just below. You can even see the value of any parameter that was passed to the script. But more important than all this, you can *control* the script as it runs. You can run just one line of the script at a time, dig into subscripts or back out to the calling script, skip over some steps completely, back up and run some steps over again, or stop the script in its tracks.

Figure 19-2:
The Script Debugger window's loaded with information about the current script. You can see the script's name at the top, and all its steps in the middle. At the bottom, you can see the script that called this script (if any). Since scripts can call scripts that call scripts, FileMaker lists the complete history here, showing which called this one, and below it, the one that called it. If a parameter was passed to any script, then it shows up in the bottom list as well.

Controlling Script Execution

Unlike most dialog boxes, Script Debugger stays on top of your work, giving you constant feedback about running scripts. As long as Script Debugger's window is open, when a script starts running, it immediately shows up in the Script Debugger, and is essentially paused. FileMaker is asking you for permission to perform the first step. You control the running script using the buttons at the top of the window. You can see them in Figure 19-3, and read about them here:

- Click **Step** to execute the current script step. (FileMaker marks the current step with a blue arrow along the left edge of the script steps.) FileMaker runs that one step, moves the arrow to the next one, and then stops, waiting for further instruction from you.

- **Step Into** works just like Step, with one caveat. If the current step happens to be a Perform Script script step, then Step Into goes into that script, and stops at its first line. This way you can step through the subscript line by line. The Step button, on the other hand, just executes the subscript in its entirety, and takes you to the next line in the calling script.

Figure 19-3:
The Script Debugger window includes a row of unlabeled buttons across the top. The buttons on the left control the running script. The buttons on the right give you quick access to other debugger features.

- When you click **Step Out**, FileMaker runs the current script to completion, takes you back to the script that called it, and then stops. If the script you're running was not called by another script, then Step Out just finishes the script normally. Use Step Out if you accidentally step into a script you don't need to see in full detail, or if you're finished investigating a subscript and want to get back to the calling script quickly.

- If you want to skip a portion of a script, or run some steps over again, select a script step, and then click **Set Next Step**. This button moves the little current step arrow to the selected step without actually running anything. For instance, if you just want to test what happens inside an If condition that you know won't be satisfied, then you can move the current step into the If and run its contents without the If step itself being run. You can also back up and run a section of code over again by moving the current step up in the list.

Warning: Any time you use the Set Next Step button, you're changing the normal flow of the script. The results you get when you use it may not match what would happen if you ran the script normally. For instance, if you back up and start part of a script over again, things may be different this time through because the script already did those parts. You may end up with a different found set or a different current record, for example. Or script variables may be different this time through. You may be bypassing If conditions that would otherwise apply. And you may be on a different layout from which the steps would normally run. Be careful, or you may end up sending the script in an inappropriate direction.

- If the script is stopped, waiting for you to click a button, then you can click **Run/ Pause** to start it running normally. It no longer stops at each step. Instead, it runs through every step in sequence. If the script is already running, then clicking this button stops the script, and lets you control its flow again. (To find out how to stop the script exactly where you want, read about *breakpoints* in the next section.)

- If you've decided you've seen enough and you just want to stop the script completely, click **Halt Script**. The Script Debugger window empties of its script-specific information and FileMaker returns to normal Browse mode behavior. The Halt Script button does not let the script finish running. Instead, it stops the script in its tracks, just like the Halt Script script step.

- You use the **Set/Clear Breakpoints** button to add or remove breakpoints in your script. You'll learn about these shortly.

- The **Edit Script** button is one of the Script Debugger's handiest buttons. If you're debugging a script that isn't quite working, and while it's running in the debugger you spot the problem, just click Edit Script. FileMaker opens the Edit Script window for the running script, and takes you straight to the step that's next in line (the one with the arrow pointing to it in the debugger window). You can easily make the change, and then run the script again to test it.

Note: When you click the Edit Script button, FileMaker opens the script for editing, but keeps it running in the Script Debugger. You're free to jump back to the Script Debugger and click any of the buttons to step the script forward further. So you can also use the Edit Script button to see more details about a script (like the exact calculation in a Set Field script step) while you are debugging. However, if you actually save a change to the script, FileMaker tells you it needs to halt the running script before it can apply the change.

- The **Open/Close Data Viewer** button shows FileMaker Pro Advanced's Data Viewer window, which is explained on page 743.

- The **Authenticate/Deauthenticate** button lets you debug a script to which you would normally not have access (because of restrictions imposed by your privilege set). Sometimes a script you create behaves differently for your users (who don't have full access to the database) than it does for you. You can log into your database as one of these restricted people to test the script, but then you can't see the contents of the script in the debugger. If you click the Authenticate/Deauthenticate button (and enter your full access account name and password), though, then FileMaker lets you see and debug the script. Importantly, the script *runs* as though you're still the restricted person. You can see exactly how it behaves for your users, and hunt down the problem.

By using the buttons in the Script Debugger, you can watch your script in action, performing each step one by one, and examining the results as it goes. This approach makes it infinitely easier to see where a script goes wrong as you try out various iterations, squashing bugs along the way.

Note: Each of the buttons in the Script Debugger window has a menu command counterpart in the Tools → Debugging Controls menu. If you prefer the menus, or want to learn the keyboard shortcuts, then this menu is your friend.

Breakpoints

In some situations, the click-the-step-button-for-each-step approach can become unacceptably tedious. For example, you may have a long script, and you know the problem part is near the end. To make your life simpler, the Script Debugger includes *breakpoints*. You set a breakpoint on any line you want, and then click the Run/Pause button. FileMaker immediately begins cruising through the script steps, running them at full speed. When it reaches the step with the breakpoint, it immediately stops so you can begin stepping manually.

You can set a breakpoint three different ways:

- In the Script Debugger window, select the script step, and then click the Set/Clear Breakpoint button.

- In the Script Debugger window, click next to the script step in the gray stripe along the left edge of the script steps.

- In FileMaker Advanced, the same gray stripe appears in the Edit Script window. You can click next to any step when editing a script to set a breakpoint. Using this method, you can set a breakpoint in a deeply nested subscript, before you debug the main script. Then, if you click Run/Pause, FileMaker runs through the script and its subscripts until it hits your breakpoint, saving you a lot of clicking.

No matter how you get it there, the breakpoint is indicated by a red arrow to the left of the script step. To remove an existing breakpoint, just click it again (or select the line in the Script Debugger, and then click the Set/Clear Breakpoint button again). The arrow disappears.

When you click the Run/Pause button, FileMaker runs to the *next* breakpoint it encounters (even if it's in one of the subscripts this script calls). If you find you've hit a breakpoint before the one you want, just click Run/Pause again to jump to the next one. In fact, adding breakpoints at key places in a complex script (and leaving them there) can make it easy to quickly debug the script later, as you Run/Pause your way through the major chunks, stopping to step through only the parts that currently interest you.

Examining Errors

In Chapter 15 you learned about checking for errors using the *Get (LastError)* function. The Script Debugger helps you tackle this job as well. As you step through your script line by line, the debugger constantly updates the Last Error display just below the list of script steps (Figure 19-4). Normally this function shows 0 (zero) because most script steps don't produce an error. But if you *do* encounter an error, the error number appears right after the step runs, making it a breeze to see what error number a certain situation produced so you can handle it in your code.

POWER USERS' CLINIC

Conditional Breakpoints

Some programs have a feature called *conditional breakpoints* that let you tell the debugger to stop on a certain line only when some condition is met. For example, you may want to stop only if the $count variable is bigger than 100, or if the found count is more than 1000.

FileMaker doesn't have built-in conditional breakpoints, but you can easily set up a similar scheme. Just add an If script step to your script that checks a meaningful condition. Then put a comment inside the If block and set a break point on the comment. FileMaker goes into the only If block when the condition is met; otherwise it skips right past it and the breakpoint it contains.

For example, you might add this to a long loop in your script, so you can break only after the loop has run 100 times:

```
If [ $count > 100 ]
  # break here
End If
```

If you set a breakpoint on the line with the "break here" comment, then you get the desired effect.

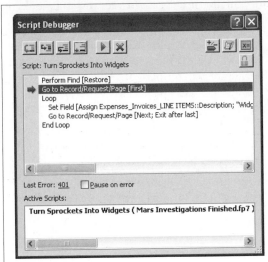

Figure 19-4:
As you step through your script, the debugger constantly updates the last error number. You can instantly see when an error happened, and what the error code is. Best of all, this error number shows up when error capture is turned on (so you can spot an otherwise silent error) and when it's turned off (so you can see the code behind the error message). So if you're looking for error numbers, watch this space. If error capture is turned on, it's the only place you can view the error condition.

You can even click right on the error number, which happens to look like a Web link, and FileMaker shows you the online help page that explains each error code.

Pause on Error

If you know your script is producing an error *somewhere* (perhaps because an error message pops up when you run it), but you don't know where it's coming from, then the "Pause on error" checkbox is your friend. Just turn this option on, and then click Run/Pause. FileMaker runs the script full speed until any step produces an error.

When that happens, it stops so you can examine your place in the script, see the error number, and use the debugger controls to manipulate execution. You can also click the Edit Script button to jump to the trouble spot in the Edit Script window.

This feature also works whether or not error capture is turned on, so it may spot errors you're already handling. If that happens, just click Run/Pause again to run to the next error. Keep going as necessary until you find the error you're looking for.

Active Scripts

The bottom part of the window shows you detail about the *active* script—in other words, the script that's running right now. It shows the name of the script, the file it lives in, and the value, if any, of the script parameter that was sent to it.

But why's this box so big if it just shows a few facts about one script? Because it can actually show a few bits about *lots* of scripts. Every time a script performs another script, it moves down in the list to make room for the new script's information. FileMaker puts the topmost—and current—script in boldface at the top of the list. Below it, you see the script *that* came before. If that script was itself run by another script, the first script's then third in the list. You can see how this looks in Figure 19-5.

Click a script in the list to switch the debugger's view to the new script. The Current Position arrow changes color (white with blue outline) to indicate you're viewing a script that doesn't include the current script step.

Figure 19-5:
When scripts call other scripts, FileMaker stacks the script names up in the Active Scripts list. On top—and in bold lettering—you see the name of the script you're currently looking at. Directly below each script is the name of the script that called it. If you have scripts calling scripts with more than three levels, then you have to scroll the list to see the oldest ones.

Working with the Debugger Window

The debugger window doesn't work like FileMaker's other dialog boxes. When it's open on the screen, you can still interact with your database window. Even when a script is running (but paused waiting for you to step), you can move database windows around, switch layouts, and even type data into records. That way, you can poke around in your database while the script runs to see how things are progressing. It also lets you totally mess up your script by putting it in a state it would normally never reach, like an inappropriate layout, or a mussed-up global field. And although you can edit existing records, you can't create new records, delete records, or create new windows.

Since all this window manipulation is possible, you're free to arrange the debugger and database windows on the screen so you can see as much as possible while your script runs. You can also resize the debugger window at any time to make more space.

Note: Before you get too hung up trying to fit your layouts on the screen so you can see field values and the like, read about the Data Viewer in the next section. It's often a better choice if you're trying to watch the data or variables change.

As long as the Script Debugger window is showing, FileMaker debugs any script that runs (even if it runs from clicking a button, or automatically when a file opens or closes). If you choose Tools → Script Debugger, then the debugger window disappears, and script execution goes back to normal. You can also simply close the debugger window to turn it off.

The Data Viewer

The *Data Viewer* grants you under-the-hood access to field data, variables, and calculations. It's usually the easiest way to watch things change as your script runs in the debugger. To show the Data Viewer, just choose Tools → Data Viewer, and it appears on your screen. You can also, in the Script Debugger window, click the Open/Close Data Viewer button. No matter how you get to it, though, it looks just like Figure 19-6.

Figure 19-6:
The Data Viewer has two tabs, Current and Watch. Current shows information related to the script that's currently running in the debugger. Under Watch, you can tell FileMaker exactly what you want to see.

The Current Tab

If you open the Data Viewer (Tools → Data Viewer) and switch to the Current tab, FileMaker strives to show you the most pertinent information about the script you're debugging. When a script starts to run in the debugger, the Data Viewer lists every field that the script uses in any way. For instance, if you use the Set Field script step to modify a field anywhere in the script, that field appears in the list in the Current tab. Likewise, if you use a field in an If condition, that field shows up, too. In addition to the name of each important field, the Data Viewer shows its current value (in the Value column) and its data type.

As you step through the script, the Data Viewer updates the value column appropriately, so it always reflects the current field value. It also helps to draw your attention to fields you should be watching, as Figure 19-7 attests.

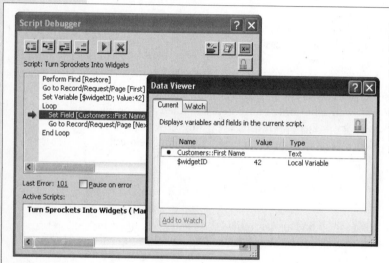

Figure 19-7:
As you step through your script in the Script Debugger, the Data Viewer keeps its list of fields up to date. Whenever you step to a new script, a little black dot appears next to any fields referenced in the current script step. You can take note of their values before moving on.

The Current tab also shows information about script variables. Instead of showing every variable the script uses as soon as the script starts, the window shows a new line for each new variable as it's created. For example, the first time you use the Set Variable script step to set a $customer Id variable, $customer Id appears in the Data Viewer, along with its type and value.

The Current tab almost always shows you just what you need to see while you debug. It can be a huge timesaver, pointing out everything your script is using and what it's doing with data, so you don't have to run calculations in your head or scramble around different layouts. Open it early and often.

The Watch Tab

The second tab in the Data Viewer, called Watch, shows the same kind of information as the Current tab, but you get to configure it yourself. Instead of magically showing the fields and variables your script is using, it shows the fields and variables you tell it to show. And it can show the result of arbitrary calculation expressions as well. You can see a sample Watch list in Figure 19-8.

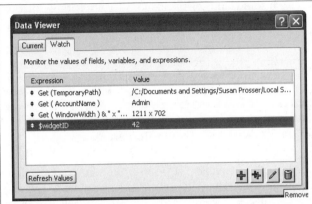

Figure 19-8:
The Data Viewer's Watch tab shows what you want to watch. You load it up with various calculation expressions, and it keeps tabs on their results for you. If you want to see a field value, then just put the field all by itself in the expression. Variables work the same way. But unlike the Current tab, you can even put complex calculations here, and watch them as things change. In this window, the second line shows the height and width of the current database window. If you resize a window, click Refresh, and the new size appears instantly.

To add an item to the Watch list, click the Add button. When you do, FileMaker shows you the Edit Expression dialog box (Figure 19-9). This window is almost an exact copy of the Specify Calculation dialog box, except it has an extra text box at the bottom labeled Result, and it has two new buttons: Evaluate and Monitor.

Figure 19-9:
The Data Viewer's Edit Expression window should look familiar—it's almost an exact replica of the Specify Calculation window. But this version can run the calculation in place and show you the result (just click Evaluate Now).

Differences aside, you can do anything here that you can do in the ordinary Specify Calculations dialog box. In the Expression box, just enter any formula you want. When you click Evaluate, FileMaker performs the calculation and shows the result in the Result box at the bottom of the window. You can use this handy feature to test a calculation and correct it without jumping in and out of the dialog box.

When you're satisfied with the formula, click Monitor. FileMaker adds the expression to the Watch list, with its value beside it. FileMaker attempts to keep the values up to date, but it can't refresh some kinds of calculations (typically those that use Get functions). If necessary, you can click Refresh Values to automatically recalculate each Watch expression.

Note: You don't *have* to click Monitor in the Edit Expression window. It's sometimes handy to use this window when you're trying to write a calculation, even if you don't need to keep an eye on the results. Just click the Add button and fiddle with the formula until you have it right (clicking Evaluate Now whenever you need to see how it's doing). When you're done, copy the formula (Edit → Copy), and then click Cancel. You can now paste the tested-and-working formula into a field calculation or a script step.

Data Viewer isn't attached to any particular file, so its Watch list contents don't change when you open and close files. The viewer can even be open while you have no databases open. Since all files and scripts share the same Watch list, it can quickly get long and hard to monitor. Select items you aren't using, and then click the Trash can icon to delete them.

Finally, if you need to see how certain calculations behave for people who don't have full access, log in as the person in question. In the Data Viewer, click the Authenticate icon to unlock its powers. You can now monitor values and edit expressions even though you don't have full access.

Disable Script Steps

The Set Next Step button in the Script Debugger lets you manually skip script steps while debugging, but it's not much help unless *you* remember to click it at the right time. Sometimes you have a script step (or several) that you always want File-Maker to skip. You could just delete them, but maybe you're not quite ready to. Perhaps it's code that isn't working yet, and you intend to come back later to fix it. Or perhaps you're moving the code somewhere else, and until you're sure you've got it moved and working, you don't want to delete the original. Whatever the reason, you may want to temporarily disable a group of steps.

To disable a script step (see Figure 19-10), in Script Maker, open the script, and then highlight the step you want to disable. In the Edit Script dialog box, click the Disable button. FileMaker puts two slashes in front of disabled script steps so you can identify them. To enable a step again, first select it. The Disable button changes to say Enable; click it, and the step is back in business. As always, you can select *multiple* script steps at once, and disable or enable them all in one shot.

Disabling script steps is useful for debugging, but it can have long-term use, too. Any step you disable in FileMaker Pro Advanced gets skipped whenever someone runs it—even in FileMaker Pro. So, say your company has a semi-regular promotion that creates discounts for a limited period.

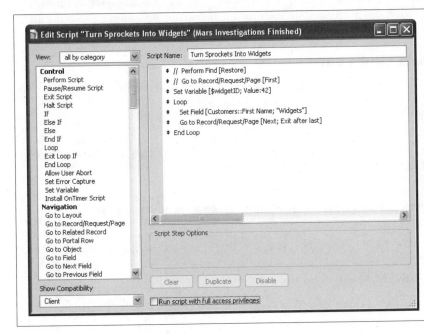

Figure 19-10:
Two steps (the Perform Find and "Go to Record/Request/Page" steps) in this script have been disabled, as you can see by the double slashes in front of the names. When a disabled script step is highlighted, the Disable button reads "Enable". FileMaker skips disabled steps when the script runs.

You don't have to write two different scripts, one with the discount and one without, and then worry about some kind of test to make them available on a button or in the script menu at the proper times. Write one script, making sure the discount creation steps are separate from the main process. Then you can enable the pertinent steps when the promotion starts and disable them when it's over, with very little fuss.

The Database Design Report

Sometimes you inherit a large database from somebody else, and you simply don't see how it comes together. (OK, be honest. Sometimes *you* create a large database and still don't understand how it's put together.) While FileMaker's point-and-click interface makes it easy to build databases, teasing things out later is a different story. You can look at a script, field, layout, table occurrence, or even an entire table in FileMaker Pro, and have no idea whether the database actually uses or needs it.

If you've shelled out for FileMaker Pro Advanced, however, you've got help. Its built-in internal analysis tool, the Database Design Report (affectionately called DDR), gives you an overview of your database, where you can easily see how database items are connected and other details, all in one place. You run the report, tell it what kinds of things you're interested in, and FileMaker presents the information in a series of Web pages.

Unlike the reports discussed in Chapter 6, the DDR is a report about the structure of your database, not about the data inside. It tells you what tables and fields you have, which fields are used on each layout, and so on, but nothing about the information in your records and fields.

Generating the DDR

The Database Design Report window lets you tell FileMaker exactly what you want it to report on. You get to pick which files and table occurrences to include, what kinds of things you want to report on, and what format you want the report to use. You also get to decide whether you want to open the report right away, or just save it for later use. To get started, choose Tools → Database Design Report. Up pops the Database Design report dialog box (Figure 19-11).

Figure 19-11:
The Database Design Report dialog box lets you tell FileMaker exactly what to include in the report. First, pick from among the open files. When you select one, all its tables appear to the right. Below these, you can decide what other elements you want to report on. Finally, you can opt for an HTML or XML report, and ask FileMaker to open it for you when it's done.

The Available Files list in this window shows every open file. To include a file in the report, turn on the checkbox by its name. FileMaker assumes you want every file at first, so you may have to do more turning off than on.

Note: If you have a lot of files to turn off, you can Shift-click to select groups. Then if you turn off one file's checkbox, every selected file turns off as well. This same approach applies to tables in the list on the right.

The report includes field information for tables in each file. Select a file in the list to see all its tables in the "Include fields from tables in selected file" list. Again, you can use the checkboxes in this list to tell FileMaker which tables you want included in the report.

The "Include in Report" section has a checkbox for each kind of database element the DDR can report on. Again, FileMaker assumes you want everything, but you're free to limit the report to just certain information. The less you report on, the faster the report runs, and the smaller the final files.

Normally, FileMaker saves the report in HTML format so you can read and navigate it in any Web browser, but it also offers a more structured XML format. XML files aren't easy for *humans* to read, but with the help of other software, you can process the XML, and integrate information about your database into other systems. Furthermore, some companies make DDR analysis tools that process the XML version of your DDR and provide extra tools for browsing, finding, and reporting on the information it contains.

When you're done making decisions, click Create. FileMaker asks you where to save the report. The DDR is made up of several files, so you probably want to make a new folder to hold the report. The more complex your files, the longer it takes to create the DDR. In a file with dozens of tables, each of which may have dozens or even hundreds of fields, this could take a minute or more. FileMaker displays a progress bar for you, so you can gauge how long the process will take.

Note: A DDR is a snapshot of the database at the moment you create it. So it's good to make periodic DDRs as your database evolves. You can create a record of when you added or changed various parts of the database. A DDR can also help with troubleshooting broken elements.

Using the DDR

If you turned on "Automatically open report when done" when you created the DDR, then FileMaker launches your browser and shows you the DDR Report Overview (Figure 19-12) as soon as the progress bar disappears.

This window shows the main report file, and it has URL links that bring up the detail pages. To view the DDR later, go to where you saved it, and open the file called Summary, or Summary.html. (You also see a folder named for each file you selected when you created the DDR.)

Figure 19-12:
Report Overview is the first thing you see when you open a DDR. It's a table, with one row for every file you included in the report, and a column for each option you checked when you created the DDR. Each "cell" contains a link leading to more information. Each DDR lists the time and date of its creation, so you can tell if the report matches the current state of your database.

On the overview page, the DDR tells you which elements you chose when you created the DDR. If you click a file name, then you see the file detail page (Figure 19-13), with lots of information about that file. The links in each column go to the same file detail page, but each link scrolls you to the relevant section. On large databases, with lots of fields, this option can save you a lot of time scrolling through the page, looking for what you want. For instance, if you click the number in the Relationships column, you see the Relationships section of the file detail page.

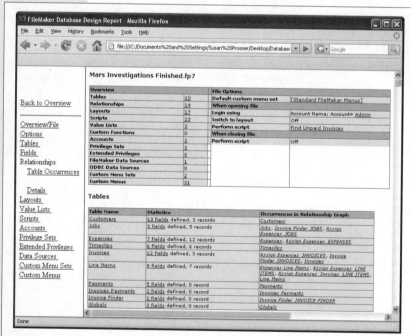

Figure 19-13:
On the Report Overview page, when you click the File Name link, you see this page. The top link on the left leads back to the Overview page. All the others just scroll the page to various important parts. The report itself is also loaded with links. You can click any link to go to more details about that item.

Use the DDR to help you figure out what parts of your database can safely be edited or deleted. Since you can so easily create tables, fields, and layouts in FileMaker, you may well end up with extras that you don't need when your database reaches completion. You can make your database easier to understand, and more efficient, by deleting these extra elements. But even if a database is the last word in efficiency, running a DDR is one of the best ways to trace the designer's thinking process.

To see if—and how—a particular element is used, look at its detail. Suppose you have a bunch of fields you'd like to delete from your database, and you want to find out whether it's safe to do so. First, click the Tables link; fields are part of tables. You see a list of tables, with information about how many fields each table contains, along with a list of occurrences of each table in the Relationship Graph (Figure 19-12). Click the link for a table's fields, and you see a list of all the fields in that table.

Details appear in the Field Name, Type, and Options columns for every field. Comments, if there are any, show up in the Comments column. Any layouts or scripts that use the field are listed in the Layout and Script columns, respectively. You see the information in the Relationship column only if it's a key field. Fields used in layouts, relationships, and scripts are called *dependencies* of those elements.

POWER USERS' CLINIC

Getting the Most from the DDR

At first glance, you may not appreciate the true value of the DDR. It appears to tell you the same things you can find out in other FileMaker windows, like Manage Database, Script Maker, and so on. But once you run your first DDR, you understand it has powers those flimsy boxes never dreamed of.

For example, the DDR information for a script helps you determine how the script functions in and interacts with the rest of the database. In a neat chart, you can see every field, layout, table, table occurrence, and custom function the script uses. More importantly, you can see every script or

layout button that runs this script. That kind of information would be very hard to nail down without the DDR. You'd basically have to go to each layout in your database, click anything that might be a button, and see if the script you're interested in is attached to it.

If you've created custom menus, you'd have to check them individually, too. The DDR gathers up all that information for you—not just for scripts but for tables, layouts, value lists, and other kinds of database elements as well.

Note: Even if you don't use a "Go to Field" script step for a specific field, a field may be listed in the scripts column. "Go to Related Record", or any other step that uses a relationship, also requires the use of that relationship's key field, so it also has that field as a dependency.

Finding Broken Elements with the DDR

Suppose you've deleted a field, unaware that it's used in a script. Your script could be run numerous times, not *quite* working, without your knowledge. The DDR is a great way to check for errors like this. Take, for example, the Find Unbilled Activity script you wrote back in Chapter 15. It searched in the Expenses::Job ID field for all unbilled expenses, but you've deleted the Job ID field.

If you examine that script in Script Maker, then you can see the words "<Field Missing>" right in the script.

```
Set Field [Expenses::<Field Missing>; "==" & Get (ScriptParameter)]
```

To spot every error like this, though, you have to open every script and read through it. FileMaker has no facility to let you search through your scripts.

But you *can* search the DDR page in your Web browser. (Pressing Ctrl+F or ⌘-F does the trick in most browsers.) In the Find field, type the text you're looking for, and then click Next (or whatever button your browser uses) to start the search. You see the first instance of your search criteria highlighted. Click the button again to find other instances.

The whole list of errors you might search for appears below. If you have any inkling what kind of error you're looking for, start with that one:

- **<Missing Field>**. Referenced field is missing.
- **<Missing Table Occurrence>**. Referenced table occurrence set is missing.
- **<Missing Base Table>**. Referenced base table is missing.
- **<Missing File Reference>**. Referenced file reference is missing.
- **<Missing Layout>**. Referenced layout is missing.
- **<Missing Valuelist>**. Referenced value list is missing.
- **<Missing Custom Function>**. Referenced custom function is missing.
- **<Missing Script>**. Referenced script is missing.
- **<Missing Account>**. Referenced account is missing.
- **<Missing Privilege Set>**. Referenced privilege set is missing.
- **<Missing Extended Privilege>**. Referenced extended privilege is missing.
- **<Missing Custom Menu>**. Referenced custom menu is missing.
- **<Missing Custom Menu Set>**. Referenced custom menu set is missing.

Once you find a broken element, return to your database, and fix it manually. The DDR doesn't update itself to show your fix until you run another one. And since you can't mark the electronic version of your DDR, a good way to keep track of your work is to print it out, and then mark off each item as you fix it. Then, when all the broken elements are fixed (or you've deleted all the unused stuff), run another DDR. This time it should be clean, but if it's not, you've got the tools to fix it.

Tooltips

Training people, either when you first launch a new database, or when new employees come into your workforce, is a big part of making your database successful. You can have beautiful layouts, bulletproof privilege sets, and complex,

Prevention is Worth a Pound of Cure

Why use the DDR to fix your mistakes when you can prevent them in the first place? Here's a technique you can use next time you want to delete a field, script, layout, or any other important element. If you're not completely certain you don't need the element, you can use the DDR to check for you.

First, in FileMaker, *rename* every element you plan to delete. Put something noticeable and consistent in each name. For example, you might put "TO_BE_DELETED" before each element's name.

Once you've renamed every doomed element, run a fresh DDR. Choose the HTML type. When the report is finished, search it for the code words you put in each name ("TO_BE_DELETED," in this example). FileMaker should find each element you've marked for deletion. But it also finds this element in the list of dependencies if it's still in use. For example, a field you're pondering deleting might show up in a script. Unless that script is also marked for deletion, you have a situation you need to investigate further. Once you're sure the things you're deleting are not used by anything else, you can delete them with confidence.

well-thought-out scripts, but if folks don't know how and when to use them, then they miss out on the benefits. To spare you the wrath of confused (or worse, frustrated) people, FileMaker Pro Advanced has a feature called *tooltips*. Like the onscreen labels that pop up in Windows and many other programs, tooltips can help guide people through the features you've created for them, and maybe even cut down on training time.

You can attach tooltips to any object, or group of objects, that you can select on a layout: fields, text, or graphics. Although you need FileMaker Pro Advanced to *create* tooltips, they work in any version of FileMaker, and even in the Web browser when you use Instant Web Publishing.

To create a tooltip, go to Layout mode, and then choose the object you want decorate. Then choose Format → Set Tooltip. Enter the text for your tooltip, and then click OK. Now people see the tooltip when the mouse hovers over the object in Browse mode. Just like tooltips in other applications, the tooltip doesn't appear immediately, so as not to inconvenience more advanced users. You can see a tooltip in action in Figure 19-14.

The Specify Tooltip dialog box has a Specify button. Click this button, and you get all the power of calculations. The result of the calculation becomes the text of the tooltip. (If the calculation has an empty result, then FileMaker doesn't show the tooltip, so you can use the If function to make the tooltip show up only when it's relevant.)

Custom Menus

FileMaker's menus are all about power. Through them, you can control—and limit—people's access to the whole feature set. As the developer, you need all those commands to do your design and development of your database, but plenty of commands give too much power to people, particularly folks who don't have much computer experience or who aren't shy about experimenting with commands, even if they aren't sure what might happen at the other end of a dialog box.

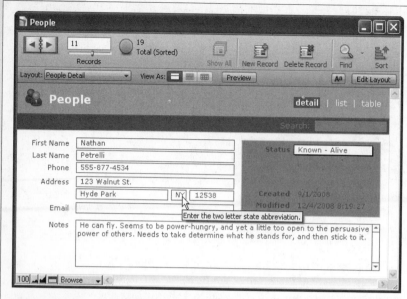

Figure 19-14:
Top: With a tooltip in place, someone needs only to point at the State field and wait a moment to get a little help. The tooltip shows just below the mouse arrow.

Bottom: In Layout mode, you can choose View → Show → Tooltips to see which elements have a tooltip assigned. In this example, the State field, in the bottom-right corner, has a little note icon, indicating an assigned tooltip.

Luckily, with FileMaker Pro Advanced, you can completely customize the menus people see. You can remove the Delete All Records and the Replace Field Contents commands for everyone, or you can remove them only from certain people's privilege sets. If you're the type of developer who likes to take charge of the user interface, custom menus are your dream come true.

Here are just a few of the things you can do:

- Remove potentially destructive items from menus: Delete All Records, for example.

- Edit menu commands: Change Modify Last Find to read Repeat Last Find, perhaps.

- Add, edit, or remove keyboard shortcuts: If you can't remember that Ctrl+S (⌘-S) does *not* mean Save in FileMaker, then you can at least prevent that pesky Sort dialog box from popping up every time.

- Remove entire menus, like the Window menu, which can be confusing for folks new to FileMaker Pro.

- Run a script from a new or edited menu item: Substitute a custom Delete Record script (complete with a custom warning) for FileMaker's normal Delete Record command.

- Change menus when a user changes layout: Create a special menu that runs commands or scripts that pertain to invoices and shows up only on the Invoice layout.

- Make one set of menus for Mac and another for Windows.

- Make menu sets that match privilege sets: Give admin-level people a special menu showing the scripts only they can run.

You can create and edit custom menus only in FileMaker Pro Advanced, but anyone can use them. These menus don't transfer to files you publish on the Web, though (Chapter 17). When you create custom menus for a database, you may want to provide a User Guide or similar documentation explaining what your custom commands do, since people can't look up the commands you add in FileMaker's online help.

You can use custom menus to supplement, and even go beyond, privilege set features. For example, if you want to limit data entry people to using the copy and paste buttons that run your scripts, then remove the Edit menu for people with that privilege set. They can't use keyboard shortcuts to cut, copy, or paste. Removing the View menu prevents the Mode pop-up menu, toolbar, and all related keyboard shortcuts from working. (But you need to do some work providing replacement commands in your buttons and menus.)

Note: As powerful as custom menus are, they're no substitute for good security practices, as discussed in Chapter 16. For example, just because you don't see a Delete command right in front of your face doesn't mean you can't delete records. (Try creating a new database, and adding an occurrence of the table into *that database*. If your privilege set allows deletion, then you can use the menus in the new database to empty out the table.) If you need to prevent someone from doing something, *you must restrict it by privilege set.*

Editing a Menu

All new files you create use FileMaker's standard menu set unless you tell them to use a custom set. Just as each new file contains three default privilege sets, you get one set of custom menus that you can edit to suit your needs. And as with privilege sets, some items are in brackets and cannot be edited or duplicated, but you're free to create new menus with the same name, and customize them.

In this exercise in customizing menus, you want to remove menu items that may confuse people. When people are just learning FileMaker, simplified menus are less intimidating than masses of unfamiliar commands. You can also help protect your database from damage by someone unwittingly choosing the wrong command. You start the process by editing the View menu so that only a few items show up:

1. **In FileMaker Pro Advanced, choose File → Manage → Custom Menus.**

    The Manage Custom Menus dialog box appears (Figure 19-15).

Figure 19-15:
You can reorder the items in the Custom Menu list with the "View by" pop-up menu. You can also click each of the four column heads to sort the list. Probably this window's most important item is the small pop-up menu at the bottom. You can do all the editing of custom menus you like, but unless you remember to switch to your custom set, you don't see any change in your file.

2. **In the Custom Menu list, click "View copy", and then click Edit.**

    Or you can double-click an item to edit it. The Edit Custom Menu window appears (Figure 19-16). Here, you tell the custom menu what it should look like, and how it should behave.

3. **Click the checkbox beside the Override Title field, and then, in the field, type *Switch*.**

    The Override Title option changes what someone sees in his menu bar. You changed it to Switch since the word "View" is too vague for beginners. Plus, you don't want them getting confused if they pick up FileMaker's manual (or this book) for help. The changed menu name should clue people in that they need to look at your custom documentation for help.

    The menu's name *in this dialog box* remains View Copy; that's how you know it originated from the normal View menu, not from scratch.

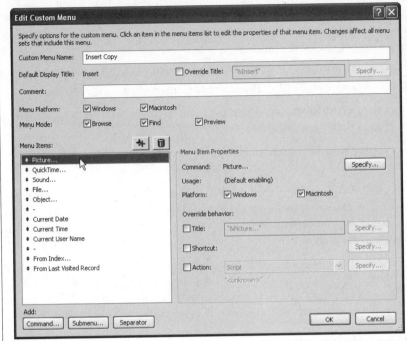

Figure 19-16:
This dialog box has many splendors. You can specify that a menu appears only when someone's on a Mac, or only when she's in Find mode. You can add, change or remove keyboard shortcuts. You can even take the liberty of replacing a command's normal action with a script.

Warning: If you customize menus even in the slightest, consider turning off the built-in Help menu as well. It opens FileMaker's online help file, which can't answer people's questions about *your* custom menus. If you need documentation, then you can add your own Help menu that leads people to the custom-crafted help on your Web site, for instance.

---

4. **Select the first hyphen in the Menu Items list below "Go to Layout >", and then press Shift as you select the last item in the list. Click the Trash can icon. Then select Layout mode, and delete it.**

   All highlighted items disappear when you click the Trash can icon (those hyphens represent divider lines in menus). You should have only three mode menu items, a hyphen, and a "Go to Layout" menu (a total of five items) remaining in the list.

5. **Click the Browse mode menu item. As with View mode in step 2, turn on the override checkbox, and then change the title to *Browse.***

   This menu item title replaces the text that appears in the list. People see a command called *Browse*, not Browse mode. Notice the quotation marks around "Browse". If you forget (or refuse) to type the quotes, FileMaker obstinately puts them back in for you. This behavior is your indication that FileMaker considers that text a character string, and that's a further cue that the Specify button gives you access to the calculation dialog box.

---

6. Repeat the previous step for Find mode, Preview mode, and "Go to Layout>". Change Find mode's title to *Find*, change Preview mode's title to *Print Preview*, and change the title of "Go to Layout>" to *Show*. When you've made these changes, click OK.

Use terms that folks can easily comprehend. Most people already understand what Print Preview does, but Preview mode's meaning is a little murky.

7. From the Default menu set for this file's pop-up menu, choose "Custom Menu Set 1", and then click OK.

You've just told FileMaker to display the customized version of your View menu.

The View menu now says "Switch". When you click it, you see only four items. Notice that the Layout tool is grayed out, and Layout mode has disappeared from the Layout pop-up menu at the bottom of your screen. Also, the commands in the pop-up menu match the changes you made in the View custom menu.

By editing menus to suppress items that might confuse those who haven't had in-depth FileMaker training, you've made your database a friendlier place to work. But don't stop there: In the next section, you'll learn how to create menus that show lists of commands, like your scripts, that you *do* want people to see.

Creating a New Menu

Using the steps described in the previous tutorial, you can edit FileMaker's menus to your heart's content, renaming them, and deleting extraneous commands to make room for new ones. If you don't necessarily want to delete any existing menus or commands, or even if you do, you can always create *additional* menus from scratch.

1. In Manage Custom Menus, click Create. In the Create Custom Menu window that appears, choose "Start with an empty menu". Click OK.

If an existing menu is similar to what you need, you can use it as a template when you create new menus. But in this case, you don't need any existing menu commands because you'll attach your scripts to a new menu. When you click OK, the Edit Custom Menu window appears, just as in Figure 19-16. This time, though, you don't edit it; you'll build the menu from the ground up.

2. In the Custom Menu Name fields, type *Invoices*. Also type *Invoices* in the Override Title field.

Since you started with an empty menu, FileMaker assumes you want a custom name. If you don't type a name, then, in your menu bar, the word "Untitled" appears.

3. Turn off the Menu Mode options for Find and Preview modes.

You don't want your scripts run from either Find or Preview modes, so by telling the menu not to even *show up* in those modes, you're adding another layer of security.

4. Click the Command button. In the Specify FileMaker Command dialog box, choose the "No command assigned" option above the list of available commands, and then click OK.

This action creates a new command, but doesn't use one of FileMaker's canned actions. You can use this method to build a new menu that picks and chooses from various default menus, but in this instance, you're going to run your scripts from the new Invoices menu.

5. In the Title field, type *Create invoice for unbilled expenses*, and then click Specify (to the right of the Action pop-up menu). From the list in the Specify Script Options window, choose the "Create Invoice for Job" script, and then click OK.

The Specify Script Options shows all the scripts you've created in this database file. To add more scripts to this menu, repeat the last two steps until you've created new commands for all the scripts you want. The arrows to the left of each item let you rearrange them. Click the Separator button to create a divider line in the menu.

6. Click Manage Custom Menus dialog box's Menu Sets tab. If necessary, select "Custom Menu Set 1" in the list, and then click Edit.

The Edit Menu Set window appears.

7. Scroll through the list of Available Custom Menus until you see Invoices. Select it, and then click the Move button. To the left of the Invoices menu, click the arrow, and move it up, so that it appears above [Scripts]. Click OK until you're back in your database.

The Invoices custom menu is now a part of the new custom menu set, and it appears between the Records and Scripts menus.

So far, you've simplified one of FileMaker's menus, and created a custom menu from scratch. Now you need to get rid of a menu that strikes fear even in the hearts of experienced FileMaker users: You're going to *completely* suppress the Window menu.

Removing a Menu

At first glance through the Manage Custom Menus dialog box, you may think you just click an item in the Custom Menu list, and then click Delete to remove it. But you run into problems if you do. First, if you highlight menus with brackets around their names, the Delete button is inactive. And if you select an item where the Delete button remains active (Help), and then delete it, you get a nasty surprise when you click OK and return to your file. You see the text "Missing Menu" inserted in the menu bar, and the Help menu stays right where it was. Despite these obstacles, you *can* remove an entire menu; you just have to dig a little deeper to do it.

Note: Troubleshoot a file for missing menu items by running a DDR (page 747), or by checking *Get (LastError)* after you load a menu set in a script.

The Window menu can cause problems for new people. For example, the Show command lists files they may not know are open. Hiding and showing windows is also perilous for new folks if they don't understand how FileMaker manages windows. Instead of bothering people with stuff they don't need to know, you can just suppress this menu entirely by removing it from the menu bar.

1. **In the Manage Custom Menus dialog box, click the Menu Sets tab. Select Custom Menu Set 1, and then click Edit.**

   The Edit Menu Set dialog box appears.

2. **In the Menu Set Name field, type *Data Entry*.**

   This descriptive name helps you remember the menu set's purpose. If you like, type additional information in the Comment box.

3. **In the "Menus in 'Data Entry'" list, click the [Window] menu. Click Clear, and then click OK until you're back in your database.**

   Usually brackets on a list item indicate you can't delete it. But you *can* delete it from the display list, as you've just done. The [Window] menu remains in the Available Custom Menus list at left. If you change your mind, you can move it back into the display list to restore it.

Back in your database, the Window menu is gone entirely from the menu bar. This menu configuration is ideal for your data entry people, but not so great for administrative people, who understand the Window menu and use it all the time. Read on to find out how to tailor *sets* of menus for people with different privilege levels.

Installing Custom Menu Sets

FileMaker Pro Advanced lets you create a set of custom menus (see Figure 19-17) and use it as the *default* for a file, meaning everyone who uses your database sees it, every time. But since the people using your database may have different levels of skill (and trust), you may want your custom menus to adapt accordingly. In fact, if you've read this book's chapters on layouts and privilege sets, you have all the tools you need to make the right menus appear to the right people at the right time. It's a simple matter of assigning menu sets to these existing features. You can conceal certain menus and commands from people who don't need them, but keep them available for everybody else. Or maybe you just want menu items to show up when they make sense for the active layout.

Once you've created menu sets using the steps outlined earlier in this chapter, you can install them in any of several ways:

- **As the default for a file.** That's what you did in the tutorial on page 755. Unless you tell FileMaker otherwise, everybody gets the same custom menus. This option works great for a runtime file, or any situation where everyone's at the same level.

Figure 19-17:
When you're editing menu sets, the field on the left lists the custom menus attached to the current set. Look in the list to see your edited View menu. The list on the right is a subset of the list on the left. Menus that aren't in the right-hand list are not displayed when this custom menu set is active. The Move, Clear, and Clear All buttons are similar to the ones in the Sort dialog box.

- **On individual layouts.** In this scenario, when someone switches layouts, either by menu command or through a script, the menu set changes to a layout-specific one of your choosing. Choose Layout → Layout Setup to attach a custom menu set to a layout.

- **By mode.** This option offers the ultimate in elegance. It lets you do things like create a set with only one menu and just a few items, and make it the *only* menu people see when they're in Find mode. Instead of a gaggle of buttons to perform and cancel finds, write the appropriate scripts, and display them in the one menu, short and sweet.

- **When a script is run.** By checking the privilege set in a script that runs when someone logs into your file, you can load a set of menus customized to that person's level of privilege. Use the *Get (PrivilegeSetName)* step to check privileges (page 656) and the Install Menu Set script step to specify which menu set installs. (If you have a re-login script, then you need to make sure the right menu set is installed each time people re-login.)

Warning: Since you're effectively removing features for people when you customize menus, thorough testing is a critical part of the process. Be sure to test menus with all affected layouts, privilege sets, and scripts, and across platforms. In FileMaker Pro Advanced, choose Tools → Custom Menus to switch among sets as you test them.

Developer Utilities

The Tools → Developer Utilities command looks insignificant and benign to the unsuspecting person, but behind it lurks a vast array of powerful features. You have developer utilities for the following techniques:

- Rename one file in a system of interconnected files, and have every file reference in the *other* files automatically update to the new name.

- Turn your database into a *kiosk* system. You can use this feature to make interactive programs that run on publicly accessible computers. In this setup, FileMaker hides the menu bars, the Windows taskbar or Macintosh Dock, and all other screen decorations that aren't part of your layouts.

- Create a *runtime solution*—a special version of your database that anyone can use, even if he doesn't have FileMaker Pro.

- Permanently remove full access to files so you can send your database to people you don't know, and be sure they can't tamper with your hard work, including your scripts, table and field definitions, and relationship graph.

- Create an error log to help you troubleshoot problems that occur when FileMaker generates runtimes.

In fact, you can (and often want to) do several of these things at once. Here's an example: You build a beautiful interactive product catalog, complete with pictures and an easy-to-use ordering screen. You then want to set up a kiosk computer at a trade show where attendees can use the database to see what you have, and place their orders. Using the developer utilities, you could do all this:

- Add "Kiosk" to the end of every file name, so you can keep this copy separate from the one you use in the office.

- Make the database run in Kiosk mode so people at the trade show can't exit FileMaker, switch to other programs, or otherwise cause mischief.

- Make the whole thing run by itself so you don't have to bother installing File-Maker on the computer you're renting just for this job.

- Lock out full access so if someone manages to steal a copy of your database while you're not looking, she can't see how it works or steal your product's beauty shots.

Using the Developer Utilities

The developer utilities' most confusing aspect is that you have to *close* your files before you work with them—just the opposite of every other command in FileMaker. So close the files you want to modify, and then choose File → Developer Utilities. You behold the Developer Utilities window (Figure 19-18).

In the Developer Utilities window, you first choose which files you want to work with. Click Add to put a file on the list. In the Open File dialog box, you can select several files at once using your Shift and Ctrl (⌘) keystrokes. Keep on adding until every file you want to change is in the list. If you accidentally add the wrong file, select it, and then click Remove.

You have to pick one file to be your *main* file. This file is the one that opens first if you create a runtime solution, for example. To set the main file, in the list, just double-click it. FileMaker shows a red square—it looks surprisingly like a script break-point—by the main file.

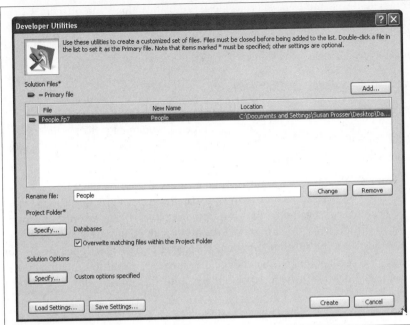

Figure 19-18:
The Developer Utilities window (File → Developer Utilities) lets you gather the files you want to change, and then tell FileMaker what changes to make. When you're done, click Create, and FileMaker builds new versions of your files (in a new location) with all the changes in place.

Renaming files

Of course, you can always rename a file in Windows Explorer or the Mac's Finder. But those interfaces let you change *only* the file name. Developer Utilities makes that look like child's play. When it changes a file name, it also looks inside the file, and updates any internal file references to match the file's new name. If you've ever tried to open two versions of a multiple file solution at the same time (to test some scripts that delete data and on a copy of the files, say), then you know FileMaker sometimes gets confused and keeps multiple copies open even after you try to close one set. You can eliminate the crossover problem by renaming one set in Developer Utilities. You can test your scripts without a problem, since the scripts in the copy files automatically inherit the correct new file names.

To rename a file or set of files, add them to the Solution File list (Figure 19-18). Select a file; in the "Rename file" box, type the new name; and then click Change. FileMaker shows the new name in the New Name column.

Next, you need to pick the *project folder*. FileMaker saves the finished files in this folder. Under "Project Folder", just click the Specify button, and then pick any folder you wish. If the folder already contains files with the same names as the ones you're about to create, then you get an error message—unless you turn on "Overwrite matching files within the Project Folder". When you click Create, FileMaker Pro Advanced makes copies of the files with their new names, leaving the originals untouched.

To complete the example above (your kiosk product catalog), you turn on "Create Runtime solution application(s)", "Remove admin access from files permanently", and "Enable Kiosk mode for non-admin accounts". You need to configure only the first option.

Create Runtime Solution application(s)

To create runtime solutions, add the files to the Solution Files list, and then select a project folder, just as you did above. Don't type a new name for the runtime in this window, though. Under Solution Options, click the Specify button. You see the Specify Solution Options dialog box, as shown in Figure 19-19.

When you tell FileMaker you want to build a runtime solution, it generates a special program you need to include with your databases. This program can do most of what FileMaker Pro can do, but it can't modify tables, fields, layouts, or scripts. You get to decide what this program is called—in the Runtime Name box, just type it. Along with the runtime program, FileMaker creates new copies of each of your files to go with it, and changes all the file name extensions to something other than .fp7. Tell FileMaker what extension to use in the Extension field.

Warning: Your computer's operating system uses file name extensions to figure out which program files belong to. The Developer Utilities let you assign any extension you want, but you should avoid common extensions like .doc, .jpg, .mp3, and so on. You know computers—they get confused easily.

The new files don't just have a new name; they're also modified internally so they're *bound* to the runtime program, and the runtime program in turn can open only properly bound files. In other words, when you send people a runtime program, they can't use it to open any old FileMaker Pro file.

To facilitate the binding process, FileMaker asks you to provide a *bindkey*. FileMaker stores this value in both the runtime program and any database files in the Developer Utilities window. The value you use for the bindkey is entirely unimportant, and you don't have to keep it secret. But if you later want to bind *new* databases to the same runtime program, then you have to use the same bindkey.

Finally, when people exit the runtime program (in other words, when they close your database system), they see a "Made with FileMaker" splash screen. Normally, this screen looks like the one in Figure 19-20. You can also control how long the splash screen shows by putting the number of seconds in the Delay box. Unfortunately, you can't make it go away entirely.

Remove admin access from files permanently

The "Remove admin access from files permanently" option doesn't actually remove the accounts that have full access. Instead, it modifies the [Full Access] privilege set so it no longer truly has full access. If you log in with an account that normally has full access, then it doesn't have access to the Manage Database window, Layout mode, or Script Maker, and its access to Accounts & Privileges is limited to the Extended Privileges tab. This option has no settings.

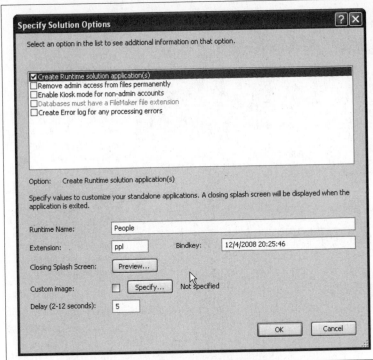

Figure 19-19:
The Specify Solution Options window lets you tell FileMaker what you want done to the files. Turn on a checkbox in the options list to tell FileMaker you want that thing done to your files. Most options need to be configured, and when you select an item in the list, the bottom half of the window lets you change the appropriate settings.

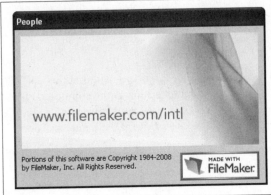

Figure 19-20:
When you quit a runtime solution, this window pops up for a few seconds. You can't get rid of the "Made with FileMaker" logo, but you can change the big FileMaker graphic to anything you want. Just turn on "Custom image," and then, from your hard drive, pick a picture file. FileMaker stretches the picture to fit in the window, so to avoid distortion, you should create a picture that's exactly 382 pixels wide and 175 pixels high.

Enable Kiosk mode for non-admin accounts

If you turn on Kiosk mode, and then open the new file using an account that has full access, then you don't see any changes. But if you log in with a lesser account, *everything* changes. The screen goes completely black, except for the content area of your database window. You can see an example in Figure 19-21.

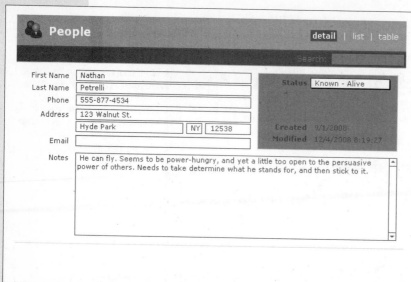

Figure 19-21:
When you open a database in Kiosk mode with an account that doesn't have full access, it looks like this example. Everything on the screen is completely black outside your layout. You can still switch layouts and otherwise interact with your database, but you can't make new windows, resize the window, exit FileMaker, or switch to other programs. You also can't print, enter Find mode, or otherwise use FileMaker's features unless buttons on the layout let you.

When you use Kiosk mode, you typically hide the Status toolbar and let people control everything using the buttons on layouts. Alternatively, you can use custom menus (page 753) to hide all the menus and commands that would let nosy people poke around in your file. Remember to troubleshoot your file before creating a custom runtime from it, because any problems in your file (broken links, missing data, bad scripts) also show up in the runtime. But once you've suppressed all the normal FileMaker commands, folks have no way of getting around these problems.

Databases must have a FileMaker file extension

Sometimes people, Mac types especially, create databases without the .fp7 file extension, only to regret that decision later. An extension is the computer's most compatible way to identify a file. So turn on "Databases must have a FileMaker file extension", and FileMaker adds ".fp7" to the end of every file name that doesn't already have it.

Create error log for any processing errors

While FileMaker processes your files, applying your options, building runtime programs, or renaming files, it may encounter problems. Turn on "Create error log for any processing errors" so you can see what went wrong. FileMaker saves error messages in a file on your hard drive (you get to pick where it goes and what it's called).

Loading and saving settings

If you maintain a database system that other people use, you may well run your files through Developer Utilities every time you send out a new version. To save you the tedium of configuring the Database Utilities dialog box again and again, FileMaker lets you save all your settings to a special file—just click Save Settings. Later, when you're ready to process your files again, click Load Settings, and then select the same file. FileMaker sets up everything in the dialog box for you. All you have to do is click Create.

Delivering a Runtime Solution

If you build a runtime solution withFileMaker Pro Advanced in Mac OS X, it runs *only* in Mac OS X. Likewise, if you build from Windows, your runtime solution is limited to Windows. If you need a runtime solution for *both* platforms, then you must buy FileMaker Pro Advanced for Mac OS X *and* for Windows, and build a separate runtime solution on each kind of computer.

Part Seven: Appendixes

7

Getting Help

This book provides a solid foundation in FileMaker and takes you well into power user territory, but it doesn't cover everything there is to know about this vastly versatile program. (You wouldn't be able to lift it if it did.) This appendix is a guide to the many resources available to help you plumb the depths of FileMaker database design and development.

Getting Help from FileMaker Itself

The installation CDs for FileMaker Pro and FileMaker Pro Advanced include online help files, electronic documentation, templates, and example files. The installer program *always* installs online help, but the others are optional. When you choose the Easy Install option in the Install panel of the installation wizard, you get *everything* installed. Choose Custom Install instead to pick and choose which of the optional files you want installed. And if FileMaker's already installed on your computer, but the helpers listed below are missing, then you can perform a Custom Install and choose the helper files you need without having to uninstall and reinstall FileMaker itself.

On Windows, you can find these helpers at Program Files → FileMaker → FileMaker Pro 10 → English Extras. And on the Mac, look in Applications → FileMaker Pro → English Extras.

The Resource Center

Your next best stop for FileMaker assistance is the FileMaker Resource Center. Just choose Help → Resource Center. FileMaker takes you to a special Web site covering many FileMaker topics. When you click a general topic, you see several related links. Not all these links are alike, though. Some are similar to the help topics FileMaker installs on your computer, but the Resource Center also has downloadable PDFs and short video demonstrations with tutorial databases. The Resource Center doesn't have everything there is to know about FileMaker, but the topics it covers, it covers in depth.

FileMaker Pro Help

If you don't have access to the Web, then you can read FileMaker's onboard help files by choosing Help → FileMaker Pro Help. You can also simply press F1 (⌘-?). If you launch Help while no dialog boxes are open, then it opens to the Contents page (Figure A-1).

If you need help with the dialog box that's open in front of you, whatever you do, don't close it! Instead, leave the dialog box open, which tells FileMaker you want context-sensitive help. For example, if you choose File → Manage → Database, then click the Relationships tab, and *then* choose Help → FileMaker Pro Help, then the file opens to the detail page called "Working with related tables and files". The detail page offers plenty of help, but if you don't find what you need, then you can use the links at the bottom to go to other pages in the section and related topics. Also, key words in the body of the help file are links to other topics (they're blue and underlined, like a Web link). The black underlined text is a link to a glossary of short definitions.

The Contents button (near the upper right), is a list of all topics grouped by subject, so you can browse them.

A comprehensive list of FileMaker's functions is one of the Help file's most useful parts. As in the Specify Calculation dialog box, the functions are listed two ways: by type, and alphabetically. The detail page for each function gives you the function name, parameter(s), data type returned, and a description of what the function does. Use these pages to help you when you're using a function for the first time.

Templates

You got a glimpse of these starter solutions in the box on page 92. You see all these template files listed in the FileMaker Quick Start dialog box—unless you've previously checked that dialog box's option to "No longer show this dialog". If you've turned this option on, but want to see the templates listed again, choose FileMaker Pro → Preferences (Mac) or Edit → Preferences (Windows), and then on the Preferences dialog box's General tab, turn on the Show FileMaker Quick Start Screen option. The next time you choose File → New Database, FileMaker's templates are listed. Pick the template you want, and FileMaker creates a new copy of the file for you. You can add data, create and edit scripts, or delete objects you don't need without affecting the original template.

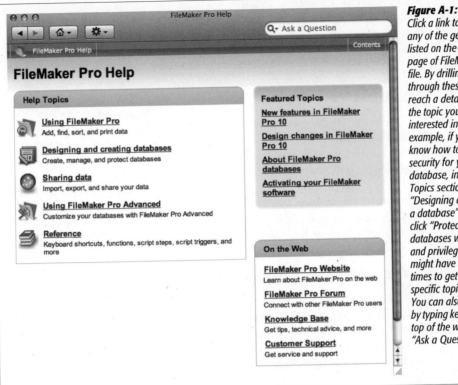

Figure A-1:
Click a link to see help on any of the general topics listed on the Contents page of FileMaker's Help file. By drilling down through these lists, you reach a detail page for the topic you're interested in. For example, if you want to know how to set up security for your database, in the Help Topics section, click "Designing and creating a database", and then click "Protecting databases with accounts and privilege sets". You might have to click a few times to get to the specific topic you need. You can also search Help by typing keywords at the top of the window, in the "Ask a Question" field.

Note: If you prefer, you can navigate to the Templates folder and launch the template you want just like any other file. When you launch a template file directly, though, you're opening the original template file, and any changes you make to the template are reflected in any new copies you make when you choose File → New Database.

These basic file templates can help you get up and running with basic data management tasks if you don't have time to figure out how things work in FileMaker's universe. But these templates also serve another purpose—as an introduction to good interface design. They have a clean, uncluttered look you can adapt for your own purposes. Feel free to copy the design as is or use it as a jumping-off point for your new database.

Each template stores different kinds of data, so it's helpful to explore several templates to get ideas for arranging and grouping your data effectively. In general, you usually see an easy-to-read name at the top of the layout, which serves to orient people to the task at hand. Underneath the name, you find a couple of rows of navigation tools and buttons grouped together by function. The largest portion of the layout is dedicated to a logical arrangement of data fields.

Finally, FileMaker's templates contain ideas you can use for creating relationships, buttons, and scripts to make your own databases more powerful. For instance, the Contact Management template contains a script that lets you swap a contact's main address data with the secondary address data. By studying these files, you can pick up tips that you can apply to your own custom solutions.

XML Examples

You find example files, including a database and sample XML and XSLT files, in the English Extras folder, in a folder called Examples. These simple files serve as a primer for working with FileMaker and XML. To get started, open the database file (*xml example.fp7*), and then run each script to see how XML import and export work. Then take a look at the steps that make up each script, paying particular attention to the options set for the Import Records and Export Records steps. Finally, take a look at the files that are imported and the files that are created by the export scripts. You see how your XML pages should be structured.

Getting Help from FileMaker, Inc.

FileMaker's Web site has the usual marketing materials you'd expect from a great software company. But there's lots of substance there, too. In its main navigation menu, Look for "Support", where you find free and fee-based help.

Updaters and Downloads

Like most programs, FileMaker's latest software versions are those on the software company's Web site. You find software updates and support files, like localized language packs at *http://www.filemaker.com/support/downloads/*. Trial software and development tools, including an XLST library and a list of recently released plug-ins, are also available from this page.

If your installation is missing some (or all) of its templates, click the Starter Solutions link to download new copies. You can also download one or all of four free, readymade solutions called Productivity Kits. You have one each for businesses, creative professionals, pupils from kindergarten through grade 12, and college students.

Even if one of these kits doesn't meet your exact need, you'll find them useful for study purposes. There's some pretty heady stuff under the hood, but the files are full of developer tricks of the trade you can analyze. Even if you don't use the exact techniques you see, you can develop your analytical skills by picking apart the files. You'll also learn different ways to approach and solve particular database problems— maybe ways you hadn't thought of!

Downloadable Resources

You can reach this list from the Downloads page above, but it's so jam-packed that it deserves a headline all its own.

- **Product Documentation.** You find all the documentation that came with your product here, plus any updates to those guides. You also have tutorial files and some extra guides on topics like security, Windows 2000 Terminal Services, and Citrix.

- **Technical Resources.** These resources don't focus on step-by-step help. Instead, they tell you about the benefits of certain technologies and the ways you can use them. You find a variety of topics, like network configuration, connectivity, security, Web publishing, and integration. You see PDFs and videos of Web seminars that you can watch on your own time.

- **FileMaker Resource Guide.** The Resource Guide lists FileMaker's complete product line, third-party products, trainers, and consultants.

Knowledge Base

Find FAQs, bug alerts, workarounds, errata, and the official word on topics that don't fit into FileMaker's other document categories. You can either search the Knowledge Base with keywords, or peruse the most recent topics to see what's new. A button at the bottom of each page lets you request email notification if the page is updated, so you can stay on top of developments with ease. A clickable list of related topics helps you wander around in case the main topic didn't fill the bill.

Forums

FileMaker Inc. provides a free user-to-user FileMaker Forum, where you can read discussions about common concerns, and post questions of your own. It has an English language section (the busiest), and also French, German, and Japanese areas. Questions range from basic topics to detailed discussions of the use of specific functions. The Forum is moderated by FileMaker staff. You can search without logging in, but you have to register to post.

Technical Support

FileMaker supports the current version of its software and one version prior. In addition to the resources listed above, you can speak with a human being to get help with specific issues. The phone number for free and fee-based tech support, plus customer service to help you decide which products you need is 1-800-325-2747. Phone tech support is available 7:00 a.m. to 5:00 p.m. Pacific Time weekdays (except holidays).

Note: If your files are in an older version for which FileMaker Inc. no longer offers support, then you need to get help from a third party, usually a consultant or a user group. See page 777 to find out how to find those animals.

Free support

You can't start making databases until FileMaker's installed, so everybody who purchases FileMaker gets unlimited tech support phone calls regarding installation or activation. Plus, you get one free troubleshooting call for each product you buy, which is helpful when you have a bunch of staffers on FileMaker Pro, a copy or two of FileMaker Server, and your very own copy of FileMaker Pro Advanced.

Paid support

Get out your credit card when you call, and then decide how you want to pay:

- You can choose a $45 flat fee and they'll solve a single issue for you, or you can roll the dice (and get multiple problems solved at once) by choosing the $3 per minute rate, with a $75 maximum.

- With Premium 800 Support, you prepay $180 for a five-pack of access codes that let you make the calls when the trouble arises. Codes are good for one year.

- Professional Support costs $899 per year. You nominate one person from your company who can call a special toll-free number as many times as needed for 12 months. Add $699 for each additional person who needs the same access. Download the order form at *http://www.filemaker.com/downloads/pdf/prof_support_form.pdf*.

Note: Technical Support deals with technical problems, like when a feature isn't working as advertised, and you need help figuring out why. Teaching you how to create databases, or writing your calculations and scripts for you are not considered technical support.

File corruption isn't common with FileMaker, but it's devastating when it happens. FileMaker offers file recovery services at $500 per file. Go to *http://www.filemaker.com/downloads/pdf/filerecovery.pdf* for more information.

Developer Programs

FileMaker runs two programs to help developers keep in touch with each other, and with FileMaker, Inc. itself. The FileMaker Technical Network (*http://www.filemaker.com/technet/*) gets you access to an email discussion forum crawling with FileMaker experts swapping ideas and helping one another. You also get access to exclusive technical white papers and how-to articles on important FileMaker topics. Finally, TechNet subscribers get free FileMaker add-on software and a special developer version of FileMaker Server Advanced for testing purposes. To call yourself a member, you just pay the dues: $99 per year.

If you're a professional FileMaker developer (meaning you build FileMaker databases for other companies for pay), you may qualify to join the FileMaker Business Alliance (FBA) instead. In addition to online discussions, technical info, and free software, FBA members get outstanding software perks. You can purchase FileMaker products for your own use (or your company's use) for deep discounts. You can also get discount pricing on FileMaker products, which you can then resell to your customers. FBA members (along with their products and services) are listed on FileMaker's Web site, and in the Resource Guide. Membership requires approval, and costs $500 per year. Find out more at *http://www.filemaker.com/fba/*.

Getting Help from the Community

Even outside the members-only programs, the FileMaker developer community is a congenial bunch. You'll find lots of resources on the Internet, including free newsgroups and Web sites. Many independent consultants' sites have free or low-cost resources, too, like lists of custom functions free for the taking or sample files that demonstrate specific techniques.

Mail Lists and Newsgroups

A listing of email lists is available at *http://www.filemaker.com/support/mailinglists. html*, but new sites are cropping up all the time, and URLs change even on established sites. So use the link above, or check your favorite search engine, to get the latest links for these groups. To get your feet wet, try general lists, like the one run by Dartmouth University or FileMaker Today. Fmpug.com is a membership-based, online user group with forums, reviews, and resources, including podcast interviews with subject-matter experts. For more specialized topics, have a look at FileMaker XML Talk, FileMaker Pro CGI Talk, and Troi FileMaker Plug-in Talk.

Training/Consultants

FileMaker's Web site lists trainers and consultants who are members of the FBA. And the FileMaker Resource Guide also lists the FBA group, plus it takes paid advertisements. Your favorite search engine will yield hundreds of results. File-Maker has a certification program, so look for the FileMaker Certified Developer logo or ask the consultant if she's been certified, as part of your selection process.

DevCon

If total FileMaker immersion is what you seek, the annual Developer's Conference (DevCon) is the way to go. Each day you can attend as many as seven sessions on about 30 different topics, ranging from running a FileMaker consulting firm to Web publishing, so you're sure to come away from the 3-day conference with a brain-pan full of new ideas. For details, see *http://www.filemaker.com/developers/ devcon/index.html*.

FileMaker Error Codes

The following table (Table B-1) lists the error codes that may pop up when File-Maker detects something out of whack in your database, especially when you're writing or running a script. Like any things written by and for computer programmers, these official descriptions may not make much sense in English, but they may provide a little more guidance than the error number alone.

Error codes marked with an asterisk (*) pertain only to Web-published databases.

Table B-1. Error codes

Error Number	Description
−1	Unknown error
0	No error
1	User canceled action
2	Memory error
3	Command is unavailable (for example, wrong operating system, wrong mode, etc.)
4	Command is unknown
5	Command is invalid (for example, a Set Field script step does not have a calculation specified)
6	File is read-only
7	Running out of memory
8	Empty result
9	Insufficient privileges
10	Requested data is missing

Table B-1. *Error codes (continued)*

Error Number	Description
11	Name is not valid
12	Name already exists
13	File or object is in use
14	Out of range
15	Can't divide by zero
16	Operation failed, request retry (for example, a user query)
17	Attempt to convert foreign character set to UTF-16 failed
18	Client must provide account information to proceed
19	String contains characters other than A–Z, a–z, 0–9 (ASCII)
20	Command/operation canceled by triggered script
100	File is missing
101	Record is missing
102	Field is missing
103	Relationship is missing
104	Script is missing
105	Layout is missing
106	Table is missing
107	Index is missing
108	Value list is missing
109	Privilege set is missing
110	Related tables are missing
111	Field repetition is invalid
112	Window is missing
113	Function is missing
114	File reference is missing
115	Specified menu set is not present
116	Specified layout object is not present
117	Specified data source is not present
130	Files are damaged or missing and must be reinstalled
131	Language pack files are missing (such as template files)
200	Record access is denied
201	Field cannot be modified
202	Field access is denied
203	No records in file to print, or password doesn't allow print access
204	No access to field(s) in sort order
205	User does not have access privileges to create new records; import will overwrite existing data

Table B-1. *Error codes (continued)*

Error Number	Description
206	User does not have password change privileges, or file is not modifiable
207	User does not have sufficient privileges to change database schema, or file is not modifiable
208	Password does not contain enough characters
209	New password must be different from existing one
210	User account is inactive
211	Password has expired
212	Invalid user account and/or password; please try again
213	User account and/or password does not exist
214	Too many login attempts
215	Administrator privileges cannot be duplicated
216	Guest account cannot be duplicated
217	User does not have sufficient privileges to modify administrator account
300	File is locked or in use
301	Record is in use by another user
302	Table is in use by another user
303	Database schema is in use by another user
304	Layout is in use by another user
306	Record modification ID does not match
400	Find criteria are empty
401	No records match the request
402	Selected field is not a match field for a lookup
403	Exceeding maximum record limit for trial version of FileMaker Pro
404	Sort order is invalid
405	Number of records specified exceeds number of records that can be omitted
406	Replace/Reserialize criteria are invalid
407	One or both match fields are missing (invalid relationship)
408	Specified field has inappropriate data type for this operation
409	Import order is invalid
410	Export order is invalid
412	Wrong version of FileMaker Pro used to recover file
413	Specified field has inappropriate field type
414	Layout cannot display the result
415	One or more required related records are not available
416	Primary key required from data source table
417	Database is not supported for ODBC operations

Table B-1. *Error codes (continued)*

Error Number	Description
500	Date value does not meet validation entry options
501	Time value does not meet validation entry options
502	Number value does not meet validation entry options
503	Value in field is not within the range specified in validation entry options
504	Value in field is not unique as required in validation entry options
505	Value in field is not an existing value in the database file as required in validation entry options
506	Value in field is not listed on the value list specified in validation entry option
507	Value in field failed calculation test of validation entry option
508	Invalid value entered in Find mode
509	Field requires a valid value
510	Related value is empty or unavailable
511	Value in field exceeds maximum number of allowed characters
512	Record was already modified by another user
513	Record must have a value in some field to be created
600	Print error has occurred
601	Combined header and footer exceed one page
602	Body doesn't fit on a page for current column setup
603	Print connection lost
700	File is of the wrong file type for import
706	EPSF file has no preview image
707	Graphic translator cannot be found
708	Can't import the file or need color monitor support to import file
709	QuickTime movie import failed
710	Unable to update QuickTime reference because the database file is read-only
711	Import translator cannot be found
714	Password privileges do not allow the operation
715	Specified Excel worksheet or named range is missing
716	A SQL query using DELETE, INSERT, or UPDATE is not allowed for ODBC import
717	There is not enough XML/XSL information to proceed with the import or export
718	Error in parsing XML file (from Xerces)
719	Error in transforming XML using XSL (from Xalan)
720	Error when exporting; intended format does not support repeating fields
721	Unknown error occurred in the parser or the transformer

Table B-1. *Error codes (continued)*

Error Number	Description
722	Cannot import data into a file that has no fields
723	You do not have permission to add records to or modify records in the target table
724	You do not have permission to add records to the target table
725	You do not have permission to modify records in the target table
726	There are more records in the import file than in the target table; not all records were imported
727	There are more records in the target table than in the import file; not all records were updated
729	Errors occurred during import; records could not be imported
730	Unsupported Excel version (convert file to Excel 7.0 [Excel 95], 97, 2000, XP, or 2007 format and try again)
731	The file you are importing from contains no data
732	This file cannot be inserted because it contains other files
733	A table cannot be imported into itself
734	This file type cannot be displayed as a picture
735	This file type cannot be displayed as a picture; it will be inserted and displayed as a file
736	Too much data to export to this format; it will be truncated
737	Bento collection or library is missing; data cannot be imported
800	Unable to create file on disk
801	Unable to create temporary file on System disk
802	Unable to open file
803	File is single user or host cannot be found
804	File cannot be opened as read-only in its current state
805	File is damaged; use Recover command
806	File cannot be opened with this version of FileMaker Pro
807	File is not a FileMaker Pro file or is severely damaged
808	Cannot open file because access privileges are damaged
809	Disk/volume is full
810	Disk/volume is locked
811	Temporary file cannot be opened as FileMaker Pro file
813	Record Synchronization error on network
814	File(s) cannot be opened because maximum number is open
815	Couldn't open lookup file
816	Unable to convert file
817	Unable to open file because it does not belong to this solution
819	Cannot save a local copy of a remote file

Table B-1. *Error codes (continued)*

Error Number	Description
820	File is in the process of being closed
821	Host forced a disconnect
822	FMI files not found; reinstall missing files
823	Cannot set file to single-user, guests are connected
824	File is damaged or not a FileMaker file
900	General spelling engine error
901	Main spelling dictionary not installed
902	Could not launch the Help system
903	Command cannot be used in a shared file
905	No active field selected; command can only be used if there is an active field
906	Current file must be shared in order to use this command
920	Can't initialize the spelling engine
921	User dictionary cannot be loaded for editing
922	User dictionary cannot be found
923	User dictionary is read-only
951	An unexpected error occurred (*)
954	Unsupported XML grammar (*)
955	No database name (*)
956	Maximum number of database sessions exceeded (*)
957	Conflicting commands (*)
958	Parameter missing (*)
1200	Generic calculation error
1201	Too few parameters in the function
1202	Too many parameters in the function
1203	Unexpected end of calculation
1204	Number, text constant, field name or "(" expected
1205	Comment is not terminated with "*/"
1206	Text constant must end with a quotation mark
1207	Unbalanced parenthesis
1208	Operator missing, function not found or "(" not expected
1209	Name (such as field name or layout name) is missing
1210	Plug-in function has already been registered
1211	List usage is not allowed in this function
1212	An operator (for example, +, −, *) is expected here
1213	This variable has already been defined in the Let function

Table B-1. *Error codes (continued)*

Error Number	Description
1214	AVERAGE, COUNT, EXTEND, GETREPETITION, MAX, MIN, NPV, STDEV, SUM and GETSUMMARY: expression found where a field alone is needed
1215	This parameter is an invalid Get function parameter
1216	Only Summary fields allowed as first argument in GETSUMMARY
1217	Break field is invalid
1218	Cannot evaluate the number
1219	A field cannot be used in its own formula
1220	Field type must be normal or calculated
1221	Data type must be number, date, time, or timestamp
1222	Calculation cannot be stored
1223	The function is not implemented
1224	The function is not defined
1225	The function is not supported in this context
1300	The specified name can't be used
1400	ODBC driver initialization failed; make sure the ODBC drivers are properly installed
1401	Failed to allocate environment (ODBC)
1402	Failed to free environment (ODBC)
1403	Failed to disconnect (ODBC)
1404	Failed to allocate connection (ODBC)
1405	Failed to free connection (ODBC)
1406	Failed check for SQL API (ODBC)
1407	Failed to allocate statement (ODBC)
1408	Extended error (ODBC)
1409	Error (ODBC)
1413	Failed communication link (ODBC)
1450	Action requires PHP privilege extension (*)
1451	Action requires that current file be remote
1501	SMTP authentication failed
1502	Connection refused by SMTP server
1503	Error with SSL
1504	SMTP server requires the connection to be encrypted
1505	Specified authentication is not supported by SMTP server
1506	Email(s) could not be sent successfully
1507	Unable to log in to the SMTP server

Index

M

Mac keystrokes, 8, 11
Mac OS X
 configuring data sources on, 669
 PDF files in, 87
Macintosh version, 11
mail lists, 777
Manage Accounts & Privileges window, 649–653
Manage Custom Functions dialog box, 480
Manage Database window
 Cancel button, 317
 Fields tab, 101, 316, 317
 Relationships tab, 321–323
 Tables tab, 316
Manage External Data Sources dialog box, 379
Manage Script dialog box, 6
Manage Scripts window, 496, 511
Manage Value Lists dialog box, 238–242
many-to-many relationships, 302, 304, 314–315
MapQuest, 211
margins, print, 225–227
Match case option, 69
matching fields, 689
mathematical operators, 404
Max() function, 432
Maximum number of character option, 116
Maximum option, 290
Member of value list option, 114–115
menu commands, 76–78, 637
menu separators, 512
menu sets, 236
menu sets, custom, 760–761
menus, 8, 19
 creating, 758–759
 custom, 753–761
 deleting, 759–760
 editing, 755–758
 pop-up, 164, 244, 245
merge fields, 195–197, 232
Merge format, 681
Microsoft SQL Server, 675
Microsoft SQL Server databases, 666
Microsoft Visio, 308
MiddleValues() function, 443
MiddleWord() function, 440–441
Min() function, 432
minimum characters, in fields, 116
Minimum option, 290
Minutes() function, 451
mirroring, 731

missing fields, 106
Mode pop-up menu, 19
modeling databases
 choosing entities, 297–299
 creating ER diagram, 305–310
 finding relationships, 300–304
 join tables, 313–315
modes
 Browse, 18
 changing, 19
 current, 19
 Find, 18, 31–35
 Layout, 18
 Preview, 19
 understanding, 18–19
modification values, for fields, 107
Modify Last Find command, 53, 62
Modify Last Find script step, 563
Modify Table View command, 50–52
modular scripting, 582–590
Month() function, 451
MonthName() function, 452
Move/Resize Window script step, 567
movies, importing, 693
moving
 between fields, 23
 fields, 147–153
 layout objects, 147–152
 windows, 566–567
multifield sorts, 37–38
multi-key relationships, 385–387
multimedia files, 84–85
multiple conditions, testing, 519–520, 612
multiple databases, systems with, 378
multiple parameters, 591
multiple sub-summary parts, 282–284
multiple tables. See tables, multiple
multiple windows, 40
multiple-window interface, 570
multipredicate relationships, 385–392
multiuser databases, 703
MySQL, 7
MySQL databases, 666, 675
MySQL drivers, 671

N

names
 account, 650
 field, 96–99, 323, 330
 global field, 372
 script variable, 591
 table, 316, 323
 table occurrences, 330